TEXTURES
of
PLACE

TEXTURES
of
PLACE

Exploring
Humanist Geographies

*Paul C. Adams, Steven Hoelscher,
and Karen E. Till, Editors*

University of Minnesota Press

Minneapolis
London

The publication of this book was assisted by a University Cooperative Society Subvention Grant awarded by the University of Texas at Austin.

Published by the University of Minnesota Press
111 Third Avenue South, Suite 290
Minneapolis, MN 55401-2520
http://www.upress.umn.edu

Library of Congress Cataloging-in-Publication Data

Textures of place : exploring humanist geographies / Paul C. Adams,
Steven Hoelscher, and Karen E. Till, editors.
    p. cm.
  Includes bibliographical references and index.
  ISBN 0-8166-3756-3 (HC) – ISBN 0-8166-3757-1 (PB)
  1. Human geography. I. Adams, Paul C. II. Hoelscher, Steven D.
III. Till, Karen E.
GF41 .T48 2001
304.2 – dc21   00-009993

To Yi-Fu

CONTENTS

ACKNOWLEDGMENTS

This book owes its inspiration and direct genesis to Yi-Fu Tuan. All the authors, despite their diverse backgrounds and perspectives, have experienced his enormous intellectual impact in their own work. Differences in generation, theoretical viewpoint, and methodology remain important and contribute to the vigorous diversity of this book. But Yi-Fu's humanist geography has touched all of us in ways seen and unseen. As editors, and as students of his at Wisconsin, we happily acknowledge that this book exists because of his untiring support and endless intellectual curiosity.

In an edited volume like this much hinges on the timeliness and thoroughness of its many contributors, and we would like to thank our authors for making this project top-priority time and time again. Each has brought a unique perspective to the study of place — a set of perspectives that, when taken together, demonstrate the continued resonance of this classic geographic concept. It has been a privilege to work with such a distinguished and hard-working group of scholars.

Several people not included in the table of contents have helped bring this book to fruition, none more so than Carrie Mullen at the University of Minnesota Press. Her contagious enthusiasm for this project is matched by her skill in shepherding it through the lengthy publication process. Mary Braun similarly was an early proponent of this book, and much of its present form is indebted to her skilled editorial advice. Kent Mathewson and Wayne Franklin read the entire manuscript and offered useful criticism that enhanced much of the book's readability. Alicia Barber's extensive knowledge of both American studies and cultural geography helped her prepare the index — no mean task for such an expansive book; and Heike Alberts helped with much of the book's early formatting. Finally, we would like to thank the anonymous reviewers of *Textures of Place* who not only supported the book's publication but helped improve it by their careful reading and suggestions.

At our home institutions, we would like to thank several funding sources. The University of Texas at Austin generously provided a University Cooperative Society Subvention Grant, for which we are most grateful. The Departments of Geography at Texas A&M University and the University of Minnesota and the Department of American Studies at the University of Texas each awarded funds to assist in the preparation of the index.

PLACE IN CONTEXT

Rethinking Humanist Geographies

Paul C. Adams, Steven Hoelscher, and Karen E. Till

A name etched in the smooth, black stone of a war memorial, a crowd of peasants captured in oil paint, a ghost town arrested intentionally in its decay, the planet we call home seen from the vantage point of space — these are a few of the infinite textures of place. What is compelling about these images is less what we see than our cross-sensory resonance with them: we nearly hear the muffled conversations in Brueghel's village square; we can almost feel the earth cool and round in our hand. Imagination makes other connections as well. Any or all of the images may remind us disturbingly of the passage of time and of our own finiteness. Since time and space are intangible and dauntingly infinite, we cling intellectually and emotionally to our experiences and memories of the material world that is so reassuringly solid. Upon close examination, however, this solidity dissolves: a ghost town, even a living town, is woven with strands of an imagined past and a fictional community, products of the time and society in which we live. And, as the Vietnam Veterans Memorial forcefully reminds its many visitors (each of whom interprets its powerful messages in different, and often competing, ways), social relations are profoundly heterogeneous and unendingly divisive.

A place's "texture" thus calls direct attention to the paradoxical nature of place. Although we may think of texture as a superficial layer, only "skin deep," its distinctive qualities may be profound. A surface is, after all, where subject and object merge;[1] the shape, feel, and texture of a place each provides a glimpse into the processes, structures, spaces, and histories that went into its making. Etymologically, texture is associated with both "textile" and "context." It derives from the Latin *texere,* meaning "to weave," which came to mean the thing woven (textile) and the feel of the weave (texture). But it also refers to a "weave" of an organized arrangement of words or other intangible things (context). A textile is created by bringing together many threads and, as such, represents ordered complexity. Language, too, is ordered complexity, and when we understand a word by its context we are discerning a pattern and filling in a gap, sewing together what is torn, extracting meaning not only from what is said but from the relationships this *act of saying* sets up with other statements, conditions, events, and situations.[2] Communication always *takes place* somewhere, in particular social and spatial contexts, and place is always "in" the communication (in the form of place-images). Similarly, "textures of place" refers not only to surfaces, processes, and structures but also to communication acts and the multiple contexts that create and are constituted by place.

When we touch a piece of fabric, the experience tells us much about the weave of the fabric, whether it is sturdy or delicate, and about the nature of the threads, either light or heavy.[3] Likewise, people's sense of place — attached variously to a movie theater, a town, a tree, a planet — reveals a great deal about the structure of each of these places in its various contexts. Place, as a topic of investigation, highlights the weaving together of social relations and human-environment interactions. Texture's simultaneous invocation of surface and depth provides a kind of pivot as we move through this book encountering themes as diverse as morality and imagination, attention and absence, personal and group identity, social structure, home, nature, and cosmos. The tramp and the poet, the professor and the graduate student, and all of the other identities discussed in these chapters are distinct in many respects, yet they all contribute to understanding the world and to the structure of society: they are part of the overall texture of place.

In using the title *Textures of Place* we therefore mean to highlight the geographic tradition of trying to understand the meanings and processes of place — their material and symbolic qualities — as well as the range of peoples and social relations that continuously define and create social and spatial contexts. We hasten to add that by highlighting "the geographic tradition" in our understanding of place we include work by both geographers and scholars from neighboring disciplines. Professional geographers, of course, enjoy no sole proprietorship in describing the earth in all its richness and textures: historians, anthropologists, and philosophers, among others, have made important contributions to this centuries-old project. Nevertheless, among the academic disciplines geographers have probably had most to say about the relationship between space and place, for, as Yi-Fu Tuan famously argued in the book of that same title, grappling with such a relationship lies at the core of geographical inquiry.[4]

Since Tuan's seminal work on the nature of space and place, a groundswell of interest, excitement, and controversy has energized geographical inquiry on these concepts — by both geographers and their colleagues from across academia. What is equally evident is the incessant reconceptualizing of a "Tuanian" perspective, an approach more generally described as "humanistic geography."[5] In what follows we examine humanistic geography in light of contemporary theoretical and methodological debates within the discipline. Then we describe how recent theoretical discussions have placed "place" at the center of research agendas inside and outside of geography, resulting in significantly reworked conceptions of place. We conclude by introducing the chapters of this book that in a wide variety of ways seek to unravel and then reweave the many textures of place.

Humanist Geographies

More than twenty years ago, humanistic geographers explored the complexities of human action and what it meant to be "placed" in the world.[6] In the classic collection of essays published in 1978 and entitled *Humanistic Geography,* David Ley and Marwyn Samuels described their perspective in this way:

> a humanistic geography is concerned to restore and make explicit the relation between knowledge and human interests. All social constructions, be they cities or geographic knowledge, reflect the values of a society and an epoch, so that humanistic philosophies reject out of hand any false claim to objectivity and pure theory in the study of man. Such claims, most notably those of contemporary positivism, negate themselves through their lack of reflexivity, their unself-conscious espousal of value positions.[7]

Beginning with this epistemological orientation, humanistic geographers studied landscape iconography, mental maps, environmental perception, and everyday geographies; they employed a range of methods, including phenomenology, ethnography, and hermeneutics. Emulating their late-nineteenth- and early-twentieth-century counterparts (George Perkins Marsh, Vidal de la Blache, J. K. Wright), they examined literary texts, art, photography, and film.[8] They focused on the richness of particular locales and explored the same topic in different cultural contexts. They emphasized writing well, even writing lyrically, as many tried to follow Wright's search for "words or phrases that carry emotional connotation."[9] Common to many of their research agendas were some central questions: What is the nature of human experience? How do place, landscape, and space define and provide the context for this experience? How do humans make the world into a home?

Many humanistic geographers turned to phenomenology (often combined with existentialism) as the philosophical basis for their investigations of "being-in-the-world."[10] Phenomenology, as defined by Edmund Husserl, is a "philosophical science" concerned with understanding "universal and absolute" laws that govern the spiritual and psychological workings of humans. Many who rejected positivism and embraced phenomenology thus adopted an approach that was thought to reveal the true essences of human experience, including everyday interactions with place. In this way, they endeavored "to peel off successive layers of a priori judgment and to transcend all preconceptions in order to arrive at a consciousness of pure essences."[11]

Other humanistic geographers emphasized the *politics* of place and place-making. Concerned with the degradation of everyday environments, Edward Relph argued that "one of the first aims of a phenomenology of geography should be to retrieve these [everyday] experiences from the academic netherworld and to return them to everyone by reawakening a sense of wonder about the earth and its places."[12] Ley's work in particular focused on "taken for granted meanings" in specific social contexts. Grounding his work in symbolic interactionism and using various qualitative methods including participant observation, he tried to understand how African Americans negotiated their lives in the concrete context of Philadelphia's inner city. For Ley, place was constructed socially and related dialectically to group identity; it became a foundational, and deeply political, concept.[13]

At the turn of the twenty-first century, geographers working within a humanities tradition (though not often self-identified as humanistic geographers) continue to explore how worlds, places, landscapes, meanings, and human experiences are socially constructed and help constitute specific cultural contexts. Continuity exists in the focal areas of interest, but the past two and a half decades have brought significant ontological, epistemological, and methodological shifts. As we discuss below, many scholars across the humanities and social sciences no longer trust the search for universal definitions; in geography one finds a shift in emphasis from theorizing place in terms of lifeworlds and dwelling (in a Heideggerian sense) to explorations that avoid such universalistic concepts. This has led some to question whether "humanistic geography" still exists. Tuan, for one, has noted that for very good reasons this term has not been used with much frequency since the late 1980s.[14] Many of the younger scholars in this volume, the editors included, consider themselves cultural and/or historical geographers (albeit working within a humanities tradition) rather than humanistic geographers per se.[15]

While humanistic geography may not be officially recognized as a subdiscipline or specialty group by geography organizations, many of its interests and concerns are nonetheless still relevant to geographers working in a humanities tradition today. One of the goals of this volume is to draw explicit connections between geography and the humanities, as well as to highlight the range of contemporary humanist geographies, including the emergence of what we would call "critical humanist geographies." The "critical" label marks a maturation, rather than complete rejection, of humanistic geography insofar as it still draws heavily on its hermeneutical traditions. In the 1970s, humanistic geographers introduced the study of interpretation and meaning to challenge empiricist and positivist approaches then dominant in human geography. Anne Buttimer, for example, suggested bringing together insider/outsider views of a place through a "dialogical approach," and Tuan proposed a reflexive approach to studying "topophilia," arguing that to know the world is to know oneself.[16] Critical humanist geographers continue to examine how signs, symbols, gestures, utterances, and local knowledges convey cultural meanings and create places. Yet they are also influenced by the more recent contributions by various social theories drawn into geography in the 1980s and 1990s, most notably from cultural materialism, feminism, and poststructuralism, and also from postmodernism and postcolonial theory.[17]

After a period of intense preoccupation with critical social theory (which, of course, continues into the present), critical humanist geographers at the turn of the millennium appear to be pursuing what Benjamin Forest has described elsewhere as a contextualist approach.[18] A contextualist approach pays explicit attention to place and language, while it rejects a dependence on standards of either "objective" geographic knowledge or radical antifoundationalism. It examines the various contexts — whether marked by differences in class, race, gender, sexuality, or nationality — within which individual meanings and social practices are produced, understood, and negotiated. Furthermore, as is demonstrated in this book, a wide range of qualitative methodologies are employed from a critical or contextual perspective including participant observation, descriptive ethnography, semiotic and textual analysis, in-depth case studies, and rigorous historical investigation.

Thus, while geographers presently interested in humanistic themes draw from a range of epistemologies and methodologies clearly distinct from their predecessors, they still share similar concerns, such as an interest in the everyday, a privileging of individuals' understandings of their physical, social, and symbolic contexts, and, most significantly, the theoretical and empirical study of place. Nonetheless, humanism's interest in revealing universal experience is tempered now with a sense of caution regarding the processes of generalization and representation. Despite claims to explore geographical differences, human subjectivity, and the creation of meaning from different philosophical positions, many humanistic geographers in the 1970s reverted to a scientific "view from nowhere," a scholarly detachment similar — though couched in different terms — to that of the spatial analysts. This was due, in no small measure, to their search for universal essences, or truths, about "man," a term that could not contain the breadth of geographical agents. By the mid-1980s feminist scholars pointed out that "humanists tend to show a *general* concern for the way in which ordinary people are subject to various forms of authority, rather than analyzing the specific forms of exploitation and oppression that occur."[19] Furthermore, the influence of critical social theory in the humanities during the 1980s and 1990s led to the exploration of "antifoundational" approaches in geography. Such approaches disclaimed grand theories (such as structural functionalism, Marxism, or idealism) and the implicit assumptions of the Enlightenment project, such as the stability of the human subject or the belief in universal political, intellectual, and moral virtues resulting from the public exercise of reason.[20]

Thus, the engagement with critical social theory demanded a reevaluation of humanistic geography in the context of revised assumptions about human subjectivity, the transparency of language, and the use of descriptive categories based upon Western traditions of understanding. Today's interest in diversity is coupled with a refusal to adopt a master discourse that can organize all that diversity. Geographical interest is shifting toward discovering both distinctive, unexplored ways of perceiving and understanding the world and the incommensurate and divergent nature of people's realities. Finally, as a number of essays in this book demonstrate, an interest in narrative and "storytelling," as opposed to analysis and explanation, is emerging.[21] Although we feel that this collection draws attention to the emergence of critical humanist geographies, it is important to point out that not all of the authors in this volume would feel comfortable with such a label or even with the project it indicates.

This book not only highlights the current work of three generations of humanist geographers but also contains valuable contributions by scholars outside the academic boundaries of professional geography. By calling attention to the connections between geography and the humanities, we explicitly recognize the increasingly fluid and interdisciplinary nature of scholarship on place, of an intense and fruitful blurring of genres.[22] Geography, like the humanities more generally, is passionately pluralist in approach and tolerant of divergent viewpoints, and nowhere is this synthetic interest felt more profoundly than in the study of place.

Place Matters

Questions of "place," it is noted with increasing frequency, are firmly back on the scholarly agenda. After decades of devaluation in orthodox social science — and within human geography itself — place has reemerged with an intellectual vigor that few would have predicted. "Locality," "region," "landscape," "territory," "area," and "place" have once again become keywords for empirical and theoretical study.[23] And it is not just within human geography that these terms constitute foci for inquiry. The New Western History has energized a traditional discipline with a notion of the American West as less a frontier than a dynamic set of interlocking places; scholars in American studies have found a "regrounding" in the concept of place; sociologists have written about "the geographical moment" and of place as "a cultural artifact of social conflict and cohesion"; within anthropology one reads of the "empowering place" and its "multilocality and multivocality"; philosophers have suggested a nuanced "understanding of the place-world"; and scholars of literature have turned increasingly to how place evokes and shapes art.[24]

The interdisciplinary nature of place's scholarly renaissance is critical, for it suggests something much more expansive and vital than merely an updating of traditional regional geography or simply an extension of humanism. With its conception of place as an "element complex" — a country-by-country, or continent-by-continent, inventory of natural resources, population, economic sectors, and the like — the chorological method confined regional geography to a museum-like status, marginalized from both social sciences and the humanities.[25] In this view, place, as a collection of objective facts that could be analyzed scientifically, contained little room for the people who inhabit places and their subjective experiences. The humanist tradition within geography, as we have suggested, emphasized a concept of place dramatically at odds with this positivistic version. Works such as Tuan's *Space and Place,* Relph's *Place and Placelessness,* and Buttimer and Seamon's *The Human Experience of Space and Place* recoiled from the abstract theorizing of space as an objective entity and emphasized the subjective qualities of place. As Relph put it: "the essence of place lies in the largely unselfconscious intentionality that defines places as profound centres of human existence."[26] The recognition of the moral, aesthetic, and experiential aspects of place was fundamental to forging links between geography and neighboring disciplines, but its limitations (as we have noted above) prevented humanistic geography from fully engaging in the tremendous varieties and textures of place.

It is precisely "the move from 'knowing about' places in an objective way, their facts and features, to 'understanding' places, in a more empathetic way, their character and meanings," that remains the hallmark of humanistic geography.[27] But today's critical humanist perspective emphasizes the tensions and contradictions of place to a degree that was little described twenty years ago. Instead of the "essence of place," most scholars today interpret its "multiplicity"; rather than focusing on "human existence," they try to unearth the many ways that place impinges on identities surrounding race, ethnicity, class, gender, and sexuality; and more than simply focusing on "unselfconscious intentionality," a critical humanist interpretation of place is equally concerned with how human creativity is hemmed in by large-scale social, political, and economic structures. "Topophobia" as much as "topophilia" has captured geographical imaginations.[28] Thinking of places in this way "implies that they are not so much bounded areas as open and porous networks of social relations," suggests Doreen Massey. "It reinforces the idea, moreover, that [place] identities will be multiple.... And this in turn implies that what is to be the dominant image of any place will be a matter of contestation and will change over time."[29]

If the study of place has received a powerful theoretical boost from the so-called cultural turn in the humanities and social sciences, its growing importance is also due to larger societal trends. Stephen Daniels makes the important point that the current focus on place is not just a current academic fad: place is central to "how the world seems to work."[30] This may be seen in two much observed, and contradictory, ways, both of which are related to forces of globalization. First, although popular writers, beginning with Lewis Mumford in the 1920s, have bemoaned the impact of modernization on place, their sense of urgency and frequency has increased dramatically. Suburban sprawl replacing fragile ecosystems and productive farmland, strip malls displacing corner grocery stores, Americans trading one city for another: such well-known trends have inspired writers like James Howard Kunstler and William Leach to denounce the contemporary "geography of nowhere," where place seems to have lost its importance. In a time when traditional social roles have collapsed, such geographical change is especially troubling because place long served as a secure anchor to stabilize personal identity.[31] The response by marketers and developers, most notably in "neotraditional" or "New Urbanist" design, has been to create willfully contrived places that imbue "a sense of place," or at least look as if they should. Or, put somewhat differently, "that is why every new restaurant is dripping with personality, and every new housing development is stiff with character."[32]

Second, such antimodern reactions in postmodern consumerism, David Harvey argues, go hand in hand with recent changes in modern capitalism. "Place-bound identities," he notes, have "become more rather than less important in a world of diminishing spatial barriers to exchange, movement, and communication."[33] At exactly the same time that critics like Kunstler decry our current state of "placelessness," the very political-economic processes that would seem to homogenize place, in fact, increase its importance. Individual localities are ever more exposed to the vagaries of global flows of investment, population, goods, and pollution. As a result of this globalization, place managers adopt multifarious strategies to attract the kinds of flows that they find attractive (like investment capital and tourist dollars) and fend off those deemed undesirable (such as prisoners and toxic waste).[34] Places, Chris Philo and Gerry Kearns suggest, have long "sold themselves" — world's fairs, the "crabgrass frontiers" of American suburbs, and the spectacular development of downtowns all attest to the well-established efforts by real estate developers, politicians, and investors of all stripes to cash in on cultural capital. What is especially intriguing today is the paradoxical acceleration of that very process. In an age of time-space compression, we are made increasingly aware, place matters.[35] And if place is subjected to the homogenizing techniques of mass production and marketing, a critical humanist perspective reminds us that the "product" may be appropriated in distinct ways by different individuals and their particular modes of habitation.

The Places of "Place" in Contemporary Humanist Geography

Given the posttraditional times in which writers on place find themselves, the reader of this volume should not be surprised to find that the authors' conceptions, methodologies, and theoretical perspectives are as varied as places themselves.[36] But there are some shared themes, too, and below we highlight three of the most important in theorizing and interpreting the textures of place.

Experience and Identity

Perhaps the most lasting contribution of humanistic geography to the idea of place, Tim Cresswell has argued, has been the reminder that we do not live in an abstract framework of geometric spatial relationships: "we live in a world of meaning. We exist in and are surrounded by places."[37] Yi-Fu Tuan, more than anyone, pioneered this "perspective of experience," as he forced us to ask of a place: What is its meaning? and How is human identity structured through place?[38] Moreover, Tuan's assertion that "home is an intimate place" leads directly to questions regarding the politics and processes of identity-formation.[39] Designating a space as "home" or "hometown" or "homeland" emphasizes the way in which one's individual and collective identities are bound to place at multiple scales. Place and place-identity are increasingly seen as significant media through which people construct an identity — whether that construction is part of a gay identity in West Hollywood, a gender-based identity in London, or an ethnic identity in rural Scotland.[40]

Imagination and Social Construction

Closely related is the view that place is socially produced and constructed and, moreover, that imagination plays a critical role in that construction. Many have followed Benedict Anderson's provocative formulation of large-scale places such as the nation as "imagined communities."[41] Furthermore, and as the chapters of this book demonstrate, places are socially constructed and produced at an enormous variety of scales, from the body to a building like a museum, to a city or suburb, to an ecosystem like a wetland, to a nation-state, to the world or cosmos. Places, like a university, can be directly experienced and concrete, or they can be more nearly metaphorical, if equally direct — as in knowing "one's place." They can appear transparently "artificial" (like the images on the movie screen, which nevertheless have deep meaning for some), or they can appear "natural" (and yet be the product of considerable artifice and domination). In every instance, however, separate groups and individuals will evoke geographical imaginations in very different, and often competing, ways in the construction of place. As such, vitally important concepts like multiculturalism, racism, nation building, and environmental destruction are linked to the making of place.

Paradox and Modernity

Despite its long-held association with stability and community, place is increasingly recognized as dynamic and fluid, as "a contested terrain."[42] Place may indeed hold out the promise as "an analeptic for individuality and the world's indifference," but, as Tuan is quick to point out, it is precisely in response to the forces of modernity that such a need has been created.[43] Similarly, place has been called upon both for a progressive political agenda and for its conservative opposite. Some, like Doreen Massey, see place as a crucial aspect of the politics of inclusion, where people form multiple identities and marginalized groups contest a dominant ideology. She has argued persuasively for the possibility of creating a "progressive sense of place," one that meets the challenges of feminism and celebrates the politics of difference. But, as Timothy Oakes has maintained, "the paradoxical qualities of modernity can just as easily yield a place-based politics which is reactionary, exclusionary, and blatantly supportive of dominant regimes."[44] One might go one step further and suggest that *place itself* is the source of such paradox, ambivalence, and contradiction. As the point where human subjectivity meets the forces of abstraction and objectification, place, due precisely to this critical quality of "betweenness," is an excellent vantage point from which to study all of the dazzling and contradictory aspects of modernity, from the building of nation-states and the elaboration of capitalism, to individual consciousness and morality.[45]

Contents of the Book

Textures of Place owes its origins to four special sessions at the 1998 Annual Meeting of the Association of American Geographers. Although the sessions were organized on the occasion of Yi-Fu Tuan's retirement, the papers presented there and the contents of this book are far removed from the usual "festschrift" fare of praise and adulation. On the contrary, each author was invited to share in a critical dialogue on the meaning of place, self, and identity. Disagreement as much as consensus, we have suggested, define a contemporary critical humanist sensibility. Some of the authors are contemporaries of Tuan, some his students, and some his colleagues outside his home discipline of geography — all, however, recognize his profound influence and share a commitment to the study of place that our esteemed colleague forged.

In keeping with the title of the book, a textile metaphor, the thread, explains the order in which we will introduce the book's chapters. To mix our metaphors a bit, as you read these chapter introductions imagine that you are overhearing a thread of conversation generated around Tuan's well-laid table, in which each participant takes a turn and picks up the loose ends left by the prior speaker. Some agree and some disagree, but they form a continuous strand of thought. That this is not the only strand among the authors should be obvious, and indeed this is emphasized by the division of the book into four parts that follow their own logic. The parts organize ideas into loose categories strongly reminiscent of Tuan's books: Landscapes of Dominance and Affection; Segmented Worlds and Selves; Moralities and Imagination; and Cosmos versus Hearth.[46] By providing the reader with two possible organizations — one the cluster and the other the strand — we hope to offer more insight into the ways the chapters relate.

We start with Karal Ann Marling. With rare literary skill she conveys the joy and magic of a public space that was lost several decades ago from the American landscape but is only now fading from collective memory. Her subject is the movie palace, the dazzling street space it created, and the alternative world it provided to several generations of Americans. These palaces have vanished not because they were tied to a medium that vanished (box office returns still increase every decade) but because they were part of a centralized urban landscape and social structure that are no more. What Marling does is help to reconstruct a collective memory of these places, linking topophilia with loss.

Miles Richardson also treats topophilia and loss, showing that this link is significant in various contexts. Places as diverse as Catholic shrines, the Vietnam Veterans Memorial, and Graceland share this tie. Here topophilia arises directly from absence, a condition many of us acknowledge by offering a presence: ourselves. We come to these places not only to see but also to bring offerings: miniature body parts, flowers, C rations, T-shirts — indeed, anything that emotionally connects us to one who is absent. Through this act, we also form bonds of solidarity with those who are present, with each other. In effect, sacred place persists in modern landscapes and forms an emotional center.

Denis Cosgrove too addresses sacred place, but through a single image. He examines a promotional poster prepared by the Jesuit order on the five-hundredth anniversary of the birth of St. Ignatius. The image juxtaposes a silver statue of the saint and a famous photograph of the earth. In this combination Cosgrove finds a mixture of attitudes toward earth and our existence on it. On the one hand, the image is overtly imperialist in its association of Christianity with the whole world — a world rendered visible by Cold War space technology. On the other hand, the distant, celestial perspective of earth resonates with oneiric (dreamlike) texts, generating a sense of awe and humility in the face of a suprahuman scale. Domination and submission are fused in one image.

James S. Duncan and Nancy G. Duncan also explore connection between an image and dominance. The image they select is not visual but mental: a collective image of a New York suburb. Bedford is a place not only of care but also of discrimination. Its residents discriminate between "us" and "them" first in a theoretical sense, determining who we are and what "our place" is like, as opposed to them and "their places." Such distinctions, based on aesthetics and an imagined community, in turn provide justifications for exclusionary practices. Zoning laws are designed to keep out at least some of the prospective in-migrants who would threaten the inhabitants' nostalgic sense of place.

Karen E. Till explores similar issues — mental images, idealized sense of place, and the fabrication of community — in a very different context. She finds that the layout, interior design, and exhibits of a German history museum reveal worldviews that are doubly partial — partial (incomplete) in their interpretation of history and geography and partial (biased) in their political and social silences. The museum attempts to script a coherent picture of several pasts, but in so doing it favors certain pasts over others and imposes a judgment on past lives. Despite its air of authority, this museum and its exhibit are not the final word; observers reinterpret the scene's "museumspeak" according to their own experiences.

Dydia DeLyser also explores museumspeak and people's interpretations of it. Her interest is in the ghost town of Bodie, which has been preserved as an open-air museum by the state of California. In a state of arrested decay, and therefore quite unlike the original Bodie, this place nevertheless evokes a sense of the West that is instantly familiar. The idealized sense of place arises through the place's sounds, smells, and sights, although these are entirely unlike the sounds, smells, and sights of the thriving mining community that once existed here. By not trying to bring the place to life, it seems that the curators better stimulate the imagination of many of the viewers.

Imagination can connect people not only through time but also across cultural divides. Steven Hoelscher traces the origins of modern multiculturalism in the "provincial cosmopolitanism" of the 1930s and 1940s. This philosophy honors or idealizes ethnic cultural differences while simultaneously envisioning a harmonious and unified society forged from that diversity. Diversity is stripped of its ethnocentrism so that this unification becomes theoretically possible. While this assumption is subject to debate — and, indeed, rests on an unspoken "whiteness" — the popularity of provincial cosmopolitanism in its time, as well as its continuing influence, indicates that the ideal blending of ethnic hearth and societal cosmos is an important element of American ideology.

Cultural difference appeared not as a virtue but as a mark of inferiority in popular writings fifty years earlier. Jonathan M. Smith's study of the nineteenth-century historian Francis Parkman reveals a worldview that applied a single scale of values to all cultures. Parkman's philosophy maintained that "the highest morality is the most effective morality," meaning that history reveals the moral condition of populations through their geographic expansion or contraction. This view of history led to the belief that society should be governed by Anglo-Saxon men of the patrician class who had accentuated their best qualities — detachment, violence, and self-reliance — as indicated by their territorial expansion in the New World and by the struggle with "raw nature."

William Howarth provides a startling contrast with this worldview — a twentieth-century vision of geography and nature. Nature has something to teach in this later formulation, but the lesson is not toughness learned through dominance; now it is the recognition of limits on human action. Geography is, for Howarth, an act that puts "a mind to land to learn what it knows." What it "knows" is process: a bear paw print filling with water, observed on a walk in the forest, is a kind of natural time-piece, a "space marking time, a presence telling of a recent absence," and therefore a source of knowledge. As a benchmark of such knowledge, Howarth explores the change in attitudes toward wetlands.

A sense of place formed through careful attention is also of interest to Paul C. Adams. He argues that walking creates a specific sense of place unlike the senses of place formed by other ways of moving through space. He calls this sense of place "peripatetic" and argues that in Western culture peripatetic comes in two versions: an optimistic or "light" peripatetic and a pessimistic or "dark" peripatetic. Both light and dark forms assume that the walker is divorced from society, through either transcendence or exile; walking is seen as passing outside the bounds, being extravagant. Adams applauds discourses of the "New Urbanism" that break with this tradition and reveal the walker as not extravagant but practical, contributing in diverse ways to the common good and the possibility of community.

Patrick McGreevy joins Howarth and Adams to reveal yet another way in which one's type of attention produces a distinctive sense of place. In this case, attention is on "the void," the unknown or unknowable. When one pays close attention to a familiar object such as a tree, he suggests, one may confront the mysterious. Its growth and movement are too slow to capture with our normal perception of time, but with patience we can become aware of them as more than just abstractions. The void confronts geographers in many other guises, such as the enormity of geologic time that we try to understand and the various parts of the world that lie beyond our experience. McGreevy therefore recalls quite eloquently the enchantment of what J. K. Wright called "terrae incognitae," unknown worlds.

Edward Relph argues that terrae incognitae are not enchanting but confusing. Whereas modern landscapes were homogenized and made "placeless," postmodern landscapes are composed of buildings and activities in a scarcely intelligible jumble. Time-space compression and technological simulations work together to disguise causal connections, while scientific theories increasingly involve uncertainty, indeterminacy, relativity, subjectivity, and chaos. Relph fears that this confusion of landscapes and epistemologies diverts attention from real problems, such as global poverty and environmental change, but he does not advocate a return to the Grand Theory of a previous era. Rather, he recommends a heterogeneous approach: respect for the particularities of place, a critical and historical perspective, a questioning of appearances, and a sense of scientific balance and practicality.

The confused world is home to confused people, according to Wilbur Zelinsky. All of the traditional foundations of personal identity are now treated as choices or options: church, locality, nation, ethnicity, profession, consumption styles, sports, and voluntary associations. Consequently virtually all external forces shaping personal identity are growing weaker. Zelinsky believes that having the freedom to deliberately construct identity in a range of ways is a major source of "confusion and angst" leading to an identity crisis as indicated by the growing preoccupation with the word and concept of "identity."

Robert D. Sack reveals that even if one feels at home in confused geographies and enjoys constructing an identity, there still may be a problem with postmodernity — namely, a need to define the foundations of moral judgment. By making morals relative (a potential consequence of postmodern geographies and identities), confused geographies open the door for immoral actions. There must be some "ground" for moral choice, and Sack argues that this ground is place. Places can obscure local and distant effects or make them clear, and by doing so they contribute to moral or immoral actions. The best places support not only "instrumental" geographical judgments but also "intrinsic" geographic judgments — those judgments based on a clear and unbiased conception of the good.

Kenneth R. Olwig cautions against looking too hard for universal order, coherence, and absolutes — a project variously enjoined by Relph, Zelinsky, and Sack. In Olwig's view, the search for order entered geography with the demise of a mythical or metaphysical worldview and covertly perpetuated much the same assumption of coherence. From Olwig's perspective, it is wrong to adopt a single abstract system that supposedly explains the relations between here and there, us and them, self and other, even if it reduces our feeling of confusion about geographies and identities. It is better to accept as primary the particularity of places.

Edward S. Casey agrees that place deserves study; he finds, however, that place is not only particular but has certain regularly occurring elements: bodies and landscapes bound together by habitus, habitation, and idiolocalization. Place is constituted through habitation by selves, and selves are constituted by the places they inhabit. The two are interconnected not in the commonly recognized sense of reciprocal influence but in the more subtle sense that each is an ingredient of the other. Self, for Casey, is indicated not only by the memory's sense of continuity in time but also by the body's physical presence in place. This physical presence of the body animates Casey's sense of self, place, and landscape.

Michael Curry joins our imaginary debate at this juncture, linking identity to neither body nor mind, but to social relations and power. Using the notion of a "professional" as his point of departure, he traces the word's associations between place and authority. In the case of the university, Curry shows that the status of one group of professionals (professors) has changed because of the increased presence of other professionals (administrators) whose authority rests astride the boundary between the place (the university) and larger social systems (the market). In opposition to Zelinsky's view, he finds an identity crisis arising not from too many choices but from the domination of a unique place by a place-negating system.

April R. Veness agrees that identity is threatened in the university but points out that it is the students, not the professors, who face the greatest challenge in this environment. From matriculation to graduation, she observes, a grad student must trace a figurative path from hearth to cosmos. The social hierarchies of this environment, including gender relations and differentials in "positional capital," can generate a sense of crisis. Especially for a female student, the incorporation of environment within body and vice versa, as Casey illuminates, can create contradictions near the crisis level. The tension of moving from hearth to cosmos is exacerbated when there are ideological and philosophical differences, as there usually are, between students and their mentors, and when the place is aesthetically oppressive.

Gillian R. Overing and Marijane Osborn reveal how this experience of moving away from the familiar world might cause a woman to feel not only lost but out of place, bizarre, monstrous. In medieval Iceland femininity was symbolically opposed to wilderness, and most women were expected to remain rooted in place. When women wandered they therefore crossed social and symbolic, as well as physical, boundaries: they changed from beautiful to ugly, from good to wicked, and from nurturers to destroyers. For all of this transgression, these troll-like women were nonetheless prized at least in imagination. They became part of the landscape in the form of *beinakerling,* sometimes translated as "bone-crones," cairns where travelers would leave messages and ribald poetry. In effect, boundary-crossing women became tangible *places* in the wilderness, a hearth in the cosmos.

Tim Cresswell shows that not only women but men too could be portrayed as abnormal and freakish if they did not stay put. He argues that terms such as "tramp" and "vagrant" defined a certain set of spatial practices as deviant or abnormal. The name, social category, and rule system were invented more or less simultaneously, so that certain persons were thereby subject to punishment and exclusion from the sedentary community. At the same time, the economic causes of homelessness and unemployment were reinscribed as individual failings or genetic flaws. This disturbing observation joins with Overing and Osborn and Curry to reveal the way in which power relations are implicated in identity-formation and oppression. Contrary to Zelinsky's argument, these authors find that *insufficient* autonomy in the sphere of identity-formation (rather than too much autonomy) is the fundamental source of concern.

This insufficient autonomy, of course, arises from domination, and David Lowenthal argues that domination is unavoidable. It is an enduring facet of human-environment relations and also of interpersonal relations. We can love what we dominate, hate what we dominate, or emotionally distance ourselves from what we dominate; but we cannot cease entirely to dominate. As cultural norms have shifted from the acceptance of domination toward "contrition for past hegemonic misdeeds," we have become uncomfortable loving the subjects of our domination. Lowenthal questions this squeamishness about domination, since domination without affection implies objectification: we end up seeing people as animals and animals as machines. Like Sack and many of the other authors, he reminds us that the ground of moral action is awareness of the world.

For all their diversity, each chapter in some sense examines the textures of place. Place can be felt, like the weave of a cloth, yet we are, after all, part of that weave. So place is also something that we are. By dominating or being dominated, seeing and being seen, moving or staying in place, remembering or engaging in flights of nostalgic imagination, people experience the places they are making as separate, "out there," already made. Yet "the void" geographers attend to, as McGreevy puts it, includes a sense that our world is a symbolic construction held in a balance between many ideological forces.

As previously mentioned, the descriptions of the chapters above are not organized according to the structure of the book. In what is to follow, the reader will find a separate clustering of original essays that cohere around four major themes in Tuan's writing. Each part is introduced by a scholar who was asked to reflect on one or more of Tuan's grand themes. These part introductions, written by David Ley, John Paul Jones III, Anne Buttimer, and Yi-Fu Tuan, do not necessarily provide detailed descriptions of individual chapters in a given part but rather represent reflections, thought pieces, and musings about topics of inquiry that continue to be important in geography and the humanities more generally. We conclude this book with J. Nicholas Entrikin's chapter. It serves as a critical assessment of Yi-Fu Tuan's humanist project, and it points the way to further work in a renewed humanist geography.

Notes

1. For a discussion of this point in relation to skin and bodies, see Judith Butler's *Gender Trouble: Feminism and the Subversion of Identity,* 2d ed. (New York: Routledge, 1999).

2. A very similar kind of ordered complexity, and the human relation to it, has been used as a model of place by Robert Sack in *Place, Modernity, and the Consumer's World: A Relational Framework for Geographical Analysis* (Baltimore: Johns Hopkins University Press, 1992). See also Robert Sack, *Homo Geographicus: A Framework for Action, Awareness, and Moral Concern* (Baltimore: Johns Hopkins University Press, 1997).

3. Gilles Deleuze and Félix Guattari contrast the texture of different materials (comparing felt, for example, to a woven cloth) to discuss what they call smooth and striated space. See Deleuze and Guattari, "1440: The Smooth and the Striated," in *A Thousand Plateaus: Capitalism and Schizophrenia,* trans. Brian Massumi (Minneapolis: University of Minnesota Press, 1987), 474–500. Edward Casey has interpreted their discussion as a poststructuralist attempt to overcome the space/place dualism. Casey, "Giving a Face to Place in the Present: Bachelard, Foucault, Deleuze and Guattari, Derrida, Irigaray," in *The Fate of Place: A Philosophical History* (Berkeley: University of California Press, 1997), 285–330.

4. Yi-Fu Tuan, *Space and Place: The Perspective of Experience* (Minneapolis: University of Minnesota Press, 1977).

5. Yi-Fu Tuan, "Humanistic Geography," *Annals of the Association of American Geographers* 66 (1976): 266–76. More recently, Tuan has described his perspective as "systematic

humanistic geography." See Yi-Fu Tuan, *Who Am I? An Autobiography of Emotion, Mind, and Spirit* (Madison: University of Wisconsin Press, 1999).

6. There are a number of edited volumes that illustrate the range of humanistic geographical inquiry. See David Ley and Marwyn Samuels, eds., *Humanistic Geography: Prospects and Problems* (Chicago: Maroufa Press, 1978); Anne Buttimer and David Seamon, eds., *The Human Experience of Space and Place* (London: Croom Helm, 1980); Peter Gould and Gunnar Olsson, eds., *A Search for Common Ground* (London: Pion, 1982); Douglas Pocock, ed., *Humanistic Geography and Literature: Essays on the Experience of Place* (London: Croom Helm, 1982); David Seamon and Robert Mugerauer, eds., *Dwelling, Place, and Environment: Towards a Phenomenology of Person and World* (New York: Columbia University Press, 1989 [1985]); and Audrey Kobayashi and Suzanne Mackenzie, eds., *Remaking Human Geography* (Boston: Unwin Hyman, 1989). For two useful discussions about the history of humanistic geography see Paul Cloke, Chris Philo, and David Sadler, *Approaching Human Geography: An Introduction to Contemporary Theoretical Debates* (New York: Guilford, 1991), chap. 3; and Anne Buttimer, "Geography and Humanism in the Late Twentieth Century," in *Companion Encyclopedia of Geography: The Environment and Humankind,* ed. Ian Douglas, Richard Huggett, and Mike Robinson (London: Routledge, 1996), 837–59. For a spirited defense of humanism more generally, see Edmunds Bunkše, "Humanism: Wisdom of the Heart and Mind," in *Concepts in Human Geography,* ed. Carville Earle, Kent Mathewson, and Martin S. Kenzer (Lanham, Md.: Rowman and Littlefield, 1996), 355–81.

7. David Ley and Marwyn Samuels, "Epistemological Orientations," in Ley and Samuels, *Humanistic Geography,* 21.

8. Buttimer, "Geography and Humanism," 837.

9. J. K. Wright, "Terrae Incognitae: The Place of the Imagination in Geography," *Annals of the Association of American Geographers* 37 (1947): 1–15. It should also be mentioned that, as Mark Billinge pointed out, turgidity became the hallmark of more than one writer. Mark Billinge, "The Mandarin Dialect: An Essay on Style in Contemporary Geographical Writing," *Transactions of the Institute of British Geographers* 8 (1983): 400–420.

10. Yi-Fu Tuan, "Geography, Phenomenology, and the Study of Human Nature," *The Canadian Geographer* 15 (1971): 181–92. For a discussion of existentialism in geography and a "spatial ontology of man," see Marwyn Samuels, "Existentialism and Human Geography," in Ley and Samuels, *Humanistic Geography,* 22–40.

11. Anne Buttimer, "Grasping the Dynamism of the Lifeworld," *Annals of the Association of American Geographers* 66 (1976): 279.

12. Edward Relph, "Geographical Experiences and Being-in-the-World: The Phenomenological Origins of Geography," in Seamon and Mugerauer, *Dwelling, Place, and Environment,* 16.

13. David Ley, *The Black Inner City as Frontier Outpost: Images and Behavior of a Philadelphia Neighborhood,* Monograph Series no. 7 (Washington, D.C.: Association of American Geographers, 1974); and Ley, "Social Geography and the Taken for Granted World," *Transactions of the Institute for British Geographers* 2 (1977): 478–512.

14. Yi-Fu Tuan, personal conversation with Steven Hoelscher and Karen E. Till, Madison, Wisconsin, June 1998.

15. See J. Nicholas Entrikin, "Geographer as Humanist," in this volume; and Entrikin, "Blurred Boundaries: Humanism and Social Science in Historical Geography," *Historical Geography* 26 (1998): 93–100.

16. Trevor J. Barnes, "Hermeneutics," in *The Dictionary of Human Geography,* ed. Ronald J. Johnston et al. (Oxford: Blackwell, 2000), 334–36; Anne Buttimer, *Values in Geography,* Commission on College Geography, Resource Paper no. 24 (Washington, D.C.: Association of American Geographers, 1974); and Yi-Fu Tuan, *Topophilia: A Study of Environmental Perception, Attitudes, and Values* (Englewood Cliffs, N.J.: Prentice-Hall, 1974). For a brief, but useful, discussion of a convergence of hermeneutics with critical theory, see Cloke, Philo, and Sadler, *Approaching Human Geography,* 142–44.

17. Several geographers have called for a similar convergence. Trevor Barnes and Derek Gregory have defined "post-humanistic geography" in ways similar to what we propose, while Cloke, Philo, and Sadler have suggested a "geographical humanism" that "in various ways abandons the strait-jackets of pre-existing philosophical positions [of a narrowly conceived phenomenology and existentialism] to make its own distinctive contributions." Finally, Kay Anderson has described a vision of a "critical human geography" that explores "the lines of conceptual and methodological convergence among cultural, political economy, and feminist perspectives." Trevor Barnes and Derek Gregory, "Agents, Subjects, and Human Geography," in *Reading Human Geography: The Poetics and Politics of Inquiry*, ed. Trevor Barnes and Derek Gregory (London: Arnold, 1997), 356–63; Cloke, Philo, and Sadler, *Approaching Human Geography*, 81; and Kay Anderson, "Sites of Difference: Beyond a Cultural Politics of Race Polarity," in *Cities of Difference*, ed. Ruth Fincher and Jane Jacobs (New York: Guilford Press, 1998), 201–25. See also Anne Buttimer, *Geography and the Human Spirit* (Baltimore: Johns Hopkins University Press, 1993); and Kobayashi and Mackenzie, *Remaking Human Geography*.

18. Benjamin Forest, "Placing the Law in Geography," *Historical Geography* 28 (2000): 5–12. Forest draws heavily from an earlier discussion by Trevor Barnes and Michael Curry, "Towards a Contextualist Approach to Geographic Knowledge," *Transactions of the Institute of British Geographers*, n.s. 8 (1983): 467–82.

19. Women and Geography Study Group, *Geography and Gender: An Introduction to Feminist Geography* (London: Hutchinson, 1984), 34. See also Gillian Rose, *Feminism and Geography: The Limits to Geographical Knowledge* (Minneapolis: University of Minnesota Press, 1993).

20. Similarly, by the late 1980s increasing concerns were voiced over the arrogance of the attempt to provide an impersonal overview of personal experience, concerns that led some to abandon the humanist project. See Stephen Pile, "Human Agency and Human Geography Revisited: A Critique of 'New Models' of the Self," *Transactions of the Institute of British Geographers*, n.s. 18 (1993): 122–39; and Derek Gregory, "Human Agency and Human Geography," *Transactions of the Institute of British Geographers*, n.s. 6 (1981): 1–18. From a slightly different perspective, see Edward Relph, *Rational Landscapes and Humanistic Geography* (London: Croom Helm, 1981). For two philosophical and historical discussions of humanism more generally that include useful critiques, see David Ehrenfeld, *The Arrogance of Humanism* (New York: Oxford University Press, 1978); and Kate Soper, *Humanism and Anti-Humanism* (London: Hutchinson, 1983).

21. Jonathan M. Smith, "Geographical Rhetoric: Modes and Tropes of Appeal," *Annals of the Association of American Geographers* 86 (1996): 1–20. See also the very useful appraisal and call for greater attention to narrative in Stephen Daniels, "Arguments for a Humanistic Geography," in *The Future of Geography*, ed. R. J. Johnston (London: Methuen, 1985), 143–58.

22. Clifford Geertz, *Local Knowledge: Further Essays in Interpretative Anthropology* (New York: Basic Books, 1983). See also D. W. Meinig, "Geography as an Art," *Transactions of the Institute of British Geographers*, n.s. 8 (1983): 314–28.

23. John Agnew and James Duncan, eds., *The Power of Place: Bringing Together the Geographical and Sociological Imaginations* (Boston: Unwin Hyman, 1989); J. Nicholas Entrikin, *The Betweenness of Place: Towards a Geography of Modernity* (Baltimore: Johns Hopkins University Press, 1991); R. J. Johnston, *A Question of Place* (Oxford: Blackwell, 1991); Kay Anderson and Fay Gale, eds., *Inventing Places: Studies in Cultural Geography* (Melbourne: Longman, 1992); James Duncan and David Ley, eds., *Place/Culture/Representation* (London: Routledge, 1993); Michael Keith and Steve Pile, eds., *Place and the Politics of Identity* (London: Routledge, 1993); Doreen Massey, *Space, Place, and Gender* (Minneapolis: University of Minnesota Press, 1994); and Sack, *Homo Geographicus*. Of course, not everyone is enamored with the recent theoretical turn to place. Edward Soja, for example, explicitly eschews an interest in place as a concept, ar-

guing instead that Henri Lefebvre's important treatment of space subsumes any meaningful statements of place. Edward Soja, *Thirdspace* (Oxford: Blackwell, 1996), 40.

24. David M. Wrobel and Michael Steiner, eds., *Many Wests: Place, Culture, and Regional Identity* (Lawrence: University Press of Kansas, 1997); Wayne Franklin and Michael Steiner, "Taking Place: Toward the Regrounding of American Studies," in *Mapping American Culture,* ed. Wayne Franklin and Michael Steiner (Iowa City: University of Iowa Press, 1992), 3–23; R. Friedland, "Space, Place, and Modernity: The Geographical Moment," *Contemporary Sociology* 21 (1992): 11–15; Sharon Zukin, *Landscapes of Power: From Detroit to Disney World* (Berkeley: University of California Press, 1992), 12; M. C. Rodman, "Empowering Place: Multilocality and Multivocality," *American Anthropologist* 94 (1992): 640–56; Akhil Bupta and James Ferguson, eds., *Culture, Power, Place: Explorations in Critical Anthropology* (Durham, N.C.: Duke University Press, 1997); Edward S. Casey, *Getting Back into Place: Toward a Renewed Understanding of the Place-World* (Bloomington: Indiana University Press, 1993); and Shelley Fisher Fishkin, "The Matter of Hannibal," in *Lighting Out for the Territory: Reflections on Mark Twain in American Culture* (New York: Oxford University Press, 1996), 13–70. The National Endowment for the Humanities' 1999 Regionalism Initiative is only the most recent example of the rejuvenated interest in study of place. Mary Lou Beatty, "A Sense of Place: Regionalism," *Humanities Magazine* (July/August 1999): 1; and William R. Ferris, "A Sense of Place," *Humanities Magazine* (January/February 1998): n.p.

25. Richard Hartshorne, *The Nature of Geography: A Critical Survey of Current Thought in Light of the Past* (Lancaster, Pa.: Association of American Geographers, 1939), 428–31. This point is presented by a number of the essays in J. Nicholas Entrikin and Stanley Brunn, eds., *Reflections on Richard Hartshorne's "The Nature of Geography"* (Washington, D.C.: Association of American Geographers, 1989), but none more effectively than in Neil Smith, "Geography as Museum: Private History and Conservative Idealism," 89–120.

26. Edward Relph, *Place and Placelessness* (London: Pion, 1976), 43.

27. Stephen Daniels, "Place and the Geographical Imagination," *Geography* 77 (1992): 311.

28. This dichotomy may be explored by comparing two essays of this book, James S. Duncan and Nancy G. Duncan's "Sense of Place as a Positional Good" and Karal Ann Marling's "Fantasies in Dark Places."

29. Massey, *Space, Place, and Gender,* 121. See also Geraldine Pratt and Susan Hanson, "Geography and the Construction of Difference," *Gender, Place, and Culture* 1, no. 1 (1994): 5–29; and Linda McDowell, *Gender, Place, and Identity: Understanding Feminist Geographies* (Minneapolis: University of Minnesota Press, 1999). In a useful review article that echoes much of our earlier argument, Edward Relph describes these changes in the interpretations of place from the early 1970s to the late 1990s as the move from "phenomenological approaches to the critical analyses of political economy." Edward Relph, "Place," in *Companion Encyclopedia of Geography: The Environment and Humankind,* ed. Ian Douglas, Richard Huggett, and Mike Robinson (London: Routledge, 1996), 906.

30. Daniels, "Place and the Geographical Imagination," 311. See also J. Nicholas Entrikin, "Place and Region 2," *Progress in Human Geography* 20 (1996): 215–21.

31. James Howard Kunstler, *The Geography of Nowhere: The Rise and Decline of America's Man-made Landscape* (New York: Simon and Schuster, 1993); and William Leach, *Country of Exiles: The Destruction of Place in American Life* (New York: Pantheon, 1999). See also Tony Hiss, *The Experience of Place* (New York: Alfred A. Knopf, 1990). Foreshadowing writers like Kunstler, Mumford warned of America's permanent crisis of modernity, of an ever more "abstract and fragmentary" landscape that left Americans in the 1920s with "a blankness, a sterility, a boredom, a despair." Lewis Mumford, *The Golden Day* (Boston: Beacon, 1957 [1926]), 275, 281, 25, 80–81. A thoughtful interpretation of this catastrophist history may be found in John L. Thomas, "The Uses of Catastrophism: Lewis Mumford, Vernon L. Parrington, Van Wyck Brooks, and the End of American Regionalism," *American Quarterly* 42 (1990): 223–51.

32. Jonathan M. Smith, Andrew Light, and David Roberts, "Introduction: Philosophies and Geographies of Place," in *Philosophy and Geography III: Philosophies of Place*, ed. Andrew Light and Jonathan M. Smith (Lanham, Md.: Rowman and Littlefield, 1998), 1–19. For a concise statement of the New Urbanist design philosophy by the best known architect-planners, see Andres Duany, Elizabeth Plater-Zyberk, and Jeff Speck, *Suburban Nation: The Rise of Sprawl and the Decline of the American Dream* (New York: Farrar, Straus, and Giroux, 2000). Geographers, unlike developers, planners, and architects, have been mostly critical of neotraditionalism and New Urbanism, in part, for reasons we mention below. See, for example, Karen Till, "Neotraditional Towns and Urban Villages: The Cultural Production of a Geography of 'Otherness,'" *Environment and Planning D: Society and Space* 11 (1993): 709–32; and Eugene J. McCann, "Neotraditional Developments: The Anatomy of a New Urban Form," *Urban Geography* 16 (1995): 210–33.

33. David Harvey, "From Space to Place and Back Again: Reflections on the Condition of Postmodernity," in *Mapping the Futures: Local Cultures, Global Change,* ed. Jon Bird et al. (London: Routledge, 1993), 4. See also David Harvey, *The Condition of Postmodernity* (Oxford: Blackwell, 1989).

34. Harvey, *Condition of Postmodernity;* and Smith, Light, and Roberts, "Introduction."

35. Chris Philo and Gerry Kearns, "Culture, History, Capital: A Critical Introduction to the Selling of Places," in *Selling Places: The City as Cultural Capital, Past and Present,* ed. Gerry Kearns and Chris Philo (Oxford: Pergamon Press, 1993), 1–32; Kenneth T. Jackson, *Crabgrass Frontier: The Suburbanization of the United States* (New York: Oxford University Press, 1985); and Massey, *Space, Place, and Gender.*

36. Anthony Giddens, "Living in a Post-traditional Society," in *Reflexive Modernization: Politics, Tradition, and Aesthetics in the Modern Social Order,* ed. Ulrich Beck, Anthony Giddens, and Scott Lash (Stanford, Calif.: Stanford University Press, 1994), 59–106.

37. Tim Cresswell, *In Place/Out of Place: Geography, Ideology, and Transgression* (Minneapolis: University of Minnesota Press, 1996), 13.

38. Tuan, *Space and Place;* and Yi-Fu Tuan, *Segmented Worlds and Self: Group Life and Individual Consciousness* (Minneapolis: University of Minnesota Press, 1982). It should be noted that none of these questions could be addressed without returning human agency to human geography and by directly questioning productions of knowledge defined by a split between subject and object. David Ley, "Geography without Human Agency: A Humanistic Critique," in *Human Geography: An Essential Anthology,* ed. John Agnew, David N. Livingstone, and Alisdair Rogers (Oxford: Blackwell, 1996 [1980]), 192–210.

39. This point is made provocatively in Peter Taylor's nuanced discussion of Tuan's *Space and Place* in his recent Progress in Human Geography lecture. Peter J. Taylor, "Places, Spaces, and Macy's: Place-Space Tensions in the Political Geography of Modernities," *Progress in Human Geography* 23 (1999): 7–26. For a critique of the humanistic fascination with "home," see Rose, *Feminism and Geography.*

40. Benjamin Forest, "West Hollywood as Symbol: The Significance of Place in the Construction of a Gay Identity," *Environment and Planning D: Society and Space* 13 (1995): 133–57; Linda McDowell and Doreen Massey, "A Woman's Place?" in *Geography Matters!* ed. Doreen Massey and John Allen (Cambridge: Cambridge University Press, 1984), 128–47; and Susan J. Smith, "Bounding the Borders: Claiming Space and Making Place in Rural Scotland," *Transactions of the Institute of British Geographers* 18 (1993): 291–308. In *Homo Geographicus,* Sack puts the matter straightforwardly: "the formation of personality [is] directly connected to the formation of place" (131).

41. Benedict Anderson, *Imagined Communities: Reflections on the Origins and Spread of Nationalism,* rev. ed. (London: Verso, 1991).

42. John Agnew, "The Devaluation of Place in Social Science," in *The Power of Place: Bringing Together the Geographical and Sociological Imaginations,* ed. John Agnew and James Duncan (Boston: Unwin Hyman, 1989), 9–28; Daniels, "Place and the Geographical Imagination," 314.

43. Yi-Fu Tuan, "Place and Culture: Analeptic for Individuality and the World's Indiffer-

ence," in *Mapping American Culture,* ed. Wayne Franklin and Michael Steiner (Iowa City: University of Iowa Press, 1992), 27–49. This is the leitmotiv of Yi-Fu Tuan, *Cosmos and Hearth: A Cosmopolite's Viewpoint* (Minneapolis: University of Minnesota Press, 1996).

44. Massey, *Gender, Place, and Culture,* 168; Timothy Oakes, "Place and the Politics of Modernity," *Annals of the Association of American Geographers* 87 (1997): 509–31. This sense of place's paradoxical ability to be both progressive and reactionary is nicely captured in Jon May, "Globalization and the Politics of Place: Place and Identity in an Inner London Neighborhood," *Transactions of the Institute of British Geographers,* n.s. 21 (1996): 194–215.

45. Entrikin, *Betweenness of Place.*

46. See Yi-Fu Tuan, *Landscapes of Fear* (New York: Pantheon Books, 1979); Tuan, *Dominance and Affection: The Making of Pets* (New Haven, Conn.: Yale University Press, 1984); Tuan, *Segmented Worlds;* Tuan, *Morality and Imagination: Paradoxes of Progress* (Madison: University of Wisconsin Press, 1989); and Tuan, *Cosmos and Hearth.*

Part I

Landscapes of Dominance and Affection

INTRODUCTION

Landscapes of Dominance and Affection

David Ley

How to circumscribe the encyclopedic? How to contain the ocean of geographic imagination? These are the challenges that confront the writer foolish enough to arm wrestle with Yi-Fu Tuan's expansive mind and seek to submit it to some rules of convention and precedent. One solution, perhaps, is the solution of all travelers who engage complexity and difference: to domesticate the wild by imposing upon it personal experiences. Of course, as David Lowenthal reminds us, such a trope does not escape one of Tuan's own metaphors — that of the appropriation and domestication of nature.[1] But domestication need not require a hostile takeover. If we think of Tuan's dualism of dominance and affection, as he encourages us to do, not only as a dichotomy but also as a dialectic, then one may arm wrestle playfully with the other within the context of respect, not subordination.

There have been two formative moments in my own encounter with Tuan's work, the first as an undergraduate, the second as a graduate student in a very different intellectual environment. Yi-Fu Tuan was a visitor to the School of Geography at Oxford University in the mid-1960s, and I attended lectures he presented on the landforms of the semiarid ("seem-eye arid," as he memorably put it) southwestern United States. This identity as a physical geographer might raise some eyebrows now, but I was reminded of it as I read William Howarth's discussion of the physicality of sympathetic interpretations of place. In Tuan's slides and narrative we engaged nature not as an abstraction but physically and also sympathetically. The second moment came a few years later as a graduate student at Pennsylvania State University. Here in one of the epicenters of the spatial science revolution that invaded human geography in the 1970s, one encountered always cosmos but never home;[2] it was always winter but never Christmas, to borrow one of the famous laments from C. S. Lewis's account of the journey from home and back again in *The Lion, the Witch, and the Wardrobe*. Geography's own experiment with "rational, abstract, decentered knowledge" might have merited a page or two of discussion in Kenneth Olwig's essay, for in a heightened manner it represented the view of the cosmopolite and of course encouraged the emergence of a resistant humanistic geography with which Professor Tuan has been closely associated. Spatial science relegated the particular in favor of the universal, while its emphasis upon tools and methods was an exact copy of the traveler's dependence upon map and chronometer (Hadn't the ubiquitous Samuel Johnson observed that every traveler measures?) to chart the edges of the known world. This land of intellectual adventure and wide open horizons was thoroughly intoxicating. But in this promise of universality there was a crude reduction of geography, no longer areal differentiation but now in the isotropic plain, areal homogeneity, and also of people, who emerged with the alienated identity of automatons. Most of all this view was thoroughly decontextualized and shed no light at all upon the political and existential dilemmas of the late 1960s, with civil rights, the draft, Vietnam, and eco-catastrophe shaping the lifeworld of many American college students. In this respect, I well remember the pleasure, no, exhilaration, in discovering Tuan's short statement " 'Environment' and 'World' " not because in a few pages it could answer much but more because it posted a direction homeward, toward knowledge that was contextual and that treated people and place as knowledgeable and complex agents.[3]

There is an irony here, for Yi-Fu Tuan, the proclaimer of local knowledge, of the irrevocably humanized nature of places, is also Professor Tuan, renaissance man, global traveler, intercultural hybrid, in many respects the consummate cosmopolite. In this respect he shares the universality of the spatial scientist, for in his intercultural travels, assembling fragments of local knowledge and local cultures, his role is that of the cosmopolite intent to compile, to compare, to comprehend, and to assert the moral imperative that in the pursuit of space we should not forget place. And like a good scholar, he gives us in this role a message that is not maudlin, scarcely ever melancholy for the world we have lost.

Or have we lost it? Certainly confinement within rural parish boundaries is the fate of scarcely anyone today, but have we not re-created new *multilocale* parishes, each one defined by the cell walls of local knowledge? Political memoirs and corporate biographies both indicate the local and limited dimensions of apparently global knowledge, while work in the social construction of scientific knowledge makes the case that even the intellectual thought traveler belongs to his/her own tribe, which purveys special, not universal, knowledge. To claim more is a case of special conceit. If we accept these arguments, then indeed we should be seeing hearth and cosmos, dominance and affection, as more nearly dialectical than dichotomous pairings.

Karal Ann Marling has uncovered a rich site to locate that dialectic, for the movie palace was (and is) a rare liminal space where everyday life is suspended for a while in order to be reconstituted as a result of an encounter with the fantastic. We return home, if the spell has done its work, caught in the wonder of the possibilities of life away. We enjoy the artifice of departure and allow it to dominate our feelings. Some of us, captured by the clever manipulations of the blockbuster movie, must repeat the experience, and, as George Lucas has admitted, the bottom-line accounting of a megaproduction like the *Star Wars* prequel, *The Phantom Menace*, depends upon pilgrims for whom once is not enough. Marling skillfully demonstrates how the architecture of the movie palace was part of a conspiracy where flattery was the means to persuasion. The names, furnishings, and spectacle of the theater made every man a king and every woman a queen, notes Marling. To what extent has the silver screen accomplished its object of refashioning identity? Indeed we wonder: To what degree has Hollywood captured the imagination of America, especially in the early decades of the century, giving shape to a dream world that was to become the American myth of upward mobility to the status of, if not king or queen, then respected burgher? For the movie palace was a site where immigrants to American cities could congregate and learn the dimensions of public culture, what it meant to grow into American identity. An issue that is implicit but not quite explicit in Marling's account is the extent to which we are witnessing a society of the spectacle, not merely an intent to dominate but also its achievement.

From movie theater to ghost town is no small shift, even if both share a status as temporary sites of public attention. As Dydia DeLyser notes, the ghost town is also a place where projection can occur as the past is reconfigured for the purposes of the present. This, of course, as many authors have observed, is the typical fate of the past, to become an archive to be appropriated for contemporary consumption. In this respect the much-maligned appropriations of postmodern design are simply achieving what has been done often more covertly before, using a memory-bank to give meaning to the present. The past has always been a vast repository of present meaning for traditional peoples — recall the repeated call to religious hope and obedience in the Old Testament as the Israelites were reminded through object lessons of God's mercies in the past. The pages of the Jewish Bible are replete with "Ebenezers" (1 Samuel 7:12), monuments to aid memory and nurture belief. What meanings then are prompted by the ghost town? DeLyser's contact with visitors is informative here, for in the empty spaces, the missing buildings, of the old town site of Bodie, California, visitors effect closure through their own imagination. They bring their meanings with them, and thus the ghost town acts as a confirmation and consolidation of what is already known.

This symbiosis between place and identity was a geographical extrapolation of symbolic interactionism, an important theoretical position that holds that reality is social and is constructed and perpetuated through the routine interactions of everyday life. This position was persuasively outlined by James S. Duncan in a series of papers in the 1970s, where he added a consideration of place as an important node of identity construction in everyday life. In a celebrated account of the upper-class commuter settlement of Bedford Village, New York, he revealed how place consolidated the contours of a social world and a shared identity.[4] Returning to Bedford twenty-five years later, James S. and

Nancy G. Duncan add an additional layer of interpretation to the earlier account. They show that like the movie palace, all that glitters is not silver or gold. The dialectic of affection and domination is brought tightly together, for the love of place, Tuan's topophilia, is predicated in Bedford upon bad faith, a plan to control land use and exclude unwelcome potential residents. Those who do not belong to the elite representation of the place — the poor, the middle class, the nouveaux riches — are not welcome. This is not *their* place. One is reminded of Tuan's portrayal in *Topophilia* of the concentric circles of meaning enveloping the Chinese empire, from the Forbidden City, the holy of holies at the center, to the "zone of cultureless savagery" at the border regions.[5] From the perspective of the long-established residents of Bedford, the realm of unmentionable incivility has penetrated the heartland, and resistance is their response.

In an elegant essay, William Howarth locates a locale of affection where we might not at first expect to find it, in the wetlands beloved of romantics and, latterly, ecologists. His example is a reminder that place serves as a multiple reality and many different kinds of projects might find their realization in a particular site. Historically, wetlands were stigmatized with the symbolism of the swamp and were invariably the object of "land improvement." If there has been a rescue operation today, its motivations are not always transparent or altruistic, for districts like Bedford around large American cities have frequently taken advantage of environmental protection to check development and buttress exclusionary intents. An important point worthy of considerable discussion is Howarth's argument in favor of respecting the physicality of place in contrast to the metaphorical use of geography in literary studies and elsewhere, which he argues too often is instrumental rather than respectful in its appropriation of spatial idiom. Indeed he sees such uses as alienated, as the commodification of place in the land market, and to each he counters with Tuan's topophilia. The oppositional tones of dominance and affection are thus laid bare, though we should not remove the possibility of instrumental uses within romanticism as well; indeed Olwig's essay provides several examples.

David Lowenthal laid a secure foundation for the meanderings of the geographical imagination in his remarkable essay on the experiential basis of geographical epistemology.[6] One of the seminal essays of the past half-century, it argued for the role of experience and imagination in the shaping of geographical knowledge. Though a major inspiration came from psychology, rather than sociology (as favored by contemporary epistemologies), it was nevertheless a radical innovation. In "Making a Pet of Nature" Lowenthal writes a clever essay that once again goes against the flow. While Howarth takes a stance unambiguously on the side of landscape affection, Lowenthal's argument is that power has been unduly maligned. We cannot avoid the will to power, for even in the most environment-friendly scenarios the tyranny of the food chain ensures that dominance and hierarchy are celebrated at every meal. Taken too far, this line of thinking could lead to a fatalistic sociobiology, but at the same time Lowenthal is surely correct that it is an error to assume that power is only oppressive. State regulations limit the power of some for the well-being of many; the Christian faith, much to Nietzsche's distaste, is based on both the ideal and (in its founder) the model of voluntary servanthood, with power a means to service.

Kenneth Olwig undertakes an ambitious tour of modernity via the concept of landscape. The essay is more of a sketch, for the ideas and linkages the author pursues need a book-length manuscript to tease out fully. Olwig charts the Renaissance reworking of the Ptolemaic cosmology to a spatialized worldview. This transition is followed through philosophy and the idea of landscape in art and civil and political life. The story moves through the romantics and then to Jean Piaget's and Louis Althusser's contemporary structuralism, to end with a return via time-space geography to the geographical view of landscape. This disparate literature and set of topics are impressive in their range and boldness and warrant fuller development. What they share in common is a detached and abstract reason that forever is concerned with space and spatiality. Several critical authors have regarded the idea of landscape to be embedded within this horizontal cosmology, with its own politics of position, indeed with an epistemology of control, for a poststructural epistemology of suspicion cannot see beyond a critique of power in the landscape concept. But Yi-Fu Tuan has succeeded in broadening that project, writes Olwig, and recovering a view of place and landscape, too long obscured, as the spontaneous achievement of a people. This "recentering" of landscape rescues it from the alien appropriation of those bearers of the horizontal worldview, authority and the market, and reconstitutes landscape as an expression of collective human identity. These are seminal thoughts that require fuller exposition and that need to include the caveats raised earlier by the Duncans and Lowenthal, while sharing Howarth's point that categorical writing must incorporate the presence of dialectical concepts. Dominance and affection, cosmos and hearth, space and place are not simply oppositional but also evoke each other.

Notes

1. Yi-Fu Tuan, *Dominance and Affection: The Making of Pets* (New Haven, Conn.: Yale University Press, 1984).

2. Yi-Fu Tuan, *Cosmos and Hearth: A Cosmopolite's Viewpoint* (Minneapolis: University of Minnesota Press, 1996).

3. Yi-Fu Tuan, " 'Environment' and 'World,' " *Professional Geographer* 17 (1965): 6–8.

4. James S. Duncan, "Landscape Taste as a Symbol of Group Identity," *Geographical Review* 63 (1973): 334–55.

5. Yi-Fu Tuan, *Topophilia: A Study of Environmental Perception, Attitudes, and Values* (Englewood Cliffs, N.J.: Prentice-Hall, 1974).

6. David Lowenthal, "Geography, Experience, and Imagination: Towards a Geographical Epistemology," *Annals of the Association of American Geographers* 51 (1961): 241–60.

FANTASIES IN DARK PLACES

The Cultural Geography of the American Movie Palace

Karal Ann Marling

America's Main Streets once marched along in serviceable blocks of barber-shops, city halls, and cafés. The bank. The coal dealer. The dress shop and the gift shop. But in among the prosaic storefronts with their twin panes of plate glass and their modest gilt letters lurked something fantastic and wonder-ful, a gaudy adjective in a sentence full of workaday nouns and verbs. Call it Dreamland. Or Paradise. The Bijou. Fairyland. The Crystal. A name outlined in lights. A phrase to conjure with: a rare jewel of a place, the gateway to a land of magical escape (Figure 1). Inside, there was no Main Street. Suddenly, it was gone, all of it, as if a genie had sucked the world of deposit slips and blue plate specials and twice-a-month haircuts into his bottle, barbershop and all. Shazaam! That's what happened every Friday night at the Aladdin. The Garden of Allah. The Rivoli. The Tivoli. The local movie palace.

The name counted, even when words like Rivoli and Tivoli failed to con-nect themselves to specific European streets and pleasure gardens. The words sounded posh anyway, like the Lux and the Ritz. High-class: Peerless, Elite, Bon Ton, Ideal. In parts of the Midwest, to call a store or a picture show after New England or Boston suggested quality and a certain decorum. The Boston. Broadway and Roxy, on the other hand, alluded to New York City, the Great White Way, big-time show biz, and Samuel "Roxy" Rothafel, the high priest/manager of Gotham's most celebrated movie houses. A famous *New Yorker* cartoon from 1929 showed a little girl and her mother adrift in the stupendous lobby of a new Roxy, built along the lines of a make-believe palace. "Mama," asks the child in innocent wonderment, "does God live here?"[1]

Some date the beginning of the picture palace era to 1913 and the opening of Roxy's gold-and-velvet Regent in New York City, with an exterior loosely based on the Palace of the Doges in Venice. Whatever the legacy of the archi-tecture, the name clearly inspired the impresarios who applied a veneer of regal respectability and grandeur to the moviegoing experience of small-town Amer-ica for years thereafter: the Princess, the Monarch, the Majestic, the Queen, the Empress. In democratic America, the movies — and the places that showed them — were fit for kings and queens. "We sell tickets to theaters, not movies,"

Figure 1. The Bijou, Minneapolis, in 1948, one of many movie houses with fancy names. Photograph courtesy of Minneapolis Public Library, Minneapolis Collection.

said Marcus Loew of MGM, head of the largest of the movie palace empires of the 1920s and 1930s.[2]

After 1922 and the discovery of the tomb of King Tutankhamen, according to some accounts, Egyptomania touched off a wave of exoticism in moviehouse decor. Sid Grauman's Egyptian Theater on Hollywood Boulevard (it opened five weeks *before* Howard Carter found King Tut!)[3] was only the beginning. There would be Chinese and Spanish theaters, Persian and Hindu models, Dutch, Aztec, Mayan, and Gothic ones. The so-called exotics strongly resembled sets for the movies that played inside them. In 1916, while filming *Intolerance,* D. W. Griffith had erected a colossal re-creation of ancient Babylon on a bare lot at 4473 Sunset Drive in Hollywood, across the street from his Majestic Reliance Studio.[4] It sat there for more than three years, guarded by giant statues of elephants balanced on their hind legs, looming over a neighborhood of ordinary little houses like some bizarre, collective dream.

The real inspiration behind the exotics may have been showmen like Sid Grauman who proposed to let the moviegoer dwell within the fictional realm of the motion picture for as long as the matinee lasted. Austrian-born architect John Eberson, who worked in the West and the Midwest in the 1920s, had that notion in mind when he invented the atmospheric theater in 1922–23, at the Majestic in Houston. The interior of an atmospheric was decorated with columns and rooftops and foliage suggesting an outdoor setting. Instead of a conventional ceiling, electric stars twinkled overhead, and, thanks to a hidden Brenograph machine, clouds sailed by (Figure 2). The Brenograph cost $290, but it created Cloudland — stars and clouds and pure enchantment: "an acre of seats in a garden of dreams."[5] "We visualize and dream a magnificent amphitheater . . . in an Italian garden, in a Persian court, in a Spanish patio, or in a mystic Egyptian temple yard, all canopied by a soft moonlit sky," wrote Eberson, where "friendly stars twinkled and wisps of clouds drifted."[6] "Please do not turn on the clouds until the show starts," read a sign in the projection booth of the Paradise Theatre in Faribault, Minnesota. "Be sure the stars are turned off when leaving."[7]

To maintain an ample supply of props, Eberson opened his own plaster factory, the Michel Angelo Studios, which churned out urns and columns and copies of Donatello Davids and Venus de Milos. In his Loew's Paradise in the Bronx, the break in the scenery that revealed the screen was flanked by plaster versions of Michelangelo's Lorenzo and Guiliano de Medici from the Church of San Lorenzo in Florence. In sixteenth-century Florence, the pair had turned toward a likeness of the Blessed Virgin. In the Bronx, they seemed to be watching the film, along with the rest of the audience. The theater and the audience had somehow become a single entity, far from Main Street or Fordham Road. And both were part of the illusion that flickered on the screen. Fantasy and wonder were no longer the exclusive property of Medici princelings. As John Eberson wrote in 1929, in the heyday of the atmospherics and the exotics, "here we find ourselves today . . . building super-cinemas of enormous capacities, excelling in splendor, in luxury and in furnishings the most palatial homes of princes and crowned kings for and on behalf of His Excellency — the American Citizen."[8]

When one of the Vanderbilt's New York mansions was demolished in the 1920s, the interiors were salvaged by decorators from the Loew's chain. A massive glass chandelier from the house turned up in the lobby of Loew's State in Syracuse, New York, in 1928. A year earlier, its celebrated Oriental Room had been crated and shipped to Kansas City, where it was reassembled as the

Figure 2. Postcard view of an "atmospheric" theater, Tampa, Florida, built around 1926. Collection of the author.

ladies' lounge of the Midland Theater.[9] So the housewife enjoying a weekday matinee became American millionaire royalty — for the duration of the show in Kansas City. A 1929 article in the *New Republic* followed milady to the pictures. That evening, she would probably be peeling onions at the kitchen sink. But this afternoon, for a few hours,

> she strolls voluptuously through lobbies and foyers that open into one another like a maze; her feet sink into soft rugs.... She enjoys the sense of leading a sophisticated, continental life with none of the practical risks. For she sees church members and respectable householders savoring the same delights about her.... She bathes in elegance and dignity; she satisfies her yearning for a "cultured" atmosphere.... The royal favor of democracy it is: for in the "de luxe" house, every man is a king and every woman a queen.[10]

The Architecture of Escapism

Movie houses had not always been so elegant.[11] Legend has it that the first commercial showing of a motion picture in the United States took place on a simple canvas screen hung in Koster and Bial's Music Hall in New York's Herald Square on April 23, 1896.[12] On the same bill were a Russian clown, an "eccentric dancer named Cora Caselli, and the Three Delevines." The film selections, projected on an Edison Vitascope, included *Kaiser Wilhelm Reviewing His Troops, Sea Waves,* and *Burlesque Boxing.* In vaudeville theaters, silent films would later be used during the lulls in the program when the audience was likely to be finding a seat or heading for the exits. At Koster and Bial's there was a formal, ten-minute intermission instead: Dr. Leo Summer's Blue Hungarian Band entertained the crowd with a selection of light classics.[13]

But movies, not vaudeville acts, were the new mechanical marvels of the age; audiences found themselves mesmerized by simple, repetitive movements, like the action of waves on the shore or a shot of crowds passing by outside the music hall. Silent movies were profoundly democratic, too. No education in the finer points of drama was needed, for example, to appreciate the 1896 sensation *The Kiss.* "For the first time in the history of the world," wrote the New York *Evening World,* "it is possible to see what a kiss looks like."[14] The movie offered a chaste enough depiction of the deed, but when viewed at huge size in a public place, the subject matter struck many critics as dangerous. Or perhaps the danger emanated from the nickelodeon, the dank, smelly storefront theater that catered to the working-class relish for the movies.

During the tide of "nickel madness," which receded around the time Roxy's Regent Theater was built, there were ten thousand nickelodeons in operation across the country — six hundred in New York City alone, mostly on the fringes of tenement neighborhoods. They were housed in rented storefront spaces, rarely larger than twenty-five by fifty feet. Inside, the "nicks" were more crowded, more intimate than any other public spaces of the period. Chairs were packed densely together facing a makeshift screen. Ventilation was poor. The room was hot. Since the price of admission was only five cents, rowdies often disrupted the show. Guardians of civic morals feared for the virtue of females who frequented such dens of iniquity. "Many liberties are taken with young girls within the theater when the place is in total or semidarkness," noted a report of the Chicago Vice Commission.[15]

The requisite darkness was achieved by removing the glass show windows, pushing the entry wall back a few feet to create a kind of sidewalk lobby, and replacing the old facade with a theater front. By 1908, Sears and Roebuck was selling pressed-tin fronts for mail-order delivery, convinced that the five-cent theater was a potential bonanza for the small-time entrepreneur. "The low price of admission," according to the catalog, "is an inducement which many people cannot resist."[16] Nor could they resist the electric lights that screwed into the tin front to spell out the evocative name of the nickelodeon. Bulbs outlined the ersatz arches and columns that lent the building a certain cut-rate elegance. Artificial light spilled out onto the sidewalk, making the street itself a part of the theater and the motion picture show. If the tiny auditorium inside was the darkest, most crowded place the average moviegoer was apt to encounter, then the sidewalk outside was surely the brightest, in a world still dominated by nature's clock. Only Coney Island, the circus, and the midway at the state fair sparkled in the nighttime gloom with such artificial gaiety. Electric lights were another modern wonder almost as entrancing as the movies themselves.

Some larger nickelodeons had fancy glass staircases at the entrance with running water and colored lights under the steps. Some were surmounted by giant metal statues of angels whose wings fluttered open when a switch was pulled. Builders' catalogs offered an eclectic assortment of cast terra cotta decorations glazed in brilliant color, specifically for use on storefront picture parlors. "A theater is its own best advertisement," noted a trade journal for exhibitors in 1905. "A picturesque and pleasing exterior, abundantly illuminated with multitudes of incandescent lights, constitutes advertising of the first order."[17] Out on the sidewalk, in the vestibule created behind the building line, the ticket window often separated itself from the facade in the form of a little column or pier that stood halfway between drab reality and glittering illusion. The box office became a familiar symbol in its own right, like a barber pole: here, under the fairyland lights — for only a nickel — was where the magic really began.

Around 1915, the movies lost their dangerous edge as well as their reputation as "the poor man's show."[18] It may well be, as some historians of film culture have recently argued, that white-collar workers had been going to nickelodeons all along.[19] But certain key events encouraged greater middle-class patronage. The medium clearly had narrative possibilities beyond the random snippets of action so often featured in nickelodeons: in 1912, Adolph Zukor leased a legitimate theater in New York for a showing of a multireel version of *Queen Elizabeth,* with Sarah Bernhardt reprising her famous stage role.[20] *Queen Elizabeth* was produced in France, but D. W. Griffith's American-made *Birth of a Nation* of 1915 was a huge hit as well and established the long, complex epic as a genre suitable for the attention of respectable people. Zukor charged one dollar for *Queen Elizabeth,* suggesting that this was no fifty-cent diversion, either. You got what you paid for.

The rise of film stars also encouraged wider movie patronage. In contrast to the anonymous figures who kissed or boxed on the screens of the nickelodeons, stars were real people with names — often romantic made-up names, to be sure — and personalities, and they appeared in a variety of roles. Public fascination with individual players was heightened by the practice of watching the actors perform in the dark and on a scale that lent them a larger-than-life stature. Movie stars became as familiar to members of the audience as their own intimate acquaintances. This new class of fans — mostly women — created a demand for new products featuring their favorites and for new, well-appointed moviegoing venues, like Roxy Rothafel's plush Regent Theater, north of Central Park, designed by Thomas W. Lamb, the inventor of the Ruritanian regal style. The era of the movie palace began in earnest.

An architect, writing in a major professional journal in 1925, recalled the day not so long ago "when it was considered degrading to attend the so-called 'movie shows....' Frequently the exteriors were adorned after the manner of a sideshow at a circus; and in the interiors the seats were arranged much as they would be in a slum mission, with flat floor and little or no ventilation."[21] But a commentator attending the opening of the opulent Regent found "an environment so pleasing, so perfect in artistic detail, that it seems as if the setting were a requisite to the pictures, that to an educated audience the two should, and must hereafter, go together."[22] The *New York Times* compared the gala opening of Roxy's New York Strand in 1914 — an establishment so grand that patrons were invited to send postcards to their friends bearing pictures of the gilded proscenium and the box seats surmounted by vast swags of drapery — to "a Presidential reception, a first night at the opera."[23] And all for twenty-five cents.

The palace era, the golden age of Hollywood, lasted until 1932, the low point in the Great Depression, when the decline in box office revenues could no longer be ignored. But from the late 1920s through 1946 — Hollywood's best pre-TV year — a new generation of movie-house architects was already producing streamlined palaces whose sleek curves, corner towers, clean lines, and dazzling white surfaces evoked the future as forcibly as Lamb's hard-tops (theaters with cloudless ceilings) had summoned up the glories of a vanished monarchy and Eberson's atmospherics had recalled the courtyards of some exotic paradise. Art Deco swept the nation, along with the talkies, in 1927. An architect from Los Angeles, S. Charles Lee, who had apprenticed with Rapp

Figure 3. An Art Deco movie palace, 1935: the elegant Westgate at Forty-fifth Street and France Avenue in exurban Minneapolis. It was described by the newspapers of the day as the "latest in contemporary construction and design." Photograph courtesy of Minneapolis Public Library, Minneapolis Collection.

& Rapp, the Chicago-based firm of palace builders, was a leader in the shift toward a simplified, airplane-age format in the Deco-Art Moderne style (Figure 3). But Lee was also a showman who understood what the American movie palace was all about, regardless of its changeable decor. "The show starts on the sidewalk," Lee declared.[24] In other words, the building is part of the show. As actor-dancer Gene Kelly, one of Hollywood's greatest stars, once remarked, "I can remember a time when where we went to the movies was just as important as the movies we went to see."[25]

The show began with the marquee, a canopy of tracer and chaser lights, of electric zigzags and curlicues suspended over the sidewalk to dazzle the passerby and announce the name of the theater. Sometimes, the name simply restated the street address at hyperbolic size or alluded to a local landmark of an earlier day: the Main, the Division, the Alabama, the Lyceum. The nomenclature confirmed the fact that the movie theater, with its splashy marquee, was making a bid to become a significant part of the fabric of the city. Unlike other nearby structures that aligned themselves with one another in modest rows, the movie palace surged out into the public space of the streetscape and claimed it noisily for its own with a marquee that pulsated and blinked and spelled out the title of the evening's attraction.

Even in broad daylight, the bulbs stayed lit on the theater's crown jewel, the terrazzo flooring gleamed, and the playbills beckoned the passerby toward the delights of the dim lobby spaces just out of sight, behind glass doors. Like the old nickelodeon, the facade of the movie palace was a tantalizing prelude to the show. But the marquee was more than a piece of flashy scenery. A roof, a sheltering room-on-the-sidewalk, a trademark, a signboard, a liminal threshold to a realm of pleasure and dreams, it also identified a place on Main Street where the ordinary rules of commerce had been suspended, and anything could happen. The stretch of Main Street under the big, cantilevered marquee — and that oasis alone — was glamorous, sophisticated, and wickedly wonderful. "With a flood of... light to blaze the trail to the theater through many blocks," one of Rapp & Rapp's house architects insisted, "the entrance must be compelling, it must be inviting, and it must overshadow everything in the immediate neighborhood. It must actually be a magnet to draw the people on foot and in vehicles to its door."[26]

Movie palaces mated the marquee with the upright — a huge vertical sign, sixty or seventy feet tall, that lifted the eye above the level of the run-of-the-mill commercial establishment (Figure 4). Novelist Meyer Levin, in *The Old Bunch,* described the surprise of stumbling upon a new upright: "As [they] turned into State Street, the Chicago sign blazed at them. Boy, was that a sign! It made daylight of the whole block. Eight stories high. Three thousand bulbs spelled CHICAGO!"[27] The size alone suggested dominance and control of the community, as the spire of a great cathedral expresses dominion over the square below it. Some exuberant promoters called the movie palaces of the 1920s and 1930s "Cathedrals of the Screen," and with good reason.[28] Once inside, the moviegoer, like the prayerful pilgrim, was cut off from the mundane cares of the world. The light was dim, or softly colored (to hide imperfections and distort spatial perception). The sound hushed. The mood, in the presence of Mrs. Vanderbilt's chandelier or some vast pseudo-throneroom appointed in the manner of Louis XVI, solemn and mysterious.

A processional path led by slow, incremental degrees through an endless series of lobbies, corridors, staircases, and anterooms to the movie screen. That passage from street to red plush seat took the form of a participatory ritual controlled by space and decor. The flamboyant appointments of the lobby and the frequent changes of floor level, said one designer, were all planned "to keep the patron's mind off the fact that he is waiting."[29] Staircases with low steps supported on mighty columns of fake marble, called "scagliola," led toward inviting vistas and the ascent to remote balcony seats moviegoers might otherwise have declined to make. There was an element of surprise within the theater, as dim rooms alternated with fitfully illuminated ones, and chambers with low ceilings opened into yawning rotundas: the building unfolded by degrees like a mystery novel or a good movie. The experience of "going to the movies" in an old-time palace was at least as interesting as what finally appeared on the screen.

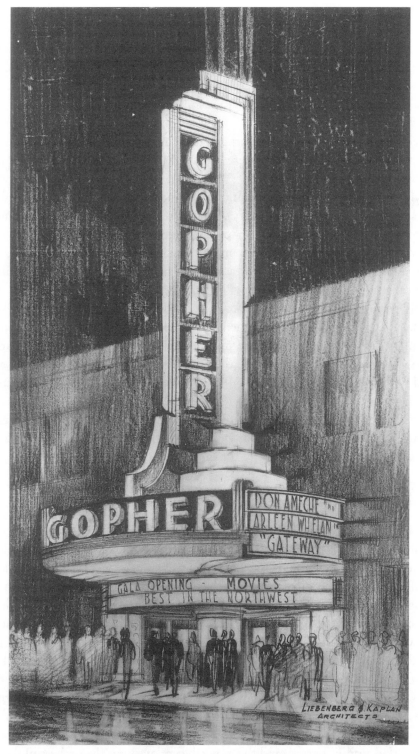

Figure 4. An "upright," or tall electric sign, proposed for the facade of the Gopher, Minneapolis, 1938. Photograph courtesy of Minneapolis Public Library, Minneapolis Collections.

The architects knew exactly what they were doing. Beaux Arts trained in many cases, they were rationalists as well as superb copyists of period detail. And so they calculated the effect of each section of the plan on the potential user: form followed function, and that function was to lull the audience into the proper mood. Thomas Lamb, describing his Loew's State Theater in Syracuse, was forthright in revealing the relationship between architectural cause and psychological effect. "The Grand Foyer is like a temple of gold set with colored jewels," he wrote. "These exotic ornaments, colors, and scenes are particularly effective in creating an atmosphere in which the mind is free to frolic and become receptive to entertainment."[30]

Movie palaces provided amenities the modern world seldom allotted to housewives, clerks, and traveling salesmen. In the men's and ladies' lounges, uniformed attendants offered fresh towels. Ushers in gold braid bowed deferentially, as though the customer were movie royalty, like Mary Pickford or Doug Fairbanks. The movie palace was a classless place — or rather, the trappings of wealth and fame were yours for the taking. Fountains tinkled. The air was subtly perfumed. Organ music wafted out of the auditorium. The carpets were thicker than those at home and the chairs softer. In the 1920s, the first functional air conditioning units were installed in urban theaters in hot-weather cities. The movie palace catered to the sensual desires of people who had only read about such pleasures in the *Saturday Evening Post*. No wonder Charles Lee believed that he was building Chartres and Notre Dame every time he opened a new picture palace. "Like the cathedral," he concluded, "the motion picture [theater] gave people what was missing from their daily lives: religion, solace, art, and most importantly, a feeling of importance."[31]

The Movies in the Movies

But it didn't take an official, full-blown, five-thousand-seat movie palace to produce mingled sensations of guilty enjoyment and awe in the ticket-holder. Although the number and size of the antechambers were greatly reduced, smaller houses — minipalaces, like the neighborhood Rex or the Royal — pleased patrons with a similar variety of experiential adventures. The flashing marquee. The ticket window. The outside vestibule with framed posters, showing coming attractions. A cool, darkish lobby where, with the onset of the depression, popcorn and candy were sold for the first time; the profits kept the old marquee lit, and the smells were grand. Then a ziggurat or two, perhaps, in gilded plaster. And finally, the theater proper: the curtain, the screen, side aisles that glowed with green and pink light puddled in sconces shaped like giant seashells or rare golden vessels fit for a king. The houselights went down, the curtains parted, and the movie began, without the orchestral themes and the showgirl preludes common in big-city palaces. But there in the dark, in Roxies and Luxes and Royals everywhere, an ephemeral community took shape as the images flickered across the screen. Because somebody else was sitting nearby, in the dark — some anonymous somebody — it was all right to laugh or to weep, to try out the emotions simulated by the actors in a make-believe world that existed inside the strange, special, make-believe world of the movie palace. It was even better, of course, if your best fella was in the next seat and those seats were in the last row of the balcony.

In his 1971 movie, *The Last Picture Show,* director Peter Bogdanovich used the community of teenagers assembled in the Royal Theater on the windswept Main Street of Anarene, Texas (pop. 1131), as a metaphor for the dying town. When the picture show closes down, after one last showing of *Red River* (1948), so does the story of the young friends and their mentor, Sam the Lion, who once owned the Royal. In the beginning of the film, the Royal is the only building left on Main Street that shows signs of life; when the marquee flickers out, at the end of the movie, so does Anarene. But the theater and the movies shown there pervade the life of the town in other ways. As *The Last Picture Show* opens, the cast is seated in the balcony of the Royal, necking and watching *Father of the Bride* (1950). The movie they watch sets the temporal limits for the story of Anarene, but it also comments on the courtship rituals being enacted on the other side of the screen. What Anarene knows of life comes straight from Hollywood and a picture-perfect vision of love that, because it fails to square with the realities of small-town lust, makes real life seem inauthentic and wrong.

At the end of *The Last Picture Show,* two boyhood friends first seen in the balcony watching *Father of the Bride* come back to the Royal for the final show. The movie is a John Wayne western: *Red River* (1948). But what we and the boys see, masquerading as the end of that picture, is really a scene from the beginning, with Wayne's cowhands setting out on their disastrous cattle drive, happy and whooping for joy. Bogdanovich has edited *Red River* to create a happy Hollywood ending, in an ironic commentary on the subtle interplay between movie make-believe and life on the dusty Texas street outside the Royal. The movement initiated at the marquee moves in two directions: inward, toward the darkness of filmic fantasy, and out again, into the pallid daylight of Main Streets everywhere.

In the 1966 novel of the same name that provided the story for *The Last Picture Show,* Larry McMurtry is even more specific about the tense dialectic between the movie theater and the street. The town whore fails to measure up to Elizabeth Taylor. The town beauty must be the star of every personal encounter.[32] Sonny and Charlene, necking in the balcony, each imagine the other to be one of the stars of the evening's feature. Sonny is less interested in Charlene than he is in the prospect that Ginger Rogers may take her clothes off in the next reel, as the poster outside suggested. And Charlene is indifferent to Sonny's fumbling advances until she tells herself that he "looked a little bit like Steve Cochran."[33] She only enjoys the kissing and petting in the picture show, where it is possible to replace Sonny with the black-and-white image of Steve, starring in *Storm Warning,* visible over her boyfriend's sweaty right shoulder. "The movies," writes McMurtry, "were Charlene's life."[34]

The plot lines of *The Purple Rose of Cairo* (1985) and *Last Action Hero* (1993) take up the themes of inside and out, daylight and darkness, illusion and reality. In Woody Allen's *Purple Rose,* Cecilia spends so much time at the local theater, evading an impoverished life and a brutal husband, that the star of "The Purple Rose of Cairo" departs from the script and speaks directly to her. "My God," Tom Baxter intones, "[y]ou must really love this picture.... You've been here...all day and I've seen you twice before."[35] And, as the audience gasps, Tom walks out of the screen and into the theater, bent on changing Cecilia's life. In *Last Action Hero,* a lonely boy spends most of his time in the Pandora, a tottering movie palace marked for replacement with a "Loew's 10" multiplex. Thanks to a magic ticket, Danny is able to pop through the screen, into the fictional world of action hero Jack Slater, and back again. But the real focus of the film is on the Pandora itself as a sort of two-way mirror or revolving door, shuttling the viewer between the twin miseries of the streets and movie violence. Danny thinks "the world stinks." But so, as it turns out, does Slater's two-dimensional universe. Pandora's box is full of woes. The villain likes the mean streets outside the Pandora's darkened marquee: "Here, in this world," he cries, "the bad guys can win!" Slater knows that to sustain the cinematic illusion — good will *always* triumph over evil — he needs somebody out there, sitting in the dark, watching and believing in him.

The edgy relationship between real life and the movies — including the theater that creates the magic aura surrounding the movie — is a favorite Hollywood theme. Sometimes the connections between film and place are perfectly straightforward: in the Gene Kelly musical *Singin' in the Rain* (1952), the movie-musical-within-a-movie premieres at Grauman's Chinese Theater (1927) because its forecourt, full of movie-star handprints and klieg lights, projects the stereotypical image of just what a Hollywood premiere ought to look like. Through its own historic service as a site of self-congratulation for the movie colony, the Chinese Theater has become a cliché that stands for the glamour, tinsel, and make-believe both celebrated and undercut in Kelly's film. *Jimmy Hollywood* (1994), directed by Barry Levinson, uses the corner of Hollywood and Vine, the marquee and upright of the El Capitan (1926), and the ruinous interior of Grauman's Egyptian Theater (1922) as the background to the story of a former siding salesman and would-be actor whose life unravels as he aspires to a fictional glamour that probably existed only within the walls of the old theaters he admires.

In *Matinee* (1993), the premiere of a horror movie takes place in the Strand, a crumbling neighborhood theater in Key West, Florida, at the height of the Cuban Missile Crisis. As the city poises itself for nuclear annihilation, enthusiastic local kids and dramatic sci-fi sound effects ("Atomo-Vision") almost destroy the Strand. When the balcony begins to collapse at the climax of the movie, the manager heads for his fall-out shelter, convinced that the Russians have attacked and the end is at hand. In *Gremlins* (1984), destructive creatures loosed on the Main Street of the idyllic town of Kingston Falls are finally thwarted when they gather in the Colony to watch *Snow White and the Seven Dwarfs* on Christmas Eve. On TV sets all over town, meanwhile, viewers see Jimmy Stewart, as George Bailey in *It's a Wonderful Life* (1946), stumbling through the streets of Bedford Falls on Christmas Eve and looking up at the marquee of the Bijou, where *The Bells of St. Mary's* is the holiday feature. In both cases, there will be a happy ending. Saved by his guardian angel, Bailey goes home — and his little girl tells him that every time a bell rings, an angel gets his wings. In Kingston Falls, the Gremlins are vanquished, and folks go back to watching old sci-fi movies on late-night television.

The old lady who inherits the little movie palace in Anarene, Texas, tells her last customers that television did in the Royal: "It's kid baseball in the summer and school in the winter. Television all the time. Nobody wants to come to shows no more."[36] In *Gremlins, The Last Picture Show,* and any number of Hollywood films made since the 1950s, old movies on TV sets act as a kind of Greek chorus, commenting on the action and warning the protagonists of dangers ahead. Yet nobody pays the slightest attention. The movies aren't real on the little screen. They aren't real without the popcorn, the usher in tarnished braid, the balcony, the bright lights outside, the old lady in the box office. Mysterious hallways and staircases. Statues peering through the gloom. The darkened auditorium with the scratchy old seats and other people, sitting there in the dark, too, crying, laughing, rigid with fear, wriggling for joy.

It's not the same at the multiplex, in a bare little screening room where everybody acts as if they're back home, talking and fooling around in front of the television. It's not the same at the drive-in, with kids in pajamas piled up in the back seat.[37] It's just not the same. You're not a king or a queen any more at the General Cinema Mall of America fourteen-plex or the Hopkins Cinema six-plex. It takes a Roxy or a Strand or a Royal, a Bijou, a Pandora to set the stage for the movie magic described by novelist John Updike: "the instant when the orange side lights, Babylonian in design, were still lit...the curtain was closed...[and] the camera had started to whir...that delicate promissory whir."[38] Without the Rivoli, the Strand, and the Lux, Main Street seems smaller, older, dingier, smaller. Diminished, somehow. As though, when Dreamland was torn down, part of the American Dream was left behind, buried in the rubble.

Notes

1. Quoted in David Nassaw, *Going Out: The Rise and Fall of Public Amusements* (New York: Basic Books, 1993), 227.

2. Quoted in John Margolies and Emily Gwathmey, *Ticket to Paradise: American Movie Theaters and How We Had Fun* (Boston: Little, Brown, 1991), 17.

3. Noted in *Grauman's Metropolitan Theatre* (Los Angeles: Los Angeles Theatre Historical Society of America, 1996), 31.

4. See illustration in Bruce T. Torrence, *Hollywood: The First Hundred Years* (New York: Zoetrope, 1982), 73.

5. Ben Hall, quoted in John C. Lindsay, *Turn Out the Stars before Leaving* (Erin, Ontario: Boston Mills Press, 1983), 45.

6. Quoted in Charlotte Kopac Herzog, "The Motion Picture Theater and Film Exhibition, 1896–1932" (Ph.D. diss., Northwestern University, 1980), 119.

7. Quoted in Maggie Valentine, *The Show Starts on the Sidewalk: An Architectural History of the Movie Theatre* (New Haven, Conn.: Yale University Press, 1994), 75.

8. Quoted in ibid., 34.

9. David Naylor, *American Picture Palaces: The Architecture of Fantasy* (New York: Van Nostrand, 1981), 38.

10. Quoted in Nassaw, *Going Out*, 239.

11. I have used the word *escapism* in the section title. The trip to Disneyland described in the preface to Yi-Fu Tuan's *Escapism* (Baltimore: Johns Hopkins University Press, 1998) was made at my request. This joint adventure was a prelude to a major exhibition on theme park architecture for which I was curator and for which Tuan wrote one of the catalog essays. But the inspiration for that project came from Professor Tuan in the first place — from his ongoing speculations on the relationship between place and human emotion, a subject to which I return here. My intellectual debt to Tuan remains enormous.

12. Herbert Scherer, *Marquee on Main Street: Jack Liebenberg's Movie Theaters, 1928–1941* (Minneapolis: University of Minnesota Art Gallery, 1982), 14.

13. The program is described in Lindsay, *Turn Out the Stars*, 7–9.

14. Quoted in Lewis A. Erenberg, *Steppin' Out: New York Nightlife and the Transformation of American Culture, 1890–1930* (New York: Greenwood Press, 1981), 70.

15. Quoted in Nassaw, *Going Out*, 181.

16. Quoted in Kathryn H. Fuller, *At the Picture Show: Small-Town Audiences and the Creation of Fan Culture* (Washington, D.C.: Smithsonian Institution Press, 1996), 24.

17. Quoted in Fuller, *At the Picture Show*, 56.

18. Quoted in Richard Charles Vincent, "The Cinema and the City: An Analysis of Motion Picture Theater Location in Selected U.S. Urban Areas" (Ph.D. diss., University of Massachusetts, 1983), 17. See also Robert Sklar, *Movie-Made America: A Cultural History of American Movies* (New York: Vintage, 1976), 16ff.

19. For a summary of recent literature, see Gregory A. Waller, *Main Street Amusements: Movies and Commercial Entertainment in a Southern City, 1896–1930* (Washington, D.C.: Smithsonian Institution Press, 1995), xvi–xvii.

20. Margolies and Gwathmey, *Ticket to Paradise*, 14.

21. Quoted in Carla Breeze, *L.A. Deco* (New York: Rizzoli, 1991), 14.

22. Quoted in Joseph M. Valerio and Daniel Friedman, *Movie Palaces: Renaissance and Reuse* (New York: Academy for Educational Development, 1982), 15.

23. Quoted in ibid., 20.

24. Quoted in Valentine, *The Show Starts on the Sidewalk*, 9.

25. Gene Kelly, foreword to David Naylor, *Great American Movie Theaters* (Washington, D.C.: Preservation Press, 1987), 9.

26. Quoted in Herzog, "The Motion Picture Theater," 91.

27. Quoted in Douglas Gomery, *Shared Pleasures: A History of Movie Presentation in the United States* (Madison: University of Wisconsin Press, 1992), 47.

28. Quoted in Herzog, "The Motion Picture Theater," 128.

29. Quoted in Naylor, *American Picture Palaces*, 26; and Naylor, *Great American Movie Theaters*, 18.

30. Quoted in Valentine, *The Show Starts on the Sidewalk*, 39.

31. Quoted in ibid., 65.

32. Roger Walton Jones, *Larry McMurtry and the Victorian Novel* (College Station: Texas A & M University Press, 1994), 98.

33. Larry McMurtry, *The Last Picture Show* (New York: Simon and Schuster, 1989), 18.

34. Ibid.

35. Quoted in Christopher Ames, *Movies about Movies: Hollywood Reflected* (Lexington: University of Kentucky Press, 1997), 128.

36. McMurtry, *The Last Picture Show*, 133. On spectatorship, see also Walker Percy, *The Moviegoer* (New York: Knopf, 1961).

37. See Chester H. Liebs, *Main Street to Miracle Mile: American Roadside Architecture* (Boston: Little, Brown, 1985), 153ff.

38. Quoted in Valentine, *The Show Starts on the Sidewalk*, 1.

WHEN LESS IS MORE

Absence and Landscape in a California Ghost Town

Dydia DeLyser

> Every sight is haunted by countless ghosts that lurk there in silence to be
> evoked or not.   — MICHEL DE CERTEAU, "Practices of Space"

Not long ago, a middle-aged man walked into the museum at Bodie State Historic Park in the remote high desert of eastern California and asked the woman
working there, "[So] how did they decide to put a ghost town here anyway?"
The woman smiled. She had heard the question many times before. She explained that gold was discovered in Bodie in 1859 but that it became a ghost
town only after World War II. "No one," she said, "*put* a ghost town here."

For this man the site could have been more conveniently located. Yet to other
visitors the rough dirt road that leads to the town takes them simultaneously
on a journey into the past in which their imaginative efforts to reconstruct
the nineteenth century are richly rewarded. Rewarded by presence but also
by absence. As this chapter will show, Bodie's landscape, with its dilapidated
miners' cabins and nineteenth-century false-fronted Main Street, provides the
park's predominantly Anglo-American visitors with reminders of a mythologized American West already familiar to them from film, fiction, and television
(see Figure 1).[1] Though what remains of Bodie is just 5 percent of the gold-
mining town that thrived in the late 1870s, the empty spaces are readily filled
in by the imaginations of visitors and staff alike and imbued with notions
of a hardy pioneer heritage. This essay, based on more than ten summers of
participant observation and interviewing,[2] explores the particular role of absence in Bodie's landscape and in the construction of the past in this California
ghost town.

"Landscape," wrote Yi-Fu Tuan, "allows and even encourages us to dream.
... Yet it can anchor our attention because it has components that we can see
and touch."[3] Thus, landscape embraces a fundamental tension between what
is, in a simplistic sense, "real" and what is "fantasy." But since landscapes are
often interpreted unwittingly or uncritically, cultural geographers have sought
to question both landscapes and the meanings we make from them, revealing
the ideological nature of their form and content.[4] In the case of historic sites
like ghost towns, these landscapes may appear to be landscapes of the past, but
they are reinterpreted by each generation and thus can convey new meanings

24

Figure 1. Bodie State Historic Park, located just east of Yosemite National Park in California's high desert, was once a booming gold-mining town. Today it is preserved as a ghost town by the state of California.

and new associations now very different from what their original users had in mind.[5] In ghost towns like Bodie, the landscape visitors see today summons images of a mythologized Western past.

Landscape and the Mythic West

The American West, alongside its role as region, has long played an important role in American social memory, that is, in the way we as (Anglo-) Americans think about our past. In fact, western historian Richard White calls it "the most *imagined* section of the United States."[6] Over the past 150 years, as the creators of film, fiction, and art took up western topics, their work evolved into the western genre — now a nearly ubiquitous presence in American popular culture — that heroicized and mythologized western landscapes and people. And as the United States became steadily more urban and industrial, its citizens sought in this mythic West an escape from the negative aspects of American society. As western historian Gerald D. Nash explains, when "the real frontier receded into time, the mythic West loomed ever larger as a stark contrast to a dolorous present."[7] But to assume that a mythic West has existed as an entity separate from some "real" West is to create a false dichotomy and to collapse a complexly intertwined history. In fact, the two can be seen as mutually constitutive, each helping to shape the other, until the people and landscapes of the "actual" West influenced those of the mythic West and vice versa.[8]

In the nineteenth century, as the mythic West was taking on many of its current popular culture forms and expressions,[9] boomtowns like Bodie fed on their mythologized reputations even as they fed their actual histories back into the myth. Penning exaggerated tales of western towns that eventually reached eastern audiences, journalists like Samuel Clemens (who visited Bodie) and Bret Harte told tales of heroic gunfights and reckless bravado that came to symbolize life in the mythic West.[10] In so doing, they, and those many westerners who strove to live up to their mythologized reputations,[11] created a mythic West where, in Nash's words, "heroes enforced the highest and purest standards of manliness and morality."[12] The result, in fiction and in numerous actual western towns, was the fumigation of original experience, as this history in the landscape became an expression of American virtues.[13] In the landscapes of western towns like Bodie, the connection to this mythic West is, for many, readily apparent. Indeed, ghost-town tourist literature is quick to promote it, promising that "the rollicking, individualistic spirit of the frontier has come to seem an antidote to urban grayness, . . . and the frail ghost towns are an obvious [destination]."[14]

Such promotions rely on the nearly ubiquitous imagery of the mythic West in American popular culture, images that are constituted largely through film, fiction, television, advertising, art, and importantly also through landscape. Literary scholars have long known that, when reading, people interpret texts not in isolation but rather in the context of other things they have read, seen, or heard: we interpret "intertextually." And landscapes, as cultural productions that are interpreted by their viewers, are no different.[15] American visitors to places like Bodie carry with them cultural knowledge about the mythic West — whether from reading Louis L'Amour or from watching *Bonanza*, whether from seeing a John Wayne western or viewing a Frederic Remington sculpture. As they gaze upon the ghost town of Bodie, their intertextual knowledges of the mythic West confirm its very existence (see Figure 2). Today, some two hundred thousand tourists visit Bodie State Historic Park annually, and, as we shall see, in the midst of the ruins of this mining town they experience the heroic and "mythic" West, for in ghost towns like Bodie, the mythic West finds a place in space, a landscape expression.

Such experiences of the mythic West are meaningful to Bodie's staff and visitors, for they provide a tangible connection to American social memory — to a past that holds meaning for them in the present. For example, one summer weekday I spoke to an older woman with bright red hair. She told me she had been to Bodie ten or fifteen years earlier but had been afraid to return because she thought it might now be "spoiled." Heading back to her car in the parking lot she was pleased that in her opinion it had not been spoiled. "This is the essence of America," she explained, "the pioneers." Clearly, she was not

Figure 2. Artifacts like these inside Bodie's buildings often remind visitors of the mythic West they know from film and fiction.

referring to the ruins of the town that she had just walked through. She did not mean that America's essence was failure, seen through the failure of this mining camp. Nor was she talking about tourism, on this crowded afternoon. This woman, and many of Bodie's other visitors and the staff as well, use the Bodie they experience today as a synecdoche, as something that stands for much more. The woman read into the remains of the town its totality. She gazed upon the ruins and *imagined* what she thought the whole had once been.

This woman's experience is not unusual, and it is experiences like hers that are the subject of this essay. Here I will examine how Bodie's landscape inspires visitors' imaginings — how an imagined landscape of the past stands in for the real landscape of the ghost town and structures experience and memory in Bodie.

Let us pause for a moment to explore the power of synecdoche, a literary stylistic figure, in landscape. As Michel de Certeau has proposed, in landscape, synecdoche "enlarges one element of space." It replaces the whole with a fragment and therefore amplifies detail.[16] In Bodie, where only 5 percent of the original town remains, it is not hard to understand that what is left for visitors (and staff) to see is a fragment. But the power of synecdoche in landscape is that such a fragment takes on greater meaning: the projected meaning of the *imagined* whole. Though the primary mode of apprehending Bodie for its visitors is the visual, what the red-headed woman's experience suggests is that one other means of understanding, though more elusive, is equally important. Visitors gaze upon the ruins of the town, and through their eyes, they engage their mind's eye, their imaginations. It is these imaginary experiences of Bodie that leave the most powerful impressions. It was her imaginary American pioneers that the red-headed woman was referring to.

Of course, as Pamela Shurmer-Smith and Kevin Hannam have pointed out, "all places are imaginary, in the sense that they cannot exist for us beyond the image we are capable of forming of them in our minds."[17] And, as Tuan has noted, this is an important aspect of landscape, for landscape "appears to us through an effort of the imagination."[18] This is how the mythic West operates in the ghost town of Bodie: visitors see things that are familiar to them from other places, other texts (films and TV programs, for example), things that evoke the mythic West. They see fragments of the town of Bodie, and in their imaginations these fragmentary details speak to much more: far beyond the actual history of the town of Bodie, the fragments of the town that remain speak to mythic images of the American West. One visitor, arriving on his Harley Davidson, explained it this way: "Here [in Bodie] you can really feel [the past]. I can walk down there [Main Street] and just hear the horses and the people. [I can] just use [my] imagination, and I have a good one, and I'm right there [in the 1880s]." This man's experience of Bodie was powerful because he could use his imagination to "feel" the 1880s. A woman visitor in her early thirties echoed the man's thoughts, "You definitely get a feel for the past. . . . You can use your imagination." One of Bodie's staff members took this idea a step further in making his imagined Bodie useful to him in daily life:

> When you're really thinking about [Bodie] you can let your imagination run and think about an 1880s town because that's one thing I do, imagine it as a working town. I sometimes try to do it when I'm working too, I see the horse and buggies going up the road. It helps me to deal with the [visitors]. I'm supposed to be here and now but technically I'm then.

This man used his imagined nineteenth-century Bodie to help him live and work in the reality of the twentieth-century ghost town. All of these people, and indeed most of Bodie's staff and visitors, see the town with their eyes, but even more powerfully through their imaginations.

That visitors see Bodie with their imaginations is suggested very strongly by the ways that they remember the town. Staff agree that many visitors who return after a number of years insist that buildings have either been added or taken away and that the two comments seem equally frequent. Actually, only two small buildings have been lost since 1962, and none has ever been added — thus the overall appearance of the town has remained essentially unchanged. But these visitors, seeing that the Bodie they imagine no longer matches the Bodie they returned to visit, assume it is the park that has changed.

Other visitors report stranger phenomena. One woman insisted that there were once wax mannequins in the windows. Another was shocked to find that the "explanatory signs" that she remembered seeing in front of each building on her last visit twenty years before had been taken away. A man who said he "knew old cars" lamented the removal of an antique fire engine. Another man insisted that staff had been sandblasting the buildings. None of these memories is based in reality, but even after the visitors were told by the park staff that they were wrong, they clung to their memories: "I'm so disappointed that the signs are gone," the woman complained after being told that the park's policy had never allowed such signs. "These buildings are a different color than they were when I was here last year," a man insisted to one of Bodie's long-time maintenance staff. "Maybe you just weren't here when they were doing the sandblasting." As time passes, it is often this imagined Bodie that leaves the strongest impression.

But what is it in Bodie that encourages visitors and staff to engage their imaginations? As John Lukacs has pointed out, certain remnants from the past carry a *potential* evocative power — potential because "their evocative power is not an inherent property of themselves; the most perfectly preserved building or document becomes evocative, indeed, 'historical,' only through our imagination."[19] In Bodie, visual understanding or interpretation is primarily stimulated by presence. Imaginative understanding, in contrast, is stimulated by absence.

Absence

Though, as noted earlier, only 5 percent of the town remains, Bodie is widely regarded by staff members, visitors, authors of ghost town guidebooks, and members of the press as "one of the best preserved western ghost towns in existence."[20] Ghost town enthusiasts know too that what remains in Bodie is much more than what remains in almost any other ghost town. But quantity is not the only key to success as a ghost town. In fact, in some towns where much remains, too much remains.

In some other ghost towns, the presence of certain elements, or rather, the lack of key absences, leads visitors to complain that the past is less accessible to them there. Much of this is associated with what are seen as contemporary intrusions on the past as presented in the ghost town. As one Bodie visitor, a southern California attorney, explained, "I'm not as excited about ghost towns with asphalt streets and stores that sell slurpies."

Some of these intrusions in other ghost towns are additions, new construction added next to or in place of the original fabric of the town. Others are alterations, major or minor changes made in the town's appearance. In Bodie, the employees of the state of California strive to carry out a policy known as arrested decay, or, in the words of one staff member, "to keep things standing but make them look like they're still falling down." Thus, obvious contemporary intrusions, including commercial operations, are kept from Bodie's landscape. One visitor, a young man from the San Francisco Bay Area, explained the effect: "*This is* a ghost town. I think you get a better feel here for life 110 years ago. It's easier for me to imagine.... You know, if you have a microbrewery right next door it makes it harder."

What this man's comment indicates is that certain *presences* interfere with his ability to fill in the absences and imagine life in another time. Comments like his are common among Bodie's visitors and staff, for the empty spaces and absences stimulate their imaginations. The man from the Bay Area explained it: "I think it's like the difference between books and television. With books you have to imagine." The southern California attorney put it like this: "You have to try to visualize the way it was. [This is] a glimpse, one-tenth [*sic*] of what was once here. You have to try to fill in the blanks."

How is it, then, that the blanks in the real geography of Bodie are filled in by visitors and staff? What images and ideas take the place of the empty space? And what is it exactly that is absent in Bodie's landscape? It is worthwhile at this point to first reconsider the power of landscape as a signifying system. As James S. Duncan writes, "a landscape does more than simply fulfill obvious, mundane functional requirements.... [B]y encoding within a landscape various conventional signs of such things as group membership and social status, individuals are able to tell morally charged 'stories' about themselves and the social structure of the society in which they live."[21] In Bodie, the landscape is as important for what is absent, what is experienced imaginatively by visitors, as for what is present, what is visually represented. Bodie's absences are significant: they form a crucial part of the town's landscape.[22] The false-fronted buildings that line the town's Main Street are punctuated by empty spaces where other buildings once stood. The firehouse topped by a bell tower stands alone in an otherwise empty field: the large commercial buildings that once surrounded it burned in the 1932 fire.[23] Bodie's residential streets are similarly composed of both clusters and gaps. Numerous houses cling to upper Green Street, but nearly all of those along intersecting Wood Street are gone. Of the tent-cabins, thrown up hurriedly in the early days of Bodie's boom, none remains.

Visitors are keyed in to these absences immediately. An interpretive poster in Bodie's parking lot at the head of the main trail into town as well as the park's self-guided tour brochure describe a boom-period population of ten thousand and explain that only a fraction of the original town remains. And the poster and the brochure both draw specific attention to some of Bodie's most important absences: while both describe the one-time presence of sixty-five saloons, today's visitors see only three buildings that resemble saloons.[24]

Indeed, some of Bodie's empty spaces represent what, to many, are the more interesting parts of the town. Bodie staff members agree that the town's red-light district is one of the primary places of interest to tourists. The questions Where was the red-light district? and Where's the whorehouse? are two of those most commonly asked by Bodie's visitors. But their desires to see this once-significant part of Bodie go unsatisfied in a concrete sense. The brochure

Figure 3. Front facade of one of Bodie's false-fronted buildings. The term *false front* refers to the squared-off front of the building, which masks a pitched roof behind it, thus creating the impression that the building is more substantial than it is.

indicates the "site" of Bonanza Street, once the red-light district, on the northern end of the town, but no tangible trace of the district remains. Even the street itself is no longer visible in a field of grass and sage brush. Imagination and a paragraph in the brochure are all that remain.

Though most of Bodie's remaining buildings contain artifacts, here too there are significant absences. As Michel de Certeau writes, "We are struck by the fact that sites that have been lived in are filled with the presence of absences. What appears designates what is no more, . . . [what] can no longer be seen."[25] In Bodie, all but two of the buildings[26] are closed to the general public. But visitors may see the contents of all of the buildings by looking in through the windows. The voyeuristic game that ensues is equally popular among children and adults as members of families describe for themselves and one another what they see inside and what they imagine about it.

At the northeast corner of Main and Green Streets, what is now perceived to be the town's main intersection, stands a two-story false-fronted building with a concrete sidewalk and tumble-down porch (see Figure 3). The words "Bodie Store" are still barely legible, painted across the west-facing facade of the second story over even fainter words, "Wheaton and Hollis." All signs of paint have weathered away from the rest of the building. A pole on the ridge of the roof, capped by a wooden ball, creates debate among visitors: Is it a flagpole or a lightning rod? At street level, the front wall of the building, made up of large windows and doors with windows in them, is almost solid glass. Many of the panes have cracked, and staff members have filled the cracks with silicon caulking, which preserves the warped glass of the original panes and enhances the spider-web appearance of the windows. The imposing front of the building, visible almost immediately upon entering the town from the parking lot, its central location (diagonally across from the museum), and the wall of glass make this one of the most looked-in buildings in Bodie.

In the center of the building's main room stands a billiard table with ornately carved legs in the shape of charging lions. The immense weight of the table with its slate top has caused the plank floor beneath it to sag uneasily: like most things in Bodie it is no longer level. Cues and balls appear ready for the next game, but a thick layer of dust obscures the green of the felt, testifying that no game has recently been played. Behind the billiard table a round, pot-bellied wood stove with nickel-plated floral foot rail and a mica window in its door hopes to heat a room this large. Old cross-country skis, most of them over six feet long, lean against the front windows testifying to summer visitors that the stove will be needed. Empty beer bottles wait on the bar against the south wall. At the north wall a long table is mostly empty, but here and there a place setting remains. Straight-backed wooden chairs stand ready—but not pushed in—at the table. Through an open doorway in the back wall visitors peer into the restaurant kitchen with its industrial-sized wood-burning cook stove. Pots, pans, and a pressure cooker clutter the cooking surfaces. Near the doorway a small chalkboard bears the message "liver and onions 30 cents." Below it, a velvet-covered fainting couch sags from overuse. Above it all, mounted on the stamped tin of the south wall, the head of a buck stares down on the empty room.

What is absent from this scene in the building, just as it is absent in the interiors of almost all of Bodie's other buildings, is any sign of life. No one is inside this building. As in Bodie's other buildings, the dust is undisturbed, presenting the impression that no one has been inside of this building for many years. Visitors with the park's tour brochure in hand may learn that this build-ing served as the U.S. Land Office after the boom, as the office of a power company, and finally as a boarding house. The brochure leaves out any more specific details, and visitors are left with their own imaginings, the visions of their mind's eye. These they freely indulge in, stimulated by the vivid images that they see with their actual eyes and guided by their intertextual knowledges of the mythic West, until the absences are filled in.

Walking past the front of the hotel it is not uncommon to overhear visitors describing not only what they see but also what they do *not* see. One man visiting with his wife and two young children narrated a scene for his family, including elements of the obvious, as well as those of the purely imagined: "There's a bar and a table and you just walked up to the kitchen and got food and then sat down." His brief narrative assumed that there was no wait staff to serve the customers and that customers did not eat standing at the bar (as they often did in boom-period Bodie), and he left out most of the history of the building as described in the brochure. It was a description composed in large part in his imagination.

But it is not only buildings or their contents that provide absences to stimulate visitors' imaginations. The absence of costumed interpreters (common in other historic sites and living-history museums)[27] inside or outside of the buildings further encourages Bodie's visitors to use their own imaginations to reconstruct individual interpretations of the town's history, its inhabitants, and the spectacular as well as mundane events that (might have) occurred there.[28] Other absences, in turn, serve to guide just how these imaginings will run. Though visitors read in the brochure that "killings occurred with monotonous regularity" and that "[r]obberies, stage holdups and street fights provided variety,"[29] now the streets of the town are crowded only with unarmed tourists. But the brochure's provocative text as well as visitors' intertextual knowledges of the mythic West assist the many visitors who wish to imaginatively fill in such absences.

For example, one summer Bodie's maintenance staff embarked on a project to lay new underground gas lines to six of the buildings used by park employees. Before we dug we marked the existing underground electrical, gas, and telephone lines with bright orange and red plastic strings, which we attached to spikes in the ground. Many visitors asked staff members what on earth these strangely out-of-place markers were. One woman didn't need to ask. She told her two curious children, "They had a clairvoyant out here and she told them where the people had been killed." Like many of Bodie's visitors, through absence, this woman and her family were able to indulge in the dangerous past from a safe distance. She drew no conclusions about the markers based on any contemporary use for them but rather linked them to an imagined geography of the mythic West.

But the dangerous past, as seen through the mythic West, is not the only past that Bodie's visitors imaginatively construct. For many, the commonly held notion that Bodie's boom-period life was rough, rowdy, and lawless supports not a connection to contemporary urban crime but a subscription to the notion of progress.[30] Since most of the park's staff and visitors do not experience daily gunfights as part of their late-twentieth-century realities, American society is seen to have "advanced" from its "Wild West state." As Eric Gable and Richard Handler observed in their fieldwork in Colonial Williamsburg, "Despite the museum's stated aim to understand the past on its own terms, the eighteenth century is often presented to visitors as a more primitive version of our own world, a version beyond which we are glad to have progressed."[31]

Whether or not the notion of progress as viewed through the lens of the early-twenty-first-century remains of a nineteenth-century gold-mining town is tenable, it is deeply held. One staff member, for example, explained what it meant to her to be able to go inside Bodie's buildings: "It's just fascinating to be able to get close to these artifacts and . . . to really be close enough to examine them and really think about what life was like and how hard it was." But while Bodie's landscape inspires some to embrace notions of progress from a difficult past, other presences and absences in that landscape guide visitors to embrace a concept of a romantic, simpler past.

During Bodie's heyday, in the late 1870s, the town was bursting with activity. Mining and milling operations went on twenty-four hours a day. The mining area on Bodie Bluff and Silver Hill held as many as fifty different mining operations. Some six stamp mills processed the ore from the mines, belching smoke from their wood-fired boilers into the air of the town below. Incoming stages carried as many as sixteen people, packed together, and they arrived twice a day. A housing shortage caused a boom in new construction, and Bodie's three daily papers documented the town's activities. Though some 450 businesses lined Bodie's streets, virtually nothing used in the town came from the town itself. Wood, for buildings, bracing in the mines, heating, and cooking, was hauled in on wagons or on the backs of mules. Food was grown in nearby Bridgeport or shipped in from as far as the San Francisco Bay Area. Machinery for the mines and mills came from San Francisco or from less-profitable mines nearer by. All of the items that stocked the shelves of Bodie's stores were made elsewhere, with the notable exception of beer and whiskey — at least four breweries and one distillery locally met the needs of a thirsty population, and Bodie's sixty-five saloons and dance halls did not even close on Sundays.[32]

Thus, despite its current Wild West reputation, boom-period Bodie was actually an urban and industrial place. Staff often mention to visitors that, with a population as high as ten thousand during its boom period, Bodie was larger than Los Angeles at that time. What remains for them to see now, however, appears rural and idyllic. During its heyday Bodie was one of a number of mining towns in this part of the eastern Sierra region. Today Bodie appears to tourists to stand quite alone and isolated, and this allows visitors and staff to embrace notions of anticommercialism and appeal to a simpler past. As Edward Bruner noted in relation to the reconstructed village where Abraham Lincoln once lived, "In the 1830s New Salem was a commercial trading center, and when Lincoln migrated there he probably thought he was moving to an urban center; but in the 1990s New Salem, for many, is rural, isolated, self-contained, rustic and folklike . . . in opposition to the commercialism . . . of 20th-century America."[33]

Perhaps the most notable aspect of Bodie's boom-period busyness, which is now also the most notably absent, was noise — not the quaint neighing of horses or the clip-clop of hooves but the deafening pounding, grinding roar of the stamp mills located on and around Bodie Bluff, where the ore hauled out of the mines was pulverized to a fine powder in order to extract its burden of gold

Figure 4. Visitors to Bodie often travel with children, creating a family-vacation atmosphere that does not accurately reflect the town's past.

and silver. Boom-period Bodie was an industrial town, filled with the sounds of its extractive industry. Today Bodie is nearly silent. The sounds of industry no longer disturb the peace. In the morning air conversations can be overheard that take place across town from the listener. Cars arriving at the park are diverted around the town to the parking lot and generally are not audible to those in the town site. Visitors talk and shout to one another. Children laugh and scream and cry. The sounds of Bodie, because of significant absences, have been sanitized. They are now the wholesome sounds of a family environment, not the industrial grind of a mining town with a population that was 90 percent male (see Figure 4).

The smells of Bodie, too, have been sanitized. Visitors, for example, are provided with modern flush-toilets in the parking lot. The availability of modern restroom facilities may seem trivial in a ghost town, but this is not the case: many visitors will walk a long way in order to avoid the outhouses provided at the center of town and to reach the more modern facilities in the parking lot. And impressions of Bodie's restrooms (either good or bad) are often lingering: one woman in her forties, standing in front of the Methodist church, was emphatic about her experience of Bodie: "I love it! No services and yet the restrooms are immaculate!" But in boom-period Bodie everyone had an outhouse. Trash accumulated behind houses and in the streets. There was no sewage system of any kind. Animals died in the winter snow, only to thaw as rotting carcasses in the spring. Today, Bodie has one overwhelming odor: that of the sage brush that dominates its hills and fields. The sights, smells, and sounds of Bodie today influence perceptions of the Bodie of the 1880s, and key absences lead visitors to project the calm and cleanliness of the present onto the past.

Landscape and Social Memory

What both visitors and staff alike describe in their imaginings of Bodie is a romantic and sanitized construction of the past closely tied to the mythic West and its concepts of American values and notions of progress. Thus, visitors and staff in Bodie engage not only with the history of the town before them but equally with important aspects of American social memory as it is represented in Bodie's landscape. Indeed, social memory is not merely a process of calling up the past but an active process of engaging with it, of making meaning for the past in the present. As such, social memory integrates elements of fantasy, reenactment, and invention.[34] While these fantasies may be individually experienced (as they were by the woman who thought our gas-line markers were for gun-shot victims), as elements of social memory they are tied to an interpretation of a perceived, shared past: in this case to the American mythic West. Though much of this mythic West is imaginary, as Shurmer-Smith and Hannam observe, "the realm of the imagination can be an extremely powerful tool in society [for] it is involved in . . . structuring both dominant and . . . transgressive myths."[35] And when such social memories are experienced in a tangible, spatial form, as they are in Bodie, their experience becomes all the more powerful.[36] In Bodie the tangible remains of an 1880s gold-mining town and, even more importantly, the significant absences in the town's original fabric provide a spatial trigger for these "flights of the imagination."[37]

Yi-Fu Tuan, in *Escapism,* poses the question, "[I]s fantasy necessarily opposed to the real?"[38] In Bodie, it is important to understand that fantasy is not the only experience visitors and staff have — it is, in fact, in part through fantasy that they create their realities. Indeed, the visible forms in Bodie's landscape work together with its absences to stimulate the fantasies and social memories out of which visitors make meaning: local geography acts as a theater for social memory,[39] encouraging the interplay between "real" and "fantasy."

Of course, different groups and different individuals likely will engage with social memory differently. Furthermore, any individual may embrace conflicting memories or fantasies.[40] In Bodie, visitors and staff must embrace the tension between notions of a difficult, or primitive, past and a simple or romantic past. They see a failed gold-mining town but imagine success and American virtues. One staff member expressed this tension in describing his feeling for Bodie: "[I have] a love for the Old West and old mining towns. [And] the traditional feeling that you should be born one hundred or so years earlier. I don't like modern times at all. But I feel like I'm in the middle of a time zone. I've gotten used to some of the conveniences. But I live in an old mining town."

As Edward Bruner explains, in a place like Bodie, these themes are not in conflict despite the fact that one evokes the simplicity of life in the past, and the other evokes the difficulty of that life: "Many visitors hold both views simultaneously. In their imagination, they yearn for a simpler life. But they are not alienated beings; they want modern 1990s conveniences, and they would not be willing to give up their 1990s lives in exchange for the [1880s]."[41] In fact, as H. U. E. Thoden van Velzen has noted, such unresolved and conflicting themes are characteristic of social memory.[42] And they are certainly common among the visitors and staff in Bodie, like the red-haired woman we met at the beginning of this essay who saw in the ruins of Bodie the "essence of America." Social memory, as it is engaged at Bodie State Historic Park, reflects visitors' attempts at understanding and manipulating the past and at intertextually engaging with narratives that hold meaning for them. In so doing, they create an imaginary space that concretizes some of the mythic images of the American West. The tensions between aspects of their imaginings, or between notions of "fantasy" and "reality" (or real history), serve to underscore the fact that reality itself is permeated by both individual and collective imaginings.[43]

Those who journey along the rough dirt road that leads to Bodie are rewarded by a chance to experience a part of the past exactly as they imagine it. In this ghost town, what can be seen and what can not be seen combine to provide each visitor with a unique "Bodie experience" that links them to their images of the mythic West in American social memory. Some see the hardiness of pioneer forefathers; others see familiar images of the Wild West; still others see the essence of America in this tumble-down town. The pasts that Bodie's staff and visitors experience may never have existed, but they are experienced just the same. As Edward Bruner puts it:

> The tourists [in New Salem] are seeking...a discourse that enables them to better reflect on their lives in the 1990s. New Salem and similar sites enact an ideology, attach tourists to a mythical collective consciousness, and commodify the past. The particular pasts that tourists create/imagine at historic sites may never have existed. But historic sites like New Salem do provide visitors with the raw material (experiences) to construct a sense of identity, meaning, attachment and stability.[44]

One summer morning, a middle-aged woman from the Bronx complained to a Bodie staff member when he told her she had to pay a five-dollar fee to see the park. "It's worth it," he told her. She frowned but paid the fee and drove on to the parking lot. Later that day he saw her again, this time in the center of the town site. "Well," he said, "Was it worth it?" A smile broadened on her face. "Oh yes," she said. And then, gesturing to the camera at her side rather than to the mine tailings behind her, she said, "There's gold in Bodie." In Bodie State

Historic Park, a landscape where gold-mining activity long ago fell silent, this woman, like many others, filled in its absence to make meaning for the town's past in her own present.

Notes

I would like to thank the visitors and staff at Bodie State Historic Park for more than a decade of support and cooperation: they made my research possible and made my life so much richer. The research for this essay could not have taken place without the additional support of the Graduate School and the Department of Geography at Syracuse University and the permission of Bodie's chief ranger, J. Bradwell Sturdivant. On top of that, the comments of several friends and colleagues helped shape this essay into its present form. In particular I would like to thank Jim Duncan, Paul Greenstein, Mark Monmonier, Anne Mosher, and Miles Richardson for sharing their insights, as well as the volume's editors, Paul C. Adams, Steve Hoelscher, and Karen E. Till for sharing theirs. Despite their help, any errors or misstatements remain mine alone. I presented an earlier version of this essay at the conference of the Association of American Geographers in Chicago in the spring of 1997.

1. Bodie's visitors are not only predominantly American but also overwhelmingly white, middle-class suburbanites. The prevalence of one relatively homogenous group of visitors helps to enable a construction of the past that reflects visitors' realities rather than boom-period Bodie's largely working-class and multiethnic past. See Dydia DeLyser, "Good, by God, We're Going to Bodie! Landscape and Social Memory in a California Ghost Town" (Ph.D. diss., Department of Geography, Syracuse University, 1998).

2. I was a participant-observer who participated very heavily indeed: alongside my research I lived in the ghost town and served as one of Bodie's seasonal maintenance workers. I explored the methodological and epistemological challenges of such a position in much more detail in Dydia DeLyser, "Authenticity on the Ground: Engaging the Past in a California Ghost Town," *Annals of the Association of American Geographers* 89 (1999): 602–32.

3. Yi-Fu Tuan, "Thought and Landscape: The Eye and the Mind's Eye," in *The Interpretation of Ordinary Landscapes,* ed. Donald W. Meinig (Oxford: Oxford University Press), 101.

4. Many geographers have engaged these ideas. See, for example, Denis Cosgrove and Stephen Daniels, *The Iconography of Landscape: Essays on the Symbolic Representation, Design, and Use of Past Environments* (Cambridge: Cambridge University Press, 1988); James S. Duncan, *The City as Text: The Politics of Landscape Interpretation in the Kandyan Kingdom* (Cambridge: Cambridge University Press, 1990); James S. Duncan and Nancy G. Duncan "(Re)reading the Landscape," *Environment and Planning D: Society and Space* 6 (1988): 117–26; James S. Duncan and David Ley, eds., *Place/Culture/Representation* (London: Routledge, 1993); Peirce Lewis, "Axioms for Reading the Landscape: Some Guides to the American Scene," in *The Interpretation of Ordinary Landscape,* ed. D. W. Meinig (Oxford: Oxford University Press, 1979), 11–32; Don Mitchell, *The Lie of the Land: Migrant Workers and the California Landscape* (Minneapolis: University of Minnesota Press, 1996); and Richard Schein, "The Place of Landscape: A Conceptual Framework for Interpreting the American Scene," *Annals of the Association of American Geographers* 87 (1997): 660–80.

5. See, among others, Åsa Boholm, "Reinvented Histories: Medieval Rome as Memorial Landscape," *Ecumene* 4 (1997): 247–72; Edward M. Bruner, "Abraham Lincoln as Authentic Reproduction: A Critique of Postmodernism," *American Anthropologist* 96 (1994): 397–415; Cosgrove and Daniels, *Iconography of Landscape;* Eric Gable and Richard Handler, "Deep Dirt: Messing Up the Past at Colonial Williamsburg," *Social Analysis* 34 (December 1993): 3–16; Eric Gable, Richard Handler, and Anna Lawson, "On the Uses of Relativism: Fact, Conjecture, and Black and White Histories at Colonial Williamsburg," *American Ethnologist* 98 (1992): 791–805; Richard Handler and Eric Gable, *The New History in an Old Museum: Creating the Past at Colonial Williamsburg* (Durham, N.C.:

Duke University Press, 1997); Eric Hobsbawm and Terence Ranger, *The Invention of Tradition* (Cambridge: Cambridge University Press, 1983); Nuala Johnson, "Where Geography and History Meet: Heritage Tourism and the Big House in Ireland," *Annals of the Association of American Geographers* 86 (1996): 551–66; David Lowenthal, "The American Way of History," *Columbia University Forum* (summer 1966): 27–32; Lowenthal, "Past Time, Present Place: Landscape and Memory," *Geographical Review* (January 1975): 1–36; Lowenthal, "The Timeless Past: Some Anglo-American Historical Preconceptions," *Journal of American History* 75 (1989): 1263–80; and Karen E. Till, "Staging the Past: Landscape Designs, Cultural Identity, and Erinnerungspolitik at Berlin's Neue Wache," *Ecumene* 6 (1999): 251–83.

6. Richard White, *"It's Your Misfortune and None of My Own": A New History of the American West* (Norman: University of Oklahoma Press, 1991), 613. Others who have written insightfully about the mythic West include Robert G. Athearn, *The Mythic West in Twentieth-Century America* (Lawrence: University of Kansas Press, 1986); Gerald D. Nash, *Creating the West: Historical Interpretations, 1890–1990* (Albuquerque: University of New Mexico Press, 1991); Richard Slotkin, *Gunfighter Nation: The Myth of the Frontier in Twentieth Century America* (New York: Athenaeum, 1992); Henry Nash Smith, *Virgin Land: The American West as Symbol and Myth* (Cambridge, Mass.: Harvard University Press, 1950).

7. Nash, *Creating the West*, 199.

8. See DeLyser, "Authenticity on the Ground"; and White, "It's Your Misfortune."

9. See Athearn, *Mythic West*; Nash, *Creating the West*; and White, "It's Your Misfortune."

10. Marvin Lewis, ed., *The Mining Frontier: Contemporary Accounts from the American West in the Nineteenth Century* (Norman: University of Oklahoma Press, 1967); Roger D. McGrath, *Gunfighters, Highwaymen, and Vigilantes: Violence on the Frontier* (Berkeley: University of California Press, 1984).

11. See DeLyser, "Authenticity on the Ground"; and White, "It's Your Misfortune."

12. Nash, *Creating the West*, 206.

13. Lowenthal, "The American Way," 28.

14. William Carter, *Ghost Towns of the West: A Sunset Pictorial* (Menlo Park, Calif.: Lane Magazine and Book Co., 1971), 7.

15. See Duncan, *City as Text*; Duncan and Duncan, "(Re)reading the Landscape"; and B. Stock, "Texts, Readers, and Enacted Narratives," *Visible Language* 20 (1986): 194–301.

16. Michel de Certeau, "Practices of Space," in *On Signs*, ed. Marshal Blonsky (Baltimore: Johns Hopkins University Press), 137.

17. Pamela Shurmer-Smith and Kevin Hannam, *Worlds of Desire, Realms of Power* (London: Edward Arnold, 1994), 59.

18. Tuan, "Thought and Landscape," 90.

19. John Lukacs, *Historical Consciousness: The Remembered Past* (New Brunswick, N.J.: Transaction Publishers, 1994 [1968]), 238.

20. California Division of Tourism, *Golden California: Visitor's Guide* (Sacramento: MH West, Inc., for the Division of Tourism, California Trade and Commerce Agency, 1993), 70.

21. James S. Duncan, "Elite Landscapes as Cultural (Re)productions: The Case of Shaughnessy Heights," in *Inventing Places: Studies in Cultural Geography*, ed. K. Anderson and F. Gale (Melbourne: Longman, 1992), 39.

22. On the meaning of absence in landscapes, see also Miles Richardson, "The Gift of Presence: The Act of Leaving Artifacts at Shrines, Memorials, and Other Tragedies," and Patrick McGreevy, "Attending to the Void: Geography and Madness," in this volume.

23. So, in fact, did the firehouse. The one visitors see today was built by the WPA in the mid-1930s.

24. These buildings became bars or restaurants only after the town's boom period had passed.

25. De Certeau, "Practices of Space," 143.

26. The two buildings are the Tom Miller House and the Miner's Union Hall.

27. Since this essay was first submitted and contrary to the park's policy (which states that "To preserve the ghost town atmosphere, park personnel should not be in 1880-period dress, but should remain in uniform" [State of California, Department of Parks and Recreation, *Bodie State Historic Park: Resource Management Plan, General Development Plan, and Environmental Impact Report* (Sacramento, Calif.: Department of Parks and Recreation, 1979)]), guides giving tours of Bodie's ore-processing stamp mill have begun to wear "period" costumes, but even now most staff member "remain in uniform."

28. Advocates of living history would disagree with me on this point, for they argue that costumed interpreters add to the experiences of visitors and interpreters alike (see, for example, Jay Anderson, *Time Machines: The World of Living History* [Nashville: American Association for State and Local History, 1984]). Anthropologists who have studied such places, as well as most of my informants in Bodie, however, seem to side with me. See Gable and Handler, "Deep Dirt."

29. California Department of Parks and Recreation, *Bodie State Historic Park* (Sacramento: Department of Parks and Recreation, 1988), 3.

30. See Bruner, "Abraham Lincoln as Authentic Reproduction"; Gable and Handler, "Deep Dirt"; and McGrath, *Gunfighters, Highwaymen, and Vigilantes.*

31. Gable and Handler, "Deep Dirt," 9.

32. This information about boom-period Bodie and a wealth of other details as well can be found in Warren Loose, *Bodie Bonanza: The True Story of a Flamboyant Past* (Las Vegas: Nevada Publications, 1979); McGrath, *Gunfighters, Highwaymen, and Vigilantes;* and Frank S. Wedertz, *Bodie 1859–1900* (Bishop, Calif.: Sierra Media, 1969).

33. Bruner, "Abraham Lincoln as Authentic Reproduction," 405.

34. Marita Sturken, *Tangled Memories: The Vietnam War, the AIDS Epidemic, and the Politics of Remembering* (Berkeley: University of California Press, 1997).

35. Shurmer-Smith and Hannam, *Worlds of Power,* 61; see also Sturken, *Tangled Memories.*

36. H. U. E. Thoden van Velzen, "Revenants That Cannot Be Shaken: Collective Fantasies in a Maroon Society," *American Anthropologist* 97 (1995): 722–32.

37. Ibid., 730.

38. Yi-Fu Tuan, *Escapism* (Baltimore: Johns Hopkins University Press, 1998).

39. See James Fentress and Chris Wickham, *Social Memory* (Oxford: Blackwell, 1992).

40. Thoden van Velzen, "Revenants"; Sturken, *Tangled Memories.*

41. Bruner, "Abraham Lincoln as Authentic Reproduction," 411.

42. Thoden van Velzen, "Revenants," 729–30.

43. Ibid., 722.

44. Bruner, "Abraham Lincoln as Authentic Reproduction," 411.

SENSE OF PLACE AS A POSITIONAL GOOD

Locating Bedford in Space and Time

James S. Duncan and Nancy G. Duncan

A quarter of a century ago, Yi-Fu Tuan coined the term *topophilia* to refer to "the affective bond between people and place."[1] He argued quite cogently that this bond varies greatly in intensity from individual to individual and that there is cross-cultural variation in its expression. Topophilia manifests itself most often in attachment to home places, places that vary in scale from the nation to the bedroom. Tuan suggests that such attachment can be based, among other things, upon memories or pride of ownership. He argues that in Europe and North America topophilia often takes the form of an aestheticization of place and landscape, that the aesthetic is one of the principal modes of relating to certain environments. Topophilia is not only an affective response to place but a practice that can actively produce places for people. Topophilia and the related idea of "sense of place" are associated with the humanistic geography of the 1970s. They were defined in opposition to the alienation produced by "placeless" modern environments. Increasing homogeneity among places was assumed to decrease attachment to particular places.[2] In this type of work, attachment to place and aestheticization of landscapes were rarely seen as anything but benign, qualities to be encouraged by planners and landscape designers.

While there continues to be much to recommend such an approach to places, there is also a more recent line of research that is more ambivalent about place-attachment.[3] Peter Jackson and Jan Penrose have explored place-based identities and argued that there is an identity politics, both progressive and reactionary, based upon attachment to place.[4] Karen E. Till has explored the negative externalities associated with the attachment to place arising from a search for distinction that depends upon explicit comparisons with other places.[5] She argues that the celebration of social and place differences through the marketing of neotraditional housing developments leads to social exclusion. David Harvey analyzes the celebration of places connected with what he sees as a "reactionary politics of an aestheticized spatiality," and Don Mitchell shows how the aestheticization of California's agricultural landscapes obscures the exploited labor embodied in them.[6] Likewise researchers have revealed a dark side of topophilia as manifested in the naturalization of the nation-state and its celebration in landscapes. In addition, aesthetic appreciation of place and landscape has been analyzed for the class and gender biases it may contain.[7]

In this essay we continue these critical lines of inquiry by interrogating the topophilia or attachments that members of a particular group have to a particular place and the role that the aesthetic plays in such attachment. We stress the particularity of the group and place because we believe that the nature of attachment to place varies and that such variation should be investigated empirically. For a group, such as the upper-middle-class Americans whom we are examining, topophilia can be fruitfully analyzed as a form of "symbolic capital" and "positional good."[8] Symbolic and cultural capital as defined by Pierre Bourdieu and others include acquired tastes, knowledge, appreciation, and consumption of aesthetically pleasing forms.[9] These types of capital are seen to supplement economic capital, lending prestige to those who acquire them. In our study, sense of place and landscape taste are offered as examples of cultural capital that is highly valued by the local population. Bourdieu argues that cultural capital serves as a subtle basis for social distinctions and the legitimation of claims to political as well as social power.

We explore these themes by drawing from interviews conducted in Bedford, New York, a suburb of New York City. Bedford residents' senses of place, we argue, are structured relationally in several revealing ways. Claims for the distinction and uniqueness of the town are attempts to show it and — through place-identification — themselves in a superior social position to other residential landscapes and populations within the New York metropolitan region.[10] When informants speak to us about Bedford as a place to live, they reveal an anxious concern for relative social position by continually making comparisons between Bedford and other places. Bedford, they tell us, is unlike this suburb or that. It is defined against those other places and is judged superior. However, for many long-term residents, Bedford's position within the metropolitan region is seen as insecure. It is not, they claim, as bucolic or different from other places as it was in the past. The implication is that the town might be losing some of its aesthetic appeal, its distinction, and hence its positional advantage.

Long-term residents tell us that new people moving into the town with different landscape and architectural tastes are decreasing the town's visual homogeneity and distinctiveness, making it less distinguishable from other suburbs. What is most feared is mimicry and reproduction, or, as Homi Bhabha says in a different context, the same but not quite.[11] An aura is associated with scarce or unique cultural productions, especially the antique and irreplaceable. The cultural capital of recognition and appreciation of this aura of distinctiveness is valued above all else. An anxiety about maintaining this aura has led to an often virulent politics of exclusion that attempts to freeze Bedford's landscape, allowing as little change as is politically feasible. Although the impetus of this politics of exclusion is more aesthetic than overtly social in intent, underlying the aesthetic are some related social issues pertaining to the fragile hegemony of the local elite — the Anglo-Saxon, Protestant establishment. Nevertheless, we would not want to underemphasize the importance of the appreciation of and attachment to a particular aesthetic. Landscapes as metaphors of cultural differentiation and achieved social status become highly valued in and of themselves. They become receptacles of great emotional investment due to the immense power of topophilia. Our point is that topophilia, too often celebrated by cultural and historical geographers, can, in the hands of some groups, have an aggressive, exclusionary component.

Between 1680 and 1727 a group of English settlers from Stamford, Connecticut, purchased six square miles of agricultural and hunting lands from the Mohicans and named it Bedford. Many descendants (around ninety) of the original settlers still live in Bedford today and are celebrated as an important part of the town's heritage. Despite its rocky soil, Bedford became a moderately prosperous subsistence- and then commercial-farming community serving the New York City market with beef and milk. By the latter third of the nineteenth century, farming was on the wane, and Bedford was rapidly becoming a rural refuge for wealthy New Yorkers who sought not only an open pastoral landscape but also wilder picturesque scenes. As active farming ceased in many parts of Bedford, the trees began to grow back on cleared land. Over time, in part because of the cost of maintaining a pastoral landscape without the availability of cheap agricultural labor, the landscape appeared more and more wild. New types of residents appeared in Bedford, ones whose relations to the national and international capitalist economy were principally through industrialism, law, and finance, rather than farming. Consequently, aesthetic rather than instrumental relations with nature became more prominent.

By the late nineteenth century, Bedford had become a romantic suburb attracting some of New York City's elite to weekend and summer gentlemen's farms and others to take up permanent residence. Because Bedford is forty-four miles from New York City, it was not too far for commuters to establish homes, but not so close that it attracted a lot of early development. But in the 1920s, as there began to be pressure to develop land, far-sighted individuals instituted highly restrictive zoning codes to protect it from what they saw as potential overdevelopment. Although some had suggested twenty-five-acre minimum lot sizes, it was decided that a four-acre minimum was more reasonable (or at least more legally defensible).

During the Great Depression of the 1930s some of the big estates began to decline and were subdivided. The second wave of settlement began slowly after World War II with some smaller houses being added to the landscape. By the 1960s, Bedford had a seedy look of elegant decay that was valued as such by many of the residents who wanted an understated and casual lifestyle. During the 1980s and 1990s, however, while Wall Street boomed, a new group of very wealthy urbanites came to buy or build estates. Along with the financiers, lawyers, and advertising executives came celebrities disillusioned with the glitzy, fast-paced life in New York and Los Angeles. All of these groups see Bedford as a quiet retreat to a more wholesome country lifestyle. Today it is an affluent bedroom community of nineteen thousand people, its landscape dominated by large, wooded estates and the open pastureland of its many horse farms and its preserved forests.

The broader study from which this essay is drawn is based on over two hundred in-depth structured and semistructured interviews of a socioeconomic cross section of residents of Bedford and surrounding towns.[12] In this essay, because we wish to focus upon how a sense of place is affected by perceived changes in that place, we have drawn principally upon our interviews with long-term residents of Bedford. What emerges from our interviews is a kind of discursive resistance to newcomers that parallels the institutional resistance that we found in the town. Our essay can be considered a critical hermeneutic interpretation of our informants' critical interpretations of the newcomers to town.

Bedford is thought by most residents to be an exceptionally beautiful landscape of rolling hills, horses grazing in sunny fields, woodlands, streams, stone walls, dirt roads lined with stone walls, and a remarkably well-preserved New England village center. The hilltops are dotted with late-nineteenth- and early-twentieth-century mansions hidden by tall trees and approached by long, winding gravel driveways. This landscape is maintained by some of the most exclusionary zoning practices in the United States. Approximately 80 percent of the town is zoned for single-family houses on a minimum of four acres, approximately 95 percent for houses on one or more acres, and less than 1 percent for two-family dwellings or apartments. Unusually stringent regulations make the subdivision of very large properties into legal four-or-more-acre lots, in most cases, prohibitively expensive. Thus the town's zoning not only effectively excludes the county's poor but also keeps out many comparatively wealthy potential residents. The perceived importance and anxiety about subtle differences in the appreciation and consumption of landscapes reveal a complex economy of identity-formation based on cultural production and consumption and the role of cultural capital in this symbolic economy. Bedford's residents are extraordinarily vigilant and at times militant in retaining the miles of dirt roads and in protecting wetlands, fields, and forests. Conservation societies and individuals set themselves up as watchdogs to ensure Bedford's full compliance with state, county, and their own town's environmental regulations. Historical preservation committees buy, maintain, restore, and/or closely regulate the most minute architectural details of the white wooden shops in the village center. Historical societies attempt to maintain the buildings and landscapes that best evoke Bedford's heritage and that invoke the idea of Bedford's history, the idea of Bedford as a traditional community. Most important, landscapes are preserved so that history and community can be consumed as good taste, as symbolic capital. Here we see not only aesthetics replacing ethics in town planning, as David Harvey has noted in contemporary American society,[13] but community ethics and values reduced to an aesthetics, and aesthetics as the highest value. It is the look of community, not the actuality, that is highly sought after.

Constructing Place-Identity: Situating Bedford in Space and Time

Residents of Bedford have a very strong place-identity. The town is known throughout the New York metropolitan area as one of the most beautiful outer suburbs and consequently is one of the most expensive. Residents not only have an emotional stake in retaining the look of the landscape but have a very large financial stake as well.

The residents we interviewed described contemporary Bedford in relation to other places and in relation to its past self. Such notions of Bedford as a unique place entail a triangulation of space and time. When speaking of Bedford, informants constantly shifted the spatial and temporal reference points. For example, the places chosen by informants to compare to Bedford reflected their own biographies. Similarly, different informants, depending upon how long they had lived in Bedford, compared Bedford in the present to Bedford at various periods in the past. The residents' conceptions of the place are clearly relational and vary according to an individual's experience, knowledge, and degree of immersion into Bedford's hegemonic culture. Interestingly, despite the variation, a certain commonality emerged in how a place like Bedford is seen by its residents. The reason for this, we argue, is that many of our informants "explain" the relational qualities of place to themselves and others in terms of an aesthetic discourse of antimodernism and antiurbanism that tends to dichotomize self and other and impose a fictitious degree of cultural homogeneity and unanimity within the boundaries of the town. An illusion of social and cultural homogeneity and integrity is an integral feature of the residents' attachment to the place. This illusion is more important than the reality. Our interviews revealed that since there is no culture of interacting "over the back fence," it doesn't matter to many of the residents who their neighbors are. What is important is preserving the landscape and excluding new housing developments for aesthetic reasons. Social identities become spatialized through topophilia. Landscapes become symbolic of social relations and the relative social standing of individuals.

The question of what is Bedford is more complex than might at first appear. Although Bedford is demarcated by a town boundary and everything within is Bedford, at the level of sense of place, parts of Bedford are more "Bedford" than others. These "most Bedford" sites loom large in people's minds, and the "less Bedford" sites or views are overlooked as much as possible. Attempts are made to erase them physically from the landscape, and, where this is not possible, they are erased in the mind. For some, Bedford is epitomized by its historic district, which includes the village green as its centerpiece, for others it is certain dirt roads and the properties situated on these roads; for still others it is centered around the large estates near the villages of Katonah and Mount Kisco.

Bedford is defined by what it is not, and most people's fears about contemporary changes in Bedford's landscape focus on the question of how to prevent Bedford from becoming too much like other surrounding towns. Newcomers who fail to appreciate differences between old buildings and reproductions, or between better and worse reproductions, cause other residents much anxiety, causing them to go to extraordinary lengths to control the aesthetic choices or to exclude those whose taste is not reflective of what they see as the essence of Bedford. Bedford need not be socially homogeneous, but it should look so, if living there is to continue to confer social capital upon the residents.

Bedford versus Elsewhere

The rural identity of Bedford and its antiurbanism are generated by the city itself. Consider for a moment the following statement by a woman who has lived in Bedford all of her life: "It's amazing that a beautiful area like this can be one mile from Mount Kisco and forty miles from Manhattan. It's extraordinary that you can't see anybody from here [a hill on her property]." Clearly much of the value of this place for this woman lies in its proximity to New York City. It is this proximity that gives it its scenic value (makes it "amazing") and simultaneously gives it its economic value. Finally, her romantic allusions to the solitude of nature can only be understood as a reaction to cities defined as crowded spaces.

The antiurbanism of Bedford residents is a flight not simply from culture to nature but from modernism. During an interview with a banker who works in New York, we asked what he thought of the postmodern style of some newly built Bedford houses. He answered by contrasting Bedford to the city: "I like postmodern architecture in a city, but I don't want Bedford to look postmodern. I don't even want it to look modern. What Bedford represents is history. Bedford for me is an escape from my world in New York." Thus, Bedford is encoded as the antithesis of urban capitalist modernity. It stands for the lost normalcy that a romantic mythology hopes to recover from late capitalism.

Bedford versus Other Suburbs

The people we interviewed thought of Bedford not only in relation to New York City but also in relation to the system of suburbs that surrounds it. For Americans, suburbs occupy a middle ground between the rural and the urban.

The residents of Bedford, it would appear from our interviews, situate their town conceptually between the rural and the suburban. Having said that, there was, within a broad band of agreement, some difference of opinion.

A real estate saleswoman said: "Bedford is less suburban than other towns. It's more rural." A homemaker claimed that "Bedford is on the borderline of the suburb." Another homemaker in trying to explain what type of place Bedford is said, "Its not suburban, that's more like Scarsdale. North Salem is rural. Bedford is in-between." Residents appear to believe that the place itself can best be described by talking about other places that it is not. But these places are taken to be local examples of types of landscapes and lifestyles. Scarsdale represents the wealthy inner suburb and North Salem the wealthy rural suburb. A number qualified what it meant to be rural. A banker who has lived in Bedford for thirty years described the town as follows:

> Parts of it are rural, but gentleman farms, because rural in America, aesthetically speaking, means it is hideous. When I think of rural — and you don't have to drive too far north of Bedford to find this — I think of trailers, abandoned equipment, and peeling paint.

A homemaker compared the rural of Bedford to that of less-affluent counties to the north: "Bedford is beautiful in comparison to Patterson and Putnam counties. They are disgusting looking; full of junk and clutter spoiling a beautiful landscape. I hate rural poverty. I don't mind city poverty so much. A city's just cement and buildings, so it's not going to look nice anyway." Here we see the aestheticized view of life, where even poverty is evaluated in aesthetic terms. To this woman, urban poverty is more acceptable than rural poverty because the urban landscape by definition is blighted anyway. Bedford to these people is the beautiful rural, the ideal of rurality rather than the reality. It is in the words of a real estate salesman "deluxe rural."

But just as Bedford was not felt to be typically rural, neither was it seen as typically suburban. Residents sought in characterizing Bedford to contrast it to other wealthy suburbs, which they saw as representing significantly different landscape types and lifestyles. One interviewee wished to distinguish it from other suburbs: "Thanks to four-acre zoning we don't have houses on top of one another like in Rye and Larchmont." The three suburbs that were most compared to Bedford were Greenwich, Scarsdale, and Chappaqua. The point of comparing them to Bedford was to use them as archetypes of both a landscape aesthetic and a distinction. Greenwich was seen as the formal, extremely affluent suburban city; Scarsdale was viewed as a more nouveau riche, manicured, and formal town; and Chappaqua was seen as a suburb that although wealthy is only a glorified middle-class suburb of tract housing, albeit with unusually well-landscaped housing developments, mature trees, and impressive houses.

The landscape of Greenwich, for example, is seen to embody different values from that of Bedford. A landscape architect said, "Greenwich is manicured. Here in Bedford we let nature do its own thing." A real estate saleswoman stressed the difference in lifestyle, "Bedford isn't flash like Greenwich. Here you don't have to wear makeup all the time and wear a fur coat. Everyone there has their Mercedes. Here we have our station wagons and jeeps." Another respondent concurred, "The biggest contrast is with Greenwich people. It's the social scene there. Few people move from there to here. It's a millionaire's ghetto." She sees the homogeneity of Greenwich as confining. In fact, this woman reveals her limited mental map of Greenwich, for as a small city it has a much more heterogeneous population than Bedford.

Scarsdale, even more than Greenwich, was used as a contrast to Bedford. For example, a local businessman contrasted the casual style of Bedford to the formality of Scarsdale: "Bedford isn't like Scarsdale with the lawn mowed right up to the street and every tree a specimen." A landscape architect generalized about the look of the landscape: "In Scarsdale every inch of property is cultivated. Here we maintain a country feeling. We are very English." The unspoken implication in this case is that Scarsdale is not "very English." Scarsdale isn't simply seen as a different landscape type (smaller lots, closer to New York City, more formal); it is also thought to have a different social ambiance (more nouveau riche, more Jewish).

Underlying all these comparisons with New York City and other suburbs is the belief that Bedford represents an elegant version of the simple (English) country life. This notion of simplicity, naturalness, and getting back to basics is central to these people's definitions of Bedford. It is closely linked to an old strain of antiurbanism that sees the city as the center of artifice and alienation of people from others and from their true natures. Another woman captured this at the level of the aesthetics of landscape when she said of one of the most fashionable roads in Bedford, "Guard Hill is elegant casual country. There are well-to-do people, but it has all the country feeling of horses and even some run-down places along the way." With her approval of "run-down places," she provided a classic statement of the picturesque with its emphasis upon charming decay.

This attitude about the casualness of the country pervades social life as well. A homemaker had this to say:

> I like the anonymity Bedford affords me. I don't want to drive a car that calls attention to myself. I love the casualness of town. People dress for who they are and what they are doing. I don't feel ashamed to go into Bedford village in jeans and green wellies if I have been gardening. I don't care who sees me.

This again draws upon deep mythologies of the power of nature as a corrective to a corrupting civilization. This is, however, a very bourgeois return to nature. It is marked by different patterns of consumption, different taste, where taste is clearly a form of social capital: a casual million-dollar property rather than a formal one, "station wagons and Jeeps" rather than a Mercedes, and English boots rather than a mink coat. While one strain of the mythology of nature and rurality signifies privacy and individualism, another has to do with community. The country is also the place where people are neighborly. It is thought of as more traditional in values and even preindustrial or premodern and therefore has "more community" than do cities.

An intriguing way of scripting Bedford as a small town took place before a national TV audience a few years ago. The actress Glenn Close, who lives in Bedford, appeared on the *David Letterman Show* with fifteen locals (including several firemen, a plumber, a garage attendant, an electrician, a grocer, and the man who renovated her house). She introduced them as the people from "my little upstate New York town" who "help me in my daily life." One might easily interpret this as the actress playing the part of the lady of the manor, by appearing with the local villagers who serve her. But this would miss the point of what she was trying to convey. For rather than using these folk to suggest that she is an exalted person, she used them to do the reverse. In fact, she operated on the assumption that the TV audience knew she was an exalted person, and she brought these "ordinary people" onto the stage to show that she is down-to-earth. Here, in this country town, she sheds all the trappings of Hollywood and New York and becomes a "real" person. For this is the little town where all sorts of people mingle. This is a community. In this way she plays out a theme central to American ideology: the classless society where all mingle as equals. The New England village is alleged to be the site of such community, as is the Jeffersonian rural.

It is interesting how a place whose identity is so class-based and driven by consumerism can be figured at the level of ideology as the rural classless society. As with most ideology, there is a kernel of truth that lies at the core of the distortion and that serves to make the ideology believable by creating a "reality effect," a small bit of truth to legitimate the large falsehood. Bedford does in fact have working-class and lower-class people living within its boundaries. These areas are segregated in Bedford Hills and the adjoining town of Mount Kisco. As another resident put it, "Bedford is so diverse. Your plumber and electrician have lived here for years." Because these people live in the area, but not within sight of the landscapes of the wealthy, people like Glenn Close can engage in fantasies of a rural society where all classes live amicably together. The segregation by class and the alienation of people are erased in the minds of those who wish to maintain and enhance the aesthetic homogeneity of Bedford. This is a mythic return to the integrated rural life shattered by the rise of urban industrialism. "And to think it's only an hour's drive from New York."

Bedford versus Its Own Past

While virtually everyone we talked to agreed that Bedford is changing, there was disagreement as to how much change had taken place. Some saw the transformation of Bedford as inevitable but still in the future: "It's still rural but modernization is coming." Here the link between the countryside and pre-modernity is made explicit. Others placed the town further along the trajectory from countryside to city: "Bedford is on the borderline of the suburb." Others thought that the town had long been a suburb but had finally begun to resemble one: "Bedford is suburbia. It's a bedroom community. It has always been suburbia, but it didn't used to feel that way." All figure these changes as a loss of individuality. They see Bedford as becoming increasingly like the places that are used to define what Bedford is not. A doctor who has lived in Bedford for thirty-five years had this to say about the changes in town:

> There are areas of Bedford that have been suburban, and by that I mean developer houses on small lots, since before I came here. But now what I see is the spirit of suburbia coming into Bedford in the form of giant million-dollar-plus developer houses which unfortunately are cropping up in some of the most beautiful parts of town. These people probably don't think that what they are creating is suburbia because they are spending so much money, but they are. Suburbia is a style.

Suburbia for this person is an aesthetic as well as a class category. It has to do not with how much money one has but with how one chooses to spend it. A businessman who has been a long-term resident was even more explicit that the changes he objects to in Bedford are changes in taste:

> Some of the new developments are in bad taste. They look like puffed-up middle-class suburban housing that has been quadrupled in size and put on a large lot. The problem is Bedford has become fashionable and people with suburban tastes and lots of money have moved here. I wish nobody had ever heard of Bedford.

Others tried to describe how Bedford is changing by claiming that it is becoming like other suburbs. For some, Bedford is becoming like Greenwich. One man who has lived in Bedford for nearly fifty years said: "The old Bedford lifestyle is slowly vanishing. People who are fixing up homes that the old Bedford people lived in are different. Bedford has become another Greenwich, which I have nothing against. They certainly have beautiful places in Greenwich."

We found no such ambivalence among those who interpreted changes in Bedford as approaching the look of Scarsdale. Scarsdale, as we pointed out earlier, is the wealthy suburb that many of our informants disdained as nouveau riche and overly formal. A stockbroker had the following to say about the small area of conservation zoning in Bedford: "I hate it. You get all the houses along the road, and it looks just like Scarsdale." Another resident compared the different aesthetic of the two places: "There are some people who move here and try and make it look like Scarsdale. They cut down trees and plant little plants. I know a woman who realized her mistake and set about correcting her property by making it look more wild,...not so manicured." Being from Scarsdale has become a term of abuse to describe people who move to Bedford with a disapproved aesthetic: "Some of these new people who have come from Scarsdale or somewhere want to change the place." Scarsdale generates such hostility in some quarters that a new word has been invented by locals to describe a disapproved aesthetic. A real estate broker described changes in town as "the Scarsdalification of Bedford with those big houses on little lots with their formal little gardens and the big tacky gates."

Others link the changes in town to the influx of people in the entertainment industry. Bedford is described as becoming like the antithesis of the rural: greater Los Angeles. One woman said she had given up on Bedford: "It's like California now. It's like Beverly Hills." Another woman said, "I hate to see Bedford beginning to look like Hollywood or some place like that." Here Los Angeles stands not so much for a particular place as for an aesthetic and a style of life.

To put this concern about development and suburbanization in perspective, note the average lot size of a subdivision that a local businesswoman referred to as representative of the transformation of Bedford: "The changes sort of creep up on you. There's been increased building and more traffic. Where I live there is a subdivision but no houses really see each other. There are seven lots on 110 acres. That's not too bad."

The Changing Village

To many people it's distressing how Bedford Village has changed. One woman reminisced, "Bedford was a wonderful place to grow up in back then [in the 1950s]. We had George's store; his wife was the post mistress. There was still a real reason to go to the village: to Sherry's Pharmacy, to Sharlach's Hardware Store." The changes in Bedford Village are linked in the minds of many to the new people who have moved into town. As one man put it, "Bedford Village went from being a place where you could sustain your family to a village full of antique shops and real estate offices." Another respondent put it even more strongly, "Look at Bedford Village. It's no longer a useful town. It used to have a purpose. There used to be many reasons to go there. Now you can go to the bank, the dry cleaners, or to the antique shops and real estate offices. You can't even find a parking space. It's a useless town now." These people draw a parallel between what they see as the transformation of a "real" village into a facade and the transformation of a "real" rural community into a suburb. The prevalence of real estate offices and antique shops in the village is seen as symbolic of this shift in values. The former are simultaneously symbols of and mechanisms for the entry of new urban and suburban people into Bedford. The antique shops, to these critics, represent the false commercialization of heritage that these wealthy newcomers purchase upon entering the town. A local village merchant put these complaints in a rather different perspective: "Those people who complain about changes to the village should have supported the stores [which left the village]. They complain but they run to the mall."

The Invention of the Decline of Community

For many people in Bedford, all of the changes in the town signify a decline of community. They argue that one can see it in the landscape. Now there are new houses cropping up every month. The styles we are told are heterogeneous now. There are so many new people, and they don't hold the same values as people used to. A man who has lived in Bedford for forty years said, "When we moved here in the fifties Bedford was a much smaller place. We knew people in town. It was like a community. It hasn't been that way for twenty years. How could it be? There are too many people now, and they are always coming and going." Whereas for this longtime resident, the decline of community took place ten to twenty years ago, for some newer arrivals it is more recent. For example, a woman who moved to Bedford with her family eleven years ago had this to say:

> It was a small community. I don't know what changed it. It has changed just in the last five years. I think a lot of the old-family-money inherited houses in the area were sold off and different types of people came into the area. I think they were new-money people and were show-offs. What you have, not who you are, is what matters to them. It's very disheartening. I'm not a materialistic person. People used to come over for tea. There was a focus on being neighborly. It's only a fluke that I know the next door neighbor. The real estate agent introduced us.

It is most interesting to hear this person talk of the recent decline of community and of the problem of "new-money people" coming in, because some longer-time residents pointed to this woman's family and others like them as examples of the new money that has been coming into Bedford and transforming the town.

Not only are places such as Bedford highly textualized, but the attitudes of the people are as well. Because Bedford looks quite rural, relative to other suburbs and the city, it brings into play textualized images of the rural. Local real estate advertisements market Bedford as the elegant rural and as the antithesis of modern urban alienation. Because Bedford is marketed as rural and certainly looks rural, it calls up for people narratives of community, individualism, privacy, neighborliness, antiurbanism, and antimodernism. But reliance on the look of the land can be misleading. It may look rural, but that does not mean that the reality of social relations in the place will correspond to the cultural narratives related to that visual image. The narratives constructed around the landscape of Bedford are largely illusory. They may conjure up images of community, but there is relatively little community there. They may conjure up images of individualism and privacy, but zoning laws control to a very large degree what one does with one's land. They may conjure up antiurban images, but most residents not only depend on the city for their livelihood but have chosen to live in Bedford precisely because it is culturally and socially part of the New York metropolitan region. The sophistication of New York City is easily accessible. Bedford isn't "Nowheresville," as one resident put it.

Conclusion

The residents of Bedford conceive of their town as a positional good. They construct Bedford discursively through relations of subordination, just as they construct it physically through social exclusion. The aesthetic appeal of Bedford is a political achievement. Underpinning the beauty of its landscape, including the village with its colonial common symbolizing New England community, is a highly exclusionary politics. The town's landscape is valued for a variety of reasons, but much of this value is generated relationally through comparisons to the city and to other suburbs. People who have lived in Bedford through much of the real estate boom of the 1980s and 1990s speak of how the town is losing its "unique" rural character and coming to resemble other affluent New York suburbs. There is a seeming contradiction that residents should perceive a loss of value at a time when land values are much higher than they were before the boom of the 1980s. But this is resolved if one distinguishes between the purely economic value of a commodity and the symbolic capital, the social value of that commodity. When residents say that Bedford is becoming like Scarsdale, they fear for the positional value of their town. In order to stop this transformation of the landscape, they organize to try to halt the subdivision of land and the construction of new houses. This is not only because the houses decrease the pastoral rurality of the town but because the new houses are seen by many to be inauthentic references to History and not truly historical, not fully "Bedford." As mimics themselves (of nineteenth-century English country gentlemen and women) many Bedford residents are anxious about small differences. Keeping aesthetic differences subtle can be an effective strategy of social distinction. However, because they are not always recognized, poor copies can threaten to spoil the whole. Mimicry can be threatening; the whole may become tarred with the same brush. Topophilia in Bedford produces anxiety and an aestheticized politics of exclusion that obscures its dependence on commercial capitalism by rejecting its modernist aesthetic.

Notes

1. Yi-Fu Tuan, *Topophilia: A Study of Environmental Perception, Attitudes, and Values* (Englewood Cliffs, N.J.: Prentice-Hall, 1974), 4.

2. Edward Relph, *Place and Placelessness* (London: Pion, 1976); David Seamon, and Robert Mugerauer, eds., *Dwelling, Place, and Environment: Towards a Phenomenology of Person and World* (Dordrecht: Martinus Nijhoff, 1985). In the latter work geographers also drew on the earlier work of Kevin Lynch, *The Image of the City* (Cambridge, Mass.: MIT Press, 1960), and Jane Jacobs, *The Death and Life of Great American Cities* (New York: Random House, 1961), who produced influential critiques of modern urban planning.

3. David Harvey, *The Condition of Postmodernity* (Oxford: Blackwell, 1989); Doreen Massey, "A Global Sense of Place," *Marxism Today* (June 1991): 24–29; Jan Penrose, "Reification in the Name of Change," in *Constructions of Place, Race, and Nation*, ed. Peter Jackson and Jan Penrose (London: University College London Press, 1993).

4. Jackson and Penrose, eds., *Constructions of Place, Race, and Nation*.

5. Karen E. Till, "Neo-traditional Towns and Urban Villages: The Cultural Production of a Geography of Otherness," *Environment and Planning D: Society and Space* 11 (1993): 709–32.

6. Harvey, *Condition of Postmodernity*; and Don Mitchell, *The Lie of the Land: Migrant Workers and the California Landscape* (Minneapolis: University of Minnesota Press, 1996).

7. Penrose, "Reification"; Nuala Johnson, "Cast in Stone: Monuments, Geography, and Nationalism," *Environment and Planning D: Society and Space* 13 (1995): 51–66; Mitchell, *Lie of the Land*; Gillian Rose, *Feminism and Geography: The Limits of Geographical Knowledge* (Cambridge: Polity, 1993).

8. In Caroline Mills, "Myths and Meanings of Gentrification," in *Place/Culture/Representation*, ed. James Duncan and David Ley (London: Routledge, 1993). Mills shows how gentrified housing and the lifestyles associated with such housing are examples of important positional goods in the establishment of upper-middle-class Canadian identities. Eugene McCann, "Neotraditional Developments: The Anatomy of a New Urban Form," *Urban Geography* 16, no. 3 (1995): 210–33, looks at a neotraditional housing style as a positional good and form of symbolic capital. Both of these authors show how a particular class fraction occupies a niche in the market for housing and show clearly some of the adverse economic and social effects of such jockeying for position and distinction.

9. Pierre Bourdieu, *Distinction: A Social Critique of the Judgement of Taste*, trans. R. Nice (Cambridge, Mass.: Harvard University Press, 1984); Edward Hirsch, *Social Limits to Growth* (Cambridge, Mass.: Harvard University Press, 1976).

10. Through what Till refers to as "otherness" or othering (Till, "Neo-traditional Towns").

11. Homi Bhabha, *The Location of Culture* (London: Routledge, 1994).

12. James Duncan and Nancy Duncan, *Suburban Pre-texts* (Baltimore: Johns Hopkins University Press, forthcoming).

13. Harvey, *Condition of Postmodernity*.

READING THE WETLANDS

William Howarth

> The odd thing, in fact, about literature as an imagined territory is that there are apparently no natural limits and hence, it would seem, there are apparently no natural limits to the field of literary criticism.
>
> — STEPHEN GREENBLATT and GILES GUNNING,
> *Redrawing the Boundaries*

Defining literature as *imagined territory* is an old habit among academic critics. Early mimetic theories of art distinguish world from text, with text neatly smoothing the earth's tangle, and this distinction has long elevated human status: we think, therefore we are sovereign; we are conscious and imaginative, hence the world is our oyster to pluck, to crack, to discard, to remake. Granted dominion for two millennia, that brand of humanism has produced a world with fewer oysters, crowded freeways, global warming, and critics who say "there are apparently no natural limits to the field of literary criticism." My purpose in this essay is to suggest that natural limits are inescapable, especially when writers use geographic metaphors or imagine physical places. I also argue that long-proclaimed distinctions between place and person, self and other, sustain the illusions known as *love* or *reverence for nature*. Nature does not need our love, but we surely need its life and health. If we accept the hard fact of natural limits, relations between terrain and imagination may turn less dominant, more respectful — bearing in mind that *respect* means to revision, or look again, which should be the purpose of critical effort.

My epigraph is from a book that raises "far-reaching questions about disciplinary mapping"[1] yet rarely examines its own geo-rhetoric. Scholars have long used spatial metaphors to fence the pastures of intellect: one occupies a *domain, province,* or *field* of knowledge, depending on rank and ambition. Today *mapping* covers a vast range of academic turf, staked with many claims about canon, period, and authorship.[2] This "imagined territory" is ostensibly beyond natural limits because its basis "is not space or territory but procedure."[3] Yet procedure is spatial, since it's a series of *steps,* a *way* of performing, to move in a desired *direction.* If our existence is so firmly bounded by space and time, what can have no natural limits? Name any object of fantasy — a centaur, Little Nell, El Dorado — and we have fictions made of natural elements. In the view of Canadian novelist Robertson Davies, imagination is "a good horse to carry you over the ground — not a flying carpet to set you free from probability."[4] Only those who know little of nature think imagination can surpass it. Researchers peer every day into mitochondria or galaxies and glimpse a nature far stranger than any previous imagining.

One poet readily grasped this insight, without the benefit of radio telescopes. In 1862 Emily Dickinson sent Thomas Wentworth Higginson, an editor in Boston, some of her early poems. Baffled by their formal oddities, Higginson wrote a polite letter of praise and inquired about her background. Dickinson replied: "You ask of my companions. Hills, sir, and the sundown, and a dog large as myself, that my father bought me. They are better than beings because they know, but do not tell; and the noise in the pool at noon excels my piano."[5] Her enigmatic response mocks his query about companions, by which he meant the friends or mentors who shaped her writings. Her answer takes a new slant: my companions are not human. In the hills, sundown, and dog (a place, time, and creature) she finds associates who are "better than beings [humans] because they know, but do not tell." This praise expresses no disregard for humans, only respect for nature's prescience. Her silent, knowing companions "do not tell" because they have no words or numbers. Yet eloquence has many forms; hence the "noise in the pool at noon" excels her "piano," the tunes she makes in verse.[6]

The assertion that knowledge is not solely human has long sustained religion and philosophy. To believers, the divine or natural forces always know more, and even skeptics agree that true knowledge begins with recognizing ignorance. Dickinson appears to side with her contemporary Ralph Waldo Emerson, who saw the relation between subject and object, mind and matter, as a process of *correspondence,* the interaction or reciprocity that resembles letters going back and forth, to exchange intelligence or secrets.[7] Dickinson calls her poetry "my letter to the World / That never wrote to me" (441), which again describes language as a human way of knowing and representing, while the world (nature) uses silence. Emerson said that language verifies human primacy, but Dickinson sees words as anterior to life.[8] From her silent companions she learns what nature *already knows,* has splendidly assembled before she happens by. The work of her poems resembles archaeology, probing to find lost places: an acre with four trees, the western hills, a plank in the kitchen floor. Places write upon the mind, and poets learn to read them. Words alone cannot make a place, any more than imagination creates territory.[9]

Readings of places have occupied many American writers, who over five centuries have witnessed drastic changes in their continent; and since 1990 a school of *ecocritics* has begun to examine place-centered texts, mainly in the Anglo-American canon. In their fledgling years, ecocritics have shared only a loose affinity. Some advocate green politics, while others evangelize for natural theology. Many long to replace literary and cultural theory with pragmatic readings, ethics favored over aesthetics. To date few have explored the highly relevant fields of ecology, geography, and environmental history. Joyce Carol Oates has mocked nature-writers for "a painfully limited set of responses...REVERENCE, AWE, PIETY, MYSTICAL ONENESS," and ecocritics too often echo that laudatory tone. Excluded from *Redrawing the Boundaries,* ecocritics have yet to persuade others that "mapping fields" also demands serious study of the relations between word and land, text and place. To recognize and accept ecocritical practice, readers will need to agree that *place* functions as a cultural and textual paradigm.[10]

Place differs from the geometrical idea of *space,* a set of points or dimensions that measure distance, area, and volume. Space has a few applied meanings, such as defining where we park, how long to wait, or the blank between these lines of type, but space is an abstraction with limited semantic reach. Place animates a broader range of human enterprise, from mathematics and logic to athletic contests. Place sustains fundamental concepts of time and space, the earth and maps, forms of writing, the sacred and profane, gardens and buildings, social order and disorder, political status, region and nation. This widely influential word has a simple, domestic origin, the neighborhoods of early Athens and Rome. In Greek, two words signified location: *topos* and *plateia* (from *platus,* broad). A *plateia* (*plattia,* in Latin) was an open square or courtyard, a shared commons surrounded by private houses. As Rome expanded, its imperial forms spread throughout Europe, creating a townscape whose components became the visual grammar of civilization: aqueduct, forum, bath, and *plattia.* The locals developed other pronunciations: *piazza, plats, plaza,* forerunners of Anglo-Norman *place,* an open space ringed by houses.

By the Renaissance, place signified doubly: it meant any physical location (a piece or plot of land) but also social position or status, because land produced wealth. To geographers, place defined external spaces where people dwell, whether in house, village, or city; and internal spaces of those structures, such as a hall, stairs, or a room. In the formal study of philosophy, history, or literature, place was a defined or bounded part of space, whether in the heavens or a book: a commonplace book was full of many places, lines copied from other books. The Greek *topos* also applied: *topikos,* of a place, became matter for rhetoricians, a commonplace argument, as in Aristotle's *Topics.* From 1500 on, place acquired especially intricate social meanings: to know one's place was to behave with proper manners; to put someone in their place was to rebuff or rebuke (in current slang, to put down); to be a place-man was to maintain social order. In the French court, status meant proximity: the Second Lord of the Stairs, the First Lord of the Antechamber; while ambitious English courtiers knew by heart the iron law of place-keeping: "Four ways at court to win men's grace / To lie, to laugh, to flatter, to face."

These meanings survive today in the notion of placement, used in schools and sports to rank performers. Place marks space and time, as events are said to take place; and by this extension, it slips from noun to verb and acquires transitive force, meaning to position, arrange, recognize, identify, and categorize.[11] Across twenty-five centuries, a city square becomes a trope for mental activity, the means of organizing perceptions into knowledge. Places write upon the mind: what began as a physical object becomes in time the work of subjectivity. As a paradigm, place is physical, social, and intellectual; it surrounds constructions like race, gender, or class because they must stand or transpire *somewhere,* within a recognizable place, though that place may range from the dateline of journalism or the venue of law to the poet's pleasure in setting: James Merrill's changing light at Sandover, T. S. Eliot's wasteland, Edgar Lee Masters's riverscape, W. H. Auden's limestone country. While the ways that places look, smell, and baffle have long intrigued writers, they are of less apparent interest to critical readers. Ecocritics could dispel that apathy by attending closely to textual places, neither skipping irritably over pages of place-description nor casually accepting how we *think* we see them.

Between Earth and Water

James Hamilton-Paterson begins *Playing with Water* (1987), his memoir of several years spent on a Philippines island, by acknowledging that such accounts are multilocal:

> The places a writer writes are always somewhere else. He may describe a journey, a foreign land; but no matter how faithfully he disposes his rocks and trees, his tokens of difference and the humdrum exotica he comes to love, certain delinquent breezes drift through landscape and writer alike, dishevelling things at their root.[12]

The "somewhere else" may be remembered or invented; it is foreign matter that writers make familiar, even as surprises and accidents, the "delinquent breezes" that stir and freshen a story, will change its direction and meaning. Literary places are never empty because they have implied observers, trying to read the stories written there. Place alone does not determine text, since the many islands, mountains, and oceans in literature are infinitely varied. Yet one locale stands out because it has a long history of ambiguous and also evolving cultural status: the wetland, in its manifold guises of bog, fen, marsh, or swamp. For thousands of years, the human attitude toward wetlands was consistently negative: they were read as dangerous, useless, fearful, filthy, diseased, noxious. Then perceptions began to change in the 1700s, gradually turning toward more positive values of beauty, fertility, variety, utility, and fluidity. Emily Dickinson covers the entire historical spectrum in a quatrain: "Sweet is the swamp with its secrets, / Until we meet a snake; / 'Tis then we sigh for houses, / And our departure take" (19). Later writers weigh in with their own readings. In his elegy "When Lilacs Last in the Dooryard Bloom'd," Walt Whitman agrees that a cedar swamp has "deep secluded recesses," but there lives the hermit thrush, a solitary daemon whose song assuages grief and despair. To Willa Cather and Ernest Hemingway, human involvement with wetlands suggests tragic decline and spiritual ruin. In *A Lost Lady* (1923) and "Big Two-Hearted River" (1925), characters who drain marshes or fish in cedar swamps must struggle against self-defeat and insanity. Recent authors are more cheerfully morbid; in *Pilgrim at Tinker Creek* (1972), Annie Dillard delights to wade in river marshes and watch a "giant waterbug" suck the life from hapless frogs. For John McPhee, the "amphibious new world" of Atchafalaya Bayou is a snake-infested morass where New Orleans began, willy-nilly.[13]

How and why these shifts occur is a problem that vexes today's cultural and environmental historians. Can the extrinsic forces of earth, water, and sky alter the intrinsic elements of language, rhetoric, and imagery? Do material realities drive these changes, or are they driven by social conditions, ideological convictions, or hegemonic systems of meaning and value? Or do aesthetic and psychological representations evolve, mapping a new status for wetlands by replacing masculine priorities of stability, coherence, and power with feminized uncertainty, inconsistency, and fluidity? Is this a canonical issue, with wetlands emerging from centuries of neglect to shine forth as empowered? In all of these responses, we rarely hear the pragmatic voice of science: perhaps the physical condition of wetlands alter, and ideas then follow? Biological determinism is unpopular with humanists because it raises the specter of systematic repression, in the name of "natural law." Ironically, natural law was a product of medieval theology, and humanism once championed science as a way to dispel dogma with the quantitative methods of mathematics, physics, and chemistry.

The current humanist disdain for science is based on partial or anachronistic knowledge, most clearly signaled by the relative indifference toward Darwin, whose ideas still validate large portions of biological science. Few humanists use Darwin as a theoretical base, even though his theory of evolution is a narrative that describes the dynamics of natural and sexual selection. Instead the hermeneutics of Marx and Freud have prevailed, and in their schemes nature is a brute or alien force. There's more and less to Darwin than humanists commonly think, and one project for ecocriticism is to reintroduce evolutionary theory to literary discourse.[14] We also need to find ways to explain why literary places change in value over time. Many disciplinary fields examine places, from anthropology and folklore to linguistics, theology, and sociology. For my present purposes, the most useful models to consider are in literature, geography, and philosophy.[15]

Since the 1970s about two dozen literary studies of space and place have appeared, most of them influenced by Gaston Bachelard, whose *The Poetics of Space* (1965) offers a graceful, neo-Freudian reading of houses, rooms, and gardens as symbolic mirrors of the human psyche. Later critics sophisticated this approach and took it outdoors, in studies that view forest, desert, or mountain as forms of cultural poetics.[16] In such readings, mental fabric is assumed to precede and fashion a natural context, much like the process of settling or building upon terrain. Yet terrain obviously plays a large role in defining where and what we may build. This causal riddle has dogged us since Descartes: Do we think, and thus shape our world, or does the world fashion our thoughts? The dissonance between subject and object gave a tragic cast to American history, as Europeans moved into a continent they called "empty," despite the presence of several million native people. Such impositions of cultural power derive from what Paul Carter calls the epistemology of spatial history: people know a continent by small increments, as they spread across its face like an ever-widening stain.[17]

Geography began in antiquity, spawned most of the earth and social sciences, and today forms with ecology the core of modern environmental studies. Simply defined, geography surveys earth forms and processes that affect natural and cultural relations. The field has three well-integrated branches: *physical* geography examines land, water, and energy resources; *human* geography studies their impact on history, culture, and society; *regional* geography analyzes political units created by those processes. Because their subject is physical, geographers use methods that are visual, spatial, and textual. They read the surface of the earth to interpret its arrangement and relations; they look for interactions that shape the environment in which all species live. Their principal descriptor is location, the placement or position of landscapes, species, cultures, and how they interact across space and time. Geography (*geographia,* earth-drawing) has many affiliations with history and literature, for all are descriptive and inscriptive, using imagery and language to read and write earthly accounts.[18]

Some human geographers have embraced recent literary theory, agreeing with David Harvey that "geographical imagination is far too pervasive and important a fact of intellectual life to be left alone to geographers."[19] Yet little reciprocity of interest is evident among literary academics, who mainly use place and space to verify notions of sign or power. Poststructural theory favors the ascendancy of reader over author or text, which to geographers is the equivalent of drawing maps in the dark. While "ground-truthing" is often required in science, empirical evidence is now commonly missing from humanistic inquiry. Ever since Michel Foucault, research has become "a space into which the writing subject constantly disappears," to cite his famous dismissal of authorship. In Marxist and cultural studies, places are social productions or constructions, while feminist, queer, and multicultural readings consistently describe place as interior or marginal, a place to reject, escape, or destroy.[20] These built or imaginary locations, of undeniable import in literature, are rarely seen as affected by physical environment. The emphasis is on severing human conduct from natural or biological conditions, a view that generates stark solipsism in readings of locations. Gillian Tindall exemplifies this approach by reading literary landscape as purely imaginative figments:

My central concern is not with actual landscapes and dwellings, surviving or vanished, but with what these physical settings have become in the minds of novelists. I am concerned with the literary uses to which places are put, the meanings they are made to bear, the roles they play when they are re-created in fiction, the psychological journeys for which they are the destinations. Actual countries become countries of the mind, their topography transformed into psychological maps, private worlds. But, in the nature of novel writing, these worlds do not remain private but are transmitted back to readers, who then, in their turn, see the original locations with changed and awakened eyes.[21]

Her reasoning is that facts matter less than stories, that fantasy is superior to actuality; and that writing changes the meaning of place, invariably for the better. Shift the emphases a little, and we have the psychology of those who buy and sell real estate: what matters is not the land or house itself, but how much profit they bring as commodities. The process Tindall describes is not enhancement or *improvement,* a word familiar to land developers, but *alienation,* a legal term that means to quit previous claims and also suggests emotional or spiritual detachment.[22] We are clearly a long way from Emily Dickinson's conviction that nature knows more than it tells. Until critics learn to read the language of land in ways that involve recognition and integration, they will continue to alienate human culture toward its only planet.[23]

Yet even as literary critics ignored them, geographers were taking a fresh look at cultural renditions of physical space. A pioneer figure in this endeavor has been Yi-Fu Tuan, whose many writings have promoted his belief that geography offers a hermeneutic for other disciplines. A political and intellectual refugee from 1948 China, Tuan wrote about his life to reveal how the division of places and people promotes anomie and migration, the hallmarks of postmodern alienation. He has proposed replacing that estrangement with *topophilia,* an affection for places, which preserves their aesthetic value and sustains ethical behavior toward the earth. His call for a sense of place that integrates feeling and thought establishes Tuan as a major interpreter of landscape in this century, one whose work provides measured political and ethical support for the natural and vernacular aesthetics of Jens Jensen and J. B. Jackson.[24]

Tuan's ideas have won support from human geographers who have worked on reading literary texts. Leonard Lutwack identifies two opposed themes that literature often expresses: that earth is a hostile, alien force, the enemy of human potential; and that it is the true home of humanity, one that best fulfills it. Both of these attitudes foreground religious convictions, which produce tensions between literal and symbolic readings of place in many literary forms, from pastoral to tragic. A parallel effort by Anne Buttimer provides an experiential grounding of concepts like place and home by examining the uses of language and narrative in small-scale communities. Efforts like these use geography as textual interpretation, with a strong focus on both empirical and moral claims.[25]

Support for Tuan is also suggested by philosophers D. W. Winnicott and Richard Rorty. Winnicott (1896–1971) worked on object relations theory, leading him to speculate about a zone between subject and object called "potential space," an area where play and aesthetics transpire. In his recasting of classical pragmatism, Rorty attacks the belief that knowledge is only mental or linguistic, arguing that literature must develop effective moral and political positions. He argues that the usual brand of realism is "an impossible attempt to view the world from Nowhere," because Somewhere always surrounds a subject, even if not well perceived.[26] This emphasis on context argues for finding a middle ground *between* two opposites, so that subject-object or mind-place becomes a synthesis of experience and imagination, a region lying amid apparent counterparts. Such a view directs the work of Nicholas Entrikin, whose "geography of modernity" affirms betweenness as the condition of place, a concept echoed (if not cited) in recent studies of women writers, who are seen to occupy liminal or marginal spaces as a condition of their gender.[27]

These ideas from geography and philosophy suggest several ways for ecocritics to read textual places. By emphasizing mediation and dialogue, we may forgo the isolating posture of alienation and learn why places like wetlands have evolved in meaning. But to build persuasive readings, and to validate the claim that places are significant in literary texts, ecocritics also need rigorous methods of analysis. Elsewhere I have urged them to use more interdisciplinary framing, with theoretical models drawn from ecology and planning.[28] Those disciplines account for change in places through a sequence called *the land-use cycle*. All inhabited land follows a cycle of change from natural to social conditions. Geographic location (latitude, longitude, and elevation) determines the sites of habitats: tundra, forest, wetland. Rain, sun, and wind erode rock into soil, which sustains plants, and they draw animals — since all life-forms follow food trails. The succession of human occupants marks phases of land tenure, secured by technology and hierarchy. If people leave, the cycle reverses; if they stay, choices must follow: neglect the land and risk its permanent damage or restore and protect it against further losses. In the latter choice, a change in cultural values occurs — as humans learn to respect what nature knows.[29]

The cycle tells a story, implying author and audience, and the ecocritical task is to apply this narrative to literary discourse. Repeating cycles in nature — like geological erosion, deposition, and uplift — have their equivalents in biological life, death, and recomposition. A sequence of energy consumption — as species use, deplete, or sustain resources — echoes the course of cultural transmission, as people acquire thoughts, give them designs, and share the results. Authors who describe these patterns are writing narratives about the geography and ecology of power. To test this theory, we might look to many imagined terrains, from Jane Austen's Hampshire to Thomas Hardy's Wessex, but in America, a prime candidate is William Faulkner, the inventor and "sole proprietor" of a land he called Yoknapatawpha County.

Faulkner wrote fourteen novels set in Yoknapatawpha, a close analogue for Lafayette County, his home in northern Mississippi. Readers often insist that Faulkner is a "universal" writer, soaring above the narrow confines of regional space and custom. This view originated with Malcolm Cowley, a veteran New Yorker, who decreed that Yoknapatawpha embodies an epic myth of Euro-American history. Later critics often divide on whether Yoknapatawpha is literal or figural, forgetting that it should be both if it is to suggest mythic dimensions.[30] In *Go Down, Moses* (1942), seven Yoknapatawpha tales portray the dispossession of Indians, the enslavement of Africans, the rebellion and destruction of the Civil War, and the impoverished years of Reconstruction. The stories repeat episodes of conquest — territorial, racial, and sexual — presented as obsessive quests for gold, power, and expiation of sin. The main rite of purification transpires in "The Bear," which tells how young Ike McCaslin finds deliverance in the Big Woods, a place described as "profound, sentient, gigantic, and brooding."[31]

Faulkner's characters call the Big Woods "wilderness," but in geographical terms it's a middle landscape, lying between lowland plains and upland Appalachians. Owned by Ike's family and now his principal legacy, Big Woods stands on piedmont, a rising country of mixed forest, conifer and deciduous, that sustains great variety of plant and animal life — and nourishes an omnivore like Old Ben, a large, elusive bear that is a legendary quarry. This piece of property is "wilderness" to men of the McCaslin clan because it represents a desire for higher ground, where they may transcend the lowland realm of farms and villages. Their annual hunts are efforts to reclaim a lost code of blood and sacrifice, thought to have ruled prehistoric time. The hunters bring food for early meals, then forage off the land. They try to preserve racial and class privileges, but in this realm, other orders prevail. On Ike's fourth hunt, he is sixteen and begins to learn about dispossession — through a rite of passage that begins in wetlands.

The story does not follow a direct chronology but slips back and forth, and as a hunter, Ike must also learn an asynchronous logic. He gives up his rifle, watch, and compass to follow tracks, wandering far from known terrain. When lost, he begins to walk a sweeping half circle, looking for a backtrack. He turns one direction and then its opposite, coming at last to a transitional zone:

> and this time it was not even the tree because there was a down log beside it which he had never seen before and beyond the log *a little swamp, a seepage of moisture somewhere between earth and water,* and he did what Sam had coached and drilled him as the next and the last, seeing as he sat down on the log the crooked print, *the warped indentation in the wet ground which while he looked at it continued to fill with water*

until it was level full and the water began to overflow and the sides of the print began to dissolve away. Even as he looked up he saw the next one, and, moving, the one beyond it; moving, not hurrying, running, but merely keeping pace with them as they appeared before him as though they were *being shaped out of thin air just one constant pace short of where he would lose them forever and be lost forever himself,* tireless, eager, without doubt or dread, panting a little above the strong rapid little hammer of his heart, emerging suddenly into a little glade, and the wilderness coalesced. It rushed, soundless, and solidified — the tree, the bush, the compass and the watch glinting where a ray of sunlight touched them. Then he saw the bear.[32]

The passage moves Ike from swamp to glade, wetland to woodland, and that change of locus transforms his identity. Lost in the woods, he finds a new track, sets aside old lessons, sees familiar terrain grow strange, keeps pace with an invisible (but also silent, knowing) quarry. The journey is a paradox, every advancing step regressing Ike from present confusion toward an ordered past, before human claims turned wilderness into land. The font of this revelation is a swamp, "somewhere between earth and water," where those twinned elements yield the sign of a paw print: a trace on soil now *in the process of filling* with water, it is space marking time, a presence telling of recent absence. Following the swamp trail to where he feels "lost forever," Ike reaches a glade, the starting point where he left compass and watch. By tracing this circuit of pursuit, he is in the right place to see the bear step out of fable and into a living moment, "and the wilderness coalesced."

This transforming moment cannot return the wilderness to its original and unitary condition, but it helps Ike see that the human claim of possession is illusory. Like that paw print, he is between earth and water, filling up and going empty, moving toward a destiny where past and future, boy and man, bear and woods, all coalesce in a single, blazing rush: wilderness. The experience is about mystical fusion, the loss of boundaries, and also about social maturation, gaining a sense of place. In later parts of "The Bear," Ike relinquishes his claim on the Big Woods to atone for its founding in racial and sexual crimes. For him, that ethic rises from the geographic identity of a place he found and lost. The tale strongly invokes geography because tracking and hunting, like surveying and mapping, are acts that put mind to land, trace nature's contours to learn what it knows.

That notion of wilderness is at odds with a view advanced by Nina Baym, that "[t]he essential quality of America" rests in "unsettled wilderness" and the opportunities it offers "the individual as a medium on which he may inscribe, unhindered, his own destiny and his own nature." Baym argues that inscribing is equivalent to owning and settling land; but Ike McCaslin is *describing* his destiny by relinquishing a claim on land, yielding to the unwritten priority of wilderness. (His cash legacy turns into worthless IOUs.) Faulkner is writing an eco-fable about the folly of possession, and his skeptical view of property has a long ancestry. As several scholars have noted, the settlement of America was fraught with nostalgic regret, as newcomers often sensed they had destroyed the Eden they had sought. Taking land was not a male obsession, since women participated in settlement, just as both genders later crowded their lives with domestic commodities. Ike's tale carries us toward a mediated view: the wilderness will coalesce when we lose old stories and read a new place, somewhere between earth and water.[33]

The Mud of the Mire

I've focused on wetlands because for thousands of years they have represented wilderness and thus help us to trace evolving readings of its status. The desert or forest might also qualify, but wetlands have experienced a more evident change in signification. To recent scientists, wetlands exemplify natural biodiversity and offer a testing ground for ecocritical practice. Most biomes correspond to climate zones: jungles in the tropics, tundra in the arctic. Wetlands are a global habitat, occurring at all latitudes and elevations, from seaboard plains to alpine ranges. Depending on location, they may have fresh, salt, or brackish water and produce high or low biotic yields. They also come in a wide variety of shapes, are seen as wild and unpredictable, yet in that diversity sustain the integrity of living systems. Described metaphorically by William Neiring as "the kidneys of the landscape," wetlands perform rites of cleansing: they transfer, settle, filter, and recharge the mingled elements of soil and water.[34] We cannot essentialize wetlands because they are hybrid and multivalent: neither land nor water alone, they are water-land, a continuum between terra and aqua. In rhetorical terms they are not syntax but *parataxis,* phrases placed side by side without apparent connection, a term Joseph Frank used to describe spatial forms that evoke great variety of response. In their wildness, wetlands dispossess readers of old codes and lead toward new syntax, where phrases may begin to reassemble.[35]

Among literary scholars, Peter A. Fritzell was the first to explore the cultural implications of this environment from an ecocritical perspective. In a journal that rarely publishes English professors, he wrote:

> Wetlands are not conventional wild areas. They do not cater to established, classical concepts of vista, horizon, and landscape. By comparison with the Smokies or the High Sierra, wetlands are claustrophobic. They force you inward, both upon yourself and upon the nonhuman world. They do not give you grand views; they humble you rather than reinforce your delusions of grandeur. . . . A wetland is nothing if not a patient environment. It reminds you more of slow, ongoing processes of change than it does of the pinnacles of evolutionary achievement.[36]

This ethical reading calls on humility and patience to master feelings of alien-ation from wilderness. A more dispassionate reader might counsel stronger action, either separation or divorce. Humans are oxic creatures, requiring oxygen-rich air, while wetlands are anoxic or noxious, producing marsh gas (methane) that has the sulfuric, fecal smell of rotted eggs. A wetland is not just alien to human life; it provides little basis for a life beyond subsistence. One may hunt or forage there, but a wetland is not solid enough to allow farming or building, the ground of civilization.

Ecologists call unstable regions of this sort *ecotones* because they contain no fixed boundaries, only a gradient slope between solid and fluid. Two terms for wetlands, *swamp* and *marsh,* are not synonyms but distinctions: a swamp has woody plants, while a marsh is mostly grasses. Swamps tend to be in-land; marshes lie on coastlines and shorelines. Yet whether called *swamp, flat, marsh,* or *bog,* these areas have come by long association to express divided values: (1) difficulty or uncertainty, as in a quagmire, or morass; (2) change, since wetlands are transition zones between water and land; and (3) contin-gency or possibility, because wetlands may foster new life. If they do not remind Fritzell of "pinnacles of evolutionary achievement," wetlands still play a vital role in ecosystem dynamics. Moving slowly through wetlands, water settles decaying organisms to create fertile bottoms, while sending a nutrient-rich effluent downstream, to nourish surface areas. Left undisturbed, wetlands transform muck into peat, methane, or coal, thus becoming useful to extrac-tive industry. They form a constellation of paradoxes: although wild and thus defining human limits, wetlands are a global ecosystem that feeds about half the world's creatures, cover 6 percent of its land surface, and exist everywhere but Antarctica.[37]

We may now begin to see why authors over time express such varying re-sponses to wetlands: yes, ideas change, but so do places, and an ecocritic should chart their reciprocity as the changes transpire. Throughout history wetlands have altered in value, at first because they impeded humanity and now because humanity is engulfing them. As a remnant of fast-receding wildness, wetlands are the landscape equivalent of extinct or endangered species, from dinosaurs and pandas to indigenous tribes. They are an anodyne for the discontents of civilization, following an inverse law of supply and demand. As they passed from original abundance to present scarcity, their meaning evolved. Somewhere along the course of history, an old reading or syntax gave way to paratactic phase, followed by a new reading that is still emerging. The transitions frame what Yi-Fu Tuan calls a *hearth* or home, places where wetlands coalesced, like Ike's wilderness, in moments of cultural revelation.[38]

Antagonism toward wetlands governed most ancient civilizations, going back to the eastern Mediterranean, where arable land was scarce and pre-cious. Early creation myths tend to form land out of water, describing the latter as a realm of demonic chaos. In Genesis 1, the world is at first a shapeless void of waters until God moves upon their face, dividing light from dark, and then waters from waters, so that dry land may appear. The great Divider thus sets a course for generations of farmers: wherever men find low, water-saturated ground, they must drain and dry it, freeing themselves from "the mud of the mire" (Psalms 40) so that plows and seeds may follow. By controlling cultivation and reproduction, men are granted dominion over earthly life (Genesis 1:28). In this old reading of wetlands, drainage is a patriarchal duty that cleanses and fertilizes the earth; it sanctions controlling land, subduing women, and training children for future security.[39]

In the year 1500, wetlands covered one-third of the North American continent, stretching along both seaboards and beside most inland waters. Early explorers described these places as hazardous, a barrier to navigation and the source of pestilential diseases. Their fears measured the ominous nature of unknown, untamed land. As Columbus traversed the coastal marshes of Cuba, and DeSoto led a forced march across the Everglades, both sought gold and found instead swampy, malaria-infested realms, unfit for all save the Arawak natives, who appeared to thrive in tropical mire. When storms blew the English Pilgrims off their course for Virginia and landed them on Cape Cod, they were dismayed to find beyond its beaches only dense marshes and boggy thickets of scrub cedar: a "howling, desolate wilderness" William Bradford recalled, where piety and practicality would be much tested. On earth their salvation lay with the Massachuset people, who revealed that the marshes held an abundance of edible plants and wild game. The old reading of wetlands began to falter, as settlers turned from ideology to direct experience. Unfortunately for the Massachuset, tales of New England plenitude attracted masses of transatlantic immigrants throughout the seventeenth century.[40]

As Europeans possessed the New World, Stephen Greenblatt writes, they also grasped its marvelous, magical possibilities. The story of America's colonial years may also be told as eco-disaster, destroying wetland habitats to build good ports and farms. William Cronon describes the fencing and draining of New England fields, ostensibly to foil wolves, as a catastrophe that erased many forms of wildlife, as well as native populations. Many of the English settlers hailed from East Anglia, a vast fenland drained to create fields and canals, dotted with windmills. As Christian farmers, they heeded a favorite allegory, *Pilgrim's Progress* (1676), wherein the hero finds his path to grace blocked by a foul mudhole. He asks a figure named Help why the place is not drained:

And he said unto me, This miry slough is such a place as cannot be mended; it is the descent whither the scum and filth that attends conviction for sin doth continually run, and therefore it is called the Slough of Despond; for still, as the sinner is awakened about his lost condition, there ariseth in his soul many fears, and doubts, and discouraging apprehensions, which all of them get together, and settle in this place.

Help says that no amount of dumping, whether cart-loads of soil or whole-some instructions, will "make good ground of the place," for it is made of despondency, the loss of faith that makes life wretched. As a figure of all things fallen, the Slough sends a clear homily to New World settlers: be of good faith, and drain thy fields.[41]

The drive for human dominion was not solely Christian, for drainage was practiced from Asia and the Fertile Crescent to the dikes of Holland. But in America, physical geography played an obvious hand in shaping wetland change. From Boston to Savannah, most coastal cities arose at fall lines, places where sand met rock and blocked easy upstream travel. Dams at those sites impounded water power for mills, and the millraces also drained wetlands. According to ecologist John Terborgh, diverting such water sources permanently destroys boundary ecosystems. Colonials read swampland as unattained capital, an outward sign of social decay. On his journey in 1729 to survey a line dividing Virginia and North Carolina, William Byrd wrote that wherever the land was "a miry pocosin," its farmers were slovenly and indolent, inclined to loaf and beget mulatto slaves.[42]

In its post-Revolutionary years, America defined itself as an agrarian republic, all progress marked by civic improvement. The federal capitol stood in a new District of Columbia, centered between North and South, on land recovered from marshes. Spokesmen for republican virtues embraced Enlightenment precepts, using rational and liberal means to justify social progress. In *Letters from an American Farmer* (1782), Hector St. John de Crèvecoeur charts the course of a civil people: "To examine how the world is gradually settled, how the howling swamp is converted into a pleasing meadow, the rough ridge into a fine field; and to hear the cheerful whistling, the rural song, where there was no sound heard before, save the yell of the savage, the screech of the owl or the hissing of the snake?" Such pastoral imagery elevated American cultural status above the reach of European jibes. Arranging his *Notes on the State of Virginia* (1782) in tidy essays on natural and social features, Thomas Jefferson disputes the French naturalist Georges Buffon, who said New World species were puny because they lived on a swampy continent. Jefferson denies the animals are smaller but also asserts that swamps have little effect on species size. He also praises the practice of draining marshes to create meadows and the unexpected cultural benefit of exposing ancient Indian mounds, like those he excavated at Rivanna, Virginia. When he later sent Lewis and Clark to find a continental route to the Pacific, Jefferson encouraged his deputies to survey river wetlands for their natural history data.[43]

Spurred by the work of Linnaeus, whose *Systema Naturae* (1734) categorized species into hierarchical order, emerging natural sciences began to alter the reading of wetlands by identifying them as homes to rare and diverse species. A literary expression of this changing view came from Quaker naturalist William Bartram, whose *Travels* (1791), which covers the Carolinas,

Georgia, and Florida, describes an unspoiled world of coastal river swamps and vigorous native tribes. Traveling on "a sylvan pilgrimage" in the Revolutionary years, Bartram happily wanders from cavernous sinkholes to alligator swamps, accepting all that he finds as emanating from the divine force of nature: "What a beautiful retreat is here! Blessed unviolated spot of earth, rising from the limpid waters of the lake: its fragrant groves and blooming lawns invested and protected by encircling ranks of the *Yucca gloriosa*." By painting and describing a large number of new plants and animals, along with the intricate customs of the Cherokee, Creek, and Choctaw nations, Bartram projected new ways to read wetlands, and his inquiring romantic spirit began to publicize the cultural value of wilderness.[44]

Even so, the early 1800s were a time of frantic national growth, when wetlands vanished at a stunning rate. By mid-century over half of the original 150 million acres were lost, mainly to increased farming. Jefferson's agrarian rhetoric held that farmers were the nation's "natural aristocrats," acquiring a sanctity from lives spent close to soil. When European immigrant populations surged, Congress negated its Indian treaties and opened western lands to settlement. Homesteaders advanced to the Alleghenies, then across the prairies to the Mississippi River. Observing in 1808 the success of squatters in clearing river bottomland, John James Audubon wrote: "Time will no doubt be, when the great valley of the Mississippi, still covered with primeval forests, interspersed with swamps, will smile with corn-fields and orchards, while crowded cities will rise at intervals along its banks, and enlightened nations will rejoice in the bounties of Providence."[45]

The rise of cities began to alter the reading of countryside. Audubon praised a cultivated landscape "interspersed with swamps" because his bird paintings sold well to urban buyers, eager to see native American wildlife. But many authors still read wetlands as unmade, slovenly aspects of rural life. The hero of Washington Irving's tale "Rip Van Winkle" (1821) seems to acquire his character from unimproved land: "The great error in Rip's composition was an insuperable aversion to all kinds of profitable labor. It could not be from the want of assiduity or perseverance....He would carry a fowling-piece on his shoulder for hours together, trudging through woods and swamps, and up hill and down dale, to shoot a few squirrels or wild pigeons." Swamps were also known to breed mosquitoes, a dangerous source of infection. Edgar Allan Poe's story "The Sphinx" recounts the horror of plague and miasma, always emanating from rural bogs. Some urban landscaping projects, Central Park in New York and Boston's Back Bay, featured well-tamed streams or ponds lined with marsh grasses, nostalgic allusions to a lost ecology. National rural policy remained firmly anti-wetland, when in 1860 Congress began to pass a series of Swamp Land Acts that ceded to the states sixty-five million acres for reclamation, draining fields for more "productive" uses.[46]

Yet as wealth promoted leisure and travel for urban dwellers, popular art began to generate ever more appealing images of wetlands. Margaret Welch notes that mass-market books by Audubon, Thomas Nuttall, and Asa Gray encouraged nature study, mainly in woods and wetlands. Henry Wadsworth Longfellow's narrative poem *Evangeline, a Tale of Acadie* (1847), tells the idyllic story of lovers separated in Acadia and reunited in the bayous of Louisiana. In Rhode Island, Martin Johnson Heade painted over one hundred scenes of salt-marsh haystacks, emphasizing the play of light upon smooth, flattened shapes of land and water. As technology diminished the old agrarian society, wetlands came to be read as what Leo Marx calls a garden, a region of beauty and fertility lying between wild and settled terrain.[47]

In Praise of Swamps

By the mid–nineteenth century, shifting attitudes changed wetlands from economic liability into cultural asset. Writers began to read places not as reflected power or virtue but as states of emotion and perception. Americans read of fen and moor, of salt marshes and tidal flats, in the poems of Wordsworth and Keats or the novels of Dickens, the Bröntes, and Hardy, and waterlands became a primary landscape of cultural imagination. Romantic esteem for joining the real and ideal, Garry Wills notes, gave fresh emphasis to images of *liminal* space, land or water that has a loose and flowing horizon. The shifting, evanescent boundaries of wetlands naturally suggested relations between actual and imagined, surface and depth. Melville writes early in *Moby-Dick* (1850), "There is a magic in water," and that magic lies in liquids, which reflect and bend light while slipping between motion and stasis. *Moby-Dick* abounds with such fluidity, using alliterative, metrical cadences and images of land to invoke a marine world:

> As morning mowers, who side by side slowly and seethingly advance their scythes through the long wet grass of marshy meads; even so these monsters swam, making a strange, grassy, cutting sound; and leaving behind them endless swaths of blue upon the yellow sea.

The rhetorical figure that conveys liminality is metaphor, which Melville uses to name a thing with another's name, transferring identity by suggesting resemblance. As we have seen with Emily Dickinson, metaphor reads a known to signify an unknown; through connections and coincidences it suggests correspondence. Metaphor also alters the meanings of words, undermining their stability until land and sea intertwine. The duality and duplicity of Melville's reading rest with its aim to perceive similarity in dissimilars.[48]

In the era when America was so profoundly divided over slavery, it was inevitable to read wetlands as evidence of cultural and political schism. John Wilmerding's exhibition catalog, *The Waters of America* (1984), equates lake and river fluidity with Yankee imagination, while David Miller concludes that wetlands absorb the sectional tensions of the Civil War. In Miller's view, Southern authors saw swamps as sanctuaries from an urbanized, technological world; while Northern writers regarded them as experimental places to test new ideas about nature and culture. Through such clashes, wetlands acquired paratactic qualities, no longer read strictly for their economic value. The writer who most advanced a new reading was Henry David Thoreau (1817–62), whose quiet life in Concord, Massachusetts, once seemed safely obscure, but today is seen as the nucleus of a "green" tradition in American writing. We can better understand that change of stature by examining his view of swamps.[49]

During the spring of 1858, Thoreau's daily excursions into Concord led him often to Beck Stow's Swamp, lying in the northeast corner of the twenty-six-square-mile township. For six weeks Thoreau studied the swamp, because a spell of warm, wet weather had produced "a remarkable spring for reptile life." Over those days he observed, and recorded at length in his Journal, the entire reproductive cycle of frogs, from earliest mating to hatching. He was keen to trace the course of amphibian metamorphosis, a slow, barely discernible succession of changes that altered quick-darting tadpoles into massive adults, sitting still and Buddha-like in the damp heat. Thoreau emulated their patience by standing motionless for hours, until one day Beck Stow happened by. For ten minutes Mr. Stow watched the unmoving Thoreau and then called out, "Father, is that you?" Upon a closer view Stow apologized, explaining that his parent often drank rum at a local tavern and then lost his way home.[50]

As told in a Journal entry, the story jokes about sobriety, contrasting one man's stimulant to another's, but it also makes telling distinctions about land use. Stow may think his swamp unfit for harvest, but Thoreau reads it as a seat of learning, the more so because it yields no material profit. Often his writings praise swamps, to celebrate land that others avoid or think useless. The story of his first trip to Maine, "Ktaadn" (1848), tells of sloshing along wet forest trails and visiting loggers in homes made of bark "and redolent of swampy odors, with that sort of vigor and perennialness even about them that toadstools suggest." In *Walden* (1854) Thoreau builds a similar home beside a glacial pond and visits swamps in the nearby woods. To him a swamp is a "savage" place, where the hidden beauty of flowering pinks and leafing black birches reveal themselves slowly to a visitor: "If there were druids whose temples were the oak groves, my temple is the swamp." Like Dickinson, he reads the inhuman swamp as a natural companion: remote and secluded, anomalous yet orderly. The swamps are cool in summer and warm in winter, as rising artesian waters keep mosses green and berries ripe for feeding partridges. Swamps are also home to owls, whose ghostly calls suggest "a vast and *undeveloped nature* which men have not recognized. They represent the stark twilight and unsatisfied thoughts which all have."[51]

Thoreau's interest in "undeveloped nature" stemmed from a lifelong fascination with wilderness, the domain that he saw as sustaining cultural vitality.

During his career he wrote about New England lakes, forests, and mountains not just to convey immediacy but to present ideas about how land changes human lives. Certainty of physical transformation and the possibility of metaphysical transcendence drive his narrative plots, which he extracted from a daily journal that recorded many years of landscape study. The similarity of this writing process to scientific experiment (observe, notate, analyze, write, revise) was not accidental, for he was a land surveyor, and his Journal entries continuously mapped the land, seasons, and ideas he encountered.

In the spring of 1858 he was studying metamorphosis, wanting to know its exact sequence, testing and correcting inferences when wrong. Within a year he was reading Darwin's *On the Origin of Species* (1859) and writing in the Journal about evolution, "the development theory." Determined to test its implications, Thoreau spent two years extracting from his Journal some final works: a paper on forest succession, "The Succession of Forest Trees" (1859); two accounts of seasonal change, "Autumnal Tints" (1860) and "Wild Apples" (1861); an essay on wilderness and history, "Walking, or the Wild" (1862); and two long manuscripts, "Wild Fruits" and "The Dispersion of Seeds," left unfinished when he died on May 6, 1862. These writings promoted evolutionary views of natural history, while urging upon Americans a new reading of undeveloped lands.[52]

In "Walking" Thoreau writes that "Wildness is the *preservation* of the world" and that America was discovered to keep the Wild alive. This radical turn away from the Puritan and Enlightenment story of wilderness locates itself in a living earth, not dead traditions, and Thoreau's new text is the swamp, because it represents "hope and the future," a place for true subsistence as opposed to cultivated gardens. Although largely unrecognized for its worth, the swamp still works a restorative power:

> When I would *recreate* myself, I seek the darkest woods, the thickest and most interminable and, to the citizen, most dismal, swamp. I enter a swamp as a sacred place, — a sanctum sanctorum. There is the strength, the marrow, of Nature. The wildwood covers the virgin mould, — and the same soil is good for men and for trees. A man's health requires as many acres of meadow to his prospect as his farm does loads of muck. There are the strong meats on which he feeds. A town is saved, not more by the righteous men in it than by the woods and swamps that surround it.[53]

The preservation of wildness defines it not for profit or leisure but for *recreation,* a word Thoreau stretches to mean spiritual health, re-creation. He also implies bodily health, with references to marrow, mold, muck, and meats all signifying metabolic process. Far from seeing the Wild as a dark enemy of civilization, Thoreau reads it as a model for dynamic change, full of intricate, seething relations between species, habitats, and natural events. His view anticipates the findings of modern ecology: that nature is interactive, self-regulating, and biologically diverse. As Dana Phillips notes, ecology reads these processes not as static or "balanced" but as unstable and mutable. Recognizing that byproduct of biodiversity, Thoreau urged farmers in "The Succession of Forest Trees" to manage their land by sustaining many habitats rather than creating one-crop fields, which erode a soil's health. He did not live to write an extended narrative on development, except in his unpublished Journal. That task fell to Darwin himself, as he composed a book on the necessity of natural change.[54]

An Entangled Bank

Darwin's "development theory" came from three sources: discoveries in the earth sciences that verified deep prehistoric time; field research on his *Beagle* voyage, confirming that species change form; and walks on the hills near his home in Kent. During the 1850s, while Thoreau stalked Concord for his Journal, Darwin daily traced his "thinking path" and pondered the sequence of species transmutation. In "Walking" Thoreau wrote that the outline of a walk "would be, not a circle, but a parabola, or rather like one of those cometary orbits which have been thought to be on non-returning curves" (607). Darwin gave a similar plot to his theory. In chapter 4 of *On the Origin of Species* he writes that development has three stages: *heredity,* what parents give offspring; *mutation,* the variations that offspring sustain; and *selection,* the survival adaptations they pass to descendants. The stages bear a strong resemblance to Melville's image, in "The Mat-Maker" chapter of *Moby-Dick,* of time as a mat woven by chance, free will, and destiny. Darwin's theory connected past, present, and future in a repeating cycle that advanced along a line. He called this chapter "Survival of the Fittest," a phrase widely misunderstood by later readers. The "fittest" species were not the strongest but those who fit best, who made the most lasting adaptations. His concluding image of nature is "an entangled bank" of linked and opposing forces, locked in competitive struggle but also laced with weblike relations. The sources of these images, which foretell ecosystem ecology, lay along his thinking path, which may explain why he read the past as a stately Victorian narrative, ever launched in a progressive direction. Later evolutionists agree that he was right about the sequence of change, but too confident it would always be improving.[55]

For the opposite case one could look to America, where a Gilded Age boom was sacking the continent with industrial speed. Barely settled to the Mississippi in 1860, the nation built a cross-country railway system and grew so rapidly that by 1900 it had drained swamps, cleared forests, and plowed grasslands from Boston to Denver. This cultural triumphalism won endorsement from historian Frederick Jackson Turner, who argued in 1893 that the settlement of frontier lands shaped early American values of independence, self-reliance, and innovation. His claim has drawn defenders and attackers, the latter noting that pioneers also eroded land, slaughtered bison, and pushed Indians into a fatal war of attrition.[56] In a saga Garrett Hardin calls "the tragedy of the commons," public resources surrendered to private greed. The urban North prospered by drawing raw materials from its poor regional cousins: grain and beef from the western Plains, timber and coal from the southern Appalachians. During its era of so-called Reconstruction, the South remained economically stagnant, and writers read that decline in their wetlands. Describing the unchanged "Marshes of Glyn" near his coastal Georgia home, Sidney Lanier broods on wartime devastation and the need to find new modes of rebuilding. In *Life on the Mississippi* (1883), Mark Twain ponders the meaning of river currents that give or take land arbitrarily, flushing it from north to south and building "the Body of the Nation," despite all the changes that scarred its regions.[57]

Darwinian theory also failed to explain changes in the status of women, as stories by or about them acclaimed social progress yet found liberty to be an enigmatic morass. In her antislavery novel *Dred* (1856), Harriet Beecher Stowe sends a black fugitive into the Great Dismal Swamp, there to become a free man, but also a violent killer. The heroine of Henry James's *Daisy Miller* (1875) defies convention with a night visit to the Roman forum, only to contract malaria from swamp air. Sarah Orne Jewett's stories of Maine, gathered in *A Marsh Island* (1885) and *The Country of the Pointed Firs* (1896), associate wetlands with female courage: an old "yarb woman" gathers medicinal herbs from swamps; in the marshes, a girl saves her beloved white heron from a plume hunter. The revisionist slant of these stories sacrificed nature to allegory. Jewett's heroine is a savior, but it's a stubborn fact that white herons never nest in Maine.[58]

The earliest attempt to read natural and cultural conflict on evolutionary terms came from George Perkins Marsh, a Vermont farmer who wrote books on language, practiced law, and traveled widely on foreign service missions. His recognition of the adverse effect of land clearance and overgrazing led to pioneering studies of conservation, *Man and Nature* (1864) and *The Earth as Modified by Human Action* (1874). In the former work, he charts many cycles of human disturbance, such as the fur trade, which destroyed beavers and their watersheds. Marsh urged halting this destruction and becoming "a co-worker with nature" by planting slopes, flooding marshes, and directing streams to reservoirs. His aim was not to return nature to its "primitive narrow channels" but to correct the damage already done, while maintaining extractive industries. These warnings helped create the United States Forestry Commission, inspired the conservation efforts of John Muir and John Burroughs, and directed many private and public actions to protect wilderness areas well into the 1920s.[59]

Conservation offered a narrative account of Darwinian change, but it told a conservative, centrist story by seeking to protect both nature and commerce. This same era saw passage of the 1902 Reclamation Act, hailed by Theodore Roosevelt because it sold public lands "for the purpose of reclaiming the waste areas of the arid West by irrigating lands otherwise worthless, and thus creating new homes upon the land." Conservation upheld the old colonial-republican reading of wetlands and made it a national template, sanctioning the destruction of a vast but fragile Western savanna. Many conservationists today still cling to the frontier hypothesis that foregrounds human sensibility, the "sense of place" or "spirit of place" they often cite in titles. As cofounder of the Wilderness Society, Wallace Stegner exemplifies that dogma: "I know no way to look at the world, settled or wild, except through my own human eyes." Conservation-minded writers tend to advance a "stewardship" or "sustainable development" model of environmental protection, as does Frederick Turner, who says writers "take imaginative possession of the land" to counteract harmful systems of land-tenure. The tendency is to cast literature as didactic, a well-intended view that overprivileges writing: books make places "special, if not sacred, because they have been the inspiration of literature."[60]

A new and quite different narrative sustained Darwin, and also Thoreau's call for preservation, with the principles of *ecology,* a term coined by Ernst Haeckel in 1869. An ardent Darwinist and socialist, Haeckel redefined the "entangled bank" of nature as a complex set of interrelations, not always progressive or beneficial to humans, that created patterns of exchange and flow between ecosystems. According to Joel B. Hagen, as ecosystem ecology developed over the next century, it became a means of narrating the abuses of land-use history and arguing for strict preservation of such wilderness habitats as wetlands, which ecologists valued as living demonstrations of theoretical metaphors like community, network, and system.[61]

Two writers at mid-twentieth-century, Aldo Leopold and Rachel Carson, invoked ecological principles to dramatize responsible wetlands policy. Both were public servants but wrote books as acts of personal testament. In *A Sand County Almanac* (1949), Leopold describes his evolution from a federal conservation ranger, paid to kill wolves, to a preservationist who designs a moral scheme for environmental protection, called "the land ethic." Leopold chose to make his case through brief nature essays, styled as segments of a seasonal almanac. In "Marshland Elegy" he describes a passing day, dawn to dusk, that portrays how a wetland evolves into habitat for nesting cranes:

> A sense of time lies thick and heavy on such a place. Yearly since the ice age it has awakened each spring to the clangor of cranes. The peat layers that comprise the bog are laid down in the basin of an ancient lake. The cranes stand, as it were, upon the sodden pages of their own history.... An endless caravan of generations has built of its own bones this bridge into the future, this habitat where the oncoming host again may live and breed and die. To what end?

With a trace of self-consciousness (as it were), this rhetoric replaces conservationist prudence with a preservationist call to dispossess. Marsh cranes are ancient and inscriptive beings, writing "the sodden pages" of their past, laying down their bones to feed the peat and keep their progeny coming on. Nature ceaselessly moves through change, and humans should preserve that process, not disturb it with farming or hunting. The core of Leopold's land ethic is to extend to nature the same rights and privileges that people enjoy: "We abuse the land because we regard it as a commodity belonging to us. When we see land as a community to which we belong, we may begin to use it with love and respect."[62]

In *Silent Spring* (1962), Rachel Carson intensifies that sense of community by analyzing the destructive force of chemical pesticides. In an incisive passage, she demonstrates how toxicity spreads through ground water, a system of transport so invisible that it is easy to ignore:

> Seldom if ever does Nature operate in closed and separate compartments, and she has not done so in distributing the earth's water supply. Rain, falling on the land, settles down through pores and cracks in soil and rock, penetrating deeper and deeper until eventually it reaches a zone where all the pores of the rock are filled with water, a dark subsurface sea, rising under hills, sinking under valleys. This groundwater is always on the move, sometimes at a pace so slow that it travels no more than 50 feet a year, sometimes rapidly, by comparison, so that it moves nearly a tenth of a mile a day. It travels by unseen waterways until here and there it comes to the surface as a spring, or perhaps it is tapped as a well. But mostly it contributes to streams and so to rivers. Except for what enters streams directly as rain or surface runoff, all the running water of the earth's surface was at one time groundwater. And so, in a very real and frightening sense, pollution of the groundwater is pollution of water everywhere.

Carson adds a feminist perspective to the evolutionary logic of preservationist discourse. Her Nature is clearly female: open and connected, she possesses both evident features and a hidden zone where water lives, "a dark subsurface sea, rising under hills, sinking beneath valleys," and constantly moves, nourishing all land and thus in equal danger of poisoning it. Her emphasis on a horizontal zone that receives and sustains the vertical is clearly sexual, the generative absorbing the seminal, like earth swallowing seed; yet Carson stresses not differences but entirety, the wholeness of a system that consists of parts, any of which may bring health or disease to all. Ecology informs her ethics through the figure of groundwater, an inverse variant of wetland. For her efforts, Carson was attacked by the petrochemical industry as hysterical and unscientific. But her logic and eloquence impressed the Kennedy administration, brought a ban on DDT and other pesticides, and eventually helped create the Environmental Protection Agency.[63]

Preservationist narrative argues for the intrinsic quality of places, as they represent ideals of beauty, sanctity, and justice. These values have made the once neglected and derided wetlands into an icon of natural health and a model for social order. In the words of Paul Errington, "Greater familiarity with marshes...[c]ould give man a truer and more wholesome view of himself in relation to Nature." Knowledge of wetlands ecology has advanced, and so has protective legislation, while on the cultural side, a new generation of writers now champion wetlands preservation. Some are scientists, like Edward O. Wilson, who writes about the marshes and swamps of Georgia and Florida, where he learned the principles of biodiversity and biogeography. Others are reporters and essayists like Barry Lopez, Peter Matthiessen, and Bill McKibben, who consistently portray American wetlands as centers of ecological harmony and rallying points for environmental action.[64]

Yet stories have no effect if they fail to reach understanding readers. Since declaring independence in 1776, Americans have destroyed over two-thirds of their continental wetlands. The current rate of loss is estimated at eight hundred acres a day (six hundred football fields), nearly all of it for tract houses or shopping malls. The surviving area is about fifty million acres, and if nothing is done, it will vanish by the year 2050.[65] If Americans lost CDs or videos at that rate, they would regard their preservation as the moral equivalent of war. If present trends continue, one day we will share only an inventory of lost wetlands, an elegy to American wilderness: the Hackensack Meadows and Tinicum Marsh; Currituck Sound and the Wet Kankakee Prairie; Indiana's Limberlost and the Black Swamp of Ohio; Horicon Marsh; the Playa Lakes of the Texas Panhandle.

Noting our long tendency to see wetlands doubly, the Australian critic Rod Giblett has called for a new bifocalism: "The challenge today is to see wetlands as regions of both life and death, as living black waters, in a kind of postmodern double vision which is both poetic (but not romantic) and ecological (but not mechanistic)."[66] His chiastic rhetoric presents not balance but stalemate, saying all forces are relative and equitable, yet dismissing romance and mechanism. I hope this essay suggests a different view of the history and meaning of wetlands, and of any place that humans attempt to read or write. Evolution occurs because every phase of development is necessary to the process of change: the ideology of dominion led to science, and science to romance; the conservation and preservation narratives, although they differ, both call for new readings of wild places. But readings alone will not save these places, especially if the readers are busy looking elsewhere. Humanists today are striving for doubled and even tripled vision, moving across old self-imposed boundaries of textual exploration. They proclaim social and cultural diversity yet spurn the biodiversity that surrounds and sustains human achievement. For many critical readers, the last acceptable prejudice is the prejudice against nature, since nature's encrypted knowledge is difficult to see, much less honor and protect. Ecocriticism seeks new ways to concur with nature, to see it as an environs, or surroundings, in which human lives transpire. If we include in our readings the wetlands with all their tangled shimmer of meanings, we will begin to imagine territory that has natural limits, for such places tell us what we may hold close, and what we must let go:

> What would the world be, once bereft
> Of wet and of wildness? Let there be left,
> O let there be left, wildness and wet;
> Long live the weeds and the wildness yet.[67]

Notes

1. Stephen Greenblatt and Giles Gunning, introduction to *Redrawing the Boundaries: The Transformation of Literary Studies* (New York: Modern Language Association, 1992), 3.

2. Geographical tropes have bloomed in many fields; see Henry A. Giroux, *Border Crossings: Cultural Workers and the Politics of Education* (New York: Routledge, 1991); Albert Borgmann, *Crossing the Postmodern Divide* (Chicago: University of Chicago Press, 1992); Helen M. Buss, *Mapping Our Selves: Canadian Women's Autobiography* (Montreal: McGill–Queen's University Press, 1993); and Philip Brian Harper, *Framing the Margins: The Social Logic of Postmodern Culture* (New York: Oxford University Press, 1994). For a study that analyzes geo-rhetoric, see Denis Wood, *The Power of Maps* (New York: Guilford Press, 1992).

3. Greenblatt and Gunning, *Redrawing the Boundaries*, 8.

4. Eugene E. Brussell, *Webster's New World Dictionary of Quotable Definitions,* 2d ed. (New York: Webster's New World, 1988), 277.

5. *Selected Poems and Letters of Emily Dickinson,* ed. Robert N. Linscott (New York: Doubleday, 1959), 7. All future references to Dickinson's letters are to this edition, by page number.

6. In 1863 she further speculates: "Nature is what we know — / Yet have no art to say — / So impotent our Wisdom is / To her Simplicity" (*The Complete Poems of Emily Dickinson,* ed. Thomas H. Johnson [Boston: Little Brown & Co, 1976], poem 668). Dickinson often used her dog Carlo, a black Newfoundland, as a corresponding medium. See an 1859 letter to Mrs. Samuel Bowles: "If I built my house I should like to call you. I talk of all these things with Carlo, and his eyes grow meaning, and his shaggy feet keep a slower pace. Are you safe to-night? I hope you may be glad" (*Selected Poems,* 271).

7. Emerson defines "correspondence" in *Nature* (1836); see *Selections from Ralph Waldo Emerson,* ed. Stephen Whicher (Boston: Houghton Mifflin, 1972), 18–63. His sources were European and Asian; see J. Baird Callecott, *Nature in Asian Traditions of Thought: Essays in Environmental Philosophy* (Albany: State University of New York Press, 1989), 38–56.

8. Poems that convey Dickinson's ideas on language include "A Thought went up my mind today — " (701), "Love — is anterior to Life — " (917), "A Word dropped careless on a Page" (1261), "Your thoughts don't have words every day" (1452), and "A Word made Flesh is seldom" (1651). The title numbers refer to *Final Harvest: Emily Dickinson's Poems,* ed. Thomas H. Johnson (Boston: Little Brown, 1961).

9. Her idea of place-knowledge is quite variable: she never saw a moor or the sea, "Yet know I how the heather looks / And what a wave must be" (*Final Harvest,* 1052). This knowledge she equates to religious faith, the certain anticipation of heaven, "As if the chart were given." Without *seeing,* she knows how a place *looks,* probably because scenes viewed elsewhere provide analogies.

10. Joyce Carol Oates, "Against Nature," in *On Nature: Nature, Landscape, and Natural History,* ed. Daniel Halpern (San Francisco: North Point Press, 1987), 236–43. For

background on ecocriticism and environmental history, see Cheryll Glotfelty and Harold Fromm, eds., *The Ecocriticism Reader: Landmarks in Literary Ecology* (Athens: University of Georgia Press, 1996); and Char Miller and Hal Rothman, eds., *Out of the Woods: Essays in Environmental History* (Pittsburgh: University of Pittsburgh Press, 1997).

11. Etymology and definitions are from the online *Oxford English Dictionary,* 2d ed., http://www.princeton.edu/oed/. Lawrence Buell defines place as "perceived or felt space, space humanized, rather than the material world taken on its own terms" (*The Environmental Imagination: Thoreau, Nature Writing, and the Formation of American Culture* [Cambridge, Mass.: Harvard University Press, 1995], 253), whereas I use place to mean both the perceived and the material world, as well as status judgments that bind the two.

12. James Hamilton-Paterson, *Playing with Water: Passion and Solitude on a Philippine Island* (New York: Amsterdam Books, 1987), 3.

13. Emily Dickinson, *Final Harvest,* poem 1740, p. 317; Walt Whitman, *Leaves of Grass* (New York: Norton, 1973), 328–37; Willa Cather, *A Lost Lady* (New York: Vintage, 1990); *The Short Stories of Ernest Hemingway* (New York: Scribners, 1938), 207–32; Annie Dillard, *A Pilgrim at Tinker Creek* (New York: Harper & Row, 1974); John McPhee, *The Control of Nature* (New York: Farrar, Straus, and Giroux, 1989).

14. Recent discussants tend to reject the New Critical reading of Stanley Edgar Hyman, *The Entangled Bank* (New York: Athenaeum, 1962), who saw Darwin as imposing "order and form on disorderly and anarchic experience." Gillian Beer, *Darwin's Plots* (Boston: Routledge & Kegan Paul, 1983), examines how writers assimilated and resisted evolutionary theory as "a determining fiction." Peter Morton, *The Vital Science* (London: George Allen & Unwin, 1984), studies the effects of post-Darwinian biology on late-Victorian fiction about heredity and eugenics. David Locke, *Science as Writing* (New Haven, Conn.: Yale University Press, 1992), discerns imaginative elements in Darwin that provide "interpenetrating laceworks of codes," while Robert Faggen, *Robert Frost and the Challenge of Darwin* (Ann Arbor: University of Michigan Press, 1997), 19, finds Darwin's use of fact and metaphor "anything but crudely reductive" or anthropomorphic. In *Mystery of Mysteries* (Cambridge, Mass.: Harvard University Press, 1999), Michael Rose takes a centrist position, arguing that evolution reports objective reality and is also embedded in cultural values.

15. I have described other resources in "Some Principles of Ecocriticism," in Glotfelty and Fromm, *Ecocriticism Reader,* 69–91, esp. 82–87.

16. Gaston Bachelard, *The Poetics of Space* (Boston: Beacon Press, 1965). Studies reflecting his influence include Judith Fryer, *Felicitous Space: The Imaginative Structures of Edith Wharton and Willa Cather* (Chapel Hill: University of North Carolina Press, 1986); Marilyn Chandler, *Dwelling in the Text: Houses in American Fiction* (Berkeley: University of California Press, 1991); Robert Pogue Harrison, *Forests: The Shadow of Civilization* (Chicago: University of Chicago Press, 1992); and Parks Lanier, *The Poetics of Appalachian Space* (Knoxville: University of Tennessee Press, 1991).

17. Paul Carter, *The Road to Botany Bay: An Exploration of Landscape and History* (Chicago: University of Chicago Press, 1987), xxi–xxiii.

18. Two useful references are George Kish, *A Source Book in Geography* (Cambridge, Mass.: Harvard University Press, 1978); and R. J. Johnston, Derek Gregory, and David M. Smith, eds., *The Dictionary of Human Geography,* 2d ed. (Oxford: Blackwell, 1986). For challenges to geographic truth-claims, see Stanley A. Schumm, *To Interpret the Earth: Ten Ways to Be Wrong* (New York: Cambridge University Press, 1991).

19. David Harvey, "Geographical Knowledge in the Eye of Power: Reflections on Derek Gregory's *Geographical Imaginations,*" *Annals of the Association of American Geographers* 85 (1995): 160–64.

20. Michel Foucault, "What Is an Author?" in *The Critical Tradition,* ed. David H. Richter, 2d ed. (Boston: Bedford Books, 1998), 950. Examples of poststructural studies include Henri Lefebvre, *The Production of Space* (Oxford: Oxford University Press, 1991); Sandra Gilbert and Susan Gubar, *No Man's Land: The Place of the Woman Writer in the Twentieth Century* (New Haven, Conn.: Yale University Press, 1987); Eve Kosofsky Sedg-

wick, *Epistemology of the Closet* (Berkeley: University of California Press, 1990); Homi K. Bhabha, *The Location of Culture* (New York: Routledge, 1992); and I. G. Simmons, *Interpreting Nature: Cultural Constructions of the Environment* (New York: Routledge, 1993).

21. Gillian Tindall, *Countries of the Mind: The Meaning of Place to Writers* (London: Hogarth Press, 1991), 9–10. See also Winifred Gallagher, *The Power of Place: How Our Surroundings Shape Our Thoughts, Emotions, and Action* (New York: Poseidon Press, 1993), which (despite its title) mainly recounts emotions that people feel about places.

22. William Cronon describes legal alienation as a land-grabbing tactic used by colonial settlers against Indian tribes; see *Changes in the Land: Indians, Colonists, and the Ecology of New England* (New York: Hill and Wang, 1982), 170.

23. See Anne Whiston Spirn, *The Language of Landscape* (New Haven, Conn.: Yale University Press, 1998), for the view that landscape possesses grammar and syntax, translated by landscape architects into aesthetic forms. Most place-writing in landscape architecture has a visual rather than textual emphasis; see William Lake Douglas, "Forming an Image of Place," *Cross Roads: A Journal of Southern Culture* (spring/summer 1994): 51–65.

24. I am paraphrasing lines of argument from Yi-Fu Tuan's works: *Landscapes of Fear* (New York: Pantheon Books, 1979); *Space and Place: The Perspective of Experience* (Minneapolis: University of Minnesota Press, 1981); *Topophilia: A Study of Environmental Perception, Attitudes, and Values* (New York: Columbia University Press, 1990); *Passing Strange & Wonderful: Aesthetics, Nature, Culture* (Washington, D.C.: Island Press, 1993); *Cosmos and Hearth: A Cosmopolite's Viewpoint* (Minneapolis: University of Minnesota Press, 1996); and *Escapism* (Baltimore: Johns Hopkins University Press, 1998). See also Jens Jensen, *Siftings* (Baltimore: Johns Hopkins University Press, 1990); and J. B. Jackson, *Discovering the Vernacular Landscape* (New Haven, Conn.: Yale University Press, 1984).

25. Leonard Lutwack, *The Role of Place in Literature* (Syracuse, N.Y.: Syracuse University Press, 1984), esp. chap. 2, "A Rhetoric of Place I: The Properties and Uses of Place in Literature"; Anne Buttimer and David Seamon, *The Human Experience of Space and Place* (New York: St. Martin's Press, 1980). Buttimer often draws on literary texts; see her survey of spatial worldviews, *Geography and the Human Spirit* (Baltimore: Johns Hopkins University Press, 1993).

26. Peter L. Rudnytsky, *Transitional Objects and Potential Spaces* (New York: Columbia University Press, 1993), esp. chap. 4, "Where Is Literature?"; Richard Rorty, *Truth and Progress* (Cambridge: Cambridge University Press, 1997); see also Rorty's *Philosophy and the Mirror of Nature* (Princeton, N.J.: Princeton University Press, 1979), and *Achieving Our Country* (Cambridge, Mass.: Harvard University Press, 1998). A useful introduction to Rorty's ideas is Carlin P. Romano, "Rortyism for Beginners," *The Nation*, July 27, 1997.

27. J. Nicholas Entrikin, *The Betweenness of Place: Towards a Geography of Modernity* (Baltimore: Johns Hopkins University Press, 1991); see also Sandra Humble Johnson, *The Space Between: Literary Epiphany in the Work of Annie Dillard* (Kent, Ohio: Kent State University Press, 1992); and Eleanor Honig Skoller, *The In-Between of Writing: Experience and Experiment in Drabble, Duras, and Arendt* (Ann Arbor: University of Michigan Press, 1993).

28. William Howarth, "Ego or Ecocriticism: Looking for Common Ground," in *Reading the Earth: New Directions in the Study of Literature and Environment*, ed. Michael P. Branch et al. (Moscow: University of Idaho Press, 1998), 7.

29. Richard Forman and Michel Godron, *Landscape Ecology* (New York: John Wiley & Sons, 1986); Rutherford Platt, *Land Use Control: Geography, Law, and Public Policy* (Amherst: University of Massachusetts Press, 1991).

30. *The Portable Faulkner*, ed. Malcolm Cowley (New York: Viking Press, 1949). Literal exegesis includes Cleanth Brooks, *The Yoknapatawpha Country* (New Haven, Conn.: Yale University Press, 1963); and Gabriele Gutting, *Yoknapatawpha: The Function of Geographical and Historical Facts in William Faulkner's Fictional Picture of the Deep South* (New York: Peter Lang, 1992). Figural readings dominate Robert Glen Dreamer, *The Importance*

of Place in the American Literature of Hawthorne, Thoreau, Crane, Adams, and Faulkner (Lewiston, N.Y.: Edwin Mellen Press, 1990); and Philip M. Weinstein, *Faulkner's Subject: A Cosmos No One Owns* (New York: Cambridge University Press, 1992).

31. William Faulkner, "The Bear," in *The Portable Faulkner*, ed. Malcolm Cowley (New York: Penguin Books, 1977), 228; hereafter cited by page number. Geographer Paul F. Starrs calls regions "among the most intelligent acts that we can work with as humans"; see his essay on the regional-universal crux, "The Importance of Places, or, a Sense of Where You Are," *Spectrum* 67 (summer 1994): 5–17.

32. Faulkner, "The Bear," 243–45; emphasis added.

33. Nina Baym, "Melodramas of Beset Manhood," *American Quarterly* 33 (1981): 128. Differing analyses of wilderness appear in Lee Clark Mitchell, *Witnesses to a Vanishing America* (Princeton, N.J.: Princeton University Press, 1981); Roderick Nash, *Wilderness and the American Mind* (New Haven, Conn.: Yale University Press, 1982); and Max Oelschlaeger, *The Idea of Wilderness* (New Haven, Conn.: Yale University Press, 1991).

34. Gareth Jones et al., *The HarperCollins Dictionary of Environmental Science* (New York: HarperCollins, 1992), 441; William A. Niering, *Wetlands* (New York: Alfred A. Knopf, 1985). See also Leslie A. Real, *Foundations of Ecology: Classic Papers with Commentaries* (Chicago: University of Chicago Press, 1991); and Ted Williams, "What Good Is a Wetland?" *Audubon* 98 (November–December 1996): 42–54, 98–100.

35. Joseph Frank, "Spatial Form in Modern Literature," in *The Widening Gyre* (New Brunswick, N.J.: Rutgers University Press, 1963).

36. Peter A. Fritzell, "American Wetlands as Cultural Symbol: Places of Wetlands in American Culture," in *Wetland Functions and Values: The State of Our Understanding* (Washington, D.C.: American Water Resources Association, November 1978), 523–24. See also his *Nature Writing and America: Essays upon a Cultural Type* (Ames: Iowa State University Press, 1990).

37. Jon Naar and Alex J. Narr, *This Land Is Your Land: A Guide to North America's Endangered Ecosystems* (New York: HarperCollins, 1993), 48–81. For accounts of contingency in nature and narrative, see Stephen Jay Gould, *Wonderful Life: The Burgess Shale and the Nature of History* (New York: W. W. Norton, 1989); and David Hackett Fischer, *Paul Revere's Ride* (New York: Oxford University Press, 1994).

38. Tuan, *Cosmos and Hearth*. For surveys of wetlands history and literature, see Anne Vilesis, *Discovering the Unknown Landscape: A History of America's Wetlands* (Washington, D.C.: Island Press, 1997); and Sam Wilson and Tom Moritz, eds., *The Sierra Club Wetlands Reader* (San Francisco: Sierra Club, 1996).

39. Hence the Jewish custom of *mikvah*, a cleansing of women thirty days after childbirth, before they may resume sexual relations. For a critique of dominion ideology, see Lynn White, "The Historical Roots of Our Ecologic Crisis," reprinted in *Classics in Environmental Studies*, ed. N. Nelissen, J. V. D. Straaten, and L. Klinkers (Utrecht: International Books, 1997). One of the few early texts to condemn marsh drainage is Virgil's *Georgics*; see Robert M. Torrance, ed., *Encompassing Nature: A Sourcebook* (Washington, D.C.: Counterpoint, 1998), 464–65.

40. William Bradford, "Of Plimoth Plantation," in *The Heath Anthology of American Literature*, ed. Paul Lauter, 2d ed. (Boston: Houghton Mifflin, 1997), 1:249; John Hay, *The Atlantic Shore: Human and Natural History from Long Island to Labrador* (New York: Harper & Row, 1966).

41. William Cronon, *Changes in the Land*, 132–33; John Bunyan, *Pilgrim's Progress* (Old Woking, Surrey: Gresham, 1978).

42. Stephen Greenblatt, *Marvelous Possessions: The Wonder of the New World* (Chicago: University of Chicago Press, 1991), 20–24; John Terborgh, *Where Have All the Birds Gone?* (Princeton, N.J.: Princeton University Press, 1989); William Byrd, "History of the Dividing Line," in Lauter, *Heath Anthology*, 546.

43. Hector St. John de Crèvecoeur, *Letters from an American Farmer*, in *Major Problems in American Environmental History*, ed. Carolyn Merchant (Lexington, Mass.: D.C. Heath,

1992), 140; Thomas Jefferson, *Notes on the State of Virginia* (New York: Harper & Row, 1964), 93.

44. William Bartram, *Travels of William Bartram,* ed. Mark Van Doren (New York: Dover Publications, 1955), 143. For Bartram's place in natural history, see Robert Mc-Cracken Peck, "Conquering the Swamps: Florida and the Southeast," in *Land of the Eagle: A Natural History of North America* (London: BBC Books, 1990), 89–118.

45. John James Audubon, in Merchant, *Major Problems,* 150.

46. Washington Irving, "Rip Van Winkle," in Lauter, *Heath Anthology,* 1296; *The Annotated Tales of Edgar Allan Poe,* ed. Stephen Peithman (Garden City, N.Y.: Doubleday, 1981); Vilesis, *Discovering the Unknown Landscape,* 71–76; Benjamin H. Hibbard, *A History of the Public Lands Policy* (Madison: University of Wisconsin Press, 1925).

47. Margaret Welch, *The Book of Nature: Natural History in the United States, 1825–1875* (Boston: Northeastern University Press, 1998), 70–89; Barbara Novak, "Martin Johnson Heade: Haystacks and Light," in *American Painting of the Nineteenth Century* (New York: Praeger, 1974), 125–37; Leo Marx, *The Machine in the Garden: Technology and the Pastoral Ideal in America* (New York: Oxford University Press, 1964).

48. Peter Ackroyd, *Dickens* (New York: HarperCollins, 1991), 19–26; Garry Wills, *Lincoln at Gettysburg: The Words That Remade America* (New York: Touchstone Books, 1992), 72–74; and Herman Melville, *Moby-Dick, or The Whale* (New York: W. W. Norton, 1967).

49. John Wilmerding, *The Waters of America: 19th-Century American Paintings of Rivers, Streams, Lakes, and Waterfalls* (New Orleans: New Orleans Museum of Art, 1984); David Miller, *Dark Eden: The Swamp in Nineteenth-Century American Culture* (New York: Cambridge University Press, 1989).

50. The incident occurred on April 28, 1858. See *The Journal of Henry D. Thoreau,* ed. Bradford Torrey and Francis H. Allen (Boston: Houghton Mifflin, 1906), x, 387.

51. Henry D. Thoreau, *Walden,* ed. J. L. Shanley (Princeton, N.J.: Princeton University Press, 1971), 125. Ten other references to swamps appear in *Walden;* see http://www.princeton.edu/batke/thoreau/ghindex.html.

52. The late natural history writings appeared in *Excursions* (Boston: Ticknor & Fields, 1862). For a history of "Wild Fruits" and "The Dispersion of Seeds," see William Howarth, *The Book of Concord: Thoreau's Life as a Writer* (New York: Viking Press, 1982), 181–219.

53. Henry D. Thoreau, "Walking," in *Walden and Other Writings* (New York: McGraw-Hill, 1980), 616–17; emphasis added.

54. Discussions of Thoreau's place in modern environmentalism include Buell, *Environmental Imagination;* William Howarth, "Where I Lived: The Environs of *Walden,*" in *Approaches to Teaching Walden and Other Works,* ed. R. J. Schneider (New York: Modern Language Association, 1996), 56–62; and Dana Phillips, "Ecocriticism, Literary Theory, and the Truth of Ecology," *New Literary History* 30 (summer 1999): 577–602.

55. Joel B. Hagen, *An Entangled Bank: The Origins of Ecosystem Ecology* (New Brunswick, N.J.: Rutgers University Press, 1992), 1–3; Janet Browne, *Charles Darwin Voyaging* (Princeton, N.J.: Princeton University Press, 1996), 441–45. Interpretations of Darwinian theory include Ernst Mayr, *One Long Argument: Charles Darwin and the Genesis of Modern Evolutionary Thought* (Cambridge, Mass.: Harvard University Press, 1991); and Daniel Dennet, *Darwin's Dangerous Idea* (New York: Touchstone Books, 1995).

56. Frederick Jackson Turner, "The Significance of the Frontier in American History," in *History, Frontier, and Section: Three Essays by Frederick Jackson Turner* (Albuquerque: University of New Mexico Press, 1993), 59–91. Literary defenders of Turner's thesis include Henry Nash Smith, *Virgin Land: The American West as Symbol and Myth* (Cambridge, Mass.: Harvard University Press, 1950); and Harold P. Simonson, *Beyond the Frontier: Writers, Western Regionalism, and a Sense of Place* (Fort Worth: Texas Christian University Press, 1989). For attacks by historians, see two essays in *The Western Historical Quarterly* (April 1987): Donald Worster, "New West, True West: Interpreting the Region's History," 141–56; and William Cronon, "Revisiting the Vanishing Frontier: The Legacy of Frederick

Jackson Turner," 157–76. Geographers Frank and Deborah Popper argue that Turner mis-read the 1890 census figures; see "The Re-emergence of the American Frontier," *Studies in History and Contemporary Culture* (March 1998): 5–11.

57. Garrett Hardin, "The Tragedy of the Commons," reprinted in Nelissen, Straaten, and Klinkers, *Classics in Environmental Studies*, 101–14; *Poems of Sidney Lanier* (New York: Charles Scribner's Sons, 1884), 14–18; Mark Twain, *Life on the Mississippi,* ed. James M. Cox (New York: Penguin, 1984), 3–5.

58. Richard Boyd, "Violence and Sacrificial Displacement in Harriet Beecher Stowe's *Dred,*" *Arizona Quarterly* 50, no. 2 (summer 1994): 51–72. Sarah Orne Jewett, "A White Heron," in *Best Stories of Sarah Orne Jewett* (Camden, Maine: Yankee Books, 1988), 81–90. Dana Phillips first noticed Jewett's problematic heron. According to Roger Tory Peterson, the only white heron in North America is the Great White, which nests in southern Florida. Herons that nest in Maine have only black, blue, or green plumage. If Jewett had in mind an albino bird, her text never says so. See Peterson, *A Field Guide to the Birds of Eastern and Central North America,* 4th ed. (Boston: Houghton Mifflin, 1980), 102, M95.

59. George Perkins Marsh, in Merchant, *Major Problems,* 340–42; Peter J. Bowler, *The Norton History of the Environmental Sciences* (New York: W. W. Norton, 1992), 318–22.

60. Theodore Roosevelt, "The Natural Resources of the Nation," in *Autobiography* (New York: Holt Rinehart, 1913); Wallace Stegner, "The Sense of Place," in *Where the Blue-bird Sings to the Lemonade Springs: Living and Writing in the West* (New York: Penguin Books, 1993), 201; Frederick Jackson Turner, *Spirit of Place: The Making of an American Literary Landscape* (San Francisco: Sierra Club, 1989), ix–x.

61. For the work of ecologists in wetlands, see Real, *Foundations of Ecology,* 5–48; and Hagen, *An Entangled Bank,* 12–15. For a geographer's view of conservation, see Bret Wal-lach, *At Odds with Progress: Americans and Conservation* (Tucson: University of Arizona Press, 1991).

62. Aldo Leopold, *The Sand County Almanac* (New York: Oxford University Press, 1949), 96. Major discussions of natural rights are Christopher D. Stone, "Should Trees Have Standing? Toward Legal Rights for Natural Objects," reprinted in Nelissen, Straaten, and Klinkers, *Classics in Environmental Studies,* 153–62; and Roderick Nash, *The Rights of Nature* (Madison: University of Wisconsin Press, 1989).

63. Rachel Carson, *Silent Spring* (Boston: Houghton Mifflin, 1962), 48–50.

64. Paul Errington, *Of Men and Marshes* (New York: Macmillan Press, 1957); Edward O. Wilson, *Naturalist* (Washington, D.C.: Island Press, 1994); Barry Lopez, *Crossing Open Ground* (New York: Vintage, 1989); Peter Matthiessen, *Sand Rivers* (New York: Viking Press, 1981); Bill McKibben, *The End of Nature* (New York: Random House, 1989).

65. John H. Cushman Jr., "Million Wetland Acres Lost in 1985–1995," *New York Times,* September 18, 1997, A24. A summary of recent wetlands history appears in Joel Makower, *The Nature Catalog* (New York: Vintage Books, 1991), 75–80. For an analysis of the future of Western wetlands, see Charles Wilkinson, *Crossing the Meridian: Land, Water, and the Future of the West* (Washington, D.C.: Island Press, 1992), 265–74.

66. Rod Giblett, *Postmodern Wetlands: Culture, History, Ecology* (Edinburgh: Edin-burgh University Press, 1996), 130. Two accounts of recent place-alienation blame the media: see Joshua Meyrowitz, *No Sense of Place: The Impact of Electronic Media on So-cial Behavior* (New York: Oxford University Press, 1985); and Bill McKibben, *The Age of Missing Information* (New York: Random House, 1992).

67. Gerard Manly Hopkins, "Inversnaid," in *The Norton Anthology of Modern Poetry,* comp. Richard Ellmann (New York: W. W. Norton, 1973), 84.

MAKING A PET OF NATURE

David Lowenthal

Fifteen years have not dimmed my delight in Yi-Fu Tuan's most enigmatically persuasive book.[1] Reviewing his topoi — gardens, domestic animals, domestic servants, zoos, dwarves, castrati, comedians, bonsai, fountains — recalls the critters frivolously categorized in Borges's Chinese encyclopedia, *The Celestial Emporium of Benevolent Knowledge:* "(a) those that belong to the emperor, (b) embalmed ones, (c) those that are trained, (d) suckling pigs, (e) mermaids, (f) fabulous ones, (g) stray dogs, (h) those that are included in this classification, (i) those that tremble as if they were mad, (j) innumerable ones, (k) those drawn with a very fine camel's hair brush, (l) others, (m) those that have just broken a flower vase, (n) those that resemble flies from a distance." Still closer to Tuan's own arena are the themes embraced by the Brussels Bibliographical Institute subdivision 179: "Cruelty to animals. Protection of animals. Moral Implications of duelling and suicide. Various vices and defects. Various virtues and qualities."[2]

Yet from Tuan's own bizarre array, marvels an encomiast, he has assembled "a creation by accretion."[3] In fact, Tuan's mode transcends accretion; it is synthesis. Its organizing principle, he tells us, is that "all these themes can be put under the broad rubric of 'man's role in changing the face of the earth' " (5). This portmanteau phrase encompasses all aspects of humanity's reshaping — and misshaping — of the face of nature.

"Man's Role in Changing the Face of the Earth" was, as every good geographer knows, the Wenner-Gren conference held in Princeton in 1955. Led by Carl Sauer, Lewis Mumford, and Marston Bates, "Man's Role" celebrated the prescient insights of George Perkins Marsh's pioneering *Man and Nature; or, Physical Geography as Modified by Human Action* (1864). Participants updated the potency of the impacts Marsh had delineated and reassessed their consequences for the ecological health and resources of the globe.[4]

As Marsh had recognized, our impingement on nature was not aberrant pathological behavior but a normal, indeed inevitable, function of being human. We are born and bred to alter the realms we inhabit and traverse. Some today are so appalled by the environmental evils they attribute to human agency — erosion, pollution, degradation, extinction — that they shrink from the exercise of any power over nature. But even the most passive stylites,

84

the most scrupulous vegans, the most gentle consumers massively affect their surroundings, reshaping them willy-nilly.

In this humans do not differ from other species. All creatures continually modify their environments: the roots sent down by every plant break up the soils beneath, altering their structure and chemistry. Humans diverge from other forms of life only in the power with which they reshape their world and in their usually conscious intent to do so. Unlike the effects of other creatures, most human impacts are not blindly instinctual but deliberately chosen, though their ultimate consequences are in large measure unintended and unforeseeable.[5]

We elect to alter the earth and its denizens for purposes that transcend the merely useful. Manipulating nature would be hardly worthwhile were its aim solely utilitarian, a mere joyless search for food and shelter. The exercise of power is simultaneously a quest for pleasure. Dominance not only implies affection; it engenders affection. Choosing to impact things and beings, we also become fond of them. We change them *because* we love them, hoping to love them all the more when we have changed them.

Power and love connote an imbalance. In Tuan's realms care feels patronizing, even condescending. The powerful seem to do most of the reshaping; the powerless are supine and passive. Is this not a perversion of true love? asks the egalitarian. Surely love ought to mean autonomy. But in fact love is characteristically assertive and coercive. Seldom is it the altruistic ideal preached by Pitrim Sorokin, as cited by Tuan at the outset (1). To imagine a beloved free from interference is a delusion. Impelled to interfere, we then admire our intervention for improving and adorning what we love.

Power and affection are conjoined not only in our relations with Tuanish pets but in most aspects of the cultural landscape. Reshaping the earth is in high degree an act of love, heightening our attachment to the achieved results — the cleared forest, the cultivated field, the cottage ornée, the city beautiful.

But if we customarily look on our work and find it good, we also react in antithetical ways. We often detest what we replace or dominate. The very act of extirpation engenders contempt and exacerbates revulsion toward the vanquished — wild jungles, savage animals, barbarous aliens, enchained slaves. "The lumberman bears no grudge against the forest, and the conqueror feels no personal hatred toward the conquered" (2), contends Tuan. I disagree. Toward those we dominate and mutilate our feelings are far from neutral. While lavishing concern and care on pets and peons, we judge them inferiors for succumbing to our will, bending to our demands. Rather than finding contemptible our violations of others, we view the victims themselves with contempt, holding them to blame for what we have done to them, how we have misshapen them.

In earlier epochs it was common to defame and to express fondness at one and the same time. The pet, the servant, the slave, the child, the woman, the aborigine inspired affection by virtue of being violated, subjugated, tormented, degraded. Few shrank from such contrarian stances — views and acts that are now condemned as condescending, perverted, often sadistic.

We have lost the endorsement of loving care formerly associated with intimate forms of domination. "What has happened to the innocence of gardening, of keeping pets, even of the feeling called affection?" (5). Gone is the eighteenth-century English lady who petted her black slave boy; "she no longer has a maid to patronize, and even if she has, the maid can hardly share her bed" (163). No longer is it acceptable to breed dogs with deformities, exhibit performing bears, castrate countertenors, have eunuchs guard harems — indeed, to keep harems at all. And even though acknowledging that children lack judgment, need protection, and require rearing, we now forbid many forms of chastisement and pretend to accord them equal status with adults; in the politically correct family, not only is dad no longer boss, but equality is absolute — kids have the same voting rights as parents.

The innocence that once tolerated loving inequality is now "tarred by the same brush of power," in Tuan's words, "tainted by the urge to dominate" (5). This trend seems to me part of a general shift of values. Normative concepts of biological and social hierarchy, with man at the apex of virtue and power, dominant over nature, are giving way to egalitarianism, hatred of all authority, and contrition for past hegemonic misdeeds. Starting with populist democracy in the nineteenth century, these changes gained further impetus with global decolonization, environmentalism, and feminism.

Normative views about how to deal with nature exemplify the shift.[6] The older view, ordained by biblical injunction and spurred by Enlightenment scientific advance, accounted man's subjugation of nature God-given and virtuous. Human progress seemed to emancipate society from the tyranny and insecurity of nature. Moreover, men were explicitly commanded to control and tame the rest of God's creation. To subdue other creatures and to bring wild nature under human dominion benefited all but primitives destined to become extinct.

How remote from current views of nature and culture were those common in the mid–nineteenth century! Here is a passage by America's then most popular historian, George Bancroft. Bancroft compares the Hudson River Valley previous to European settlement with the scene of his own day. As Henrik Hudson first encountered it in 1607,

> trees might everywhere be seen breaking from their root in the marshy soil, and threatening to fall with the first rude gust; while the ground was strewn with the ruins of former forests, over which a profusion of wildflowers wasted their freshness in the mockery of the gloom. Reptiles sported in the stagnant pools, or crawled unharmed over piles of mouldering trees; masses of decaying vegetation fed the exhalations with the seeds of pestilence.... Vegetable life and death were mingled hideously

together. The horrors of corruption frowned on the fruitless fertility of uncultivated nature.

But now, in 1837, exulted Bancroft,

> how changed is the scene from that on which Hudson gazed. The earth glows with the colors of civilization; the banks of the streams are enamelled with the richest grasses; woodlands and cultivated fields are harmoniously blended.... The yeoman, living like a good neighbor near the fields he cultivates, glories in the fruitfulness of the valleys.... The thorn has given way to the rosebush; the cultivated vine clambers over rocks where the brood of serpents used to nestle; while industry smiles at the changes she has wrought, and inhales the bland air which now has health on its wings. And man is still in harmony with nature, which he has subdued, cultivated, and adorned.

In Bancroft's eyes, deforestation, the railroad, mineral extraction, and commerce spell aesthetic progress and spiritual regeneration; the conquest of nature assured harmony with it.[7]

At least outside America, Bancroft's man-centered hubris is not wholly supplanted. "If you could get through the bogs and jungles and the thickets [that covered] this country one million years ago, you would say, 'What a dreadful place this is,'" 1980s environment minister Nicholas Ridley admonished Green primitivists in Britain. "The valleys were mosquito-ridden swamps; the mountains were covered in hideous oak thickets and there were just a few shacks, where miserable people attempted to live. Now this is a country full of wonderful landscape, full of beautiful buildings, superb cities and towns, all built by man, [and] we are constantly enhancing it."[8] But in today's environmentalist climate such preferences are seldom expressed. What was once enhancement is now adjudged degradation.

For most of human history few seriously queried that their manipulations of nature were anything but benign. So evident and paramount were the benefits of conquest that any adverse side-effects were dismissed as inconsequential, evanescent, easily reparable. Supporting such confidence was the belief that human impact, however technologically enhanced, was still puny compared with geological and other natural agencies; mankind's impacts were ultimately constrained by all-powerful nature.

Even reformers like Marsh, who warned that human blindness and greed threatened environmental health and global resources, believed that timely reform could rectify such abuses. But to reform was not to exert less control over nature; on the contrary, human dominion must become more thoroughgoing and farsighted. As Marsh put it, "wherever man fails to master nature, he can but be her slave."[9] Nature was no mere passive pet, but a potential avenging demon.

What a contrast with current views! Along with slavery, imperialism, and ethnic, racial, and patriarchal hegemony, the subjugation of nature now seems morally wrong and socially disastrous. Every species if not every creature is accorded equal rights to autonomous existence. Hierarchy, domination, and subordination are immoral; social and natural harmony are egalitarian, democratic, nonaggressive.

Environmentalists today abnegate control both for nature's sake and for our own. Fearful of technology's mounting might, they shun dominion over nature both as moral evil and as ecological disaster. They preach that nature is best where least affected by culture. Most human agency is ill-intended, uninformed, or misapplied. A sacred sense of organic unity endures only among tribal indigenes, who coexist as nature's respectful partners rather than ruthless extirpators.

In the burgeoning cult of wilderness, former symbols of triumphant conquest became emblems of horrendous desecration. The logger's ax and the hewn stump no longer meant the advance of civilization; they came to denote the rape of innocent nature.[10] Even landscaped gardens had to seem "natural." In New York's Central Park the landscape architect Frederick Law Olmsted "planted trees to look like 'natural scenery,'" Anne Whiston Spirn wryly observes, with such success that those who accepted "the scenery as 'natural', objected to cutting the trees he had planned to cull."[11]

Nature as sacred pet is exemplified in the best-seller *The Trail of the Lonesome Pine* (1908). Desecrated by soulless loggers, Cumberland Gap's once crystal-clear stream was laden with sawdust and "black as soot." At Lonesome Cove

> the cruel deadly work of civilization had already begun. . . . A buzzing monster, creaking and snorting, sent a flashing disk rimmed with sharp teeth, biting a savage way through a log, that screamed with pain as the brutal thing tore through its vitals, and gave up its life with a ghost-like cry of agony.

The novel's protagonist, a mining engineer turned nature lover, tells his fiancée he will restore Lonesome Cove:

> "I'll tear down those mining shacks, . . . stock the river with bass again. And I'll plant young poplars to cover the sight of every bit of uptorn earth along the mountain there. I'll bury every bottle and tin can in the Cove. I'll take away every sign of civilization. . . . "
> "And leave old Mother Nature to cover up the scars," said June.
> "So that Lonesome Cove will be just as it was."
> "Just as it was in the beginning," echoed June.
> "And shall be to the end."[12]

Nature is both maternal and eternal. The contrast with George Bancroft's image could not be more stark.

Along with the worship of wilderness, revulsion against inequity leads many reformers to condemn hierarchy in toto. Any exercise of power — over other people, other creatures, even inanimate nature — comes to seem morally and socially iniquitous. But dominance and hierarchy are not policies that can simply be disowned at will; they are conditions integral to the nature, life cycles, and interactions of all beings, human beings included. Part and parcel of mammalian social behavior, patterns of dominance and submission are unlikely to have been wholly bred out of the human constitution.

Moreover, infantile dependence profoundly marks the human species. Adult dominance and childhood submission are ingrained over many years of obedience and emulation. Unusually prolonged intimacy between the mature and the immature reinforces habits of both dominance and affection.

We also remain at the mercy of an enduring Great Chain of Being — the food chain. Among all of animal creation, predation is essential to life. Creatures consume other creatures, but ingestion is asymmetric. The food chain operates on the basis not of mutual equivalence but of hierarchical dominion, the instinct and power of certain creatures to corral and eat certain others.

Mankind's place in this hierarchy is indubitable, though consciousness and culture also make it exceptional. Although carnivorous, few humans rely mainly on hunting game; we now mostly defang and breed it. Some urbanites, remote from farm reality, turn vegetarian. They see domestic animals as victimized pets, differing from cats and dogs only in being lamentably culled for carnivores. A case in point is the filmic popularity of "Babe," Dick King-Smith's fictional pig whose sheepherding exploits saved him from the slaughterhouse.

But the slaughterhouse is indispensable if pigs are to exist. Popular adjuncts of heritage today are Rare Breeds Survival Trusts, bent on retrieving and husbanding past livestock diversity. To the consternation of animal rightists, the consumption of exotic sheep and goats is promoted for their gamy flavor. However cuddly or appealing such breeds may be, they would soon become extinct if we did not eat them.[13] Moreover, domestic species thrive precisely because their appealing juvenile traits elicit our stewardly care.[14]

To moralize about our relations with pets and other creatures we dominate is risky. How we feel and how we deal with them varies with culture and circumstance, often unexpectedly. What antebellum American would have dreamed of today's protective concern for bison and wolves? Some landscape tastes prove at odds with traditional precepts. The demilitarized zone of Korea and the no-man's-land created by the Berlin Wall became precious nature reserves, precisely because humans could not safely venture there; analogous hazards protect the lethal landscapes of minefields. In Queenstown, Tasmania, and Røros, Norway, sites that mining effluent makes toxic to much vegetation are now enjoyed, even protected, for their bizarre topography and floristic communities.[15]

One new enhancement of the making of pets now looms as an offshoot of genetic cloning. When Dolly proved viable, "Mary Had a Little Lamb" was revised to mark the occasion:

THE CLONING OF DOLLY

Mary had a little lamb
its fleece was slightly grey,
It didn't have a father,
just some borrowed DNA.
It sort of had a mother,
though the ovum was on loan,
It was not so much a lambkin,
as a little lamby clone.
And soon it had a fellow clone,
and soon it had some more,
They followed her to school one day,
all cramming through the door.

It made the children laugh and sing,
the teachers found it droll,
There were far too many lamby clones
for Mary to control.
No other could control the sheep,
since their programs didn't vary,
So the scientists resolved it all,
by simply cloning Mary.
But now they feel quite sheepish,
those scientists unwary,
One problem solved, but what to do,
with Mary, Mary, Mary.[16]

As the reduplication of Mary implies, the making and keeping of pets remolds not only dependent creatures but also their masters and mistresses. "It has sometimes been said that the owners have become domesticated and enslaved by their pets," Tuan notes, "so much work do they put in to keep their pets healthy and happy" (171). But the effort of caring for pets and other subordinates is only a small part of this reciprocal effect. The exercise of power transforms the potent no less than the weaker partner. It is not the hapless subject whom power famously corrupts, but the despot wielding it — like the Duke of Omnium in Anthony Trollope's *The Prime Minister*.

The iniquities wreaked by those in charge of slaves and servants, pets and prostitutes, and by extension on all animate and inanimate nature, have first claim on our concern. But we should not ignore the self-inflicted injuries of the mighty, the effects on human nature of habitual exercise of power. Children at play pretend objects are creatures and creatures are human. Domineering adults reverse this, treating people as animals, animals as inanimate things, both as commodities. Power dehumanizes the mental set along with the subjugated victims of tyrants, slaveholders, absolute rulers. They grow incapable of relating to others either as intimate companions or as fellow beings.

Yet inequality is not innately iniquitous, unless predation, parental control, and anatomical gender anomalies be deemed intolerable. In stressing playfulness, Tuan invites us to reconsider how power may fructify not only the garden but the gardener, enlarge the sympathy of the caretaker along with the lot of the indigent, expand the affection of the parent while rearing the child, and revivify the master of nature, reformed from heedless despoiler into empathetic steward.

Notes

1. Yi-Fu Tuan, *Dominance and Affection: The Making of Pets* (New Haven, Conn.: Yale University Press, 1984); subsequent page references are given in the text.

2. Jorge Luis Borges, "The Analytical Language of John Wilkins," in *Other Inquisitions 1937–1952* (New York: Washington Square Press, 1966), 108–9.

3. William Kessen, dust jacket of Tuan, *Dominance and Affection*.

4. George Perkins Marsh, *Man and Nature; or, Physical Geography as Modified by Human Action*, ed. David Lowenthal [1864] (Cambridge, Mass.: Harvard University Press, 1965); William L. Thomas Jr., ed., *Man's Role in Changing the Face of the Earth* (Chicago: University of Chicago Press, 1956).

5. R. C. Lewontin, *Biology as Ideology: The Doctrine of DNA* (Concord, Ontario: CBC/Anansi, 1991), 86–89.

6. I detail these changes in "Awareness of Human Impacts: Changing Attitudes and Emphases," in B. L. Turner et al., *The Earth as Transformed by Human Action* (New York: Cambridge University Press, 1990), 121–35. As Tuan notes, prior to the Enlightenment "submission to nature and acceptance of a permanent state of childhood were the common posture" (*Dominance and Affection*, 173), and notions of nature taking its revenge on disobedient humans have survived into our own day.

7. George Bancroft, *History of the United States from the Discovery of the American Continent* [1837], 10th ed. (Boston, 1842–74), 2:271–72.

8. Nicholas Ridley, in *The Future of the Public Heritage*, Cubitt Trust Panel conference, October 15, 1986 (London: Royal Society of Arts, 1987), 92.

9. Clarence Glacken, *Traces on the Rhodian Shore: Nature and Culture in Western Thought from Ancient Times to the End of the Eighteenth Century* (Berkeley: University of California Press, 1967); Marsh, *Man and Nature*, 465; Marsh, "The Study of Nature," *Christian Examiner* 68 (1860): 34.

10. Thomas R. Cox et al., *This Well-Wooded Land: Americans and Their Forests from Colonial Times to the Present* (Lincoln: University of Nebraska Press, 1985), 144–47; Nicolai Cikovsky, " 'The Ravages of the Axe': The Meaning of the Tree Stump in Nineteenth-Century American Art," *Art Bulletin* 61 (1971): 613.

11. Anne Whiston Spirn, "Constructing Nature: The Legacy of Frederick Law Olmsted," in *Uncommon Ground: Toward Reinventing Nature*, ed. William Cronon (New York: W. W. Norton, 1995), 111–12.

12. John Fox Jr., *The Trail of the Lonesome Pine* (New York: Grosset and Dunlap, 1908), 201–2.

13. Warren Hoge, "To Save Rare Livestock, Put Them on the Menu," *International Herald Tribune,* January 30, 1997.

14. Stephen Budiansky, *The Covenant of the Wild: Why Animals Choose Domestication,* rev. ed. (New Haven, Conn.: Yale University Press, 1999), 17, 107–10.

15. Mary Jordan, "Where Wildlife Thrives in No-Man's-Land," *International Herald Tribune,* October 9, 1997; Ian Anderson, "Environmental Cleanup? No Thanks," *New Scientist,* November 13, 1993, 6; Dan Charles, "Wasteworld," *New Scientist,* January 31, 1998, 32–35.

16. *New Scientist,* April 5, 1997.

LANDSCAPE AS A CONTESTED TOPOS OF PLACE, COMMUNITY, AND SELF

Kenneth R. Olwig

> As location place is one unit among other units to which it is linked by a circulation net; the analysis of location is subsumed under the geographer's concept and analysis of space. Place, however, has more substance than the word location suggests: it is a unique entity, a "special ensemble" (Lukermann, 1964, 170); it has a history and meaning. Place incarnates the experiences and aspirations of a people. Place is not only a fact to be explained in the broader frame of space, but it is also a reality to be clarified and understood from the perspectives of the people who have given it meaning.
>
> — Yi-Fu Tuan, "Space and Place"

The notion of place that emerges in the above quotation is one in which the meaning of place is, to use Tuan's term, "tensive."[1] There is a certain *tension* in the usage of the concept of place. On the one hand, it can be reduced to mere location and subsumed under the "geographer's" concept of space. On the other hand, it is not as insubstantial as location because it is also a special ensemble, with a history and meaning, incarnating the experiences and aspirations of a people.

Place is not simply a locus in space for Tuan; it constitutes a substantial dialectical opposite to the cosmic emptiness of space. People, he argues, "cannot live in a space-time continuum. The world, to be livable, must be reconstituted to reflect the human need for privileged location and boundaries."[2] The counterpoising of place to space is key to understanding Tuan's elucidation of the idea of landscape. The following passage, from Tuan's *Topophilia* (1974), will be cited here in full because it prefigures much of the present-day debate on landscape and place and because it is central to the argument of this essay.[3] According to Tuan,

> Scenery and landscape are now nearly synonymous. The slight differences in meaning they retain reflect their dissimilar origin. Scenery has traditionally been associated with the world of illusion which is the theater. The expression "behind the scenes" reveals the unreality of scenes. We are not bidden to look "behind the landscape," although a landscaped garden can

93

be as contrived as a stage scene, and as little enmeshed with the life of the owner as the stage paraphernalia with the life of the actor. The difference is that landscape, in its original sense, referred to the real world, not to the world of art and make-believe. In its native Dutch, "landschap" designated such commonplaces as "a collection of farms or fenced fields, sometimes a small domain or administrative unit." Only when it was transplanted to England toward the end of the sixteenth century did the word shed its earthbound roots and acquire the precious meaning of art. Landscape came to mean a prospect seen from a specific standpoint. Then it was the artistic representation of that prospect. Landscape was also the background of an official portrait; the "scene" of a "pose." As such it became fully integrated with the world of make-believe.[4]

Landscape, on the one hand, has substantive meaning as used in the native Dutch to refer to such common*places* as a collection of farms or administrative unit, which are concrete domains having a history and meaning. The *spatial* illusion of landscape as scenery, on the other hand, makes up an insubstantial world of "make-believe" that constitutes "the world of illusion which is the theater." The identification of the scenic concept of landscape with a world of "make-believe" raises fundamental questions concerning what it is that is being made believable. Tuan provides a leverage point, by which to seek an answer to this question, through his reexamination of the concept of landscape. "A scene," in Tuan's analysis, "may be of a place but the scene itself is not a place. It lacks stability: it is in the nature of a scene to shift with every change of perspective. A scene is defined by its perspective whereas this is not true of place: it is in the nature of place to appear to have a stable existence independent of the perceiver."[5]

The above-quoted passage on landscape refers to the native Dutch meaning of landscape as designating certain "commonplaces." The Greek for commonplace is *Koinos topos*. It literally means common place, but it is also used figuratively to refer to a central rhetorical trope, which is usually shortened as *topos*. This trope is a traditional or conventional figure of speech in Greek rhetoric that is largely concerned with forms of argument that are widely applicable.[6] In this essay landscape is regarded as a contested, tensive, *topos* of place, community, and self in both the literal and the figurative sense of topos. The landscape is thus contested both as an actual place and as the figurative site of an ongoing sociopolitical discourse concerning the relations between community, self, and place. The chunks of text (along with the illustrations) that infuse this essay both explicate and illustrate the tensive character of this discourse and should therefore also be regarded as having something of the status of graphs and tables in scientific texts — they are, hence, something to be pored over, rather than skipped over.

Space and Place in Early Geographical Discourse

The contested, tensive, meaning of place, caught between being a substantial, historically constituted domain and being reduced to an insubstantial location in space, has a long epistemic history. This history, I will argue, is key to the construction of landscape as scenic space. Fundamental to this history is the genesis of that which Tuan termed "the geographer's" concept of space. In order to understand how landscape has become a contested topos of place, community, and self, it is necessary to take a closer look at the origins of the geographic concept of space. I will argue that the discursive key to this concept can be found in the work of the Alexandrian astronomer, astrologist, and geographer Claudius Ptolemy (ca. A.D. 90–168). It was he who wove the threads of ancient discourse on space and place into a textual whole that has literally mapped geographical thinking ever since.

The story begins with the early-fifteenth-century rediscovery of Ptolemy's *Guide to Geography*.[7] As the Greek author of the *Almagest*, Ptolemy had long been established as the leading ancient astronomical authority of the Middle Ages. As the author of the *Tetrabiblos*, he was the master of an astrological *"science"* that the geographer of ideas Clarence J. Glacken has described as "an incredible melange" producing "an important and depressing literature."[8] Ptolemy's importance lay not so much in his originality but in the fact that his residency at the library in Alexandria put him in a position to create a brilliant summary of ancient astronomical and astrological wisdom at a time when the age of the classics was drawing to a close. Now, as if in a stroke of fate, the leading ancient authority on the heavens suddenly gave posthumous birth to a book on the relation between the heavens and the earth.[9] Joan Gadol, a Renaissance scholar, places this discovery at the heart of the Italian Renaissance:

> The systematic origins of Renaissance art and of the Copernican astronomy can be found in a movement of thought which may be properly called a "Ptolemaic renaissance" even though Ptolemy was to be deprived of his authority because of it. We have seen how Alberti established the rules of artistic representation by modifying Ptolemy's principles of projection. When scientific "pictures" of the world came to be constructed according to these same principles, modern astronomy and geography began their rise.[10]

It was the application of Ptolemy's principles of projection to drawing by Renaissance architects (called "surveyors" in Renaissance English), such as Fillipo Brunelleschi, and art theorists, such as Brunelleschi's friend Leon Battista Alberti, that made possible the development of single-point perspective in art and hence the representation of landscape as scenery. There is, thus, a direct relationship between the Greek Platonist's guide to geography and the construction of the scenic conception of landscape by Renaissance Neoplatonists.[11] This suggests that if we are to trace the geographical meanings of the contested meaning of place it might be wise to take a closer look at Ptolemy's influential text.

The use of geographical science to create pictorial representations of the globe was integral to Ptolemy's cosmology. Ptolemy divided geographical knowledge into three subdisciplines: (1) geography proper, (2) topography, and (3) chorography. The Ptolemaic map provided the structure behind this division. As Ptolemy put it: "Geography is the representation, by a map [*diagraphos*], of the portion of the earth known to us, together with its general features."[12] The map of the earth was created by plotting the geometries of the heavens onto the globe in the form of the lines of longitude and latitude. Once a map is projected according to the cosmic principles of geometry, it then becomes possible to undertake a *topographical* study of any given location on this map or, alternatively, connect such points together so that they create an enclosed *chorographical* form, such as the shape of a country. This triadic structure has arguably pervaded the study of geography up until the present time.[13] The persistent importance of the Ptolemaic map, and the triadic structure derived from it, suggests that it might be useful to explore the role of place and space in Ptolemy's *Guide to Geography* in relation to the development of the idea of landscape as scenery. This, in turn, should provide clues to understanding the reason why place, when viewed in the context of geographic space, has a tendency to become reduced to an insubstantial locus within a set of coordinates.

The root of *chorography* is the Greek word *choros,* which, according to *Merriam-Webster's Collegiate Dictionary,* simply means "place" in ancient Greek.[14] Liddell and Scott's standard *Oxford Greek-English Lexicon* elaborates upon this meaning, defining it as "a definite space, piece of ground, place," and makes particular reference to "the lower world," defining it also as "land or country."[15] *Choros* is thus very much the sort of place that Tuan, as cited above, would define as "a 'special ensemble'" with history and meaning, incarnating "the experiences and aspirations of a people." The phrase "special ensemble" is, as noted by Tuan, from Fred Lukermann, an American geographer and polyhistor.[16] Lukermann himself has defined *choros* as "literally meaning room," and he states that it "may safely be translated in context as area, region (*regio*), country (*pays*) or space/place — if in the sense of the boundary of an area. *Choros* technically means the boundary of the extension of some thing or things, it is the container or receptacle of a body." Insofar as chorography was concerned with location, it was, in Lukermann's words, "referent solely to the total relational content within a given area." *Choros,* according to Lukermann, should never be translated as space (*spatium*) if the connotation of that word is "empty" or "absolute" space, that is, implies extension or duration without the presence of a body or thing. The Greek word for absolute or empty space was *kenos* (void) or *chaos*.[17] Ptolemy, as has been seen, used the word *topography* for studies that focus upon particular locations within the geometric coordinates of the absolute, geographical space constituted by the map.[18] Topography, in Lukermann's words, was defined as "the order of discrete units one to the other." Geography, finally, is concerned with "processes of world-wide pervasiveness," or to use a more contemporary phrase, it was concerned with the *global.*[19]

It is the map that facilitates the reduction of the roomlike *place* of *choros* to location. As location, it remains a form of place, but it is a place that has been reduced to a spatial coordinate. This redefinition of place, facilitated by being plotted within the geographical space of the map, generates an unstable, *tensive,* meaning. Is place to be defined in areal terms as the field defined historically by a people (its "land or country"), or is it a location within the topographical coordinates of an absolute and atemporal space? Place can mean both, depending upon the context. It can be defined as the *choros* of a historically specific country or land, or it can be defined topographically as "the *places* of a country" with relation, for example, to their *"geographical position."*[20]

Space, Place, and Landscape

The geographic principles elucidated in Ptolemy's *Guide to Geography,* which was termed a *cosmography* in Renaissance translations, was illustrated in some sixteenth-century cosmographies by a form of *world-picture* involving a *diagraphic* sketch of two globes or worlds (see Figure 1 on the following page).[21] The first is the macrocosm of the universe, in which the heavenly regions are drawn upon lines of celestial longitude and latitude. From this macrocosm are projected the lines of longitude and latitude upon the microcosmic earthly world.[22] This whole diagram represents the overarching field of geography. The globe of the earth is compared to the human head, and the face of this earth, with its features (eye and ear), forms the domain of chorography and topography. Whereas the measuring of the earth (i.e., geography) was the domain of the mathematician and scientist, the depiction of the face of the earth was, in Ptolemy's view, a fitting task for an artist:

> Geography looks at the position rather than the quality, noting the relation of distances everywhere, and emulating the art of painting only in some of its major descriptions. Chorography needs an artist, and no one presents it rightly unless he is an artist. Geography does not call for the same requirements, as any one, by means of lines and plain notations, can fix positions and draw general outlines. Moreover Chorography does not have need of mathematics, which is an important part of Geography.[23]

Ptolemy specifically calls for an artistic approach to the graphic depiction of *choros.* The Renaissance application of perspective drawing techniques deriving from Ptolemaic cartography to the depiction of places can thus also be

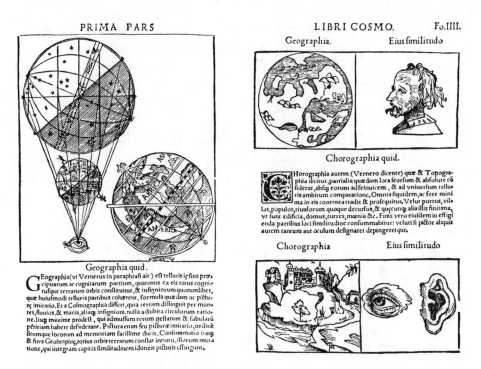

PRIMA PARS

LIBRI COSMO.   Fo.IIII.

Geographia.   Eius similitudo

Chorographia quid.

Horographia autem (Vernero dicente) quæ & Topographia dicitur, partialia quædam loca seorsum & absolute cõfiderat, absq̃ eorum ad sethnuicem , & ad vniuersum telluris ambitum comparatione, Omnia fiquidem, ac fere minima in eis contenta tradit & profequitur. Velut portus, villas, populos, riuulorum quoque decurfus, & quęcunq̃ alia illis finitima, vt funt ædificia, domus, turres, mœnia &c. Finis vero eiufdem in effigienda partibus loci fimilitudine confummabitur: veluti fi pictor aliquis aurem tantum aut oculum defignaret depingeretque.

Chorographia   Eius similitudo

Geographia quid.

GEographia (vt Vernerus in paraphrafi ait) eft telluris ipfius præ, cipuarum ac cognitarum partium, quatenus ex eis totus cogni, tufque terrarum orbis conftituitur, & infigniorum quorumlibet, quæ huiufmodi telluris partibus cohærent, formula quædam ac pictu, rę imitario. Et a Cofmographia differt, quia terram diftinguit per montes, fluuios, & maria, aliaq̃ infigniora, nulla adhibita circulorum ratio, ne, lisq̃ maxime prodeft, qui admuffum rerum geftarum & fabularũ peritiam habere defvderant. Pictura enim feu picturæ imitatio, ordine fitumque locorum ad memoriam facillime ducit. Confummatio itaq̃ & finis Geohraphie, totius orbis terrarum conftat intuitu, illorum imita tione, qui integram capitis fimilitudinem idoneis picturis effingunt.

Figure 1. Illustration of Ptolemy's conception of geography (left) and of chorography and topography (right), from Peter Apianus, *Cosmographia* (Antwerp, 1540).

seen to combine Ptolemaic cosmographic principles drawn from both descriptive chorography and the mathematics used by the geographer/cartographer to delimit and frame *choros*. It was appropriate that such paintings be described as scenes of "landscape" because the root of the word *landscape* is *land,* in the sense of *country,* and one of the meanings of *choros,* of course, is "land" in this sense.[24] A landscape, as Tuan argued earlier, is the sort of common place that has a history and meaning, incarnating the experiences and aspirations of a people. The areal sense of *choros* might be regarded as an expression of its sociopolitical meaning, in which the areal form of *choros* is the juridical field shaped by a political community. The term *choros* was thus often applied to the sort of place that the Greek and Roman imperial city-states sought to bring under their dominance and control.[25] The incorporation of the *choros* of these places within the geometric space of Ptolemy's globalizing map thus has sociopolitical implications, just as the imposition of the grid of a globalizing Roman empire upon the spatial organization of conquered territories also has sociopolitical implications. When brought within the absolute space of a Ptolemaic map, the roomlike place of *choros* becomes reduced to a locality within the hierarchical spatial coordinates of a larger unbounded and expansive imperial space.[26]

Space, Place, and Body

For Ptolemy, as we have seen, chorography was the description of the areal phenomena of tangible place, whereas geography was a generalizing science, just as astronomy and astrology were generalizing sciences. The mathematical/geometrical science of geography is inherently superior to descriptive chorography when seen from the perspective of these sciences, especially when they are combined with a Platonist cosmology. As the art historian E. H. Gombrich puts it:

> For Plato, the universal is the idea, the perfect pattern of the tree exists somewhere in a place beyond the heavens, or, to use the technical term, in the intelligible world. . . . It was on these grounds that Plato himself denied art its validity, for what value can there be in copying an imperfect copy of the idea? But on the same grounds, Neoplatonism tried to assign to art a new place that was eagerly seized upon by the emerging academies. It is just the point, they argued, that the painter, unlike ordinary mortals, is a person endowed with the divine gift of perceiving, not the imperfect and shifting world of individuals, but the external patterns themselves. . . . He is aided in this by the knowledge of the laws of beauty, which are those of harmonious simple geometrical relations.[27]

In Plato's dualistic philosophy it is the idea that impresses itself upon the material receptacle of the *chora*. *Chora* is often translated simply as "space," but it is actually a variant of *choros* that, as Lukermann pointed out earlier, should be distinguished from *kenos*.[28] A look at the original Platonic text shows that this "receptacle" is decidedly feminine for Plato. We may, as Plato puts it, "liken the receiving principle [*chora*] to a mother, and the source or spring to a father."[29] According to the semiotician Julia Kristeva, the *chora* remains amorphous and unknown until it is given position and ordered according to the principles of geometry, which marks and "fixes it in place and reduces it."[30] Ptolemy, a Platonist, might well have seen geo-*graphy* as a means by which one engraves, with the help of geometry, a meaningful, rational representational form upon the *chora* of the earth. It is through this effort that *chora* (see Figure 2 on the following page) is fixed and given position as a *topos* (or *locus* [Latin]) within an absolute geometric space. The forms treated in Ptolemy's *chorography,* whether or not they were conceived of as being particularly feminine in character, did have a decidedly enclosed, bodily quality.[31] *Choros,* as Lukermann states above, "technically means the boundary of the extension of some thing or things, it is the container or receptacle of a body." When the principles of Ptolemaic cartography are applied to the depiction of a land or country, then, by this same logic, the tangible body of the land is transformed into the illusory space of scenery.

Figure 2. *Ur Underweysung der Messung,* by Albrecht Dürer, 1525. This is an apt illustration of the way perspective drawing reduces *chora* to an abstract coordinate space.

Landscape as Theatrical Stage

Yi-Fu Tuan observed, in a quotation cited at the beginning of this essay: "Scenery has traditionally been associated with the world of illusion which is the theater." The word *theater* ultimately derives from the Greek word *theasthai,* meaning "to view," with the root *thea,* meaning "the act of seeing," which, in turn, is akin to the word *thauma,* which means "miracle." Renaissance architects and artists applied the visual principles of perspective to elevated "world landscapes" that were seen to "mirror" the world and be "pregnant with whole provinces." Renaissance architects used these same principles in the creation of both theaters and their stage scenery, whereby they create visions of infinite depth, *mir*roring the depth of cosmic space in a way that was seen to be *mir*aculous by contemporaries. Cartographic works were correspondingly titled "theaters" or "mirrors."[32] An example of such a "theater" was John Speed's 1611 *The Theatre of the Empire of Great Britaine,* which encompassed the various separate lands of the British Isles within the uniform geometric space of the map.[33] At this time William Camden was making a parallel effort through the development of his pioneering chorographic classic *Brittania,* which helped revive the memory of the Roman name and heritage of the isles.[34] This geographical work served the needs of King James, who himself financed elaborate and fabulously expensive theater productions, called *masques,* to represent a union of his English and Scottish realms as a revived imagined Roman-era British state. This theater of state was to be under a body of "natural" statutory law, inspired by Roman law, that members of James's court (particularly Francis Bacon) believed to be superior to the law of the English Parliament, which was rooted in custom.[35] The monarch's theater was so structured that the head of state's elevated throne commanded a privileged perspective for the surveillance of the staged "landscape" scene and the persona located upon it. These masques represented perhaps the earliest use of perspective scenery in Britain and one of the earliest and most influential modern English uses of the word *landscape* to refer to scenery. This, of course, was the era when landscape was "transplanted to England," to repeat Tuan's words, and thus we see that this British spin on the concept of landscape was, from the very beginning, "fully integrated with the world of make-believe." In this case it was used to make believe that the differing lands under James's crown formed a unity within the space of a British state. Thomas Hobbes immortalized the landscaped image of the state with the famous 1651 frontispiece to his classic work on the state, *Leviathan* (see Figure 3 on the following page). In this frontispiece, the head of state surveys a stagelike landscape scene of the territory under his control. The "body politic," which supports the head, is made up of an assemblage of individualized Hobbesian "persona" (meaning theater "mask" in Latin) who, without the sword and scepter in the hands of the state, would have a life that is "nasty, brutal and short."[36]

Ptolemaic Cosmology and the Kantian *Vorbegriff*

The idea of the world as stage was powerful enough to outlive the Renaissance. It can be seen, for example, in the work of such a foundational figure in modern philosophy as Immanuel Kant (1724–1804) — who, not incidentally, taught geography.[37] For Kant this stage formed a kind of preexistent scene upon which the theater of our existence was played.

Kant was particularly impressed by the ability of geography to predict the outcome of a journey into the unknown, before actually making that journey. When Kant described geography as a "propaedeutic" discipline that allows one to generate a *Vorbegriff,* or preconceptualization, of the world, he situated himself in the Ptolemaic tradition.[38] Kant saw cosmography as foundational to knowledge of humankind, referring specifically to the division between *geography, topography,* and *chorography.*[39]

For Kant the conception of the world as scenery acted as a "systematic" (or *structural,* to use the equivalent modern term) *Vorbegriff.* According to Kant,

> The world is the substratum and the stage [*Schauplatz*] on which the play [*Spiel*] of our abilities takes place. It is the foundation upon which our modes of knowledge [*Erkenntnisse*] are acquired and used.... In addition we must get to know the objects of our experience as a whole, so that our modes of knowledge do not constitute an aggregate but a system [structure]. Because in the system [structure] the whole precedes the parts; in the aggregate, however, the parts precede [the whole].... The whole is here the world, the scene upon which all our experiences are placed.

Through knowledge of the geography of this scene, Kant argued, "we anticipate our future experience, which we will later encounter in the world," and, in this way, gain "a pre-conceptualization of everything.... [T]he perception of the world requires more than merely seeing the world." The idea of the whole as *Vorbegriff* is, for Kant, "architectural; it creates the sciences."[40] This idea of

Figure 3. Frontispiece to the 1651 edition of Thomas Hobbes's *Leviathan*. Reproduced by permission of Cornell University Library, Division of Rare Books and Manuscript Collections.

the world as a scene or stage springs from the scenic conception of landscape and the cosmology that it expressed. The surface of the stage is known through our senses (the focus of the then-new study of aesthetics), whereas the system or structure behind the aesthetics of the stage is analogous to the geometries that prestructure the Ptolemaic map (and the perspective drawing) and give it the form of a global totality. The changing scenes upon which the play takes place represent, in turn, the staged movement of *time*. The metaphor of the theater stage thus proves the spatial and temporal epistemological structure for knowledge gained upon the world scene and, ultimately, for the idea that the world develops through stages.[41] The conceptualization of the world as landscape scene, or stage, in turn helped create a philosophical background for the preconceptualization of the nation-state as something preordained to fill the preexisting space of the map.

The Landscape of the Nation-State

At the time Kant was writing, Germany was divided into a myriad of independent lands and quasi-independent "landscape" territories. The threat of the centralized power of the French nation-state became more and more manifest as Napoleon rose to power. The call for German national unity, which emerged at this time, culminated with the rise of a centralized nation-state under Prussian hegemony. One of those who helped set this process of national consolidation in motion was the Danish/German geoscientist and natural philosopher Henrik Steffens (1773–1845). His work exemplifies the way in which the picturing of the world as stage scenery worked to envision the progressive development of a unity of nation and individual:

> Just as the individual human's existence is a string of incidences, which have as an internal unifying principle the inner being of the individual itself, in the same way the history of nations consists of a string of changing events, *which* involves not only that of the single individual, but all of mankind.... Through this interaction of the whole upon the individual, and the individual upon the whole, is generated an identical picture-history, which presupposes the entirety of nature as the foundation for all final existence, and all of humanity as the expression of this interaction itself. The expression of the coexistence of all these individuals' interaction in history and nature is *space* — eternity's continually *recumbent* picture. But the whole *is* only an eternal chain of changing events. Yes it *is* this constant alternating exchange, this eternal succession of transformations itself. The constant type of these changes is *time* — eternity's constant moving, flowing and changing picture.[42]

The metaphor of the picture linked Steffens's argument to a larger Germanic realm of ideas in which the ideas of "picturing," creation, and development were conflated. The German word for picture, *Bild,* and the verb *bilden* (meaning to shape, form, or create and, by extension, to educate and develop) had been identified with each other at least since the era of the Renaissance cosmographers, and this identification culminated with the Romantics.[43]

The art theorist Carl Gustav Carus (1789–1869), who belonged to the same intellectual circles as Steffens, developed an influential theory concerning the origins of landscape art as an expression of cultural and social development. This was published in his well-known *Neun Briefe über die Landschaftsmalerei* (1815–1834). According to E. H. Gombrich, Carus described the history of art as "a movement from touch to vision":

> Wanting to plead for the recognition of landscape painting as the great art of the future, he based his advocacy on the laws of historical inevitability: "The development of the senses in any organism begins with feeling, with touch. The more subtle senses of hearing and seeing emerge only when the organism perfects itself. In almost the same manner, mankind began with sculpture. What man formed had to be massive, solid, tangible. This is the reason why painting ... always belongs to a later phase. ... Landscape art ... pre-supposes a higher degree of development."[44]

Carus's ideas, in Gombrich's opinion, prefigured a questionable form of modern thinking in which art becomes the measure of a society's stage of development. "By inculcating the habit of talking in terms of collectives, of 'mankind,' 'races,' or 'ages,'" this mode of thought, according to Gombrich, "weakens resistance to totalitarian habits of mind."[45] The nation-state thereby becomes the whole that precedes the parts. This whole, in the hands of Steffens and Carus, becomes the natural national stage upon which the drama of individual and national development, from one stratified stage of superior *Bildung* to the next, takes form. It thereby creates a form of "myth," in the sense analyzed by Roland Barthes, which "transforms history into nature."[46] This idea of *Bildung* enables the development of a "total history" that, according to Michel Foucault, seeks to link together the events of "a well-defined spatio-temporal area" so that history itself may be articulated into great units — stages or phases — that contain within themselves their own principle of cohesion": the "'face' of a period."[47]

The conception of landscape that developed at this time has been described as "imperial" by the art historian W. J. T. Mitchell. This landscape is imperious because it legitimizes "the claim that not merely landscape *painting,* but the visual perception of landscape is a revolutionary historical discovery of the European Renaissance that marks, in Ruskin's words, 'the simple fact that we are, in some strange way, different from all the great races that existed before us.'" This form of argument exemplifies that which Mitchell has termed "the 'natural history' of modernity" or "the teleology of modernism" or, alternatively, "the teleology of landscape" — for example, the idea that phylogenesis recapitulates ontogenesis in the stratified development of a mature civilization that is capable of comprehending its world as a horizontal landscape scene, controlled by abstract laws.[48]

Mitchell focuses upon the teleology of landscape as a central tenet of modernity, but it might be more precise to focus upon the structural premises that underlay this conception of landscape. Gyorgy Kepes, professor of visual design at MIT, thus tells us: "Each historical era seeks and needs a central model of understanding. Structure seems central to our time — the unique substance of our vision."[49] The relation between *Bildung,* as a pictorialized notion of individual and national development, and the underlying principles that structure the landscape scene is highly apparent in the work of the prophet of structuralism and developmental psychology, the Swiss historian of science and educator, Jean Piaget.

The Pictorial Structure of Development

The art historian Samuel Edgerton has remarked upon the inspiration that Piaget derived from the Renaissance rise of perspective art in developing his ideas concerning the stages of development of the individual mind:

> In recent years Swiss psychologist Jean Piaget has been studying the change in children's perceptual development from an egocentric, nonperspectival viewpoint to a growing understanding of "space structuration" after the age of about eight. He has related this developmental change to the history of mankind generally: phylogenesis recapitulates ontogenesis. Admittedly, Piaget has only experimented with Western children in this regard...and the parallel he draws between the growth of the child's perception and that of the human race as a whole necessarily reflects his own Western values and predispositions.[50]

Piaget's theories give a modern form to the pedagogical implications of the *Bildung* ideal's pictorial premises.

For Piaget the development of the child's cognitive abilities parallels the development of the collective mental capacities of society, much as they are described by Carus. According to Piaget's model, which echoes the Ptolemaic trinity of topography, chorography, and geography, "perceptual space is organized in three successive stages. The first of these is based on topological, the second on metric and projective, the third on overall relationships bearing upon displacement of objects relative to one another."[51] One of the most famous tests developed by Piaget, to plot the cognitive development of the child, was the use of landscape models, or pictures, in which the child is asked to describe the objects in the landscape.[52] The test is based on the idea that the "egocentric" mind-set of the child (or, by extension, the childlike primitive human) relates to the world in terms of the position of his or her body in relation to other body-like, or sculptural, shapes. This brings to mind Lukermann's reference, quoted above, to *choros* as being "referent solely to the total relational content within a given area." The development of the child's cognition is measured against the ability of the child to "decenter" and reorient the self according to the abstract underlying spatial coordinates of a maplike landscape. This would then be equivalent to the orientation of *topography*, described above by Lukermann, as "the order of discrete units one to the other."

Structuralist *Bildung*

Piaget was not only a historian of science and a cognitive psychologist but also one of the founders of modern structural theory in the human sciences. As a structural theorist his ideas merged with those of the Marxist structuralists. Piaget thus openly declared his sympathy for the dialectics of structural Marxism as espoused by the French philosopher Louis Althusser. Piaget was particularly taken by Althusser's notion of "overdetermination," which he termed "the sociological counterpart to certain forms of causality in physics." According to Piaget, it is the concept of overdetermination "which prompts Althusser to insert the contradictions inherent in the relations of production or the contradictions between these and the forces of production, in short, all the apparatus of Marxist economics, into a transformational system whose structure and principles of formalization he tries to articulate."[53] Althusser's notion of overdetermination (*surdétermination*) can be traced back to the Austrian psychologist Sigmund Freud, who used it (*Überdeterminierung*) to describe the way dream thoughts can create privileged images that condense many thoughts into the single totality of a picture. The mode of production is similarly a picturelike totality that embodies within it the contradictions that will bring about its transformation. It is the overdetermined structure of this "ever-pre-given" structure (*structure toujours-déjà-donnée*) that brings about its transformation, rather than the central activity of an essential agent or subject. This agent or subject is thus seen to be "decentered" (*décentrée*) in Marxist structuralist theory.[54] Piaget defends this decentering of the individual in Marxist structuralism, noting that "the chief objection urged against him [Althusser] is that — at least in the eyes of some critics — he has too low an estimate of things human; but if the values of the 'person' (often regrettably confused with those of the ego) are taken to be less important than the constructive activities of the epistemic subject, the characterization of knowledge as production is in agreement with one of the best established traditions of classical Marxism."[55] Classical Marxism, of course, is a classical example of a historicist modernist teleology.

"The individual or *existential* subject," as Yi-Fu Tuan explains, "does not in fact have a role in structuralism; but what Jean Piaget (1970) calls the *epistemic* subject does. The epistemic subject is that cognitive nucleus which is common to all subjects at a certain level of abstraction."[56] Piaget's affinity for Althusser is understandable given the fact that he, like Althusser, conceptualized his structural system in terms of a picturelike totality in which the progressive decentering of cognition, on the part of the "epistemic subject," is the mark of mental development. Piaget's emphasis upon the construction of this form of rational, abstract, decentered knowledge made him the guru of the science-centered national curricula that developed in the wake of the space race of the 1960s at all levels of education.[57] The structural principles described by Piaget link these ideas both back to the theorists of *Bildung* and forward to present-day structuralist and structurationist approaches to landscape and social theory. Much contemporary social theory has been influenced during its formation by this type of neo-Marxist structuralism and has subsequently struggled to find a *locale* for a rehabilitated decentered epistemic subject.[58]

The Place of Place in a "Nonmodern" Landscape

A characteristic of the "imperial landscape," with its "teleology of modernism," is that it defines a linear developmental progression. This teleology can be seen to permeate modernist thinking concerning everything from social development to individual cognitive development. This is a teleology that classifies certain modes of cognition, as well as certain conceptions of place, as being necessarily primitive, or at least "premodern" (or "traditional") as opposed to modern. The *is* of this mode of thought easily becomes a prescriptive *ought,* due to its teleological character. "Modernity 'dis-places,' " as the sociologist Anthony Giddens puts it in the context of a discussion of "the contrasts between the premodern and the modern." The consequence of this displacement is that "place becomes phantasmagoric."[59] Is this necessarily the case, or does it reflect a hidden teleology? The latter is suggested by Foucault, who has criticized such premodern/modern dualisms by noting how the notion of "tradition enables us to isolate the new against a background of permanence."[60] This results in what Barthes might term a "miraculous evaporation of history" that is "another form of a concept common to most bourgeois myths: the irresponsibility of man."[61]

The teleology of modernism, with its inherent decentering of both people and place, depends upon the notion of linear development through stages. The questioning of this teleology thus leads to other questions concerning the related status of place and people. Are, for example, "decentering," "disembodiment," or "dis-placement" necessary correlates to the bettering of social conditions? Must place necessarily become a phantasmagoric locus in an insubstantial space for this to be achieved? Must place necessarily be reduced simply to "[a] portion of geographical SPACE occupied by a person or thing"? If the importance of place is to be recognized in the modern world, can it only be as a subjective, vaguely effeminate, "structure of feeling"? — the proper realm of the artist, as in the case of Ptolemy's *choros.*[62] To answer these questions it is useful to reexamine the historical meaning of landscape as a substantial place with a history and meaning, which Tuan sketched at the beginning of this essay.

The conception of landscape as a form of scenery has gained such power that it is easily forgotten that, at the time the scenic idea of landscape was developed in the Renaissance, the words *land* and *landscape* (*Landschaft* in German) had a complex and contested meaning that persists to the present.[63] The historian Otto Brunner gives the following description of this contestation:

> The *Land* comprised its lord and people, working together in the military and judicial spheres. But in other matters we see the two as opposing parties and negotiating with each other. Here the Estates appear as the "Land" in a new sense, counterpoised to the prince, and through this opposition they eventually formed the corporate community of the territorial Estates, the *Landschaft*. At this point the old unity of the *Land* threatened to break down into a duality, posing the key question that became crucial beginning in the sixteenth century: who represented the *Land*, the prince or the Estates? If the prince, then the *Landschaft* would become a privileged corporation; if the *Landschaft*, then it would become lord of the *Land*.[64]

Variants of the situation described by Brunner in the context of Austria could be found throughout Europe, particularly in those areas like the most mountainous regions of the Alps or the marshy coasts of the North Sea that were difficult for a centralized, hierarchically stratified state to control.[65] These same areas were often, simultaneously, regions of economic growth and social change that threatened the hegemony of the feudal state at a time when the economic fulcrum of Europe was moving from the Mediterranean to the North Atlantic.[66] These political and economic transformations must be seen, furthermore, as part of a larger spectrum of change. The *Landstandschaft,* the estates *(Stände)* of a land, were the equivalent of the law-abiding and tax-paying citizens who, by virtue of their good *standing*, have the right to vote. Standing meant being *somebody,* or to have a "place" as *some body,* within an independent landscape domain conceived as place (or *choros*). This place, to paraphrase Lukermann's earlier definition, is referent to the totality of relations within the jurisdictional field of the landscape. This jurisdictional field defined the domain of the landscape from the inside out, as the place of a *choros,* rather than from the outside in, as is the case with the map's geographic space. The *Landschaft*/landscape was important as an expression of community and place-identity at a time when the medieval ascetic ideal was being replaced by the ideal of the active, engaged citizen.[67] This was a time of ferment, throughout Europe, in which the modern state was emerging, and countries experienced dramatic shifts between more representative forms of government and more autocratic forms—and this is still an ongoing process.

The key question asked by Brunner above was, "who represented the *Land,* the prince or the Estates?" The concept of *representation* lay at the heart of the contestation over landscape as a topos of place, community, and self. King James, as noted earlier, represented his vision of autocratic rule, over the various separate lands found on the British Isles, in terms of a staged landscape scene under the surveillance of his central monarchical gaze. James had little use for representative political bodies founded on custom, such as the English Parliament. Italianate central-point perspective was not, however, the only means of visually representing the *Landschaft,* or landscape, as a body politic. Forms of artistic representation that differed in important respects from the Italian Renaissance tradition can be seen to have reinforced the complex place-identity of the Netherlands.[68] They allowed for a form of place-identity that was intensely local yet cosmopolitan and tolerant.

The *Landschaft* claimed its right to representation in a parliamentary body on the basis of common law founded on custom.[69] This form of representation is also, despite the efforts of King James, still characteristic of legal and political organization in Eng*land* and most of the places settled by the English, including the United States. These are places, of course, that are by no means characterized by backward social development, though the leadership of more centralized, autocratic states might think so. Customary law is built up into a body of common law through a process of generalization based upon the precedence of particular concrete cases in particular places. This form of representation, it could be argued, also characterizes the principles used to create northern landscape art. These principles have been elucidated by Gombrich through reference to the work of the painter Jan van Eyck (1390?–1441):

> The southern artists of his generation, the Florentine masters of Brunelleschi's circle, had developed a method by which nature could be represented in a picture with almost scientific accuracy. They began with the framework of perspective lines, and they built up the human body through their knowledge of anatomy and the laws of foreshortening. Van Eyck took the opposite way. He achieved the illusion of nature by patiently adding detail upon detail.[70]

The art historian Svetlana Alpers complements Gombrich's analysis of artistic technique with an approach that focuses upon artistic form. She notes how "pictures in the north were related to graphic description rather than to rhetorical persuasion, as was the case with pictures in Italy." "Northern mapmakers and artists," in Alpers's view, "persisted in conceiving of a picture as a surface on which to set forth or inscribe the world rather than as a stage for significant human action" — for example, the action of history conceived as theater.[71] For the painters of the lowlands, by contrast, the goal appears to have been to inscribe the canvas with the landscape place of a community whose generic

Figure 4. *Haymaking,* by Pieter Brueghel, from the mid–sixteenth century, shows a landscape shaped by custom.

workings are based on custom (Figure 4). The difference is brought out in the art historian Max Friedländer's distinction between the role of "genre" and that of history in painting:

> Custom means: the form of life to which we are used, to which we have been educated, which is enjoined on us. But the genre-painter is concerned with what people are accustomed to do not merely because custom prescribes it but from instinct and inclination as well.... The interest which an historical event arouses rests on its extraordinariness, its uniqueness.... In the genre-picture the particular case points to other cases, so that a certain happening or state is illustrated as an example or, to put it philosophically, as an "idea." The historical picture says: *that* happened once; the genre picture says: *this* happens often.[72]

The approach to the representation and construction of concrete place-identity developed by Netherlands painters contrasts vividly with the Ptolemaic-Florentine tradition that posits, as Alpers puts it, "a viewer at a certain distance looking through a framed window to a putative substitute world."[73] The perspective gained through this window is that of infinite horizons in space, whereas seventeenth-century Netherlands art sought to capture the life of a place with history and meaning.[74] The cognitive significance of the difference between the two conceptions of landscape, with respect to place-identity, can be elucidated by a reexamination of Piaget's cognitive landscape.

Cognitive Recentering

Piaget, like Plato, looked down upon the figurative, concrete forms of knowledge typical of plastic representation in the arts. Terence Turner, an anthropologist, has pointed out a sharp distinction in Piaget's epistemology between what are called "figurative" and "operative" modes of thought. The former comprises perception, imitation, mental imagery, and "symbolic signifiers." Operational thought, on the other hand, consists of logical manipulations of a dynamic character, for example, inverse or reciprocal transformations. Operational thought relies upon nonfigurative signs that are arbitrary, collectively standardized tokens that typically denote general concepts. This epistemological model, in Turner's view, "is for all intents and purposes exclusively a model of the development of operational thought" in which "figurative thought is passed over as a lower form of mental activity." This means, in turn, that Piaget's approach does not give adequate consideration to "the analysis of art, religion, or other symbolic forms of a nonscientific nature (i.e., those that characteristically employ figurative symbolism or modes of thought)."[75]

Figurative modes of thought, according to Turner, are important to the process by which the individual cognitively "recenters." Recentering, as Turner writes, is "in many ways the opposite of the 'decentering' process which constitutes the leitmotiv of Piaget's model of mental development, but should not be confused with the primitive egocentricity of childhood. On the contrary, it presupposes that 'decentering' has already occurred."[76] Recentering occurs through the medium of "art and religion, including myth, ritual, magic, poetry, painting, etc." The above analysis of Netherlands painting suggests that place and community identity was generated through custom as reinforced by the recentering effect of art. Such art has this effect, according to Turner, because it imposes "forms upon objective reality which serve, at the same time, as models for the subject's affective and cognitive orientation to that reality." In this way "the symbolic structure of a myth, ritual, painting, or poem, interpreted as a figurative model of an objective situation, functions much as an objective template for the molding of subjective experience and the restructuring of subjective identity as a projection of subjective states onto the objective environment."[77]

The pictorial and stagelike landscape ideal promoted by Steffens and Carus favors a form of *Bildung* that encourages the person to decenter his or her identity, reducing it to that of an individualized actor in an abstract, spatialized, national landscape. The place of this actor is defined "topographically," again to paraphrase Lukermann's earlier definition, within an order of discrete units, one to the other.[78] Personal identity is thereby removed from the concrete context of local community and transferred to the imagined (or "make-believe") community of the nation-state. This form of *Bildung* thus helps create the basis for the transferal of concrete local loyalties to larger, more abstract, territorial entities. Historically, this form of identity *Bildung* has proved to be an effective means of creating a rooted blood-and-soil loyalty to the central state.[79] The process of recentering, by contrast, provides a means by which a person can develop a reflected sense of place that is capable of encompassing multiple place identities (such as those developed at the time of the Dutch struggle for independence).[80]

Conclusion

Ptolemy's "science," though it belonged to the ancient realms of astrology and astronomy, was also critical to the forming of a modern pictorial idea of landscape as both a picture of the world and the world as picture. It is this notion that makes possible the envisioning of the world in terms of a (theater) stage or stages, an episteme that has inspired globalizing thinkers ranging from Renaissance cosmographers to modern structuralists. The ability to comprehend and conform to this world-picture has come to be seen as a mark of modern individual and collective national development, or *Bildung*. Yi-Fu Tuan's counterpoising of space and place breaks the hegemony of the scenic, spatialized conception of the social landscape by recognizing that the development of place-identity also has a substantive, historical dynamic of its own. The landscape prospect creates an illusory substantiality that Tuan's dissection effectively punctures, thereby forcing us to confront the discordant, tensive meanings encompassed by the historically constituted concepts of landscape and place. In this way, Tuan helps free us from the modernist teleologies tied to the landscape as the progressive scene of a history that dis-places people. Once freed from the make-believe of modernist illusions of progress, place can be made manifest as being more than a location in space. It can then be seen for what it has been through a long period of history, a contested topos of place, community, and self. And we, as embodied subjects, have a rightful place in this contestation.

Notes

For help with the illustrations I would like to thank Terje Semb and Radmil Popvic. For help with the manuscript I wish to thank Michael Jones, Karen Fog Olwig, and the volume editors, who deserve special thanks for putting together an excellent conference seminar and book for Yi-Fu Tuan.

1. Tuan applies the term *tensive* in a discussion of *landscape*'s "diaphoric" status as a metaphor because it combines "two dissimilar appearances or ideas," thereby generating its "tensive meaning." This tension derives from the fact that the differing meanings of landscape as "domain" and as "scenery" belong to two different discourses: that of politics and economics, on the one hand, and that of aesthetics, on the other. This differentiation is also pertinent to the following discussion of landscape in this essay. See Yi-Fu Tuan, "Sign and Metaphor," *Annals of the Association of American Geographers* 68, no. 3 (1978): 366, 370.

2. Yi-Fu Tuan, *Man and Nature* (Washington, D.C.: Association of American Geographers, 1971), 18.

3. On landscape, see Denis Cosgrove and Stephen Daniels, *The Iconography of Landscape* (Cambridge: Cambridge University Press, 1988); Kenneth Robert Olwig, "Recovering the Substantive Nature of Landscape," *Annals of the Association of American Geographers* 86, no. 4 (1996): 630–53. On place, see Robert David Sack, *Homo Geographicus: A Framework for Action, Awareness, and Moral Concern* (Baltimore: Johns Hopkins University Press, 1997); and J. Nicholas Entrikin, *The Betweenness of Place: Towards a Geography of Modernity* (Baltimore: Johns Hopkins University Press, 1991).

4. Yi-Fu Tuan, *Topophilia: A Study of Environmental Perception, Attitudes, and Values* (Englewood Cliffs, N.J.: Prentice-Hall, 1974), 133.

5. Yi-Fu Tuan, "Space and Place: Humanistic Perspective," *Progress in Geography* 6 (1974): 236.

6. Tormod Eide, "Retorisk Topos & Gresk Geometri," *Rhetorica Scandinavica* 2 (1997): 20–27. The term *common place* (*koinos topos*), as used in Greek rhetoric, did not mean a trite comment or truism.

7. Samuel Edgerton, *The Renaissance Rediscovery of Linear Perspective* (New York: Basic Books, 1975), 91–123; Claudius Ptolemy, *The Geography,* ed. Edward Luther Stevenson (New York: Dover, 1991).

8. Clarence J. Glacken, *Traces on the Rhodian Shore: Nature and Culture in Western Thought from Ancient Times to the End of the Eighteenth Century* (Berkeley: University of California Press, 1967), 111–15.

9. On Ptolemy's influence, see John Kirtland Wright, *The Geographical Lore of the Time of the Crusades: A Study in the History of Medieval Science and Tradition in Western Europe* (New York: Dover, 1965), 10, 19, 34, 48, 78.

10. Joan Gadol, *Leon Battista Alberti: Universal Man of the Early Renaissance* (Chicago: University of Chicago Press, 1969), 157.

11. On this subject, see Edgerton, *Renaissance Rediscovery.*

12. Quoted in Fred Lukermann, "The Concept of Location in Classical Geography," in *Introduction to Geography: Selected Readings,* ed. Lawrence M. Sommers and Fred E. Dohrs (New York: Thomas Y. Crowell Company, 1967 [1961]), 55; see also 58.

13. Ibid., 56. See also Kenneth R. Olwig, "Nature — Mapping the 'Ghostly' Traces of a Concept," in *Concepts in Human Geography*, ed. Carville Earl, Kent Mathewson, and Martin S. Kenzer (Savage, Md.: Rowman and Littlefield., 1996), 63–96. Ptolemy's distinction between geography, chorography, and topography was preserved in the influential system of Bernhardus Varenius (1622–50), a German scholar living in Amsterdam, who defined "the mixt mathematical science" of geography in his 1650 treatise *Geographia Generalis,* which was eventually published in England under the auspices of Sir Isaac Newton. Through the influence of Varenius the field termed "geography" by Ptolemy became known as "general geography," whereas chorography came to be know as "special geography," though Ptolemy's *choros* persists in the present-day use of the term *chorology.*

14. *Merriam-Webster's Collegiate Dictionary* (Springfield, Mass.: Merriam-Webster, 1995), s.v. "chorography."

15. Henry George Liddell and Robert Scott, *A Greek-English Lexicon* (Oxford: Clarendon Press, 1940), 2016, s.v. "choros."

16. Fred Lukermann, "Geography as a Formal Intellectual Discipline and the Way in Which It Contributes to Human Knowledge," *Canadian Geographer* 8 (1964): 170.

17. Lukermann, "Concept of Location," 55, 64.

18. Eide, in "Retorisk Topos," has argued that the rhetorical use of topos derives from the concept of the "geometric place" as used in geometry, with the connotation of being an element in a structure. This would fit in well with Ptolemy's geometric use of the term. My thanks to the Bergen rhetorician Tom Are Trippestad for pointing this out to me.

19. Lukermann, "Concept of Location," 55.

20. The word *topos* is sometimes applied to a larger region, but most definitions in Liddell and Scott define *topos* as "place" in the senses listed here: (Liddell and Scott, *Greek-English Lexicon*, s.v. "topos").

21. Gerald Strauss, *Sixteenth-Century Germany: Its Topography and Topographers* (Madison: University of Wisconsin Press, 1959), 55–56.

22. A. J. Gurevich, *Categories of Medieval Culture* (London: Routledge & Kegan Paul, 1985), 57–59.

23. Ptolemy, *The Geography*, 26. This passage foreshadows, or perhaps foreordains, the modern debate between proponents of geography as an ideographic chorologic study and proponents of geography as a nomothetic, quantitative, spatial science. The roomlike space of chorology is translated as *Raum* in German, but it means both room, in the areal sense, and space, in the abstract, Euclidean sense. It can lead to confusion when geographical theorists, such as Richard Hartshorne, use German definitions to define geography as a science concerned with space. The modernist quantitative geographers of the 1960s accepted the Hartshornian definition of geography as a science of space but rejected his interest in *chorology*. They focused instead upon a study of "locational analysis" that effectively reduced place to a coordinate in absolute "geographic" space, and this tendency persists among their successors in geography to this day. See Richard Hartshorne, "The Concept of Geography as a Science of Space, from Kant and Humboldt to Hettner," *Annals of the Association of American Geographers* 40 (1958): 97–108.

24. Olwig, "Recovering the Substantive Nature."

25. This is the subject of an extensive literature, of which a classic study is Numa Denis Fustel de Coulanges, *The Ancient City* (Garden City, N.Y.: Doubleday Anchor, n.d. [1864]); see also Ian Morris, "The Early Polis as City and State," in *City and Country in the Ancient World*, ed. Andrew Wallace-Hadrill and John Rich (London: Routledge, 1991), 24–57; and François Polignac, *Cults, Territory, and the Origins of the Greek City-State* (Chicago: University of Chicago Press, 1995).

26. Samuel Edgerton, "From Mental Matrix to *Mappa Mundi* to Christian Empire: The Heritage of Ptolemaic Cartography in the Renaissance," in *Art and Cartography: Six Historical Essays*, ed. David Woodward (Chicago: University of Chicago Press, 1987), 10–50. It is interesting to note that the great Ptolemy-inspired cosmographies of the 1500s were largely initiated to serve imperial efforts to consolidate the Holy Roman Empire; see Strauss, *Sixteenth-Century Germany*, 7.

27. E. H. Gombrich, *Art and Illusion: A Study in the Psychology of Pictorial Representation*, 3d ed., Bollingen Series 35.5 (Princeton, N.J.: Princeton University Press, 1969 [1959]), 155–56.

28. On the meanings of *choros/chora*, see Liddell and Scott, *A Greek-English Lexicon*, s.v. "choros, chora." My thanks to Professor, dr. phil., Minna Skafte Jensen, Odense University, for her patient help in explaining to me what *choros* does *not* mean (it is not, for example, etymologically related to the word *chorus*). She cannot, however, be held responsible for my ruminations concerning what it does mean.

29. Plato (1961), "Timaeus," in *The Collected Dialogues of Plato*, ed. Edith Hamilton and Huntington Cairns (New York: Pantheon, 1961), 1177–79.

30. Julia Kristeva, *Revolution in Poetic Language* (New York: Columbia University Press, 1984), 25–27, 239–40. For a different approach to *chora*, see Inger Birkeland, "The Mytho-Poetic in Northern Travel," in *Leisure/Tourism Geographies: Practices and Geographical Knowledge*, ed. David Crouch (London: Routledge, 1999), 17–33. On the perception of the earth as predominantly feminine as opposed to a masculine celestial realm, see Kenneth Robert Olwig, "Sexual Cosmology: Nation and Landscape at the Conceptual Interstices of Nature and Culture, or: What does Landscape Really Mean?" in *Landscape: Politics and Perspectives*, ed. Barbara Bender (Oxford: Berg, 1993), 307–43.

31. The "face of the earth" depicted in the sixteenth-century cosmographical literature, referred to above, might well be male. See Figure 1.

32. The words *mirror* and *miracle* both derive from the Latin *mirrari,* meaning "to wonder at." For these etymologies, see *Merriam-Webster's Collegiate Dictionary,* s.v., "theater," "mirror," "miracle." On the perception of landscape and maps as theaters and maps, see Walter S. Gibson, *"Mirror of the Earth": The World Landscape in Sixteenth-Century Flemish Painting* (Princeton, N.J.: Princeton University Press, 1989).

33. John Speed, *The Theatre of the Empire of Great Britaine* (London: John Sudbury and George Humble, 1611). For a more detailed discussion of the masques and the concept of landscape, see Kenneth R. Olwig, *Landscape, Nature, and the Body Politic* (working title) (Madison: University of Wisconsin Press, forthcoming).

34. William Camden, *Britannia* (London: John Stockdale, 1806 [1607]).

35. The distinction between natural justice and conventional justice can be traced back to Aristotle (the teacher of Alexander the Great), who wrote: "There are two kinds of political [as distinguished from domestic] justice: the natural and the conventional. Natural justice has the same force everywhere and it does not depend upon its being agreed upon or not. Conventional justice is justice whose provisions are originally indifferent, but once these have been established they are important" (Aristotle, *The Nicomachean Ethics* [Cambridge, Mass: Harvard University Press, 1934], 295–98). This principle was also important in Roman imperial law, where a distinction was made between customary law, which varied from place to place according to local historical circumstances, and the Roman law that applied everywhere.

36. Thomas Hobbes, *Leviathan (orig. title Leviathan, or The Matter, Forme, & Power of a Common-wealth ECCLESIASTICALL AND CIVILL)* (Cambridge: Cambridge University Press, 1991 [1651]), 9, 89, 112–13. Michel Foucault has written brilliantly about the penetrating power of this surveillant gaze, but he focuses on a later period and thereby does not take cognizance of landscape scenery's role in the process of early state-building; see Michel Foucault, *Discipline and Punish: The Birth of the Prison* (Harmondsworth, Eng.: Penguin, 1979 [1975]).

37. Hartshorne, "Concept of Geography."

38. Immanuel Kant, "Physische Geographie: Auf Verlangen des Verfassers aus seiner Handschrift herausgegeben und zum Teil bearbeitet von D. Friedrich Theodor Rink," in *Kant's gesammelte Schriften* (Berlin and Leipzig: Walter de Gruyter, 1923 [1802]), 9:156–65; J. A. May, *Kant's Concept of Geography and Its Relation to Recent Geographical Thought,* University of Toronto Department of Geography Research Publications 4 (Toronto: University of Toronto Press, 1970), 101, 257. As Kant wrote: "In regard to the summation of our knowledge we must direct our attention to the sources or origin. Following this we must search for the plan of how it is arranged or for the form, that is, how this knowledge can be organized" (Immanuel Kant, *Unpublished Translation of Introduction to Physische Geographie,* trans. L. Seidler for B. and F. Lukermann, eds., *Kant's Gesammelte Schriften,* 24 vols. [Berlin and Leipzig: Der Königlich Preussischen Akademie der Wissenschaften, 1923 (1802)], 9:1); the translations from Kant are based on Seidler's translation. My wife, Karen Fog Olwig, and I have compared this translation with the original in Kant, "Physische Geographie," and made changes where we thought this would bring the translation closer to the original.

39. Lukermann, "Concept of Location," 56.

40. Kant, *Unpublished Translation,* 9:2–3. It is interesting to note, in light of the following discussion of structuralism, that the founder of modern linguistic structuralism, Ferdinand de Saussure (1857–1913), used the word *system,* not the word *structure,* as also was the case with Kant.

41. Kenneth R. Olwig, "Landscape, Place, and the State of Progress," in *Progress* (working title), ed. Robert David Sack (Baltimore: Johns Hopkins University Press, forthcoming). On the relationship between the infinitude in the projection of space in scenic depictions of landscape and a progressive conception of time, see Yi-Fu Tuan, *Space and Place: The Perspective of Experience* (Minneapolis: University of Minnesota Press, 1977), 122–24.

42. Henrik Steffens, *Indledning til Philosophiske Forelæsninger i København 1803* (Copenhagen: Gyldendal, 1905), 91; my trans.

43. Gyorgy Markus, "Culture: The Making and the Make-up of a Concept (An Essay in Historical Semantics)," *Dialectical Anthropology* 18 (1993): 14–15. The suffix in Land*schaft* can mean *shape* or *create* and therefore is parallel to the meaning of *bilden,* thus strengthening the parallel between the picturing of landscape and *bilden/Bildung.* See Olwig, "Sexual Cosmology."

44. Gombrich, *Art and Illusion,* 19–20.

45. Ibid.

46. Roland Barthes, *Mythologies* (New York: Hill and Wang, 1972 [1957], 129).

47. Michel Foucault, *The Archaeology of Knowledge, and The Discourse on Language* (New York: Harper & Row, 1972), 9–10.

48. W. J. T. Mitchell, "Gombrich and the Rise of Landscape," in *The Consumption of Culture 1600–1800: Image, Object, Text,* ed. John Brewer and Ann Bermingham (London: Routledge, 1995), 104; see also W. J. T. Mitchell, "Imperial Landscape," in *Landscape and Power,* ed. W. J. T. Mitchell (Chicago: University of Chicago Press, 1994), 5–34.

49. Gyorgy Kepes, introduction to *Structure in Art and in Science,* ed. Gyorgy Kepes (London: Studio Vista, 1965), ii.

50. Edgerton, *Renaissance Rediscovery,* 22.

51. Jean Piaget and Bärbel Inhelder, *The Child's Conception of Space,* trans. F. J. Langdon and J. L. Lunzer (New York: W. W. Norton, 1967 [1948]), 244.

52. Ibid., 209–46, 419–46.

53. Jean Piaget, *Structuralism,* trans. Chaninah Maschler (London: Routledge and Kegan Paul, 1971 [1968]), 120–35; quote on 126.

54. Louis Althusser, *For Marx,* trans. Ben Brewster (New York: Vintage Books, 1970 [1965]), 252–55.

55. Piaget, *Structuralism,* 126–27.

56. Yi-Fu Tuan, "Structuralism, Existentialism, and Environmental Perception," *Environment and Behavior* 4 (September 1972): 321.

57. Jean Piaget, *Science Education and the Psychology of the Child,* trans. Derek Coltman (Harmondsworth, Eng.: Penguin, 1977 [1969]).

58. For a geographical approach to the study of landscape and "social formation," a key structural Marxist concept, see Denis Cosgrove, *Social Formation and Symbolic Landscape* (London: Croom Helm, 1984). The geographer David Harvey and the sociologist Anthony Giddens are examples of modern-day social theorists who have been inspired by Piaget's and/or Althusser's structuralism. Giddens has also drawn upon the cartography-inspired picturing techniques used by time geography; see Paul Cloke, David Sadler, and Chris Philo, *Approaching Human Geography: An Introduction to Contemporary Theoretical Debates* (London: Paul Chapman, 1991). It would be interesting to tease out the structural similarities between Giddens's notion of a duality of structure and the duality of Piaget's structuralism (in which the child alternates between structural accommodation and assimilation), but there is not room for this here. The ideas of George Orwell on the role of *doublethink* in totalizing forms of thought would also be interesting to explore in this context.

59. Anthony Giddens, *The Consequences of Modernity* (London: Polity Press, 1990), 140.

60. Foucault, *Archaeology of Knowledge,* 21.

61. Barthes, *Mythologies,* 151.

62. These quotations are from the definition of *place* found in a standard British geographical reference work, R. J. Johnston, David M. Smith, and Derek Gregory, eds., *The Dictionary of Human Geography* (Oxford: Blackwell, 1994), 442.

63. Among the definitions of *landscape, Merriam-Webster's Collegiate Dictionary* includes "political landscape" as an "area of activity," as well as "scene." The meanings "vista" and "prospect" are now listed as being "obsolete" (*Merriam-Webster's Collegiate Dictionary,* s.v. "landscape").

64. Otto Brunner, *Land and Lordship: Structures of Governance in Medieval Austria,* trans. Howard Kaminsky and James Van Horn Melton, 5th ed., Middle Ages Series (Philadelphia: University of Pennsylvania Press, 1992 [1965]), 341.

65. Olwig, "Recovering the Substantive Nature of Landscape."

66. Simon Schama, *The Embarrassment of Riches: An Interpretation of Dutch Culture in the Golden Age* (London: Collins, 1987); Immanuel Wallerstein, *The Modern World-System: Capitalist Agriculture and the Origins of the European World-Economy in the Sixteenth Century* (New York: Academic Press, 1974).

67. Henri Pirenne, *A History of Europe: From the Thirteenth Century to the Renaissance and Reformation* (Garden City, N.Y.: Doubleday Anchor, 1958), 2:221–69.

68. Simon Schama, "Dutch Landscapes: Culture as Foreground," in *Masters of 17th-Century Dutch Landscape Painting,* ed. Peter C. Sutton (London: Herbert Press, 1987), 64–83.

69. For a relevant and more detailed treatment of this conflicting notion of law and representation, see Olwig, "Recovering the Substantive Nature of Landscape."

70. E. H. Gombrich, *The Story of Art,* 12th ed. (London: Phaidon, 1972), 178–79.

71. Svetlana Alpers, *The Art of Describing: Dutch Art in the Seventeenth Century* (Chicago: University of Chicago Press, 1983), 137.

72. Max J. Friedländer, *Landscape, Portrait, Still-Life: Their Origin and Development,* trans. R. F. C. Hull (Oxford: Bruno Cassirer, 1949), 154–55.

73. Alpers, *Art of Describing,* 138.

74. Friedländer, *Landscape,* 88.

75. Terence Turner, "Review of Piaget's Structuralism," *American Anthropologist* 75, no. 2 (1973): 351–73.

76. Ibid., 353.

77. Ibid.

78. This is the idea of place focused upon in Michel de Certeau, *The Practice of Everyday Life* (Berkeley: University of California Press, 1984).

79. Olwig, "Nature — Mapping the 'Ghostly' Traces of a Concept," 63–96.

80. Kenneth R. Olwig, "Childhood, Artistic Creation, and the Educated Sense of Place," *Children's Environments Quarterly* 8, no. 2 (1991): 4–18.

Part II

Segmented Worlds and Selves

INTRODUCTION

Segmented Worlds and Selves

John Paul Jones III

The relationships between "worlds" and "selves" — and their equivalents, places and peoples, spaces and identities — are central in human geography, in all its historical, substantive, theoretical, and methodological diversity.[1] Reflecting broadly on the theoretical issues surrounding these terms brings forth a set of interconnected questions: How have worlds and selves been defined in human geography? How have they been theorized in relation to one another? And, more subtly, how should we conjoin these terms — with an "and," with a dash, with a slash? — such that these relations can even be investigated? In what follows I briefly sketch some responses to these questions as they have been addressed in twentieth-century geography: I discuss different understandings of worlds and selves; I make note of how their relations have been theorized over time; I attempt to account for these changes; and I interpret the essays in this part of the volume in light of these reflections.

The constituent elements and meanings of both terms has varied considerably. In the first part of the twentieth century, "worlds" of inquiry included both physical and built environments. Carl O. Sauer managed to combine these into the cultural landscape,[2] but most geographers were content to define the world as consisting of two separate sets of features. These material and visible features of the world were in turn separated from human thought and practices, thereby establishing a triadic model of land, cultural artifacts, and social life that continues to hold sway to this day. Richard Hartshorne, writing in 1939,[3] widened our understanding of worldly elements to include virtually all patterns of regional differentiation and their connections, even those that were not patently visible on the landscape.[4] The geographer's task was to investigate these patterns and interconnections as they varied over the earth's surface. The school of spatial analysis extended Hartshorne's approach, offering less a new theory of the world than a methodology that helped formalize the study of patterns and the relations among them.[5]

Partly in reaction to the segmentation of the world that is implicit in the Hartshornian/spatial-analysis ontology, humanistic geographers in the 1970s posed yet another world, the lifeworld, which, it was held, would connect place, meaning, and the human body. These ontological elements were argued to be the ground zero of geographic investigation: the segmentations found in previous schools of thought were not foundational but rather the outcome of a mechanistic and technocratic process that delineates the world prior to actually theorizing it.[6] The late 1970s and 1980s saw the arrival of a world of socio-spatial structures, with spatially dependent social relations — first of class, but then of gender and race — forming the bedrock for investigation.[7] And, in the 1990s, under the influence of poststructuralism, attention turned to the examination of socially constructed worlds that are simultaneously material and representational.[8] Often eschewing ontological foundations in favor of epistemological inquiries into how the world becomes known as such, these researchers widened once again the range of objects studied in human geography, extending their analyses beyond built environments into texts of various types, including film, print, and electronic media. Excepting protestations by the confident, who claim to know geography when they see (and read) it, the "world" in twentieth-century geography is shown to be an unsettled concept. It would seem that the "thing-itself" can logically only be glimpsed within a set of categories, and history has shown that geographers set few limits on their plurality.

Conceptualizations of our "selves" have likewise varied over time. Early-twentieth-century groupings usually followed national or other political borders, cultural (e.g., ethnic, linguistic, and "racial") patterns, or homogeneity in the means for securing livelihood. Researchers tended to define their substantive allegiances (e.g., political, cultural, or economic geography) in terms of the groupings they favored. Though less susceptible to overwriting diversity than the aspatial self of location theory, *homo economicus,* all such groupings may ultimately be complicit in a process that marks "a people" in the singular. Part of the rationale behind both behavioral and humanistic geography was based in the effort to recover the individual, whose identity had largely been annulled in previous schools of thought; both schools also stratified cultural or other groups into more precise categorical designations. Behavioral geographers investigated individual-level decision making, while their larger-scale studies were reported according to respondents' memberships in various socio-demographic groupings.[9] Humanistic geographers undertook both individual and culture-group studies, but in contrast to behavioral geographers, they were more attuned to the meanings they or their research subjects held of the world.[10]

Arguably, it was the early feminist geography, with its focus on women's lives, that gave the search for diversity a sharp analytical and empirical edge.[11] Diversity, however, only complicates the category by reference to an other that lies within the categorical boundary (culture, "race," women); as a concept, it does not deconstruct the boundary-making process.[12] For this we need the concept of difference, a poststructuralist term that directs attention to the discursive processes by which categories are formed and by which selves achieve identity through the performance of the category.[13] Poststructuralist feminist and postcolonial theory shows that the "self" *is not one,* not simply through a denial of the singularity of the self ("one") but through a denial of any true essence ("is not"). In poststructuralism, the category is suspect, including the category of the self.[14]

This brief history of worlds and selves has a parallel in the development of methodologies that provide the grounds for studying their relations. Throughout most of the last century, worlds and selves, however defined, were conceived in terms sufficiently separate that geographers could map, as in regional geography, or even calculate, as in spatial analysis, their correlation. By assuming ontologically separate but interacting entities, untold variations among groups, whether based on culture, nation, region, or some other category, could be analyzed with respect to variations in worldly spaces, whether physical or "man-made." A persuasive counter to this assumption was Martin Heidegger's ontology of immersion, "being-in-the-world."[15] As developed by humanistic geographers, the concept of lifeworld sublates the conjunction that separates world and self, thereby undermining the simplistic recursivity of correlative methodologies. The lifeworld conjoins the world to the self, making the world a repository of meaning and the self a meaning-full actor whose intentionality is directed toward and thoroughly interpenetrated by the world.[16] This retheorization enabled humanistic geographers to extend geographic analysis into the interpretative methods characteristic of the humanities, as the lifeworld infuses all products of human invention, from the log cabin and modern skyscraper to the poem and the photograph. Meanwhile, the research approach adopted by the early dialecticians of space and social relations was extended through Henri Lefebvre's triadic model of perceived, conceived, and lived space, which similarly widened the objects of analysis from "real" to represented spaces.[17] And poststructuralists, always critical of foundational definitions, were inclined to put the very terms "world" and "self" under genealogical and deconstructive analysis.[18] How, for example, did the concepts of world and self arise?[19] What exclusionary processes produce the meanings our of worldly constituents, such as nature, community, and nations, as well as our self-based ones, such as culture, "race," gender, and sexuality? And, from a geographic perspective, how does space, "real," represented, and imagined, work in these constructions and stabilizations, and to whose benefit?

This reading of the definitions and methodologies of worlds and selves, though necessarily synoptic, shows that late-twentieth-century geography offers a rich response to the questions posed at the outset of this introduction. We might be seduced into attributing this growing complexity to the natural evolution of the discipline. But have our interpretations and analyses of worlds and selves become more complex as a result of geography's maturity? its engagement with philosophical questions over the past thirty years? its increasing interdisciplinarity? Or should we also look outside the discipline for the answer?

I am inclined to respond yes to this last question, and I am affirmed in that assessment by the essays that follow. As each of the essayists demonstrate, there have been profound changes in the twentieth century's segmentation of worlds and selves, and it is partly these trends that have led to more complex theories. For example, the infusion of the modernist grid in social space — in our neighborhoods and streets, our maps, our technology, and our time-space routines — has increased spatiotemporal juxtapositions to the degree that correlation analyses are no longer tenable.[20] The simultaneous fragmentations and flows set in motion by the globalization of capital and culture have so undermined previously secure definitions of space that to speak with certainty of any such grouping (such as community, region, or nation), one risks being labeled a romantic.[21] The rise of transmigration, telecommunication, and the Internet has complicated subject positions to such an extent that we no longer have faith in well-established categories, such as "citizen." And contemporary politics become fragmented: the proliferation of identity positions (remember when there were only three — race, class, and gender?) seems to know no end.

The relationship between these shifts and theories of worlds and selves goes to the heart of the essays in this part, and no more so than in the fast-paced historical survey offered by Wilbur Zelinsky. After a very useful survey of the rise of identity as a concept, he attempts to make sense of the proliferation of identity positions through an explicit theorization of three social "forces" (Force I: adhesive, which solidified identification; Force II: improvisational, which led to experimentation; and Force III: hierarchical, which I interpret, adapting Habermas's phrasing, as the "colonization of identity"). These forces, in turn, are said to be tied to three landscape types (Landscape I: organic communities; Landscape II: modern nation-state; and Landscape III: postmodern dislocations). Zelinsky finds, somewhat pessimistically, that our contemporary alignments of forces and landscapes find us "caged in a world of contradictions, of unprecedented personal and group anxieties." In response to this postmodern identity crisis, and in an effort to secure the lost moorings of selfhood, Zelinsky looks to, but ultimately rejects, regionalism, voluntary associations, sport, occupation, religion, consumerism, and the nation-state. It is ethnicity, however tenuous and contingent, that might hold the primary ground for identification, but Zelinsky is rightly suspicious of its social and political consequences and possibilities.

Edward Relph locates his essay around Yi-Fu Tuan's geographic question: "What is this world like, and how do we describe it?" For Relph, postmodernism is real: its hyperkinetic unraveling in theoretical, political, and spatial spheres has unleashed a set of mystifying uncertainties, and he is uneasy with other critics' responses to them. Attempts to recenter critical analysis and practice through global or cosmopolitan values only end up reinscribing elements of modernism that he has consistently criticized. Nor can he stand with David Harvey,[22] who explains the postmodern malaise in terms of disruptions to our spatiotemporal understandings caused by the rapidity of change within late capitalism (this in spite of the fact that Relph is, like Harvey, a critic of contemporary economic inequality). Echoing Zelinsky's pessimism, he maintains that the postmodern age has seriously strained our capacity to theorize it, for it "continually outruns theories and descriptions of it." For example, his now-classic analytic lever, "place and placelessness,"[23] was effective in distinguishing between, on the one hand, landscapes of authenticity organically tied to the social contexts and natural environments in which they were developed and, on the other hand, those placeless modern landscapes of the suburb, mall, and shopping strip that lack any context and could just as well be placed anywhere. But postmodernism puts authenticity in quotation marks, jumping over the place and placelessness distinction, and as a consequence, new forms of description are required. In searching for a middle ground characterized by practical wisdom and a balanced avoidance of excess, Relph directs our attention to "critical descriptions" rooted in the empirical world of everyday landscapes, attentive to the deceptions of surface appearances, and grounded in historical analysis.

In two other well-connected papers, Tim Cresswell and Paul Adams take on the central spatial concept of mobility and its relation to identity. Cresswell outlines a social constructivist stance toward identity, one that should be required reading for anyone who dismisses poststructuralist approaches as having no concern with, or grounding in, the "real." For Cresswell, the "real" and the categories by which we describe it go hand in hand, and, in a parallel fashion, so too do space and identity. His empirical site is the invention of the tramp — a wanderer through space who holds no interest in securing employment. The tramp was codified in the popular press and legislation and then regulated through the state apparatus in the nineteenth and early twentieth centuries. The discursive construction of the tramp, in turn, had a productive effect on both U.S. sociology and the eugenics movement. Tramps legitimated sociology by offering a concrete social problem for the emerging discipline, while the eugenicists gained support for their "science" through the tramp's medicalization. Cresswell presents an intriguing case study of modern America's insecurity over dislocation — an insecurity suggestively reflected in the two essays that precede his own.

If Cresswell's account reminds us that spatiality is fundamental to the social construction of identity, Paul Adams's essay, "Peripatetic Imagery and Peripatetic Sense of Place," further elaborates the importance of movement. His historical survey of walking is rooted in the phenomenology of the body and in the sensory experience and perceptions that contrast this form of movement with that of the automobile. Drawing on literary and archival sources, he offers evidence of two sides of a "peripatetic sense of place," one of which, through its density of connections to the world, is akin to spiritual practice (and, we could add, geographic practice: Carl O. Sauer wrote that "Locomotion should be slow, the slower the better").[24] Adams uncovers another side to walking, "dark peripatetic," that suggestively links to Cresswell's constructed tramp: a "mobility, which ties blindness, nakedness, and madness together in a signature of the outcast." Adams updates his survey through readings of contemporary advertisements, where urbanites are shown attempting to recover Thoreau's ambulatory serenity, and he works through the dialectics of suburban design, urban decay, and social anonymity catalogued by Jane Jacobs, as well as efforts by some planners to restore walking through neotraditional urban design.

Finally, Michael Curry takes us inside the academy, asking us to reflect with him on the relationship between the professional academic and the place of the university. The latter has traditionally been conceived of as a house of refuge from the tainted world of markets, bureaucratization, and instrumental knowledge. As a result, the identity of the professor was universalized into spheres of knowledge, codes of ethics, and disciplinary associations, all of which sealed off the professoriate from the particularistic, everyday, "real world." This combination of institutional form, place meaning, and individual identity, Curry notes, is now under assault by the growing professionalization of university administrators, whose job it is to manage the internal affairs of the institution and to provide accountability to its constituents. As the professors' places of work have changed—a development paralleled for doctors, judges, and other professionals—the aura of their work has diminished and their attachment to their colleges and universities has been undermined. In this essay, the segmentation of place reveals its effects at the level of the subject: the new university professor.

What, finally, ties these essays together? I have a sense that, notwithstanding Relph's acknowledgment that postmodernism demands a new approach, many of these essays resonate with the sensibilities of early humanistic geography. That school developed a trenchant critique of modernism's hierarchical, bureaucratic, mechanistic, standardized, and technocratic rationality, which, it was held, infused scholarly thought, social practices, and the built environment. The essays of Adams, Curry, Relph, and Zelinsky appear, in part, to be informed by this line of analysis, suggesting that some of what we now call postmodernism is actually a deepening of modernism's rationality, rather than a wholesale shift to a new paradigm.[25] Another alignment with early humanistic geography can be found in the manner in which some of these essays express a longing for a return: to real identities and places, to walking, and to the ideal university.

Frankly, it is difficult not to be sympathetic to some of these impulses. (Take Curry's critique of the university: as I write this essay I am also being pressed to compile and enter departmental information on several sets of forms; this information will go into a university strategic plan and from there to an external accreditation agency; yet I doubt the evening's work will actually be read.) I also think, however, that like any other era, the contemporary period holds special opportunities for oppositional politics; and I believe that we should look into these cracks in the mortar for our politics, rather than bemoan what has been lost in the past. Consider, for example, the postmodern self's attempts to disentangle from identity. Zelinsky sees dangers in this refusal of the core self. But if categories of identity (Zelinsky analyzes ethnicity, religion, consumerism, region, and more) are products of dominant sociopolitical powers, does it not follow that in the process of disidentifying from them we might also activate some sense of freedom for the individual (a person, though, differently theorized)? Notwithstanding the complications posed to collective politics from such a position, would not disidentification mark one route toward constructing a world less troubled by racial, ethnic, religious, and regional divisions?[26]

Consider also the contemporary dynamics of places. Though no critical geographer would affirm gated communities, rapacious gentrification, or the purely ornamental affectivity of box-and-hat architecture, a potentially progressive landscape trend might be found in the "postmodern" mixing of spaces brought about by the translocation of cultures and their close juxtaposition in social space. I am thinking here of the alternative spaces that have recently proliferated in the most unlikely middle-American cities. The "ethnic" shops and neighborhoods in my adopted city, Lexington, Kentucky, have in a few short years helped to cut through an oppressive, unspoken whiteness that long dominated the city's landscape. The key to these landscape changes is movement. As Cresswell shows for the tramp, movement tends more to disrupt than reinforce existing power relations. For it is through movement that centers — of both worlds and the selves — are destabilized, unraveling as they are displaced from one context to another. Movement offers some hope that the textures of world and self can be enhanced in the postmodern era. This would be a texture born not of a return to authenticity and centering, such as was aimed for in the early models of humanistic inquiry, but one emerging from the juxtaposition, recombination, and destabilization of centers, which puts the very notion of a center in question, thereby propounding difference and increasing texture. Put most generally: for every segmentation there is always a disobedient flow.

Notes

1. The title of this part recognizes the important contribution of Yi-Fu Tuan, *Segmented Worlds and Self: Group Life and Individual Consciousness* (Minneapolis: University of Minnesota Press, 1982).

2. Carl O. Sauer, "The Morphology of Landscape," *University of California Publications in Geography* 2 (1925): 19–53.

3. Richard Hartshorne, *The Nature of Geography* (Lancaster, Penn.: Association of American Geographers, 1939).

4. For an account of Hartshorne's rejection of Sauer's focus on the visible landscape, see John Paul Jones III, "Making Geography Objectively: Ocularity, Representation, and *The Nature of Geography*," in *Objectivity and Its Other*, ed. Wolfgang Natter, Theodore Schatzki, and John Paul Jones III (New York: Guilford, 1995), 67–92.

5. A good account of the methodology of spatial analysis is found in Brian J. L. Berry, "Approaches to Regional Analysis: A Synthesis," *Annals of the Association of American Geographers* 54 (1964): 2–11.

6. Influential in this regard are Anne Buttimer, "Grasping the Dynamism of the Life-world," *Annals of the Association of American Geographers* 66 (1976): 277–92; Edward Relph, "An Inquiry into the Relations between Phenomenology and Geography," *Canadian Geographer* 14 (1970): 193–201; Yi-Fu Tuan, "Geography, Phenomenology, and the Study of Human Nature," *Canadian Geographer* 15 (1971): 181–92; David Seamon, *Geography of the Lifeworld: Movement, Rest, Encounter* (London: Croom Helm, 1976).

7. The definitive early statement is found in Edward Soja, "The Socio-spatial Dialectic," *Annals of the Association of American Geographers* 70 (1980): 207–25.

8. See Derek Gregory, *Geographical Imaginations* (Oxford: Blackwell, 1994).

9. A representative sample can be found in Kevin R. Cox and Reginald G. Golledge, eds., *Behavioral Problems in Geography: A Symposium,* Northwestern University Studies in Geography, no. 17 (Evanston, Ill.: Department of Geography, Northwestern University, 1969).

10. Seamon, *Geography of the Lifeworld.* We should also acknowledge that Anne Buttimer encouraged self-reflexivity before the concept was formally introduced in geography; see Anne Buttimer, *Values in Geography,* Resource Paper 24 (Washington, D.C.: Association of American Geographers, 1974).

11. Probably the most influential early essay is Jan Monk and Susan Hanson, "On Not Excluding Half of the Human in Human Geography," *Professional Geographer* 34 (1982): 11–23; readers might find interesting the essays in John Paul Jones III, Heidi J. Nast, and Susan M. Roberts, eds., *Thresholds in Feminist Geography* (Lanham, Md.: Rowman and Littlefield, 1997).

12. In developing the distinction between diversity and, below, difference, I follow Homi Bhabha, *The Location of Culture* (London: Routledge, 1994).

13. Judith Butler, *Gender Trouble* (London: Routledge, 1993).

14. See Wolfgang Natter and John Paul Jones III, "Identity, Space, and Other Uncertainties," in *Space and Social Theory,* ed. Georges Benko and Ulf Strohmayer (Oxford: Blackwell, 1997), 141–61.

15. Martin Heidegger, *Being and Time,* trans. J. MacQuarrie and E. Robinson (New York: Harper and Row, 1962).

16. Buttimer, "Grasping the Dynamism"; Seamon, *Geography of the Lifeworld.*

17. Henri Lefebvre, *The Production of Space,* trans. David Nicholson-Smith (Oxford: Blackwell, 1991); interpretations can be found in Edward Soja, *Thirdspace* (Oxford: Blackwell, 1996); Gregory, *Geographical Imaginations;* and David Harvey, *The Condition of Postmodernity* (Oxford: Blackwell, 1989).

18. Natter and Jones, "Space, Identity, and Other Uncertainties"; Deborah Dixon and John Paul Jones III, "My Dinner with Derrida, or Spatial Analysis and Poststructuralism Do Lunch," *Environment and Planning, A* 30 (1998): 247–60.

19. Zelinsky offers one such analysis for "identity" in the chapter that follows.

20. Gregory, *Geographical Imaginations;* Dixon and Jones, "My Dinner with Derrida."

21. Arjun Appadurai, *Modernity at Large* (Minneapolis: University of Minnesota Press, 1996).

22. Harvey, *Condition of Postmodernity.*

23. Edward Relph, *Place and Placelessness* (London: Pion, 1976).

24. Carl O. Sauer, "The Education of a Geographer," *Annals of the Association of American Geographers* 46 (1956): 287–99.

25. On this point, see Edward Soja, "Postmodern Geographies and the Critique of Historicism," in *Postmodern Contentions,* ed. John Paul Jones III, Wolfgang Natter, and Theodore Schatzki (New York: Guildford, 1993), 113–36.

26. This argument is developed further in Natter and Jones, "Identity, Space, and Other Uncertainties."

THE WORLD AND ITS IDENTITY CRISIS

Wilbur Zelinsky

> [W]e should be as suspicious of "identity" as we have learned to be of "culture," "tradition" and "ethnic group." ... [T]he concept of "identity" is peculiar to the modern Western ... World.
>
> — RICHARD HANDLER,
> "Is 'Identity' a Useful Cross-Cultural Concept?"

And, verily, after looking into the matter, we do indeed discover that *identity* is one of a surprisingly large set of concepts we have mistakenly come to take for granted as timeless components of our familiar world. In actuality, it happens to be a relatively recent invention.

The historical fact is that *identity* is modern in origin as both word and idea. You will not find it in the Bible, and it did not form part of Shakespeare's capacious lexicon. The *OED*'s earliest citation of the term in anything resembling its current sense is dated 1638, and its definition is as good as any: "The sameness of a person or thing at all times or in all circumstances; the condition or fact that a person or thing is itself and not something else; individuality; personality."

The birth or maturation of a word, that is, concept, such as *identity* is not a casual occurrence; it usually signifies a novel development in social history. My impression is that, during the first three centuries of its existence, *identity* remained a rather inconspicuous item in both our vernacular and scholarly vocabularies. Symptomatic of its initial obscurity is the absence of any entry on the topic in the truly encyclopedic *Encyclopedia of the Social Sciences*.[1] In addition to other indicators, a spectacular upsurge in usage that began roughly fifty years ago offers quantitative evidence that a large, rapidly increasing portion of the world's population — and many of the places they inhabit — have begun agonizing quite recently over just who or what they are. Table 1 on the following page reveals the recency of this unprecedented pandemic *identity crisis*.[2] (*Identity angst* is a more meaningful term, but *identity crisis* seems to have caught the public fancy.)

We have in this tabulation the per-annum incidence of entries appearing under the heading "Identity" (but not "Identities") in the compendious *Social Sciences Citation Index* during the period 1956–98. It is quite likely that a count of titles of books and articles in the humanities would generate similar

129

Table 1
Entries under the heading "Identity"
in *Social Sciences Citation Index,* 1956–98

	No.	Per-Annum
1956–65	688	69
1966–70	1,131	226
1971–75	1,360	272
1976–80	2,739	548
1981–85	3,270	654
1986–90	3,813	763
1991	780	780
1992	1,202	1,202
1993	1,355	1,355
1994	1,479	1,479
1995	1,653	1,653
1996	2,219	2,219
1997	2,232	2,232
1998	2,413	2,413

results, and doing a content analysis of items published in newspapers and other popular periodicals during the years in question might also document an explosion in the popularity of *identity* comparable to that in the social science journals.

Although Raymond Williams bypassed the opportunity to discuss *identity* in his admirable *Keywords,*[3] we are most fortunate in having Philip Gleason's searching inquiry into the semantic history of the term, one too subtle and detailed to recapitulate here.[4] It is not by chance that its recent meteoric career began in the United States, the country in the vanguard of contemporary social evolution. It was here that the brachiation of connotations rapidly luxuriated, then presumably diffused to other First World countries. But, interestingly, it was immigrant psychologist Erik Erikson who coined the term *identity crisis* and did more than anyone else to popularize identity.[5]

Identity in Historical Context

But, whatever the paternity of the term might be, the astonishing efflorescence of *identity* and related usages in the scholarly literature and in vernacular parlance, this seemingly abrupt development over the past half-century, calls for the most thoughtful sort of interrogation. In order to make some sense of the phenomenon, I offer some speculative, but plausible, hypotheses, while insisting on situating our current dilemma within the broadest possible sweep of human history and prehistory — a metanarrative, if you please. Let me postulate the existence within human beings and societies of three distinct drives, tendencies, impulses, or forces — I am unable to find any single noun that fully expresses the idea in question. The oldest, indeed one we share with certain animal species, I call Force I, the tendency to cling together, to huddle with our ilk. Its expression varies greatly over time and from community to community, but this is the universal adhesive, however it may be eroded today, binding together kinship, friendship, and neighborhood groups and intimate bands of co-workers, a concept roughly conveyed by the term *Gemeinschaft.*

The second item, Force II, is unique to our species and indeed is one of the attributes that make human beings human, but whose strength varies widely among individuals: the tendency to experiment, improvise, innovate, dissent, fantasize, to test the limits, to probe whatever possibilities are kindled by imagination and personal appetites. Force II has been seriously cribbed and confined by social and environmental circumstances throughout nearly all of human existence. But it is its occasional expression that brings about those technological advances and personal, social, and cultural speciations that have made the human chronicle so dynamic and unpredictable.

If the first two of our forces are presumably somehow resident in our individual genomes, Force III is quite different in origin and nature, and I must apply to it that controversial term "superorganic." It comes into being only after a society has grown past a certain threshold in terms of complexity of organization and of technological prowess; and it operates over and beyond individual wills and only by means of corporate entities. A handful of nouns and adjectives may help characterize the concept, namely: hierarchy, dominance, stratification, conformity, bureaucracy, regimentation, authoritarian, centripetal, militarization.

In a final burst of foolrushery, I propose dividing our metanarrative into three qualitatively distinct epochs, three *longues durées,* to use Fernand Braudel's apt expression. For each of these periods I also suggest the designations Landscapes I, II, and III, following the seminal explorations of the American scene by the late J. B. Jackson.[6] Although in Jacksonian parlance "landscape" refers only to the visible humanized tracts of the earth's surface, I use the term metaphorically so as to include the entire social fabric as well as physically tangible objects.

Landscape I is the most protracted of the *longues durées* by some orders of magnitude. During this lengthy prelude to the arrival of agriculture and its momentous consequences, there was no opportunity for Force III to manifest itself, while Force II was at low ebb, rarely flickering into some weak semblance of life. Over the millennia in question, *Homo sapiens* subsisted at the hunting-gathering-scavenging stage. Society was cellular, essentially egalitarian, and gender, age, lineage, physical condition, and perhaps special skills may have been the only important attributes distinguishing individuals.

Our current concept of identity would have been utterly meaningless to such folks. Imagine a time machine whisking us back to some typical community twenty-five thousand years ago so that we were able to converse with the brightest person in the band. Would it be possible for him or her to grasp the meaning of identity—or of alimony, vacation, boredom, alienation, underdevelopment, graft, or isotopes? I seriously doubt it. And, of course, some of their most central, "primitive" concepts would be utterly incomprehensible to us.

After the arrival of plant and animal domestication in several regions of the Old and New Worlds and the growth of dense sedentary populations, larger, more complex societies gradually arose. There begins a slow, but irreversible, evolution of centralized, stratified, hierarchical societies. Landscape II had materialized. This is also the time when "uneven development" first manifests itself, as certain favored regions advance into Landscape II, leaving the peripheral zones of humankind languishing in a relatively timeless Landscape I. It is the genesis of a zonation that has intensified and become more complex over the succeeding millennia. Within the "advanced" areas, a world had come into being where identity was implicit, so deeply a component of the social fabric it needed no comment or naming. Hereditary class, caste, and occupation were universal, along with subservience of female to male. Establishing one's locus within the human realm was merely a matter of citing place of residence, gender, social station, kinship ties, and mode of livelihood.

With the ushering in of the modern age some five hundred years ago, we see a radical energizing and intensification of Landscape II. Space is not available for even the sketchiest account of the many facets and strands of the process, but the supreme achievement, the ultimate chapter in the biography of Landscape II, was the fabrication of the nation-state, a process begun in earnest some two hundred years ago. What sets this novel political institution apart from its predecessors is the appearance, for the first and probably last time in history, of strong emotional identification with the state on the part of the citizenry. A sense of common peoplehood, of a shared history and destiny, had been engendered, however artificial it might be; and it replaces the forcible exploitation of a subjugated population that regarded their overlords with resignation or dread if not outright loathing.

Despite the gradual rousing of Force II during the first centuries of the modern age, Force III and Landscape II moved ahead even more vigorously. With the maturation of capitalism and state socialism, an imperialist world-order, the nation-state system, and nationalism in Europe and its outliers, and the belated, if imperfect, export of the package to the rest of the world, Landscape II reached its climax during the early twentieth century. Its supremacy seemed beyond challenge. During this heyday, any potential question as to identity was a nonquestion (and keep in mind that the term *identity* was still a minor item in the lexicon). One was automatically, primarily, and proudly a Frenchman, German, American, Japanese, Italian, Swede, or whatever.

So successful was the implementation of the nation-state program that, at its apogee, many of its adherents would willingly, even joyously, volunteer to sacrifice life, limb, and property in encounters with hostile powers. Furthermore, there was acceptance, as a set of necessary evils for the smooth operation of the complex national apparatus, of passports and various identity cards (social security, driver's license, insurance, voting registration, etc.), along with fingerprint files and all manner of regulations.[7]

Whatever rigidities the modern nation-state may have invented and imposed upon its citizens, the issue of choice of individual life-projects and of personal identity had begun to emerge:

> In modernity, identity becomes more mobile, multiple, personal, self-reflective and subject to change and revision. Yet identity in modernity is also social and Other-related.... [T]he forms of identity ... are also relatively substantial and fixed; identity still comes from a circumscribed set of roles and norms: one is a mother, a son, a Texan, a Scot, a professor, a socialist, a Catholic, a lesbian — or rather a combination of these social roles and possibilities. Identities are thus still relatively circumscribed, fixed and limited, though the boundaries of possible identities, of new identities, are continually expanding.[8]

Despite the apparent triumph of Landscape II in the early twentieth century, rapid, profound change was just around the corner: the arrival of our third *longue durée,* whose duration or ending is beyond our powers of prediction or imagining. The full unleashing of Force II, and thus the genesis of Landscape III, depended upon an interlocking series of technological and social developments. The most palpable of proximate factors, it seems, were major innovations in communications and transportation.

The invention of writing several millennia ago initially and exclusively served the interests of rulers and merchants; and, as a skill monopolized by a small minority, including the clerisy, literacy continued to do so for many centuries. As a device for standardizing and stabilizing language, or at least retarding changes therein, writing also tended to strengthen the corporate structure of society.

However, eternally latent in the written word have been subversive opportunities for challenging or circumventing authority. This potentiality became obvious with the advent of printing. Once again, a new technology was recruited immediately to bolster the power of state, church, and market. But, just as promptly, agents of dissent learned how potent a weapon the printing press could be in countering conformity and the establishment. The truly pivotal event was the realization of universal literacy, a process essentially consummated in the First World by the early twentieth century. What ensued was a reshaping of the minds and imagination of individuals and of humanity in general. Now it became feasible for Everyman to don mental seven-league boots, so to speak, to vault backward and forward through time, to visit real or imagined places far removed from one's humdrum surroundings, and perhaps to enter vicariously into other identities. Progress toward Landscape III was also greatly facilitated by the advent of automotive and air transport and of electronic media, beginning with the telegraph, cable, and telephone, then the brave new world of television, tape cassettes, e-mail, the Internet, web sites, and their inevitable even glitzier successors, not to mention photography and movies.

As causative as the obvious technological developments in the transition from Landscape II to its successor have been related alterations in social, demographic, economic, and psychological conditions. In terms of ultimate psychological impact, perhaps no single event was to have a larger role in preparing the ground for Landscape III than World War I. Until July 1914, Landscape II, based as it was on the nation-state system, had been promising utopia and seemed to have perfection almost within its grasp. But, then, the horrific, senseless, massive slaughter of the following four years inculcated a quite different lesson as the nation-state and its world began to look distinctly dystopian. Although the system remained intact and Landscape II lurched on-ward for a few more decades, disenchantment and a certain numbness had set in, most noticeably in the arts and letters among the intelligentsia in gen-eral. An even more cataclysmic World War II finally set Landscape II on a decisively downward course.[9] Be reminded that it was during the presumably placid 1950s, the decade when it is likely that Force II had finally caught up with Force III, that *identity* began its meteoric rise from relative obscurity.

Among the varied social and demographic developments endangering the well-being of Landscape II perhaps none is more directly threatening than the sheer vigor of population redistribution within, but, more menacingly, among, our various sovereign states. Setting aside the less-than-voluntary movements of refugees, asylum-seekers, and the products of other accidents of history, which show no signs of abating, we have witnessed in recent times an extraor-dinary increase in the voluntary mobility of individuals and families in terms of frequency and distances as well as volume. One result has been a substantial influx of unfamiliar ethnic and racial groups (and adherents of alien faiths) into not just the settler countries with their tradition of liberal hospitality for famil-iar types of immigrants but also into a good many European lands previously characterized only as exporters of their surplus inhabitants. Even xenophobic Japan has begun to relax the barriers against non-Japanese sojourners, however reluctant the process. And compounding the situation has been the appearance of a nontrivial number of those footloose persons called transmigrants. In any case, this novel population mix in First World states, those with the most ad-vanced claims to a mature Landscape II, has raised doubts about the wholeness and purity of the national community and has generated troubling questions concerning national identity.

Identity in Cultural Context

Symptomatic of a deep, metastasizing malaise among the inmates of Land-scape II are various developments in the psychic realm. Most revealingly, we have those individual and collective attempts at escape. An especially compelling example is that of science fiction. In its initial nineteenth-century incarnation, perhaps best exemplified by the works of Jules Verne, it may have been an affirmation of the wonders of science and technology. But, in recent decades, as the genre has grown in popularity and sophistication, it has generally taken on a more somber tone. Consciously or otherwise, the authors and their readers and viewers, as science fiction has migrated into film, comic books, and television, as they concoct alternative worlds, histories, and life-forms, are expressing a decided discontent with the felicities of Landscape II.

In parallel fashion, we have in the imagining of time travel another mode of exit from a less-than-optimal here and now. Interestingly enough, the earliest fictional embodiment of the notion of which I am aware, *A Connecticut Yankee in King Arthur's Court* (in 1879, some eighteen years ahead of H. G. Wells's *Time Machine*), was the doing of Mark Twain, who matured into one of the most caustic of all commentators on his contemporary America. Then, more recently, we have seen the boom in historic preservation, the pervasive cultivation of heritage, genealogy, historical museums, and other manifestations of nostalgia and antiquarianism, including the ancient music and period instrument craze in classical music circles and perhaps the many backward-glancing gestures in postmodern architecture.[10] One might also argue that one of the factors contributing to the recent surge of environmental activism is a traditionalist yearning to turn back the calendar to a mythical past when humankind and ecosystem coexisted in salubrious balance.[11] Whether wittingly or not, those who indulge in such activities are voting against the present while seeking emotional refuge and a more meaningful personal identity in other (largely imaginary) eras.

By the 1960s, various cultural, social, and psychological tendencies that had been germinating and festering below the surface of public awareness erupted into view rather abruptly. We have entered what, by general consensus — and for lack of a better term — we must call the postmodern era, as Landscape III challenges the hegemony of Landscape II. Although we are still much too close to the event, this seemingly radical transformation of human affairs, to see or to judge it with the cool rationality of some ideal twenty-second-century historian, some interim observations seem feasible. The new mode of perceiving, feeling, thinking, creating, and behaving may be most readily noted in architecture, literature, literary criticism, and much of popular culture, but postmodern sensibilities and anxieties have begun to reach into all departments of present-day existence, most visibly in the United States but in other lands as well. Still, if there is any single pervasive theme articulated or implicit in the relevant discourse, it is the dilemma of identity.[12]

At this point I can do no better than quote some characterizations of this dilemma more acute and eloquent that anything I am capable of:

identity disturbance in general terms [is] part of a *meaning vacuum* which results from defective symbolic responses of one kind or another. We do not usually receive the kinds of responses from our fellow that will permit us to feel ourselves deeply (in warm relationships or strenuous tests) as a unity or whole (continuously as the same kind of person), of inherent worth (creatively fulfilling inner potential), and living "for" something (a cause, value, or ideology in which one deeply believes).[13]

Or, as Zygmunt Bauman would have it:

Postmodernity is the point at which modern untying (dis-embedding, dis-encumbering) of tied (embedded, situated) identities reaches its completion: *it is now all too easy to choose identity, but no longer possible to hold it.* At the moment of its ultimate triumph, the liberation succeeds in annihilating its object. . . . Freedom . . . has given the postmodern seekers of identity all the powers of a Sisyphus.[14]

For a concrete example of the growing identity quandary, we have in Fred Davis's historical account titled *Fashion, Culture, and Identity* (1992) a richly informative illustration of how one important department of material culture has evolved over time in form and meaning in tandem with the permutations of personal identity. During the earlier phases of Landscape II, fashion, as we have come to know it in recent times, had not yet been born. With barely perceptible shifts from generation to generation, one's dress denoted occupation, gender, localized culture, and perhaps season. Then, in a development that was a harbinger of the gestating modern age, "fashion in the modern sense began in late medieval Europe, probably in Burgundy [logically enough in historical-geographic terms] in the late 13th, early 14th Century."[15] If members of the upper class throughout Europe and, later, its overseas outposts zealously adhered to the slow swings and cycles of style, "The common people were for the most part excluded from fashion's orbit until the nineteenth century."[16]

Then, in recent decades, as the "other-directed" individual of the high noon of modernism yielded to the "inner-directed" type, to adopt David Riesman's valuable insights,[17] and the unleashing of Force II, "the classic 'long wave' fashion cycle, which formerly would in time dragoon all into the same stylistic camp, fell victim somehow, most certainly by the late 1960's, to the identity-defining reactivity elicited by late capitalist consumer culture."[18]

The result has been our anarchic, carnivalesque situation today in which individuals from childhood onward enjoy virtually unlimited options as to dress and personal adornment. Thus one can perform a wide repertory of identities, flitting from one costume to another following whim or circumstance. Paradoxically, the persons who strive to create a unique persona by means of personal appearance do so usually by assembling a mix of mass-produced commodities. In any case, we have reached the point where it is now often literally impossible to distinguish pauper from millionaire by their garments or to use her garb in guessing a stranger's ethnic background, class, or mode of employment. But the most convincing evidence of the blurring of the semantic value of garments and accessories may be the difficulty of ascertaining the genders of many young adults nowadays merely by looking at apparel, hair style, jewelry, or even tattoos.

We find ourselves caged in a curious world of contradictions, of unprecedented personal and group anxieties. The freedom to comparison-shop among lifestyles, to rotate among multiple identities, this culmination of millennia of human struggle and progress, such power and flexibility, all this has failed to generate the bliss one might have anticipated or hoped for. Instead an increasingly large segment of First World populations, and incipiently others as well, has begun to wonder who or what they are, or should be.[19]

But, of course, the process of realizing, acquiring, fabricating, or shedding one's personal identity is hardly a straightforward, unidirectional phenomenon. A simple, relentlessly evolutionary model, such as the one postulated here, does not do justice to the ambiguities or crosscurrents of the situation, perplexities set forth provocatively and with such characteristic eloquence by Yi-Fu Tuan elsewhere in this volume.

Entry into Landscape III has been a mixed blessing for inhabitants of the First World, something actively resisted or feared by many, and the new dispensation has certainly brought us no end of social and psychological miseries. It is not surprising, then, that few of us are wholly immune to pangs of nostalgia, to daydreaming about the delights of returning to Landscape I. In doing so, we tend to overlook all the many drawbacks, the constraints, the multiple physical perils of that primordial existence. Such unpleasantries may have been bearable in the premodern past when no alternatives were at hand. (In parallel fashion, in many autobiographical accounts by subsequently upwardly mobile individuals we learn that they failed to perceive at the time how wretched their poverty-stricken childhoods must have been in objective terms; they were oblivious while doing all those kid things. Ontogeny recapitulating social phylogeny?)

But today, thanks to the pervasiveness of advanced communications and heightened mobility, those who dwell in the so-called Third and Fourth Worlds are keenly appreciative of the joys of joining an affluent advanced society. One of the major blessings of such a transition, whether in situ or via migration, is the escape from an indelibly ascribed identity, a condition that is no longer tolerable. Thus, for the escapees, the new freedom and flexibility, the option of rotating among identities, are positively exhilarating. Eventually, however, they, or their offspring, may realize that they have traded the frying pan for the fire. The quest for genuine bliss or certitude is Sisyphean.

In any event, choice has bred confusion, neuroses, and anomie rather than certitude.[20] But, obviously, not everyone is a full-time victim of this latter-day pandemic. Many millions are too preoccupied with the business of staying alive, of being fed, clothed, housed, and medicated, to fret about anything beyond the daily grind. And, then, there is that blithe, talented fraction of humankind that revels in its late modern or postmodern opportunities as they enjoy personal fulfillment in cultivating creative arts, crafts, science, advanced technologies, or social activism in the company of their planetwide confreres, or simply luxuriate in the euphoria of personal anarchy. But few such folks are wholly immune to the general angst when they look up from their work or frolic.

An additional source of nervousness, one seemingly quite opposite to the unbridled expression of Force II, is the ongoing globalization of all realms of human affairs, including material and nonmaterial culture as well as the economy.[21] Subconsciously or otherwise, we have begun to worry whether we are all being ground down into universal sameness and anonymity. Hence the urge to be different, to find one's authentic self. This concern is observed readily enough in all those many cities, towns, and other localities that have reacted to the perils of placelessness and labor to sustain or fabricate some semblance of distinctiveness.

Refuges from Identity Crisis

What to do? There are two general strategies — the individual and the collective — but they frequently operate in tandem. Beginning at the personal level, the most immediate question in constructing one's identity for all but the beneficiaries of inherited wealth is choice of occupation or means of livelihood. Gone are the days when one was simply born into (or married into) a particular line of work. Perhaps as decisive a moment as any in human history was the one when adults began to ask youngsters, "What do you plan to be when you grow up?" (Alas, we shall never be able to pinpoint date or place.) Whatever the juvenile response, during their working years, more and more individuals switch employers, types of job, or entire career paths, and are doing so with ever greater frequency. Such occupational churning has been eroding the ideal rigidities of Landscape II and also magnifying the dilemma of personal identity. We must conclude that, except for that lucky minority with a lifelong passion for a given vocation, profession, or craft, describing one's employment does not pin down one's identity.

In the past, admittedly, successful business firms offered a seemingly solid, durable core of reality for their employees, their dependents, and frequently entire cities. But nowadays, in our advanced (and final?) stage of capitalism, such intimate bonds have been badly frayed or severed. Footloose and driven by the bottom line, more and more companies have abandoned their natal sites and long-term workforce. In the process, many towns have lost much of whatever uniqueness they claimed previously. (Think of Akron and rubber, Pittsburgh or Bethlehem and steel, Manchester and textiles, Belfast and shipbuilding, Lynn and shoes.) And the same must be said of the corporation in terms of geographic specificity. What places, if any, spring to mind when you hear the names IBM, Exxon, Pepsi-Cola, Xerox, Shell, Nike, Burger King, Time Warner, or AT&T? And the firms themselves are not inoculated against identity angst, so that many go to great lengths to invent some sort of instantly recognizable image via logo and cunningly crafted print and TV ads.

Another popular option involves territorial mobility. The person engaged in an identity quest may realize a certain measure of satisfaction by migrating to a place whose physical and/or social qualities are consonant with his or her inner proclivities.[22] Created thereby are "voluntary regions" or specialized cities or smaller tracts blessed with unquestionable individuality. Such places may have some degree of permanence or may only be transient gatherings. By partaking in this geographic specialness he or she has helped form, the migrant has nestled within a compatible nest where, wittingly or not, one can nurture whatever special appetites and qualities may have only been latent previously. Of all the stratagems to be reviewed here, this may be the only one that, partially or temporarily, assuages the craving for an authentic identity. But not everyone has the knowledge or means to gravitate to such exceptional sites, and even those who do cannot totally evade the perplexities, the identity challenges, of the wider world beyond their enclave.

Much more widespread is a ploy generated by our consumerist, postindustrial economy with its relentless pressures to seek personal fulfillment by buying, and presumably enjoying, more and more commodities and experiences. Thus many of us classify ourselves and others by the autos we drive, the style and price of the houses we inhabit, the beverages we drink, the things we smoke, the entertainments we indulge ourselves in, the designer clothes we wear, or the vacation spots we frequent. But all such items, houses partially excepted, are essentially ephemeral and faddish and thus subject to swift obsolescence. The shifting sands of our purchases do not make for solid foundations of personal identity. There is, however, one quite costly acquisition that can mark us for life: a college education. During the four years or more of residence, the young person certainly partakes of a quite specific collective identity, something a persistent alumni organization will never permit the grad to ignore. But for even the most devoted alumnus, this bygone experience does not supply all the ingredients for postcollege identity-formation.

Still another way to create personal identity that has flourished in recent years is membership in one or more of those countless voluntary associations catering to every imaginable form of human interest and curiosity. Such quasi-communities can now congregate in cyberspace with gay abandon in addition to the traditional conventions, newsletters, and other publications. The proliferation of such flocks of far-flung individuals with shared appetites and impulses is an intriguing paradox. Here we have as full an expression of Force II as one could desire, as the atomized person casts about to realize a unique destiny within Landscape III while, at the same time, he or she seeks to satisfy a primordial craving that harks back to Landscape I. But such pseudo-identities fall short of meeting the need even, or especially, when a person affiliates with several of the organizations in question. Total immersion of self into any such groups is difficult to realize.

If solo efforts to forge a meaningful personal identity in an increasingly unstable world are proving fruitless, the questing individual might logically turn to grander entities to learn who he or she really is, or should be. As we have seen, two of the more obvious options, the large business corporation and the special-interest voluntary association, are less-than-ideal solutions to the dilemma. We are still left with that ultimate mass institution of the recent past, the nation-state. Until quite lately, for almost the entire citizenry, this was the absolute, rock-solid core of group and individual identity. But that was then. Today, as Landscape III encompasses more and more of our social, cultural, and economic terrain, the legitimacy of the nation-state, its monopolistic title to loyalty and shared identity, has been mortally compromised.

Perhaps no one has diagnosed the plight of the nation-state and the ongoing transition to some sort of postnational world more insightfully and disturbingly than Jean-Marie Guéhenno.[23] Although we twentieth-century creatures find it mind-boggling to try imagining a world bereft of the nation-state, he rightfully characterizes it and its two-century career as no more than a transient episode within the vaster flow of human history, while documenting all of its incurable weaknesses at the end of the millennium. In any event, the nation-state can be a leaky vessel on which to embark on an identity quest at this late date. With such rare exceptions as serenely self-assured Japan, Korea, Iceland, and (the Republic of) Ireland, the present-day nation-state is agonizing through its own identity crisis. Thus, for example, Canadians have been squabbling about Canadianness ever since their country was cobbled together in 1867; Israelis are at odds as to whether they dwell in a secular state or theocracy; and Mexicans are still not sure how to merge their Hispanic and indigenous heritages.

We have already noted how the debacle of World War I began the demystification of the nation-state, how doubts were sown concerning its goodness and inevitability. But more directly damaging is the threat posed by a chronic social and economic crisis that had become impossible to ignore as of 1973 and has no end in sight. And there has been a remarkable sea-change in the popular disposition toward the state and its governmental apparatus. I am old enough to recall the period when national leaders were accorded considerable deference by the masses. Today, in contrast, I have trouble citing a single example (perhaps the Czech Republic's Havel or South Africa's Mandela?) where admiration or adulation describes the general attitude of the ruled toward their rulers. Instead, almost universally, we find the rank and file envisioning those at the top of the political heap as incompetents or scoundrels, as self-serving, meretricious, or worse, as objects of suspicion, derision, or contempt.

A good many observers have pointed out other serious challenges to the integrity of the nation-state.[24] Most often cited are the multinational corporations with their global reach and mighty accumulations of wealth and power. Then there are the many NGOs, including grassroots environmental and social-issues organizations, whose missions and activities may run counter to the interests of sovereign states, and various international treaties and conventions that circumscribe their operations.

Nevertheless, reports of the imminent demise of the nation-state are greatly exaggerated. However shaky its emotional hold may have become, the state still monopolizes police and military power, along with the judicial system, and remains the decisive agent in many phases of economic and social life; and recent technological advances in surveillance and control have meant an even greater potential for manipulating the behavior of its citizens. Not even the mightiest of multinational firms or the most ambitious of international agencies have the capacity, or desire, to manage all of humankind's affairs. Thus, despite its current deficiencies, we dare not ignore the huge facticity of the nation-state, that looming presence that is still so much with us. In lieu of any obvious substitute, it still serves as a *nominal* label for the great majority of the world's population, but with ever diminishing emotional salience, and may do so for some time to come. Consequently, more and more human beings today find themselves groping for alternative sustenance, some safe anchorage of identity.

A venerable choice is offered by the church, despite the fact that it was so often co-opted by the state. A striking development in recent times has been a virtually worldwide resurgence of fundamentalism (another form of time travel?) among great numbers of worshipers. We are also witnessing the spawning of many new denominations and cults, groups ranging along the entire spectrum from the most traditional all the way to the most esoteric and outlandish. Such rekindled religiosity might be characterized as a side-effect of globalization, as a response to the shortcomings of the modernization project.[25] But, however interesting such stirrings may be, the truth remains that the truly devout, who may attain the personal-cum-group identity they crave, account for only a small fraction of humankind. Secularism continues to claim more and more nonbelievers. Furthermore, most relatively observant, churchgoing (but not-yet-born-again) parishioners are unlikely to think of themselves primarily in religious terms.

Another expedient revolves around region or locality. The recent efflorescence of regional sentiment in the United States and some European countries, often in the absence of a political agenda, has yet to be studied definitively, but one can speculate about a yearning for rootedness in place, for a shred of geographic identity, as one causative factor. In any case, many cities have indulged in some interesting, if rather desperate, ploys to proclaim their, and thus their inhabitants', particularity. Some localities can capitalize on the fame of their illustrious dead. Such examples as Bayreuth, Weimar, Stratford, Salzburg, Arles, Lourdes, Hannibal (Mo.), Springfield (Ill.), Oxford (Miss.), Charlottesville (Va.), Jim Thorpe (Pa.), Salinas (remember Steinbeck?), and Memphis (of Elvis renown) spring readily to mind. Or the strategy may depend upon a recurrent spectacle, for example, New Orleans's Mardi Gras, Edmonton's Stampede, Charleston's Spoleto Festival, or Pasadena's Rose Bowl Parade. But almost every less-favored town or city can conjure up some claim to uniqueness by virtue of its being the birthplace of some minor celebrity, the gateway to, or center of, some region, or the "capital" of some unusual activity; and such credentials will be flaunted via logos, distinctive monuments, slogans, welcoming signs, billboards, and other forms of publicity.[26]

An almost universal program for fabrication of group identity is based on spectator sports, arguably the last vestige of old-fashioned community. Beginning gradually in the late nineteenth century but reaching an almost hysterical climax lately is a deep emotional commitment to the local professional football, baseball, hockey, basketball, or soccer team or, in the case of the nominally amateur college football or basketball program, the enmeshment of entire states or regions. And, of course, during the periodic Olympic and World Cup excitements, the nation's identity and manhood seem to hang upon the fortunes of its athletes. What is truly disturbing about this ersatz type of belongingness, one that excludes all those bystanders lacking interest in sport, is its willful, open-eyed self-deception. Even the most fanatic of fans realizes that the players are mobile professionals, or subsidized amateurs, usually born and reared elsewhere, with their eye on the main chance, and that indeed (except for the collegiate) the franchise itself is portable and can be whisked away at any time at the whim of the owners. Such blind devotion to a business enterprise with no lasting commitment to the locality reveals more than a little desperation.

Community or Neotribalism?

The quandary remains. The individual adrift alone in Landscape III can nowhere espy the stable, identity-affirming mooring so avidly sought. All the larger aggregations, the quasi-ideal communities we have examined thus far — nation-state, business firm, college class, other voluntary associations, born-again congregation, sport-fandom, boosterish town — seem to meet the identity needs of far fewer than the totality of any society, or perhaps do so only temporarily and imperfectly. Is there any other option, any potential magic formula, still waiting to be considered? Perhaps.

> The sweet warmth of the community, with its one-dimensional simplicity, is...a very natural temptation. To those who see the idea of the nation becoming more and more abstract, to those who do not participate in the integration of the enterprise, to those that the enterprise isolates, rather

than unites, the community is likely to appear as the natural framework within which everyone may rediscover his identity. Without any links to a territory, "nomadic," and nevertheless imprisoned in a function, without an overarching perspective to give a meaning to a given task, modern man, a social module infinitely reproduced and nevertheless always single, solitary, is condemned to find in a search for origins a difference that he needs in order to share with others, as different as he is, a feeling of common heritage.[27]

And so we seek refuge in the latter-day ethnic community. Is this the unbreakable safety net in which, when all else fails (to muddle metaphors), we find our bearings?

There are those who would like to have us think so. However, it is readily demonstrated that the self-conscious ethnic group is a modern social construct that may or may not have some claim to primordiality.[28] Looked at coolly and objectively, any campaign to mobilize latent ethnic sentiment into some semblance of genuine community is a quixotic enterprise. "The search for community turns into a major obstacle to its formation."[29] What is created, following the ethnic strategy, is what Michel Maffesoli[30] and Zygmunt Bauman label as "neo-tribalism."[31] "Such communities will never be anything like Tönnies' cosy and unreflective (cosy because unreflective) homes of unanimity. Tönnies-style communities fall apart from the moment they know of themselves as communities."[32] These latter-day neo-tribes are products of willful effort, not the Tönnies-style communities of remote, Landscape I antiquity; but however fragile or temporary they may prove to be, such recent social constructs can and do have substantial political and other consequences.

Their instigators, too often with ignoble motives in mind, have been able to capitalize on the tensions engendered by modernism and, more acutely of late, by globalization. Much of the appeal derives from recovered or invented traditions and also the fiction that their popular movement, as a corrective to the coercive top-down homogenization mandated by the nation-state, is a spontaneous people-based phenomenon.

Rather ironically, the nation-state has been an active agent in initiating neotribes. For a variety of administrative, political, and other reasons, the bureaucracy, in all but the most homogenous of states, has found it necessary to categorize the population into convenient pigeonholes. Such standard measures as age, sex, residence, class, and occupation do not suffice. Almost always the preferred option has been an ethnic/racial taxonomy (although religion can be equally important in some countries). In many instances, designations and definitions are arbitrary and may have only a tenuous relationship, if any, with anthropological actualities. But the impact of administrative fiat can be substantial. The case of South Africa during the apartheid era may be extreme, but in the United States, as elsewhere, the census classification scheme has certainly been a factor in channeling the collective behavior of various constituencies. If you are officially informed that you belong to a given group, you may begin to believe it.

How well has the ethnic strategy worked in packaging individual and group identity? The partial successes of ethnic mobilization have been apparent in, inter alia, various portions of France, Spain, the United Kingdom, Canada, Romania, Bulgaria, Yugoslavia, India, and the former Soviet Union — in all cases, populations with venerable claims to particular territories. But, by their very nature, neotribes are transient, subject to corrosion and beset by centrifugal tendencies.

Not all eligible persons are willing to buy into the scheme, and the increasing incidence of intermarriage reduces the pool of candidates. Then there is the basic contradiction between a backward-glancing mind-set and the lived realities of our current future-oriented age. The complex movements and action-spaces of the neotribal folk, the transnationalization of information and all manner of cultural items, and the globalization of the economy all militate against the snugness of self-contained, territorially defined ethnic cocoons. And, finally, the most nagging problem of all: If one must stop and ask oneself, as our postmodern ethnic wanna-bes are obliged to do periodically, Who am I? how trustworthy is the response?

Despite such reservations, we must acknowledge the intensity, even fanaticism, of devotion to the ethnic cause among *some* members of certain societies in Europe, Asia, and Africa, for example, Catalans, Basques, Afrikaners, Tamils, Albanians in Serbia, Moros, Transylvanian Magyars, and Palestinians. For them there is no doubting the personal primacy of the ethnic label. Nothing fully comparable is to be found in the United States at the subnational level, and we must ask why. One answer concerns territory. If all the examples cited above involve claimants to ancestral lands, the only American possibilities (with the marginal exception of the Cajuns) involve non-European peoples. Although some immigrant groups from Europe have maintained a heavy multigeneration presence in some tracts, it has never been to the exclusion of other communities. Thus, in contrast to the social geography of the Old World, no authentic Euro-American "homelands" have come to pass.[33] And, given the relative tranquillity we enjoy as a result of this situation, Americans might well be thankful.

The situation of Native Americans is, of course, quite different but not fully comparable to the case of, say, the Chechens, Québecois, or Basques. Many of these aboriginal communities were nomadic or frequenters of territories with vague, contested boundaries; and since the disastrous encounter with the invaders from overseas, shifts hither and yon, voluntary or otherwise, followed by much miscegenation and rapid urbanization have weakened or broken attachments to ancestral locales. If, however belatedly, territorial claims are being advanced in courts and legislatures, for only a minority of these nations is identification with place the dominant component of ethnic identity. A parallel statement applies to the burgeoning Latino population. Outside some Chicanos in the Southwest, for whom a mythical homeland shines brightly in the imagination, location is incidental or irrelevant in building a sense of Hispanic-American peoplehood. And its relevance is probably even less for African Americans despite historic concentrations in the South. For Asian Americans the territorial issue is a nonissue. But vital though it may be for many communities, place-bonding is not an absolute requirement for the existence of an ethnic group. The diasporic Gypsies, Jews, and Lebanese are obvious counterexamples of robust peoplehood, if not full-fledged ethnic identity, in all its modern dimensions.

If the immigrant Europeans fail to furnish any convincing exceptions, we must still consider the abortive Euro-American "ethnic revival" of the 1970s. Why did it fizzle by the 1980s even though other ethnic movements in the United States and abroad have continued to display some vitality? Two or three reasons come to mind. First there was the initial encounter of the European immigrant with an overpowering American cultural system; thus any transatlantic cultural heritage was quickly and mortally compromised as soon as assimilation got under way. By the latter half of the twentieth century, the process was so far along that symbolic ethnicity was the dominant condition for those nth-generation persons of foreign stock who gave the matter any thought at all. The coup de grâce may well have been the invention of the idea of ethnicity. The sublimation of specific ethnic complexes into a transcendent entity whereby various cultures become essentially interchangeable has meant discrediting the campaign of an individual Euro-American group for gaining autonomy or special recognition.

Must we conclude that the ethnic option is missing from the inventory of identity alternatives available to the modal American? Not at all. Membership in the national cultural community means participation in a macroethnic group. But, as it happens, unlike such contentious cases as Bosnia or Lebanon, few U.S. citizens have reason to think about this crucial affiliation in the course of their everyday activities. It is only during episodes of international strife or in their travels abroad that most Americans are jolted into some appreciation of their identity. A more reasonable conclusion is that, as in the case of other advanced nation-states, being an American is only one of the many ways residents of the United States can use to define themselves — at least those Euro-Americans who still comprise a majority of the population — but, under normal circumstances, it is far from a definitive, soul-nourishing answer to that persistent, postmodern query: Who am I really?

If this essay, or something like it, were being composed in 1965, this would be a fitting place to write finis. And the final comment might have been that, for Americans at least, ethnic identity had dwindled into insignificance, while other options for identity-formation had come to the fore. But, by the 1980s and 1990s, ethnic issues had come roaring back in the United States and most other First World states because of two developments. First, in the American case, the native subordinate groups — peoples of color — had become vociferous in demanding their place in the sun; and, second, a massive, predominantly non-Caucasian influx of immigrants and sojourners, so alien in appearance and frequently also unfamiliar in terms of religion, language, and other cultural attributes, had made their presence felt. In neither category does numerical growth show any signs of slackening. Furthermore, the rate and extent of assimilation remain problematic.

Indeed there is no assurance that ultimate amalgamation is possible. We see, then, that what had become a moribund issue, the concern with ethnic groups, has taken on a new, extended lease on life, more than incidentally a development concurrent with the invention of ethnicity. This turn of events is not confined to the United States. Similar situations have arisen in other neo-European lands, notably Canada and Australia, and in Europe itself with such instances as Pakistanis in Britain, Surinamese in the Netherlands, Turks in Germany, Albanians in Italy, and Algerians in France. The subaltern groups in question may or may not welcome recognition of their ethnic distinctiveness, but they have little choice in the matter. If they do not cherish and cultivate their identity themselves, it is thrust upon them by official designation or by the attitudes of the host population. Under the conditions of American life, hardly a day (or hour?) goes by when an African American, a Latina, or a Chinese American is not reminded of her ethnic/racial status, especially in dealings with gentiles. The reverse situation is uncommon: whatever the company, the Euro-American, whether hyphenated or old stock, is seldom obliged to contemplate the ethnic label that is so visible to the Other.

What must we conclude from all this? The most obvious conclusion is that in posing the question How relevant are ethnic considerations in finding solutions or palliatives for our pandemic identity angst? the answer is tentative and unsatisfactory. Quite important in some cases, trivial in others. But, unlike the other alternatives previously reviewed, the ethnic option is one of considerable urgency with wide-ranging social, cultural, and political consequences quite apart from whatever efficacy it may have in coping with the identity dilemma. Indeed, if there is a larger message embedded in the preceding pages, it is that latter-day ethnic identity is deeply interwoven not just with the currently unanswerable questions Who am I? and What are we? but with most of the more pressing societal problems of our day.[34]

In any event, the frustrating conclusion to this inquiry into the contemporary world's identity crisis is that there are no effective general solutions available at either the individual or social level, nor are any likely in the foreseeable future. The confusion and angst I have sketched are endemic to, inescapable features of, the postmodern condition. They will pass away or be replaced by some other pathology only when or if humankind enters another utterly unpredictable phase of social evolution.

Notes

1. But some three decades later the *International Encyclopedia of the Social Sciences,* ed. David L. Sills (New York: Macmillan and Free Press, 1968–70), included two relevant articles: "Identity, Psycho Social," and "Identification, Political."

2. The earliest lexicographic notice of *identity crisis* I have come across is dated 1954 in the 1993 edition of *Merriam-Webster's Collegiate Dictionary.* Both of its definitions are apposite to this discussion: "1: personal psychological conflict esp. in adolescence that involves confusion about one's social role and often a sense of loss of continuity to one's personality. 2: a state of confusion in an institution or organization regarding its nature or direction."

3. Raymond Williams, *Keywords: A Vocabulary of Culture and Society,* rev. ed. (New York: Oxford University Press, 1983).

4. Philip Gleason, *Speaking of Diversity: Language and Ethnicity in Twentieth Century America* (Baltimore: Johns Hopkins University Press, 1992), 123–49.

5. Ibid., 127.

6. John Brinckerhoff Jackson, *Discovering the Vernacular Landscape* (New Haven, Conn.: Yale University Press, 1984). In a rather polemical essay, Timothy Luke sets forth a succession of three "natures" that rather closely parallels Jackson's scheme ("Identity, Meaning, and Globalization: Detraditionalization in Postmodern Space-Time Compression," in *Detraditionalization: Critical Reflections on Authority and Identity,* ed. Paul Heelas, Scott Lash, and Paul Morris [Oxford and Cambridge, Mass.: Blackwell, 1996]).

7. For a lavish and most illuminating account of the phenomenon as it developed in nineteenth-century France, see Alain Corbin, "The Secret of the Individual," in *A History of Private Life,* vol. 4, *From the French Revolution to the Great War,* ed. Michelle Perrot (Cambridge, Mass.: Harvard University Press, 1990), 447–57.

8. Douglas Kellner, "Popular Culture and the Construction of Postmodern Identities," in *Modernity and Identity,* ed. Scott Lash and Jonathan Friedman (Oxford: Blackwell, 1992), 141.

9. Among the many consequences of the two world wars were the initiation of the decolonialization of the European and American overseas empires and, at least within Europe, the reshaping of new nation-states along ethnic lines. In general, the liberationist impulses sparked by the two conflicts subverted the rationale of Force III.

10. David Lowenthal, *The Past Is a Foreign Country* (New York: Cambridge University Press, 1985); and Lowenthal, *Possessed by the Past: The Heritage Crusade and the Spoils of History* (New York: Free Press, 1996).

11. Jonathan Friedman, "Narcissism, Roots, and Postmodernity: The Constitution of Selfhood in the Global Crisis," in Lash and Friedman, *Modernity and Identity,* 361.

12. The scholarly literature treating questions of contemporary personal and group identity has been growing at an alarming rate in recent years. I cannot pretend to have read and digested more than a modest fraction of these publications, but much of the time spent in perusal was time wasted. All too many of these books and essays are confused or confusing, written in nearly incomprehensible jargon. It would be too unkind to cite examples, but the worst of them sound like spoofs. On the positive side, I have encountered several items that are lucid, illuminating, and useful. In addition to the writings of Douglas Kellner ("Popular Culture," 141–77) and Nikolas Rose ("Authority and the Genealogy of Subjectivity," in Heelas, Lash, and Morris, *Detraditionalization,* 294–327), I have found especially valuable what seems to be the earliest, but still highly stimulating, book-length treatment of postmodern identity: Orrin Klapp's *Collective Search for Identity* (New York: Holt, Rinehart and Winston, 1969). Virtually no mention of ethnicity, but Klapp does discuss fads, fashions, cults, crusades, hero and celebrity worship, and the pursuit of fun in all its forms. Also recommended for its provocative, sprightly examination of the fluidity and uncertainties of personal identity is Kenneth Gergen's *The Saturated Self* (New York: Basic Books, 1991), and for acute insights into not only identity issues but larger contemporary sociological questions, the works of Zygmunt Bauman (e.g., "Morality in the Age of Con-

tingency," in Heelas, Lash, and Morris, *Detraditionalization*, 49–58) offer rich helpings of food for thought. For deep historical-cum-philosophical disquisitions on identity, see Dieter Hoffman-Axthelm ("Identity and Reality: The End of the Philosophical Immigration Officer," in Lash and Friedman, *Modernity and Identity*, 196–217) and Charles Taylor's massive and erudite *Sources of the Self* (Cambridge, Mass.: Harvard University Press, 1989).

13. Klapp, *Collective Search for Identity*, 19–20. Emphasis in original.

14. Bauman, "Morality in the Age of Contingency," 50–51. Emphasis in original.

15. Fred Davis, *Fashion, Culture, and Identity* (Chicago: University of Chicago Press, 1992), 28–29.

16. Ibid., 33.

17. David Riesman, *The Lonely Crowd: A Study of the Changing American Character* (Garden City, N.Y.: Doubleday, 1953).

18. Davis, *Fashion, Culture, and Identity*, 158.

19. "But freedom and globalization has also brought in its wake a need for cultural and ethnic self-identification, as people become uncomfortable with the borderless global community and feel a loss of control" (Michael A. Burayidi, "Multicultural Nations in a Monocultural World: An Introduction," in *Multiculturalism in a Cross-National Perspective*, ed. Michael A. Burayidi [Lanham, Md.: University Press of America, 1997], 1). "[T]he old essentialisms, such as the Marxist idea that social identity could be reduced to class identity, are now redundant. Rather gender, age, disability, race, religion, ethnicity, nationality, civil status, even musical styles and dress codes, are also very potent axes of organization and identification. These different forms of identity appear to be upheld simultaneously, successively or separately and with different degrees of force, conviction and enthusiasm" (Robin Cohen, *Global Diasporas: An Introduction* [Seattle: University of Washington Press, 1997], 129).

20. It is almost needless to point out how psychotherapy in all its varied forms has become a growth industry in recent decades.

21. Richard J. Barnet and John Cavanagh, *Global Dreams: Imperial Corporations and the New World Order* (New York: Simon & Schuster, 1994), 13–22, 25–41.

22. Wilbur Zelinsky, "Selfward Bound? Personal Preference Patterns and the Changing Map of American Society," *Economic Geography* 50 (1974): 144–79.

23. Jean-Marie Guéhenno, *The End of the Nation-State* (Minneapolis: University of Minnesota Press, 1995).

24. Orlando Patterson, "The Emerging West Atlantic System: Migration, Culture, and Underdevelopment in the United States and the Circum-Caribbean Region," in *Population in an Interacting World*, ed. William Alonso (Cambridge, Mass.: Harvard University Press, 1987), 260.

25. Roland Robertson and JoAnn Chirico, "Humanity, Globalization, and Worldwide Religious Resurgence: A Theoretical Perspective," *Sociological Analysis* 46 (1985): 219–42.

26. Wilbur Zelinsky, *Nation into State: The Shifting Symbolic Foundations of American Nationalism* (Chapel Hill: University of North Carolina Press, 1988); and Zelinsky, "Where Every Town Is above Average: Welcoming Signs along America's Highways," *Landscape* 30 (1988): 1–10.

27. Guéhenno, *End of the Nation-State*, 45.

28. Nathan Glazer and Daniel P. Moynihan, introduction to *Ethnicity: Theory and Experience*, ed. Nathan Glazer and Daniel P. Moynihan (Cambridge, Mass.: Harvard University Press, 1988), 20.

29. Zygmunt Bauman, *Intimations of Postmodernity* (London: Routledge, 1992), 139.

30. Michel Maffesoli, *The Time of the Tribes: The Decline of Individualism in Mass Society* (London: Sage, 1996).

31. Bauman, *Intimations of Postmodernity*, 136–37.

32. Ibid., 138.

33. This rather controversial topic is explored in definitive fashion by Michael Conzen in "Culture Regions, Homelands, and Ethnic Archipelagos in the United States: Methodologi-

cal Considerations," *Journal of Cultural Geography* 13, no. 2 (1993): 13–25; and Conzen, "The German-Speaking Ethnic Archipelago in America," in *Ethnic Persistence and Change in Europe and America: Traces in Landscape and Society,* ed. Klaus Frantz and Robert Sauder (Innsbruck: Veröffentlichungen der Universität Innsbruck, 1995), 67–92.

34. "[C]ultural/political identity is a processual configuration of historically given elements — including race, culture, class, gender, and sexuality — different combinations of which may be featured in different conjunctures. These elements may, in some conjunctures, cross-cut and bring each other to crisis. What components of identity are 'deep' and what 'superficial'? What 'central' and what 'peripheral'? What elements are good for traveling and what for dwelling? What will be articulated within the 'community'? What in coalition work? How do these elements interact historically, in tension and dialogue? Questions like these do not lend themselves to systematic or definitive answers; they are what cultural politics are all about" (James Clifford, *Routes: Travel and Translation in the Late Twentieth Century* [Cambridge, Mass.: Harvard University Press, 1997], 46).

THE CRITICAL DESCRIPTION
OF CONFUSED GEOGRAPHIES

Edward Relph

Geographical description has been made surprisingly difficult by the confusions of postmodernity. Cultures, landscapes, and styles are being mixed up and redeposited like detritus in a terminal moraine at precisely the same time that significant doubts have arisen about the legitimacy of rational knowledge. Even if we can find concepts to describe the new blends of landscapes, it seems that there are no firm grounds for claiming that our account of them is true or more legitimate than some other account. These confusions certainly present intellectual challenges, but they also simultaneously undermine confidence in strategies for dealing with deepening problems, such as widespread poverty and environmental change, that have a deep impact on the lives of people regardless of who describes them. I accept Terry Eagleton's charge that it would be worse than dishonest to give up the vision of a just society simply because the postmodern world is a mess.[1] But description is an essential part of the process of making sense of things, and I do not see how it is possible to develop this vision and advocate social reforms if we cannot even be clear about how to describe the world. This essay is therefore an attempt to clarify the possibilities for describing landscapes and places in the context of postmodernity.

What Is This World Like, and How Do We Describe It?

Somewhere near what appears to be the end of Italo Calvino's book *If on a Winter's Night a Traveler*...several bibliophiles meet in a library and discuss possible ways to read books. One of them samples a few lines at a time in order to stimulate his thoughts; another scours the entire text to glean every possible insight from it. A third claims that the act of reading is its own reward and a book is a mere accessory to this. A fourth reads chiefly to recover memories of childhood. Another enjoys the anticipation of reading and a book's opening sentences, but a sixth reader prefers conclusions and what follows in the spaces beyond. Finally, the narrator interjects: "I must say that in books I like to read only what is written, and to connect the details with the whole, and to consider certain readings as definitive, and I like to keep one book distinct from the other, each for what it has that is different and new; and I especially like books to be read from beginning to end."[2]

It is difficult not to feel a sense of relief. Here is a comprehensive and sensible approach. We even suspect it must be Calvino's own opinion. Then, after a moment's reflection, doubts arise. This apparently sensible way of reading does not apply to the very book in which we are reading it. *If on a Winter's Night a Traveler*...is a collection of abandoned beginnings of stories and of details that evoke memories of childhood; it seems to consist of loose ends rather than to have an end, and it is far from clear that there is a coherent whole that would allow a definitive reading. We seem to be trapped in a maze.

Yi-Fu Tuan has offered advice about description that could be a paraphrase of the advice of Calvino's narrator about reading. In his essay "Surface Phenomena and Aesthetic Experience," Tuan asks, "What is this world like, and how do we describe it?"[3] Since the precise context is a discussion of aesthetics, his question refers specifically to "the pleasing world" pervaded with beauty and significance, which, he suggests, in some form all people imagine and all people want. He proposes that descriptions of it should attend to details as well as the grand scaffoldings of ideas and should see both of them as products of an effort to build something fair and right rather than merely necessary. Descriptions should note contradictions and ambiguities, consider how cultures differ in their degree of expressivity, and be alert to whether the surfaces of landscapes reveal or hide what lies behind them.

Tuan's question is a penetrating one, and his advice about description seems eminently sensible. Yet I have difficulties with them. First, I can untangle neither the question nor his methodological advice from the confusions of *this* world, that is to say the everyday one in which we have to live regardless of whether it is pleasant or unpleasant. My preference is to try to understand the everyday world by examining its landscapes, and I have trouble separating the nice side of aesthetic imagination from what is, quite frankly, a plethora of ugliness and utilitarianism — parking lots, airports, gutters, intersections of arterial roads, farmyards, and so on. And even the landscapes that appear pleasant, such as tourist areas in the Caribbean, often disguise deep social inequalities or some other nastiness. Second, while I agree with Tuan that worthwhile answers must begin with careful description, in practice I find that description is no more straightforward than reading. There are no firm criteria for deciding whose world this is or what constitutes a definitive account of it. Like Calvino's stories, the everyday world is filled with beginnings and loose ends and details that do not necessarily connect with some larger whole. It, too, appears to have become a maze.

The Age of Uncertainty

In *The Order of Things* Michel Foucault wrote of "the thought that bears the stamp of our age and our geography."[4] It helps to know that this vaguely deterministic statement is part of a discussion of "heterotopia." If, Foucault argued, utopias are untroubled regions where values are shared, then heterotopias are their opposite — the expression of multiple visions and plural rationalities, filled with visual non sequiturs and "fragments of a large number of possible orders that glitter separately without law or geometry." Foucault was not exactly enchanted with our age, so the best sense I can make of his remark is that he considered our thought, our age, and our geography all to be uncertain and confused. They interact, of course, but there is no common logic or order to these interactions and the patterns they create.

This is not an unreasonable assertion. The twentieth century could justifiably be called the Age of Uncertainty. From its beginning, traditions have been cast aside, intellectual barriers pulled down, geographical boundaries crossed, methodological conventions undermined, and cultural traditions blended. Relativity, abstract art, Heisenberg's uncertainty principle, indeterminacy, Wittgenstein's failure to find a firm foundation for meaning in language, the category-obliterating destruction of nuclear weapons, huge migrations and cultural exchanges, the women's movement that has begun to overturn centuries of social practices, decontructionism, and chaos theory — all of these have brought into doubt assumptions that once were beyond question.

In spite of the range of its manifestations and its depth, this sense of uncertainty is not universally shared. To present the issue very simply, it seems to be just one-half of a two-sided mask. On one side lie the epistemological and geographical turmoil that have followed the erosion of assumptions and the mixing of cultures. On the other side are those attitudes and practices that are apparently unaffected by uncertainty. Fundamentalist religions are an obvious example, as are the rationalist convictions that seem to govern the behavior of economic corporations and engineering firms. And on this side are also what might be called the actual conditions of everyday life, including hamburgers, houses, running shoes, environmental contaminants, malnutrition, and the gap between wealth and poverty.

Those who look through the mask of uncertainty see that the logical foundations of rational and fundamentalist knowledge have been mostly gnawed away and that the current social and political order is based on systems of power that have no underlying justification. They believe that the great social edifice founded on science and reason is slowly collapsing. On the other side, those who wear the rationalist mask are unimpeded by doubts about logical underpinnings; they have a clear sense of purpose and unbridled confidence; religious and economic fundamentalisms thrive and global corporations flourish on the basis of unrestrained technological development. And for those who experience the consequences of this, who enjoy a late-model car or a fully equipped home in a gated community, who suffer the wounds caused by the latest generation of antipersonnel land mines, or who are condemned to deep poverty because of shifts in international money markets, there is little that is uncertain about their condition.

Postmodernism and Heterotopia

The various uncertainties of the past century have culminated in postmodernism, a widespread conviction, at least among academics, that the world is contingent, unstable, indeterminate, and consists of a set of disunified structures.[5] From this perspective there are no solid facts and no definitive accounts of the world or anything in it. The world is as it is, neither because it is the product of universal natural processes nor because it was ordained by God, but because this is the best sense we can make of it for the moment, or, from a more political angle, because powerful and knowledgeable groups have convinced everybody else to accept that this is how it should be.

Much writing about postmodernism is burdened by jargon and obscure theories, but for all that it would be a mistake to regard it as some passing intellectual fashion. There are substantial indications, including the uncertainties of the twentieth century, that it represents a profound epistemological and geographical shift. Epistemologically it is as though many strands of thought have simultaneously slipped anchor and are now drifting aimlessly, so that explanations about causes, and judgments about what is good or right or true, depend more on context than on universal principles of reason or logic. Philosophers who have examined the progression of Western thought over the last century cannot find a logical way to question the conclusions that there are no objective foundations for scientific methods,[6] no a priori privileged methods to sort things out, and no definitive readings of books or landscapes. In contrast with the modernist perspective that offered clear answers about what is true and what is false, and about the right ways to think, act, and pass judgment, this is profoundly disturbing. Nevertheless it is not without merits. Terry Eagleton, who is otherwise not a fan, notes that postmodernism has a very positive aspect as "the ideology of a special historical epoch in the West, when long reviled and humiliated groups are beginning to recover something of their history and identity."[7] Gianni Vattimo, an Italian philosopher who is a fan, calls postmodern understanding "weak thought" and regards this as a positive attribute.[8] It is the descendant of the former strong categories of thought such as logic and truth that have lost their power. Strong thought was a dogma that imposed its own view and dismissed all others; in contrast, weak thought makes everything a type of fiction and it acknowledges other voices. This very weakness, Vattimo argues, offers possibilities for discovering new forms of creativity and cooperation.

Current geographies and their landscapes are no less indeterminate, dislocated, and perplexing than postmodern epistemologies. *Heterotopia* seems to be an accurate word[9] to embrace the arbitrary geography of the juxtaposed elements of Las Vegas, with its fake Egyptian pyramids, reproductions of the landmarks of world cities, suburban tracts, artificial volcano, and palm trees in the high desert. Las Vegas seems to be emerging as an archetype, but heterotopia can be found in more diluted forms in megamalls, themed and gated communities, and the cultural hodgepodge of inner cities. In all of these there are spatial conjunctions of otherwise disconnected activities, and super-imposed fragments of different cultures and histories, arranged in ways that defy conventional description.

The processes of transferring bits of geography elsewhere, and of cultural exchange, are not exactly new, but in premodern times the processes were sufficiently slow and inefficient that there was almost always some adaptation to local circumstances. It made sense to describe that traditional world in terms of places, regions, and distinct cultures. In contrast, over the last two hundred years the force and rate of diffusion of the deliberately standardizing practices of modernism have allowed little local adaptation. New, uniform landscapes were imposed on top of or adjacent to older, diverse geographies, creating differences as abrupt and distinct as that between an ornately carved, late-nineteenth-century sandstone commercial building and the sleek glass-and-metal, international-style skyscraper across the street. These sorts of contrasts between premodern and modern can be accurately represented in terms of place and placelessness.

The heterotopian geographies of postmodernity are different again. The sophisticated communications technologies of the global economy have simultaneously intensified and diversified the interchange of ideas, practices, people, and images. Paul Virilio suggests that we have leapt from a world of places to the "sudden bewildering Babel clamor of the world-city, the untimely mix of the global and the local."[10] In the suburbs of San Pedro Sula in Honduras a nominally American Burger King is located next to the putatively British Lloyd's Bank, just down the road from a Korean-owned *maquiladora* where young Honduran women work twelve hours a day for insignificant wages, unseen by the ecotourists from Europe and North America on their way to Copan, a restored Mayan city that is also a world heritage site. In the high-tech outer suburbs of Toronto an edge-city development of reflecting glass offices is set next to the protected historical village of Buttonville; a few hundred meters away a new Chinese shopping center, where even the *P*s indicating parking areas have translations, is located across the road from a development of neo-Georgian houses called "The Enclave," which overlook the gleaming onion domes of a recently built Eastern Orthodox cathedral situated in a field behind locked gates and a chain-link fence.

Neither the old geographical language of regions nor the newer dialect of place and placelessness has much value for describing this postmodern world. It seems possible to do little more than list its features in some sort of trivial inventory or to call it a heterotopia as though something defined as lacking law or geometry is a clarification. It appears that postmodern landscapes consist of people, things, and bits of geographies, histories, and cultures that have been uprooted, franchised, spun around above the earth, topologically transformed, remixed, deposited elsewhere, linked by electronic networks, and given distinctive facades to distinguish them from all the other equally confused places. Virilio calls the process "glocalization," a suitably awkward contraction to express the paradox of local identities based on generalized and unrooted interactivity.[11]

Corporatism, Technology, and Problems without Apparent Solutions

Money is deeply implicated in the processes of heterotopia, perhaps a primary cause of them. Capitalism, Eagleton proposes, "is the most pluralistic order history has ever known, restlessly transgressing boundaries and dismantling oppositions, pitching together diverse life forms and continually overflowing the measure."[12] That may sound like something characteristically postmodern, and David Harvey, among others, has indeed interpreted postmodernism as an expression of what he calls "late capitalism."[13] That is, I think, a wrong interpretation. Although capitalism in its corporate form has the ability to affect many disguises, it is really a type of fundamentalism based on the specific and unwavering goals of development, productivity, profit, short-term gain, and power exercised on behalf of self-interest.[14] The uncertainties suffered by those imbued with postmodernism are apparently not shared by the corporate managers of the global economy.

Twentieth- and twenty-first-century technologies also affect disguises. Many of these work invisibly at the scale of genes or electrons; they penetrate and then change cells, atoms, chemical structures, genes, and minds; they modify, record, manipulate, and pollute in ways that are difficult, perhaps impossible, to detect. As a result it is no longer possible to be sure what anything is, whether it is made of plastic, whether we or our food have been irradiated, whether images have been electronically reprocessed, or whether strawberries, carrots, and sheep have been genetically modified. The technologies of the late twentieth century and early twenty-first century have the power to transmit people, things, and ideas with unprecedented speed and have annihilated the mediating properties of distance and space. In the context of such profound possibilities for transformation it is hard to know whether the terms *real* or *fake* or *natural* or *artificial* have any meaning left or if geography has any significance. It is part of the deep perplexity of postmodernity that these transforming changes are based on the strong thought of measurement and the logic of an enduring material reality. Philosophers, it seems, merely talk about the uncertainties of the world; the point is that technicians and corporate managers are confidently changing it in ways that actually make it uncertain.

In short, neither capitalism (in its various forms of international finance and corporate management) nor modern technology shares the unease that infuses postmodernism. Both are positivistic, driven by measurements of productivity and efficiency; both are confident and often self-righteous, constantly striving to grow and innovate. This confidence is justified to the extent that together they have raised the material conditions of life, improved health, and increased life expectancy. They have, however, not distributed their benefits well. Statistical evidence (that is, evidence that is consistent with their own assumptions and methods) indicates that more than a billion people suffer from chronic malnutrition and live in abject poverty.[15] Furthermore, the gap between rich and poor is widening rapidly both within the developed world and between the developed and less-developed countries.[16] Additional systemic problems are revealed in ragged wars that persist for decades, in the international marketing of young women from poverty-stricken families to fuel the global sex trade, and in increasing international violence engendered by resource scarcities.[17] In the North I suppose it is easy to overlook these problems because we are protected from them by numerous indications of well-being, but once they are noticed it is hard to understand how they can be interpreted as anything other than indications of profound social and political failure.

It is little wonder that the economic historian Eric Hobsbawm concludes his magisterial survey of the history of the twentieth century with the grim observation that it is ending in "problems for which nobody has or even claimed to have solutions."[18] Any attempt to resolve these will clearly require a firm challenge to corporatist power and careless technological innovation, as well as a resilient commitment to justice toward those with whom we share the planet and toward future generations. In the postmodern world of uncertainty and confusion it is difficult to see where this purpose and commitment might come from, but it would be a serious evasion of responsibility not to look at all.

Three Proposals for Transcending Uncertainty

Postmodernism, suggests Terry Eagleton, is like the living dead — it can neither resuscitate itself nor decently die.[19] It cannot, however, be ignored, because it surrounds us in the confused landscapes in which we live, because its relativisms are now insinuated into patterns of thought, and because it emasculates possibilities for resolving deep social inequities and environmental problems.

Some of the philosophers and social scientists who have considered the enfeebling consequences of postmodernism dismiss it as an aberration and argue for a return to the strong principles of modernist thought.[20] Others find the logic leading to postmodernism irrefutable, in spite of their best efforts, and end up arguing for what is essentially a personal ethic.[21] Yet others celebrate postmodernity for its liberating qualities and the opportunities it affords for the revision of the social order.[22] These three different types of argument have been made, in part with a geographical twist, by Yi-Fu Tuan, James Edwards, and David Harvey. An assessment of them reveals some possibilities for approaches to the description of the postmodern world.

Cosmos before Hearth

In *Cosmos and Hearth: A Cosmopolite's Viewpoint,* Yi-Fu Tuan explores the tension between the ends of the geographic spectrum. Hearth represents home, tradition, familiarity; cosmos stands for reason, modernization, science. He recognizes that reason has recently been under attack and there has been a "resurgence of pride in local culture," probably because science has become arrogant and a threat to diversity. Rather than simply side with this resurgence (which is part of postmodernism), Tuan argues for "high modernism," an attitude that still aspires to a modern and just world but has a strong sense of the limitations of science. This attitude looks to the past for a balance of reason and tradition, and it sees merit in both hearth and cosmos. Nonetheless, Tuan writes that when a choice must be made he sees the life path of a human moving from hearth to cosmos. Plants have roots while human beings have feet and minds, and thinking can take us to visions and imaginings beyond the constraints of tradition and place. He recognizes that the choice is never an easy one, for it leads to isolation from locality and home, but "a cosmopolite is one who considers the gain greater than the loss."[23]

This is an attractive argument. Apart from anything else, it cannot be quickly dismissed because without the benefits of modernity many of us would probably have died from simple infections. Furthermore, our crowded world of cities and megacities, with their heterotopias of juxtaposed differences and blended cultures, needs the breadth of vision and tolerance of the cosmopolite more than ever.

Put the Local First

In an essay on Wittgenstein's ethics, James Edwards, a philosopher, makes an argument similar to that of Tuan, then reaches exactly the opposite conclusion. First he identifies a "diseased understanding" that is manifest in the bifurcation between the debilitating relativism of postmodernity and the dogmatic fundamentalisms of science and religion. Then he proposes that this might be overcome by adopting an attitude that is tolerant and that preserves the best practices and thought of the past while avoiding their rigidities. Thus far his argument could support Tuan's notion of high modernism. Yet Edwards, on the basis of his reading of Wittgenstein, who regarded most of what can be said by science and logic as trivial because it offers no support for ethics, proposes that this tolerant attitude has to be grounded in a sense of wonder about the details of the world. Direct and unimpeded action to help one's neighbor only becomes possible when the neighbor has been noticed, he writes, and not through a rational search for universal principles. Accordingly, "we should abandon the global for the local, the abstract for the concrete, the willful for the self-effacing."[24]

It is befuddling that an analysis of the current situation that has a strong family resemblance to Tuan's argument can lead to the opposite conclusion. Nevertheless, those who have extolled the virtues of sense of place, topophilia, and local action should applaud Edwards's advice. As a sometime phenomenologist, I support it because it is clear to me that all abstract principles must be grounded in the specific situations of the lived world. When a choice has to be made, my inclination is to make it for real people in particular places. On the other hand, I am well aware that single-minded attention to locality and place can become insular, poisoned, and exclusionary. Michael Ignatieff, a political philosopher who describes himself as a cosmopolitan, has visited the scenes of many ethnic conflicts and observed how love of place has been corrupted into vicious intolerance and ethnic cleansing.[25] In the absence of a civil society based in principles of order and reason, the descent into geographically based brutality can be rapid indeed.

The Just Production of Just Geographical Differences

There is a third possibility. Tuan notes that modernism is sometimes denounced because it has trampled on diverse cultures,[26] and it is undeniable that modern civilization has been a cause of repression and destruction. Its narrative of progress and growth has suppressed ethnic voices and geographical variety, first in colonization and industrialization, then through the many devices of placelessness. Recently, however, corporate capitalism and other forces of modernism have come to realize that diversity has value, and they have therefore re-created it for the dubious ends of profit and further progress. The combined, somewhat paradoxical result of these different processes has been the replacement of former regional differences by a mixture of economic inequality and contrived variety.

It is the inequality that most concerns David Harvey. In his book *Justice, Nature, and the Geography of Difference,* he argues for the need to transcend the competing discourses and deconstructionist theories of postmodernity in order to consider "the just production of just geographical differences." Postmodernism for him is either the handmaiden or the product of global capital. Harvey argues that Marxism and socialism, in spite of their weakened credibility following the collapse of the Soviet empire, still offer the best possibility for confronting capitalism and therefore for addressing postmodernism. He is, however, careful to stress that old experiences should not be reused uncritically, and we "cannot trust in dead dreams resurrected from the past." Historical materialism has to be critically reconstructed and selectively used to provide the foundations for "a political commitment to feed, nourish, clothe and sustain the poor and the weak" and to imagine "possible urban worlds" in which geographical differences would be just differences. Achieving this will not be easy. "It will," he declares in language that blends socialist manifesto with phenomenological insight, "take imagination and political guts, a surge of revolutionary fervor and revolutionary change (in thinking as well as in politics) to construct a requisite poetics of understanding for our urbanizing world, a charter for civilization, a trajectory for our species being, out of the raw material of the present."[27]

This is a clarion call. Given everything I have claimed about the depths of postmodern confusion and current social injustice I have to agree with its thrust even if I question its details. There is a pronounced political aspect to postmodernity that demands a political as well as an intellectual solution. At the same time I find that I am apprehensive that historical materialism draws so heavily on economics. I find it difficult to grasp how the undesirable consequences of one type of economics (capitalist) can be corrected by the application of a different type of economics (socialist), both with origins in the universalist principles of eighteenth-century rationalism that have been undermined in postmodernity. I acknowledge that economics is an important aspect of social existence, but in the possible and pleasing worlds that I imagine it is not a primary or determining factor. In the 1860s John Ruskin took a stand against the utilitarian economists of his time because he found them to be excessively consumed by notions of wealth and to have nothing of substance to say about happiness, justice, truth, or beauty. The power of his criticism is scarcely diminished. In capital letters he exclaimed, "THERE IS NO WEALTH BUT LIFE. Life, including all its powers of love, of joy, and of admiration."[28]

Critical Description

I suppose it is symptomatic of what Terry Eagleton calls "the appalling mess that is the contemporary world"[29] that there can be three contradictory suggestions about how to deal with it and that there are good grounds for agreeing and disagreeing with each of them. One of the reasons for my apparently paradoxical reactions lies, I think, in the fact that arguments based on opposites such as local-global or socialist-capitalist do not map well onto the postmodern world.[30] I know it is fashionable to refer to the local and the global as though these are clearly defined and opposing forces, so localities can resist the forces of globalization in order to preserve their identities, or globalization can rescue places from backwardness. This is simplistic. Even brief observation of specific places will suffice to show that these are vague abstractions; things local and those with remote origins intersect in countless subtle ways.

The world continually outruns theories and descriptions of it, and in the twentieth and twenty-first centuries the pace of social and technological change has created a sort of theoretical vacuum that is now filling with simple concepts that are not always well connected with the everyday world. If they are not to be misleading, attempts to clarify these concepts have to occur in concert with descriptions that are responsive to the perplexities of postmodernity. I suggest four strategies to accomplish this. First, accounts must be grounded in the subtleties of everyday places and specific situations. Second, there is a need to maintain a critical historical perspective. Third, given the breadth of deception in postmodern landscapes it is essential to question appearances. And fourth, it is necessary to argue forcefully for balance and for practical wisdom that can address the injustices of the present age.

This critical way of description therefore aims to be empirical, local, historical, skeptical, and reasonable. It is "critical" in the sense that in making descriptions we need always to be as aware as possible of our motives and biases and how we might be imposing those. But it does not and cannot overcome the logical difficulty at the root of postmodernism that the world is contingent and there is no best way to account for it. Instead it adopts the pragmatic view that at some point it is necessary to take actions and these should be thoughtful, careful, and considerate of others. From those actions, in due course, some epistemological clarification may emerge.

The Complexity of Everyday Landscapes

The section of Yonge Street near where I live in Toronto is part of one of the oldest roads in Ontario, and a few banners from a celebration held a couple of years ago announce that it is "200 Years Yonge." Though the road is older, this part of the city was developed as a streetcar suburb in the first decades of the twentieth century; the surrounding streets are lined with mature maple trees and tastefully renovated houses, many of them occupied by professional couples working for financial and engineering companies in the city core. Yonge Street itself is mostly lined with undistinguished two story, brick commercial blocks, divided into small stores. I know of four or five stores owned by families who have lived in the neighborhood for sixty or seventy years, but most have changed hands in the last decade. There are several Italian restaurants, a sushi bar, a pseudo-English pub called "The Sailor's Dickey," some international coffee bars including Starbucks, a number of convenience stores run mostly by Koreans or Filipinos, four travel agencies plus a specialized Australian travel center, and a small park to mark the boundary of what used to be the City of Toronto. In 1997 the provincial government mandated a change in municipal boundaries and also imposed a change in property taxation that is intended to correct an inequity between the overtaxed outer suburbs and the supposedly undertaxed areas of the old city. On the morning I was leaving to present a version of this essay at a conference in Boston, the local store owners closed Yonge Street to traffic in a protest against the injustice of this tax reform; many of them could have property taxes raised by five or six times and may be driven out of business.

This fragment of Toronto is at once unique and unexceptional. Similar complexities exist in urban streets everywhere. My point in listing some of its features is simply to demonstrate that concepts such as local and global, tradition and cosmopolitanism, justice and injustice, when they are considered in actual places, are murky and elusive. They are always interwoven and often ambiguous. It is the warp and woof of the interweaving that is apparent, not the opposition of theoretical entities. Here it is clear that a policy to correct one injustice can generate a different injustice; local stores are run by people from all over the world while restaurants serve foods from around the globe; and the residents who work in international finance and employ nannies from the Philippines are creating a local version of the international division of labor. Here cosmopolitanism and global culture are integrated into daily local life.

This, then, is the first principle of critical description — that theoretical constructs of postmodernism should be tested against the complexities of specific situations. Our world has been shrunk by air travel and mixed up by migration. Differences of race, culture, and religion that were once geographically separate are now piled against one another. Neat theoretical distinctions made on the basis of obsolete assumptions about geography have little to offer as guides to these landscapes, so in confronting heterotopia I choose not to choose *between* the approaches of the cosmopolite, the localist, and the socialist but rather to choose *from* them whatever ideas offer some promise of clarity.

A Historical Perspective; or, Recuperating from Modernity

In spite of their other differences, Tuan, Edwards, and Harvey concur that a historical perspective is essential in attempting to overcome the confusions of postmodernism. They also are clear that historical experience has to be considered critically — in other words the lessons of the past should not be mindlessly applied to the postmodern present. This second principle of critical description ought to be uncontroversial, not least because the landscapes of the 1990s borrow so heavily from history, for instance in architecture and New Urbanist planning, and therefore cannot be understood even in a trivial way without some grasp of historical precedent. However, it is precisely because so much of this borrowing involves casual cutting and pasting from different traditions that a critical appreciation of history is warranted. By this I do not intend to advocate some historical purism, only to suggest that the absence of historical knowledge necessarily leads to superficial understanding. Since postmodern landscapes also borrow freely from landscapes and traditions around the world, a similar argument can be made for the importance of a critical geographical perspective.

There is a different reason why a historical perspective is essential in postmodernity. In the modernist perspective time is understood as a linear progression. Gianni Vattimo writes of this as persistent overcoming, in which "the new rapidly grows old and is immediately replaced by something still newer in an unstoppable movement."[31] His view, based on his interpretation of Nietzsche and Heidegger, is that this is like an addiction — ever more progress is needed to correct the problems created by progress. As an addiction it has become part of consciousness and cannot be easily replaced by some more moderate view, nor neatly sidestepped or forgotten. It has to be faced up to. Vattimo argues that the narrow illusions of this view of time and history first have to be exposed; then we have to try to recuperate from them, as though from a sickness, and to take responsibility for the social and environmental consequences of actions and ideas. A critical historical perspective is an essential part of this recuperation both because it clarifies how this situation emerged and because recuperation from an addiction to constant progress that depends on original solutions would obviously be self-defeating.

Questioning Appearances

The Biodome in Montreal contains scientific displays of ecosystems from around the world. In the tropical section there are huge trees — possibly ceibas, the great sacred tree of the Mayans — growing right next to the path. How did these grow here? The Biodome is in a renovated cycling stadium built for the Montreal Olympics in 1976. As if to test their doubts visitors have reached out to touch the trees so frequently that the surface has worn away and bits of fiberglass core can be seen glowing orange and cream. If they looked up they would have seen that the tree trunk has a ventilation grill and stops abruptly at the ceiling; this is not a tree at all, but a heating and ventilation device.

The construction of landscapes and buildings that deceive has a long history. In the postmodern world deceptions have intensified because new technologies have made fakery easy and because there are now entire industries intent upon turning cities into theme parks and citizens into audiences.[32] If we do not want to be duped by landscapes, it is essential to touch the trees, to look behind ornate brick facades to see if they are no more than a skin over concrete blocks, and to examine the picket fences in neotraditional developments to find out whether they are made of plastic.[33] Even more fundamental than these are the deceptions associated with remote production and remote control, especially those of powerful institutions and corporations that masquerade as being sensitive to local circumstances. Elegant facades for stores and glossy advertisements belie the harsh realities of chemical pollution or exploited employees in some far-off country. In a world of cosmetic surgery and contrived identities it would be naive indeed not to be skeptical about appearances.

Jacques Ellul writes that efforts to make things seem what they are not constitute a form of "propaganda."[34] They are associated with the exercise of power and the need to hide something, and if we are unaware of propaganda we become pawns in somebody else's game. "Doubt," John Ralston Saul has written, "is the only human activity capable of controlling power in a positive way. Doubt is central to understanding."[35] By power, Saul means political and corporate hegemonies, arrogance, domination, and self-righteousness. To doubt is to contemplate and weigh carefully the actions and accomplishments, including the landscapes, of others and to bring their claims for authority into question. Doubt is an essential part of the critical description of the postmodern world.

On the other hand, relentless doubt can lead to cynicism and turn the world into a bitter and ugly place. Tuan warns that critical probing is not always advisable, that behind every face there is a skull.[36] This is a valuable caution, for it reminds us that the surface is as significant as what lies behind it; skin and skeleton are both essential even though we usually notice faces and not skulls. The relationships between surface appearances and hidden structures are often complex and can only be grasped through careful observation and reflection.[37] The purpose of doubt is not to dismiss surface appearance but to avoid being deceived. From this point of view a well-executed deception may even warrant admiration. Ruskin wrote that "there is no action so slight nor so mean" that it may not be considered "well or truly done."[38] It requires a high level of skill to paint stucco to appear like marble and considerable imagination to design a themed casino-hotel in Las Vegas that looks like an Egyptian pyramid. It is always well to remember that these are the work of individuals who take pride in their work and whose work is widely appreciated and enjoyed. It is also well to question the ends for which those skills are used.

Forceful Balance and Practical Wisdom

A difficulty faced by postmodern critical description, one alluded to by Harvey, is that fundamentalism and corporatism have their own strong arguments for what is good and right and just. A description is an *account* of something, and, to take the literal meaning of that word, it therefore attributes responsibilities. Any accounts of the postmodern world that hope to change current practice have to be made forcefully in order to challenge these strong arguments. Yet, if they are not to exacerbate the excesses they describe and criticize, they must also be moderate and balanced.

What I mean here by *balance* is the humanist virtue that involves acceptance of contradiction, change, and difference. From this perspective the world is approached as a series of complex tensions and interactions rather than simple oppositions. Balance manifest as tolerance is necessary for the maintenance of a civil society, and balance manifest as thoughtfulness is needed to ensure that the details of specific lives in specific places are not forgotten in the rush to make profits. Balance requires time and care; it embraces uncertainty, common sense, imagination, creativity, memory, and experience. It has no definite goal or master plan but rather is a way of continually accommodating change. "The question," Saul proposes, "is not whether we could ever achieve a humanist equilibrium, but whether we are attempting to achieve it."[39]

Ideas of balance and moderation have a long and distinguished history. For instance, in *The Nichomachean Ethics* Aristotle argued that excellence is to be found through pursuing the intermediate way, the way that avoids excess.[40] He gave numerous cases to support his view: drink or food that is above or below a certain point destroys the health; in a work of art excellence is to be found when one can neither add to it nor take away from it; bravery lies between foolhardiness and cowardice.[41] Aristotle maintained that the good life based in moderation and balance could be achieved through what he called practical wisdom. This form of knowledge applies for things human and things that are changeable (as opposed to knowledge of universals, such as those of mathematics) and is concerned with particulars and a sense of judgment about appropriate actions. "Practical wisdom," he proposed, "is the quality of mind concerned with things just and noble and good."[42] Balance provides a standard by which to judge the world; practical wisdom is the means by which we can hope to attain that standard.

It is helpful here to recall Harvey's caution that dead dreams cannot be resurrected from the past. Social and political contexts are changeable; our world bears scant resemblance to the Athens of Aristotle. Nevertheless, it is important to know that ideas of moderation, balance, and practical wisdom have endured for more than two millennia.[43] They have adapted and changed and persisted through many epistemological and political upheavals. They are valuable in working through the peculiar confusions and injustices of post-modernity. However, it should be remembered that the history of moderate views being brushed aside or suppressed is equally long. Saul, from whom I have adapted several of these ideas about balance, suggests that it is easier to believe in absolutes and regurgitate received ideas than to strive for equilibrium and moderation. It is necessary to argue forcefully, tenaciously, and repeatedly for balance and moderation because these are qualities of mind and behavior that can be easily lost or taken away.

I have written elsewhere about a method that is responsive to the qualities of landscapes and places.[44] The three elements of this method are unprejudiced observation, reflective thought, and careful description, or more briefly, seeing, thinking, and describing. This essay has suggested revisions and qualifications to that method, mostly by suggesting what has to be achieved in description so that it can come to terms with the complexities associated with postmodernity. In particular I think these descriptions have to be grounded in everyday land-scapes, expose deceptions, use a critical historical perspective, and adopt a standard of balance and moderation.

It is easy to propose critical description. It is less easy to accomplish. In accounts of actual places the old oppositions of local and global, tradition and progress, natural and artificial, will try to reassert themselves because they are so deeply engrained in thought and language. To counter this tendency it is necessary to be vigilant about our own values so we do not impose them unwittingly, and that is difficult. Furthermore, it is probable that the various fundamentalisms of religion, global economic growth, and relentless technological innovation will persist and that the social and environmental problems attendant upon these will worsen. The critical description of landscapes offers no handbook solutions to these problems and no grand theories of social change. What it does do is to attend to the landscape evidence of what is happening around us, and this can help to clear a path through the confusing underbrush of postmodernity that leads toward geographies that are more just than those that now prevail.

Notes

1. Terry Eagleton, *The Illusions of Postmodernism* (Oxford: Blackwell, 1996), ix.
2. Italo Calvino, *If on a Winter's Night a Traveller...* (Toronto: Lester and Orpen Dennys, 1981), 256–57.
3. Yi-Fu Tuan, "Surface Phenomena and Aesthetic Experience," *Annals of the Association of American Geographers* 79, no. 2 (1989): 233–41.
4. Michel Foucault, *The Order of Things* (London: Tavistock, 1970), xv, xvii.
5. Eagleton, *Illusions of Postmodernism*, vii.
6. Richard Rorty, *Philosophy and the Mirror of Nature* (Princeton, N.J.: Princeton University Press, 1979). Rorty is a philosopher of science, and my interpretation of his writing is that he would prefer not to advance the case for the lack of a firm foundation for scientific method, but he finds the logic that leads to this position unavoidable.
7. Eagleton, *Illusions of Postmodernism*, 121.
8. Gianni Vattimo, *The End of Modernity* (Baltimore: Johns Hopkins University Press, 1988).
9. The term *heterotopia* is used elsewhere by Foucault ("Of Other Spaces," *Diacritics* [1986]: 16, 22–27) in a more specific sense to mean somewhere or something that imaginatively contains many other places and therefore stands apart from them; a ship is a heterotopia par excellence. It is used in this sense by Ed Soja in *Thirdspace* (Oxford: Blackwell, 1996), chap. 5, 145–63. I think this is a less rich meaning than that of heterotopia as the juxtaposition of many spaces and places, without logic or geometry, because it is really little more than a secular reworking of familiar notions of sacred places that stand apart from profane space.
10. Paul Virilio, *Open Sky* (London: Verso, 1997), 56.
11. Ibid., 144.
12. Eagleton, *Illusions of Postmodernism*, 133.
13. David Harvey, *The Condition of Postmodernity* (Oxford: Blackwell, 1989).
14. John Ralston Saul, *The Unconscious Civilization* (Toronto: Anansi, 1995), 86 and throughout.
15. United Nations, Research Institute for Social Development, *States of Disarray: The Social Effects of Globalization* (New York: United Nations, 1995), 24. This and numerous other systemic problems of similar severity are discussed in, for example, Jerry Mander and Edward Goldsmith, eds., *The Case against the Global Economy* (San Francisco: Sierra Club Books, 1996); and William Greider, *One World, Ready or Not: The Manic Logic of Global Capitalism* (New York: Simon and Schuster, 1997).
16. Robert Reich, *The Work of Nations* (New York: Alfred Knopf, 1991), 282 and throughout; Mark Kingwell, *Dreams of Millennium* (Toronto: Viking Penguin, 1996), 101, suggests that the gap between rich and poor is now greater than at any time since the Middle Ages. See also the polemical account — by a former adviser to François Mitterand — of a possible future if this gap is not closed: Jacques Attali, *Millennium: Winners and Losers in the New World Order* (New York: Times Books, Random House, 1990).
17. Robert Kaplan, "The Coming Anarchy," *Atlantic Monthly,* May 1994; Thomas

Homer-Dixon, "On the Threshold: Environmental Changes as Causes of Acute Conflict," *International Security* 16, no. 2 (1991): 76–116.

18. Eric Hobsbawm, *The Age of Extremes: A History of the World 1914–91* (New York: Pantheon, 1994), 558.

19. Eagleton, *Illusions of Postmodernism,* 134.

20. Ernest Gellner, *Postmodernism, Reason, and Religion* (London: Routledge, 1992); Jürgen Habermas, *The New Conservatism* (Cambridge, Mass.: MIT Press, 1989).

21. Richard Rorty, *Contingency, Irony, Solidarity* (New York: Cambridge University Press, 1989).

22. Wolfgang Sachs, ed., *The Development Dictionary* (London: Zed Books, 1992); see especially Sachs's entry titled "One World"; see also Serge LaTouche, *In the Wake of the Affluent Society: An Exploration of Post-Development* (London: Zed Books, 1993).

23. Yi-Fu Tuan, *Cosmos and Hearth: A Cosmopolite's Viewpoint* (Minneapolis: University of Minnesota Press, 1996), 134, 179, 184, 187.

24. James C. Edwards, *Ethics without Philosophy: Wittgenstein and the Moral Life* (Tampa: University Presses of Florida, 1985), 225, 243.

25. Michael Ignatieff, *Blood and Belonging* (Toronto: Viking Penguin, 1993), 189.

26. Tuan, *Cosmos and Hearth,* 179.

27. David Harvey, *Justice, Nature, and the Geography of Difference* (Oxford: Blackwell, 1996), 6, 438, 5, 403ff., 438.

28. John Ruskin, *Unto This Last* (London: J. M. Dent 1907), 185. The original essay was published in *Cornhill Magazine* in 1860; this famous quotation is from the chapter "Ad Valorem."

29. Eagleton, *Illusions of Postmodernism,* ix.

30. The summaries I have made of the arguments of Harvey, Tuan, and Edwards do not, of course, do justice to their subtleties and complexities. I acknowledge that I am, in part, using these three books somewhat unfairly to represent what I believe is a widespread and simplistic type of argument through opposing concepts.

31. Vattimo, *End of Modernity,* 1988, 166.

32. Michael Sorkin, ed., *Variations on a Theme Park* (New York: Noonday Press, 1992).

33. The neotraditional town of Cornell, near Toronto; Andres Duany and Elizabeth Plater-Zyberk were consultants.

34. Jacques Ellul, *Propaganda* (New York: Alfred Knopf, 1965).

35. John Ralston Saul, *The Doubter's Companion: A Dictionary of Aggressive Common Sense* (Toronto: Viking Penguin, 1995), 109.

36. Tuan, "Surface Phenomena," 237.

37. This is excellently demonstrated in the seminal work by Clifford Geertz, "Deep Play: Notes on the Balinese Cockfight," in *The Interpretation of Cultures* (New York: Basic Books, 1973), 412–53, in which he shows that rituals of the cockfight have to be understood at many levels of significance, none of which substitutes for the others.

38. John Ruskin, *The Seven Lamps of Architecture* (London: J. M. Dent, 1907), 5.

39. Saul, *Doubter's Companion,* 167.

40. Aristotle, *Nichomachean Ethics,* in *The Complete Works of Aristotle,* ed. Jonathan Barnes, vol. 2 (Princeton, N.J.: Princeton University Press, 1984), 1106b27; see esp. books 5 and 6.

41. These examples are respectively from ibid., 1103a15, 1106b14, and 1108b.

42. Ibid., 1141b8, 1143a26ff, 1143b21.

43. Ideas of moderation and balance are to be found, for example, in Buddhism and in several Chinese philosophies such as the Doctrine of the Mean. In recent Western thought, as it might relate to landscape, I find that Ruskin, Thoreau, Kropotkin, and Geddes implicitly or explicitly argued for balance.

44. Edward Relph, "Seeing, Thinking, and Describing Landscapes," in *Environmental Perception and Behavior,* ed. T. Saarinen, D. Seamon, and J. Sell, Research Paper 209 (Chicago: Department of Geography, University of Chicago, 1984, 209–23).

MAKING UP THE TRAMP

Toward a Critical Geosophy

Tim Cresswell

It is well known that visionary geographer John Kirkland Wright called for a geography of knowledge, which he called geosophy — an understanding of the way in which people knew the world.[1] Geographers, he told us, would benefit from an engagement with the knowledges of sailors, farmers, travelers, and all manner of other people. I want to take this opportunity to extend the project of geosophy and examine how some ways of knowing have had particularly powerful effects on the objects of knowledge. In this essay I apply my own thoughts on a geography of knowledge to the definition of tramps and hobos in turn-of-the-century America and the ways in which they were made up, counted, tabulated, and categorized. There are three main theses I will pursue:

1. That the tramp was "made up" in the United States during the period 1870–1940.

2. That forms of knowledge that claimed to be *about* the tramp actually served to bring the tramp into existence.

3. That these forms of knowledge were themselves informed by a particular *geographical* imagination about the meanings of mobility.

One expression that appears to neatly summarize the perspective I use here is *social construction*. But to simply claim that the tramp and the mobility of the tramp were socially produced is, to me, banal. Human mobility, however it is embodied, could never be anything other than social. What is interesting is how particular social constructions, which are implicated in relations of power, come to be formed and how, in turn, they interact with the objects of knowledge. In the case of the tramp I am interested in how knowledges come to interact with people called tramps and with larger ideas about what is "normal" and what is "pathological" in human geographical behavior.

I am informed here by the Canadian philosopher Ian Hacking. Hacking has suggested a framework for thinking about the construction of individuals and social types. He distinguishes between a realist, a nominalist, and a dynamic nominalist perspective. A realist argument, he suggests, rests on the assumption that conditions, categories, and types exist in the world waiting to be patiently discovered and analyzed. People come presorted:

Some are thick, some thin, some dead, some alive. It may be a fact about human beings that we notice who is fat and who is dead, but the fact itself that some of our fellows are fat and others are dead has nothing to do with our schemes of classification.[2]

Similarly the realist will argue that stable human dichotomies such as male and female are simply facts to be noticed and discussed, but not invented. There may be some individuals such as "hermaphrodites" to complicate the issue, but gender and sex are almost identical and real distinctions. Nominalists, on the other hand, believe in nothing but invention — all we have are names. Hobbes's question, "How can any man imagine that the names of things were imposed by their natures?" succinctly makes the nominalist's case. Following Hobbes, the nominalist believes that all classifications, categories, and names are human creations, not "natural" ones, and that once invented, they hang around and have effects.

Hacking invents a third position he calls "dynamic nominalism," which insists that kinds of people "come into being at the same time as the kind itself was being invented."[3] In this respect human types are like manufactured objects such as gloves and not like other things such as horses. While horses exist before our thinking about them and it would be strange to think that the only thing all horses have in common is that we call them horses, a glove can only be seen to exist hand in hand with the observation that we made it. The category "glove" and the thing "glove" emerged more or less simultaneously. Hacking's argument, then, is that categories and the people "in" them emerge together. We could extend this claim to most forms of knowledge about humanity — human action is often dependent upon and created by the things we describe it as. As Hacking states: "if new models of description come into being, new possibilities for action come into being in consequence."[4] Hacking's argument is very much in line with Roy D'Andrade when he states that

> Probably every cultural category "creates" an entity in the sense that what is understood to be out there is affected by the culturally based associations built into the category system.... The cultural categories of marriage, money, theft, are created solely by adherence to the constitutive rule systems that define them. Without these rule systems these objects would not exist.[5]

Much the same could be said of vagrancy and the tramp. Tramps, as we shall see, were the product of systems of rules and codes created by sociologists, lawmakers, and others. Tramps, in this sense if no other, were more like gloves than horses. The implication of Hacking's argument is that individuals (as members of social groups) have new possibilities — new potential ways of being — when new categories are invented. Some time during the 1870s in the United States it became possible to be a tramp.

In the remainder of this essay I sketch some of the ways in which tramps were "made up" in the United States in the years following 1870. There are many kinds of knowledge involved in the making up of the tramp. Here I focus on definitions of tramps, legal discussions of tramps, and the way in which the tramp was subjected to the knowledge of early sociology and eugenics. In each case there is a clear moral geographical imagination of mobility involved.

Definitions

Every student knows that one of the most basic forms of knowledge is the definition. Definitions are supposed to make things clear, to provide exactness and precision, to mitigate against vagueness and ambiguity. The connected word *definitive* also denotes authority — the definitive text. The definition of the tramp then is a supposedly precise and authoritative marker that tells us who we are talking about when we are talking about tramps.

The definition of what constitutes a tramp, though, is hardly the clear and distinct image that the word suggests. One of the first uses of the word *tramp* as a noun appeared in the *New York Times* in February 1875 and was used to describe the homeless unemployed.[6] While such people had previously been referred to as vagrants, the use of the word *tramp* had not been common.[7] It was in the period following the crash of 1873 that *tramp* became part of common usage in the United States. The most famous and often repeated (formal) definition is said to originate from the work of Chicago anarchist and tramp Ben Reitman. Reitman claimed that the general condition of vagrancy is divided into three main classes: bums, tramps, and hobos. "A tramp is a man who doesn't work, who apparently doesn't want to work, who lives without working and who is constantly travelling. A hobo is a non-skilled, non-employed labourer without money, looking for work. A bum is a man who hangs around a low class saloon and begs or earns a few pennies a day in order to obtain drink. He is usually an inebriate."[8] This definition was a more elaborate version of that used by men on the road and repeated in a number of contemporary accounts: the hobo was a migratory worker, the tramp a migratory nonworker, and the bum a nonmigratory nonworker. Nels Anderson, the noted sociologist of tramp and hobo life, referred to several variations on this theme from a number of sources. Nicholas Klein, president of the hobo college in Chicago, for instance, wrote the following:

> A hobo is one who travels in search of work, the migratory worker who must go about to find employment.... The name originated from the words *hoe-boy* plainly derived from work on the farm. A tramp is one who travels but does not work, and a bum is a man who stays in one place and does not work. Between these grades there is a great gulf of social distinction. Don't get tramps and hobos mixed. They are quite

different in many respects. The chief difference being that the hobo will work and the tramp will not, preferring to live on what he can pick up at back doors as he makes his way through the country.[9]

Such subtle differences were often lost on outside observers who took anyone riding a freight train to be a tramp and dealt with him accordingly. Similarly, texts concerning tramps often slip between the words *tramp* and *hobo* for no apparent reason.

If there were no people called tramps before the 1870s, then there were no tramps. The act of definition is a foundational moment in the making up of a social type. I do not mean by this that tramps were simply fabricated. I mean that both the meaning and the materiality of the life of people who came to be called tramps changed when the word *tramp* and its meanings started to be used. A new model of description came into being, and new possibilities for action arose as a consequence. These working definitions of the tramp were combined with the geographical fact of mobility and ideas about work to differentiate between those mobilities that were to be applauded and those mobilities that were suspect.

Definitions in Law

In case anyone is wondering whether arguments over definitions are merely semantic, consider the way in which definitions become reified in law. It is important to make this point because, as we shall see, the general definition of the tramp that emerged in the 1870s quickly became part of the legal fabric of nineteen states and, as such, had starkly real effects on the lives of those so defined. Once tramps have been made up they can be acted upon, argued over, confined, made to work on log piles, and disenfranchised. Again arguments over mobility are key.

In 1876, seven years after the completion of the transcontinental railroad, the first of many state "Tramp Laws" was passed in New Jersey. A tramp was defined as an idle person without employment, a transient person who roamed from place to place, and who had no lawful occasion to wander.[10] Tramp laws were not the first laws at the state level to intervene in the lives of the mobile unemployed. Indeed vagrancy laws had been on the books of most states since their inception. For the most part these had been borrowed wholesale from Great Britain, which had a long history of antivagrancy laws.[11] As A. L. Beier has noted, the legal concept of vagabondage originated in England in the long-standing distinction between the able-bodied and the non-able-bodied poor. As early as the fourteenth century the British Parliament had made it an offense to have no master (and thus no "place").

It was a combination of the British 1824 Vagrancy Act and earlier vagrancy acts that formed the basis for most state vagrancy laws in the United States before 1876. The legal definition of vagrancy (and later tramphood) hinges on both geography — the lack of home — and work. In addition, vagrancy laws typically specified three further characteristics of vagrants — that they were able-bodied, poor, and potentially dangerous. As Beier remarks in relation to early English vagrancy laws, the underlying fear was that of a generalized form of disorder that threatened the ruling elites.

The history of vagrancy law in the United States reflects the variety of European and particularly English vagrancy law. Vagrancy laws in colonial America were used as tools to deal with perceived moral threats to small and isolated communities. As Adler has argued, "drifters challenged both the moral character of small-town society and the delicate web of mutual obligation that provided relief for the poor in country settings."[12] The problem of vagrancy was, for the most part, a local, or at most regional, problem. Local institutions were obliged to look after their own poor but not the poor from somewhere else. During the nineteenth century vagrancy laws were increasingly used to counter the threat of an industrial poor who would gather in nearby cities during economic downturns hoping for relief. As they increased in number and visibility vagrants were increasingly seen as a threat to social order and moral standards, and vagrancy law was used to attempt to disperse the perceived threat. Vagrancy laws were very broadly written and used to apprehend a diverse array of potential troublemakers. Often American vagrancy laws, like British ones before them, included many different types of offenders against society including vagabonds, wanderers, rogues, prostitutes, pimps, gamblers, and people who refused to work for wages. Some laws were explicitly referred to as vagabond laws and were marginally more specific than vagrancy laws. Illinois's vagabond laws of 1874 defined vagabonds as "idle and dissolute persons who went about and begged, runaways, pilferers, drunkards, night-walkers, lewd people, wanton and lascivious persons, railers and brawlers, persons without a calling or profession, visitors of tippling houses and houses of ill-fame, and wanderers."[13]

The question arises as to why nineteen states found it necessary in the ten years following 1876 to rewrite their established vagrancy laws as "tramp laws." No law explicitly defined tramps until New Jersey's law of 1876, which was little changed from earlier vagrancy laws on both sides of the Atlantic.[14] Attempts to differentiate tramps from vagrants were occasionally made in court. In *Des Moines v Polk County* in 1899 the court held that tramps were a division of the genus vagrant, which included the usual range of "worthless and wandering people."[15] In an Ohio Supreme Court review of an appeal against a tramp law conviction, the judgment clearly illustrates the role of specific categorization in the legislation enacted against tramps:

Speaking of the class, the genus tramp, in this country, is a public enemy. He is numerous and he is dangerous. He is a nomad, wanderer on the face of the earth, with his hand against every honest man, woman and child in so far as they do not, promptly and fully, supply his demands. He is a thief, a robber, often a murderer, and always a nuisance. . . . It will not be understood that there may not be differences in tramps. There may be. Some may be less worthless and vicious than others; but all pirates are not alike brutal and bloody. . . . Is there not sufficient difference between the condition . . . of a pauper in his own country, and the same character abroad, and between the situation of the people of the country where the pauper resides and those of distinct neighbourhoods, to warrant a legal distinction? . . . In short, tramping makes a different class of the same person. And why may they not, when thus grouped, be regarded as a class?[16]

Here the judges are attempting to justify the legal definition of tramp. Their argument is that there is, in fact, a difference between paupers who are local and those who travel that warrants different treatments under the law. "The objection that the act prescribes a cruel and unusual punishment we think not well taken. Imprisonment at hard labor is neither cruel or unusual."[17]

Key to this differentiation between tramps and other vagrants and paupers was a specifically geographical factor — that of mobility. The first transcontinental railroad had been completed in 1869, and this made it possible for unemployed migrants to travel much greater differences in a much shorter time. The new technologies of modernity — so connected in American myth to democracy and the story of Manifest Destiny — also created new forms of deviance and new repressions. As the Massachusetts assistant relief officer stated in 1900 with reference to the tramp:

No one will deny that he is one of very latest fruits of civilisation so far as our own state is concerned. . . . Various causes contributed to this change. Among them is the great increase in the facility of cheap travel, by which a man may come from the centre of Russia for less that it cost our grandfathers to travel to New York.[18]

The well-known tramp turned investigator, Josiah Flynt, was asked by the Pennsylvania Railroad to undertake a kind of ethnographic investigation of tramp life on the railroad in order to ascertain the extent of the tramp "problem." It was Flynt's view that the tramp was the product of the Civil War. Demobbed soldiers had become used to life on the road, including the railroad, and had simply continued to live in the manner to which they had become accustomed. By 1875, he claimed, ten thousand tramps would ride for free every night on the railroads of the United States.

The railroads spread the tramp nuisance over a much greater stretch of territory than would be the case if the tramps were limited to turnpikes. As matters now stand, however, you may see a beggar one day on fifth avenue in New York City, and a fortnight later he will accost you in Market Street in San Francisco.[19]

Making the connection between tramps and long-distance mobility explicit, the vagrancy law of Massachusetts made riding a freight prima facie evidence of tramphood.

Most states went to great lengths to precisely define who counted as a tramp. Chapter 159 of the 1902 general statutes of Connecticut, for instance, states that "All transient persons who rove about from place to place begging, and all vagrants, living without labor or visible means of support, who stroll over the country without lawful occasion, shall be deemed tramps."[20] Section 1337 makes the link with excessive mobility explicit by stating that "Any act of begging, or vagrancy, by any person not a resident of this state, shall be *prima facie* evidence that such a person is a tramp." Finally, section 1341 points out that "These provisions shall not apply to any female, or minor under the age of 16 years, nor to any blind person, nor to any beggar roving within the limits of the town in which he resides."[21] Technically and interestingly, the tramp laws of Connecticut excluded women, children, blind people, and local vagrants, who legally could not be tramps. Punishment for convicted tramps varied from ninety days of hard labor in New Mexico to being sold into servitude for up to a year in Kentucky. In Missouri, the tramp could be hired out to the highest bidder with cash in hand. Tramps were usually released with no provision for the future, thus making them liable to be immediately rearrested on the same charges. New York's Tramp Act was passed in 1879 immediately following the depression of 1877. It was further strengthened in 1885 following the 1884 depression. Significantly, the Tramp Act transformed what were misdemeanors when committed by most people into felonies when committed by tramps. The immediate material effect of this distinction was to prescribe considerably harsher penalties for the traveling unemployed, who could be sentenced to up to three years of hard labor.[22] Being defined as a tramp clearly had severe consequences.

As law, the tramp laws were clearly contestable in court. It is not that surprising, however, that this rarely happened. As one Maryland judge noted, "if these vagabonds do not think the tramp law is constitutional let them raise the fund and carry their case to the appellate."[23] The tramp was not completely without support. A prominent supporter of the rights of tramps, Governor Lewelling of Kansas, reacted to the "tramp evil" by issuing a circular (which became known as the Tramp Circular) to his police chiefs suggesting they be lenient on tramps in the state. Lewelling maintained that "the right to go freely from place to place in search of employment, or even in obedience of a mere whim, is a part of that personal liberty guaranteed by the constitution of the United States to every human being on American soil. Even voluntary idleness is not forbidden."[24] This defense of tramps was subjected to ridicule by newspapers in Kansas and around the United States. Newspapers accused Lewelling of consorting with anarchists and communists and raising the potential of tramps flooding into Kansas from other states.

A contemporary observer, Elbert Hubbard, supported Lewelling and satirized the tramp laws that were being formulated around the country. He pointed out that the tramp laws were rooted in English common law designed centuries earlier to suppress vagrancy. Section 1 of the Vagrancy Act of Kansas read:

> All beggars and vagabonds who roam about from place to place without any lawful occupation, sleeping in barns, sheds, outhouses or in the open air, not giving a good account of themselves, and all persons roaming about commonly known as gypsies, shall be deemed vagrants and be liable to the penalties of the act.[25]

The penalty for those found guilty of vagrancy was imprisonment in jail or hard labor not to exceed sixty days. On release the person could be rearrested immediately for the same crime. If a person wished to contest the sentencing he was entitled to redress by jury after paying a bond of approximately five hundred dollars. Hubbard found the whole process ridiculous:

> Beside not being able to "give an account of himself," if it can be proven that he "slept in the open air" the night before his arrest, and that, being hungry, he asked for food, both counts are construed against him as a proof of his guilt. The state legally regards him as a criminal, and being such, the state has the right to confiscate his labor. The taking of food by force to satisfy the demands of hunger is not a crime, but the asking for food is. Hunger in the United States of America, is crime.[26]

And further:

> In this country we say every man is assumed to be innocent until he be proven guilty. *This applies only to men who have money.* No peaceable decent man with money is asked to "give an account of himself." But let him have no place to lay his head, and ask for a cup of cold water, immediately we may legally assume his guilt and drag him before the notary, who shall demand that he "give a satisfactory account of himself." Satisfactory to whom forsooth?[27]

Unusually for the time, Hubbard argued that tramps were a symptom of economic downturns and legal formulations. He pointed toward the economic downturn of 1873 as a reason for the wandering tramps, alongside seasonal agricultural work in states such as Delaware. In that state, he argued, migrants would arrive to work during the fruit season and offer to work for lower wages than Delaware workers. As a result of this, Delaware introduced a tramp law in 1879. Section 1 of this law defined a tramp as "Any person without a home in the town in which he may be found wandering about without employment."[28] A person no longer had to beg, sleep in the open air, or have no money to be convicted. So a person who did not beg, was seeking work, and carried a little money could now be arrested, found guilty of being a tramp, and sent to work for up to thirty days. In other words, just to have no home and seek employment was a crime. "A tramp may be a criminal and he may not," Hubbard wrote. "If he is a criminal punish him for his crimes, but do not punish him for being a tramp; to do this may be only to chastise him for his misfortunes."[29] Lewelling's circular, in Hubbard's view, was a bold and noble refusal to create a whole class of criminals out of people who had already been subjected to great misfortune.

The voice of Lewelling was a voice in the wilderness as tramp laws were created across the states. The tramp laws, as we have seen, were far more than simple definitions. As legal discourse they had very material effects on those defined as tramps. The tramp laws also made the explicit connection between the tramp identity and long-distance travel, usually on trains. The main characteristics of the tramp were thus mobility over a large, possibly continental, area and lack of work. It was the mobility in particular that distinguished the tramp from the earlier figure of the vagrant. People didn't use the word *tramp* to refer to homeless people before tramps were able to travel the kind of distances that the new railroads allowed. If persons could be defined as tramps for the purposes of law, they could receive far more severe sentences than if they were merely vagrants, since in the latter case the local community would owe them public charity. Definitions, as a form of knowledge, have their consequences, particularly when they become imbedded in the law.[30]

My argument is that knowledge is not simply a representation of tramps but a way of acting on and against them. Legal knowledge is a particularly powerful form of knowledge because it has direct and pernicious effects on the way people defined as tramps were treated. The term *social construction* is often used to describe how objects, beliefs, and actions are the product of society and not simply "natural." The implication of using this term is that the thing (the tramp) is the product of a society. It is not just society in a generalized sense, however, but particular parts of society that are implicated in this process of production. Some people have more power to name and to act than others. Those who create laws and then prosecute people for transgressing them are particularly powerful as they, in a limited but important way, define the things people can and cannot do. The issue of social construction, in a legal context, is quite literal.[31] There is a tendency to think of law, in a liberal Western tradition, as in some way separate from society — as a high-minded and independent abstraction. Recent work in critical legal theory has questioned this assumption and argued instead that law is embedded in society both in the sense that law plays an important role in making society what it is and in the sense that law is itself constructed within particular arrangements of power within a given society. As David Delaney has argued, "Legal and social phenomena are inseparable whether the point of their interpretation...is on the street, in the workplace, in the home, in law schools, or on the bench."[32] This is particularly clear in issues of vagrancy, which is nothing if not a construction of the law.

Vagrancy laws and tramp laws both produce crimes of status. The threat of the vagabond and the tramp is a virtual threat because they have not committed any crimes above and beyond that which makes them a vagabond or a tramp. In connection with vagrants in France, Kristin Ross has argued that "their 'way of life' places them in a state of *eventual* violation of laws: vagabonds are always virtual, anticipatory."[33] Beier refers to vagrancy as a "classic crime of status, the social crime *par excellence.*"[34] Vagrants since the fourteenth century in Europe had been arrested and punished not for an act they had committed but because of who they were and the threat to order that they represented. The "crime" of vagrancy is, most important, not a quality of an act a vagrant commits but a consequence of the application of rules and sanctions to an offender. Law and legal definitions created the legal type "vagrant" and the legal type "tramp."

Pathologizing the Tramp

Law was not the only form of knowledge making up the tramp. Two important bodies of thought in the late nineteenth and early twentieth centuries were sociology and eugenics. Once the tramp was brought into being he or she quickly became the object of these forms of knowledge that, in their different ways, labeled the tramp and his or her lifestyle as "pathological." Of particular importance here is the Chicago School of Sociology. It was Chicago that became the site of both early urban sociology and an enormous number of tramps and hobos riding the rails in and out of the important railroad hub. It is no surprise, then, that the life and actions of the tramp fell under the watchful gaze of Robert Park and his acolytes.

Sociology

Just as mobility was central to the general and legal definitions of the tramp, so it was to the likes of Robert Park, Ernest Burgess, and Nels Anderson. On the one hand, mobility was seen to be the motor of civilization, but, on the other, mobility threatened to undo place to such a degree that the city was threatened by chaos. "The mobility of the city," Anderson wrote, "detaches and undomesticates the city man. By it he is released from his primary group associations, the family or the neighborhood. With this independence come a loss of loyalty. The city man gains freedom, but the individualism he achieves is often at the cost of his locus."[35] In addition to Anderson's book and field notes there is the often-overlooked short essay written by Park called "The Mind of the Hobo: Reflections upon the Relation between Mentality and Locomotion." In this essay, Park considers the roles of both place and mobility in constructing what he calls "human mentality." Animals are distinguished from plants, he asserts, by their mobility.

Park links the human fact of motion to the other human characteristics of intelligence and imagination. "Mind," he argues, "is an incident of locomotion."[36] It is only through the ability to change location — to be mobile — that humans were enabled to develop the ability to think abstractly. Park enlarges this argument still further by asserting that it is in "locomotion" that forms of organization between and among individual people develop. Thus mobility, in addition to being responsible for abstract thought, is implicated in the development of the social. The social, to Park, is made up of individuals who are capable of locomotion.

Where, then, do the tramp and the hobo enter this equation? Clearly Park was familiar with the vast armies of tramps and hobos passing through Chicago who in many ways embodied the "locomotion" that Park believed constituted both mind and society. Why then, he asked, were these itinerants not more philosophical? His answer revolved around the idea of directedness and destination. While the hobo was certainly mobile, he was not going anywhere in particular. His life was marked, according to Park, by a lack of vocation, direction, and destination. His mobility was for its own sake. He invoked the semimedical diagnosis of wanderlust to label this type of mobility:

> Wanderlust, which is the most elementary expression of the romantic temperament and the romantic interest in life, has assumed for him, as for so many others, the character of a vice. He has gained his freedom, but he has lost his direction.[37]

The problem with the mobility of the tramp, in Park's terms, was that it never stopped. Because of this, the tramp was doomed to live an unorganized life on the margins of society without the benefits of organization and association.

In "The Growth of the City," Burgess makes mobility a central part of his ecological model of city-form. He contrasts mobility with movement. While movement is "a fixed and unchanging order of motion, designed to control a constant situation, as in routine movement,"[38] mobility is a change of routine movement in response to new stimuli and situations. So while movement appears to be a relatively mundane and everyday activity, such as commuting, mobility is more exceptional — moving house or having adventures. The activities that Burgess labels mobility have implications of potential for progress or regression — opportunity and threat. Burgess sees mobility as a central stimulus to the successful growth of both the individual and the city but warns that when the mobility of individuals becomes detached from and unorganized by the whole (city, society) it becomes dangerous and pathological. It is of course the "zone in transition" that is most marked by this unattached mobility:

The mobility of city life, with its increase in the number and intensity of stimulations, tends inevitably to confuse and to demoralize the person. For an essential element in the mores and in personal morality is constancy, consistency of the type that is natural in the social control of the primary group. Where mobility is the greatest, and where in consequence primary controls break down completely, as in the zone of deterioration in the modern city, there develop areas of demoralization, of promiscuity, and of vice.[39]

Burgess was clearly fascinated with the consequences of mobility on the city because he believed that areas of high mobility were characterized by multiple pathologies such as prostitution, gangs, crime, poverty, wife desertion, and alcoholism. He recounts how train rides per capita in Chicago had risen from 164 in 1890 to 320 in 1910. Someone standing on the corner of State and Madison (an area of extremely high land values that lay alongside the area most frequented by tramps and hobos), he believed, would be passed by thirty-one thousand people an hour on average over a day.

Throughout the work of Park, Burgess, and Anderson there is a clear concern for the negative effects of mobility on city life. While directed mobility was clearly an important factor in the production of everything from city-form to society itself, mobility in its extreme forms was linked to the idea of pathology and vice. Just as mobility distinguished the tramp from the mere vagrant in tramp laws, so we see a politics of mobility in the distinction between the mobility of the "normal" urban dweller and that of the tramp/hobo.

Sociology (and other social sciences) records itself as much as it records the world. The production of sociological texts is part of the way in which society produces a set of social problems that seem self-evidently worthy of debate. As Pierre Bourdieu points out, the production of categories by academics is a way of "officializing" a problem and making it a matter of public concern. Sociology in particular needs to have "social problems" in order to legitimize itself and generate opportunities for funding, contracts, and the production of research bodies. Anderson's book on the hobo is a case in point. The title page states that *The Hobo* is "a study prepared for the Chicago Council of Social Agencies under the direction of the Committee on Homeless Men." The preface to the book includes a statement by the committee that includes the following:

The object of this inquiry, from the standpoint of the Committee, was to secure those facts which would enable social agencies to deal intelligently with the problems created by the continuous ebb and flow, out of and into Chicago, of tens of thousands of foot-loose and homeless men. Only through an understanding both of the human nature of the migratory casual worker, and of the economic and social forces which have shaped his personality, could there be devised any fundamental program for social agencies interested in his welfare.[40]

Clearly the work of Anderson was, in part, implicated in the production of the tramp as a social problem; that is, his work helped produce the problem he was allegedly reporting. Many of the objects of social science are "social problems" made formal in an academic arena. We need only think of contemporary catchphrases such as *globalization* or *social exclusion* to realize that the products of social science are quickly institutionalized into social facts that are subsequently used to legitimate themselves. Just by directing funding at a problem it is possible to create it as a social fact. Many of the norms of social science, both at the time of the Chicago School and now, are implicated in quite unconscious ways in the production of social reality. Anderson, Park, and others were deeply implicated in the production of problems that needed experts to solve them and committees to fund the research. Sociology, through the production of the tramp, was producing itself.

Eugenics

Another group of people who took pathologies particularly seriously were eugenicists. Charles Davenport, a leader of the American eugenics movement, had been to Britain and studied with Karl Pearson, the eugenicist and statistician. One of Davenport's early explorations of Mandelian ratios in people was his book *The Feebly Inhibited*, which was published in 1915. It included his work *Nomadism; or, The Wandering Impulse, with Special Reference to Heredity.*[41] Davenport believed that tramps suffered from an inbred desire to wander that he referred to as nomadism. In this work, Davenport considers a number of medico-psychological conditions related to the desire to move. Wanderlust he describes as a mild form of desire for travel that we all exhibit from time to time but that, for the most part, remains under control. At the other end of his spectrum lies the condition known as "fugue," which he describes as an extreme and markedly pathological inability to stop moving. In addition to, and somewhere between, these two is the condition known as "dromomania," a form of ambulatory automatism. In preference to all of these, Davenport chooses to talk about "nomadism," which he describes as a racial or tribal tendency to wander. "On the whole," he says, "I am inclined to use the word 'nomadism' just because it has a racial connotation. From a modern point of view all hereditary characteristics are racial."[42]

Davenport develops his thesis via a discussion of the wandering tendency as a normal characteristic of man and animals that sets them apart from plants. He traces nomadism through a kind of evolutionary hierarchy, noting the "wandering instinct" in anthropoid apes, in "primitive" people, in young children, and in adolescents. By tracing these connections Davenport seeks to show how nomadism is a primitive trait exhibited most frequently in those who have not fully enjoyed the benefits of civilization. Apes, "primitive peoples," babies, and adolescents all suffer from an excess of primitive urges and a lack of civilized constraints and are thus likely to wander. He spends the greatest effort discussing so-called primitive people in order to reveal how all of the most primitive people are nomadic. At the bottom of this hierarchy are "Fuegians, Australians, Bushman and Hottentots," all of whom are nomadic. He refutes the suggestion that they are nomadic because they are hunters and instead asserts that they are forced into hunting by their nomadic traits. He continues up his hierarchy of peoples, noting the nomadism of Cossacks, Turkomans, Mongols, Polynesians, and Gypsies. Indeed, his central contention is that non-nomadic lifestyles are a very recent phenomenon in human history. Davenport's favored term, though, is *nomadism*, which slotted neatly into his eugenicist theorizing. Nomadism, to Davenport, indicates a racial tendency to wander that, somewhat bizarrely, but in keeping with American ideology about mobility, he saw as an expression of Americanness. Quoting Lowell's *Fireside Travels*, he points out that "The American is nomadic in religion, in ideas, in morals, and leaves his faith and opinions with as much indifference as the house in which he lives."[43] Americans, he argues, are descendants of those restless elements of other, mainly European, nations who chose to leave their ancestral homes, and so it is surely no surprise that many American families would show nomadic traits.

Using the findings of his fieldworkers, Davenport comes to the conclusion that nomadism is the result of a simple recessive sex-linked gene associated with these psychoses. In the extreme case of tramps and vagabonds, Davenport suggests, "the inhibitory mechanism is so poorly developed that the nomadic tendency shows itself without waiting, as it were, for the paralysis of the inhibitions."[44] In other words, people who lead a nomadic lifestyle are in the same category as babies, "primitive people," and others who have none of the inhibitions typical of intelligent adults and "civilized" people.

As an appendix to his work he provides details of one hundred family histories of his nomads. Some of them read as bizarre litanies of pathological traits inevitably linked to nomadic lifestyles:

(4) Propositus is a *restless visionary. He has always been shifting from one position to another. Left home some months ago saying he was going West; has not been heard from since.* Sibs: 1, female, died 14 years. 2, male, died in infancy. 3, female, works in a factory; is getting divorced. 4, male, has a *roving disposition;* is a nurse and companion; accompanies various patients on their trips for health. 5, female, has long been lawless and violent in her actions; *she ran away from home* while in a commercial school; had been there only a few weeks when she got the principal to refund her tuition, which had been paid in advance; with this money she

went to L——— and became a telephone operator, later she *ran away again to marry,* and since her marriage she has *run away;* she loses her temper.

Father, unknown

Mother, unknown. Sibs: 1, male, unknown; 2, male, drowned when 7 years old.

Mother's father. — Was a stage-driver between Salem and Boston and kept a tavern or "roadhouse" in what is now an outskirt of L———. Some of his descendants suggest that the *wanderlust* and frequently erratic character of his descendants come through this ancestor.

Mother's mother, unknown.... [45]

(11) Propositus, born 1895 in Missouri, is (1914) a wanderer and *has left home repeatedly and been away for months at a time,* returning home for rest and clothes, then he goes away again; works some, but does not save or provide for the future — a disobedient boy.... Smokes a pipe and cigarettes, drinks whiskey, and has used cocaine considerably.... Is irregular and uncertain in his habits, *does not like to stay in one place long; likes to bum and tramp around to see the world....* Has flat feet, crooked toes, crooked spine, and one shoulder is higher than the other.[46]

In these family histories anything from headaches to drinking to having crooked feet is considered evidence for the pathological nature of human wandering. The one hundred entries are a remarkable route-map of the prejudices and paranoias of early-twentieth-century social science. Clearly the knowledge embodied in these family histories collected by fieldworkers from the Center for Experimental Evolution was a knowledge with potentially devastating consequences for the men who were counted, labeled, recorded, mapped, and defined as tramps.

The kinds of knowledge about tramps being constructed in Chicago and by eugenicists rested on earlier, pre-twentieth-century developments in knowledge that made possible the use of terms such as *pathological, normal,* and *deviant.* Such is the momentum that words such as these carry with them that we are often unsure as to where they came from. *Normal* only acquired its present meaning in the 1820s. Before that it had been used to refer to right angles in geometry — a synonym for *orthogonal.* Even at this stage the word *normal* had a normative function. Ian Hacking makes this point well:

It is just a fact that an angle is a right angle, but it is also a "right" angle, a good one. Orthodontists straighten the teeth of children; they make the crooked straight. But they also put the teeth right, make them better. Orthopaedic surgeons straighten bones. Orthopsychiatry is the study of mental disorders chiefly in children. It aims at making the child normal. The orthodox conform to standards.[47]

The modern (post-1820) use of the word comes from medicine and is opposed to *pathological*. These words very quickly moved out of the realm of medicine and colonized many other realms of life in the nineteenth century. *Normal* is a word that joins together fact and value, claiming that the normal and the right are the same thing.

Pathology also underwent a curious mutation in the early nineteenth century as it went from a word denoting the study of diseased organs to a term used to mark the deviation from the normal state, a limitless variety of possibilities. Most famously Émile Durkheim used the term *pathological* to refer to extreme deviation from a norm or average that was thought of as good. In this sense *pathology* became linked to *deviance* — a word with origins in statistics, marking the difference from the mean along a normal distribution curve. Not surprisingly, the origin of the statistics in the social sciences was firmly connected to social and eugenicist concerns with marginal members of society in western Europe — particularly vagrants.

Conclusion

In his essay "Strangers and Strangeness," Yi-Fu Tuan reflects on the role of the outsider in the construction of culture. "Outsiders, by implication, belong to a lower order. They are strangers who have not submitted to culture at its best. They are raw, unpredictable, and dangerous."[48] He goes on to suggest that the existence of outsiders is a result of the prior existence of classificatory systems that inscribe familiarity and order in an otherwise chaotic world. He also points out that the stranger and the strange can be seen as positive or even romantic. The tramp is a case in point. The strangeness of the tramp is a product of ways of thinking, such as law and sociology, that attempt to reinscribe order into the world — to make it legible. They have no place for enchantment. In other forms of knowledge, particularly in the writing of Jack London and Jack Kerouac and in the films of Charlie Chaplin, the tramp was made into a romantic figure whose disruptions of the mundane were welcomed. Whether the tramp is made up as a pathological or deviant identity depends on how the tramp is known and how the type of knowledge that is mobilized relates the practices of the person called a tramp to the places he or she travels through. A truly inclusive account of the geography of knowledge about the tramp would have to include all of these. Here I have focused on the more negative representations of the tramp.

The geographical imaginations implicit in the knowledges of law, sociology, and eugenics helped constitute the tramp as a subject, and each made the tramp a particularly geographical actor marked by pathological mobility. These knowledges not only produced the tramp and underlined a general moral panic about tramps in the late nineteenth and early twentieth centuries but also produced material effects. Once the tramp existed he or she could be acted upon, counted, subjected to numerical, legal, and medical procedures. A geography of knowledges is not simply a catalog of ideas and imaginations but a critical examination of practices and consequences that affect the way people can lead their lives. As Pierre Bourdieu has written: "Each society, at each moment, elaborated a body of social problems taken to be legitimate, worthy of being debated, of being made public and sometimes officialized and, in a sense, guaranteed by the state."[49] Such knowledge has effects within academia as it leads to funding, contracts, grants, and the creation of research bodies. The funding that follows each newly defined problem helps to reaffirm it as a social fact. It thus follows that one of the most powerful instruments of rupture lies in a geography of knowledges, that is, with the history of the work of sociogeographical constructions of reality. Geosophy thus conceived takes as its task not the colorful description of knowledge for its own sake but the understanding of why and how one understands and how this understanding goes on to have effects on the objects of knowledge.

Notes

1. J. K. Wright, "Terrae Incognitae: The Place of the Imagination in Geography," *Annals of the Association of American Geographers* 37 (1947): 1–15.

2. Ian Hacking, "Making Up People," in *Reconstructing Individualism: Autonomy, Individuality, and the Self in Western Thought,* ed. T. Heller, M. Sosna, and D. Wellbery (Stanford, Calif.: Stanford University Press, 1986), 227.

3. Ibid., 228.

4. Ibid., 231.

5. Roy D'Andrade, "Cultural Meaning Systems," in *Cultural Theory: Essays on Mind, Self, and Emotion,* ed. R. Shweder and R. Levine (Cambridge: Cambridge University Press, 1987), 91.

6. Paul Ringenbach, *Tramps and Reformers 1873–1916* (Westport, Conn.: Greenwood Press, 1973).

7. The word *tramp* had, however, been used as a verb to denote various forms of movement. It was, for instance, used to refer to the act of marching long distances during the Civil War.

8. Quoted in Roger Bruns, *The Damndest Radical: The Life and World of Ben Reitman, Chicago's Celebrated Social Reformer, Hobo King, and Whorehouse Physician* (Urbana Ill.: University of Illinois Press, 1987), 44.

9. Quoted in Nels Anderson, *The Hobo* (Chicago: University of Chicago Press, 1925), 89.

10. For accounts of tramp law and vagrancy law in the United States, see Orlando Lewis, *Vagrancy in the United States* (New York: [self-published], 1907); Michigan State Library, *Laws of the Various States relating to Vagrancy* (Lansing: Michigan State Library, Legislative Reference Department, 1916); Jeffrey S. Adler, "A Historical Analysis of the Law of Vagrancy," *Criminology* 27, no. 2 (1989): 209–29; Elbert Hubbard, "The Rights of Tramps," *Arena* 9 (April 1894): 593–600.

11. See A. L. Beier, *Masterless Men: The Vagrancy Problem in England 1560–1640*

(London: Methuen, 1985) for the classic account of sixteenth-century vagrancy laws in Britain.

12. Adler, "Historical Analysis," 214.

13. Victor Hoffman, "The American Tramp, 1870–1900" (Master's thesis, University of Chicago, 1953), 57.

14. A tramp was defined here as an idle person without employment, a transient person who roamed from place to place and who had no lawful occasion to wander.

15. Hoffman, "American Tramp," 58.

16. *State v. Hogan,* 63 Ohio (1900), 215–18, cited in Michael Davis, "Forced to Tramp: The Perspective of the Labor Press, 1870–1900," in *Walking to Work: Tramps in America 1790–1935,* ed. Eric H. Monkkonen (Lincoln: University of Nebraska Press, 1984), 162.

17. Ibid., 162.

18. Lewis, *Vagrancy in the Unites States,* 33.

19. Josiah Flynt, "The Tramp and the Railroad," *Century Magazine* 58 (1899): 265.

20. Lewis, *Vagrancy in the United States,* 13.

21. Ibid.

22. Sidney Harring, "Class Conflict and the Suppression of Tramps in Buffalo, 1892–1894," *Law and Society Review* 11 (summer 1977): 873–911.

23. Hubbard, "Rights of Tramps," 597.

24. Ibid., 593.

25. Ibid., 593–94.

26. Ibid., 594.

27. Ibid., 595.

28. Ibid., 598.

29. Ibid., 599.

30. Don Mitchell, "The Annihilation of Space by Law: The Roots and Implications of Anti-homeless Laws in the United States," *Antipode* 29, no. 3 (1997): 303–35, provides an astute analysis of what he calls "anti-homeless laws" in the United States in the 1990s. Clearly the story of the war against vagrancy does not end with the tramp laws.

31. The classic essay on social construction is Peter Berger and Thomas Luckmann, *The Social Construction of Reality: A Treatise in the Sociology of Knowledge* (New York: Doubleday, 1966). For a recent set of essays on the issue of social construction, see Irving Velody and Robin Williams, eds., *The Politics of Constructionism* (London: Sage, 1998). For a perceptive account of the role of language in constructing social institutions, see John Searle, *The Construction of Social Reality* (London: Allen Lane, 1995). For discussions of legal process within a geographical context, see Gordon Clark, *Judges and the Cities: Interpreting Local Autonomy* (Chicago: University of Chicago Press, 1985); Nick Blomley, *Law, Space, and the Geographies of Power* (New York: Guilford, 1994); and David Delaney, *Race, Place, and the Law* (Austin: University of Texas Press, 1998).

32. David Delaney, "Geographies of Judgment: The Doctrine of Changed Conditions and the Geopolitics of Race," *Annals of the Association of American Geographers* 83, no. 1 (1993): 50.

33. Kristin Ross, *The Emergence of Social Space: Rimbaud and the Paris Commune* (Minneapolis: University of Minnesota Press, 1988), 57.

34. Beier, *Masterless Men,* xxii.

35. Nels Anderson, "The Trends of Urban Sociology," p. 14 in the Ernest Burgess papers, box 126, Special Collections Division, University of Chicago.

36. Robert Park, "The Mind of the Hobo: Reflections upon the Relation between Mentality and Locomotion," in *The City: Suggestions for Investigation of Human Behavior in the Urban Environment,* ed. Robert Park and Ernest Burgess (Chicago: University of Chicago Press, 1925), 156.

37. Ibid., 158.

38. Ernest Burgess, "The Growth of the City: An Introduction to a Research Project," in Park and Burgess, *The City,* 58.

39. Ibid., 59.

40. Anderson, *The Hobo*, xxvi–xxvii.

41. Charles B. Davenport, *The Feebly Inhibited: Nomadism; or, The Wandering Impulse, with Special Reference to Heredity* (Washington, D.C.: Carnegie Institution, 1915).

42. Ibid., 7.

43. Ibid.

44. Ibid., 25.

45. Ibid., 28–29.

46. Ibid., 31.

47. Ian Hacking, *The Taming of Chance* (Cambridge: Cambridge University Press, 1990), 163.

48. Yi-Fu Tuan, "Strangers and Strangeness," *Geographical Review* 76, no. 1 (1986): 11.

49. Pierre Bourdieu, "The Practice of Reflexive Sociology," in *An Invitation to Reflexive Sociology,* ed. Pierre Bourdieu and Loic Wacquant (Chicago: University of Chicago Press, 1992), 236.

PERIPATETIC IMAGERY AND PERIPATETIC SENSE OF PLACE

Paul C. Adams

> We should go forth on the shortest walk, perchance, in the spirit of undying adventure, never to return — prepared to send back our embalmed hearts only as relics to our desolate kingdoms.
>
> — HENRY DAVID THOREAU, "Walking"

This quote about walking gestures toward a vanishing experience and also, less obviously, a vanishing sense of place. Fifty years ago John K. Wright used the term *terra incognita* to indicate the geographical unknown, a realm that is filled primarily by the imagination. His concept was nuanced according to various types of knowledge and scales of social organization so that despite the virtually complete mapping of the world's gross features by the date of his comments, geographers were still faced with "an immense patchwork of miniature *terrae incognitae.*"[1] By drawing attention to the unknown Wright intended to exhort geographers to further explore the subjective aspects of reality.

We can carry this project forward by asserting that terrae incognitae do not constitute a receding horizon constantly pushed back by the accumulation of scientific knowledge, a conquerable space of the unknown as conceived in modernist views. History involves contradictions and reversals; a place-experience that is familiar in one period may be unfamiliar in the next; what is once known can later become terra incognita through the abandonment of normal or frequent relations with a place (as was the case with East Germany for West Germans, and vice versa, during the Cold War).[2] The same occurs on an individual level through the abandonment of certain paths and routes over the course of a lifetime. Furthermore, place-experience is not binary, a simple matter of knowing or not knowing; knowledge arises from actions, and place-experiences thus present innumerable shades of differentiation depending on what one is doing in a place. Accordingly, terrae incognitae can emerge when any way of interacting with the world is changed and, what is most important for our purposes here, when *paths are no longer traveled in the same way.*

In the late twentieth century in affluent countries, particularly the United States, walking, once the commonest of place-experiences, is now becoming a rarity. The labor force of the information economy sits at the breakfast table, takes a few steps to the car, drives to work, takes a few steps to and from the elevator, sits at a desk until noon, and similarly passes the rest of the day sitting, with only fleeting moments on their feet. If walking is engaged in at all, it is likely to be structured as a special kind of work, "getting in shape," an endeavor clearly indicated to observers on the street by an uncomfortably rapid pace, a fixed forward gaze, and pumping L-shaped arms; but increasingly often it is relegated to treadmills in climate-controlled workout spaces.[3] This reduction of walking to a purely utilitarian activity recognizes only one aspect of mobility and supports a shift to machine-oriented modes of being-in-place that have various costs that are beyond the scope of this essay to explore.[4] Aside from the formal "workout," walking is now avoided with surprising intensity.[5] This radical change in the structure of daily life, a change in both place and self, is a product of a set of ideologies about mobility. Yet because its effects are experienced by virtually all segments of society, it has thus far escaped the attention of geographers interested in deconstructing the ways that ideology creates social differences and landscapes. As neither landscape nor "social interaction" per se, walking is no more apparent in place as theorized in the United States than in place as lived in the United States.

What is disappearing, to be specific, is the stroll as a source of pleasure and the foot as a means of serious transportation, which together were for a long time at the root of a strong and deep sense of place. These varieties of walking produced a sense of place that I call *peripatetic,* from the Greek *peri,* meaning around, and *patein,* meaning to walk. The disappearance of walks — the walk to work, the walk to the store, the walk to the park, and the pleasure walk — directly contributes to the often observed thinning out of the meaning of place frequently associated with modernity and the reduction of sensory involvement in one's surroundings, as well as weakening place-based forms of community.[6] In an attempt to elucidate the loss of a peripatetic sense of place and to reveal the forces that are driving its disappearance, this essay begins with an analysis of peripatetic symbolism in literature, then turns to ways of framing place that may help to resuscitate a peripatetic sense of place, particularly those of neotraditional urban design.

One purpose of my essay is romantic (a term used pejoratively by the social scientists but one that I embrace for its radical potential). Romantic ideas and ideologies indicate a means of "release from, or transcendence over, ignominious or uncomfortable circumstances."[7] If one's senses are deprived of stimuli and if one's body becomes an unnecessary appendage to a mechanized system that demands immobility for the sake of production (not unlike the logic that guides the rearing of veal calves and chickens), then the romantic urge to envision walking as part of the "good life" is not an indulgence but a strategic response to the ideology of bodily immobility as a *necessary* adjunct of the good life.[8]

The degree to which American culture has incorporated Thoreau's antiurban model of the good life is indicated by suburbanization itself: the passion for a rural idyll finds its ironic expression in the lifestyle of the long-distance commuter — a life from which Thoreau's passion, walking, is essentially absent. The problem is not the car. Ideologies more than technologies have shaped this socio-spatial evolution. Ideologies have, for example, guided the appropriation and accommodation of various technologies to construct a car-dependent society. Principal among these ideologies is peripatetic imagery: a set of polarized ideologies that sometimes glorify but ultimately discourage the act of walking. The loss of a peripatetic sense of place is related most directly to peripatetic imagery situating the walker outside the social fabric.

Following a brief discussion of the sensory and social dimensions of walking we progress to the opposing yet complementary views of walking held by Western culture — light peripatetic and dark peripatetic — that are also implicated in the marginalization of the walker by late modernity. We end with some recent symbolic gestures toward a renaissance of a peripatetic sense of place, the kernels of a peripatetic ideology that must diffuse if a peripatetic sense of place is once again to become *terra cognita*.

Walking and Sensation

To walk through a place is to become involved in that place with sight, hearing, touch, smell, the kinetic sense called proprioception, and even taste. Auditory sensations range from the calls of birds to the sounds of traffic and horns. Tactile sensations include the brush of tall grass, the spray of passing cars on wet roads, and the jostling of strangers in crowded places. Olfactory sensations range from the scent of apple blossoms to the stench of paper mills to the pleasing and unpleasing odors of passing strangers. Proprioceptive stimuli, signals from the muscles, indicate among other things the slope underfoot and one's rate of movement. Even taste can be involved in a walk, if the mouth intercepts berry bushes or bakeries. These various sensations, as trivial as they may seem to a person habituated to mechanized transportation, are the basis of a close connection to place and are likely to be recalled with great fondness when one thinks back on the places one has loved. The reduction of experience from such multisensory intake to the scanning gaze is fundamental to the loosening of ties between person and place that have preoccupied more than one generation of human geographers.

To pick the least understood of the senses and highlight its role in peripatetic sense of place: through proprioception a hill is *felt* by the leg muscles, as resistance (when climbing) or as a persistent acceleration (when descending). To climb and descend a hill on foot is therefore to establish a kind of dialogue with the earth, a direct imprinting of place on self; this physical dialogue becomes silent when one moves by merely pressing on a gas pedal. In peripatetic place-experience lies the basis of a special kind of knowledge of the world and one's place in it.[9]

A sense of place can, of course, be constructed purely through sight and, as I have argued elsewhere, even through mediated visual experiences such as television and computer networks.[10] Notwithstanding this important phenomenon, I want to recall here an important assertion made by Yi-Fu Tuan, that multisensory apprehension of one's surroundings is qualitatively different than vision or mediated vision — it is a more profound mode of experiencing place.[11] As common as mediated experiences are, and as seamlessly woven as they are in our daily lives and experiences of place, they are sensorially impoverished in comparison with a peripatetic sense of place. Walking brings persons more directly into contact with their environment than mediated experiences or driving and thus presents a striking contrast with the climate-controlled, sterilized, and deodorized environmental experiences of American suburbs and "edge cities," not to mention the "virtual environments" one can access through the various media installed in these environments.[12]

Habituation to a "motorized metal box"[13] reduces one's environment to a visual tableau, an abstract play of angles and light. The sound-proofing of vehicles combines with sophisticated stereo systems to immerse the driver in a bubble of acoustic space that is entirely separate from his or her surroundings, heightening this effect. The music emerges from a different time and place, and its presence helps reduce the surrounding landscape to scenery, which in turn encourages an emotional detachment from one's surroundings, so the many subtle pleasures of place are lost. A self-perpetuating process of substitution leads to dependency on vehicles: as walking disappears from the human-environment interaction, the multisensory qualities of the landscapes experienced by the remaining walkers are increasingly degraded with the sounds, smells, dust, and spray of traffic. Furthermore, an absence of positive social interactions in transit spaces prompts a psychological retreat from public space as that space is increasingly accessed remotely, not only from media in places but also from mobile media such as the on-board stereo and cellular phone. The blurring of the distinction between virtual place and physical place is not only (as I have argued elsewhere) a product of new technologies; it is also a product of the evisceration of our unmediated experience through the presence of machines in the landscape and elsewhere in daily life.

Walking and Social Transformation

The loss of peripatetic sense of place is part of a long-term historical transformation featuring three general components:

1. urbanization;

2. increasing spatial flows of commodities, people, information, and capital; and

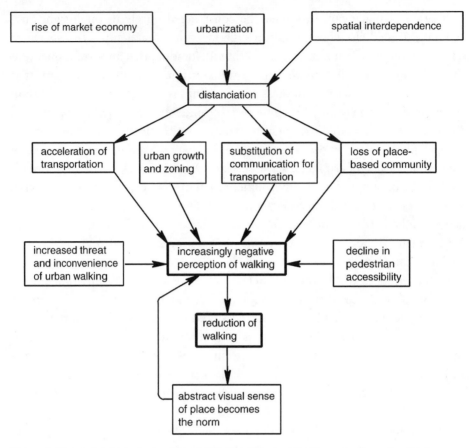

Figure 1. The social, historical, and technological context for the reduction of walking.

3. a growing spatial interdependence that manifests itself through distanciation — the stretching out of human interactions and projects across space.[14]

These transformations have been widely examined by geographers, but seldom with an eye to their impacts on daily life and, particularly, to the subjective experiences of movement and communication. Even time-geography overlooked the phenomenon of distanciation, the stretching out of social relations across space, so that physical proximity was thought to be necessary for interaction.[15] Distanciation generally increases the rate, volume, distance, and frequency of communication and transportation flows between places (Figure 1). As landscapes are reorganized to support greater mobility, facilities become larger and farther apart, reducing walkers' accessibility, demanding technologically assisted mobility, and contributing to a more vehicular lifestyle. In technical terms, one must become more mobile simply to retain the same level of accessibility.[16] In this nexus of technological dependency, urban growth, and increasing functional interdependence among places, the diverse values of walking (physiological, social, and aesthetic) are overshadowed by a single one of its attributes, its slowness, which when inserted within a time = money rationality becomes nothing more than a high transportation cost. This is only one of many ways that a complex world apprehended through all of the senses gives way to a sterilized "scopic regime"[17] that abstracts and devalues both physical and social places, reducing the world to an image. In this visual space, distance is conceived negatively as an obstacle (rather than a sequence of places) and one's sense of self-worth becomes dependent on the power of one's vehicle. More generally, the place-self relationship already loosened by the increasing *amount* of mobility is further weakened by the *nature* of the mobility.

The cultural transformations attending one technological diffusion, the diffusion of vehicles, parallel the cultural transformations linked to other technological diffusions. Computer simulations, video games, World Wide Web experiences, and other "virtual worlds" are overwhelmingly visual, and in their foundation in instantaneous connection they both reflect and reinforce the dislocated worldview of the driver. Although simulations and "virtual place" are sensorially thin (vision alone or vision and distorted sound), they may not be experienced as thin (for example, tedious and unsatisfying) by persons accustomed to the sensory sparseness of modern offices, houses, streets, and shopping environments. Again, the ubiquity of the machine (itself a product of certain shifts in ideology) is at the heart of the process.

Dependence on technology is a precondition for the loss of a peripatetic sense of place, but technology is not a determining force. Lewis Mumford overstates the case when he argues that

> In so far as the phonograph and the radio do away with the impulse to sing, in so far as the camera does away with the impulse to see, *in so far as the automobile does away with the impulse to walk, the machine leads to a lapse of function which is but one step away from paralysis.*[18]

The error in this line of reasoning is that the habit of immobility is not an inevitable consequence of any particular technological development but rather is a cultural development; it is technologically enabled but not technologically driven. The driving force is culture, which shapes the social incorporation of new technologies within an infinite range of possibilities. Habituation to a certain technological apparatus may encourage certain types of thought—certain ideologies — as intriguingly suggested by Marshall McLuhan, but to address (and perhaps cure) the "paralysis" in question we must direct our attention to cultural values and ideologies.[19]

Peripatetic Imagery

The pleasure walk, a cultural form ranging from expeditions in the wilderness to saunters in the country, has deep resonance with the themes of European and American romanticism. In the literature of the early nineteenth century and afterward, walking is presented *in opposition* to urbanization, industrialization, and modernization—a response to the shock of rapid social and environmental change. Perhaps the most direct stimulus for this set of associations was the enclosure of agricultural land, which blocked access to common holdings previously allocated under the feudal system. Most noticeably, in the period from 1750 to 1850 in England (somewhat later in other parts of Europe), the landscape of open strip fields, pastures, and forests inhabited by generations of peasants was gradually replaced by a patchwork of privately held fields closed to foot travelers and linked by a new system of roads designed to hasten the shipping of goods to urban markets. By the mid–nineteenth century, some villagers could not find any commonly held land within a day's road travel.[20] Multitudes who had depended on the commons for the acquisition of usable or salable commodities (as well as for purposes of leisure and access to various activities) were pressed into poverty and migrated to the city. Those who remained in the countryside found themselves effectively impoverished by loss of access to a wide range of resources previously obtained at no cost from the commons. In addition to this economic hardship, emotional disorientation resulted from attachment to a landscape that no longer existed and the loss of opportunities for walking as a social and individual activity.

Of continuing importance to the oppositional and marginal connotations pervading varieties of peripatetic imagery is the fact that after enclosure common law protected walking paths from privatization if they were used regularly. Walking thus became not simply a form of recreation or transportation but also a means of preserving public access, both to paths and to whatever lay at their end. It became a link in both time and space, since it joined the present to the pre-enclosure past both imaginatively and pragmatically. These connections in turn spawned associations between walking and antimodernism: walkers knit together distance in space (travel), distance in time (history), and distance in social space (marginality). As a kind of labor itself, walking became a symbol of rural laborers and their lives. But these laborers were increasingly marginal, and as the wanderer became an emblem of resistance to blind progress the measured movement of footsteps was placed metaphorically as well as physically "outside" the spaces of modernity.

Anne D. Wallace argues: "although pedestrian reappropriation of footpaths could not reverse [rural impoverishment], it could preserve an important topographical expression of the older economy (in which everyday walking played a significant part) and so establish a formal site for the cultural values ideally associated with self-sustaining rural labour."[21] But walking had become more symbolic than utilitarian. There is a certain irony in the fact that *popular* walking was declining at this time through the loss of access to public spaces, even as walking was becoming fashionable among the upper strata of society. Two forms of peripatetic sense of place, one popular and the other elite, could be discerned. Thus, Leslie Stephen, a romantic poet, advocated "a little judicious trespassing," but the meaning of "judicious" depends, of course, on the judgment of the landowner. An educated man or woman, even a romantic poet, was less likely to incur the wrath of a landowner by trespassing than a common laborer who might be obtaining wood or game from the land. Excursions became "an uncertain guerrilla tactic"[22] after enclosure, and for the poor the uncertainty was always greater. Despite these class distinctions, attempts to link romantic poets and landlords to a single process of upper-class appropriation, both material and symbolic,[23] essentialize class as a measure of the individual.

Thus, no sooner had the modernist aesthetics of speed, restlessness, change, and materialism begun to take hold than a potent countervailing aesthetic of deliberation, reflection, permanence, and simplicity was elaborated, in no small part through peripatetic imagery. While the symbolic associations with walking are quite diverse,[24] I will focus here on a central distinction that dominates much of the peripatetic literature. This is a continuum from what I call "light peripatetic" to "dark peripatetic."

Probably the central authors constructing light peripatetic are William and Dorothy Wordsworth. This motif linked walking to an experience of solitude, simplicity, and moral transcendence. Modern attitudes toward walking still reflect this romantic idyll, passed down by authors such as Henry David Thoreau and Walt Whitman and naturalists such as John Muir and Edward Abbey. In the modern media, this motif is most often seen in advertisements that link products to the leisure, independence, and presumed elevated status of the walker. A countervailing current, dark peripatetic, portrays such romantic associations of walking as delusions or distractions and demonstrates the downfall of characters who dare to separate themselves from community or society. While these forms of peripatetic are opposed in more than one sense, they are in agreement on the marginal and oppositional character of pedestrian mobility, a view that obscures the ways walking may fit into a civilized life. We can find occasional exceptions, as in Alfred Kazin's *A Walker in the City,* but the preponderance of literature on walking works to show the walker as antisocial, whether framed in the light or dark peripatetic motif.[25]

Light Peripatetic

In light peripatetic, walking is a kind of ritual whereby one attunes oneself bodily and mentally with the universe and especially with nature. To become attuned has two meanings: to be sensitive to something and to harmonize with it. The walker's movement *through* his or her environment, a kind of rhythmic harmonization, produces a heightened sensitivity to the environment, as well as a heightened or special sense of self. Examining Eastern and Western literature, John Elder finds that "the landscape and the imagination may be united through the process of walking" so that "walking becomes an emblem of wholeness."[26] This wholeness derives not from a dominating gaze[27] but rather from a multisensory experience, an intertwining of person and place.

Light peripatetic often evokes a sense of the walker's environment *unfolding,* or what Wallace calls "the representation of successive, limited viewpoints."[28] These viewpoints are organized in a somewhat arbitrary but pleasant way, like a string of beads rather than a typically directional realist narrative. Also unlike modernist panoramas and their constitutive gaze, the antimodernist motif of the walk avoids collapsing the world into a single perspective. Wordsworth's "An Evening Walk," for instance, carries the reader past the sounds and sights of various rural environments and livelihoods:

> Sole light admitted here, a small cascade,
> Illumes with sparkling foam the twilight shade.
> Beyond, along the vista of the brook,
> Where antique roots its bustling path o'erlook,
> The eye reposes on a secret bridge
> Half grey, half shagg'd with ivy to its ridge.
> . . . .
> Their panneir'd train a groupe of potters goad,
> Winding from side to side up the steep road;
> The peasant from yon cliff of fearful edge
> Shot, down the headlong pathway darts his sledge;
> . . . .
> Sounds from the waterside the hammer'd boat;
> And blasted quarry thunders heard remote.[29]

The setting is presented as a still life, a bucolic collage of loosely related impressions. Starting with a visual motif (the light of the setting sun) the poet shifts to a kinetic rendition of the potters ascending a slope and a peasant descending the same slope; then he shifts sensory modes again to an auditory impression of the place. Although described in a sequence, bridge, cliff, and peasants all exist at once in a particular place at a particular time and are placed in sequence only by the observer, a parallel to the act of walking, which is a way of carving a transect through a place. The peripatetic frame therefore invites contemplation of a place (and a social reality) where permanence and simultaneity are more evident than change and sequence. This antilinear (antimodern) sense of place can not be captured all at once, through a quasi-omniscient perspective, but only over time, so walking is interpreted as wandering:

> How pleased [a walker] is to hear the murmuring stream,
> The many Voices, from he knows not where,
> To have about him, which way e'er he goes,
> Something on every side concealed from view,
> In every quarter some thing visible,

Half-seen or wholly, lost and found again —
Alternate progress and impediment,
And yet a growing prospect in the main.[30]

Thus a comprehensive view is constructed in the mind rather than the eye. This presentation of walk-as-discovery is found also in Robert Frost's "The Wood-pile," William Carlos Williams's "The Desert Music," and countless other walking poems.[31] Such a place-conception opposes both the visual appropriation of landscape with its aristocratic or bureaucratic desire to control and dominate territory and the modernist construction of time as an arrow.[32] Light peripatetic constructs place as something that is not neatly contained and controlled but rather messy, complicated, and random — built up of sounds, physical movements, and other odd impressions — a multisensory collage celebrating values that are at odds with the societal norms of modernity and late modernity; it is *extravagant* in the literal sense, that is, a step off the beaten path.

One of the most notable American expressions of light peripatetic is Thoreau's essay "Walking," composed in the 1850s. This essay presents walking as an essential daily routine: "I think that I cannot preserve my health and spirits, unless I spend four hours a day at least — and it is commonly more than that — sauntering through the woods and over the hills and fields, absolutely free from all worldly engagements."[33] Among the reasons he gives for this extravagant behavior are love of nature, habit, adventure, disdain for people and their affairs, and the search for an ideal: "we would fain take that walk, never yet taken by us through this actual world, which is perfectly symbolical of the path which we love to travel in the interior and ideal world."[34] Thoreau's walking is a kind of externalization, a "walking out" of his ideals. His purpose is to attain "absolute freedom and wildness, as contrasted with a freedom and culture merely civil."[35] In the opposition between nature and society, Thoreau uses the motif of walking to side with nature and oppose the ideology of human control. He asks: "what would become of us, if we walked only in a garden or a mall?"[36] and suggests that exercise for its own sake, without the concomitant attunement to nature, is repugnant: "think of a man's swinging dumbbells for his health, when those springs are bubbling up in far-off pastures unsought by him!"[37]

Thoreau's peripatetic imagery finds an echo in the twentieth-century naturalist Edward Abbey, who calls walking "the one and only mode of locomotion in which a man proceeds entirely on his own, upright, as a human being should be, fully erect rather than sitting on his rear end."[38] Here the walker's freedom is contrasted with technological-dependence; the driver has not empowered himself but rather subjugated himself with technology.

Cultural texts of various kinds continue to be framed in the trope of light peripatetic, even advertisements. For example, an ad for Timex Expedition®

watches shows a man, woman, and young child, casually but expensively dressed, on a hike in the foothills of the Rockies or Black Hills. The caption reads, "10 million acres that couldn't care less what a big shot you are at the office." The watches are shown below this image, strapped to a rock, with the slogan: "The watch you wear out there." Taken as a whole, the ad addresses the successful career man who wears an expensive watch during the week and wants a sturdier, less-expensive watch for his weekend outings. Despite the ad's thinly veiled appeal to ambition, the implication is that walking outdoors is a way to escape the pressures of one's societal role. Likewise, a boot ad proclaims simply, "Nature wins," against a gray urban backdrop, while in the foreground a flower is breaking through the pavement, and an inset shows a pair of feet in Havana Joe® boots walking on yellow pine needles (Figure 2).

These versions of peripatetic implicitly question the validity of human society. Their emphasis is on the wellsprings of hope in the countryside that are accessible to the walker. Light peripatetic is, in short, optimistic but alienated: the walker arrives "in the community as a stranger."[39] And more generally: "the walker becomes the person whose relationship to society has been thrown into question."[40] In rhetorical terms, the walker is an ironist.

In contrast, societal constraints may be the central motif with the walker still opposed, but now vulnerable because of that opposition, in which case peripatetic becomes dark: pessimistic, cynical, or tragic. An excursion beyond the boundary of the civilized world then becomes an experience of, or at least a flirtation with, one's own rejection from society. Walking becomes an existential encounter with nonbeing in one or more of the following guises: disgrace, guilt, insanity, sickness, or death.[41]

Dark Peripatetic

In literature we often find what Wallace describes as "a fevered, haunted, misdirecting, unilluminated, and unilluminating walking."[42] Call to mind King Lear and Gloucester wandering on the heath after being reduced to indigence by their own foolishness and their ungrateful children.[43] Their outcast state is neatly dramatized by their desperate form of mobility, which ties blindness, nakedness, and madness together in a signature of the outcast and discarded condition. The dark peripatetic motif signifies that the bonds of society have been torn, or a character's identity is beginning to dissolve, or both. Walking is, on this account, an ominous excursion: out of doors, out of society, out of community, out of normal reality, and perhaps even out of life itself. Here as in the ad nature wins, but apparently to the detriment of the protagonist. Nevertheless — as in the character of Lear — such a state may also be associated with a fleeting encounter with an intense awareness of self and world, a kind of clairvoyance that goes beyond the province of optical knowledge.

A primary expression of the association between walking and otherness is a

Figure 2. Advertisement for Havana Joe® boots. Courtesy of Havana Joe.

fallen moral state. In James Joyce's *Portrait of the Artist as a Young Man,* for example, Stephen Dedalus literally strays into the company of prostitutes:

> He had wandered into a maze of narrow and dirty streets. From the foul laneways he heard bursts of hoarse riot and wrangling and the drawling of drunken singers. He walked onward, undismayed, wondering whether he had strayed into the quarter of the jews. Women and girls dressed

in long vivid gowns traversed the street from house to house. They were leisurely and perfumed. A trembling seized him and his eyes grew dim. . . .

He stood still in the middle of the roadway, his heart clamouring against his bosom in a tumult. A young woman dressed in a long pink gown laid her hand on his arm to detain him and gazed into his face. She said gaily:

—Good night, Willie dear![44]

After the moment of extravagance that follows, Stephen wanders (emotionally) into a hell of self-recrimination and fear, a mental excursion beyond the sphere of his family and his entire community.

While Dedalus's excursion eventually leads to his self-discovery as an artist (one type of transcendence and clairvoyance), other versions of the dark peripatetic do not end as happily. In Kafka's exploration of guilt, *The Trial*, K., the protagonist, finds himself trapped in the maze of an obscure criminal investigation. Ultimately he is escorted to the edge of town and executed. His denouement occurs at "a small stone quarry, deserted and desolate [which] lay quite near to a still completely urban house."[45] This ambiguous location, in a certain sense both inside and outside, both here and there, is an emblem of the fallen status of one who strays off the beaten path. The final scene of the story begins predictably with a forced march in which K.'s arms are held by his escorts, but ends with K. mysteriously racing these men to the place of execution. As in Joyce's novel, the act of voluntarily leaving familiar territory is emblematic of guilt, but here guilt leads inevitably to death.

Dark peripatetic may also present walking as a sign of wrongful exclusion from society. In Dickens's *The Old Curiosity Shop*, for example, an old man flees London with his granddaughter, Nell. The girl is a veritable angel — cheerful despite her poverty, uncomplaining when the stones in the road cut her feet, eternally humble, quiet, and charitable. Before leaving the city, the pair ponders the urban streets:

[S]tunned and bewildered by the hurry they beheld but had no part in, [they] looked mournfully on; feeling, amidst the crowd, a solitude which has no parallel but in the thirst of the shipwrecked mariner, who, tost [*sic*] to and fro upon the billows of a mighty ocean, his red eyes blinded by looking on the water which hems him in on every side, has not one drop to cool his burning tongue.[46]

Watching the well-to-do citizens hurrying past them on the city streets magnifies their sense of deprivation, so they become a different kind of walker and leave the city, drawn by Wordsworthian images of an idyllic pastoral life and a community that will sustain them. Although they do find a place to live in the country, the change in fate comes too late for Nell, who succumbs to a sickness precipitated by years of work, hardship, and malnutrition. Her pleasure in a few final walks in the country cannot forestall death. Dickens offers the walk only as a kind of sop to the wretched and the outcast, while also, in keeping with the peripatetic tradition, passing a bitter judgment on the costs of urbanization and industrialization.

The German poet and novelist Rainer Maria Rilke employs yet another type of dark peripatetic. His character Malte Laurids Brigge pursues a mentally ill man through the streets of Paris as the man's bizarre walk betrays the confusion of his mind. Malte notices the man because others are pointing at him and laughing:

> I was sure that there was nothing laughable about this man's clothing or behavior, and was already trying to look past him down the boulevard, when he tripped over something. Since I was walking close behind him I was on my guard, but when I came to the place, there was nothing there, absolutely nothing.[47]

After a second mysterious stumble, the observed man hops several steps on one foot, then begins obsessively to straighten and unstraighten his collar while continuing to walk as normally as possible. As the compulsive movements continue, the man resorts to holding his back against his cane, as a kind of splint, but eventually is overcome by compulsive movements. He is engulfed at this point by a crowd of curious onlookers that has suddenly formed. Rilke, who probably witnessed something similar while living in Paris in the summer of 1902, uses the bizarre walk as a symbol of the loneliness of an individual in the big city.

A similar observation motivates the French poet Charles Baudelaire, in "Les petites vieilles" (The little old women). Likewise set in Paris (the epitome of urban civilization at this time) the poem scrutinizes the walking styles of old women with a gaze that is alternately cold and affectionate but always unflinching:

> They trot, just like marionettes,
> Or drag along like wounded deer,
> Or dance against their will, as if
> A devil were swinging in the belfry of their bones.
> . . . .
> But I, who watch you affectionately from a distance,
> A nervous eye on your faltering steps,
> Just as if I were your father (to think!)
> Enjoy forbidden pleasures on your behalf.[48]

Baudelaire, like Rilke, is haunted by the unusual walk, the *marked* walk, as a manifestation of human solitude. In watching such a walk he feels his own solitude more sharply, even as he knows that part of his solitude entails the ability to enjoy pleasures that are not accessible to all. It is precisely because the city is a "world of strangers"[49] that the walk becomes an emblem of loneliness.

While these authors present a dark subject in a serious manner, dark peripatetic can also be ironic or grimly humorous. Particularly adept at this approach was Robert Frost. In "Away," he flippantly dismisses all the associations of dark peripatetic that have been discussed thus far:

> Now I out walking
> The world desert,
> And my shoe and my stocking
> Do me no hurt.
>
> I leave behind
> Good friends in town
> Let them get well-wined
> And go lie down.
>
> Don't think that I leave
> For the outer dark
> Like Adam and Eve
> Put out of the Park.
>
> Forget the myth.
> There is no one I
> Am put out with
> Or put out by.
>
> Unless I'm wrong
> I but obey
> The urge of a song:
> I'm — bound — away!
>
> And I may return
> If dissatisfied
> With what I learn
> From having died.[50]

Although insisting that he has not been put out (exiled) from society, and he is not put out (annoyed), he nonetheless raises the prospect of death and banishment by the act of flippantly denying these prospects.

If dark peripatetic resonates less with modern urban dwellers than it once did, this is perhaps because it is so deeply engrained in daily life, in the avoidance of walking. Ads for vehicles continue to suggest that one is not a complete person, and has no place, if one is not the owner of a particularly impressive vehicle. Off-road vehicles, for example, appropriate elements of dark peripatetic to encourage a nonpedestrian departure from society. Like Frost, the ads both acknowledge the departure from the human world and deny it. Suzuki's all terrain vehicle, the Quadrunner® 500, is shown in a magazine ad parked in a wild-looking forest with leaves stuck to its giant knobby tires. The text declares: "It's a world with three hundred television channels, get as far away from it as you can." The ad's text argues, as well, that a "return to the basics" requires "exceptional ground clearance and a massive engine with the performance to take you where you need to go." Paradoxically, the desire to escape technology is inverted, transformed to the need for technology; meanwhile one's escape from society is linked to the display of a (socially constructed) status symbol. The common thread joining modern four-wheel-drive ads to the dark peripatetic of the cited works is the suspicion that stepping beyond borders is a threat to one's life and identity. Technology is required for this dangerous pursuit, and the appeal to ambition suggests that nature has been inscribed as a part of identity that you may own as a badge of virility. If you can not walk away from insecurity, then perhaps you can ride.[51]

Urban Space, Modernity, and Walking

Uniting these disparate peripatetic images and the two categories into which they fall is the opposition between walking, on the one hand, and society, on the other. A representation of walking as a basis of society is not, however, completely absent from the literature. Jane Jacobs's classic *The Death and Life of Great American Cities,* for example, not only echoes romantic concerns regarding the destruction of a sense of place but also focuses attention on the walker in an urban context, the pedestrian.[52] This work emerged in a period of technological optimism and rapid change in the United States not unlike that of the first industrial revolution that horrified Wordsworth and Thoreau. For Jacobs, however, the walker is essential to the preservation of society, not a symbol of a return to nature. This view departs from the peripatetic imagery discussed thus far because the walker here is neither a happy nor an unhappy outcast; he or she is an integral member of society. If Jacobs is remembered for her views on built form, this interest in pedestrian mobility is certainly an important subtext.

In a series of three chapters on "the uses of sidewalks," which focus in turn on safety, social contact, and the socialization of children, Jacobs makes the following claims. In regard to safety: "Sidewalks, their bordering uses, and their users, are active participants in the drama of civilization versus barbarism in cities. To keep the city safe is a fundamental task of a city's streets and its sidewalks."[53] In regard to social contact: "The trust of a city street is formed over time from many, many little public sidewalk contacts. It grows out of people stopping by at the bar for a beer, getting advice from the grocer and giving advice to the newsstand man, comparing opinions with other customers at the bakery and nodding hello to the two boys drinking pop on the stoop, eyeing the girls while waiting to be called for dinner, admonishing the children, hearing about a job from the hardware man and borrowing a dollar from the druggist, admiring the new babies and sympathizing over the way a coat faded."[54] In regard to socializing children: "The people of cities who have other jobs and duties, and who lack, too, the training needed, cannot volunteer as teachers or registered nurses or librarians or museum guards or social workers. But at least they can, and on lively diversified sidewalks they do, supervise the incidental play of children and assimilate the children into city society. They do it *in the course of carrying on their other pursuits.*"[55]

To understand pedestrianism in this way we must see it in a context where it is part of a way of life, and sadly these days many people in their twenties and older — who have grown up in automobile-dependent cities like Houston and Los Angeles and even in suburbs of livelier cities like Boston — may never have seen it. By the 1950s, liberal and conservative planners alike saw little value in older urban landscapes that had been designed for access by foot. Such spaces were demolished, and housing developments, shopping malls, freeway interchanges, and housing projects were all designed for "convenience," which meant the avoidance of bipedal locomotion. In the new environments they helped create, driving was easier and pedestrians had to contend with greater distances between goals, faster vehicles, discontinuous sidewalks, and the proliferation of parking lots, so that walking was ever more difficult. The rewards of walking were simultaneously diminished as the diverse functions of the street were "thinned out" to form single-function zones of residential, industrial, office, and retail land uses. Aesthetically, the urban landscape became monotonous and intimidating; socially, it became threatening, as pedestrians were too sparse to render the streets safe by regular and continual presence.

One of Jacobs's most important insights was that the street's role derives from circulation but is not identical to it. "The first thing to understand is that the public peace — the sidewalk and street peace — of cities is not kept primarily by the police, necessary as the police are"; instead it is kept by "an intricate, almost unconscious, network of voluntary controls and standards among the people themselves, and enforced by the people themselves." Walkers in urban environments provide "eyes on the street," that is, surveillance, hence her preoccupation with sidewalks. A flow of pedestrians on lively, functional sidewalks also invites people-watching, effectively providing more eyes on the street. Pedestrians alone are not sufficient, of course: land uses should be mixed; there should be a clear demarcation between public and private space; and residents must be committed to their neighborhood. In such environments, pedestrian use becomes part of a self-perpetuating cycle: the more pedestrians, the safer the streets; the safer the streets, the more businesses; the more businesses, the more destinations; and the more destinations, the more pedestrians.[56] Her argument was novel not only in its spatial implications but also in its representation of walking.[57]

In recent years, concern about the rapid consumption of agricultural land and wildlife habitat, the use of petroleum, the accumulation of carbon dioxide, the loss of a sense of community, and the unhealthiness of prevalent lifestyles has prompted a type of urban design and planning called "neotraditional" urban planning, or simply "New Urbanism," that belatedly incorporates the ideas of Jacobs and a few other luminaries.[58] Its proponents reject many of the principles of architecture and urban design promulgated in the grandiose plans of modernist architects such as Le Corbusier and Mies Van der Rohe and put in place by the transportation planners of the postwar era.

As elaborated by Peter Calthorpe, neotraditional planning depends on pedestrians:

> Pedestrians are the catalyst which makes the essential qualities of communities meaningful. They create the place and the time for casual encounters.... Without the pedestrian, a community's common ground — its parks, sidewalks, squares, and plazas — become useless obstructions to the car. *Pedestrians are the lost measure of a community,* they set the scale for both center and edge of our neighborhoods. Without the pedestrian, an area's focus can be easily lost. Commerce and civic uses are easily decentralized into distant chain store destinations and government centers. Homes and jobs are isolated in subdivisions and office parks.[59]

There is some rescripting of history here, for the pedestrian, as shown thus far, has not been a respected member of community as framed by Western discourses. He (and occasionally she — see Overing and Osborn, in this volume) is an extravagant wanderer, prone to cross boundaries and stray in all sorts of symbolic ways. Nonetheless, neotraditional planning does recapture something traditional: certain design principles of earlier eras, including those that created the kind of streetscapes that Jacobs extolled.[60] While the form is, to some degree, a return to the prefreeway landscape, the textual articulation of this form *as a pedestrian space, and as an ideal social space for that reason,* is something new. We have, then, the explicit creation of new peripatetic imagery along a completely different line than the light-dark opposition, as an adjunct to certain landscape design practices.

The receptivity of American culture to such an "invented tradition"[61] certainly remains in question. If there is no resonance with this portrayal of walking as a basis of urban society in popular discourses such as novels and films, can the idea diffuse into popular consciousness? Can this countercurrent of ideology stake out a "place" for the walker when vehicles lie at the center of so much of consumer culture? How can people be induced to build community ties in physical spaces like sidewalks and parks when so much of public life is conducted in the virtual space of the electronic media? What are the moral opportunities and risks associated with neotraditional urban spaces, in particular conjunction with their emphasis on the pedestrian? These questions cannot be answered at present, but I predict that as neotraditional planning (and its rhetoric) diffuses because of concern with the environmental and aesthetic impacts of an automobile-dominated lifestyle, they will be raised with increasing frequency. It will be interesting to see if the timeworn moral narratives constructing the walker as good and society as bad, or the walker as bad and society as good, or both (most disturbingly) as bad, can be resolved (for a time) to indicate how the walker and society can both be good. The peripatetic sense of place is likely to remain terra incognita unless this symbolic reconciliation is achieved.

Notes

1. John K. Wright, "Terrae Incognitae: The Place of the Imagination in Geography," *Annals of the Association of American Geographers* 37, no. 1 (1947): 3.

2. See Karen E. Till's essay in this volume.

3. Upward of three billion dollars are spent by Americans annually on indoor exercise equipment, more than a quarter on indoor treadmills alone ("The Year in Review," *Sporting Goods Business* 29, no. 11 [November 1996]: 40).

4. Consider, for example, that cardiovascular disease is the leading cause of death for both women and men in the United States, causing more deaths than cancer, AIDS, and accidents combined (Texas Heart Institute, *How to Be Heart Healthy* [Houston: St. Luke's Hospital, Texas Heart Institute, June 1998; online file at www.tmc.edu/thi/matters.html).

5. Parking fees in a medium-sized city range as high as five dollars a day in certain locations while within a distance of only four blocks from such locations free parking can be found. This steep gradient indicates that people are willing to spend five dollars to avoid a five-minute walk to and from their car, or one hundred dollars a month since many of the persons in question are commuters. In other words, people in an average American city would pay fifty cents per minute *not* to walk. The data are from Denver. My thanks to Darryl and Kathryn Adams for this information.

6. For a description of these processes, see Edward Relph, *Place and Placelessness* (London: Pion, 1976), 90–121; and Relph, *The Modern Urban Landscape* (Baltimore: Johns Hopkins University Press, 1987), 238–67; as well as Yi-Fu Tuan, *Topophilia: A Study of Environmental Perception, Attitudes, and Values,* with new preface (New York: Columbia University Press, 1990), 11.

7. Jonathan Smith, "Geographical Rhetoric: Modes and Tropes of Appeal," *Annals of the Association of American Geographers* 86, no. 1 (1996): 6.

8. For a full analysis of the relation between space, place, and the good life, see Yi-Fu Tuan, *The Good Life* (Madison: University of Wisconsin Press, 1986).

9. For a more detailed view of the mechanisms involved, see Edward Casey, "Body, Self, and Landscape: A Geophilosophical Inquiry into the Place-World," in this volume.

10. Paul C. Adams, "Television as Gathering Place," *Annals of the Association of American Geographers* 82 (1992): 117–35; Adams, "Computer Networks and Virtual Place Metaphors," *Geographical Review* 87 (1997) (special issue on cyberspace and geographical space, guest editors, Paul C. Adams and B. Warf), 155–71; Adams, "Network Topologies and Virtual Place," *Annals of the Association of American Geographers* 88 (1998): 88–106.

11. Tuan, *Topophilia*, 10.

12. Joel Garreau, *Edge City: Life on the New Frontier* (New York: Doubleday, 1988).

13. Tuan, *Topophilia*, 175.

14. Anthony Giddens, *The Constitution of Society: Outline of the Theory of Structuration* (Berkeley: University of California Press, 1984).

15. See Paul C. Adams, "A Reconsideration of Personal Boundaries in Space-Time," *Annals of the Association of American Geographers* 85 (1995): 267–85.

16. Susan Hanson, "Getting There: Urban Transportation in Context," in *The Geography of Urban Transportation,* ed. Susan Hanson, 2d ed. (New York: Guilford Press, 1995), 3–25.

17. M. Jay, "Scopic Regimes of Modernity," in *Vision and Visuality: Discussions in Contemporary Culture,* ed. H. Foster (Seattle: Bay Press, 1988), 3–28.

18. Lewis Mumford, *Technics and Civilization* (New York: Harcourt, Brace & World, 1963), 343–44; emphasis added.

19. Marshall McLuhan, *Understanding Media: The Extensions of Man* (New York and Scarborough, Ontario: Mentor/New American Library, 1964).

20. Anne D. Wallace, *Walking, Literature, and English Culture: The Origins and Uses of Peripatetic in the Nineteenth Century* (Oxford: Clarendon, 1993), 169.

21. Ibid., 11.

22. Ibid., 114.

23. Raymond Williams, *The Country and the City* (New York: Oxford University Press, 1973).

24. Jeffrey C. Robinson, *The Walk: Notes on a Romantic Image* (Norman: University of Oklahoma Press, 1989); Roger Gilbert, *Walks in the World: Representation and Experience in Modern American Poetry* (Princeton, N.J.: Princeton University Press, 1991).

25. Alfred Kazin, *A Walker in the City* (New York: Harcourt, Brace, 1951).

26. John Elder, *Imagining the Earth: Poetry and the Vision of Nature* (Urbana: University of Illinois Press, 1985), 93.

27. Stephen Daniels, "Marxism, Culture, and the Duplicity of Landscape," in *New Models in Geography,* vol. 2, ed. Richard Peet and Nigel Thrift (London: Unwin Hyman, 1987).

28. Wallace, *Walking,* 89.

29. *Poems by William Wordsworth,* ed. George McLean Harper (New York: Charles Scribner's Sons, 1923), 4–5.

30. William Wordsworth, *Home at Grasmere,* part first, book first, of *The Recluse,* ed. Beth Darlington (Ithaca, N.Y.: Cornell University Press), 82.

31. Gilbert, *Walks in the World,* 54–57, 129–47, 261.

32. Daniels, "Marxism, Culture, and the Duplicity of Landscape."

33. Henry David Thoreau "Walking," in *The Portable Thoreau* (New York: Viking Penguin, 1975), 593.

34. Ibid., 602–3.

35. Ibid., 592.

36. Ibid., 597.

37. Ibid., 596.

38. Edward Abbey, "A Walk in the Desert Hills," in *Beyond the Wall* (New York: Holt, Rinehart and Winston, 1983), 35.

39. Robinson, *The Walk,* 55.

40. Ibid.

41. I leave aside the Taoist or Zen conception of nonbeing, which appears predictably in the peripatetic poems of Japanese and Chinese authors, such as the great haiku artist Basho.

42. Wallace, *Walking,* 229.

43. William Shakespeare, *King Lear,* in *The Illustrated Shakespeare* (New York: Park Lane/Crown Publishers, 1979), 3:53–122.

44. James Joyce, *A Portrait of the Artist as a Young Man,* in *The Portable James Joyce* (New York: Viking Press, 1967), 351–52.

45. Franz Kafka, *The Trial* (New York: Penguin Books, 1953).

46. Charles Dickens, *The Old Curiosity Shop* (New York: Heritage Press, 1941).

47. Rainer Maria Rilke, *The Notebooks of Malte Laurids Brigge,* trans. Stephen Mitchell (New York: Vintage Books/Random House, 1982), 66–67.

48. Charles Baudelaire, "Les petites vieilles," in *Les fleurs du mal et autres poèmes* (Paris: Garnier-Flammarion, 1964); my translation from the French.

49. Lyn Lofland, *A World of Strangers: Order and Action in Urban Public Space* (New York: Basic Books, 1973).

50. Robert Frost, "Away," in *In the Clearing* (New York: Holt, Rinehart and Winston, 1962), 15.

51. A sign of the instrumentality of this ideology is that the Suzuki Company refused to grant permission to show the ad in this essay.

52. Jane Jacobs, *The Death and Life of Great American Cities* (New York: Vintage Books/Random House, 1961).

53. Ibid., 30.

54. Ibid., 56.

55. Ibid., 81–82.

56. Ibid., 31–32, 35.

57. Despite academic interest in Jacobs's observations, little attention was paid in the United States to the creation or maintenance of pedestrian spaces. Indeed, by the 1990s, the majority of new jobs and construction had shifted to the beltways outside the built-up part of the city (or in some cases to a second or third beltway) where agricultural land could be converted quickly to shopping malls, condominiums, million-dollar estates, and office buildings surrounded by fashionable "greenfields." These "edge cities" are overwhelmingly oriented toward motor vehicle traffic, as indicated by a growth rate in vehicle miles traveled (VMT) in the United States that is three times population growth, and an average of 2.3 cars per household in the suburbs; see Garreau, *Edge City;* and Peter Calthorpe, *The Next American Metropolis: Ecology, Community, and the American Dream* (Princeton, N.J.: Princeton Architectural Press, 1993), 20.

58. See, for example, Christopher Alexander, *A Pattern Language* (New York: Oxford University Press, 1977).

59. Calthorpe, *Next American Metropolis,* 17; emphasis added.

60. Its four basic principles are that urban environments should be mixed-use, transit-oriented, walkable, and diverse; see ibid. Specifically, the new Transit-Oriented Developments (TODs) would focus retail and services (and sometimes offices and industry) in small pockets rather than strips or large agglomerations. Each pocket of public activity would concentrate activity around (and hence help to protect) a park or greenspace. All residences would be located within walking distance of such an activity center with a transit stop, thus alleviating the need for driving, and traffic would be diffused and slowed in residential areas on a network of through streets rather than concentrated by the currently popular treelike road pattern. At least in theory, a full range of housing types from inexpensive to expensive would be mixed to reduce spatial stratification by class.

61. What is "traditional" is not simply a matter of fact but is a social construction: see Eric Hobsbawm and Terence Ranger, *The Invention of Tradition* (New York: Cambridge University Press, 1983).

THE FRAGMENTED INDIVIDUAL AND THE ACADEMIC REALM

Michael Curry

We have heard a great deal lately about "distance learning" in higher education. And we have heard, too, about other developments occurring within the university, changes as seemingly diverse as the rise of postmodernism, the penetration of corporate money into the interstices of the institution, the focus on new technologies, and pressures for and against affirmative action.

If these developments have occurred against the background of the idea of the university as an "ivory tower," those who have commented on them have in fact typically failed to see that the traditional ivory tower was a *place*. And they have failed in the process to see that it was only within the ivory tower *as* a place that certain of the features that we see as most characteristic of academics could make sense.

In what follows, I shall argue that the university has at least over the last one hundred years been a place of a very special sort, one in which academic professionals were able to represent themselves as in some sense "placeless," and that recent developments have in various ways begun to undercut the possibility of its remaining such a place.

On the Professions

As Bruce Kimball has shown, there have been

> six "moments" in the rhetoric of "profession," six changes in the usage of "profession" and its cognates. First was the extension of "profession" from referring to a religious vow to denoting the group who made the vow, especially, the "secular" clergy. Second was the shift in reference from the clergy to dignified, non-religious occupations. Third was the introduction of the terms "learned professions" and "liberal professions," which identified certain dignified occupations. Fourth was the displacement of "professed" by "professional" as the adjective denoting "occupational" or "vocational." Fifth was the introduction of the noun "professional" to replace "professor," which was narrowed to the field of education. The sixth moment in the rhetoric of "profession" was the sloughing away of the terms "learned professions" and "liberal profes-

sions" in the early twentieth century, as "professions" began to refer to many vocations, just as it had in sixteenth-century English.[1]

For Kimball the era of greatest ferment, of the most rapid changes in the rhetoric of "the profession," was the nineteenth century. This was, of course, the era of dramatic growth of what Karl Polanyi termed a "new way of life," centered around capitalism and individualism:

> That system developed in leaps and bounds; it engulfed space and time. . . . By the time it reached its maximum extent, around 1914, every part of the globe, all its inhabitants and unborn generations, physical persons as well as huge fictitious bodies called corporations, were comprised in it. A new way of life spread over the planet with a claim to universality unparalleled since the age when Christianity started out on its career, only this time the movement was on a purely material level.[2]

And this is just the era in which was to be found, as Thomas L. Haskell has shown, a countermovement:

> What Durkheim had in mind when he spoke of improving "professional ethics" was what Tawney meant [i.e., in *The Acquisitive Society*] when he spoke of transforming occupations into professions, namely, the establishment or reinforcement of a collegial mode of occupational control. . . . [W]herever applied it meant an intensification of collegial discipline and a struggle for autonomy against patrons, clients, and other forces outside occupational ranks.[3]

In one sense, then, the goal of the professions was to establish for themselves a set of spaces metaphorically outside of the Weberian iron cage, spaces within which the professional might escape the deforming forces of the market.

Professional Places

But from the point of view of the geographer, one very interesting feature of the way in which the professions made that attempt was the way in which they relied on the construction of sets of *non*metaphorical places. Indeed, this has been symptomatic of the strategy used by the professions, from the clergy in the early eighteenth century, through lawyers, professors, and now physicians. In each case the professional laid claim to a status metaphorically outside everyday self-interest by operating from within a set of places whose scope and scale the professions attempted at every turn to control. If the clergy had the church and the sanctuary, the attorney the law office and the courtroom, and the physician the hospital and clinic, the professor had the "ivory tower." And like these other professional places, the ivory tower has been widely seen, from within and without, as isolated, cut off from the forces of the outside world.

If the maintenance of these professional places as places has relied on the view of them as symbolically isolated, as separate from the rest of the world, this isolation has been maintained in a number of ways. Some are as simple as the building of a wall or fence or the location of the institution in a physically remote place. But more important — and certainly more interesting — have been other means. As Kimball notes, for example, in early New England local parishioners were expected both to construct the minister's dwelling and to maintain stores of firewood; there the minister's dwelling, like the parish church, established the professional status of the minister just through these ritualized practices.

At the same time, the institutionalized location of judge and attorney in the courtroom is a means by which the professional status of both is maintained; only they can occupy those positions and be said to belong there. This sense of who belongs where is further cemented in courtroom, operating room, classroom, and church alike by the existence of defined places that the audience may occupy and from which they may see and hear, but not touch, those occupying the places of professionals.

In each of these cases those operating within their appropriate places become actors in a system for the collection and organization of knowledge. The judge and attorney speak from their own positions; the defendant, typically, only from the witness box. The surgeon collects information, but only through the appropriate channels. Noise from the gallery, talk radio, and the like are merely that, noise. And, of course, the professor, when lecturing or doing research, is very much a part of a system for the acquisition and distribution of knowledge.

At the same time, in each of these cases the place of the professional is one not simply wherein information is transmitted from professional to audience; rather, the professional engages in actions and in discourse that is fundamentally performative. The minister declares a couple married, and in declaring it makes it so; the judge declares a defendant not guilty, and makes it so. And the professor does not merely pass along information, but rather performs it, constructing the truth in the telling.

The Universal Professional

But if the professional becomes a professional only by virtue of actions carried out in the appropriate place, to be a professional, at least according to the model supported by nineteenth-century writers like Durkheim and Tawney, is in a sense to step beyond the constraints of those places. In other words, the professional is universally a professional.

This is the case for several reasons. Just to the extent that professionalism is associated with licensing, and licensing, in turn, with governments, the establishment of professions regulated by systems of credentials establishes the state as an open space, within which the professional has the right of free movement and, at least in principle, the right to be treated *as* a professional within the boundaries of that state and in all others with which it has established the appropriate agreements.[4]

At the same time, the almost universal establishment, within those credentialing systems, of ethical standards for practitioners of professions suggests another form of universality within which the professional operates; the professional is never "off duty."[5] The behavior of the professional is always relevant to the question of whether he or she is truly a professional. Indeed, so important is this fact that if it has been formalized in the codes of ethics of groups that have been granted exclusive rights over certain forms of activities, as in the case of attorneys and physicians, more marginalized or aspiring professions have used their adherence to such codes as a means of demonstrating the validity of their claims to professional status. This is precisely what has happened recently in computer science[6] and within geography, in the case of geographic information systems.[7]

This form of universality is shown in another way, in the means that professionals have used to market themselves. This is perhaps most starkly the case in academics, where the job application, traditionally a listing of relevant experience, and the résumé, focusing on experience and skills, have been replaced by the curriculum vitae. If the other documents assume that the applicant has picked and chosen among his or her experiences, the curriculum vitae is generally assumed to be a comprehensive statement of the professional's life, at least since leaving secondary school. The life of the professional is imagined to have a trajectory, a path of development from education to entry into a professional position, and on up the ladder; gaps, exceptions, changes of heart, all need to be explained, as all seem to suggest the lack of just what the code of conduct implies, a collegial spirit and an unalloyed moral will.

And in fact, in those cases in which the professional violates the code of conduct, and does so in a way that is seen as seriously jeopardizing the status of the profession, he or she is cast out, exiled, paradoxically, into the larger community of particular and particularistic individuals. In many cases — of physicians, military officers, and members of the clergy — this involves a kind of inverse marking; the individual is marked by the larger community as special just to the extent that the identifying uniform can no longer be worn.

The Fragmented Individual and the Academic Realm

The preceding has been merely a sketch, an attempt in a very preliminary way to lay out some of the features of the geography of the professions. I make no claim that it is wholly accurate, and it is surely not comprehensive. Yet I would argue that in its lineaments it is a reasonably accurate portrayal of the place of the professional in contemporary American society. I would at the same time argue that over the last several decades each of the professions has in a different way faced challenges to this model of professionalism. Further, those challenges can be seen as involving a dual recasting, of the nature of the places within which the professions operate and of the ways in which they have been able to represent themselves as universal, as placeless.

The examples of these changes are manifold. First television and now almost-instant, Internet-based transcripts have breached the walls of the courtroom where before the printed word and the artist's sketch were the primary means by which the workings of the legal profession were made clear. At the same time, the development of entertainment programs, such as those on Court TV, and of alternative, private judicial proceedings, using judges hired by the parties, has blurred the distinction between the judicial and the nonjudicial, the professional judge and attorney, and the TV actor.

Similarly, the joint introduction of government-funded health insurance, managed care, and computer-based, networked medical-record systems has transformed the doctor's office. What was once imagined as a refuge within which a professional and his (or occasionally her) patient could discuss matters of life and death has now become porous, as everything that is said becomes possible fodder for pharmaceutical companies, insurance companies, law-enforcement agencies, and mass marketers. And, indeed, it ought to come as no surprise that similar changes have been felt in the realm of the academic professional.

The Academic Realm

In the nineteenth century, it is said, the ideal of the institution of higher education was Mark Hopkins at one end of a log and a student at the other. Stark as is this image, it points to just the claim that I have been making about the professions. For, on the one hand, the professor and student are "right there," engaging in the sort of dialogical project that requires that those involved be together, in a place. And, on the other hand, just to the extent that this is a place without ornament, the sort of place within which Plato put Socrates and his friends, the activities that occur are represented as universal.

And, in fact, this second, universalistic feature of academic life has come to be associated with the idea that scholars operate in a realm of "pure thought." If the average person needs to work at it in order to transcend the vicissitudes of everyday life — the barking dog, the bill collector, the reactionary senator, and the common cold — the scholar works in a place that allows just that sort of thinking to go on, and to go on routinely.

This idea of the scholar has, in turn, and in rather complicated ways, been incorporated into common sense about academic practice. As is commonly known, since the sixteenth, and especially the eighteenth, century this way of thinking about scholarship as pure thought has come to be associated with an idea, most familiarly formulated in the romantic reaction to modernism, of the author as someone who by the very fact of authorship attains a kind of aura.[8] That notion of the author has come to be the groundwork for the principle of intellectual property known as the idea of moral right, a notion that is, of course, at the center of European intellectual property law and is incorporated into the laws of all members of the World Intellectual Property Organization.[9]

It is easy here to imagine that because the creations of the scholar are characterized in the law as *intellectual* property, they are conceived in the moral-right tradition strictly as intellectual. And, in fact, this way of thinking would seem to make sense, just because it is very much in accord with a pair of ideas, about scientific knowledge as being a product of reason and scientific practice as involving the attempt to achieve scientific discoveries, to discover the nature of the world. Here, reason is very often construed as instrumental in nature; to use reason in science is to move from previously known facts and principles to that which was always there but remained unrecognized. It is in this way that science has been seen, too, as a matter of discovery, of truths that have existed but have not been known. Here science is seen as a product of Cartesian, extensionless minds, minds that need be neither here nor there. The acts of scientific reasoning and discovery can be seen as fundamentally placeless. And the relationship between the place where scientific work is carried out and that work itself is only contingent.

As it happened, this view of the relationship between science and the places wherein it is carried out was reinforced by the development of the vernacular science that by the sixteenth century had increasingly augmented — and threatened — more theoretical forms of learning. Written in other languages — Spanish, English, Italian, Portuguese, French, and Dutch — this literature focused less on the theoretical than on the practical and created results in the forms, familiar to geographers, of atlases and other compendia.[10] If this work did not share in the developing appeal to instrumental reason among theoretically minded scientists, by representing the world itself as a laboratory and the scientist as a peripatetic laborer using universally applicable tools, the more vernacular science did promote the view of the relationship between the scientist and particular places as a contingent one.

Of course, even in the early eighteenth century advocates of moral right were fighting a rearguard action, for by then alternatives to the moral-right approach to intellectual property were well established. One of these, the Lockean labor theory of property, has been a particularly visible element of Anglo-American thinking about the nature of intellectual property and of scientific practice. And central to this view is the belief that labor is a form of human activity that creates a set of property rights, where those rights are contingent and alienable. Here too, the work of the laborer is conceived of as only contingently related to the places in which it is created. Indeed, after Frederick W. Taylor and Frank B. Gilbreth,[11] one can conceive labor as the product of only *parts* of the laboring body, products purely of habit and not of consciously directed labor.

So if for Marx the modern laborer was special because he had no property, common sense has come to imagine that the scientist, as intellectual laborer, has no proper place. But, in fact, it is a mistake to see the moral-right approach to intellectual property as centrally focused on a person, the intellectual. On the contrary, the moral-right theory is romantic in intent; its roots extend back to Vico — to the critique of the then-new Cartesian sundering of the mind and the body and to later attacks on the sundering of the human and the natural worlds.[12] In fact, it sees a central feature of a work as its place within a community, so that a work created is a work that becomes part of one's identity.[13] Indeed, it sees the creations of the artist or scholar as needing to be protected just because they are the products of a whole individual, who inhabits a community — and a place.

The Fragmented Professional

Now, I would like to suggest that over the last twenty years this way of thinking about the scholar and scientist, which in spite of prevailing common sense has been right at the heart of the way in which these universal professionals have thought about themselves, has been undercut in a number of ways. Although these changes have roots in a variety of political, economic, and social phenomena, I would like to limit my attention here to the relationship between the university as a place, and a place within places, and a series of technological changes. Perhaps the best place to start, oddly enough, is with Jeremy Bentham.[14]

If we recall the two predominant ways of conceptualizing property — the labor theory and the moral-right theory — we see that in both cases the focus of discourse about property rights is on legitimacy. And in both cases theorists, like G. W. F. Hegel and John Locke, have justified their favored conceptions by appealing to stories about places. In the case of Hegel these are stories about people operating within communities, creating their identities through their possessions. As Hegel put it, "The rationale of property is to be found not in the satisfaction of needs but in the supersession of the pure subjectivity of personality. In his property a person exists for the first time as reason."[15] And for Locke, "Thus labour, in the beginning, gave a right of property wherever anyone was pleased to employ it upon what was common."[16]

Whatever their — very substantial — differences, proponents of the labor and moral-right theories share one thing in their discussions of private property. They treat property as something that has a "real" existence. It is tangible, people have visceral connections with it, it is out there in the world. For Locke, a worker invests labor in an object, and the object is suffused with that labor. It is as though, with Walter Benjamin, property has a kind of aura.[17]

But for Bentham, property has value "[o]n account of the pleasures of all kinds which it enables a man to produce, and what comes to the same thing the pains of all kinds which it enables him to avert."[18] Although, granted,

> the value of such an article is universally understood to rise or fall according to the length or shortness of the time which a man has in it: the certainty or uncertainty of its coming into possession: and the nearness or remoteness of the time at which, if at all, it is to come into possession.[19]

Now, the interesting thing is this, that even though he uses words like "nearness" and "remoteness," words that might be seen as appealing to the object just as they do in Hegel and Locke, in the end property is valuable *only* to the extent that it makes a person happy. And that means that the relationship between a person and his or her property is always contingent, always subject to reinterpretation and renegotiation.

So the real news is that with Bentham, as with the more recent Benthamite theories of value implicit in neoclassical economics, the object has lost its aura. In Thomas C. Grey's memorable phrase, we have seen "the disintegration of property."[20] Property is no longer of value because it is an outward expression of character, nor because the creator has insinuated her or his labor into it. Rather, a piece of property has value because of the pleasure that its owners imagine that it can create, and the transfer of property is in the end a contractual matter, where a piece of property is valued in terms of another measure, most often today, of money.

The New Academic Professionals

And, in fact, this process of contractualization has undercut the possibility of seeing the university as a place within which a group of academic professionals can be said to belong. At the same time, this process has been a part of the creation of a new set of academic professionals and a new model of professionalization.

The emergence of these new professionals has not occurred overnight. Indeed, in an important sense we can see that emergence as accompanying the rise of what Derek J. de Solla Price called "big science," beginning early in this century.[21] Central to the growth of big science was, of course, a substantial increase in the use of outside funding for research. But perhaps more important was the formalization of this support in government organizations,[22] and geographers have long been a part of this process.[23]

Funding for science is increasingly derived from organizations that are bureaucratically organized. Such funding sources typically work very much within the contractual model, seeing their provision of funds as reasonably requiring a reciprocal provision of scientific output, where that output, in turn, is expected to give credit to the source of funding. This system is now so much a part of scientists' daily lives that it hardly needs mentioning. But we should be reminded that under the moral-right tradition the author could not be held legally liable for not having produced a contracted work; there it was believed that to force an author to produce a work would be at times to require that author to publish a work not representative of his or her personality; and under the moral-right theory to do so would be to run counter to the very foundations that underpinned that system of intellectual property.

Governments have been involved in other ways in the transformation of universities. The creation beginning in the 1940s of the GI Bill, and then in the 1960s of massive financial aid programs, such as the National Defense Student Loan Program, a part of the Cold War attempt to out-educate the Soviet Union, and then later a long list of other programs, has provided government with an opportunity to exert indirect control over teaching in the same way that it has over research. Martin Duberman, for example, describes in his study of Black Mountain College the way in which the failing institution was shored up by money provided to veterans under the GI Bill.[24] The cost to Black Mountain was rather meager; the college merely had to have an official catalog, with a listing of appropriate courses.

But by the 1960s, the increasing influx into educational institutions of government funds led governments to develop a more formal and rigorous means of determining whether their money was being well spent; they required that institutions receiving federal aid funds be accredited by an appropriate association. If such associations, like the North Central Association, had in the past been controlled by academics and teachers, the list of accredited accreditation associations was now supervised from the government. And so, albeit indirectly, the government began to have the authority to set the standards that a curriculum would need to meet in order to be acceptable.

If teaching and research were increasingly required because of their funding sources to operate in accordance with accepted standards for the use of money, those standards themselves were undergoing change. The creation of the Financial Accounting Standards Board (FASB) (established 1973) and the Governmental Accounting Standards Board (GASB) (established 1984) helped institute those standards.

In each of these cases — of government funding of research and of teaching, and of the authority of accreditation associations and of standards boards — the issue is *not* one of growing external control of the university. Or rather, that is only part of the story. Central to the story is the way in which educational institutions came to have operating within them groups of people who have closer ties to those outside the university than to those within, groups of people who see themselves as professionals.

As universities have come increasingly to be connected with governments, funding agencies, and the like, institutional representatives from within universities have found themselves forced to operate in accordance with technical standards set from without. And not unreasonably, they have seen as a means to the adequate carrying on of their duties the involvement with organizations like the National Association of College and University Business Officers (NACUBO), whose "mission is to promote sound management and financial practices at colleges and universities"[25] and whose Benchmark Program attempts to "provide an organized forum for higher education institutions to identify opportunities to improve their operating efficiency and effectiveness."[26]

Similarly, the National Association of Student Financial Aid Administrators (NASFAA) "supports financial aid professionals at colleges, universities, and career schools. NASFAA is the only national association with a primary focus on student aid legislation, regulatory analysis, and professional development for financial aid administrators."[27] These and other organizations, dealing with issues as diverse as intellectual property and human subjects in research, provide means through which administrators can synchronize their work not only with that of other administrators but also with government officials, lobbying organizations, and suppliers of support technologies.

The End of the Universal Professional

Indeed, here we begin to see the process that Michel Callon has called "enrolment," where around a particular object or idea grow a range of actors, all of whom see their interests as best served by the maintenance of that object, that financial aid form or audit report.[28] And so, where the university could once be seen as a place in which only one person — the faculty member — had a rightful place, today there is a proliferation of new professionals, each of whom occupies a position that straddles the boundary that separates the university from the outside world. But these are not the universal professionals that have come before. These are not the ministers and lawyers, physicians and professors who both occupied visible places and were accorded the status of professional well beyond that place. In a range of ways they fail to meet the standards that those professionals were at least claimed to have met. In part because so many of them are right in the thick of issues having to do with finances and property, they cannot so easily claim to be operating, as did the universal professionals before them, in an enclave separate from the market. Neither can they be said to operate in terms of the collegial form of interaction privileged by Durkheim and Tawney.

But from the perspective of the universal professional, whether the professor or the physician or the attorney, the rise of the new professional is of significance for another reason. The new professionals are by and large involved in the task of the collection, organization, and analysis of information relevant to the operation of their organizations. It is now of course a commonplace that in the medical profession the physician is required to report to a wide range of institutions, governmental and private. It is equally accepted that a result of this reporting requirement has been the undercutting of the professional autonomy held by physicians.

The same system of increasing data collection and reporting is at work in the university. I would argue that it has been more destructive of the universal professionalism valued there than have been recent developments in the medical profession. This is the case just because the image of the professional in the university has been one of a person who embodied a range of skills, of researcher, author, lecturer, and counselor. What is relevant here is not whether any person ever truly filled all of these roles, but that the roles were seen as intrinsic parts of the profession and that they formed a kind of ideal against which the actual might be gauged.

This ideal is undercut in three ways by the rise of the new professionals. First, they in various ways are involved in tasks that were previously performed by the "traditional" professional. Whether in the case of billing in the medical office or counseling in the university, there are now separate offices and individuals to whom those needing the services are expected to turn. Putting the matter crudely, there has been a battle for turf, and in many areas the new professionals have won.

Second, in large measure as a consequence of their positions at the interface with external service providers, the new professionals have established themselves as collectors of information and, indeed, as managers of the systems that are used for that collection. Whether in the case of the collection of data concerning medical diagnoses, to be used for establishing insurance rates, or of the collection of information about teaching, research, and the like, they have effectively established systems that ensure and rely upon the routine reporting of data. Just as libraries have always as a matter of procedure tracked the reading habits of their users, hospitals and universities are increasingly using such systems. The new professionals have been effective at adapting older systems, developed for other purposes, such as student grading or the evaluation of the teaching of faculty or even the curriculum vitae, to new technological systems that allow the data contained within them to be used for new and different purposes.

One of the most controversial of such developments has accompanied the development of systems of electronic mail. Within corporations and universities alike there is both a movement toward requiring the use of electronic mail for more and more purposes and an explicit claim, from a group of new professionals, that any messages sent via such a system are the property of the institution and appropriate for its reading and analysis.[29] And so, the traditional professionals find themselves unable to maintain the traditional forms of collegial control, just because always at hand are sets of data that suggest the need to appeal to a model of decision making that incorporates a model of technical rationality.

Finally, and here I return to my earlier remarks about intellectual property, the creation of the new professionals has supported an increasing contractual-ization of relationships within the professions. If in the traditional model the research professional was remunerated almost entirely in the form of status, today universities have begun to argue, in teaching as well as research, that the remuneration can better be seen as a contractual, financial matter, where the professor is seen as a sort of consultant, helping to create courseware that will be the property of the institution.

From the point of view that I have taken here, all of these developments can fruitfully be seen as matters of the loosening of the connections between professionals and the places that they have occupied *as* professionals. This loosening — in which elements of the roles traditionally taken by these pro-fessionals are taken up by the new professionals — has served to undercut the ability of those professionals to represent themselves as outside of the mar-ket, just because they have been implicated in such a range of contractually organized activities. And in that way, it has undercut their ability to repre-sent themselves as able to approach their area of expertise from an unbiased perspective.

Many have seen this apparent failure of objectivity as simply another conse-quence of the 1960s, of the professorate's embracing of a radical relativism. But if what I have suggested here is true we need to see the possibility of objectivity as having been undercut by a longer series of events and a more fundamen-tal set of processes. As Yi-Fu Tuan has shown, the process of segmentation of group life has a long history.[30] And a central feature of that segmentation has been the development of new ways of thinking about who has a right to say what. In a segmented household, for example, the authority of individuals is increasingly associated with places that are their own, and they at the same time lose the right to speak authoritatively when they are outside of their own places.

It is just this segmentation that has occurred in the contemporary university. If the development of larger academic institutions in the past involved what might be seen as a similar segmentation, there was a crucial difference; it was at least possible for physicists and historians, for example, to claim that their differences could be bridged. But if this claim was typically couched in terms of an appeal to shared scholarly values, it makes as much sense to see it as relying on the possibility of a physicist walking into a historian's lecture hall and saying something that did not seem dramatically out of place. But the segmentation of the university today has developed in a different direction, and few would argue that a physicist and financial officer could easily trade roles or places. Indeed, if what I have said is true, we may have as a consequence moved into a world in which the traditional forms of professionalism are simply not possible. And we may have moved into a world in which one very important means of judging — accurately or not — the objectivity of those making claims about the nature of things has been lost to us.

Notes

1. Bruce Kimball, *The "True Professional Ideal" in America: A History* (Cambridge: Blackwells, 1992).

2. Karl Polanyi, *The Great Transformation* (Boston: Beacon, 1944).

3. Thomas L. Haskell, "Professionalism versus Capitalism: R. H. Tawney, Émile Durkheim, and C. S. Peirce on the Disinterestedness of Professional Communities," in *The Authority of Experts: Studies in History and Theory,* ed. Thomas L. Haskell (Bloomington: Indiana University Press, 1984), 180–225; the reference is to Émile Durkheim, *Professional Ethics and Civic Morals,* trans. Cornelia Brookfield (Glencoe, Ill.: Free Press, 1958), and to Richard H. Tawney, *The Acquisitive Society* (New York: Harcourt Brace, 1921).

4. Peter M. Blau and Marshall W. Meyer, *Bureaucracy in Modern Society,* 2d ed. (New York: Random House, 1971); Magali Sarfatti Larson, *The Rise of Professionalism: A Sociological Analysis* (Berkeley: University of California Press, 1977); Shoukrey Roweis, "Knowledge-Power and Professional Practice," in *The Design Professions and the Built Environment,* ed. Paul L. Knox (London: Croom Helm, 1988), 175–207; Randall Collins, *The Credential Society: An Historical Sociology of Education and Stratification* (New York: Academic Press, 1979); and Haskell, "Professionalism versus Capitalism."

5. "Code of Practice," *Network* 43 (1989): 4–5.

6. Ronald E. Anderson, "Social Impacts of Computing: Codes of Professional Ethics," *Social Science Computer Review* 10 (1992): 453–69.

7. William J. Craig, "A GIS Code of Ethics: What Can We Learn from Other Organizations?" (paper presented at the URISA 1993 Annual Conference Proceedings, Atlanta, 1993), 1–9.

8. John Feather, "From Rights in Copies to Copyright: The Recognition of Authors' Rights in English Law and Practice in the Sixteenth and Seventeenth Centuries," *Cardozo Arts and Entertainment Law Journal* 10, no. 2 (1992): 455–74; Mark Rose, *Authors and Owners: The Invention of Copyright* (Cambridge, Mass.: Harvard University Press, 1993).

9. Sam Ricketson, *The Berne Convention for the Protection of Literary and Artistic Works: 1886–1986* (London: Centre for Commercial Law Studies, Queen Mary College, 1987); Jane C. Ginsburg, "French Copyright Law: A Comparative Overview," *Journal of the Copyright Society of the USA* 4 (1989): 269–85; Ginsburg, "A Tale of Two Copyrights: Literary Property in Revolutionary France and America," *Tulane Law Review* 64 (1990): 991–1031.

10. Edgar Zilsel, "The Sociological Roots of Science," *American Journal of Sociology* 47 (1942): 544–62.

11. Frederick W. Taylor, *The Principles of Scientific Management* (New York: Harper and Row, 1947); Frank B. Gilbreth, *Motion Study: A Method for Increasing the Efficiency of the Workman* (New York: Van Nostrand, 1911).

12. Giambatista Vico, *The New Science of Giambatista Vico,* trans. T. G. Bergin and M. H. Fisch (Ithaca, N.Y.: Cornell University Press, 1970); Isaiah Berlin, *Vico and Herder: Two Studies in the History of Ideas* (New York: Random House, 1970).

13. G. W. F. Hegel, *Philosophy of Right,* trans. T. M. Knox (London: Oxford University Press, 1967 [1821]); Pierre Masse, *Le droit moral de l'auteur sur son oeuvre littéraire ou artistique* (Paris: Arthur Rousseau, 1906).

14. Jeremy Bentham, *An Introduction to the Principles of Morals and Legislation* (New York: Hafner, 1948 [1789]).

15. Hegel, *Philosophy of Right,* addition, paragraph 41.

16. John Locke, "Second Treatise of Government," in *Two Treatises of Government* (New York: Hafner, 1947 [1690]), 121–247, chap. 5, sec. 44.

17. Walter Benjamin, "The Work of Art in the Age of Mechanical Reproduction," in *Illuminations* (New York: Schocken, 1969), 217–51.

18. Bentham, *Introduction.*

19. Ibid.

20. Thomas C. Grey, "The Disintegration of Property," in *Property*, ed. J. Roland Pennock and John William Chapman (New York: New York University Press, 1980), 69–85.

21. Derek J. de Solla Price, *Little Science, Big Science* (New York: Columbia University Press, 1963).

22. Terence J. Johnson, *Professions and Power* (London: Macmillan, 1972); Michael D. Reagan, *Science and the Federal Patron* (New York: Oxford University Press, 1969); Terry N. Clark, *Prophets and Patrons: The French University and the Emergence of the Social Sciences* (Cambridge, Mass.: Harvard University Press, 1973).

23. Evelyn Pruitt, "The Office of Naval Research and Geography," *Annals of the Association of American Geographers* 69, no. 1 (1979): 103–8.

24. Martin Duberman, *Black Mountain: An Exploration in Community* (Garden City, N.Y.: Doubleday, 1973).

25. See http://www.nacubo.org/website/aboutnac.html.

26. See http://www.nacubo.org/website/benchmarking/index.html.

27. See http://www.nasfaa.org.

28. Michel Callon and John Law, "On Interests and Their Transformation: Enrolment and Counter-Enrolment," *Social Studies of Science* 12 (1982): 615–25; see also Bruno Latour, "The Powers of Association," in *Power, Action, Belief: A New Sociology of Knowledge?* ed. John Law, Sociological Review Monographs (London: Routledge, 1986), 264–80.

29. Janice C. Sipior and Burke T. Ward, "The Ethical and Legal Quandary of Email Privacy," *Communications of the ACM* 38, no. 12 (1995): 48–54; Suzanne P. Weisband and Bruce A. Reinig, "Managing User Perceptions of Email Privacy," *Communications of the ACM* 38, no. 12 (1995): 40–47.

30. Yi-Fu Tuan, *Segmented Worlds and Self: Group Life and Individual Consciousness* (Minneapolis: University of Minnesota Press, 1982).

Part III

Moralities and
Imagination

INTRODUCTION

Moralities and Imagination

Anne Buttimer

> Civilization is an achievement that transforms raw nature into orderly
> worlds and crude humanity into civil, moral, and enlightened beings.
> ...However, if human achievement is to be measured by the quality
> of human relationship — by the depth of the affectional and intellectual
> exchanges between persons — one may well wonder how much of the ma-
> terial and institutional wealth of civilization is really necessary....Here
> we return to [the issue of] the degree of congruence between morality and
> imagination: the one implies restraint and the other is naturally inclined
> toward excess. — YI-FU TUAN, *Morality and Imagination*

Morality and imagination are commonly regarded as counterpoised: morality
establishing fixed definitions and often claiming culture-specific imperatives,
imagination always seeking new horizons. And what kinds of "fresh air" might
geography have to offer on this domain of inquiry? The five essays in this
section respond courageously to this challenge. They speak of monuments,
madness, morality, and memories: a panorama of themes.

Monuments, madness, morality, and memories are geographically interesting in that they all relate to place. All are definable in terms of being in place or
out of place. Once constituted, places define what behavior may be appropriate
there; some are welcome, others shunned. Places indeed serve a useful focus for
studies on morality and imagination. For as all the following essays illustrate,
places are constructed. And in place-making, as Tuan's writings continuously
note, "moral issues arise at every point if only because, to make any change
at all, force must be used and this raises questions of right and wrong, good
and bad."[1]

Each of the following essays addresses questions of moralities and imagination. The first and last place emphasis on morality, two others emphasize
imagination, and a fifth explores both themes in representations of cultural history and the shaping of identities. Robert D. Sack deals with questions of the
real and the good — themes that are central in Tuan's own work — and develops a geographical theory of morality. Jonathan M. Smith explicates the work
of a nineteenth-century American historian, Francis Parkman, who believed

223

that environment had much to do with the sustenance and eventual superiority of early-nineteenth-century Yankee morality. Two essays deal with the poetics of place and some intriguing imaginings. Miles Richardson's visits to sacred sites and memorials lead him to hypotheses about their universal significance and connections with death, while Patrick McGreevy tells how a slow-motion film taught him how to pay attention to trees. Karen E. Till introduces "social constructionist" perspectives in visiting the Deutsches Historisches Museum (German Historical Museum) in Berlin, assessing the effectiveness of recently crafted narratives on German identity through representations in an exhibition titled *Lebensstationen in Deutschland, 1900–1993* (*Chapters of Life in Germany, 1900–1993*). Each essay presents fresh and evocative reflections on everyday life and experience: "What is real may not be good, but what is good must be real.... The real, despite the fuzziness of the idea, is still an anchor among aspirants toward the good."[2]

First among the essays here, and perhaps closest to themes addressed in Tuan's *Morality and Imagination*, is Sack's "Place, Power, and the Good." All places are real, he notes, but some places increase and enrich reality; others may contract and diminish our awareness of reality. These two elements — levels of complexity within places and human awareness of reality — constitute the essential components for a "geographical theory of morality" on the basis of which one could evaluate places.

Most geographers import moral theories to evaluate geographical conditions, Sack notes. Why not instead develop geographical principles of judging that are drawn from geography's interest in the real and the good? he asks. "A moral person," Tuan wrote, "is someone irresistibly drawn by the good."[3] A moral place, in Sack's view, is one that helps us to see through to the real. Analogues between place and person thus extend to the moral domain. Both authors agree that the good is ineffable — a luminous horizon toward which humans aspire — and this essay outlines ways in which geography could contribute toward elucidating such horizons. Concepts of place are central in the construction of a geographical theory of morality.

From this theory, two distinct types of geographical judgment emerge: "intrinsic" and "instrumental." While "instrumental geographical judgment" can assess the efficacy of places for the achievement of particular projects, "intrinsic geographical judgment" aims at a much more basic and general assessment. Two of its cardinal features are (1) seeing through to the real and (2) valuing a varied and complex reality. The morality of places may thus be approached via cognitive and aesthetic routes. First, the cognitive route: assuming that the "true" is identifiable with the "real," "goodness" definable in terms of knowledge, and "evil" in terms of ignorance, one is led logically to an identification of truth and goodness. There are Platonic and Augustinian precedents for this suggestion. Second, the aesthetic route: "the goodness of a plenitudinous reality — a more varied and complex reality is better than a simpler and duller one." Cultural variations in definitions of "reality," "goodness," and "diversity" are not explored.

"Place, Power, and the Good" holds out an ideal, a desire that geographers could contribute toward the making of a better world. Coherence and reasonableness are among the claims to credibility for this moral theory. As developed more fully in *Homo Geographicus,* Sack seeks to show that a focus on place can "provide an antidote to the often unreal and dissociated quality of current a-geographic theory."[4] The distinction between "intrinsic" and "instrumental" geographical judgments does indeed afford a fresh look at the questions raised in *Morality and Imagination.* How "intrinsic geographical judgments" could be reached without specifying the contexts of culture, space, and time where the discipline is practiced, however, remains unclear. This geographical theory of morality propounds a universal set of values, that is, those proclaimed in the so-called Western Enlightenment, held forth in the 1789 French Revolution, and enshrined in the American Constitution. How the basic values underlying this morality might eventually be harmonized with the diverse and equally cherished values underlying culturally enshrined moralities in other parts of the world remains surely an unaddressed question.

Evoking keener awareness of our surroundings and our everyday behavior has been one of Tuan's enduring gifts to geography. Attention to features of everyday life and landscape is the central concern of Patrick McGreevy's essay. Each of us occupies a tiny circumscribed niche in time-space; all around — behind us and before us — is the void. Attention to the boundaries between our habitat and the terrae incognitae beyond enables us to recognize the extent to which our identities and rationalities, our moralities and imaginings, have been defined in terms that differentiate us from that Other beyond the boundary. A critically important "geography lesson" is contained here. The central goal of humanist education, Tuan wrote, "is to transform one limited self into a rich concourse of selves, one narrow world of direct experience into many worlds, a creature of one time into a seasoned time traveler."[5]

McGreevy's essay evokes several insights. The term "attention" evokes a meaning that is virtually identical with the phenomenological slogan of "letting things reveal themselves in their own terms." At-tention is like a window open to admit[ting] the presencing of things. The journey toward understanding, McGreevy notes, involves more than cerebral analysis: it involves emotion and will, desire to understand. Then the question arises: How does at-tention relate to thinking? Does each individual arrive at at-tention in his/her own way? And if so, are there ways in which such insights could be shared and lead to a more general knowledge of environment?

Delight in understanding, however, is associated with a fear of its consequences. As awareness expands, there is a sharper sense of one's own finitude, one's "thrownness" toward death, to use Heidegger's phrase; our creations are "like sandcastles that can be erased by the next tide."[6] To venture beyond the familiar — intellectually and emotionally — is a potential invitation to madness. One could ask if indeed any creative discovery is possible without a little madness (*Daimon*). "Predating the child is the fool," Tuan wrote. "Ignorance of the world enables him to see truth behind the meretricious facades of culture."[7] On the fine line between genius and madness societal commentary has varied much through history. "The world and the void," McGreevy notes, "like reason and madness, come as a pair."[8]

In this essay places are viewed less for their morality than for their temporality. Places are dynamic, some aspects changing ever so slowly, others more rapidly. Attention is about noticing the vitality of all creation — trees, hills, valleys — *omnia in lapsu,* as Heraclitus is credited to have said. The essay speaks most forcibly to individual rather than social concerns, to the contemplative/reflective rather than the analytical/calculative ways of being in the world: "the more diversified and individualized the world appears to a person the more that world is for him imbued with the beauty and worth of actualized presences, however fleeting, and the more these presences call for some kind of response — contemplative, appreciative, or in physical action."[9]

Omnia in lapsu. Ever-present media sound bites stir attention to events, wars, murders, and obscenities. At places where such tragedies have occurred, Miles Richardson's presentation reveals how people frequently erect shrines and memorials, perhaps as efforts to halt the perpetual fluctuations of Heraclitean flux or the Borgesian "book of sands." People also like to visit such shrines and leave objects behind, thereby establishing the location as a place. Shrines, memorials, graves, he claims, are all places of death. Objects deposited there signify presence in the face of absence. Death — the definitive absence — is what makes presence and self possible, just as the void in McGreevy's essay makes awareness of home and identity possible.

Anyone who witnessed the volumes of floral bouquets lining Stockholm's Sveavägen after the murder of Olof Palme in 1986 or the million bouquets deposited around Windsor Castle after the death of Diana, princess of Wales, in a car crash in Paris 1997 will acknowledge the enormous significance of this topic. The scenes presented by Richardson amply document the importance of symbolic landscapes — artifacts left at shrines and memorials all evoke reflections on the reciprocity of absence and presence in human experience. Symbolic transformations indeed, Hannah Arendt reminded us, are among the unique features of *Homo sapiens.*[10] Symbols convey absence yearning for presence. Presence means the immediate, face-to-face, experience of this unique moment — the gift of oneself in place — in the reverential atmosphere at a shrine that marks the absence of a loved one. "Presence...turns us...into a gift," Richardson writes.

This transposition of nouns to verbs — a typical Heideggerian knack — affords fascinating common denominators between the essays of Miles Richardson and Patrick McGreevy. McGreevy's "attention" seems close to Richardson's "presence." Both involve action. McGreevy's attending to the subtle vitality of trees demands an opening of sensitivity to a "letting-be"; Richardson's offer of gifts at a shrine is a "presencing." Neither would be possible without a recognition that our conventional distinctions between subject and object, action and passivity, in the learning process are legacies of questionable value. Both essays stand in potentially creative counterposition to the preceding and following ones.

A reader might well pose the question as to whether places with memorials to bombings and shootings should be regarded in the same terms as places that were deemed (or constructed) as sacred sites. Monuments and artifacts may be shrines for those who erect them, but for subsequent generations, they may become contested symbols, targets at times for graffiti or dynamite. Their physicality does not always guarantee the denial of absence; in some cases they invite a celebration of that absence. Sacred sites, on the other hand, tend to have more enduring appeal, not only to believers. Consider Delphi, Ise Shrine, the Dome of the Rock, Bethlehem, Medina, or Compostella. The experience of presence at such sites is quite different from presence among the flower bouquets to Diana or the various war memorials that stud the walls of Reformed European cathedrals. As Richardson's essay so elegantly puts it, a visit to a shrine or memorial could be regarded as a gift of self to the absent Other. But the religious experience of being in a sacred place can be an occasion of receiving the gift of presence — a reminder of ever-present and infinite goodness (God) in this everyday world, an epiphany of the wholeness toward which one could hope for in life.

What both varieties have in common, and something only briefly touched upon in the essay, is the commercial element. Once the memorial at the bomb-site in Oklahoma City has been built, it is noted, "no doubt replicas of it will be available." Then the shrine can be taken home with you, and maybe you will never again feel the need to gift that place with your presence. In England these days there are worries about the Elvisization of Diana. Could it be that all this concern over monuments could become exploited for commercially induced amnesia in an era when many of the previous certainties and identity grounds have lost their stability?

Themes of identity and morality are explored further in the final two essays. Both also touch on the poetics of narration, geographical representations, and their political significance: "place-centered narration not only refocuses our attention on the ways in which place is political: it necessitates the geographic equivalent of the ghost story — an awareness of the irreducible strangeness of space and a narrative capable of addressing its encryption."[11]

Karen E. Till's essay extends the themes of monument and memory, introducing wider issues of identity, symbolism, and representation of place and public space. During the early 1990s East and West Germans, having lived for forty years in separate worlds, faced the challenge of rediscovering (or reinventing) a sense of common national identity. The physical dismantling of the Berlin Wall took little time, but what of the perceptual wall (*die Mauer im Kopf*) that lingered?

The challenge of evoking bases for common identity was one eagerly accepted by the German Historical Museum in Berlin. Like its nineteenth- and early-twentieth-century antecedents, it recognized the powerful role of visual display in shaping images of self and other. As Till remarks, "Exhibitions localize and spatially communicate dominant discourses of time and identity." But the 1990s exhibit was different. "Chapters" of German life (*Lebensstationen*) between 1900 and 1993 displayed "typical" life experiences such as birth, schooling, youth, marriage, military service, and death for four distinct periods: Kaiserreich (ca. 1900), National Socialist Germany (NS), the German Democratic Republic (GDR) (East Germany), and the Federal Republic of Germany (FRG) (West Germany). Visitors were led through these "stations" as though "it were a large family album."

Interviews with visitors as well as with authors of exhibits revealed a complex set of responses. Far from promoting a common sense of German (national) identity, some displays evoked rather a sense of separateness. But the intention of authors was to evoke awareness of difference and to promote dialogue among diverse types of viewer: " . . . *we* have presented *our* construction, against which many of the visitors are now placing *their own,* likewise constructed remembrance, without it being possible to arrive at a uniform view or indeed at an *identity.*" The overwhelming conclusion — one very much in tune with postmodern cultural discourses — is one that, in Till's words, emphasizes difference and pleads for "more inclusive and interactive exhibition spaces for a range of social groups and individuals."[12]

The final essay returns to issues of morality, "moral maps," and "moral places." In vivid and elegant prose Jonathan M. Smith interprets the work of Francis Parkman, one of the most famous nineteenth-century American historians, a man whose work was admired by Ellen Churchill Semple and Carl O. Sauer. His lifework focused on the history of French and English colonists of North America, and from this story he derived general principles regarding morality and imagination. And his narrative style made ample use of scenes from diverse landscapes and lifeways to render accounts gripping and evocative.

Parkman's "moral geography" involved a "precise sense of place" and "an intuitive grasp of the significance of site and situation." These were particularly relevant for military strategies, which need to adapt themselves to particular topographic and physiographic contexts and also to avail themselves of locational networks and linkages across continental space. Success in wars and in colonization projects was for Parkman the historical grounds for moral judgment. There is an interesting analogue here to the "geographical judgments" of Sack's essay — endurance over time rather than conformity to place — but

Parkman makes no distinction between "instrumental" and "intrinsic" (historical) judgment. Contests for territory decide not only the "prevalence of races" but also the "triumph of principles." It was not only successful territorial expansion that revealed the superiority of energetic English colonists; it was also their ability to transform landscapes. The third vital element of Parkman's "moral geography" also involved places — sites where "the vital qualities of the system are reproduced," for example, institutions that reflect free and spontaneous political vitality or machine-like socialistic despotism, such as athletic fields that encourage "competition, teamwork, impartial rules and regulated aggression."

To unravel the basic principles of civilization — the "natural laws" that could explain the moral superiority of one over the other — was, in Parkman's view, one of the primary tasks of the historian. North America was portrayed as the arena on which contrasting civilizations (only two) laid moral and political claims to territory: a democratic, industrious, and Protestant English civilization versus an absolutist, militarist, and Catholic France. "Imbecile" moral systems could be recognized in their inability to populate territories or spawn colonies, whereas "fruitful moral systems" were those exemplified in the British colonial empire. Compared with the "masculine race" of New Englanders, for example, New France was "barren." But there was ultimately a note of grand tragedy in the story. Parkman believed that America had reached its apogee in the early nineteenth century and was headed for a cataclysmic decline in the century's latter decades.

Francis Parkman's "geographical imagination" had apparently both idealist and organicist elements, at times echoing the racial theories of Johan von Herder (early nineteenth century), the evolutionist theories emanating from Darwin's *Origin of Species*, the ethical principles in Adam Smith's *Wealth of Nations,* and the fatalism/harsh judgments of Marlowe's *Doctor Faustus.*

Of all five essays, it is perhaps this one that grapples most explicitly with issues Tuan calls "paradoxes of progress." Parkman's "moral geography" would appear to be a stark contrast to Tuan's more ecumenical stance. In fact there are hints in Tuan's writing that tensions between morality and imagination could never be resolved if one were to follow strictly the "moral maps" sketched by Parkman:

> It may be that the tension between morality and imagination exists only
> if morality is conceived as proper conduct that one learns once and for
> all or as a gift of nature — golden rules engraved in the heart; and if
> imagination is conceived either as license or as the method for attaining
> a permanent state of wisdom. But what if morality is an ideal toward
> which individuals and society must endlessly strive? What if the effort to
> imagine the moral and the good, boldly and yet responsibly, is itself an
> endless moral undertaking?[13]

The essays contained in part III of this book all resonate to fundamental themes broached in the writings of Yi-Fu Tuan. Issues of morality and imagination are mostly construed in terms of individual persons and their relationships with the world. Social dimensions are more explicitly addressed in the essays by Till and Smith. Yet it is in the essays by McGreevy and Richardson — the two essays most "humanistic" in style — that there is a hint of Tuan's deepest concern, namely, the source of inspiration for morality and the "irresistible lure of the good." "In the final analysis" Tuan wrote, "we cannot remain moral in any recognizable sense of the word, nor can our projects and creations — including homes, cities, and landscapes — retain any sort of moral earnestness, without somewhere in the background the support of a deeply felt mythopoeic or religious model of reality."[14] *Religio,* as Heidegger often reminded his readers, means "to bind"; its opposite is *negligio,* to unloose or unbind. Morality implies a bonding; immorality implies indifference. From the vantage point of *Homo geographicus,* what is remarkable is not so much the demise of traditional "morality" but rather the rise of new "moralities," all of which have potential geographical implications (from Green Parties and nature-loving sects at one extreme to global marketeering of eco-products at the other extreme) and all of which have been launched as offers not to be refused by an increasingly docile public.

Apart from the first and last essays, little reference is made to the impacts of Western Enlightenment moralities on the natural environment. Yet such issues would seem to be central in Yi-Fu Tuan's life quest. "Unlike the propounding of a moral philosophy or religion, and unlike the making of poems and paintings, the construction of a material world must confront the issue of the damage that the use of force inflicts on nature, on laborers, and on the people who must be evicted to make way for the new.... We are thus brought to human relations which lie at the heart of morality."[15] Till's interviews with visitors and authors of displays at Berlin's German Historical Museum yield some insight into social differences in perspective, but the environmental implications of twentieth-century "progress" raised in Tuan's book merit attention as well.

Despite their differences, the presentations have revealed one resounding common denominator, that is, their poetic character and challenge. "Poets sing of the absence," Heidegger wrote, "because they have been touched by presence." It is therefore to Yi-Fu Tuan, a veritable presence, that one hearkens for a concluding sentiment:

> One *becomes* more moral, society becomes more moral, with the help of an imagination, disciplined by respect for the real. This stress on "becoming" forces us to entertain the possibility of genuine progress, which can be exhilarating.... If the challenge is nevertheless taken up by conscientious people, as I believe it is, one possible reason... is the irresistible lure of the good.[16]

Notes

1. Yi-Fu Tuan, *Morality and Imagination: Paradoxes of Progress* (Madison: University of Wisconsin Press, 1989), vii.

2. Ibid., 159.

3. Ibid., 3.

4. Robert D. Sack, *Homo Geographicus: A Framework for Action, Awareness, and Moral Concern* (Baltimore: Johns Hopkins University Press, 1997), 28.

5. Yi-Fu Tuan, *The Good Life* (Madison: University of Wisconsin Press, 1986), 161.

6. Martin Heidegger, *Aus der Erfahrung des Denkens* (Pfullingen: Neske, 1954).

7. Tuan, *Morality and Imagination*, 5.

8. See McGreevy's essay in this volume, p. 254.

9. Tuan, *Morality and Imagination*, 163.

10. Hannah Arendt, *The Human Condition* (Chicago: University of Chicago Press, 1958).

11. Patricia Yaeger, ed., *The Geography of Identity* (Ann Arbor: University of Michigan Press, 1996), 5.

12. See Till's essay in this volume, p. 294.

13. Tuan, *Morality and Imagination*, 10.

14. Ibid., 174–5.

15. Ibid., 9.

16. Ibid., 10.

PLACE, POWER, AND THE GOOD

Robert D. Sack

Power takes many forms. I want to explore the *real* and the *good* and how they are sources of power, and how geography, primarily through the instrument of place, enables us to see this and to engage in their pursuit. The central issue is therefore the relationships among geography, the real, and the good. Understanding these connections provides the foundation for a geographical theory of morality that draws upon Yi-Fu Tuan's work. Let us begin with geography.

Geography

Geography has two levels of meaning. At one level, it concerns our role as geographical agents transforming the world and making it into a home. This need to transform is in fact a geographical problematic: we seem to be constitutionally incapable of accepting reality as it is, and so we continuously transform it, and our creation and use of place are fundamental and inescapable tools in this process of transformation. Place in fact is our principal geographical tool, and I will often use the term *place* to represent what is essentially geographical. By place I do not mean the location of things in space, though places like everything else have locations. Rather place here refers to the countless areas of space that we have bounded and controlled. These humanly constructed and maintained places — or places-as-territories, many of which can be virtually identical in their look and function and found repeatedly over the landscape — range in scale from a room to a continent and support the innumerable projects we undertake: a kitchen, as a delimited area of space, is supported by rules about what may or may not take place that help make possible food preparation; and a very large area of space, such as Antarctica, because it is bounded and thus partly constructed by international treaties, helps maintain and even restore what we think of as elements of nature. We create and use places as tools because they provide a means for us to undertake projects, and in so doing, places add to the nature of the projects. That is, projects not only require place in the sense that they need a place to occur, but the place becomes an active agent in the project and thereby affects it.[1]

(It may appear, from the "spatial" vocabulary of many works in geography, that most geographical theorizing examines space, not place. Space is a natu-

232

ral science concept that is part of the foundation of the universe. Everything happens within and through it. Even places are in this space. But an often neglected fact is that for humans, both the effects of space on our behavior and our use of space are mediated by place. Places are the primary means by which we are able to use space and turn it into a humanized landscape. The popular emphases on the "social construction of space" and "spatiality" are at bottom allusions to this humanized landscape and to the significance of places and their interconnections. In other words, the arguments about spatiality and the social construction of space are really about the effects that places have on creating and sustaining projects.)

At the second level, geography is about our awareness of our place-making activity and our reflections upon it. This level includes our role as professional geographers who theorize about place, space, and landscape as part of the human transformation of the world. By no means do we have to be professional geographers to be aware of our geographical agency, but being trained in geography can help. Awareness of our geographical agency in turn can influence how we transform the world. The ideas we possess about place can lead us to change the places we make and the projects we undertake.

Place will be the focus of our attention, but it should be made clear that places require human agents. We are the ones who delimit an area of space with rules about what should or should not take place. And we are the ones who enforce or transgress these rules. Places cannot exist without us. But equally important, we cannot exist without places. They enable and empower us by helping to organize reality. In so doing they have effects and thereby exhibit causal properties, in the same sense that the languages we speak enable us and have effects on what we think and do. People and places are then mutually constitutive. We can say that "we make" things happen, but still we need places to help us; and we can say "places make" things happen, but of course they need us as agents. Since this is a geographical discussion, place will take center stage. We will focus on the power of places and assume that humans are involved, but their role will remain in the background. We must also make clear that when we talk about places we often mean a system of places and their flows and interactions through space.

With this idea of agency in mind, we can see that place and reality are linked. Places exist. They are part of the reality we wish to explore. As we destroy, create, and change places we are also destroying, creating, and changing portions of reality. Reality of course includes the entire universe, but most of us are intensely interested in the reality that we find on the earth, and it is in this very important corner of reality that place plays such a vital role.

Places then contribute to the reality we wish to explore, and as we shall see they also expand and constrain our awareness of that reality. Let us now focus our attention on these connections between geography and the real.

Geography and the Real

We are place-makers because place undergirds our projects. The places we construct are part of reality, and as we construct places we are altering our world or reality. A central point is understanding how the places we construct can expand and enhance or contract and diminish reality.

Place clears things away to allow other things to occur. In so doing place helps create and destroy some things and displaces others so that we can undertake projects. If the places or projects are more complex and numerous than before, then, in a crude sense, places are expanding the real. But reality is diminished if the number and variety of places or projects diminish. Number and complexity of places are ways in which place is linked to the real and can expand or contract it.

How place affects our awareness of reality is an equally important connection. Some places attempt to encourage our awareness of reality. I take this to be the ideal purpose of schools and universities. This is not to say that they always meet their ideals, but when a school diminishes or distorts a pupil's view of reality, we know that it is not functioning properly.

Other places attempt to encourage us to escape from an awareness of reality. They pretend that there is no reality to view. Theme parks, tourist attractions, and the general theatricality of place are cases in point. And some places intentionally obscure our vision. These include places that censor information and places that are secret. These remove parts of the world from view.

To sum up so far, we know that as geographical agents we affect reality and our awareness of reality through the places we construct. This is a realist view of the world that accepts the fact that human constructions, such as places, are part of, and also alter, that reality.[2] All places are equally real, but some places may increase and enrich reality, others may contract and diminish it, and others may expand or contract our awareness of reality. These connections between geography and the real become even more complex when issues of the good are added. We have said that all places are real, but are all places good?

Geography, the Real, and the Good

Places are constantly evaluated. We think of them as good or bad, or combinations of both, and we try to improve them. Places are complex, and when we judge them we must be careful to recognize that our evaluations focus on one or more of their facets. Still these may so overwhelm the place that the rest of what takes place is not enough to prevent us from censuring or praising the place as a whole. The same is true of people. Even the most evil of us may possess a few positive qualities, but these may not be sufficient to prevent moral condemnation.

Moral evaluation can be made by using moral theories from outside geography. This is in fact what most geographers do. We import moral theories to evaluate geographical conditions. And in doing so, we have focused primarily on theories of justice. There is however another alternative. By incorporating several of Yi-Fu Tuan's themes, it is possible to construct a theory of morality that begins with geography's own concerns.[3] That is, we can see how geography sheds light on parts of the real and the good that would not be directly illuminated by other approaches and how these facets help us understand issues of justice and broader facets of morality. Indeed, the theory can show that principles of justice, and its instruments of rights and duties, rest on conceptions of the good, so it makes sense to begin there. What then are the conceptions of the good and their relationship to the real that geography illuminates?

The argument I wish to make has several steps. At the most general, the theory is realist in two senses. It assumes that reality exists (and that we contribute to it), and it also assumes that the good exists, and so is part of the real. That is, we do not make up what is good, though, through our own actions we instantiate the good, and there are countless ways of doing so. The good is part of the real, but not all of the real is good. Though the real and the good exist, they are ultimately ineffable. We can discern facets of both, but the two are never completely accessible or knowable. The models of science can be said to have come closer to representing the real, but its ultimate nature seems to still be beyond our grasp. And the good, though real, seems to be even more difficult to know. Still, both the real and the good draw us to them like magnetic forces, in large measure because they are ineffable.

The theory also assumes that the good must be understood in relation to evil and that most evil stems from a lack of awareness of the consequences of our actions and of the possibilities that exist to do better. This lack of awareness is both a cause and a consequence of evil. The lack occurs at the individual or personal level, and it is also a product of the behavior of institutions that make it difficult if not impossible for us to be aware. Understanding evil as a lack has deep roots in Western moral theory. We find it in Platonists (who argue that no one willingly does evil) and in Kantians (who understand it to be a lack of will and reason). These positions see the good as real and compelling, that people generally prefer good to evil, and that evil's prevalence is due to some form of ignorance. This assumption does not apply to all cases, but I believe (optimistically) that it applies to most. Not being aware does not absolve our bad actions; it explains them.

With these as assumptions about the real and the good, I will argue that geography helps us to see how facets of the real and the good can be engaged in and through place. It draws attention to two particular qualities that can then be used to guide us in our creation and use of place. Because geography can illuminate and draw these together, making them central to our geographical agency, I will call them a geographical conception of the good, though I do not intend the word *conception* to mean they are invented or made up by geography. Rather they exist as facets of the good that geography helps us to see clearly. They are intrinsically good, and geographical judgments that use them will be called *intrinsic* geographical judgments.

Intrinsic geographical judgments are the ones that the theory promotes. But the theory recognizes another kind that is not about the good in an intrinsic sense but is still part of how we do behave and so part of geographical reality. This kind of judgment is used to evaluate the effectiveness of one or more places as instruments in particular projects. If geographical activity (namely, place-making) is used effectively to attain the goals of a project, then it is judged to be good. The school, as a place, may be effective in furthering the aims of education. In this way the place — the school — is good instrumentally. This *instrumental* geographical judgment is directly related to the real. The grounds, the buildings, and the organization of activities that take place within help instantiate the process of education. Place helps make it a reality.

But instrumental geographical judgments are relative to the goals of projects. If the school is part of the system of segregated or "separate but equal" education, as was the case in the pre-1950s United States where until then such practices were legally sanctioned (although since then we still have de facto segregation), then part of the place's effectiveness instrumentally will mean that it is good at keeping the races apart and in privileging one group over another. In this case, it still may be effective in helping to expand intellectual horizons in some areas, but it closes them off in others. This is why instrumental geographical judgments are relative to the goals of projects. If segregation and racism are part of the goals of these projects, then to the extent the place promotes these, the place is good instrumentally.

To avoid this relativity, the theory argues for intrinsic geographical judgments. They provide a nonrelativistic means of evaluating and judging the moral qualities of these instrumental judgments. Intrinsic geographical judgments trump instrumental ones. So the problem of the theory then is to describe instrumental judgments, to describe intrinsic geographical judgments, and to understand how intrinsic geographical judgments can be used to evaluate instrumental geographical judgments. Moral improvement and progress occur when instrumental geographical judgments become more like intrinsic geographical ones.

Instrumental Geographical Judgments

Instrumental geographical judgments are based on how effectively geography is used to support particular projects. To judge properly requires that we understand how geography is a tool and what it can do. The role of place is especially important, and its capacity to undergird our agency and thereby produce effects has been discussed at length in my *Homo Geographicus*. Here I will simply assume that we know how place works, how it is related to space, and how and why it is an essential instrument in projects. Then I will apply this general and assumed knowledge to particular cases.

Consider for example the Iron Curtain that, in Churchill's words, descended across the continent. Of course this event is situated in a complex historical context that is open to many interpretations, yet, at the risk of historical over-simplification, I wish to make a few geographical points. The boundaries of the Soviet Union did in fact make it extremely difficult if not impossible for most of those on the inside to see out and those on the outside to see in. Stalin used this as an instrument to attain his goals, which, let us suppose, were the preservation of socialism. Without going into the complex geographical details of how place works, we can argue that the Iron Curtain was an effective geographical instrument. It helped Stalin accomplish his goal of securing socialism. Instrumentally, it was good. And instrumentally effective uses of geography are directly linked to the real. They help projects take place. The Iron Curtain helped create a new element of reality. It added to the geographical variety and complexity of the world.

We can make similar evaluations of any other place. The use of a classroom could be assessed, and we might claim that it is effective in terms of the project we are undertaking: it could be facilitating discussions about geography. Or we can evaluate the use of place in our homes, factories, farms, and cities. And of course we can also say that Nazi Germany used places such as concentration camps extremely effectively to annihilate Jews and that the American South before the Civil War used plantations effectively to enslave blacks. Each of these cases may be using different aspects of place, but we may conclude that in each, place was used effectively as an instrument and thus contributed to facets of reality.

The difficulty with instrumental judgments is that they are always relative to the goals of the projects. Of course the projects can be embedded in larger ones, so that justification can appeal to what seems to be a more general concern, but if these are still projects, then the justification is still instrumental and relative to them. Can we evaluate projects more generally and nonrelativistically? Many would argue that we cannot escape the cycle of instrumental judgments. What is right or wrong depends on our goals.

The point I want to make here is that geography itself opens up the possibility of identifying qualities of the good that are independent of any particular project and that lead to intrinsic geographical judgments that can be used to evaluate projects. As is the case in assessing all moral theories, the claim that these judgments are indeed worthy of application (that they do in fact draw attention to qualities of the good) should be based on their coherence and reasonableness and on their conformity to the way things are — that is, on the degree to which they point in the direction of the real and the good. These I would trust are the grounds for accepting or rejecting the validity of intrinsic geographical judgments.

Intrinsic Geographical Judgments

The theory argues that there are two related kinds of intrinsic geographical judgments, and each draws on a facet of the good. The first kind recognizes the good that lies in a heightened and expanded awareness of reality and recognizes that a major source of evil is a lack of awareness. Being aware is better than not being aware, and being more aware is even better. The second is based on the goodness of a plenitudinous reality — a more varied and complex reality is better than a simpler and duller one.

These facets of the good are widely held, but they are drawn together and made especially vivid by geography, and so this is why I call them "geographical conceptions" of the good. They are employed jointly by the theory to evaluate places and instrumental geographical judgments.

Geography takes the first moral quality — the value of being more rather than less aware — and turns it into the geographical value of encouraging us to create and value places that heighten our awareness of the real and that share this awareness openly and publicly. This open communication of knowledge is extremely important, for it provides a check on whether our ideas are based on reality or fantasy. It also encourages us to think of our practices as providing gifts of awareness to others. The geographical judgment based on the goodness of being more aware and seeing more clearly will be called *seeing through to the real*. Wanting to learn as much as we can about the world is a deeply held geographical value and is often expressed as a desire to see the world and its places as clearly and comprehensively as possible and to understand how these places make up the world. We find this geographical value in all cultures and times as witnessed by the fact that virtually every culture has attempted to cartographically render this relationship of the whole (the world) and its parts (the places).

The second intrinsic geographical judgment draws from the goodness of a plenitudinous reality and encourages us to create and value places that increase the complexity and variety of the real. We will call this the value of *variety and complexity* for short. A varied and complex reality is compelling. The mysteries of an inexhaustible and complex reality beckon us to see the real, while a simple, dull, and monotonous world does not.

Variety and complexity must not be completely impervious to understanding. Parts of reality must yield to comprehension, or else the real would be something from which we would want only to escape. Understanding this variety and complexity leads us to the assumption that everything in reality is ultimately connected as a single whole; we become more confident that we have made progress in knowing the real when we see the complex relations among parts and whole to be generated by less complex ones. These become the underlying processes that clarify reality.

As geographical agents we create places not only that can help or hinder our awareness of the world but that can also expand or contract its variety and complexity. The two are internally complex, and so are their interrelationships. For example, while it is important to have places that help us see through to the real, we must recognize that by their very nature even the best of places help focus our attention on only a part of reality by temporarily narrowing our vision and obscuring the real for others. This is because places contain boundaries that create varying degrees of opacity in order to permit only certain things in and out. An astronomy observatory expands our horizons, but to accomplish this only those qualified to work there are admitted. Its doors are shut to all others. The science laboratory helps us discover new processes at the same time that only a very few are allowed in to see what is taking place. All places then to some degree obscure our vision. The first intrinsic geographical judgment justifies a place and its opacity if these ultimately enhance our collective ability to see through to the real. On these grounds, a scientific laboratory, a classroom, and a library all have the potential of being good places, for though their walls, doors, and boundaries set up some degree of opacity, the outcomes of what takes place for the most part increase our collective understanding of reality.

Place also complicates the aims of variety and complexity. By its very nature, place allows some things to happen and not others. Even though we may judge things to be good or bad, we have no idea if the things that were prevented could have turned out to be better or worse than the things that were allowed to occur. All we can do is assess what has happened. So place by necessity is selective in how it can increase variety and complexity, and most of our choices are among possibilities that could all be good.

The theory not only must bear these complications in mind but must apply the two intrinsic geographical judgments jointly. The first (seeing through to the real) and the second (valuing a varied and complex reality) are mutually reinforcing. A varied and complex reality is more interesting than a simple and dull one. It piques our curiosity and spurs us to explore and discover. It also enables us to undertake more complex projects and to increase our life chances. It is good then for geographical actions to contribute to a complex and diverse reality, and it is also good for geographical actions to allow us to see and understand this reality. Together, the two encourage us to create places that increase the real and our awareness of the real. Not only do the two complement each other—each checks the other's extremes.

For example, if we are concerned only with "seeing through to the real," then we may have places become so transparent that "variety and complexity" would point out that nothing of importance can take place. Such a landscape is open to inspection but is devoid of real content. At this extreme, "variety and complexity" would trump "seeing through." And if we focus only on "variety and complexity," we may arrive at the point where boundaries become so important that they prevent us from "seeing through to the real." For example, places of poverty, crack houses, and areas that encourage superstitious life can all be thought of as contributing to the diversity and complexity of the world — and to those on the outside they may appear exotic and intriguing — but again, this diversity would be outweighed by the fact that such places are clearly curtailing awareness of those within; for them these places are prisons. So here, "seeing through to the real" trumps "variety and complexity."

Most places are morally mixed; they contribute to neither aspect of intrinsic judgments very much. Some places are clearly good in that they contribute to both. And some places are clearly evil, for they violate both criteria or one of them to the point where the other cannot offset it. Any place would serve as an example of how the joint applications of the intrinsic geographical judgments can help assess the instrumental use of place. But in order to illustrate the paramount importance of an expanded awareness to the theory, I want to consider again the Iron Curtain.

From the point of view of variety and complexity, the Iron Curtain is of considerable merit. It helped sustain a different political-economic form than existed before. But the theory requires that we apply both qualities of intrinsic geographical judgment jointly, and so the criterion of "seeing through to the real" would not judge the Iron Curtain to be good. It obscured so much of reality for so many that it made it almost impossible for people to understand the consequences of their actions and thus the possibility of acting responsibly. So in this case, not being able to see through to the real overweighed whatever variety and complexity the Iron Curtain may have added to the world. Other places also violate the principle of "seeing through" to such a degree that the lack of this principle overrides all other considerations. Such is the case with Nazi concentration camps and slave plantations.

The theory uses intrinsic geographical judgments to evaluate place, but it also encourages us to incorporate these values as reasons for creating all of our places. That is, if the intrinsic values become part of our instrumental judgments, or if instrumental judgments come to look more like intrinsic ones, then places will be better and we will be making moral progress.

The two intrinsic geographical judgments point us in the direction of the good, but the theory also provides a sketch of the landscape that lies in the opposite direction — a sketch of what may be called the geographical criteria of evil. Evil is the absence of the intrinsic geographical values. A place can be bad because it lacks one, or the other, or both.

The Iron Curtain example certainly lacked the capacity of "seeing through to the real." So do all places that try to be autarkic, secret, and that employ censorship. Certain places attempt to deny variety and complexity by imposing one model of place on all others. Such a tyranny of place can occur through such well-known forms as conquest and colonization, but it can also occur in subtler ways. Recently it appears as though schools and hospitals are striving to become more like businesses. The business model of cost effectiveness and efficiency pervades these places to the point where students become customers, and patients become clients. The pervasiveness of this model diminishes the essential differences between these places. And finally there are places that involve the absence of both "seeing through" and "variety and complexity." The result is a chaos or anarchy, a constant transgression so that no projects can be undertaken. Autarky and secrecy, tyranny, and chaos are the three prototypes of geographical evil. The Iron Curtain may have been more heavily weighted in the direction of the first, but other places of evil, like Nazi Germany, combined all three in virtually equal amounts.

These are geographical qualities of evil, and the intrinsic geographical judgments point to qualities of the good that are illuminated by geography. Still, one might argue that Stalin's Soviet Union, Hitler's Germany, and slavery in the American South, as well as a host of other evils, can be condemned on more direct and humanitarian grounds — they were places in which people were murdered, tortured, humiliated, and, in general, treated unjustly. This is all true, but the essential point is that concepts of justice (and injustice) and theories about them, in the last instance, rest on principles of the good, which is where this theory begins. How then do our conceptions of the good lead us to principles of justice and to their stipulation in rights?

To understand this connection we must remind ourselves of two points: the good is compelling and ineffable, and much of evil is based on a lack of awareness. Both of these lead to the principle that human beings are never to be treated solely as means to an end (as Kant would say) but as ends in themselves. That is, human beings are of intrinsic value. Consider the first — that the good is compelling and ineffable. Of all possible things, the good is the most important. It exists as a powerful lure, but it also cannot exist only as an abstraction. It must also be exemplified or instantiated by the good acts of human beings. To act according to the good or to be good is to in some sense possess the good. Because this is within every individual's capacity, it makes human life itself, its preservation and nurture, the highest goal, for life itself always has the potential of possessing the good.

To pursue the good requires a desire or will to do so and an honest evaluation of our own position, our motivations, and the effects of our actions. In other words, we must see clearly, and this requires that we possess the greatest degree of awareness. If we understand the consequences of our actions, we would be more alert to the harm we do and become more responsible agents. Certainly we are gripped by vices such as greed, envy, and sloth, and there are cruel streaks in many of us, but being aware of these and their consequences can help hold them in check. We are more likely to do better when we know that our lack of care, our inattention, and our narrow-minded focus on our own needs lead to the humiliation, degradation, and death of others. The good is compelling, but it is often difficult to discern, and so we must also be aware of the opinions of others so that our view of the good can be checked with theirs to make sure that we are seeing truly.

Being geographically aware and having places that increase this awareness make it easier for us to understand not only how our actions affect other human beings but also their effects on the elements of nature and even on the search for truth. Truth and the natural are as important components of morality as is justice, and geography alerts us to this fact. Even though it is issues of justice that are immediately invoked by concentration camps and slave plantations, we must remember that questions of justice ultimately rest on theories of the good. Because this theory is based on place, it reminds us that the good involves justice, truth, and nature, and its stress on awareness leads to a regard of human life as the highest end of all. Intrinsic geographical judgments are intended to make us more aware of the moral connections of our actions in order to nurture the dignity and creativity of human life.

The values of the theory translate into specific issues of justice and rights. The theory supports the right of human beings to become as aware of the world as possible, and the obligation to see that these heightened and expanded views are shared by all. A full, free, public, and unshrinking awareness of the implications of our actions is essential to curb the worst qualities of our nature. This crucial role of public awareness means that the theory supports free and open access to knowledge and information. It values diversity of projects and viewpoints, for that is the means by which we both increase reality and check our opinions against reality. It supports the elimination of suffering, malnutrition, and disease, because these diminish our human qualities; they narrow our world and reduce our capacities to see it clearly. Caring about the welfare of others is not limited by distance. Care and concern are universal because of the intrinsic value of human life and the need for everyone to pursue the good. In short, the theory's focus on the real and the good and its stress on awareness lead to virtually the same conceptions of justice that are found in liberal democracy, the Bill of Rights, and the United Nations charter on human rights. But it does so by specifying the foundations of these rights. They become not only things that should not be denied others, or negative rights as they are called, but also a starting point for moving to the good — rights that lead to positive action.

Implications

There is much more to say about the logic of the theory and how it addresses particular places, but I want now to turn to some of its more general implications. I want to make two points here. The first concerns the universality of the theory. The second is its implications about nature.

Universality

The theory shows how geography can base its judgments on place and the particular but not be relative. Relativity would result if the theory were confined only to instrumental geographical judgments, for these are entirely context-dependent, and the context is stipulated by the relationship of places and the projects undertaken. Instrumental judgments look inward. They bend the ideas of truth, justice, and the natural to suit the needs of projects. The Iron Curtain was good instrumentally because it was effective in attaining Stalin's goals. Truth and meaning had to conform to what these goals required, and so did justice. The same is the case with Nazi Germany or the American slave system. Concentration camps were instrumentally effective in removing huge numbers of people. They were instruments of Nazi justice because they eliminated groups of people who were seen as racially inferior. And slave plantations were instrumentally good and just because, according to their adherents, they provided a paternalistic environment for a racially inferior group.

Intrinsic geographical judgments are able to place these instrumental judgments in perspective. They can tell us what was geographically immoral about slave plantations, concentration camps, and gulags. In so doing, they take account of the rich and complex contexts that places create, but they also show that places can help us point outward to the real and the good. Helping us discern these qualities makes it possible for intrinsic geographical judgments to evaluate the instrumental ones. Geography then plays a central role in revealing that the good is real and not made up or dependent only on context and that the good depends on our using place to create an increasingly varied and complex world that can make us ever more aware. The intrinsic geographical judgments of the theory correct the all-too-frequently mistaken belief that because the core of geography concerns place, this focus necessarily leads only to the particular, situational, and contextual. This theory, along with *Homo Geographicus,* points out how that is not the case. The structure and dynamics of place can lead us to real moral qualities that are independent of particular places and projects and that can be used to judge these places and projects.

Still, the ineffability of the good and the qualities emphasized by the theory make it clear that the best we can do is point in a direction that is better than another. We cannot rank places in terms of their moral qualities, nor can we make the theory into a formula. It can only provide us with criteria that help us judge and evaluate and that, if followed, can move us in a better direction or have us come closer to it. The ineffable quality means that the theory can never be written as a series of rules or commandments, for that would diminish the good and make it more like a yoke around our necks than a magnetic and compelling image toward which we strive.

Nature

The theory has much to say about our relation to nature, but here I want to mention only one general point. Because the theory emphasizes place, and place mixes nature and culture and hybridizes both, the natural is always part of our considerations at both the instrumental and the intrinsic level. Place is central to our use of nature because place allows it to become part of our projects, even when the project is "protecting or preserving" nature. That is, even to protect nature we must make it into a place (i.e., bound and control at least some of the things that take place) and thereby hybridize it. But instrumental judgments cannot tell us what competing uses of nature are better than others. For that we need intrinsic judgments.

Intrinsic geographical judgments can justify a multiplicity of uses (though not necessarily the same ones that would be supported by instrumental judgments alone). These uses have in common the purpose of creating places that increase both the variety and complexity of the world and our awareness of the world. If the new places we create endanger the capacity of nature to support these undertakings — if our transformation of the world impoverishes natural variety and complexity to the point where we no longer can increase the variety and complexity of places and our awareness of the world — then we are not moving in the right direction. Indeed, preserving and protecting natural diversity can then become a major imperative of the theory, for such preservation could ensure a richer reality, which is a precondition for our own abilities to be as aware as possible. Still, this raises numerous intriguing problems regarding what is meant by natural or biological diversity and how to trade this off against cultural diversity. For example, it may be the case that a primary means of preserving biodiversity is to encourage cultural diversity, but this poses the danger of having these cultures become static means to particular ends.

The theory has many more implications, but in closing I want to stress that its underlying assumptions about the reality of the empirical and the moral are most clearly articulated in Yi-Fu Tuan's own research. In his more recent works, such as *Morality and Imagination, The Good Life, Passing Strange and Wonderful,* and *Escapism,* we find deep, insightful, and provoking discussions of the connections between the real and the good and their association with truth, beauty, and fantasy or illusion. Tuan is the first geographer to make clear that the good is real and ineffable and that these are precisely the qualities appropriate to our age of individualism and skepticism. A recognition of the ineffability of the good is "a safeguard against intolerance and moral stasis. [It is] a powerful lure which limits the indecisiveness of freedom and yet does not enslave or bind."[4] As lures, or magnetic forces, the real and the good have power to draw us to them, and places exert a positive or moral power when they help us become aware of the real and the good. Providing us with a discerning and lucid understanding of the relationship among geography, the real, and the good is one of Tuan's many gifts. His clear-sightedness is the source of his power and exemplifies how disclosing the truth is the strongest force of all.

Notes

I would like to acknowledge that portions of the research for this essay were based on works supported by the National Science Foundation under Grant SBR-9802637 and that sections of this essay are drawn from "A Sketch of a Geographical Theory of Morality," *Annals of the Association of American Geographers* 89, no. 1 (March 1998): 26–44.

1. My arguments about how place is a necessary instrument that has effects are found in Robert Sack, *Homo Geographicus: A Framework for Action, Awareness, and Moral Concern* (Baltimore: Johns Hopkins University Press, 1997).

2. This is a critical realism that assumes the real exists, that it is ultimately unknowable in its range and depth, that we alter it, and that what we know of it is through a glass darkly.

3. The fuller development of these ideas can be found in my essay "A Sketch of a Geographical Theory of Morality," *Annals of the Association of American Geographers* 89, no. 1 (March 1999): 26–44.

4. Yi-Fu Tuan, *Morality and Imagination: Paradoxes of Progress* (Madison: University of Wisconsin Press, 1989), 80.

ATTENDING TO THE VOID

Geography and Madness

Patrick McGreevy

> Our earth is but an ant-hill's form,
> A thing of fleeting fantasies;
> The lightning and the thunderstorm
> Are Will-o'-wisp and murmuring bees;
> Proud history is but a breath,
> The brief vibration of a sigh;
> All glory is a mist of death,
> And epochs like a bubble die.
> — FERENCE KÖLCSEY,
> "Vanitatum Vanitas"

My purpose in this essay is to pose some fundamental questions about how geographers understand places. Since these questions presented themselves to me in the context of two related personal experiences, I will take these experiences as my points of departure.

The first experience came upon me gradually. I began to notice that when I looked at the face of, say, a middle-aged person, I could not help but imagine that same face in youth, childhood, and old age. At any particular moment, a face seemed unstable, part of a process of growth and decay. It was as if my eyes wanted to speed up the process, like an effect in some horror film in which a face ages and melts from its skull in seconds or a time-lapse sequence showing a plant growing, blooming, and withering. In short, I became much more aware of the ephemerality of the individual human life. This perception is hardly new or unique. Samuel Beckett, for instance, was profoundly impressed by the fact that, as his character Lucky puts it, existence dwindles toward "the great cold the great dark," a void about which no statement from any human voice can tell us anything.[1]

The second experience grew out of my habit of taking long walks beyond the edges of my town and into the forested landscape of western Pennsylvania. The Allegheny Plateau consists of rounded hilltops and deeply incised, steep-sided valleys. It is a topography shaped primarily by the slow action of water and gravity, unaffected by mountain-folding, glaciers, earthquakes, or other catastrophic processes. Yet it did not seem stable to me. In my walks I often encountered abandoned railroad beds, shacks, mining equipment, and other evidence of human occupation now overcome with vegetation and the erosion resulting from steady precipitation and fluvial processes. Everything seemed to be sliding downhill. And again, as in a sped-up film sequence, I could almost see the entire landscape flowing toward the sea. Ultimately, I thought, it is as if we are all living on the San Andreas Fault. And what, then, of the human settlements, the towns atop the rounded hills? Their geometric structures and street patterns began to seem a mere birdcage of provisional architecture in relation to the void that circumscribed them. In *Mason & Dixon,* novelist Thomas Pynchon highlights this void by shifting the reader's frame of reference. He tells a story about a concave world inside the globe whose inhabitants ask: "How many of us, I wonder, could live the other way, the way you People do, so exposed to the outer darkness? . . . And wherever you may stand, given the Convexity, each of you is slightly *pointed away* from everybody else, out into that void that most of you seldom notice."[2]

It seems to me that there is a tradition in geography of attending to this void. We try to understand the worlds humans create by placing them in the most comprehensive framework, the broadest context. We tend to be acutely aware of how circumscribed all human worlds are. The geographer's keen interest in scale reveals that all places occupy a tiny portion of space and time. We are fond of startling undergraduates with statements such as this: if the age of the earth were a twenty-four-hour day, all of human history would occupy only three-tenths of a second.[3] We present them with images of our fragile planet from space and with world maps showing humans to be confined not only to this planet but to the dry quarter of its surface and — for the most part — to the arable 3 percent. If it is true that we geographers are particularly aware of the void that encircles all our worlds, at every scale, how does this knowledge inform our understanding of those worlds?

In considering this question, I think it is useful to compare the worlds geographers investigate to the situation of the individual, for the condition of humans, individually and collectively, is the same in this sense: to use Richard Coe's words, "around us on every side, in space, lies the Void; behind us, before us, in time, lies the Void."[4]

Before we can examine the relation of either individuals or worlds to the void, we must consider what separates both from the void: boundaries. "A living thing," writes Nietzsche, "can only be healthy, strong and productive within a certain horizon: if it be incapable of drawing one around itself . . . it will come to an untimely end."[5] Maintaining a sense of identity depends on limits. Or as Freud would have it, psychological health depends on repressing some parts of reality (creative self-restriction), which begins with the infantile recognition of the distinction between I and not I.[6] In *Landscapes of Fear,* Yi-Fu Tuan recounts the widespread anxiety in many cultures about violation of boundaries, whether of the body, the house, or the political/cultural domain.

Tuan also suggests that the willingness to reach out beyond boundaries is the fruit of a certain level of security.[7] There is a distinction to be made between the sort of boundary that defines a particular political/cultural domain vis-à-vis other cultures and the boundary that distinguishes the human from the nonhuman, but there is also a sense in which all that is beyond a cultural boundary, whether human or nonhuman, functions as a counterpart to group identity. European settlers, for example, often classified Native Americans as part and parcel of the natural landscape. In this sense, other human groups can also represent the void. This is also true on the level of individual identity, for, as one of Sartre's characters reminds us, "There's no need for red-hot pokers. Hell is — other people."[8]

Pynchon's *Mason & Dixon* is a novel that turns on the central metaphor of the boundary: "It goes back [he writes] to the second Day of Creation when 'God . . . divided the waters which were under the Firmament, from the waters which were above the Firmament,' thus the first boundary line. All else after that, in all History, is but sub-division."[9]

In Genesis, God creates the world out of the formless void by *speaking* it into being. Words divide what we experience into discrete units, they dismember, yet we can only create cultural worlds with them. Creation is distinction, though the reality of inside and outside, we and they, may be illusory. "We . . . have dreamt the world," Borges writes, "we have dreamt it as firm, mysterious, visible, ubiquitous in space and durable in time; but in its architecture we have allowed tenuous and eternal crevices of unreason which tell us it is false."[10]

The last thing we want to admit is that our worlds are arbitrary, provisional creations — bastions against the void. Yet a tacit acknowledgment of the immensity of what our worlds exclude justifies the maintenance of boundaries and helps to define these worlds by contrast. When the ancient Greeks banished anthropophagi, amazons, and centaurs to the edge of the ecumene, they were defining their own culture by what it was not. Twentieth-century geographers have promoted themselves as experts in this matter of defining worlds, and they too have used the notion of contrast between inside and outside as a way of casting identity into sharper relief. Hence Carl O. Sauer contrasts the non-human natural landscape with the cultural landscape,[11] or John K. Wright contrasts the known world with terrae incognitae.[12] The metaphorical boundaries implied by these conceptual frameworks suggest that what is outside is inherently and entirely different from that within.

Because boundary drawing is a process of limitation, what is excluded may be rendered a realm of infinite possibility. The space within the boundary may even seem confining, a cage.

Again, Pynchon's character Mason muses:

Does Britannia, when she sleeps, dream? Is America her dream? — in which all that cannot pass in the metropolitan Wakefulness is allow'd

Expression away in the restless Slumber of these Provinces, and on West-ward, wherever 'tis not yet mapp'd, nor written down . . . ever behind the sunset, safe till the next Territory to the West be seen and recorded, mea-sur'd and tied in, back into the Net-Work of Points already known, that slowly triangulates its Way into the Continent, changing all from sub-junctive to declarative, reducing Possibilities to Simplicities that serve the ends of Governments, — winning away from the realm of the Sacred, its Borderlands one by one, and assuming them unto the bare mortal World that is our home, and our Despair.[13]

Compared with the view of the ancient Greeks, Mason's image of what lies beyond the boundary of the "bare mortal World" is less fearful, more cosmopolitan, but like the Greek view, it cannot help but assign particular meanings to the excluded realm. Our worlds and even what we imagine beyond them are constructed largely with our own words. Nevertheless, this does not mean that what is real is limited by our linguistic abilities. "The *real,*" Ashley L. Preston suggests, "might be described as that elusive *other* whose description, by definition, always exceeds our linguistic abilities, but whose existence is undeniable at the level of immediate experience."[14] Preston points to those "unexpected moments" when a tornado or an avalanche "intrudes without the benefit of mediation" and leaves us speechless.[15] Using the word *real* in this sense suggests that there is more to the world than we expected or imagined. It does not necessarily imply that there is some neutral point from which all that is would be clearly visible. Robert Sack, in this volume, argues that expanding awareness of the real is always a moral good.[16] The "aim of liberal education," Tuan writes, "is to transform one limited self into a rich concourse of selves, one narrow world of direct experience into many worlds, a creature of one time into a seasoned time traveler."[17] This constitutes an attempt to be open to the real, to pay attention to what lies beyond the boundaries.

But what exactly is this thing called attention? I want to relate another ex-perience — one that showed me how a work of art can help us develop the ability to attend. *Fog Line* is a short independent film by Larry Gottheim,[18] a central figure of the movement known as Avant Garde or Critical Cinema.[19] Gottheim simply turned on a single stationary camera and let it run for eleven minutes with no panning, zooming, or sound. Through a misty fog, the viewer sees a solitary leafy tree in the middle distance (see Figure 1 on the following page). An electrical line divides the scene horizontally. I watched this film with a group of academics at an institute focusing on the graphic and literary rep-resentation of nature. During the first few minutes of the film, it seemed we were looking at a photograph. Then many people began to get restless; some started talking. Eventually several got up, complaining, and left. The rest of us grew gradually more quiet and simply stared at the screen — wondering what Gottheim could possibly have in mind. About halfway through the film I began

Figure 1. Still from Larry Gottheim's independent film *Fog Line*, 1970. The camera never moves in this eleven-minute, silent film. Viewers who are not outraged may become very attentive to small movements of limbs and leaves in the slight breeze.

to notice slight movement among the leafy limbs of the tree. I remembered this was a *film*, not a photograph. This encouraged me to attend more closely, and slowly more and more movement became perceptible. Finally I could see the tree pulsating, breathing like a lung. This film made me want to go out and stare at trees, and I must admit, it genuinely changed the way I looked at them. I began to see a subtle vitality that I had entirely missed.

Learning to attend, according to Nietzsche, should be one of the central goals of education:

> Learning to *see* [means] — accustoming the eye to calmness, to patience, to letting things come up to it; postponing judgment, learning to go around and grasp each individual case from all sides.... Not to react at once to a stimulus, but to gain control of all the inhibiting, excluding instincts.[20]

But for Nietzsche there is also something ignoble, even dangerous, about what he calls "the famous modern 'objectivity.'" In the same passage about seeing, he continues:

> As a learner, one will have become altogether slow, mistrustful ... to have all doors standing open, to lie servilely on one's stomach before every little

fact, always to be prepared for the leap of putting oneself in the place of, or of *plunging* into, others and other things.[21]

The Spanish philosopher José Ortega y Gasset takes a different approach to attention:

[F]or the discovery of a new thing, intellectual keenness is not enough. One must have enthusiasm for this, a previous love for this very thing. Understanding is a lantern which must go directed by a hand, and the hand must be moved by a pre-existent eagerness for this or that type of possible things.[22]

In *The Good Life* Tuan takes an intermediate position. Attending to the experience of another individual or culture is enriching only if one can minimize one's own desires and fantasies. "One must be able to attend selflessly," he writes, but this attention is "necessarily discriminatory." He continues: "Some things naturally command our attention, others do not, and only those things for which we have a natural affinity — however strange they may appear at first — can truly feed and enlarge our being."[23]

There is a paradox here. We have to be able to imagine, to think something, before we can grasp it or perhaps even see it, but even this ability to imagine and think is formed within our limited, contingent experience. Moreover, thought is the very thing that calls into question the status of boundaries. Hannah Arendt writes:

The thinking ego — summoning into its presence whatever it pleases from any distance in time or space, which thought harnesses with a velocity greater than light's — is nowhere . . . , a void. . . . [I]t is homeless in an emphatic sense — which may explain the early rise of a cosmopolitan spirit among the philosophers.[24]

Thinking, even as it reveals and sometimes undermines the arbitrary limitedness of concepts like home and nation, also ironically demonstrates the inevitability of limits. Again, Hannah Arendt points out that "man's finitude, irrevocably given by virtue of his own short time span set in an infinity of time stretching into both past and future, . . . manifests itself as the only reality of which thinking qua thinking is aware."[25] Pynchon's Mason and Dixon, triangulating their way into the continent, bursting again and again through the boundary between the known and the unknown, finally discover a border they cannot penetrate. Mason pines for his dead wife who dwells in "that other Tract, across the Border . . . that very essence of division" (his ellipses). One night her ghost accosts him, complaining about the feeble hubris of imposing order upon the void: "Dare you calculate me? Dead-reckon your course into the Wilderness that is now my home, as my exile?"[26]

A heightened awareness of personal finitude is one of the bitter fruits of thought, of the sort of attention that penetrates boundaries. Especially since the Enlightenment, there has been a gradual erosion of traditional collective certainties in the Christian West — a failure, we might say, of shared illusions. This has left many of the most thoughtful individuals acutely aware of their personal finitude. "Terror, perdition and annihilation," Kierkegaard reminds us, "dwell next door to every man."[27] We are surrounded by a void of nonexistence: the horizon-to-horizon face of death. But there are a variety of reactions to this knowledge. For Nietzsche, the heroic human response is "to *live danger-ously!* Build your cities under Vesuvius! Send your ships into uncharted seas."[28] Jacques Derrida, and a number of existentialists before him, argue that death gives us our singularity and that this awareness, in turn, makes us truly free.[29] Peter Koestenbaum contends that "the thought of death suffuses . . . life with a liberating sense of urgency."[30] For others, however, death deprives life of mean-ing.[31] Some existentialists, staring unflinchingly into the face of death, see only oblivion, while others see heroic or Promethean possibilities.

The thought and attention that, I have suggested, geographers often direct toward the boundaries of geographical domains enable us, Tuan writes, "to ac-cept a human condition that we have always been tempted by fear and anxiety to deny, namely, the impermanence of our state wherever we are, our ultimate homelessness."[32] Our creations are like sandcastles that can be erased by the next tide, though this may elude the casual glance. As in the case of the indi-vidual confronting death, this knowledge of the void can lead to a number of different perspectives on human creations.

One perspective is to conclude that human agency is so limited and frail that it is insignificant compared to the forces confronting it. An extreme expression of this view is the recurring geographical idea of determinism. In practice, of course, many determinisms represent attempts less to attend to the real beyond cultural borders than to bolster cultural pride by discounting the agency and value of those beyond.[33]

A second possibility is that the geographer who sees human worlds as ar-bitrary impositions upon a foundation of ceaseless flux finds these creations nonetheless expressions of an appealing, courageous sort of madness: heroic gestures of freedom. We cobble together intricate webs of meaning in the very face of the void. We make an ecumene, a life-world, while recognizing that it is ultimately a mere pea pod upon the Pacific. For Sartre, the human individ-ual's freedom comes with the recognition of its nothingness, which compels it to make itself into something.[34] The void, like the ocean in Kant's view of the sublime, can be both a midwife and a mirror: a spur to human creativity and to the recognition of its worth.[35] In recent years, geographers have turned more and more to the investigation of the worlds of the apparently powerless and voiceless. They have learned to appreciate the heroic efforts these people make to create homes and communities in the face of powerful erosive forces.

A third response is to purposely breach the boundaries and try to reestablish them at a more inclusive level. The narrator of Nikos Kazantzakis's *Zorba the Greek* tells of his grandfather who, though he never left his native Cretan village, invited every stranger he met to his home, provided "an abundance of food and drink," and made the stranger talk about everything and every place that person had experienced.[36] Cosmopolitanism, in the sense of attending to and recognizing the value of what lies beyond parochial boundaries, has nothing necessarily to do with travel. "The desire for objectivity," Richard Rorty argues, need not be "the desire to escape the limitations of one's community, but simply the desire for as much intersubjective agreement as possible, the desire to extend the reference of 'us' as far as we can."[37] We are all located within limited worlds, limited communities, no matter how broadly or idiosyncratically we define them. Attending to the real is a matter of stretching and negotiating at the borders, of reimagining one's community more comprehensively. Certainly this cosmopolitan impulse to extend the world's boundaries provides the impetus for much geographical and anthropological work. Political, cultural, and social geographers are able to transcend the narrow political, cultural, and social categories of their own nations by imagining themselves members of a community of inquirers — international in scope and perhaps centuries old — who agree on the value of such aspirations.

There is also the possibility that the breach in the circle may defy healing. "Venturing beyond the familiar circle," Tuan reminds us, "entails the risk of pushing to the edge of madness."[38] Pynchon's Mason recognizes that it was a heightened attention that led to Herschel's discovery of Uranus in 1781. "Suddenly the family of planets had a new member, tho' previously observ'd by Bradley, Halley, Flamsteed, Le Monnier, the Chinese, the Arabs, everyone it seemed, yet attended to by none of them." But this is deeply troubling to Mason, who feels that the boundary separating the familiar world from something profane and terrifying has been broken. He is hounded "by summonings from beyond the Horizons, by Spirits who dwell a little over the line between Day and its annihilation, between the number'd and the unimagin'd — between common safety and Ruin ever solitary...."[39] In *Nausea*, Sartre's character Roquentin makes a similar point: "Contingency is not a false appearance which can be dissipated.... [E]verything is gratuitous — this garden, this town, I, myself. When we realize this, then it turns our hearts, everything begins to float."[40] Attending to the void, while it can make one aware of personal limitations — of the need, as Nietzsche says, to be enclosed in some kind of circle — can also dislodge the world from its moorings, and in that moment of floating relativity, madness is a possibility. My point is not to explain how the desire for the exotic might lead the occasional graduate researcher or senior professor into an inescapable labyrinth or even suicide but rather to underscore the tension that accompanies all attempts to transgress sustaining boundaries in search of the real. The "extreme geography" that David J. Nemeth has recently advocated would consciously engage the void and embrace relativity.[41] Perhaps it would function as Michel Foucault says a work of art does. "By the madness which interrupts it," Foucault writes, "a work of art opens a void, a moment of silence, a question without answer, provokes a breach without reconciliation where the world is forced to question itself."[42]

Of course, there is a much older way for a structured world to question itself. "Almost all human societies," Tuan writes in *Passing Strange and Wonderful,* "exhibit a need to shatter periodically the bonds and boundaries of culture in riotous carnivals... and bursts of iconoclasm in religion and art."[43] In such moments, which Victor Turner has labeled liminal, the ordinary structure of the world is abolished or inverted. Whether liminality is truly transformational or simply serves to "let off steam" is an open question.[44] In carnival, normal cultural boundaries and distinctions are breached, but within a well-defined temporal boundary. The irony of such moments, as Victor Turner and Mikhail Bakhtin both point out, is that despite the breach of boundaries, a strong sense of group camaraderie usually obtains, as well as a sense of timelessness.[45] The participants are no longer curious about horizons: they are no longer thinking, in Arendt's sense of being aware of finitude. "In the presence of extraordinary actuality," Wallace Stevens tells us, "consciousness takes the place of imagination."[46] Or Ludwig Wittgenstein: "Eternal life belongs to those who live in the present."[47]

One might conclude that such an experience is very different from that of attending to the void where one seems to be alone. Yet if this essay itself is an attempt to attend to the void, I must concede that its very form implies the void's counterpart: a human world. The chaos of carnival is tolerable because it is embedded within the ordinary structured world represented by the rest of the calendar. So also, "the meditative temperateness of an essay," Cynthia Ozick has recently argued, "requires a desk and a chair, a musing and a mooning, a connection to a civilized surround; even when the subject itself is a wilderness of lions and tigers, mulling is the way of it."[48] Though we may venture toward horizons and voids, in a sense we are never alone, for we always venture from the locus of "we": a human world. The void is nothing and almost everything, but it only has meaning in relation to what we create against it. The world and the void, like reason and madness, come as a pair. It is the act of creation, of division — though the boundary line may be arbitrary, leaky, and false — that brings into existence not only the world but also the void.

Notes

1. Samuel Beckett, *Waiting for Godot: A Tragicomedy in Two Acts* (New York: Grove Press, 1954), 29.

2. Thomas Pynchon, *Mason & Dixon* (New York: Henry Holt, 1997), 741.

3. Peter Koestenbaum, *The Vitality of Death: Essays in Existential Psychology and Philosophy* (Westport, Conn.: Greenwood Press, 1971), 10.

4. Richard N. Coe, *Samuel Beckett* (New York: Grove Press, 1964), 3.

5. Friedrich Nietzsche, *The Use and Abuse of History,* part 2 of *Thoughts Out of Season* (New York: Russell and Russell, 1964), 10.

6. Ernest Becker, *The Denial of Death* (New York: Free Press, 1973), 177–78.

7. Yi-Fu Tuan, *Landscapes of Fear* (New York: Pantheon, 1979), 205.

8. Jean-Paul Sartre, *No Exit: And Other Plays* (New York: Vintage Books, 1955 [1946]), 47.

9. Pynchon, *Mason & Dixon,* 360–61.

10. Jorge Luis Borges, *Labyrinths* (New York: New Directions, 1964), 208.

11. Carl O. Sauer, "The Morphology of Landscape," *University of California Publications in Geography* 2 (1925): 19–53.

12. John K. Wright, "*Terrae Incognitae:* The Place of Imagination in Geography," *Annals of the Association of American Geographers* 37 (1947): 1–15.

13. Pynchon, *Mason & Dixon,* 345.

14. Ashley L. Preston, "Nature Conservation in a Deconstructed World," *Humanities and Technology Review* 16 (fall 1997): 32.

15. Ibid., 27.

16. Robert D. Sack, "Place, Power, and the Good," in this volume.

17. Yi-Fu Tuan, *The Good Life* (Madison: University of Wisconsin Press, 1986), 161.

18. Larry Gottheim, *Fog Line,* independent film, 16mm, 11 minutes, color, silent, 1970.

19. Scott MacDonald, *A Critical Cinema: Interviews with Independent Filmmakers* (Berkeley: University of California Press, 1988); MacDonald, "The Garden in the Machine: Two American Avant-Garde Films and the Nineteenth-Century Visual Arts," *Prospects* 22 (1997): 239–69.

20. Friedrich Nietzsche, *Twilight of the Idols,* in *The Portable Nietzsche,* ed. Walter Kaufmann (New York: Viking, 1968), 463–563, 511–12.

21. Ibid., 512.

22. José Ortega y Gasset, *What Is Philosophy?* trans. Mildred Adams (New York: W. W. Norton, 1960), 171.

23. Tuan, *The Good Life,* 162.

24. Hannah Arendt, *The Life of the Mind* (New York: Harcourt Brace Jovanovich, 1978), 200, 199.

25. Ibid., 201.

26. Pynchon, *Mason & Dixon,* 702–3.

27. Søren Kierkegaard, *The Concept of Dread,* trans. Walter Lowrie (Princeton, N.J.: University Press Edition, 1957 [1844]), 140.

28. Friedrich Nietzsche, *The Gay Science,* in *The Portable Nietzsche,* 97.

29. Miles Richardson, "The Gift of Presence: The Act of Leaving Artifacts at Shrines, Memorials, and Other Tragedies," in this volume; Jacques Derrida, *The Gift of Death* (Chicago: University of Chicago Press, 1995), 15.

30. Koestenbaum, *Vitality of Death,* 19.

31. Alfred Stern, *Sartre: His Philosophy and Existential Psychoanalysis,* 2d ed. (New York: Delta, 1967), 103; Jacques Choron, *Modern Man and Mortality* (New York: Macmillan, 1964), 160–68.

32. Yi-Fu Tuan, *Cosmos and Hearth: A Cosmopolite's View* (Minneapolis: University of Minnesota Press, 1996), 188.

33. Richard Peet, "The Social Origins of Environmental Determinism," *Annals of the Association of American Geographers* 75 (1985): 309–33; George Tatham, "Environmentalism and Possibilism," in *Geography in the Twentieth Century,* ed. G. Taylor (London: Methuen, 1953), 128–64.

34. Stern, *Sartre,* 65.

35. Immanuel Kant, *Critique of Judgement,* trans. J. H. Bernard (1935; reprint, New York: Macmillan, 1951), 1790.

36. Nikos Kazantzakis, *Zorba the Greek,* trans. Carl Wildman (New York: Simon and Schuster, 1952), 49.

37. Richard Rorty, "Solidarity or Objectivity?" in *From Modernism to Postmodernism: An Anthology,* ed. Lawrence E. Cahoone (Oxford: Blackwell, 1997), 575.

38. Tuan, *Landscapes of Fear,* 205.

39. Pynchon, *Mason & Dixon,* 769.

40. Jean-Paul Sartre, *Nausea* (Norfolk, Conn.: n.p., 1957 [1949]), 171.

41. David J. Nemeth, "Extreme Geography," *California Geographer* 37 (1997): 11–30.

42. Michel Foucault, *Madness and Civilization: A History of Insanity in the Age of Reason,* trans. Richard Howard (New York: Pantheon, 1965), 208.

43. Yi-Fu Tuan, *Passing Strange and Wonderful: Aesthetics, Nature, and Culture* (Washington, D.C.: Island Press, 1993), 238.

44. Patrick McGreevy, "Place in the American Christmas," *Geographical Review* 80 (1990): 32.

45. Mikhail Bakhtin, *Rabelais and His World,* trans. Helene Iswolsky (Cambridge, Mass.: MIT Press, 1965); Victor Turner, "The Center out There: Pilgrim's Goal," *History of Religions* 12 (1973): 191–230; Victor Turner and Edith Turner, *Image and Pilgrimage in Christian Culture* (New York: Columbia University Press, 1978).

46. Wallace Steven's, quoted in Joyce Carol Oates, "Against Nature," in *On Nature: Nature, Landscape, and Natural History,* ed. Daniel Halpern (San Francisco: North Point Press, 1987), 242.

47. Ludwig Wittgenstein, *Tractatus Logico-Philosophicus,* trans. D. F. Pears and B. F. McGuiness (London: Routledge and Kegan Paul, 1972), 147.

48. Cynthia Ozick, "She: Portrait of the Essay as a Warm Body," *Atlantic* (September 1998): 118.

THE GIFT OF PRESENCE

The Act of Leaving Artifacts at Shrines, Memorials, and Other Tragedies

Miles Richardson

At Christian shrines in Catholic countries in Europe and Latin America, pilgrims come to leave objects. Called in Spanish America at some locations *milagritos,* little miracles, the objects portray the body part that the pilgrim is thanking the shrine figure for curing. So along the walls or in cabinets hang tiny hearts, lungs, arms, and legs. But there are other objects as well. Photographs, letters, paintings, crutches, and even a mannequin's head all express gratitude for the assistance received. Placing objects at holy places no doubt extends back centuries and perhaps serves as a model for other, more recent practices of leaving objects at significant, if not holy, places. An example of the latter is the Vietnam Veterans Memorial in Washington, D.C. (see Figure 1 on the following page). At any visit to the "Wall," the anthropologist-geographer may well find flags, wreaths, messages, C rations, and medals.[1]

Apart from shrines and memorials, it is not uncommon for relatives to take flowers to the grave of a loved one. The leaving takes on another dimension when the grave is the resting place of a rock star, like Elvis Presley (Figure 2). At Graceland in Memphis, Tennessee, in the Meditation Garden where the King lies among his closest kin, the faithful leave flowers sprouting from vases and wreathed into hearts and flags, but also into teddy bears and hound dogs. Significantly, the day the fans descend upon Memphis is not Elvis's birthday but his death day, August 16.[2]

In addition to shrines, memorials, and graves, the site of an unexpected, senseless death may become a location where people leave objects. In the early spring of 1995, at the University of North Carolina in Chapel Hill, a student on his way to class walked into the sights of another student's M-1 rifle as that student slipped over the edge and pulled the trigger. Overnight, the location where the murdered student fell became a place for leaving things, which included flowers, a UNC lacrosse cap, a can of chewing tobacco, and a Bible (Figure 3). With the unspoken cooperation of the street cleaners, the objects lay there for a week, protesting in their silence the insanity of the event. Augment the sound of a single rifle shot to that of a truck bomb and we visualize the Alfred P. Murrah building, in Oklahoma City on April 19, 1995, exploding in

Figure 1. Vietnam Veterans Memorial, Washington, D.C.

Figure 2. Graceland, in Memphis, Tennessee, the resting place of Elvis Presley.

Figure 3. The location where a murdered student died, University of North Carolina, Chapel Hill.

its horror of 168 deaths. Long after the last bodies were taken from the rubble and the building was razed, people continued to place items on the chain-link fence that cordoned off the disaster site. Today, among the items they leave (flowers, photographs, crosses, and autographed T-shirts of sport teams passing through), the most poignant are the baby garments and dolls, recalling the occupants of the day-care center inside the building (Figure 4).

But wait, you say, wait. What do these have in common? What do shrines, memorials, graves of media stars, and sites of senseless killing share that would make anyone say they belong together? A lot of variation, to be sure. Yet at each location, people leave things. And in their leaving they establish the location as a place. So, you say again, a place. But what is the location a place of? The place of a public event. And the public event is a death. Thus, all the places — shrine, memorial, grave, and sites — are places of death. They are places where people leave objects in the face of death.

All right, you agree, the Oklahoma site, the street of the UNC incident, the grave at Graceland, and the memorial in Washington, D.C., are all connected to death, although in different ways. What about shrines? What are their connections? In Spanish America, among the shrines devoted to Christ, those that predominate by far are the ones devoted to the crucified Christ. And the Christ on the cross is frequently at the point of death or has died, his eyes closed, his head slumped, the blood from his wounds slowing in its flow. Several of

Figure 4. Site of the Alfred P. Murrah building, Oklahoma City.

the Christs are dark, and even called *negro*, black, like the famous shrine at Esquipulas, Guatemala. And what they are dark with is death.[3]

True, you reluctantly concur. But what about Mary? Both in Europe and in Spanish America shrines to the Blessed Mother outnumber those to Christ. And the Mary of the shrines is not dead. No, she is not. But while she may reign, as she does at Lourdes, France, as the Crowned Virgin, the Queen of Heaven, an air of melancholy never escapes her. As La Madre Dolorosa, she grieves, her eyes filled with sorrow for her dead son (Figure 5).

And the saints? The saints are not saints until they have died, and more than a few have died violently. Their violent deaths gave them the capacity to act saintly. In the early days of Christianity, when memory of the martyrs was still fresh, people believed the pain the saints endured in their dying cured illnesses. In an "emotional inversion of suffering," the objects that tortured the saints, the mallet that crushed the bones, the thongs that rip the flesh, had the power to heal.[4]

Okay, you are nearly ready to concede when you recall el Niño. And the Niño you recall is not the el Niño that is the current darling of TV weather forecasters, but el Niño, for example, of Atocha, at the shrine at Plateros, in northern Mexico, who, dressed in the flowing hat and dress of a medieval pilgrim, is very far from being dead, especially farther north, in Chimayó, New Mexico, where he is said to walk around at night and so is constantly in need of new shoes. And in response, I can only agree you are correct, but call upon

Figure 5. As La Madre Dolorosa, the Virgin Mary grieves for her dead son.

your generosity, for which you are justly famous, to allow me to set the Child of Atocha and his like aside, and continue.[5]

In all cases, the death the objects are left in the face of is violent, and the violence is public. Upon hearing of, or even in some cases seeing, the death, we, you and I and all those around us, stand aghast at its appearance. It rises before us at the crucifixion, battlefield, casket, street, and building. We recognize its familiar face as the mirror image of our own.

The face of death is a mirror image of our own what? It is the mirror image, the other side, of the self. And the self is what makes us human.[6] The capacity to reflect back upon the flow of experience permits us to reify that experience into an entity and give it a name. Me. You. Us. Words give us this power to name. But the same reflexive power that resides in words also resides in artifacts. "The significance of the artifact," to cite the scholar this book celebrates,[7] lies in its ability to recall and reconstitute experience. In a manner similar to the way speech joins together ideas and behavior, artifacts likewise unify ideation and action into concrete objects that signify.[8] And what the objects left at shrines, memorials, graves, and sites signify is presence in the face of absence.

Pairing presence with absence suggests a relationship between those two that is as fundamental as the one between self and death. That is, absence and death, what we ordinarily avoid, makes possible presence and self, what we surely treasure. This inversion, this convolution of everyday thought, you recognize immediately and impatiently and with some disgust as the bête noire of all of us romantic, humanistic truth-seekers, deconstructionism. Despite our built-in antagonism toward the likes of "phonocentricism," "logocentricism," and, a personal favorite, the "absence of the transcendental signified," the insights of Jacques Derrida seem especially appropriate for the examination of tragedies. This appears particularly true when we read according to one interpreter that "If there is a masterword for Derrida, that word is death."[9] And indeed, Derrida himself, in pointing to Rousseau's equation of humanity, passion, imagination, speech, and liberty, may well be voicing his own position when he says that the series "indirectly name the danger itself, the horizon and source of all determined dangers, the abyss from which all menaces announce themselves," that is, death.[10]

Death resides in the vacant space of words. Words, or more generally symbols, claim to be more than what they are. They claim reality, but in fact they are only symbols. Symbols stand at some distance from reality, otherwise they would not be symbols. Despite the protest of poets, biblical literalists, and other true believers, their meaning is never fixed in their sounds, but their meaning is implemented in one another. Symbols yearn for presence, but in their presence, in their difference from what they purport to symbolize, and in their constant deferral of meaning, they convey absence. When we became human, we primates spoke and discovered absence — which is another name for loneliness.

264 • *Miles Richardson*

Apart from the loneliness, this paragraph is my outrageously condensed interpretation of Derrida's concept of *différance*. Any signifier differs from the concept it signifies, its signified; consequently, the meaning of the signifier can only be determined from the presence of other signifiers; that is, its meaning is deferred. Derrida puts together *difference* and *defer* into the neologism *différance*. "This means that differance makes the opposition of presence and absence possible. Without the possibility of differance, the desire of presence as such would not find its breathing-space. That means by the same token that this desire carries in itself the destiny of its non-satisfaction. Differance produces what it forbids, makes possible the very thing that it makes impossible."[11] The center, Derrida explains in another work, "has no natural site, [but it is] a sort of nonlocus in which a number of sign substitutions come into play; [consequently,] the central signified, the original or transcendental signified is never absolutely present outside a system of differences. The absence of the transcendental signified [there's my favorite!] extends the domain and play of signification infinitely."[12]

Various writers have found Derrida's insistence that we have no central rock upon which to anchor ourselves disturbing.[13] They overlook the fact that the rock can be a millstone we drag about wherever we venture. Its absence frees us, even in our loneliness, to create a joyous world of affirmation.[14] They also overlook that an entirely different writer, Kenneth Burke, who has a much more congenial reputation among humanists, also noted a decade earlier that words are "sheer emptiness."[15] Since words are not the things they stand for, their very use implies a negativity, an absence. Burke maintains that it was the invention of the negative that heralded our birth as humans, and indeed he wonders if it might be more accurate to say that the negative, the classic symbol, invented us. That two writers, so separate from each other as Derrida and Burke, both find the human secret, as it were, in absence, strengthens the arguments of each.

In regard to the loneliness that absence brings, I can do no better than direct you toward the songs of Hank Williams, the patron saint of all us redneck existentialists.[16]

The discovery of absence turns presence into a quality more precious than our everyday language of "We are here, where else?" suggests. Presence in the face of absence turns us from a factual given, from simply being here as objects occupying space, into a gift. Presence is the immediate, face-to-face, muscular experience of this unique moment. Presence requires the presence of the body, but the body not as an object but as the self made flesh, equipped with the seeing hand, the listening eye, the comprehending ear, the beseeching mouth, and the empathetic skin. Presence also requires language, but not language as *la langue*, the disembodied structure of code sending and receiving, but language as *la parole*, the speech of one flesh-and-blood self to another. For when we speak, you and I, it is not from one mind to another, but from one bipedal dealer in symbols to another. Spoken in this manner, language "does not *presuppose* its table of correspondence; it unveils its secrets itself."[17]

Presence also requires another. I cannot be the Miles I claim I am without you. Conversely, you, no matter your flights of megalomania, require me to support your you. The self is not a bundle of neurons buried deep in the brain's cortex and antecedent to presence, but it is a social construction arising out the exchanges between us.[18] Even in my solitude, I know you are alongside. Indeed, it is often when I am apart from you that I hear your voice most clearly, for as Miguel de Unamuno tells us, in solitude, the heavy shell of conventional discourse that entraps us like an exoskeleton encasing a crustacean gradually softens until our interior selves may touch in ecstatic communion.[19] Together, then, kneeling before the crucifix, approaching the memorial, bowing at the grave, or staring at the baby clothes on the chain-link fence in Oklahoma City, we, you and I, offer our gift of being.

In offering our gift of being, we may kneel, with head bowed, or we may stand almost rigid with attention and gaze at the sight before us. Rarely are we physically alone, with no one else at arm's length, yet universally, we speak softly, if at all. Silence during our giving bespeaks of intense interest and, we often say, of respect. In staring at the names on black marble at the Vietnam Memorial, are we offering respect? Maybe. But at the crucified figure bent in frozen agony? Or at dolls on the chain-link fence? No, you shake your head in disbelief. Here, the normal sound of talk seems blasphemous. Silence, on the other hand, you point out, and lowering our voices far below the conversational level in some mysterious way augment our offering.

In offering our gift of being we encounter the artifacts that others have left. Among the objects most commonly left are flowers. These flowers, however, are not those casually plucked from the roadside, but ones secured for a price from the florist, or perhaps in rare cases taken from one's own garden. Although objects of nature's beauty, the flowers share the same shaping quality that characterizes the other items, such as medals, dolls, dog tags. Thus, along with giving the presence of being we are also offering culture, the item most distinctive of humans.

There is more, you insist. Yes, but just what I am not sure. Of all the images of Princess Diana's funeral, the one of people tossing bouquets of flowers upon the hearse as it rolled past on its way to the grave stirred me the deepest — me, a Yellow Dog Democrat, who stands about as far removed from princesses as it is possible to be. What was it? Was it the flowers themselves? Or was it the sight of people, so moved that they, in an elegant gesture of arm and hand, toss an offering to a memory? Yes, the gift of presence is there, in the rising arm, the releasing hand, and the letting go. To be sure, but what they let go of was flowers.

Jack Goody has much to offer in his massive *The Culture of Flowers*.[20] His examination reveals that the so-called language of flowers, which purports to be a lexicon of what flowers symbolize, was a compilation begun in the nineteenth century that expressed the taste of the authors more than it actually interpreted the semiotics of floral displays. And while he documents, in what he calls "the americanization of a foreign mind," the presence of flowers at funerals and graves, he hesitates to address what flowers accomplish at burials or — in our case — at the sites of violence. It has something to do with their beauty, doesn't it? Beauty and death. A strange, compelling joining, one that resonates in a beguiling way with a book a colleague wrote on the Romantic image of the beautiful death.[21] Unable to pursue that tantalizing clue at this time, I await your research.

Apart from flowers, we also find messages, some carefully typed, others apparently written on the spot. At shrines, these messages typically begin with a formulaic statement of thanks to the shrine figure for favors granted. They may continue to describe the incident in which the Señor or the Virgin rendered assistance, curing a sick child, healing a bad wound, or confusing the border patrol so the pilgrim could escape detection. They end with a name, Diego Gonzáles García, Lola Montoya Flores, so as to identify the person in the message. Names too appear on the sports T-shirts that hang from the fence in Oklahoma City — Jim Strickland, Bill Ferguson. The names attempt to tell us who was here, to separate out these particular gifts from the anonymous hearts, crutches, or wreaths.

In all cases, the objects left are more powerful than the words that their givers might have spoken. They are more powerful in the sense that their very physicality denies absence. While speech is our most direct and forceful presentation of being, it is also the most ephemeral. The words we speak at these locations, no matter how heartfelt, last only for the few seconds it takes us to say them. The objects we leave continue to speak that we were here and made this gift, long after we have gone. The written artifacts seek to combine the voicing of speech with the physical permanence of objects. So messages left by others seek to attest to the now-lost presence in a fuller, more intimate manner. The writing makes their particular claim to presence stronger.

Despite their permanence, these gifts by people who have left, who are no longer present, signify a kind of presence that is absence. Consequently, we find ourselves in the presence of a double absence: the absence of the person or people that death has made permanent and the absence of those who were here, left us a sign, and then departed. It's as if they have joined their absence with the larger absence that drew us here in the first place. And still another paradox: The objects themselves announce absence. At the street in Chapel Hill and at the Alfred P. Murrah building, at least, they tell us here is the spot, here is the location where people die, suddenly, violently, and without cause. If the objects were not here, would we even know where to go? They are, in Karen Mills-Courts's term, epitaphic.[22] Like an epitaph on a tombstone, the objects announce here is what is no longer here.[23]

Finally, we arrive at the most crucial aspect of our giving: What do we receive in return?

Drawing upon Marcel Mauss's celebrated *The Gift*,[24] in which he analyzes the reciprocal flow of artifacts among members of "archaic societies," several authors have recently distinguished between what we in "modern societies" receive from an exchange of commodities and from an exchange of gifts.[25] Both exchanges call for the transfer of objects, and both necessitate social interaction. The differences, however, lie in the greater links between members in gift exchange. These links begin with the obligation to give, the obligation not to buy, but to give. The giver must give. Second, the gift is linked to the giver. The present I give, or the object I place alongside the wall at the Vietnam Veterans Memorial or hang on the fence at Oklahoma City, bears my identity. The identity may be private in the sense that few may know those are your flowers on the sidewalk in Chapel Hill, or the identity may be almost blatantly public and, as we have just discussed, carry the name and message of the giver. Finally, and perhaps most important, the gift implies a relationship between the two parties in a manner that a purchase may not. As applied to our cases, we might better say the gift *seeks* a relationship. To be sure, at the shrine, when we leave an arm in gratitude for the curing, we are continuing a relation we already have, but even here we are *seeking* a continuation, while at the Wall or in the Meditation Garden, the search of our seeking is clearly evident even if its goal is obscure. Furthermore, our search is not that of abstract individuals whose existence can be substituted for others without loss, but the search of moral persons. Mary Douglas, in her foreword to Mauss's treatise, is succinctly forthright: "The theory of the gift is the theory of human solidarity."[26] Assuming that reciprocity and solidarity are the same, what do we receive for our gift of presence?

At the shrine, where reciprocity rules the day, nothing could be more clearcut. I ask for a miracle. On its receipt, I travel to the shrine and place an object as near to the figure as the officials will allow. I then purchase items, including images of the shrine figure, which I attempt to put in contact with the sacred figure or at least have the priest bless it. I return home with my shrine image. At the Wall, upon finding a certain name inscribed on its black marble, I make a rubbing of the name to take home or to my office. Thus, at the Wall you and I take home names rather than icons. At both shrine and Wall, however, what we take back has come into contact with the sacredness or holiness of the place and in so doing has acquired a metonymic quality.

When we visit Graceland, we come back with postcards, slides, knickknacks of one thing or another, but all imprinted with Elvis's name and, frequently, his likeness, all of which we have purchased away from the actual grave.[27] But what do we return with from the site of the former Alfred P. Murrah building? What I took away you see here. We take away in cameras images of our presence and then attempt to transfer those visual images into a verbal

Figure 6. Reflections of the living in the Vietnam Veterans Memorial.

one. Once the memorial planned at the bomb site is finished, no doubt replicas of it will become available.

But if a gift suggests reciprocity, does that not imply the places we visit give us something back in a more direct fashion than the objects we purchase to take home? In response, I ask you to return once more to Derrida. In perfect fulfillment of your expectation for something convoluted, he offers us a book titled *The Gift of Death*.

The gift that death gives us is our singularity, our irreplaceability, or in other words, our own unique self — in my case, my Miles, in your case, your own I. In accepting death's gift, we become morally responsible, and the emerging "conscience that looks death in the face is another name for freedom."[28] Citing with approval Martin Heidegger's *Being and Time*, Derrida insists that while I can offer my death for another, I cannot die the other person's death. Each of us dies our own death; the gift is uniquely ours alone.

Do the locations we visit offer us their deaths? Is that their gift? In the Spanish American shrine, as Christ hangs before us, is he offering us his death? Here, in complete opposition to Derrida, a Christian of any persuasion might assert that what separates Christ's death from any other is that he in fact died our death. Is it not perfectly orthodox for the Christian to say that Christ died so that each Christian would have eternal life?

What of the other locations? Staring at the names on the Vietnam Veterans

Memorial, we may feel that yes, in distant Vietnam, those we see before us offered us their death.

What about the grave at Graceland? Did the man who sang, "You Ain't Nothing but a Hound Dog," die for you and me? The tens of thousands who that gather on Elvis's death day apparently would say, if not shout, "Yes."

But no one can, in their right mind, say that the student in Chapel Hill or the babies in Oklahoma City offered us their death.

"The theory of the gift is the theory of human solidarity," Douglas reminds us. In return for death we give presence. At these places that fill us with sad nostalgia for what has gone, we arrive at the moment to which we knew all along we were heading. In the artifacts that we leave we address less the death before us and more one another. I who stand before these places do not speak to an it out front but instead address the you who are sometimes in my head, not uncommonly in my face, but now a Thou who abides alongside.[29] You as Thou remain you, in your flesh-and-blood glory, but now you exist in a relation whose warmth melts away the shell of conventional being and opens you to my heart. With Thou, the I you call Miles becomes I who smiles unafraid. Standing together, the mystery we know so well and understand so little, and dare not name, comes. In the space that resides between I who am and Thou who art we create the gift of hope for what awaits. Here, reaching for your hand I say to you, both of us facing the black marble of the Vietnam Memorial, join me in solidarity before death (Figure 6).

Notes

I am grateful to Paul C. Adams, Steven Hoelscher, and Karen E. Till for their kind invitation to participate in this honoring of Yi-Fu Tuan. We all have our own personal debts to Yi-Fu. Mine increased tenfold at a conference he and I attended back in the early 1980s on drama and theater held in New York City. It was a wonderful occasion. All the big names were there, but Yi-Fu was the only real geographer present. It did not take long, however, for the big names to discover the calm, clear, revealing insights that are Yi-Fu's trademark. On the other hand, I was intimidated. All that intellectual power turned me into a lump on a log. Eventually, I screwed up enough courage to offer a comment. No sooner had I opened my mouth when people looked around as if to ask, "Who let this guy in? Anyone who talks like Jed Clampett can't be serious." But then Yi-Fu, being a gifted linguist, translated for me, and they said, "Oh, that's what he meant. Of course. Right on the mark." And from then on the conference took a much more friendly turn. I would present an observation. Yi-Fu would translate. And the big names would beam.

1. "At first, National Park Service rangers did not know what to do with the things they were finding each day at the Vietnam Veterans Memorial. . . . The rangers gathered up flags and roses, letters and teddy bears, toy cars and birthday cards, dog tags and service medals, cans of C ration and packets of Army-issue toilet paper. For a time, everyone was puzzled by the status of the objects, many of which were obviously valuable, yet purposely abandoned. But an awareness grew that there was something almost sacred about these objects. They were like tangible bonds between those who fell in Vietnam and those who remembered, a mystic communion with the dead. Everyone who touched these offerings at the Wall knew that they had to be kept — forever" (Thomas B. Allen, *Offerings at the Wall: Artifacts from*

the Vietnam Veterans Memorial Collection [Atlanta: Turner Publishing, 1995], 5). Given the widely recognized power of the Vietnam Memorial, we forget the furious controversy surrounding the unveiling of the design. "A black gash of shame" and "a tribute to Jane Fonda" were some of the more restrained assessments. See Kathleen Elsa Kennedy, "Reflecting Darkly: Face to Face with the Vietnam Veterans Memorial" (master's thesis, Louisiana State University, 1991); and Miles Richardson and Robert Dunton, "Culture in Its Places: A Humanistic Presentation," in *The Relevance of Culture,* ed. Morris Freilich (New York: Bergin & Garvey, 1989), 75–90.

2. Karal Ann Marling, *Graceland: Going Home with Elvis* (Cambridge, Mass.: Harvard University Press, 1996).

3. Miles Richardson, "Clarifying the Dark in Black Christs: The Play of Icon, Narrative, and Experience in the Construction of Presence," in *Yearbook of the Conference of Latin Americanist Geographers,* ed. David J. Robinson (Austin: University of Texas Press, 1995), 107–20.

4. Peter Brown, *The Cult of the Saints: Its Rise and Function in Latin Christianity* (Chicago: University of Chicago Press, 1981), 84. The ability of objects to absorb the violence associated with their use continues today. Kenneth Foote, in his excellent study, notes that paraphernalia associated with the likes of Bonnie and Clyde and John Dillinger "can attract high prices" (Kenneth Foote, *Shadowed Ground: America's Landscape of Violence and Tragedy* [Austin: University of Texas Press, 1977], 210). Visitors, such as you and I, to the grave of Billy the Kid at Fort Sumner, New Mexico, will find it enclosed in an iron cage. The tombstone has been stolen so many times, the rangers in charge of the cemetery have had to lock it up. This absorptive ability appears closely linked with the manner in which objects pilgrims purchase at shrines and place against the shrine figure take on its sacred qualities. The diffusion of the sacred from shrine to artifact and of violence to tombstones, and so on, is in ways still unclear to me related to the quality of presence I am striving to portray.

5. One direction to continue is to note that British scholars are also puzzling about the current practice of leaving objects at the site of tragedies. See George Monger, "Modern Wayside Shrines," *Folklore* 108 (1997): 113–14.

6. This is a point carefully developed by Robert Sack. In addition, Sack stresses the intertwining of self and place; they are "mutually constitutive" (Robert David Sack, *Homo Geographicus* [Baltimore: Johns Hopkins University Press, 1997], 127).

7. Yi-Fu Tuan, "The Significance of the Artifact" *Geographical Review* 70 (1980): 462–72.

8. In any consideration of artifacts, we think, first and foremost, or at least I do — being from Louisiana State University — of Fred B. Kniffen. In Kniffen's work at LSU, artifacts on the landscape, particularly domestic house styles, testify to the presence of the past. See, for example, Fred B. Kniffen, "Material Culture in the Geographic Interpretation of the Landscape," in *The Human Mirror: Material and Spatial Images of Man,* ed. Miles Richardson (Baton Rouge: Louisiana State University Press, 1974), 252–67. Inspired by Kniffen but also by George Herbert Mead and his concept of objects as "collapsed acts," I have tried to develop the process whereby artifacts unify concepts and action into concrete signifiers. See Miles Richardson, "A Social (Ideational-Behavioral) Interpretation of Material Culture and Its Application to Archaeology," in *Mirror and Metaphor: Material and Social Constructions of Reality,* ed. Daniel W. Ingersoll Jr. and Gordon Bronitsky (Lanham, Md.: University Press of America, 1987), 381–403.

9. Karen Mills-Courts, *Poetry as Epitaph: Representation and Poetic Language* (Baton Rouge: Louisiana State University Press, 1990), 261.

10. Jacques Derrida, *Of Grammatology* (Baltimore: Johns Hopkins University Press, 1976), 183.

11. Ibid., 143.

12. Jacques Derrida, *Writing and Difference* (Chicago: University of Chicago Press, 1978), 280.

13. For example, Sack, *Homo Geographicus,* but also see Daniel W. Ingersoll Jr., ed., *Personal Meaning and Cultural Commitment: Critical Reactions to Post-modernism,* special issue of *Journal of Steward Anthropological Society* 22 (1994).

14. For further development of this point, see Miles Richardson, "Unamuno and the Flesh-and-Blood, Celebratory Critique of the Postmodern Play of Signification," in Ingersoll, *Personal Meaning,* 177–94.

15. Kenneth Burke, *Language as Symbolic Action* (Berkeley: University of California Press, 1966), 6.

16. Hank Williams, *The Complete Work of Hank Williams* (Nashville: Acuff-Rose, 1983); Colin Escott, *Hank Williams: The Original Singles Collection* (New York: PolyGram Records, 1990).

17. Maurice Merleau-Ponty, *Signs* (Evanston, Ill.: Northwestern University Press, 1964), 42. The classic distinction between *la langue,* commonly translated "language," and *la parole,* "speech," was made by Ferdinand de Saussure, *Course in General Linguistics* (La Salle, Ill.: Open Court, 1986). Saussure, in developing a science of linguistics, privileged the more consistent *langue* over the more idiosyncratic *parole* and in so doing laid the foundations for structuralism, an endeavor quite opposite from the phenomenology of Merleau-Ponty.

18. This dialogic theory of the self comes from George Herbert Mead. See Anselm Strauss, ed., *George Herbert Mead on Social Psychology* (Chicago: University of Chicago Press, 1964). For the application of Mead's ideas to place, see Richardson, "A Social (Ideational-Behavioral) Interpretation"; and Richardson and Dunton, "Culture in Its Places."

19. Miguel de Unamuno, *Soledad* (Madrid: Espasa Calpe, 1974).

20. Jack Goody, *The Culture of Flowers* (New York: Cambridge University Press, 1993).

21. J. Gerald Kennedy, *Poe, Death, and the Life of Writing* (New Haven, Conn.: Yale University Press, 1987). With all this talk about flowers and death, I believe we should also keep in mind the sight of graves in folk cemeteries in the American South. Even into the recent past, the graves, often scraped clean of grass, had on top of their mounds flowers to be sure, but also shells, dishes, mugs, eyeglasses, and medicine bottles. Those of children were adorned with toys, marbles, and stuffed animals. For the most part, these items were the personal possessions of the deceased and served to guard the identity of the dead as opposed to expressing that of the living. See Gregory D. Jeane, "Cemeteries," in *Encyclopedia of Southern Culture,* ed. Charles Reagan Wilson (Chapel Hill: University of North Carolina 1989), 463–65.

22. Mills-Courts, *Poetry as Epitaph.*

23. Or, as Karen Till remarked in a personal observation, the presence of absence.

24. Marcel Mauss, *The Gift: The Form and Reason of Exchange in Archaic Societies* (New York: W. W. Norton, 1990).

25. These include C. A. Gregory, *Gifts and Commodities* (London and New York: Academic Press, 1982); Arjun Appadurai, ed., *The Social Life of Things: Commodities in Cultural Perspective* (Cambridge: Cambridge University Press, 1986); Marilyn Strathern, *The Gender of the Gift* (Berkeley: University of California Press, 1988); David Cheal, *The Gift Economy* (London: Routledge, 1988); and James Carrier, *Gifts and Commodities: Exchange and Western Capitalism since 1700* (London: Routledge, 1995). Carrier, in particular, clarifies both the similarity and differences between the two exchanges and how one type may take on some of the characteristics of the other. The purchasing of *milagritos* to give to the shine figure is certainly a blend of the two. Derrida, himself, has taken it upon himself to criticize Mauss's concept of the gift as gift. Since a gift is by definition unfettered, how can Mauss speak of the gift of reciprocity? At my initial readings, this distinction seems to be too much of a philosopher's obsession for logical niceties to be useful in the real world of imperfect give and take. See Jacques Derrida, *Given Time, I: Counterfeit Money* (Chicago: University of Chicago Press, 1992).

26. Mary Douglas, foreword to Mauss, *The Gift,* x.

27. Sue Birdwell Beckham, "Death, Resurrection, and Transfiguration: The Religious

Folklore in Elvis Presley Shrines and Souvenirs," *International Folklore Review* 5 (1987): 88–95.

28. Jacques Derrida, *The Gift of Death* (Chicago: University of Chicago Press, 1995), 15.

29. The I, It, and Thou come, of course, from Martin Buber, *I and Thou*, 2d ed. (New York: Macmillan, 1987 [1958]). Scholars as diverse as Victor Turner, *The Ritual Process: Structure and Anti-Structure* (Chicago: Aldine, 1969), and Shlomo Hasson, "Humanistic Geography from the Perspective of Martin Buber's Philosophy," *Professional Geographer* 36 (1984): 11–18, find in the dialogic quality of Buber's work an appealing strategy for addressing those qualities of human interaction that conventional social science tends to flee from — in the name of scientific rigor. Both Buber and Mead stress the "*parole,* speech" component in the making of our world as opposed to the "*langue,* language" aspect. This essay does likewise by its very plotting of the conversation between you and me.

REIMAGINING NATIONAL IDENTITY

"Chapters of Life" at the German Historical Museum in Berlin

Karen E. Till

Germany recently celebrated the tenth anniversary of the fall of the Berlin Wall. Yet many former East German citizens, known as *Ossis,* felt little reason to celebrate in 1999: unemployment rates were high, feelings of foreignness remain, and official recognition of the role of East German citizens in creating a new Germany was minimal. Although the physical barrier dividing the two Germanys was quickly dismantled in 1989, *die Mauer im Kopf* (the Wall in one's mind) stands solidly in place at the turn of the new millennium.

One way to understand the psychological barriers between former East and West Germans is to examine distinctive social experiences at particular places of memory (such as the Berlin Wall, national museums, or Holocaust memorials) at different moments in time. Groups create places of social memory to authenticate and legitimate selective stories about the past and thereby construct a collective identity in the present. When the present is socially perceived to be in turmoil, the process of establishing memory in place may become more noticeable. Following the fall of the Wall, for example, landscapes of the postwar division quickly began to disappear in the public spaces of Berlin, a city that historically has functioned as a stage for imagining the nation. Furthermore, in the former East, memorials dedicated to socialist leaders were torn down, street names celebrating communist resistance fighters were changed, and many historical buildings were renovated. Former German Democratic Republic (GDR) government buildings, including the Palace of the Republic (the People's Parliament), the Marxist-Leninist Institute, and the Museum of German History were closed.[1]

Why the move to change East Berlin landscapes? These sites were understood by Western officials as places of GDR memory that promoted Eastern values, pride, and truths. They were quickly closed or renovated because they were perceived as a threat to the legitimacy of a new Germany. Museums, monuments, and memorials have traditionally functioned as "theaters of memory" for officials of the state because they provide a spatial context within which stories and rituals of citizenship are performed, enacted, understood, and contested. As Lauren Berlant explains, national culture becomes local and tangible "through the images, narratives, monuments, and sites that circulate through personal-collective consciousness." When competing understandings exist about what national past should be remembered at a particular site or how a place should function to define or represent a "people," the constructed nature of the nation — as an "imagined" rather than a "natural" community — becomes more conspicuous. Thus, in times of immense social upheaval, officials of the state may move quickly to communicate a singular understanding of what it means to belong to a particular nation-state through places of memory.[2]

The physical presence of traditional places like the museum, archive, and memorial provides a tangible marker of historical continuity and stability in times of perceived dramatic change. In 1990, the German Historical Museum (Deutsches Historisches Museum) in Berlin replaced the GDR Museum of German History and "inherited" the latter's collections, building (the historic Prussian armory building, or Zeughaus), and staff.[3] One of the first unified national state-sponsored exhibitions that displayed the history of the divided Germany in the new/old museum was the Chapters of Life in Germany, 1900–1993 (Lebensstationen in Deutschland, 1900–1993) exhibition, which opened in 1993. Local and national newspapers described the exhibit as the autobiography of the German nation: "With more than 700 objects, the visitor is led through the individual life sections as though it were a large family album." The Frankfurter Allgemeine Zeitung reported: "Admittedly, only collective memories are saved in the exhibit. We're looking at the album of the great family Germany." The main focus of the exhibition became, as the museum director described, "a large-scale comparison with the old Federal Republic and the former GDR." One museum staff member described the exhibit as a "family reunion" between East and West Germans: "individuals have lost sight of themselves, see themselves again, talk about it, and come closer again — or now at least know more exactly where the differences and foreignness lie."[4]

In this essay, I examine the Chapters of Life exhibition as a tangible expression of national history housed in an official place of memory during a period of postunification transition.[5] To discuss the complex and diverse ways individuals and social groups responded to unification and to the new German nation, I describe the narratives, spaces, and visitor experiences of the exhibition.[6] In particular, I discuss the normative representations of the nation in the exhibition and pay attention to which social groups were "excluded" from being represented as "typical" Germans. I argue that while East Germany was exhibited as a relic of the past — reinforcing the notion that the FRG was the inevitable model for a unified Germany — all Germans (both East and West) were represented as belonging to a "family" defined by kinship relations. Visitors, of course, had a range of responses to the exhibition, especially in their reactions to how the GDR was exhibited. Before describing the exhibition and visitor responses, I first discuss briefly the national history museum as an official place of memory.

The National History Museum as a Place of Social Memory

Place is the cultural and spatial context within which we construct and locate our individual and collective identities. As Yi-Fu Tuan has eloquently argued, the ways in which individuals and groups perceive and represent the everyday settings of human actions contribute to a sense of self and being located in the world. It is through and within places that we frame our social memories. By social memory, I mean the process by which groups "map" their myths (in an anthropological sense) and values onto particular times and places. Societies build places like history museums and memorials because groups and officials assume that a particular type of place can shape the public memory of the past and that this memory, in turn, can influence social understandings of the present moment.[7]

Museums are particularly dense centers of meaning and social memory due to their multiple functions and histories. Scholars have described museums as memory palaces, secular temples, shrines, private sanctuaries of a wealthy, white society, storehouses of dead artifacts, rooms of inquiry, and ceremonial time capsules. These descriptions denote the history of the museum as a type of place, one linked to Western traditions of political thought, science, colonialism, and nationalism.

Although museums began as cabinets of curiosities by wealthy collectors, by the eighteenth and nineteenth century officials of new nation-states used collections of artifacts symbolically to replace a lost medieval cosmos with a rational one. Objects in the museum were linked to ancient civilizations to demonstrate that the rise of the European nation-state was historically inevitable. During the colonial period, cultural objects were classified in museums according to moral, spatial, and temporal hierarchies that supported hegemonic notions of identity based upon differences *and* distances between self/Other, West/East, civilized/savage, and masculine/feminine. These organizational schemes, including taxonomies and associational groups, were based upon Western traditions in the natural sciences that were biased toward vision. History was presented as progressive, and objects came to signify the cultural and technological achievements of a "nation," or people.[8]

Today, museums have multiple social functions as educational institutions, tourist sites, and cultural centers of valuable objects. At a symbolic-economic level, museums may continue to function as national public monuments and even, like the Louvre in Paris, symbolize a city or nation. At museums, just as at other national places of memory with long-standing cultural histories, tensions may exist between more traditional, and often ceremonial, uses and more contemporary educational activities, that is, between the ritualistic and pedagogical aspects of collective memory and group identity. Sometimes these tensions may result in practical constraints. For example, museum experts may be limited in what projects they can propose or realize due to traditional collection and exhibition practices and economic and political relationships to museum sponsors, donors, and diverse publics. Furthermore, because there is a range of museum professionals, including academics, design experts, educational specialists, and public relations officials, understandings by experts as to what should take place in the museum may vary quite dramatically.[9]

Although museums have many social functions, a central defining feature is its "inscapes," or the spaces, architecture, material objects, texts, and meanings of exhibitions. Exhibitions are theatrical, staged spaces that perform selective versions of the past. Exhibition authors interpret the past by relating spaces, objects, and written texts in distinct combinations that can, in turn, be interpreted by visitors in various ways. As Masao Yamaguchi explains, "the relationships of objects in time are transposed into a spatial context, and that regrouping is imprinted in the memory of the visitors.... [The museums'] ability to function as machines for turning time into space, enables them to be used as an apparatus of social memory."[10]

Yamaguchi hints at two facets of museum exhibitions that are still not well understood by scholars and museum experts: spatiality and experience. Exhibition spatiality includes the range of meanings created by the social groups, sites, and spaces around, between, and at displayed material objects (including interpretive texts). To analyze different spatial representations of the past, the scholar must pay special attention to architecture, layout, design, objects, and texts in an exhibition and then situate these constellations within the larger contemporary cultural and political contexts of a society to understand their meanings. Furthermore, the multiple interpretive spaces, times, and power relations between the various groups involved in an exhibition (as well as their relationships to what is on display) must be considered. Museum visitors (and the "public" if it is a state institution), exhibition authors, curators, designers, museum collectors (and other experts), and the individuals who made, used, and previously owned the artifacts and objects displayed all take part in the creation and experience of a given museum exhibition.[11]

Acknowledging the complexity of exhibition spatiality and the groups involved in the creation of exhibition meanings entails recognizing the scales at which social experiences take place in a museum. In exploring the significance of the artifact for visitors, for example, Tuan has argued that the actual material object is not what is meaningful but rather the human experience it reifies. Artifacts, he explains, "have the power to stabilize life. Transient feelings and thoughts gain permanence and objectivity in things — in the jugs and chairs that endure." Not only do artifacts communicate stability and permanence, so too do museum exhibitions, their buildings, and their locations. Robert Foster argues that when school groups visit a national museum on a field trip, for example, historical consciousness and everyday life come together to inform the visitors' sense of what is "normal, appropriate, or possible" in their society. Of course the relationships between visitor experiences and representations of national identity at exhibitions are far from straightforward. As we shall see in the final section of this essay, when tourists go to museums, they do not passively accept the narratives presented or automatically change their conceptions of nation or self.[12]

The history museum, then, is a complex type of place that localizes and spatially communicates narratives of time and identity. In the next section, I describe one particular exhibition, *Chapters of Life,* to explore how German memory and identity were represented after unification.

Lebensstationen: Chapters of German Life, 1990–1993

Walking into the elegant lobby of the Zeughaus, the visitor would have seen a banner with a wall-size black-and-white wedding photo that declared the entrance to the exhibition. Once inside, banners in French, German, and English announced the exhibit's theme: the presentation of "typical" life experiences for four societies, the Kaiserreich (around 1900), National Socialist Germany (NS), the German Democratic Republic (GDR), and the Federal Republic (FRG). In each of the four historical periods, the chapters displayed included birth, education, youth, military duty, marriage, old age, and death. According to exhibition authors, the exhibit did not attempt to depict the minutiae of everyday life but rather illustrated the "underlying structures and frames of reference" for the majority of Germans living during these times.

As illustrated in Figure 1 on the following page, the spatial layouts for the Kaiserreich, National Socialist, and GDR sections were linear, whereas the FRG section was fractured. Through this spatial organization, exhibition authors wanted to depict the general change in German society from an ordered, predictable life to an increasingly fragmented one. Although a section may have covered anywhere from twelve to forty years, display techniques transformed the fluidity of time into a static representation of history — each period, with perhaps the exception of the FRG, was like an image, photo, or memory of a place and time. Visitors were also encouraged to identify personally with the exhibition through the quotidian artifacts on display in each section, including birth certificates, confirmation photos (Figure 2), wedding invitations, photo albums, clothing, schoolbooks, popular magazines, children's backpacks, anniversary trays, greeting cards, and coffins.[13]

Germany around 1900: The Kaiserreich Section

In the Kaiserreich section, chapters were displayed in open black-framed spaces, what one exhibition author described as "picture-rooms." The main colors used were brown, black, and gold, colors that evoked the everyday experiences of the turn of the century, such as the dark brown of the floors in Berlin's *Altbauten* (older buildings). The artifacts exhibited almost smelled of

Figure 1. Spatial layout of the *Lebensstationen* exhibition, 1993. Illustration courtesy of Deutsches Historisches Museum. Entwurf: Daniele Schneider-Wessling.

times past, such as the yellowing certificates with old German script that summoned forth pungent odors of dust and mildew in the mind of the visitor. Brown-and-white photos (Figure 2) and china with old German script also evoked the nostalgia of the turn of the century. The dim lighting of this section enhanced the sensation one has when a memory comes back: the image is a bit hazy, and the edges are not clearly defined.

Designers envisioned visitors moving through the space of the exhibition by metaphorically stepping back in time as they entered a room/chapter. Many

Figure 2. Kaiserreich section: exhibit display for the chapter "Confirmation." Photograph of exhibition room by author, 1993.

visitors, however, preferred to view the framed rooms from the outside, as though these were distant images from the past to be looked at in photos or paintings. The chapters of life — from birth to death — were presented as a progression of square rooms. One exhibition author described this spatial layout in this way:

> When one leaves a chapter to move to the next one, the last one is gone and there is a new station. There is no going back. . . . The socially expected life path ran in a straight line; there were no deviations. Or when there were deviations from this linear, expected path, they were seen as problems, scandals, or were very difficult.[14]

The deviations from this linear progression were titled "Youth," "Between Occupation and Marriage" (which referred to women), and "Separated Women and Single Mothers." Unlike the picture-rooms, the green circular area for "Youth" stood to the side of the path and represented a new socially recognized life chapter for bourgeois groups at the end of the 1800s. After this brief detraction, the linear progression of picture-rooms continued, leading to military duty and marriage:

> Everyone had to go to [the life station of] marriage — it was very difficult to get around it, and although it was possible, it was not normal. There were very few single women and mothers, [a theme] which is presented off to the side in the hall.

On the backside of the "Marriage" picture-room, women who didn't fit that chapter, such as single mothers, were displayed. Yet even these social outsiders, according to exhibition authors, ultimately had to go back to the path: "One went directly to death from the old-age station; it was ever-present and unavoidable." Death was dramatically symbolized by a looming black-iron coffin at the end of the path.[15]

National Socialist Germany

Upon leaving the Kaiserreich section, visitors entered a room with an immense black wall that seemed to symbolize memories so monstrous that they had been intentionally forgotten or confined to a part of the self that was better left untouched. All of the walls in this section were dark charcoal grey, almost black, and were as tall as the museum, about twenty feet high. A framed series of thirty small black-and-white identity card photographs were mounted, their smallness exaggerated by the height of the looming, dark wall, suggesting their inability to fight the NS system. It was as though these people were under some kind of interrogation in the past and present with a single overhead light burning onto their faces.

In the constricted exhibition space of this section, the main colors used were associated with fascism: black, white, and red. Third Reich propaganda posters towered overhead, diminishing the presence of the more personal artifacts and photos illuminated in the small glass cases. The spatial design of the NS section reflected what exhibition authors viewed as the extreme level of state control in all aspects of everyday life during this time. This oppressive architecture, shaped into a half-swastika, was intentionally designed to show that

> individuality was only possible through conformity and adaptation to the state's ideology and conceptions. So there are not well-defined chapters of life, like in 1900 or the GDR [sections of the exhibit], but rather one level. We see signposts of these chapters, but the life path was completely defined by the state. There are no deviations and breaks, it is completely linear. It is a closed system. All the chapters are in glass cases and exhibited in the same way; it is all part of one hermetic system — it is very strict.

Once a visitor entered this restricted space, he or she would not easily be able to turn back. After the "Education" chapter, visitors had to make a ninety-degree turn to the right and enter a narrow corridor with a slight uphill incline. Again this effect was intentionally designed:

> Humans were like robots in this time. Everyone had to follow the procession. They had do what they were told; therefore the right angles of the exhibit. Visitors shouldn't be comfortable in this part of the exhibit. Also the small incline is uncomfortable.

Figure 3. National Socialist Germany: exhibit display for "Hitler Youth" and "Year of Duty." Photograph of exhibition room by author, 1993.

Text panels and artifacts depicted the influence of the state on everyday life. In the "Entering School" chapter, for example, "fatherland studies," biology, and racial studies textbooks were displayed. Nearby stood a wall-size photograph of a Hitler Youth rally in Berlin, and around the corner were Hitler Youth uniforms, posters, and board games (Figure 3).[16] In both "Birth" and "Marriage and Family," texts explained how NS ideology excluded women from public life to emphasize their "natural responsibilities" as wives and mothers.

At the end of the path stood "Death," symbolized by a wall-sized stylized soldier's head upon which large white crosses were painted (Figure 4). According to exhibition authors, the state even controlled dying:

> We wanted to show that the state's hold on the population ultimately was to be able to further the war, to create death as defined by the state.... We therefore decided not to focus upon the individuality of death.... Death was a social duty.

Yet exhibition authors wanted to "contrast the heroic, exalted death with what this really meant for the people" by having visitors walk down three small steps to look at soldiers' passes and letters before exiting. As one author explained:

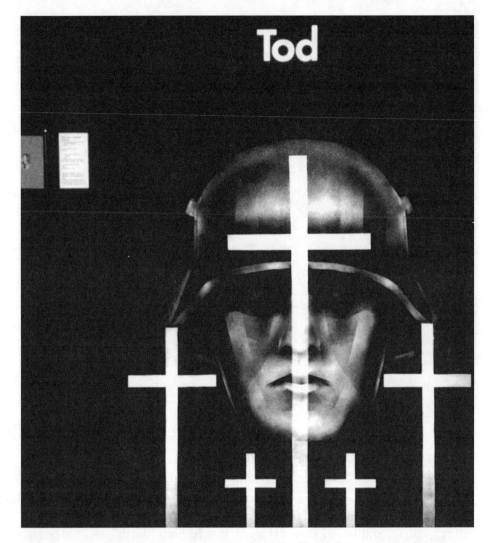

Figure 4. National Socialist Germany: exhibit display for "Death." Photograph of exhibition room by author, 1993.

The only thing that remained was the soldier's pass that was sent back to the family. It was a very bureaucratic process: a red line written across the middle with the word "fallen." No one had the chance to escape this ordered system.

The German Democratic Republic

After coming out of the darkness of the National Socialist section, visitors had to choose which period they would go through first, East or West Germany. In my survey, most West Germans explained that they decided to go to the GDR section first because it was the "Other" to them — the East was unknown and foreign. On the other hand, East Germans went "home" first

Figure 5. The German Democratic Republic: exhibition display for "Kindergarten." Photograph of exhibition room by author, 1993.

because they wanted to see how *Wessis* (West Germans) represented their "nation."[17] Although the GDR and FRG sections covered the same time period, the appearance of the respective entrances may have also influenced the visitor's choice to go East first. As I describe below, the GDR section to the left evoked the hazy nostalgia of the recent postwar past (the 1950s to the 1970s), whereas the FRG section to the right declared the modernity of the recent present.

In the East German section, the lemon-yellow walls and light-turquoise-blue floors harked back to the 1950s and 1960s. The lighting was diffused, and artifacts elicited a vague, yet familiar image of a period in the not-too-distant past that was no longer part of the present. Objects from the "Childbirth" and "Kindergarten" sections (Figure 5), mostly daycare furniture, children's toys and clothing, gave the section a dated feeling. The "Youth" and "Jugendweihe" (Youth Initiation Ceremony) chapters communicated the 1970s with the plastic purses for girls and photos of youth and adults in tightly fitted polyester outfits with long-collared shirts. In the "Work" chapter, a documentary film ran on a 1950s-style television that depicted young East German women textile workers with clothing and haircuts from the 1970s.[18]

The *Chapters of Life* exhibition poster itself was from the "Old Age" section in the GDR, a 1956 photo of a "veteran's club" that depicted elderly people wearing suits and relaxing in lawn chairs. This wonderfully nostalgic image was hung as a poster advertisement in metro and train stations, communicating the notion that the tourist could safely visit the past/place of the GDR in the museum. This representation of the GDR resonated with postunification *Ostolgie* (nostalgia for the East), whereby many *Wessi* tourists visited the East as a place from the postwar past. As Mary Fulbrook explained, the GDR had "an archaic, old-fashioned feel to it" after unification because East German community sizes were not so dissimilar to the immediate post- and even prewar period, whereas West German urban and rural configurations changed dramatically from 1945 to 1990.[19]

The GDR not only was presented in terms of a nostalgic past but was also exhibited as a totalitarian space. Visitors' movements were restricted to a linear path (Figure 1), to the left of which were small cubicles (the chapters) and to the right of which stood a ten-foot (Berlin) Wall with a "Going West" chapter. As an exhibit author explained, the GDR section was designed to show that

> the life path was ordered, clearly laid out, and there were very few variations. When one was 14, one went to Jugendweihe; when one was 20, one got married; when one turned 65, one retired.... There was a typical life path, and we wanted to show that typical way. That's why one sees the general overview of the chapters of life in the orderly architecture.

When placed within this spatial frame, artifacts could be interpreted as belonging to a socialist order. For example, in "Birth," two open side-by-side rooms simulated a regimented daycare nursery room and a kindergarten (Figure 5), and interpretive texts explained that 80 percent of children aged one to three attended state-run centers by 1980. In "Youth," uniforms, oaths ("True to our salute I am always prepared for freedom and socialism"), artwork, and texts described student activities in the state youth political organizations of the Free German Youth (FDJ), Young Pioneers, and Thälman Pioneers (98 percent of all GDR students participated in these groups). The selection of artifacts and texts thus emphasized GDR state control through contrasts to the West. As one author explained: "There were no surprises. Everything was planned....After unification, that's what many people from the East feel they lost — the general overview, the security, the expected."

Comparisons: The Federal Republic of Germany

After going through the GDR section, visitors walked over the Wall, which also functioned as a bridge, to get back to the entrance of the FRG section. Tour guides encouraged visitors to make comparisons between East and West from this "distanced" vantage point by looking from the bridge down onto the two exhibition sections. Unlike the GDR section, the FRG section looked colorful and modern, with flashing neon lights.[20] Each chapter had multiple entries and exits so that it was physically impossible to move along a straight path, a layout described by one author as "perfectly normal chaos" (Figure 1):

> We wanted to show in the FRG section that this security [in the GDR] doesn't exist, no security in education, job/career, or marriage. There are marriages without certificates; children have parents who live together but aren't married; children don't necessarily live with their mother or father. There are very different life patterns. We wanted to show this with the architecture.

The layout, architecture, and artifacts of the GDR and FRG periods were intended to help visitors visualize the different life paths and experiences of citizens in authoritarian or democratic states. One exhibition author described the contrasts between East and West Germany according to these chapters: "Youth, or being young, is an ideal in the FRG, and that wasn't true in the GDR. It is also a phase that lasts very long. Education is pushed to a later age. People marry later, and have children later [in the FRG]." In "Youth," a variety of spaces and artifacts communicated rebellion and individual choice, such as the poster of the Rolling Stones, pictures of West German youth, an electric guitar, a black-and-white Palestinian scarf, teen magazines dealing with sexual themes, and a 1950s style blue dress (see Figure 6 on the following page).[21] A large, royal-blue wall with an open-ended question, "When is a person grown-up?" and different answers to the question served as a backdrop for the chapter. After "Youth," there was no clear spatial progression to subsequent chapters. "Marriage and Partnership" similarly suggested many possible individual decisions through its depiction of a large traditional, tiered wedding cake with angular-shaped sections cutting into this symbol. To the right, a bright green cage exhibited books and texts about partnerships and marriage alternatives. Another wedged corner displayed posters and magazine covers about birth control and abortion, and to the left of the cake artifacts like soft-core pornographic magazines, posters, and books represented the sexual revolution of the 1960s and 1970s.

Unlike the "old-fashioned," yet authoritarian, GDR section, the FRG section was represented as the space of an advanced modernity and even postmodernity. Indeed, the first chapter surrounded visitors with technology — a hospital delivery room of the 1970s and 1980s — and the last chapter created

Figure 6. The Federal Republic of Germany: exhibition display for the chapter "Youth." Photograph of exhibition room by author, 1993.

the "eco-friendly" death of the 1990s. Time in the FRG section was represented as a pastiche of past images, bold colors, neon lights, and fractured spaces. Flickering TV film-clips of weddings from various decades were exhibited in "Marriage," and artifacts and photos in "Youth" evoked the rebellions from the 1968 hippie generation to the punk rockers of the 1980s. A strong sense of postmodern irony permeated the final chapter, where the visitor found him or herself viewing a politically correct "Death" of the 1990s. As one author explained:

> There are two tendencies: the environmentally sound death — there are not only environmentally friendly coffins, but also ecologically friendly clothing — and the anonymous death. These tendencies take death away,

so to speak.... This is also different than in the GDR. Death in the GDR was shabbier.

Leaving the FRG section and its beeswax covered pine coffins, the visitor left with the eco-mentality and cynicism of the (Western?) present, of the here and now.

Who Is the "Typical" German? Interpreting Artifacts and Identity through *Chapters of Life*

While visitors certainly disagreed with parts of the exhibition (as I discuss below), within each period "typical" life chapters encouraged identification with the abstract cultural notion of a German nation. An assumption of the exhibition was that all Germans, irrespective of where or when they lived, had similar life experiences: everyone was born and died, so in each period, there were pictures of mothers and babies, and actual coffins. All Germans received candies on their first day of school, so each period had candy cornets (*Schultüten*) in the "Education" chapter. This idea of a "typical" German life path reflects what Homi Bhabha describes as the pedagogical aspect of national culture, or the representation of a group's history that is assumed to reflect the experiences of the nation. The *Chapters of Life* narrative, in deploying the idea of "typical" experience, created a singular voice — a "we" — to speak for the "imagined community" of Germany. In the exhibit, this "we" was defined by exclusive notions of kinship, in particular by ethnicity, and by gender and sexuality.[22]

Kinship Relations I: Ethnicity

Statistical data for the "majority" of Germans defined what was exhibited and interpreted in *Chapters of Life*. Minority experiences and those not officially classified as Germans (i.e., noncitizens) were not presented. When considering the recent history of Germany, such an approach to define "typical" German experiences (or a "we") is problematic because it may reinforce neo-conservative images of the German past. According to Jürgen Habermas, "the neo-conservatives see their role as, on the one hand, mobilizing pasts which can be accepted approvingly and, on the other, morally neutralizing other pasts that would provoke only criticism and rejection."[23]

The most striking example of pasts neutralized in the exhibit was the National Socialist period. Although exhibition authors displayed the ideologically racist concept of Aryan heritage through two propaganda posters in the "Marriage" section, the history of the Holocaust was not mentioned. Even in the chapter of "Death" there was no presentation of the systematic forced labor, persecution, and murder of the millions of individuals that were central to the existence of the Nazi state. Without representing Nazi state-defined "Others," museum visitors may have overidentified with the exhibit and assigned personal and collective responsibility for the Holocaust to the stylized black-box of the NS System. Many visitors, when responding to this period in surveys and visitor books, commented on "how horrible that time was," indicating a sense of guilt, but also a sense of suffering, as though Germans similarly were victims of an oppressive system.

Personal experiences of the past, as well as contemporary images and representations, are always reframed in the interpretative spaces of the exhibition. For any representation of the NS past in Germany, visitors may (re)experience conflicting and very strong emotions such as denial, guilt, mourning, and suffering. Due to visitors' preconceptions and experiences, I would question the assumption that all visitors could critically contemplate the consequences of state-defined notions of being German, particularly due to exhibition aesthetics in this section. When an exhibit represents the NS past and the Holocaust in an abstract form (as a "black box"), concrete historical loss (in terms of human life) is conceptualized as either metaphysical absence (the Holocaust is exhibited as unrepresentable and thus unknowable) or presence (the Nazi terror system is represented as a force that was larger than life). From an ethical perspective such a strategy may be problematic because human responsibility (either individual or collective) for past actions is ignored, and perpetrators of the Holocaust can be considered "victims" of the system. A visitor might argue, for example, while standing in front of the looming charcoal walls, that the overwhelmingly abstract, bureaucratic, NS organizational structure was so powerful that individuals were reduced to passive subjects who could only follow orders. If someone were to challenge such an interpretation, as did one young female guide on a tour by mentioning specific historical details about the Holocaust in front of the "Death" section, the result may be aggression and denial, as was articulated by two older male tourists on this tour. (Emotional defensiveness and hostility should not be necessarily associated with an older generation, as postunification neo-Nazi and xenophobic violence in 1993 and thereafter indicated.) Silence may also be a response: the rest of the group was quiet as one male continued aggressively to harass the guide and attempted to undermine her authority throughout the rest of the tour.[24]

Using state-defined categories of citizenship excludes the perspectives of some social groups in Germany and reinforces the notion that German identity (nation-ness) and German citizenship (nationality) are the same. For example, in the FRG period, no minority group experiences (in particular foreign guest workers) were presented despite the significance of these groups for postwar and present-day German prosperity. In the context of 1993, citizenship was still based upon a modified 1913 law according to descent (*jus sanguinis*) not territory (*jus soli*). Yet to be classified as non-German after unification may have meant living in fear. A poll taken of West Germans in 1992 indicated that resentment of foreigners ran high, from the least despised, former GDR citizens, to the most despised, Sinti and Roma Gypsies. This xenophobia was expressed in the numerous violent attacks on foreigners in 1993, some deadly, and many directed toward second- and third-generation West German Turkish guest workers (*Gastarbeiter*) and political and economic refugees from the former East Bloc and former Yugoslavia.[25]

Despite this violence, and in the context of an increasingly multiethnic Germany and Europe, categories of a West German national imagination based on exclusionary kinship relations were retained by officials in 1993 when the German Parliament changed Article 16 of the Basic Law (German constitution). This generous clause, written from the experience of Germany's Nazi past, ensured asylum to any political refugees. While Germany was burdened economically by former East Bloc refugees after 1989, by changing only asylum and *not* citizenship laws, officials represented Germany as a nation of ethnics, not of immigrants.[26] The *Chapters of Life* exhibit reinforced this exclusive representation of the nation, one that extended backward in time, as displayed by the invisibility of ethnic Others in the NS section.

Kinship Relations II: Gender and Sexuality

According to Karen Jankowsky, another way the nation is imagined is through gender roles, in particular the opposition of middle-class male and female roles. At the *Chapters of Life* exhibit, the German "family" was defined by exclusive gendered, heterosexual social roles and spaces. From the moment the visitor passed by the wedding entrance banner and walked into the exhibit, he or she would have seen, in every section but the GDR, images of "the mother" fulfilling her "biological" role — having children and breast-feeding — in her "natural" place, at home (the "private" sphere). The ideal images of heterosexual couples or of "woman as mother" in "Birth" chapters excluded all nonreproductively oriented sexualities from the discourse of the nation; even "atypical" women on exhibit did not include (at least explicitly) lesbians or bisexual women. Males were shown as active with other men in the public world via the chapters "Education," "Apprenticeships," and "Military Obligation." In particular, the "Military" chapter presented male-male relations in terms of a brotherhood, a "proper" homosociality or fraternity that contained male-male sexuality. Through the coupling of the "Military" and "Marriage" chapters in each section, a gendered image of the nation was promoted: the ideal bride nurtured her husband and offspring in the private sphere so that the male could participate in the public sphere with other men to defend the family/nation.[27]

While exhibit authors included the biases of gender roles in the Kaiserreich and NS sections, for the GDR and FRG sections Cold War categories of identity were uncritically displayed.[28] Historically, West Germany defined protecting women as mothers in the private sphere as a national duty. East German women were viewed as a threat to this duty and were portrayed as masculine workers. This Western interpretation of women was exhibited in the GDR "Birth" chapter without including information about Cold War politics. "Data" were understood as statistics of women's labor participation: in 1950, 50 percent of all East German women worked; in 1960, 70 percent; in 1970, 82 percent; and by 1989, 90 percent—the highest percent of working women in the world. I do not want to suggest that these numbers are "false," but they are far from politically neutral. A more "objective" representation would have "situated" this data for a diverse public by providing distinctive Cold War Eastern and Western understandings of these numbers in both the GDR and FRG sections.[29]

In a more subtle aesthetic form, the exhibition also implied that East German women were bad mothers *because they worked*. Next to the work data, texts described the amount of time East German children spent in state-run centers, places negatively portrayed by a daycare table with restrictive, bolted down chairs that communicated a notion of compliance.[30] While there were problems with the quality of GDR daycare, similar information was missing about the FRG, such as the lack of affordable daycare options for West German families that resulted in more women staying home than men. For both Germanys, the role of men as "natural" parents was not displayed in "Birth."[31]

Information and artifacts in all periods also reinforced the historic naturalness of gendered Western private/public spheres. Even in the FRG section, in which "marriage" was questioned (albeit in heterosexual terms), I suggest that exhibition authors assumed an a priori exclusion of women in the public sphere, what Isabella Hull describes as an "emancipatory framework." In such a narrative structure, women's history "is the history of their 'progress' measured against male standards masquerading as universal or human: access to the 'public sphere,' paid work, education, political rights, and so forth." Of course such a representation of the past would have been especially ironic for former GDR female visitors, a social group in the new Germany that has described the social *losses* they experienced after 1990, including job security, financial support, and, significantly, independence. Many of these women felt as though they suddenly had to make a *Western* choice between work (the public sphere) and family (the private sphere). If information was included about how socialist and democratic states structured and defined gender (and sexual) roles and spaces, the data and historical events on display may have been more accessible to all visitors.[32]

Visitors' Experiences and Comments

Thus far I have presented how *Chapters of Life* excluded particular social groups from being imagined as part of the German "nation" or family. But what about visitors' responses and experiences? What might their comments tell me about my interpretations? Visitors wrote a lot about this exhibit, filling six large guest books in six months, and writing extensive comments on the backsides and margins of voluntary surveys.[33] Although one cannot "quantify" these visitor comments, they reflect to some degree the larger ongoing discussions of what it meant to be German in the 1990s. More generally, I found that in surveys and visitor books, individuals contested those parts of the display that did not correspond to their cultural and personal understandings of self.

What was the general nature of visitor comments and surveys? As one exhibition author described, visitors wrote of

> many *personal* experiences.... Many people commented on our comparison between East Germany and West Germany. Simply leafing through six large tomes of comments gives you the impression of a discordant babble of voices — there's no harmony, and particularly not with regard to the interpretation of the GDR. The Eastern and Western viewpoints are extremely different — and that is also true of the assessment of our exhibition.

In surveys, when asked about their impression of the FRG section, most visitors from both the East and the West had nothing to say. Perhaps East Germans were still trying to figure out the West. West Germans wrote little perhaps because of their familiarity with the FRG period. But I would argue it was also because of their unease with identifying with the concept of "nation," as the voice of a forty-one-year-old woman from a residential district in West Berlin described: "I believe that 'it' cannot be documented [in a museum]. Points are emphasized [in the exhibit] that closely represent 'it.' I find it interesting that I identify myself with a particular vantage point, but I don't identify with 'it.' " The visitor explicitly set "it" off with quotes and symbolically and linguistically distanced herself from the concepts of "national identity" and "nation." Her use of language suggests a culturally specific West German rejection of such categories. Similarly, one exhibition author, when reviewing an earlier version of this essay, responded negatively to my emphasis on examining representations of the "nation." The intent of the exhibition, the author explained, was to represent different *societies* and not *nation-states* because "the word 'nation' in the FRG is a taboo concept." Due to the negative associations of extreme German nationalisms in the recent past that resulted in a "divided" nation, the cultural frameworks through which FRG citizens came to identify their democracy were federalism and the region, both of which symbolized a European, rather than national, identity.

Some visitors were critical of the normative spatial organization of the exhibition. One journalist asked:

> Was life in the old Federal Republic really so confused and free? . . . Does
> the GDR correspond to the boring little yellow packed cubicles? . . . Some-
> times it seems as though the exhibition makers gave too much credit to
> the claims of both sides. The ideology, however, surely looked different
> than the reality.[34]

Visitors (some of whom were not German) were also critical of the similarities
portrayed between the NS and GDR periods, a representation that indicated
(even if unintentionally) that East Germany, not the FRG, inherited the NS
past. The "West," displayed so differently from the "Other" Germanys, was
exhibited as breaking sharply from Prussian and fascist pasts (known as the
Stunde Null [Zero Hour] narrative by historians) and as the inevitable historical precursor to the unified Germany. In the context of 1993, this subtle
suggestion would have had a strong resonance. In postunification newspaper
articles, official political investigations, and criminal trials, parallels were often
made between the GDR and Nazi Germany. Some authors have argued that
Germans became obsessed with the Stasi (GDR secret police) because the organization's "past has become a metaphor for the Nazi past, and for German
complicity in that past."[35] In addition, popular media implied that neo-Nazi
violence after 1990 was evidence that East Germans — not West Germans —
needed to confront their recent pasts. While the history of the GDR certainly
needed (and needs) to be critically addressed after unification, the implied and
direct parallels made between the GDR and Nazi Germany in the popular
imagination, and as exhibited, distanced the history and future of the Federal
Republic from both of those pasts.

Wessis, while reluctant to discuss the FRG section, had no problems in writing about the East, even though one has to assume that some of these visitors
may not have known *Ossis* or had access to recent scholarship about the GDR.
Visitor book comments suggest that some responses were informed by media
descriptions. To quote an exhibition author:

> A 63-year-old cabinet-maker from Berlin-Charlottenburg in the West
> noted: "It was much, much worse over there," and another man asked:
> "Where are the Stasi informers, stoolpigeons and so on?" There is a con-
> spicuous lack of such remarks by former GDR citizens (as far as can be
> determined).

In contrast, *Ossi* visitor book remarks about the GDR section included such
comments as, "There was also joy and laughter in the GDR!" Visitor comments
indicated that many Easterners felt that persons who lived in the GDR had
more direct knowledge of that period than did Western museum experts. The
differences in opinion on how the East was represented by *Ossis* and *Wessis*
relate to larger concerns about who should have the right to represent GDR
"history" in the new Germany.

Concluding Comments: Out of Oblivions Spring Narratives

By displaying the divided German history in a national museum so soon after unification, the message was communicated to citizens and visitors that this division, and in particular East Germany, had become an artifact. As Benedict Anderson reminds us, when notions of identity undergo dramatic change, new narratives are forged and aspects of the past/present forgotten: "All profound changes in consciousness, by their very nature, bring with them characteristic amnesias. Out of such oblivions, in specific historical circumstances, spring narratives." In the *Chapters of Life* exhibition, Germans were represented as citizens belonging to a seemingly natural, timeless, kin-based family. Yet this family, or "imagined community," was defined by the experience of West Germany. As I have already suggested, in the context of 1993 the representation of "typical" German experiences — according to hegemonic Western narratives at a national history museum — reinforced social boundaries between an "us" (ethnic, gendered, heterosexual Germans) and "them" (Eastern Others).[36]

Here I think it is helpful to consider briefly the views of the exhibition authors:

> As scientifically trained historians occupied with real culture, we see ourselves suddenly confronted with an entirely different stock of objects in the museum. The little pennants used by the traffic police, the blue shirts of the Free German Youth, the [Thälmann] Pioneer neckerchief, etc., etc., are objects that are familiar to our colleagues from the East and were often a part of their daily lives, but we so-called *Wessis* only knew them by hearsay, and they often seemed very strange to us.

In describing what it felt like when the German Historical Museum acquired GDR artifacts in 1990, this exhibition author viewed objects as exotic and as belonging to a socialist past. This author located Western museum experts in the space of rationality and the time of the present; they are scientists who examine everyday artifacts that came from a "foreign country."

From this situated position, exhibition authors described GDR visitor responses to the exhibition as emotional:

> The representation of this straight-lined, ordered path of life was hardly bearable for many visitors from the East.... The former citizens of the GDR still implicitly insist on brushing aside the official, regulated side of their lives as the nonintrinsic, nonauthentic part. This part of their lives is their "not-remembered history." The life stations regulated by the state and society are for many of them the "nonessential" ones. They would like to ignore this part and forget about it. And so you find many entries in the visitor books by people who lived in East Germany who try to play off the daily life that in retrospect seems to have been pleasant against the dimensions of life that structured this everyday life. Is this then an

expression of nostalgia, a transfiguration of history, or is it perhaps even the "true" identity of GDR citizens? We simply don't know.

In the exhibit—and in Berlin in 1993—*Ossis* were lumped into one category of identity as "not" Western. Suddenly faced with being classified as foreign Others, some of these individuals may have felt the need to rebuke popular and official images of the East. In surveys and visitor books, some sought to claim the right to (re)define the GDR on the basis of their personal experience, whereas others entirely cast off any relationship they may have once had with their former home. This process of negotiating one's identity to both a non-existent state and a new nation-state is far from straightforward, particularly when individuals have mixed feelings about their "home" in the recent past and present. Consequently, many of these individuals may have felt it important to rewrite this part of the exhibit the "right" way in visitor books and surveys, that is, the way they experienced it, to make sense of a confusing present. In their writings, they also directly challenged the popular notion that all East Germans were the same, robotic "citizens" defined by the state. They contested many, if not most, "official" representations and Western expert understandings of their (former) state by offering multiple, contradictory, and alternative stories about their pasts through their writings.[37]

More generally, visitor responses indicated that tourists take exhibitions seriously. Their written comments, in fact, should be considered as part of the exhibition's meaning and experience, an idea that one exhibition author supported, noting that

> . . . every identity shown in the museum and in exhibitions is a construct. Here it's the construct of the people who made up the exhibition, based on the material that is supplied on the one hand by the relics of the object world and produced, on the other hand, by the social sciences, contemporary history, the mass media, statistics, etc. And thus *we* have presented *our* construction, against which many of the visitors are now placing *their own*, likewise constructed remembrance, without it being possible to arrive at a uniform view or indeed at an *identity*. The chasms— as well as many a bridge—will remain, for we are not able to return to the past in order to reconstruct the way it "really" was [emphasis added].

This author suggests that the museum space can become an active forum for discussion to find the "bridges" and "chasms" between groups. Museum spaces and experiences do include the "discordant babble of voices" that, at least for this exhibit, may have caused museum experts to reassess critically the diverse experiences of "Others" and to create more inclusive and interactive exhibition spaces for a range of social groups and individuals.[38]

Notes

This essay is a revised version of "After the Wall: The German History Museum in Unified Berlin," from my Ph.D. dissertation. Rosmarie Beier, Yi-Fu Tuan, Karen Jankowsky, Ana Schmidt, Steven Hoelscher, Paul Adams, Heike Alberts, and the members of the geography department at the University of Lampeter, Wales, provided helpful comments on earlier versions and presentations of this essay. I am indebted to the generosity of many staff members at the Deutsches Historisches Museum, especially one *Lebensstationen* exhibition author and the press relations director, for providing assistance with my visitor survey and supporting my research. This research would not have been possible without the financial support of the Alexander von Humboldt Foundation (which funded research in 1993–94 and 1997), an Association of American Geographers' Dissertation Research Grant, and the Louisiana State University Summer Stipend Program.

1. Hermine de Soto, "(Re)inventing Berlin: Dialectics of Power, Symbols, and Pasts, 1990–1995," *City and Society* 1 (1996): 29–49; John Borneman, *After the Wall: East Meets West in the New Berlin* (New York: Basic Books, 1991); Karen E. Till, "Place and the Politics of Memory: A Geo-Ethnography of Museums and Memorials in Berlin" (Ph.D. diss., University of Wisconsin, 1996); Till, "Staging the Past: Landscape Designs, Cultural Identity, and 'Erinnerungspolitik' at Berlin's Neue Wache," *Ecumene* 6 (1999): 251–83. About places of memory, see also A. Charlesworth, "Contesting Places of Memory: The Case of Auschwitz," *Environment and Planning D: Society and Space* 12 (1994): 579–93.

2. Lauren Berlant, *The Anatomy of National Fantasy: Hawthorne, Utopia, and Everyday Life* (Chicago: University of Chicago Press, 1991), 37; Carol Duncan, "Art Museums and the Ritual of Citizenship," in *Exhibiting Cultures*, ed. I. Karp and S. Lavine (Washington, D.C.: Smithsonian Institution Press, 1994), 90–91; Christine Boyer, *The City of Collective Memory* (Cambridge, Mass.: MIT Press, 1994); Till, *Place and the Politics of Memory*; Till, "Staging the Past"; and Benedict Anderson, *Imagined Communities* (London: Verso, 1991).

3. The political context of the German Historical Museum was heavily contested before unification. See Charles Maier, *The Unmasterable Past: History, Holocaust, and German National Identity* (Cambridge, Mass.: Harvard University Press, 1988); Christoph Stölzl, ed., *Deutsches Historisches Museum: Ideen-Kontroversen-Perspektiven* (Berlin: Propyläen, 1988); Till, *Place and the Politics of Memory*, chap. 2.

4. Christoph Stölzl quoted in S. Maier, "Lebensstationen: Eine Ausstellung im Deutschen Historischen Museum," *B.Z.* 26 (March 1993); "Blättern im deutschen Familienalbum," *Berliner Wochenblatt*, April 7, 1993; J. Ross, "Am Ende steht der Umweltssarg: Deutschland, eine Großfamilie," *Frankfurter Allgemeine Zeitung*, April 21, 1993; "Lebensstationen in Deutschland," *Der Tagesspiegel*, May 2, 1993. The *Lebensstationen* exhibit ran from March 25 to June 15 and was extended until November 9, 1993. The exhibit was conceived of before 1990, but after 1990, with the new artifacts from the GDR, the emphasis changed to focus on the East/West histories (interview with exhibition author, Berlin, 1993).

5. This information stems from the results of qualitative methods during 1993 and 1997 in Berlin and includes the following: personal interviews with one of the exhibit authors/staff curators; participant observation of tours and of visitors going through the exhibition individually; interviews with two museum guides; and textual analyses of the following: the exhibit catalog (Rosmarie Beier and Bettina Biedermann, eds., *Lebensstationen in Deutschland 1900 bis 1993, Katalog- und Aufsatzband zur Ausstellung des Deutschen Historischen Museums 26 März bis 15. Juni 1993 im Zeughaus Berlin* [Giessen: Anabas, 1993]), exhibition text panels, open-ended volunteer visitor surveys conducted in June 1993, remarks written in one of the six visitor books, and newspaper articles about the exhibit. Newspaper articles from the German Historical Museum Press Archive about the exhibition have no page numbers and may not have titles and complete names of authors. All translations from the German are my own.

6. By narrative, I mean a story that integrates and links disparate elements by the very structure of the story itself; see Trevor Barnes and Derek Gregory, eds., *Reading Human Geography* (London and New York: Arnold, 1997), 510.

7. Yi-Fu Tuan, *Space and Place: The Perspective of Experience* (Minneapolis: University of Minnesota Press, 1977); Till, *Place and the Politics of Memory;* Maurice Halbwachs, *On Collective Memory* (Chicago: University of Chicago Press, 1992 [1952]); Paul Connerton, *How Societies Remember* (Cambridge: Cambridge University Press, 1989); Marita Sturken, *Tangled Memories: The Vietnam War, the AIDS Epidemic, and the Politics of Remembering* (Berkeley: University of California Press, 1997); compare with James Young, *The Texture of Memory: Holocaust Memorials and Meaning* (New Haven, Conn.: Yale University Press, 1993).

8. Warren Leon and Roy Rosenzweig, eds., *History Museums in the United States: A Critical Assessment* (Urbana: University of Illinois Press, 1989); Steven Toulmin, *Cosmopolis: The Hidden Agenda of Modernity* (Chicago: University of Chicago Press, 1990); Anderson, *Imagined Communities;* Richard Handler, *Nationalism and the Politics of Culture in Quebec* (Madison: University of Wisconsin Press, 1988); David Lowenthal, *The Past Is a Foreign Country* (Cambridge: Cambridge University Press, 1985); Johannes Fabian, *Time and the Other: How Anthropology Makes Its Object* (New York: Columbia University Press, 1983); James Clifford, *The Predicament of Culture: Twentieth Century Ethnography, Literature, and Art* (Cambridge, Mass.: Harvard University Press, 1988); Gary Kulik, "Designing the Past: History-Museum Exhibitions from Peale to the Present," in Leon and Rosenzweig, *History Museums*, 3–37.

9. Connerton argues that commemorative ceremonies are performative, involving habit and bodily memory to reenact the narratives of a group. So the places at which ceremonial social activities occur have a symbolic life and history, or place myths, and are, at the same time, concrete (Connerton, *How Societies Remember*). For a discussion of "public monuments," see Tuan, *Space and Place*. For a discussion of the limits of exhibition practice, see James Oliver Horton and Spencer Crew, "Afro-Americans as Museums: Towards a Policy of Inclusion," in Leon and Rosenzweig, *History Museums*, 215–36; Neil Harris, "Exhibiting Controversy," *Museum News* (September/October) 1993: 37–39; and Barbara Melosh, "Speaking of Women: Representations of Women's History," in Leon and Rosenzweig, *History Museums*, 183–214.

10. Masao Yamaguchi, "The Poetics of Exhibition in Japanese Culture," in Karp and Lavine, *Exhibiting Cultures*, 61.

11. Michael Wallace, "Visiting the Past: History Museums in the United States," in *Professionalizing the Past: Essays on History and the Public,* ed. S. Porter Benson, S. Brier, and R. Rosenzweig (Philadelphia: Temple University Press, 1986), 137–61; Thomas Schlereth, "History Museums and Material Culture," Leon and Rosenzweig, *History Museums*, 294–320; Joseph Corn, "Tools, Technologies, and Contexts: Interpreting the History of American Technics," in Leon and Rosenzweig, *History Museums*, 237–61; Paul Sant Cassia, "Ways of Displaying," *Museums Journal* (January 1992): 28–31; Yamaguchi, "Poetics"; and Barbara Kirshenblatt-Gimblett, *Destination Culture* (Berkeley: University of California Press, 1998).

12. Yi-Fu Tuan, "The significance of the artifact," *Geographical Review* 70 (1980): 463; Robert Foster, "Making National Cultures in the Global Ecumene," *Annual Review of Anthropology* 20 (1991): 243; Ivan Karp, "Culture and Representation," in Karp and Lavine, *Exhibiting Cultures*, 11–24.

13. When I prepared the questions for a visitor survey, one of the exhibition authors specifically requested that I include a question ("Haben Sie das Gefühl, daß die Ausstellung etwas mit Ihrer eigenen Biographie zu tun hat?") asking whether or not the visitor could personally relate his or her own biography to the exhibit.

14. Unless otherwise stated, quoted information comes from personal interviews with one of the exhibition authors in November 1993 and June 1997, in Berlin, and informal personal communications from 1993 to 1997.

15. The looming coffin, which could be seen from about midway in the hall, was a deluxe

model, which few people could actually afford. In surveys, this coffin was one of the objects visitors remembered most after having gone through the exhibit.

16. In surveys, many visitors cited the uniforms and posters in this section as standing out in their minds.

17. In addition, some visitors from both East and West said their decision was arbitrary, whereas others said they went to the East section first because of the layout of the exhibit. The shortest distance was from the NS section to the GDR section.

18. The film *Mädchen in Wittstock* was made by Volker Koepp in the GDR in 1975. The filmmaker produced *Neues in Wittstock* in 1992 as a follow-up. The latter film was part of an accompanying film series that ran at the German Historical Museum in April 1993 and included *Heimat* (1979–84, FRG) and *Die zweite Heimat* (1992) by Edgar Reitz; *Lebensläufe* (1981, GDR) and *Drehbuch: Die Zeiten* (1993) by Winfried Junge; and *Abschied von Gestern* (1966, FRG) by Alexander Kluge.

19. Mary Fulbrook, *Divided Nation: A History of Germany 1918–1990* (New York: Oxford University Press, 1991), 222–23. See also Daphne Berdahl, *Where the World Ended: Re-unification and Identity in the German Borderland* (Berkeley: University of California Press, 1999). On *Ostolgie*, see Michael Rutschky, "Wie erst jetzt die DDR entsteht," *Merkur* 9/10 (September/October 1995): 851–64.

20. One exhibition author explained that the FRG section was conceived of as an advertisement, bright on the outside but gray on the inside. Many visitors on tours did not notice this color system until guides pointed it out.

21. In surveys, visitors cited the Rolling Stones poster as standing out in their minds for the FRG section.

22. Homi Bhabha, *Nation and Narration* (New York: Routledge, 1990). I use John Borneman's definition of kinship to mean state-structured patterns of group membership that define everyday relations and an expected life path. Borneman suggests that kinship relations have served as a naturalistic model for structuring nationality and citizenship, perhaps because of the many different territories the German nation-state has occupied (John Borneman, *Belonging in the Two Berlins: Kin, State, Nation* [New York: Cambridge University Press, 1992]). Not surprisingly, visitors to *Chapters of Life* specifically noted the lack of regional categories in the exhibition. One critic argued that the notion of "typical" was based upon the "folkloric illusion of 'average,'" a misconception that corresponded to placelessness — "no state and no city, neither north or south, neither Berlin nor Bebenhausen, but rather a vacuum, Germany, an airless space" (Sibylle Wirsing, "Wer soll des Ortes Hüter sein?" *Frankfurter Allgemeine Zeitung*, July 2, 1993).

23. Jürgen Habermas, *The New Conservatism: Cultural Criticism and the Historians' Debate*, ed. and trans. Shierry Weber Nicolsen (Cambridge, Mass.: MIT Press, 1989), xiii.

24. I attended tours given by two female guides and one by one of the exhibition authors. Only one person mentioned the Holocaust in the NS section. I would like to thank Stephanie Endlich for encouraging me to reconsider the politics of aesthetically representing National Socialism through such a "black-box" approach. For a discussion about historical loss versus metaphysical absence, see Dominick LaCapra, "Trauma, Absence, Loss," *Critical Inquiry* 25 (1999): 696–727.

25. Between January 1991 and April 1992, 610 xenophobic criminal acts were committed in former East Germany and 790 in former West Germany (data from FRG Ministry for Women and Youth, in Heinrich August Winkler, "Rebuilding of a Nation," *Daedalus* 123 [1994]: 107–27). Evidence of hostility toward East European refugees and Turkish and Vietnamese guest workers includes numerous violent attacks in 1992 and 1993, often led by East German neo-Nazis, but also applauded by local citizens. See Ian Buruma, "Outsiders," *New York Review of Books*, April 9, 1992, 15–19; Timothy Garten Ash, *In Europe's Name* (New York: Vintage Books, 1993); and Ingo Hasselbach with Tom Reiss, "How Nazis Are Made," *New Yorker*, January 8, 1996, 36–56.

26. At the time this essay was being revised, new citizenship laws under the Social Democratic–Green administration of Chancellor Gerhard Schröder went into effect — on

January 1, 2000. The main law stipulates that citizenship will be by "soil" and replaces the 1913 law that defined citizenship by blood. Originally, permanent dual citizenship was also proposed. What passed stipulates that all those born in Germany may have more than one nationality until age twenty-three, when they must choose one or the other. Also, the period for naturalization will be cut from fifteen to eight years. Thanks to Daniel Williams and Heike Alberts for this information. See Roger Cohen, "The German 'Volk' Seem Set to Let Outsiders In," *New York Times,* October 16, 1998, A4; "German Parties Reach Deal to Relax Law on Citizenship," *New York Times,* October 15, 1998, A11; Martina Fietz, "Bundesrat stimmt neuem Staatsbürgerrecht zu," *Die Welt,* May 22, 1999.

27. Karen Jankowsky, "Between 'Inner Bohemia' and 'Outer Siberia': Libuše Mónikóvá Destabilizes Notions of Gender and Nation," in *Other Germanies: Questioning Identity in Women's Literature and Art,* ed. K. Jankowsky and C. Love (Albany: State University of New York Press, 1997), 119–46. See also Andrew Parker et al., eds., *Nationalisms and Sexualities* (New York: Routledge, 1992); George Mosse, *Nationalism and Sexuality: Middle-Class Morality and Sexual Norms in Modern Europe* (Madison: University of Wisconsin Press, 1985); Joanne Sharp, "Gendering Nationhood: A Feminist Engagement with National Identity," in *Bodyspace: Destabilizing Geographies of Gender and Sexuality,* ed. N. Duncan (New York: Routledge, 1997), 97–108. "Marriage" was presented as a (if not *the*) significant defining chapter in the exhibit, as evidenced by the opening banner portraying the newly wed couple.

28. Texts described how few women went on to higher education around 1900 because they were socially viewed as wives and mothers only. Motherhood, as defined by the NS state, was displayed by the iron crosses awarded for the ability to reproduce in Nazi Germany — bronze if the mother had four or five children, silver for those who had six or seven, and gold for eight or more children. The critical nature of these objects and texts, however, was often overshadowed by other artifacts. For example, in the Kaiserreich section, many visitors skipped by the small text that explained that legally binding patriarchal-Christian-based laws of marriage weren't changed until 1957 and 1977 in the FRG; the visitors went instead to the two bridal gowns centrally displayed. (There was no mention of the GDR, and this information was not included in the FRG section.) Continuities between the FRG and the NS past were also not displayed. To take but one example, in the FRG "Marriage" chapter there was no mention that Nazi laws criminalizing birth control and abortion, as well as the coercion of "racially inferior women" to abort, were nullified only in 1960. Abortion itself was not legalized until 1976, and even then certain restrictions remained; see Borneman, *Belonging in Two Berlins.* After unification, abortion was one of the most heated topics discussed, with the Supreme Court overturning earlier decisions to allow for the more liberal East German laws.

29. Donna Haraway, *Simians, Cyborgs, and Women: The Reinvention of Nature* (New York: Routledge, 1991).

30. In the surveys, many visitors mentioned that the table with its connected chairs in the "Daycare" section stood out in their minds.

31. As one early official FRG report proclaimed: "[If our growing economy] ... continues to absorb women into the workplace, we must soon fear that in the near future the majority of all young mothers will be working outside the home. That will surely lead — certainly against the will of those involved — down another road to the same social order that already is regnant in the countries of the Eastern ilk" (*Familienlastenausgleich* [report of the FRG Ministry for Family Questions, Bonn, 1955], 23, quoted in Borneman, *Belonging in Two Berlins,* 86). Certainly, the relationship between East German women and their workplace was problematic. Furthermore, although women were more strongly encouraged in the GDR to participate in paid labor through educational and professional training programs, by not recognizing the role of fathers in childcare, both the East *and* West German states structured the maternal roles as being "natural" for women. Programs for maternal vacation reinforced the role of mothering, just as these programs did in the FRG. See John Borneman, *Belonging in Two Berlins;* Nanette Funk and Magda Mueller, *Gender Politics and Post-communism:*

Reflections from Eastern Europe and the former Soviet Union (New York: Routledge, 1993); and Sharp, "Gendering Nationhood."

32. Isabella Hull, "Feminist and Gender History through the Literary Looking Glass: German Historiography in Postmodern Times," *Central European History* 22 (1989): 282; Funk and Mueller, *Gender Politics;* and Dinah Dodds and Pam Allen-Thompson, eds., *The Wall in My Backyard: East German Women in Transition* (Amherst: University of Massachusetts Press, 1994).

33. Discussing these comments in their entirety would be the topic of another essay. See Rosmarie Beier, "The Relationship between the Museum and National Identity; or, Facing History and Ourselves," paper delivered at the Annual Conference of the Dansk Kulturhistorisk Museums Forening, Fuglsocentret/Aarhus, November 18, 1993, and Rosmarie Beier, "Bericht zur (mentalen) Lage der Nation: Was die Besucher einer Berliner Ausstellung über die deutsch-deutsche Vergangenheit, Gegenwart und Zukunft denken," *Aus Politik und Zeitgeschichte* 27 (June 30, 1995): 10–27.

34. S. Stosch, *Hannoversche Allgemeine Zeitung,* April 14, 1993.

35. Jane Kramer, "The Politics of Memory," *New Yorker,* August 14, 1995, 63; see also Mary Fulbrook, "Aspects of Society and Identity in the New Germany," *Daedalus* 123 (1994): 211–34.

36. Anderson, *Imagined Communities,* 204.

37. Berdahl, *Where the World Ended.*

38. Julian Spalding, "Communicating Generously," *Museums Journal* (February 1992): 28–31.

MORAL MAPS AND MORAL PLACES IN THE WORK OF FRANCIS PARKMAN

Jonathan M. Smith

Francis Parkman formed his intention to write a history of France and England in North America in 1841, when he was eighteen years old. He released the last of the nine volumes in 1892, one year before his death, and in so doing completed one of the more prodigious and engrossing works of nineteenth-century American historiography and literature. The theme had obvious appeal for Parkman, who in 1878 recalled that it had promised to reconcile and draw upon the two consuming passions of his youth, "books and the woods." This promise was in large part fulfilled, as he was able to write near the end of his life that he had studied his subject "as much from life and in the open air as at the library table."[1]

The concreteness of these metonomies is characteristic of Parkman and well illustrates his lifelong preference for images of tangible things such as books, woods, and library tables. This picturesque and verisimilar quality has, unfortunately, misled many readers into supposing Parkman little more than a gifted writer of bellicose adventure stories. Such a shallow reading is only slightly improved by recognition that, in Parkman's imagination, the contest for North America was an object lesson in political philosophy, a conclusive demonstration of the weakness of autocratic government and the vigor of societies that allow some measure of individual liberty. This political reading is correct, given substantial qualification, but it is also far from perfect because it overlooks large and important elements of the poetic and philosophic worldview that Parkman formed in youth and held "with great firmness" for the remainder of his life.[2]

To adequately appreciate the shape of Parkman's imagination, one must read more deeply and discover his object lessons in the philosophy of history and moral philosophy. One must see that Parkman imagined the cosmos governed by a universal principle of tragedy by which every instance of greatness was brought to ruin and that Parkman, betraying his lifelong debt to Byron, imagined moral duty to inhere in the desperate and improbable acts with which heroes protested or forestalled tragic collapse. One must understand the relations between these themes of limited political liberty, cosmic tragedy, and moral heroism, their mutual modifications, their deductive necessity, their ironic paradoxes. One must understand the relation of these themes to Parkman's pictorial prose, particularly to his vivid images of maps and landscapes. This essay attempts to aid an adequate appreciation of the shape of Parkman's imagination by disclosing some of the mythic structure that supports his historical narrative. In the course of doing so, it may well elucidate at least some of the general ways in which the shape of an individual's imagination is linked to the stuff of geography and the practice of literature.

It must be allowed at the outset that Parkman's moral and political philosophy is deeply conservative, even by the standards of the nineteenth century. The modern reader will find in it much to condemn, just as Parkman would, no doubt, find much to condemn in the modern reader. Imperfect sympathy must be expected. We are, after all, products of the trends — egalitarianism and industrialization — that Parkman most deeply deplored. This does not mean that I wish to present Parkman as a trogloditic crank whom I have flushed from the past to exhilarate modern readers with the seductive pleasure of moral reprehension. He is sometimes wrong, but he is never ridiculous. Moreover, his ideas are far from dead; they live on, some deservedly, in the American geographical imagination.

Evocation and Tragedy

Parkman wrote literary history, which is to say history as a species of literature rather than science. Thus Parkman moved easily from his early intention of writing poetry and novels to his mature work as a historian. Throughout his life he returned to Shakespeare and Byron to renew his command of language and powers of expression, and he showed at least as much interest in novelists as he did in historians. Such "literary research," to use David Levin's term, was meant to enlarge a historian's sympathies by exposing him to a great range of human experiences, passions, and motives, and to enhance a historian's eloquence by exposing him to the great models of written expression. Parkman studied, emulated, and adapted to his own use the diction of Edward Gibbon, Edmund Burke, James Fenimore Cooper, and Sir Walter Scott. He also appreciated the simplicity of explorers' accounts and often copied their terse style to good effect.[3]

Literary history was decidedly a gentleman's craft. It rests on the assumption that high-born and well-bred males possess unique powers of insight and expression and are therefore entitled to serve as mythmakers, storytellers, and poets, interpreting a people to itself. It is easy, and today almost automatic, to condemn the arrogance of this pretense, but such criticism overlooks the extent to which literary history is a symptom of democratization. Literary histories were popular. Their authors necessarily followed the path opened by Thomas Macaulay, "the first English writer to make history interesting."[4] They had to. It was the only way the people could any longer be made to listen to the opinions of a gentleman.

Parkman's histories have two pronounced literary qualities that allow him to remain true to his literary exemplars and write like a gentleman, and yet at the same time attract the attention of a popular audience. First, he learned from novelists the value of discussing ideas in terms of concrete objects, striking personalities, and dramatic actions. This is why Howard Doughty claims that Parkman's writing relies on "vivification of its ideational content." From Scott, Parkman had learned "portrait making," "picturesque groupings," and "dramatic narrative." From Cooper, he learned the compelling power of "characters [who] were no mere abstract ideas, or insubstantial images, but solid embodiments in living flesh and blood." Cooper also taught Parkman how to paint a scene, a "tangible presence of rock, river, and forest," and how, through violence, action, suspense, and surprise, to compel the reader "to play a part in the scene."[5]

The literally sensational quality of Parkman's prose is also attributable to the historian's poor eyesight, an affliction that often confined him to a heavily shaded room, where others read aloud to him or took down his dictation. These circumstances seem to have enhanced Parkman's already vivid imagination and apparently encouraged him to picture clearly in his mind the scenes that were described to him. "The narrator must seek to imbue himself with the life and spirit of the time," he wrote in the introduction to his first volume, and "must himself be a sharer or spectator of the action he describes." As one of his friends wrote, Parkman was able to "reproduce what he saw in his mind so that his readers also could see it," and therefore his was "an historical style which gain[ed] the ears of the people."[6]

Parkman's vivid descriptions were also applauded by contemporary critics, who unanimously praised his power to evoke pictures. The novelist William Dean Howells likened Parkman's scenes to "a vigorous sketch made by some quick-eyed, sure-handed painter." Other critics wrote that his scenes "seem to have been photographed," that his books provided "a photographic record of a state of things which has passed away never to return." Cinematographed would have been a better analogy, could these critics have known it, because Parkman's landscapes were less often panoramas than active settings for action. At some points the reader moves through a landscape: "An open country; a rude cultivation; the tall palisades of an Indian town." At other points the landscape moves around the reader: "Slaughter, pillage, flame." This is why contemporary critics so often commented that a reader of Parkman's histories seemed to have "passed through the events and scenes" or at least to have observed them with "the intense interest of one who has friends or acquaintances there." Carl O. Sauer admired this skill and in 1956 asked of his fellow geographers, "Who has not been ... with Parkman over the Oregon Trail?"[7]

The second great literary quality of Parkman's work is its pervasive mood of tragedy. This is routinely misread by nationalists and other superficial readers, who discover in Parkman's histories a monument to "the glory of the race to which he belongs." If, as another nationalist claimed, Parkman actually celebrated the story of how "the Anglo-Saxon race rose to its full power," the historian's enthusiasm was tempered by his profoundly equivocal attitude toward that group's past and present members. "I recognize some most respectable and valuable qualities in the settlers of New England," Parkman wrote in a letter, "but do not think them or their system to be praised without great qualification." And, of course, tragedy is all in the qualifications. The tragic mood originates in recognition that the virtues, aptitudes, and excellencies of any people are necessarily and inextricably tied to their weaknesses, limitations, and shortcomings, in recognition that they create their world only by destroying a predecessor that was finer in many respects, if not altogether.[8] "Plants devour each other," Parkman wrote in his first volume, "and play their silent part in the universal tragedy of nature." Except that the parts they play are far from silent, the same can be said of moral and political systems. "Civilization has a destroying as well as a creative power," Parkman noted early in life. The new obliterates the old; the gain is not always perceptible. Thus he ended his last volume on a note of tragic ambivalence about the United States: "it remains for her to prove, if she can, . . . that democracy can give the world a civilization as mature and pregnant, ideas as energetic and vitalizing, and types of manhood as lofty and strong, as any of the systems it boasts to supplant."[9]

The tragic mood must not be confused with fatalism. Fatalism denies the efficacy of human acts; tragedy denies the purity of human acts. A fatalist faces no real choices because she believes that her acts are effected by distant causes; a tragedian faces no easy choices because he believes that his acts cause distant effects and that at least some of these effects must be ill effects. The tragic character is thus loaded with a tremendous moral weight of responsibility and uncertainty that threatens to sink him in indecision. The heroes respond with audacity and impetuosity, such as the "immense moral force" that bore up the frail body of Parkman's great paragon, Brigadier General James Wolfe, "and forced it to its work."[10]

Parkman's Moral Geography

Parkman was keenly interested in geography; he amassed a large cartographic collection and illustrated his histories with large-scale maps and topographical sketches of pivotal sites. He conscientiously visited most of the major places he described, a diligence remarkable in his day, and used these forays to verify documentary evidence and gather impressions of local color. The fruit of this careful research is what Levin calls Parkman's "precise sense of place" and "acute awareness of geography," what Otis A. Pease, writing in a similar vein, describes as Parkman's "sense of over-all geography with the reality of a specific place."[11] Parkman had an intuitive grasp of the significance of site and situation.

This appreciation grew out of Parkman's military interests. As he noted in the greatest of his histories, *Montcalm and Wolfe* (1884): " 'Geography' says Von Moltke, 'is three-fourths of military science,' and never was the truth of his words more fully exemplified [than in the British assault on Canada]."[12] For Parkman, a geography is primarily an array of locations and a network of linkages: Indian towns, missions, colonial settlements, and fortified positions connected by rough roads, lakes, rivers, and portage-points or passes. His view of geography is, in other words, strategic and concerned primarily with the deployment, support, movement, and coordination of military forces. As a friend of the historian wrote, Parkman pored over a map of a place seeking to understand

> the elements that affect life there, especially the means of subsistence and the exigencies of travel. Lakes, streams, swamps, ranges of mountains, windfalls, tangled undergrowth, laurel thickets, game and fish, the trails of animals and men — he delighted in all such features.[13]

Parkman's grasp of strategic geography was recognized and praised by Ellen Churchill Semple, and modern historians have found in it little to modify.[14]

Parkman nowhere dilates upon his moral views, and he scorned the idea that his histories were politically motivated. Despite his own reputation as a romantic, he regretted the "romantic haze" that obscured the subject of a historian like William Prescott and preferred "the actual record made in the thick of the conflict" to the "decorous paraphrase." Since Parkman refused to primp his characters, and thereby impart to them an undeserved refinement or an improbable perspicuity, he could not write comfortable myths. Indeed he ridiculed the mythic Indians of Cooper and Thomas Campbell as "aboriginal heroes, lovers, and sages who have long formed a petty nuisance in our literature," and he distanced himself from historians like his mentor, Jared Sparks, who had altered George Washington's published correspondence in order that the man should more exactly match the myth. He criticized George Bancroft for writing history that was overly dignified. Dignified and decorous history makes the past distant rather than present; it makes it into a place of noble acts and eloquent orations, a place compared with which the present can only appear grievously degenerate. Exaltation of the past also tempts writers to "theory and speculation," to "sermons, sentiments, or personal opinions," all of which Parkman scorned as "sophomoric wisdom."[15]

Parkman's reticence in these matters has caused his histories to age far more slowly than those of his moralizing contemporaries, but it does not prevent him from presenting a morality. His moral meaning is simply "beyond the reach of overt comment and explicit statement," borne to the reader by carefully crafted content and style. This is why historian John Fisk claimed, at the time of Parkman's death, that his "pages are alive with political philosophy"; it simply took the form of an "object lesson" in which the facts were left to speak for themselves. Parkman allows "the course of events to carry its own philosophy," another contemporary wrote, and does not pause to point out the moral of those remarkable and edifying instances when events conclude as they should.[16]

The primary if unspoken moral point of any object lesson — what we today might call empiricism or positivism — is that the virtue of an act is entirely determined by objects, by the material consequences of that act in time and space. As described in the secular morality of David Hume, the virtuous act is one that excites a sentiment of affection, esteem, or approbation in the heart of an unbiased spectator who contemplates the whole and thereby perceives the ultimately favorable balance of human pain and pleasure effected by that act. To regard as virtuous any action that lacked desirable material consequences was, for Hume, the very essence of superstition.[17] Another way to say this is to say that history and science — Hume's "contemplation of the whole" — are the sole grounds of moral judgment.

In Parkman, objective history is the ground of moral judgment; because one of the most objective elements of history is territory, as documented by treaties and maps, we might even say that historical geography is the ground of moral judgment. This is how Parkman is able to write what his readers recognize as a history of the "contest of ideas" with almost no explicit discussion of the ideas that are being contested. History itself makes the moral judgment. Parkman's "spatial vision" reduces the entire philosophical debate to a question of "which subspecies of Western civilization was to master the new continent."[18] Stated crudely, although perhaps not too crudely, in this view the highest morality is the most effective morality, and the most objective proof of effectiveness is accumulation of some finite good, such as territory. Ellen Churchill Semple employed the same geographical appraisal of morality:

> Evolution needs room but finds the Earth's surface limited. Everywhere old and new forms of life live side by side in deadly competition; but the later improved variety multiplies and spreads at the cost of the less fa-vored types. The struggle for existence means a struggle for space. . . . The superiority of such expansionists consists primarily in their greater ability to appropriate, thoroughly utilize and populate a territory.[19]

Like Semple, Parkman makes his moral argument in terms of a historical change, and he substantiates this change by describing a geographical change in the size of the territory controlled by the new form of life. Contests for territory decide not only "the prevalence of races" but also "the triumph of principles."[20]

Parkman further substantiates the historical change (moral vindication) by describing the transformation of landscape. His landscapes are, therefore, emblematic. For example, the "three vital principles" of New France, "war, religion, and trade," are personified in a ruling triumvirate of "commandant, chaplain, and storekeeper" and emblematized in a landscape of "chapel, fortifications, and storehouses." Indians and French bushrangers move easily through the primeval forest, obsolescent peoples in an obsolescent landscape, "biding its own day of doom" and vainly resisting "the process of improvement." Meanwhile the English colonists "plodded at their workshops, their farms, or their fisheries" and with prosaic diligence slowly and ineluctably enlarged their utilitarian landscape. Deforestation, expulsion of the French, removal of the Indians: these are concrete geographical expressions that prove, in one sense, the superiority of the expansionists, the practical and energetic English colonists with their powerful political and moral philosophies of "regulated freedom" and "practical activism."[21]

Parkman uses juxtaposed images of landscapes past, present, and future to convey not only the fact but also the meaning of historical change. He describes, for example, the newly constructed Fort Duquesne in 1755 as "the first intrusion of men upon a scene which, a few months before, breathed the repose of virgin wilderness" and in the same paragraph describes, as though in a vision, late-nineteenth-century Pittsburgh, "with its swarming populations, its restless industries, the clang of its forges, and its chimneys vomiting foul smoke into the face of heaven." Like territorial expansion, environmental modification is proof of a sort of moral triumph. "The West in English hands meant farms, villages, cities, the ruin of the forest, the extermination of the game, and the expulsion of those who lived on it," Parkman wrote, "while the West in French hands meant but scattered posts of war and trade."[22]

Territorial acquisition and loss, and the creation and destruction of emblematic landscapes, compose two-thirds of Parkman's moral geography. The third component is based on recognition that the territory of a moral system must contain places where the vital qualities of that system are reproduced. We might call these places moral crucibles. They are the sites of core institutions and formative experiences. Across much of present-day America, the athletic field is such a place, as it is widely supposed to infuse citizens with an informing love of competition, teamwork, impartial rules, and regulated aggression.

Vital and Sterile Civilizations

Parkman was intrigued by human variety, by the way in which what he took to be an essential human nature is shaped and differentiated by experience and the way in which that experience is itself shaped by social institutions and everyday practices. "Does not education make the most essential distinctions?" he writes in his journal, and by this he certainly means "the mighty educational powers which spring out of life itself" and not the comparatively feeble tutelage of pedagogues. Parkman's sensitivity to the formation of character by milieu gave him a lifelong interest in details of daily life in the past, in those "things of lesser importance" that take one to the heart of a people, a period, or a place.[23]

Among the peoples Parkman classifies as civilized, the mightiest educational powers originate in institutions, whereas factors of race and environment are throughout his work subordinate, if never categorically denied. When he describes England and its colonies as peoples united by "laws, language, and blood," the word *order* is significant. From his repeated readings of Sismondi, Parkman had learned that "government and laws were the most essential factors in the character of people, not climate or race."[24]

The Acadians, for instance, were in no sense naturally ignorant, credulous, and indecisive but were made so by paternalistic government and a dogmatic church that had left them "unused for generations to think for themselves" and therefore "enfeebled by hereditary mental subjection." Any institutional environment encourages development of some human capacities while it discourages development of others. The process is not fundamentally different than that at work among peoples who Parkman presents as somehow closer to nature. Describing the Native Americans gathered at Fort Duquesne in 1755, Parkman writes: "The law of the survival of the fittest had wrought on this heterogeneous crew through countless generations; and with the primitive Indian, the fittest was the hardiest, fiercest, most adroit, and most wily."[25]

Among character-shaping institutions, the law is dominant. Parkman studied law and, though never obliged to practice it, retained from this experience a profound and abiding regard for the character-shaping power of constitutions and legal systems. These give basic shape to national character and are the foundation of what Parkman calls civilizations. Parkman describes these civilizations as organisms or at least makes recourse to organic metaphors when describing them. He claims that every civilization follows "its natural laws of growth" and comes in the end "to its natural result": corruption, vitiation, and collapse. "All nations have in them some element of decay"; to believe otherwise is "futile optimism."[26]

The corruption and decline of civilizations occur in one of two ways, either the essential principles are carried to excess or the essential principles are rendered obsolete by changed circumstances. The first theory stands behind Parkman's bleak diagnosis of the nineteenth-century United States, where the principles of democracy and industry were pursued to a degree far removed from the practical realities of "every sound and wholesome society." The second theory stands behind his analysis of the collapse of monarchical Catholicism, which had fulfilled its historical purpose with the propagation of Christian ethics throughout Europe, and the final defense of European civilization against Islamic attack at Lepanto in 1571 and Vienna in 1683. Writing in the same vein, Parkman describes the mid-eighteenth-century Whigs as "a great party, which had fulfilled its mission and done its work."[27]

Yet obsolete moral systems persist. The "prostrate Middle Ages," for instance, lingered on in Spain and was for more than a century the "incubus of Europe." These systems persist because they are taken over by what Parkman describes as bigots, individuals attached to the creed with irrational tenacity and ferocity, often for low and self-serving reasons. Parkman's sixteenth-century Spaniard is, for instance, "bigotry incarnate." To Parkman, who was a man without religious convictions, all theological controversies seemed quibbles absurdly magnified by fanatical bigots or pretenses exploited by impostors to further their worldly ambition. The automatic, unthinking nature of these champions of a dead moral system is conveyed by Parkman in metaphors that compare them to swarms of insects, packs of wolves, and ant-like armies of Myrmidons. The soldiers of Spain are "dark masses of organized ferocity."[28]

Allegiance to the lost cause of a doomed civilization is difficult to explain, even after the loyal have been dehumanized to automatons. This is why Parkman relentlessly emphasizes dishonesty, duplicity, and deceit among defenders of tradition. New France is infested with "official jackals," "indigenous and imported scoundrels" who "fatten on the general distress." Dishonesty and crafty dealing by these "forces of knavery" spread like a contagion through the colony, "and to resist it required no common share of moral robustness." Peculation and maleversation are but one aspect of a more general hypocrisy. Parkman also finds it in Catholic missionaries who connive at, or even incite, the "midnight onslaughts" of "baptized savages." He finds it in the French government's ready use of "flattering illusions" to perpetuate in the minds of citizens a groundless confidence in the viability of their system. "By indefatigable lying, by exaggerating every success and covering over every reverse," the Canadian Governor Vaudreuil "deceived the people and in some measure himself." Parkman finds it in "the Canadian gift of gasconade."[29]

A moral system may be dying and yet long retain a capacity for destruction. Its morbidity is betrayed by its inability to create, a failing that Parkman represents in careful metaphors of attenuated masculinity and sexual impotence.[30] The decay of the eighteenth-century French nobility is evident to Parkman from the fact that "the two sexes were never more alike"; masculinity had virtually disappeared from the "silken nobility, whose ancestors rode cased in iron." Of this epicene lot, the most peccant is Louis XV, "the pampered Sardanapalus of Versailles," a listless, lazy, and licentious man whose procreative powers were vitiated by "effeminate libertinism." In Parkman's day effeminate meant weak as well as womanish, and with it he meant to portray the French monarch as a creature governed by appetite and unrestrained by manly forbearance. Parkman also describes the king's "fatuity," connoting by this not only foolishness but also deficient vital force. He also describes the king's "imbecility," a word that in Parkman's day carried the clear sense, now entirely lost, of male loss of procreative power.[31]

The physical evidence of the sterility of the old moral system is its inability to populate territory, spawn colonies, and transform environments. In Florida, the Spanish can resist "the vast scheme of encroachment" by Protestant peoples, but they can foster no vigorous colonies of their own. Unlike the "fruitful" system of the British colonies, particularly the "masculine race" of New England that "spread itself in swarming millions over half a continent," New France was "barren." The contest for North America is thus in Parkman an unequal rivalry between "barren absolutism" and "liberty . . . full of prolific life." After seventy years under the Bourbons and the pope, the Ohio country remained "a realm of wild and waste fertility," a fecund bride unjustly wed to a sterile dotard.[32]

A corrupt and sterile system thus fights a hopeless rearguard action against the vital and prolific moral system of the future. North America is the theater of the contest; the future is the prize. To possess North American space is to possess future time. But it is not to escape tragedy. Nineteenth-century weaknesses grew from eighteenth-century strengths, and in Parkman's view the United States was threatened by "excess and perversion of the principles that made her great." Democracy had degenerated to demagoguery, "organized ignorance, led by unscrupulous craft." Practical industry had degenerated to "a too exclusive pursuit of material wealth," a routinized "morality of commerce" practiced by swarms of bigots who were mindlessly locked in "overstrained and morbid activity." Parkman found bigotry even in forest destruction. "The early settlers regarded the forest as an enemy to be overcome by any means, fair or foul," he wrote, and the tradition is thoughtlessly perpetuated by the settlers' descendants who "do not yet comprehend how completely the conditions are changed."[33]

The physical evidence of the sterility of the new moral system of liberal democracy was, for Parkman, its inability to produce great individuals. He saw in nineteenth-century America a vast "aggregate of mediocrity," a mass of "little devils of human beings" preoccupied by "little pranks" and "little thoughts," men and women who appeared to him as "thin, weak, tottering figures" whose principal characteristics were "vulgarity and helplessness." The country lacked great leaders, generals, artists, and intellectuals; it was "a parvenu nation with the faults of a parvenu," and "no expansion of territory, no accumulation of wealth, no growth of population, can compensate for the decline of individual greatness."[34]

The Moral Crucible of Manliness

What was wanting, in Parkman's opinion, was manliness, a nearly ineffable quality that combines the virtues of endurance, fortitude, courage, self-devotion, and competence (in the senses of ability and independent means of subsistence). In the words of his first biographer, manliness was Parkman's "ruling ideal"; it was "what he demanded first and last." As Fellow of the Corporation of Harvard College, Parkman "sought especially the welfare of the students in regard to developing manliness," and as a historian he wrote to counteract what he perceived as a pervading "lack of manliness" in nineteenth-century U.S. society. This is why his histories accentuate heroes like Massachusetts governor William Shirley, who persevere though "bitterly criticized" and the "butt of adversity," or British secretary of state William Pitt, who "held his purpose regardless of the gathering storm."[35]

Few today will approve of Parkman's term, or of the fundamental sexism (he called it "sexual reciprocity") that it betrays, but moral distaste should not muddle our understanding of the concept's general political significance. Parkman's manliness is a patrician quality that serves less to distinguish men from women than to distinguish men from men. It is the quality of a class of men who do not constantly crave "the stimulus of success" and who are sheltered from the vicissitudes of public opinion by private incomes, emotional detachment, and a strongly developed sense of their own superiority. They are, in other words, self-sufficient or self-reliant to an extraordinary degree and thus able to rise above the "perverse and exasperating narrowness" of ordinary people and their "purblind representatives" and take a longer view.[36]

Parkman's call for manliness is, in other words, an argument in favor of unique political influence for men drawn largely, although not exclusively, from his own patrician class. A central political object lesson of Parkman's histories is that for democracy to survive, and not disintegrate into "discordant communities" or "semi-republics" incapable of concerted action, it must grant "the preponderance of power to character and intelligence" and remain "ballasted...by strong traditions of respect for established worth and ability, as well as by families prominent in affairs for generations." A friend of Parkman called this "led democracy" guided by "men of light," led by what Parkman himself called "leading minds," "master minds," or "the culture of the nation."[37]

It is important to see that writing in the tragic mood always contains an implicit argument for establishment of such a class of leaders, political ballast to use Parkman's term. The heart of tragic narrative is crisis, with ruin and destruction all but certain and reprieve a slender possibility. This is the moment when the hero steps forward to save the day (only the day, mind you, since tragedy allows no escape from ultimate fate); the figure of the hero is thus a creature of crisis, just as crisis is a creature of the mood of tragedy. This is because there are in tragedy no easy choices and all acts have distant effects, some of which must be ill effects. Only an extraordinary human — a hero — is capable of making such choices, of assuming responsibility for such equivocal effects. Any fool can do the right thing in stories written in the mode of romance or comedy, since in these modes right action leads to public praise and happy endings.[38] More is demanded in tragedy; much less is given in return. The tragic hero thus performs a public service, but he is seldom popular.

This is why an implicit moral lesson of the tragic mood, and of Parkman's entire work, is that civilization never outgrows its need for "great men." For example, when Parkman describes General James Abercrombie's disastrous attack on Ticonderoga in 1758, he insists that it is Abercrombie's assistant, Brigadier Lord Howe, who possesses "the qualities of a leader of men." When Howe, the "soul" of the army, is shot dead in the opening stage of the assault, disaster ensues: "The death of one man was the ruin of fifteen thousand."[39] Tragic narrative pivots on the acts of extraordinary individuals who act (or fail to act) in the moment of crisis, and thus it serves to naturalize consolidation of deliberative authority in the hands of a superhuman elite. This is why the same rhetoric of crisis is employed today to augment the powers of technocrats and experts.

The problem, as Parkman saw it, was that heroic qualities and manliness were not encouraged by the dominant institutions of liberal democratic society, but required other "favorable associations and surroundings." Ordinary life in the republic did not routinely demand courage, fortitude, and endurance but rather seemed to call forth and reward sheepish conformity and petty self-interest in the market and at the ballot box. The manly virtues required "a rougher school," where a man was "thrown more completely on his own resources." Parkman wrote these lines from the Great Plains, where he ventured to undertake just such an education in 1846. Adam Smith had made the same observation a century earlier: "The general security and happiness which prevail in ages of civility and politeness, afford little exercise to the contempt of danger, to patience in enduring labour, hunger, and pain."[40]

Like Smith, Parkman believed that a person's character develops in the same way as a person's body, through use and exercise. Virtues such as courage, fortitude, and endurance develop only where they are useful, that is to say in places where possession of such traits is a positive advantage. Where they are not useful, they are seldom practiced; where they are seldom practiced, they become increasingly difficult and uncommon. This is the idea behind Hume's claim that governments should seek to change the customs of a people "primarily by varying the utility of those customs" and thereby occasioning "a proportionable effect on the sentiments of mankind." Moral character is shaped by incentives, not exhortations or imperatives. The idea is as old as Hippocrates, who in the fifth century B.C. explained that courage is stunted by the institution of despotic government because there is no incentive to run risks that can only benefit another. The idea stands behind Hume's criticism of charity, which serves as "encouragement...to idleness and debauchery," and his defense of private property, which serves as "encouragement to such useful habits and accomplishments" as "art, care, and industry." The idea appears explicitly in Parkman when he writes that a society will produce characters who possess the virtues and behaviors that that society rewards, because in this as in other cases, "demand and supply act and react with inevitable and deadly reciprocity."[41]

It may be needless to point out that similar ideas about adaptive behavior remain very much alive in the works of contemporary social theorists, liberal and conservative.[42]

For Parkman, the woods was the greatest moral crucible of manliness that North America has known. This is the old woods of peril, action, and conflict, the "savage" woods, to use Parkman's preferred adjective. It is not the poet's woods of Wordsworth or Thoreau, men whom Parkman reportedly despised for their pantheism and "affectation of being natural"; it is not the therapeutic woods of William Cullen Bryant or Thomas Cole, to which tired and harassed businessmen were encouraged to retire periodically and restore their souls: it is "the wilderness which wakens the dormant savage in the breasts of men" and recalls to their minds "scenes of fear and blood."[43]

Parkman went to the woods as a young man "to taste the half-savage kind of life." He was "fond of hardships and vain of enduring them" and eager to exercise these stoic virtues. He believed that "a wider diffusion of Pottawatomie tastes was the grand desideratum of a bookish age" that seemed to swarm with stoop-shouldered weaklings who resembled "the outcasts of a hospital." The woods was for him, as it remains for many, a great reservoir of the three requisites of Spartan vitality: "fresh air, cold water, and exercise." But Parkman's woods is more than an enormous open-air gymnasium. It is also a place of sudden, violent death. As such, it is a place of fear and of opportunities to exercise mastery over fear. It is a place of "appalling loneliness," "a leafy maze, a mystery of shade, a universal hiding place, where murder might lurk unseen at its victim's side, and nature seemed formed to nurse the mind with wild and dark imaginings," with "nightmares of horror." It is a place of "insidious warfare" wrapped in the "shadows of the tomb," a place "silent with death, yet haunted everywhere with ambushed danger." In this "tomb-like silence . . . the ranger strode . . . and like Dürer's knight, a ghastly death stalked at every side."[44]

The old woods posed a physical, mental, and in some respects spiritual ordeal, a formative and critical experience. It was a uniquely grim and fearsome moral crucible, but one that selected and cultivated traits that Parkman admired and believed necessary to national survival. With the passing of the old woods and its ways, all that remained was war, for which Parkman remained a lifelong enthusiast. Nowhere in Parkman is there "a word of reprobation for the cruelty of war," and he welcomed the Civil War as "the resurrection of our manhood." The idea is not unique to Parkman. A century earlier, Adam Smith also saw "war as the great school for acquiring and exercising . . . magnanimity, . . . for forming every man to this hardiness and firmness of temper." In the decades after Parkman's death, the idea informed a persistent admiration for the martial virtues and a novel preoccupation with sports and the strenuous life.[45] Moral crucibles of manliness, although now largely coeducational, have by no means disappeared from the American landscape.

Impossible Places, Improbable Places

Parkman's forest is an imagined place. It is not an imaginary place of his fancy but rather a real place partially pictured in his mind's eye. Imaginary places do not exist outside of imagination; they are invented, figmental, fictitious. They are creations of fantasy, places to which one escapes from the present, with its limits, constraints, and finite possibilities. In many cases, imaginary places cannot exist outside of imagination, because in them seemingly permanent exactions of the human condition are suspended or abridged. They are, in other words, impossible places.

Impossible places are, however, but one sort of imagined place. As I write these lines, I imagine a dozen places, all of which have or had existence independent of my imagination: a pond where I played as a boy, my chair in the garden, St. Peter's in Rome (where I've never been), Little Round Top during the Battle of Gettysburg. These are creations of memory, not fantasy, and are therefore limited by the spirit of fidelity to what actually is, or was. When I imagine my chair in the garden, it is green; an imaginary chair in an imaginary garden might be any color I fancy; it might also fly through the air or grant to those who sit in it superhuman powers. But the spirit of fidelity ensures that the places to which I repair by way of memory are always possible places. They are also, however, by definition memorable, which is to say extraordinary, and this makes them improbable places.

When Parkman elected to write history rather than poetry, he turned from imagining impossible places to imagining improbable places, most notably the scenes of crisis in which tragic heroes act. This was a moral choice consonant with Parkman's general moral vision. Impossible places, of the sort one finds in fairy tales or poetry, stimulate in the beholder a desire for something other than the present, yet at the same time by their patent impossibility make it clear that they are not themselves true images of that desired something. A child who imagines flying on a magic carpet soon understands that what he wants is not an impossible carpet but rather freedom; the carpet is only an image. Another child, who imagines flying in an airplane, cannot get past the object so easily; she thinks she wants an airplane, and should she some day get one will very likely discover that an airplane is after all not exactly what she desired. Like an impossible carpet, an impossible place can stimulate in those who behold its image a desire for some quality, but it does not propose a possible object or form of life with which that individual might hope to quench that desire.[46]

The unquenchable longings stimulated by impossible places should prevent moral complacency without building false expectations of perfection in this world. However, in Parkman's day (as in our own), it was becoming increasingly difficult to speak with certainty about the limits of possibility. Anything might be possible, sooner or later, through technological innovation and social change. This meant that it was increasingly difficult to imagine an impossible place that would stimulate desires without seeming to promise satisfaction. The wildest figments of imagination were, indeed, taken as attainable objects of desire, as goals for technological advancement and progressive politics, the very tendencies that Parkman most deeply deplored. Parkman did not wish to excite further enthusiasm for the future, and so turned to history, a form of memory, written in the tragic mode. With poetry degraded to utopias, and impossible places widely viewed as blueprints of the future, Parkman turned to writing cautionary tales. He took for his themes limits, fate, unintended consequences, and the ineluctable tragedy of corruption, vitiation, and collapse. There are, however, points of light in his lugubrious landscape: those improbable but not impossible places and moments of crisis in which individuals are given the chance to rise to moral greatness.

Notes

1. Wilbur R. Jacobs, ed., *Letters of Francis Parkman* (Norman: University of Oklahoma Press, 1960), 2:124; Francis Parkman, *Montcalm and Wolfe* (Boston: Little, Brown, and Co., 1902), 1:74, 68.

2. Charles Haight Farnham, *A Life of Francis Parkman* (1900; reprint, Boston: Little, Brown and Co., 1910), 212, 296.

3. Wilbur R. Jacobs, *Francis Parkman: Historian as Hero* (Austin: University of Texas Press, 1991), 117; David Levin, *History as Romantic Art: Bancroft, Prescott, Motley, and Parkman* (Stanford, Cal.: Stanford University Press, 1959), 6; Mason Wade, ed., *The Journals of Francis Parkman* (New York: Harper and Brothers, 1947), 2:539.

4. G. P. Gooch, *History and Historians in the Nineteenth Century,* 2d ed. (Boston: Beacon Press, 1959), 279.

5. Howard Doughty, *Francis Parkman* (New York: Macmillan, 1962), 165, 179; Bliss Perry, "Francis Parkman," in *Later Years of the Saturday Club, 1870–1920,* ed. Mark Anthony De Wolfe Howe (1927; reprint, Freeport, N.Y.: Books for Libraries Press, 1968), 25; Francis Parkman, "The Works of James Fenimore Cooper," *North American Review* 74 (1852): 148.

6. Francis Parkman, *Pioneers of France in the New World* (Boston: Little Brown, 1902), 1:c; Julius H. Ward, "Francis Parkman and His Work," *The Forum* 16 (1893): 427.

7. W. D. Howells, "Mr. Parkman's Histories," *Atlantic* 34 (1874): 607; F. H. Underwood, "Francis Parkman," *Contemporary Review* 53 (1887): 658; Edward G. Mason, "Francis Parkman," *The Dial* 1 (1880): 149; Francis Parkman, "The Fleur-de-Lis in Florida," *Atlantic* 12 (1863): 231; Underwood, "Parkman," 659; James Russell Lowell, "Francis Parkman," *The Century Magazine* 45 (1892): 45; Carl O. Sauer, "The Education of a Geographer," in *Land and Life: A Selection from the Writings of Carl Ortwin Sauer,* ed. John Leighly (Berkeley: University of California Press, 1963), 391.

8. "A Half Century of Conflict," *Atlantic* 70 (1892): 416; Ward, "Parkman," 422; Jacobs, *Letters,* 2:82; Doughty, *Parkman,* 267.

9. Parkman, *Pioneers,* 1:67; Parkman, "Cooper," 151; Parkman, *Montcalm,* 3:261.

10. Parkman, *Montcalm,* 3:121.

11. Farnham, *Life,* 344; Jacobs, *Letters,* 2:18, 97; Levin, *Romantic Art,* 211, 223; Otis A. Pease, *Parkman's History: The Historian as Literary Artist* (New Haven, Conn.: Archon, 1968), 57.

12. Parkman, *Montcalm,* 3:227.

13. Farnham, *Life,* 65.

14. Ellen Churchill Semple and Clarence F. Jones, *American History and Its Geographical*

Conditions, rev. ed. (Boston: Houghton Mifflin, 1933), 34, 444–45; John Keegan, *Fields of Conquest: The Wars for North America* (New York: Alfred A. Knopf, 1996), 63, 112.

15. Jacobs, *Letters,* 2:102, 14; Justin Winsor, "Francis Parkman," *Atlantic* 73 (1894): 662; Parkman, "Cooper," 150; Parkman, "Dr. Sparks and the Washington Letters," *The Nation* 46 (1887): 136–37; Farnham, *Life,* 212; Francis Parkman, "Indian Antiquities in North America," *Christian Examiner* 50 (1851): 417; Farnham, *Life,* 183–85.

16. Doughty, *Parkman,* 168; John Fisk, "Francis Parkman," *Atlantic* 73 (1894): 674; Winsor, "Parkman," 660.

17. David Hume, *An Enquiry concerning the Principles of Morals* (1751; reprint, Chicago: Open Court, 1907), 131, 31–32.

18. "Parkman's *Half Century of Conflict,*" *The Nation* 55 (1892): 9; Doughty, *Parkman,* 178–79.

19. Ellen Churchill Semple, *The Influences of Geographic Environment* (New York: Henry Holt and Co., 1911), 170.

20. Parkman, *Pioneers,* 1:xcv.

21. Parkman, *Montcalm,* 1:74, 68, 20, 130, xcv; Doughty, *Parkman,* 196.

22. Parkman, *Montcalm,* 1:215, 2:355.

23. Wade, *Journals,* 2:408; Jacobs, *Letters,* 1:164, 2:113, 1:9, 29, 31.

24. Parkman, *Montcalm,* 3:258; Mason Wade, *Francis Parkman: Heroic Historian* (New York: Viking Press, 1942), 341; Gooch, *History and Historians,* 160.

25. Parkman, *Montcalm,* 1:127, 269, 217.

26. Parkman, *Pioneers,* 1:xcvi; Parkman, "The Failure of Universal Suffrage," *North American Review* 128 (1878): 12; Farnham, *Life,* 297.

27. Francis Parkman, "The Woman Question Again," *North American Review* 16 (1880): 29; Parkman, "The Woman Question," *North American Review* 129 (1879): 312; Levin, *Romantic Art,* 100–106; Parkman, *Montcalm,* 2:185.

28. Francis Parkman, "The Spaniard and the Heretic," *Atlantic* 12 (1863): 539; Parkman, *Pioneers,* 1:20–21; Parkman, "Spaniard," 539; Parkman, *Pioneers,* 1:20, 22, 49; Parkman, *Montcalm,* 1:92, 304, 14, 41; Parkman, *Pioneers,* 1:32.

29. Parkman, *Montcalm,* 2:234, 3:12, 44, 2:221, 232, 195, 353, 3:9–10.

30. John Spencer Bassett, "Francis Parkman, the Man," *Sewanee Review* 10 (1902): 297.

31. Parkman, *Montcalm,* 1:14, 17, 42, 2:249; Levin, *Romantic Art,* 40; Parkman, *Montcalm,* 1:4, 5, 2:323–34.

32. Parkman, "Spaniard," 554; Parkman, *Pioneers,* 1:9–18, xcvi; Parkman, *Montcalm,* 1:29, 38, 44.

33. Parkman, *Montcalm,* 3:260; Parkman, "Universal Suffrage," 2; Jacobs, *Letters,* 1:143; Parkman, *Montcalm,* 1:215; Parkman, "Woman Question," 311; Parkman, "The Forests and the Census," *Atlantic Monthly* 55 (1885): 837.

34. Jacobs, *Letters,* 1:145; Wade, *Journals,* 1:312, 2:405; Jacobs, *Letters,* 1:143, 146.

35. Levin, *Romantic Art,* 61–71; Farnham, *Life,* 309–14, 301, 114, 258, 207; Parkman, *Montcalm,* 2:80, 71, 3:238.

36. Parkman, "Woman Question," 306; Parkman, *Montcalm,* 3:11, 1:205.

37. Parkman, *Montcalm,* 3:260, 2:105, 1:28; Parkman, "Universal Suffrage," 6; E[dwin] L. G[oodkin], "Francis Parkman," *The Nation* 71 (1900): 441; Parkman, "Universal Suffrage," 5; Jacobs, *Letters,* 1:48, 165.

38. Jonathan M. Smith, "Geographical Rhetoric: Modes and Tropes of Appeal," *Annals of the Association of American Geographers* 86 (1996): 1–20.

39. Jacobs, *Letters,* 1:145; Parkman, *Montcalm,* 2:304.

40. Jacobs, *Letters,* 1:155, 161, 44, 48; Adam Smith, *The Theory of Moral Sentiments* (1759; reprint, New York: Augustus M. Kelly, 1966), 297.

41. Hume, *Enquiry,* 85; Hippocrates, "Airs, Waters, and Places," in *Hippocrates,* Loeb Classical Library (1957), 1:133; Hume, *Enquiry,* 66, 117, 131, 13, 28, 27; Jacobs, *Letters,* 1:145.

42. William Julius Wilson, *When Work Disappears: The World of the New Urban Poor* (New York: Vintage, 1992), 70–72; Charles Murray, *Loosing Ground: American Social Policy, 1950–1980* (New York: Basic Books, 1984), 154–91.

43. Wade, *Journals,* 1:14, 56, 60, 76, 209; Parkman, *Pioneers,* 1:44; Wade, *Journals,* 1:256–57.

44. Wade, *Journals,* 1:31; Jacobs, *Letters,* 1:177; Francis Parkman, "Exploring the Magalloway," *Harper's New Monthly Magazine* 24 (1864): 736; Wade, *Journals,* 1:223–24; Jacobs, *Letters,* 1:83; Parkman, *Montcalm,* 2:19, 21, 342, 7, 121.

45. "Francis Parkman," *The Nation* 79 (1904): 82; Jacobs, *Letters,* 1:157; Smith, *Moral Sentiments,* 352, 361; T. J. Jackson Lears, *No Place of Grace: Antimodernism and the Transformation of American Culture, 1880–1920* (New York: Pantheon, 1981), 98–139.

46. C. S. Lewis, *Of Other Worlds,* ed. Walter Hooper (New York: Harcourt, Brace and World, 1966), 28–30.

Part IV

Cosmos versus Hearth

INTRODUCTION

Cosmos versus Hearth

Yi-Fu Tuan

"Cosmos" and "hearth" stand for two scales as well as for two sets of values. Hearth is local, cozy, familiar, nurturing — and all these words imply a small, circumscribed place, accessible to the sort of direct experience in which all the senses are engaged. Cosmos, by contrast, implies the large, the abstract, and the impersonal, accessible only to mediated experience — to the eye, possibly, to the mind's eye, essentially.

These two terms (hearth and cosmos) correspond to our dual nature, to the fact that we are both body and mind. The body requires, yearns for, the nurturing intimacy of the hearth; the mind the air and light, the capaciousness, of the cosmos. Ontogenetically, hearth precedes cosmos, for in the first year of life we all need, above all, nurturing intimacy. In this sense and also in the sense that the mind is unlikely to function well without a sound body, hearth is basic — basic to physical survival. On the other hand, conceptually, cosmos has primacy, for only someone capable of standing outside of hearth can see it, consciously appreciate it, compare it with other hearths, and contrast it with cosmos.

In my book *Cosmos and Hearth,* I have polarized the terms for the sake of simplicity and clarity. In actuality, the worlds and experiences that these terms conjure often overlap. I would even say that, under certain circumstances, they ideally overlap. Consider a small child being read to on the lap of her parent. The small child is in the ideal overlapping worlds of cosmos and hearth: her body is nestled in hearth, her mind is elsewhere — in sparkling fairyland. When we are older, few indulgences are more delectable than to sink into an upholstered wing chair and in that sheltered environment read a book of adventure. Cannot seminars in graduate school be conducted that way? April Veness subtly raises this question in her essay, one of the five in this part. My answer is yes, ideally. The seminar room should be a hearth, with paneled walls, comfortable chairs, and perhaps even coffee and banana bread on the table. Why not? But the discussion itself must attempt to probe the heights and the depths — positions that may not be comfortable or homelike. The professor herself, while courteous and attentive, is not mother; she ought not interrupt cosmic exploration with a solicitous, "Another piece of banana bread?" that threatens to break the line of thought.

Hearth is traditionally woman's world; beyond lies man's. A striking example of this division, widely recognized in different parts of the world, is recorded in Icelandic literature, as Marijane Osborn and Gillian Overing show. Hearth is an ordered world, peaceful and civilized. Woman is in her element there. When she moves beyond hearth, she moves into a region of dishevelment and disorder, where she is vulnerable to rapacious men — to rape; or she herself becomes disheveled and wild and may even become a troll, "at home" in the wilds. On the other hand, a man, violent and murderous in the wilds, upon returning home may be content to farm his land and leave people in peace (*Egil's Saga*).

"Hearth," so interpreted, has a positive meaning. But, increasingly in modern times, its negative meaning — hitherto repressed — comes to the fore, exposed by unsentimental storytellers and social scientists. On the dark side, hearth is a place of constraint, a prison. A cozy prison, maybe, but still a prison. The feminist movement in the last two centuries is torn by a contradiction: on the one hand, hearth, a center of order and civility, is a feminine achievement that should be spread with missionary zeal into man's chaotic sphere; on the other hand, hearth as dollhouse prison is horribly confining. Women should strive to escape, even if it is into danger and chaos. Why not? So what if one has to lose certain attributes of femininity, even discard them all and become a troll, so as to feel "at home" in the wilds? Why shouldn't women, like men, become disheveled and carefree?

But is hearth even a cozy prison? Verbal violence, either outright or in the subtler form of cruel put-downs, is not unknown in the family living room or bedroom; indeed, it may be more common there than in the boardroom or marketplace. As to physical violence, its shocking frequency in even "good" homes has only recently been exposed. By contrast, the streets are relatively safe — and safest of all is wilderness. So the meanings are subject to reversal: hearth is emotional repression, with violent outbreak an ever-present threat, whereas the great outdoors (wilderness) is liberating and harmonious.

I have used the words *wilds* or *wilderness* as the polar opposite of hearth and home. What has happened to *cosmos*? How does it fit in with the other key terms? Cosmos is the opposite of wilderness in that word's literal and original sense. Yet the two have one characteristic in common — *size;* and the sense of freedom and exhilaration that goes with size. Cosmos, though like wilderness in its projection of size, is unlike it in its exemplary definition; cosmos is a clearly demarcated, harmonious whole. Hearth or home is also such a whole; hence it is sometimes called a microcosm. Hearth is a world in miniature. There is beauty, comfort, and goodness in miniatures, in small worlds. Women have created them, men have benefited from them. Human beings — above all, children — need them. A sign of modern times is that women have rebelled against confinement to microcosms. They want to break out to taste the exhilaration of size and power, not only those to be found in the wilderness but also those to be found in the cosmos; that is, they want to be full participants of political and intellectual life in public forums, in society and world, hitherto almost the exclusive spheres of men.

Men may have more command over space than do women, but the actual extent and degree of their domination depend on their status in society and on the society to which they belong. Societies themselves differ — have differed — markedly in power, especially from (say) 1500 onward, when European society surged forward, leaving others behind and forgotten, or alongside and exploited. Within Europe, while most people remained poor, those already well off gained new wealth, and with it new signs of confidence and power. One such sign was the advent of landscape painting and of gardening at an ambitious scale — forms of art that emphasized sight over the other senses. Sight commanded space — panoramic views and regions. One could envisage a potentate, most likely male, standing on a hill and casting his proprietary gaze over a large and handsomely landscaped domain. One could also envisage a potentate poring over an assortment of maps. Cartographic science and the art of globe-making proceeded apace from the Renaissance onward, as Denis Cosgrove shows. The map and the globe became standard furniture in the merchant prince's study. They indicated his rightful place in the cosmos. Landscape painting and gardening were obviously not just about power; they also appealed to the viewer's sense of beauty and evoked natural/societal ideals. Maps and globes, by contrast, were more clearly about power. But, as again Cosgrove shows, they were in themselves works of art; they exhibited beauty. Moreover, the globes, the emblematic pictures of the world, and their textual descriptions directed attention to wonder and goodness, to antiquity's harmony of the spheres and Christianity's hint that it was the Sacred Heart's power of love that moved the universe.

"Hearth" and "cosmos" can take on figurative meanings such that "hearth" stands for locality, community, and ethnicity; and "cosmos" for space, society or world, and cosmopolitanism. Confused arguments over their relative merits may eventually find some kind of resolution if we start by recognizing that both are necessary — as necessary as body and mind — to the development of our full humanity. Moreover, although we can treat "cosmos" and "hearth" as polar opposites, yet they do have the ideal of order or harmony in common; and also, as we have noted, full human contentment seems to require that both be present and mutually supportive. April Veness reminds us of this fact at the personal level. Steven Hoelscher, for his part, takes us beyond the personal to the level of nation and state. His expression "provincial cosmopolitanism" neatly captures the possibility of a cooperative fusion, despite certain oppositional characteristics, between cosmos and hearth. At a still higher level of abstraction, philosopher Edward Casey warns us — me especially! — against a tendency to polarize "cosmos" and "hearth" such that the more people have of the one, the less they can, or even want to, have of the other. Not necessarily so, Casey argues. He observes that people may yearn all the more for hearth as they move into the "thinned-out" places of the global economy. For Casey, place rather than the abstract space of the philosophers is primary and crucial to embodied human beings. Landscape is thus not "open space out there," as some writers may put it, but rather a place larger than the ones normally experienced in day-to-day living. And cosmos is not "space" but "place-world."

Cosmos and hearth can be overlapping worlds, enriching each other, as I have noted. Let me add two more examples at a scale larger than "child in mother's lap and adult reading in a wing chair." During Christmas Eve, an American family gathers around the decorated fireplace; a more cozy and satisfying world is hard to imagine. Yet its perfection depends on elements from the cosmos — the ice of the North Pole, a figure of universal goodwill riding out of the firmament on a reindeer sledge, the bizarre entry down the chimney rather than through the door. Without hints of fresh air from the empyrean beyond, even good experiences behind drawn curtains could eventually come to feel limiting, stuffy. If lovers of the hearth need the cosmos, so do lovers of the cosmos need the hearth. Consider starry-eyed scientists, outstanding creatures of the cosmos. They are right in their element as they argue and exchange ideas at an international conference. Yet they look forward to returning to their home laboratory, with its distinctive way of doing things, for it is there rather than at the international conference that their best ideas first begin to stir; and beyond their home laboratory, they no doubt look forward to home itself, to home-cooking, with its inimitable flavor, and to their own comfortable bed, where in sleep the subconscious does its important work.

Although both hearth and cosmos contribute to a sense of self, they do so in different ways — sometimes in harmonious fusion, more often (I believe) in tension. The tension is created by the fact that experiencing the hearth is not at all the same as experiencing the cosmos. Complementarity, after all, presupposes difference. Hearth offers security, cosmos adventure. One reason why hearth offers security is that one's identity there is not an effect of personal struggle and definition; rather, one is born into it and raised to have it. Identity is bestowed by one's kin and neighbor and by material objects that one's ancestors, rather than oneself, have made. If, for some reason, one's sense of self dims, one can simply rekindle it by foraging in the attic: everything needed — photographs of dead worthies, discarded customs and objects — is already there. By contrast, identity gained through adventure in the cosmos requires effort, individual or group; and it is effort with no guarantee of success. One may fail badly and become totally disoriented. If, however, one *is* successful, a strong sense of self accrues; moreover, it is a sense that grows stronger with each new success — with each new action completed, each new knowledge mastered.

Some scholars — Hoelscher among them — have wisely pointed out that a qualification is necessary, for the way of the hearth, too, can be a process of discovery and invention. Yes, the attic is there, but what to make of the objects in it is a project of present seekers after identity, and it is directed to the future: one *becomes* (note the word's future orientation) a Swiss or Italian American through dramatizations of the past — dramatizations that may or may not correspond with historical reality, that may or may not succeed.

Nevertheless, the two routes differ sufficiently so that if one people pursues the route of the cosmos or, better still, pursues both with vigor, whereas another people pursues the route of the hearth and minimally, if at all, the route of the cosmos, the result will be a widening knowledge gap between the groups. Such a gap can be even more damaging to a democratic society than the widely acknowledged, growing economic gap. After all, is there really such a difference in quality of life between the greatly rich, living in gated minds in gated communities, and the well-educated poor, living in a city tenement, exposed to the noise and smells, but also experiences and ideas, of the cosmos?

The educational "haves" — a disproportionately large number of whom are white Americans from good schools — enjoy the luxury of following both routes to self-identity and confidence. They can play at heritage, derive satisfaction from a reinvented hearth, and at the same time aspire to be full members of the cosmos — successful business entrepreneurs with global links, astrophysicists, or even genuine historians; and by genuine historians I mean students of the past who, thanks to their training in critical scholarship, are able to protect themselves against the grosser forms of self-indulgent nostalgia and wishful thinking. By contrast, many (too many) of the educational "have-nots" are members of minority groups that have suffered, historically, from acute economic discrimination and racism. Lacking the educational background even now to follow both routes, they pick the easier one of the hearth, often (sad to say) with the encouragement of privileged whites. Unchecked by history, hearth leads all but inevitably to a cult of heritage. What begins as imaginative recovery ends as sentimental illusion. The semieducated risk locking themselves into an unreal world of their own making. Immersion in unreality may provide temporary relief, but it destroys sooner or later a sense of self that is already made fragile by overt and subtle forms of condescension on the part of those in power. Matters are actually worse, for added to self-manufactured illusions are the mass-produced ones of global capitalism. In a modern society where the stars are no longer visible, the poorly educated people's only daily dosage of the cosmos is in the degraded (that is, passive) form of drugs, cheap consumer goods, and entertainments.

There are many ways of exploring "cosmos" and "hearth," as the five essays of this part demonstrate. I would like to give a final fillip to my introduction by presenting a disturbing dream. Disturbing to whom? Disturbing to well-educated and well-traveled people like you and me who want the rest of the world to have the opportunities we have had, but who also realize that such an eventuality could endanger not only the earth's ecological health but also its glorious diversity that, up to this point, has provided a feast for our cosmopolitan eyes.

In the dream, I am the curator of a well-endowed museum. Its pride is a succession of long dark corridors on the walls of which are dioramas that vividly illustrate, in clever three-dimensional constructions, the range and variety of animals and human beings. Through well-lit windows I can see, successively, dinosaurs frolicking on the edge of the Cretaceous Sea, mammoths breasting the wind in an Ice age blizzard, koala bears chewing leaves on eucalyptus trees, seals resting on ice floes, and so on; and then, without a break, through other well-lit windows I can see human beings and their habitats — hunter-gatherers in a rainforest, Eskimos in an igloo participating in a family meal, slash-and-burn farmers in central Africa, fishermen hauling in their net on the shores of an Indonesian island, and so on. An inevitable result of this organization, common to many museums, is to make the distinctions between one human group and another seem as sharp as those between different animal species.

In the dream, I am not surprised to find that the figures in the dioramas move about, make sounds, and, in the case of human beings, speak. Each human group speaks its own language, making the separate languages sound, to an untrained ear, almost as different as that between a tiger's growl, a seal's bark, a horse's whinny.

The museum is filled with visitors, admiring the multinatural and multicultural richness of life. As I, monitoring my domain, walk by the Eskimo diorama, I pause to listen to the conversation in the igloo. Imagine my displeasure when I find that they are speaking not Iglulik or Inuit but English, a language that may well be understood by other figures in the exhibition and surely by visitors. Worse, one Eskimo says to the other that he is tired of hunting and that he is thinking of moving south to experiment with another way of life. I quickly skip to the next diorama, hoping to find frozen normality there. It shows Indonesian fishermen hauling in the net. One fisherman says to another that, tired as he is of fishing, he has no wish to change to farming, which he can see exhibited in a diorama across the hall. What he really yearns for — he points to the swarming crowd on the other side of the glass — is the life of a museum tourist, at liberty to survey and enjoy animals and human beings who do not themselves have that liberty. And how does the other fisherman respond? He says, "Sure, it's good to be a tourist, but why stop there? Why not be the all-powerful curator of the museum himself!"

In shock, I realize that a rebellion is brewing. My animals may be happy to remain true to type behind their glass plates, but my humans refuse to be confined; they want the choices open to the tourists and even my own God-like freedom! What if they succeed? They will, of course, destroy the museum and with it my position as curator. Interestingly enough, they themselves cannot be curator, or even tourists, because for there to be tourists there must also be colorful natives willing to be seen but not see. I wake up drenched in sweat, more determined than ever to maintain my museum and the integrity of its rich collection; and I wisely see that the only way to do so is to persuade the natives to know and stay in their place.

GEOGRAPHY'S COSMOS

The Dream and the Whole Round Earth

Denis Cosgrove

Ignem veni mittere in terram.
— St. Ignatius Loyola

Yi-Fu's Cosmos and the Aesthetic Moment

Cosmos has been a recurrent theme in Yi-Fu Tuan's writings. Already in *The Hydrological Cycle and the Wisdom of God*, Tuan's first book, he dealt with a historical turning point in the transformation of premodern European cosmography and sacred geography, when theologically generated questions concerning the relative areas of land and water on the globe generated the secular and "natural" theory of the hydrological cycle, while in *Topophilia* he devoted a significant discussion to the comparative summary of cosmological schemes among literate and nonliterate cultures in different parts of the world.[1] Elsewhere, I show how Western cosmographic thinking has sought consistently to coordinate local experiences (of climate, topography, ecology, and modes of subsistence) with the observation of a cosmic regularity in the heavens (solar, lunar, planetary, and stellar).[2] Recording cosmic harmony and mobilizing it to underwrite temporal power, authority and empire is a recurrent theme in his writing, but Tuan acknowledges also a more individual, private, but no less consistent human urge to reach toward the heavens and grasp an order and meaning beyond the contingencies and failings of a mundane life and the apparent chaos of local incident. In later writings too, Tuan has turned to cosmographic schemes — Chinese, Indian, pre-Columbian — in dissecting the spaces of fear, to illustrate utopias, to reveal human images of the good life. He has deployed these schemata in order to maneuver a sensibility of the local alongside an attachment to a more universal order, and thereby explore the dialectics that connect them. At the scale of the individual, he has pointed out more than once that to harmonize local, contingent experience with the sense of a more symphonic order requires an act of imaginative apprehension that characteristically follows intense concentration: physical or mental. In his "Topophilia" essay of 1961, for example, he places a town planner at a newsstand on Fifth Avenue, New York, relaxing briefly from an effort of intensive fieldwork, the senses suddenly overwhelmed with the majesty of the whole:

The color of the buildings, the traffic noises, the heat of the pavement burning through the soles of his shoes, the symphony of odors from the succession of coffee houses, shoe shops and air-conditioned department stores, together move in upon him as a coherent piece of reality.[3]

Between the local and the cosmic a space is opened for the "effort of imagination," for aesthesis.

In "Surface Phenomena and Aesthetic Experience," Tuan returns to this theme, noting how the beauty of appearances yields to the sense of a greater harmony beyond: even more wonderful than such appearances is the unseen order that sustains them. Plato, more eloquently and persuasively than other thinkers, has argued for the idea of successive layers of beauty, each more abstract and splendid than the other, that stand behind (as it were) the sensible particulars.[4] He points out that the language conventionally deemed most appropriate to this order is mathematics. The connection between mathematical order and musical harmony (captured in the German word *Stimmung*) is an enduring feature of cosmological thought, both in ancient Greek philosophy and contemporary physics. Mathematical regularity provides the architectonics of cosmic space. Tuan reminds us of the philosopher Anaxagoras's answer to the question of life's purpose: humans are born "for the sake of viewing the heavens and the things there, stars, moon and sun."[5]

In *Cosmos and Hearth*, Tuan brings to these themes the precision and elegance of a lifetime's sustained scholarly reflection — reworking his long-standing geographical project to construct and reflect the examined life. In this text he addresses the question in terms of current debates on localism and cultural cosmopolitanism, drawing upon the two national cultures of which he has most intimate knowledge: China and modern America. The former, he claims, seeks order in a vertically structured cosmos, the latter in a horizontal framing, a two-dimensional surface, more characteristic of modernity, as Tuan noted many years ago in a finely drawn comparison between the spires of medieval university towns such as Oxford or Heidelberg and the flat-roofed dormitories and interdenominational chapel of a midwestern campus. Accepting, it seems, the inevitability of a modernity that ignores the planetary cosmos for an earthbound, surface existence, in *Cosmos and Hearth*, Tuan seeks to resolve current dilemmas of cultural pluralism, situated knowledge, and cosmopolitan life through the concept of a cosmopolitan hearth, an oxymoron that he believes allows us to be "at home in the cosmos."[6]

What pulls together the two modes of experience captured by the "cosmopolitan hearth" remains the act of imagination, that aesthetic imperative that Tuan has long recognized as a stimulus to geographical inquiry and that finds a characteristic expression in those apparently disinterested and objectively scientific activities of fieldwork and mapwork. Each can yield a form of reverie and prompt dreams of order, apprehensions that, as Tuan has also noted, find characteristic expression in the visual image — the material and product of imagination, as the connections between the words "image" and "imagination" remind us. These activities are geographical, restricted to the earth's surface, as Tuan recognizes in his rubric that geographers do not raise their heads too far above the earth's surface or delve too deeply below it. Sustained examination of the vertical axis, the cosmographic link between the earthly globe and the heavens, which Tuan associates with premodern Europe and contemporary China, is relatively absent in his work. In *Cosmos and Hearth*, it yields to an entirely horizontal modernism wherein cosmopolitanism is conceived in the Erasmian or Cartesian sense of citizenship within a world conceived as extensive surface.[7]

Equally absent in Tuan's work is sustained reflection on graphic images. His own output is overwhelmingly textual: actual maps are rare, as are diagrams, formulas, or mathematical equations. The texts only occasionally interrogate individual images; in *Cosmos and Hearth* the one shared aesthetic experience (other than erotic love) that Tuan emphasizes is conversation. Yet the cosmos as an object of study in the sense that Anaxagoras spoke of it has an ancient connection with geography through the study of cosmography, a synthetic study of the whole earth in relation to the heavens whose movements differentiate its surface features.[8] Cosmographic science relied heavily on images — as much as on words and narratives — and its harmonies expressed themselves in the mathematical music of planetary motion. Cosmography was conventionally the imaginative and poetic expression of a home in the created world. The oneiric, a concern with dream and reverie, has always been closely connected to the cosmographic project. In what follows I explore a contemporary image, one that connects the themes of individual and world and of cosmography, to suggest that their association still inflects contemporary discourse of earth's surface. I shall use for this discussion a modern image of the globe in space, the NASA photograph A17–22727 of the whole earth, which I have examined itself and in detail elsewhere.[9]

Photomontages of 22727: "To Love and Serve in All Things"

The *Apollo* photo of the globe taken from space not only refocused attention on the planetary surface but also has become iconic within debates about a whole earth, a global destiny, and planetary-scale ecological vulnerability. As such, it is reproduced not only alone, or with textual additions intended to enhance its meanings, but in juxtaposition with other images. The British artist Peter Kennard has exploited this aspect of the cosmographic image in a series of photomontages in which the NASA image acts as frame and background for other elementary, symbolic forms superimposed upon it: tree, atomic bomb, bullet, and human fetus, for example. Each of his monochrome, low-contrast, and poor resolution images works entirely with the grain of liberal, secular, whole-earth values that have come to be associated with 22727. But against the grain of this conventional exploitation of the original photograph, I want to examine another, more difficult, photomontage that I think gives us pause to reflect — as Tuan himself might — on how framing of the good life remains more complex and fractured in a world of human difference rather than harmony and how the horizontalism that has shaped modernity — the cosmopolitan hearth — still coexists for many, even in the West, with an active urge toward the transcendental.

"In tutto amare e servire" is the slogan on a poster published by the Jesuit Order to celebrate the Jesuit Year of 1991, the five-hundredth anniversary of the birth of its founder, St. Ignatius Loyola. This poster (see Figure 1 on the following page) is a composite image of St. Ignatius's statue that stands over the saint's tomb in the Jesuit mother church at Rome and NASA photo 22727, the latter geographically inverted with the white of Antarctica at the top. The poster's message is both unambiguous and consistent with the aims and role of the Jesuits since their foundation as a Counter-Reformation global missionary order in 1540. Jesuits have spearheaded Catholicism's engagement in Europe's global modernization since its origins in Renaissance oceanic discovery. This image places Ignatius within a vacuum of black space, beyond an earth to which he both gestures and that he appears to offer up to God in a classic gesture of prayerful presentation, his eyes turned along the axis between heaven and earth. It is a cosmic image of a very particular kind, and it prompts us to ask what it is about and how it works.

I suggest here two readings of this image; they are neither unconnected nor mutually exclusive. The first is a familiar critical reading of subjecting the globe to a distanced, mastering, and colonizing Eurocentric gaze that appropriates the surface of the earth to a universal monotheism. The second is a more nuanced reading that does not entirely ignore the first but treats seriously, in the manner that Tuan's work might prompt, that aspect of vision and imagination that is concerned, through contemplation and self-reflection, with the examined life. Both readings locate the poster in a long genealogy of Western global images that have connected the poetics of a spherical earth to both imperial globalism and a more personal, imaginative vision, especially the dream.

Imperial Image: Contemplative Emblem

The most immediate response of a critically sensitive contemporary geographer is that this is an imperial, Eurocentric, and hegemonic image. It stands squarely in the tradition of Western cultural projects that proselytize universal space on behalf of a monotheistic religion, whose offer of universal redemption erases cultural difference and masks the historical actualities of capitalist imperialism.[10] There is much in the image itself to support this. The statue and tomb of Ignatius in the Gesù near the Piazza Venezia in Rome were constructed in

Figure 1. "In tutto amare et servire." Photomontage (1991) of the *Apollo* whole-earth image and the statue of St. Ignatius Loyola celebrating the five-hundredth anniversary of his birth.

1695–97 from solid silver, that imperial tribute extracted by Catholic Spain from the same American colonies where Jesuit missionaries were most actively present. Photo 22727 is the token of the United States's signal Cold War ideological achievement: victory in the space race. It remains the icon of hegemonic American one-worldism. Located beyond this image of earth, Ignatius adopts that patriarchal, mastering position that marks the view from nowhere so profoundly criticized today from the perspective of situated knowledges and polyvocalities.[11] Since their creation, the Jesuits have been regarded by many as the theological storm troops of the papal imperium: in Portuguese India, in China and Japan, as well as across Latin America and the Canadas. Their college in seventeenth-century Rome was the center of a global network of science, an empire of knowledge through which they intervened strategically in the parturition of intellectual modernity.[12] The seventeenth-century Jesuit attempt to "develop a moral, religious, and philosophical framework that connected *all* the different regions of the world" incorporated a geography that was profoundly cosmographic, based on empirical observation, with a special interest in the physics and metaphysics of light and illumination.[13] For the Jesuit Order, scientific knowledge was a dimension of their central mission, captured in Ignatius's motto: "I came to bring light into the world" (Ignem veni mittere in terram). It is an implicitly imperial, monovocal conception of mission, as Athanasius Kircher's illustrations, such as his *Universal Jesuit Horoscope,* showing the global network of provinces spreading the light of faith to the four corners of the earth, make clear. In this reading, then, the image of St. Ignatius with photo 22727 connects past and present within a single and powerful image of Western cultural hegemony.[14]

My second reading suggests a rather softer set of meanings, more vertical than horizontal in their spatiality and more sympathetic to the individualist, humanist tradition in which so much of Tuan's work has been presented (although I do not mean to suggest that this would be his reading of this particular image). This approaches the photomontage as an emblem or icon, in the sense of an object of contemplation through which the individual viewer meditates upon his/her self and life in this world and destiny within eternity. As aids to concentration in the difficult work of meditation, sacred images have a long tradition, especially in the Counter-Reformation Catholic culture from which the Jesuit Order emerged. Ignatius thus stands in the role of mediator, bringing divine illumination to earth in a gesture of faith and love: "I came to bring light into the world." Here too there is internal support within the photomontage for the reading: Ignatius is robed for the celebration of the Catholic Mass, the ritual in which the body of a redeeming God/Man becomes really present at a mundane locale. The saint's gaze is directed not at earth but toward the heavens; one hand passes across the globe as if in a gesture of humility, penitence, and pity. Ignatius thus acts as a mediating individual (as the Christ/Apollo or God/Man himself), located in a liminal space between earth and heaven, a space often figured as that of dreams and transports of ecstasy. Within this reading too, the spatialities of the image have deep historical connections with Western mapping and picturing of the globe, within a tradition that represents the earth as an object of contemplation. I want to examine the genealogy of this emblematic image, for it connects closely to some of Yi-Fu Tuan's aesthetic and imaginative concerns.

The originating text for the emblematic globe is Cicero's *Somnium Scipionis* (Dream of Scipio), from the final book of the Roman writer's *De Re Publica*, in which Scipio Africanus (imperial conqueror of Carthage) falls into a dream during which he is raised into the Milky Way and gains sight of the whole earth at rest, at the center of the celestial spheres. Scipio occupies the same cosmic position as Ignatius in the more contemporary image and is offered an insight into his divine destiny:

> When I gazed in every direction from that point, all else appeared won-derfully beautiful. There were stars which we never see from the earth, and they were all larger than we have ever imagined. The smallest of them was that furthest from heaven and the nearest the earth that shone with a borrowed light. The starry spheres were much larger than the earth; in-deed the earth itself appeared so small that I was scornful of our empire, which covers only a single point, as it were, upon its surface.[15]

The extended surface of the whole earth is a thing of wonder, rendering pathetic the pretensions of even the greatest empire — it is a humbling moment for one of Rome's imperial heroes.

Scipio is shown the structure of the heavens, perfect in form and motion, and Cicero offers his reader a Platonic-Pythagorean explanation of the harmony of their movements, continuing to emphasize Scipio's mediating location between heaven and earth:

> While gazing at these wonders, I was repeatedly turning my eyes back to earth. Then Africanus resumed: "I see that you are still directing your gaze upon the habitation and abode of men. If it seems small to you, as it actually is, keep your gaze fixed upon these heavenly things, and scorn the earthly. For what fame can you gain from the speech of men, or what glory that is worth the seeking? You see that the earth is inhabited in only a few portions, and these very small, while vast deserts lie between those inhabited patches.... [T]he inhabitants are so widely separated that there can be no communication whatever among the different areas."[16]

The passage, indeed the entire text, is a classic statement of Stoic philosophy, of the need for an examined life, of self-awareness and humble recognition of one's telos or destiny.

In the West, the historical and cultural significance of Cicero's text has been considerable, especially during the medieval and early modern periods. This derived in no small measure from the commentary written on it by a late-fourth-century Neoplatonist writer, Macrobius, who used it as evidence for the physical structure of the cosmos and the geographical patterning of the earth's surface. Numerous manuscripts and early printed editions of Macrobius's *Commentary* exist, characteristically illustrated by a world map, which has been closely studied by historians of cartography.[17] In the history of geography the text is usually interpreted as an example of the "four ecumene" theory, which suggested that the known land area of Eurasia was believed to be balanced by similar habitable spaces in western and southern hemispheres of the round earth, and as an example of how classical cosmographic knowledge passed into the medieval world in a corrupted and pastiched way.[18] But here I want to focus on two rather different aspects of Macrobius's *Commentary*: its place as an oneiric text in the evolution of dream theory and, closely connected with this, it significance as a rendering of the Neoplatonic theory of harmony between stable earth and moving planetary and crystalline spheres.

Until well into the seventeenth century, Macrobius remained the key text for Western theorizing on dreams (indeed Jung's dream analyses could be said for some still to give it contemporary credence). The work classifies five dream types, of which three are significant for interpreting the self, one's future, and destiny. These are the *visium* or prophetic dream, the *oraculum* or revelatory dream, and the *somnium* or enigmatic dream.[19] According to Macrobius, Scipio's dream of earth is a *somnium,* but it contains elements of all three, thus placing it in the realm of Macrobius's fifth and broadest category of enigmatic dreams, the universal:

> [B]y gazing up and down he was initiated into the wonders of the heavens, the great celestial circles, and the harmony of the revolving spheres, things strange and unknown to mortals before this; in addition he witnessed the movements of the stars and planets and was able to survey the whole earth.[20]

In other words the dream tells us about both the individual destiny of the dreamer and the nature of material creation itself as an object of conscious contemplation.

Macrobius's classification of dreams was particularly influential in utopian and speculative literature in early modern Europe, where the *somnium* was used as a literary form for the expression of cosmographic theories. Perhaps the best example is Johannes Kepler's *Somnium Seu de Astronomia Lunari* (Lunar dream), in which the early modern astronomer describes the geography of the moon and the utopian society that exists on its surface, among whose greatest delights is "the most beautiful of all sights on Levania...the view of its [the Moon's] Volva [the Earth]. This they enjoy to make up for our Moon."[21] NASA's famous "Earthrise" photo captures on film the vision enjoyed by Kepler's Levanians.

Macrobius's *Commentary* was also a key Neoplatonic text that elaborates the Pythagorean echoes to be found in Cicero's original text. The cosmos is imbued with a Universal Soul, made evident in the harmonious motion that produces the music of its spheres. Commenting on that passage in the *Dream of Scipio* where Cicero claims that

> Men were created with the understanding that they were to look after that sphere called Earth which you see in the middle of the temple. Minds have been given to them out of the eternal fires you call fixed stars and planets, those spherical solids which, quickened with the divine mind's journey through their orbits and circuits with amazing speeds, . . . [22]

Macrobius suggests that Cicero's designation of the universe as a "temple" signifies those visible objects that testify to an omnipotent but invisible Creator and that "whoever is inducted into the privileges of this temple might know that he has to live in the manner of a priest." Further, he states: "in the above passage we are also informed . . . that such a divinity is present in the human race that we are all of us ennobled by our kinship with the heavenly mind."[23] The material surface of the unmoving earth always threatens to distract the human spirit from its true mission, while the vision of the heavens prompts the soul toward self-motion and harmony with the cosmos. This is a standard rendering of the principal features of Neoplatonism: a metaphysics of cosmic harmony, hidden, obscure, arcane, and hermetic to the mundane eye, but made available to the contemplative vision of the intellectual soul operating through the agency of images, number, and symbol that create universal language, for example, the uniquely expressive Hebrew *Tetragrammaton*. This complex of ideas establishes a moral relationship between the human soul and the globe by means of contemplation, poeisis, reverie, and dreaming.

The Macrobian vision continued to attract the attention of philologists and humanists in the mid-fifteenth-century decades when the West was rediscovering and reapplying techniques of number and measure to representations of the terrestrial globe, stimulated by the invention of the printing press and the dissemination of Ptolemy's *Geography* with its tables of location and techniques for constructing the graticule, and by studies in spherical geometry from students such as Brunelleschi and Regiomontanus. We should not therefore be surprised to find poetic translations of Ptolemy's work such as that in 1464 by Francesco Berlinghieri, a member of the group of Medicean scholars led by Marcello Ficino, Lorenzo di Medici's classical Greek scholar and philosopher, who himself was then engaged in a Latin translation of the central texts of hermetic Neoplatonism: Hermes Trismegistus's *Prisca theologia*, supposedly the common source for the three world religions: Christianity, Judaism, and Islam. These were also of course the initial years of oceanic European expansion and of the first terrestrial globes to be produced in the West. The explosion of globe-making and picturing after 1500 coincided not only with Magellan's circumnavigation but with a burgeoning interest in cosmography, incorporating hermetic knowledge, alchemy, and mysticism, signaled by Cornelius Agrippa's *De Occulta Philosophia* (1510/1533). These were also the early years of emblem-making, initiated by Alciati's *Emblematica* (1531), which exploited the connections between visual image, enigmatic text, and contemplative knowledge, while Copernicus's decentering of the Aristotelian globe in favor of a heliocentric cosmos (*De Revolutionibus*, 1536) initiated an eventually revolutionary reexamination of creation and cosmos. The Jesuit Order, founded in 1540 and profoundly engaged from its origins in exploration, knowledge, and observational science, emerged from this complex cultural and intellectual context.

Jesuit Cosmography

The revolutionary impact of Copernicus's work stemmed not merely from its heliocentrism but also from its anti-Aristotelian claim that the earth moves. If the earth moves, it too must have spirit (*anima*); it is one of the spheres; and therefore it becomes appropriate as an object of contemplation and a contributor to the greater harmony of creation. The earth, then, becomes more lovely as an object of contemplation. There is evidence that both Copernicus and many of the church's most thoughtful scholars — the commitment of the Jesuits to education securely placed them in this group — were sympathetic to heliocentrism in part through their attachment to Neoplatonic metaphysics, at least until the theory was decisively rejected by the church at Galileo's trial. Indeed, learned seventeenth-century Jesuits such as Athanasius Kircher, while embracing Tychonian planetary theory as the middle way in the cosmographic dispute of early modernity, seem almost to accept heliocentrism. Thus in the frontispiece to Kircher's *Itinerarium Exstaticum* of 1656, the Jesuit holds his compass and stands next to his angelic guide to the heavens. He is shown against a Tychonian cosmos, rendered at an angle that allows it easily to be read as Copernican (see Figure 2 on the following page). Most immediately significant for the present discussion is that the composition of this frontispiece image is remarkably similar to that of Ignatius and the globe in the contemporary poster.

The *Itinerarium Exstaticum* narrates an ecstatic journey that commences with Kircher being lulled into a dreamlike reverie by sacred music. He is guided angelically on a journey through the heavens, a passage of contemplation and learning that includes a long description of his vision of earth from above. The narrative structure is modeled upon the conventional trope of the *somnia*, dating back through Kepler, Cicero, and Plato. The goal of the dream is enlightenment, that recurrent theme in Jesuit discourse and iconography: "I came to bring light into the world." For Kircher and his fellow Jesuits, the study of light generated complex layers of meaning. It encompassed not only the physics

Figure 2. Athanasius Kircher's cosmographic journey: the frontispiece to *Itinerarium Exstaticum* (1656).

of solar light but more significantly the metaphysics of divine illumination and, most important, the individual light of insight, which yielded illumination and Christian love. To become thus enlightened involved prayerful contemplation, self-examination, and intellectual commitment. This is aided above all through the contemplation of holy images and emblems, perhaps most memorably for the Jesuits the Sacred Heart, whose love is capable of moving the cosmos, as so many Jesuit emblems indicate. This is a rather distinct vision from the "patriarchal gaze" and the analytic optics of Cartesian modernity, one that is closer to the Macrobian, Neoplatonic idea of the *visio* and the *somnium:* an internal vision within the liminal space and time of universal, cosmic, and divine harmony, to which the soul responds. It is characteristic of Jesuit thought as it was refined through the course of the critical seventeenth-century debates with modern thought.

In the light of these considerations we may return to that deceptively simple photomontage of the early 1990s and recognize within it a more complex visual play, one in which "In tutto amare et servire" is at once globalizing and personalizing, both imperial and contemplative. The photomontage may be regarded as an emblem, an object of contemplation in which Ignatius holds his conventional position within Jesuit iconography, bringing light to the world, but a light that is as much interior as missionary. The role of photo 22727 within secular discourse is already ambiguous enough — given the response of both the astronauts who filmed the whole earth and the photo's iconic status as a quasi-sacred image (able to be cast by Kennard as a womb for the human fetus) — for Jesuit artists to place it within the heritage of their own tradition of sacred emblems. The density and impact of the poster derive from this, despite its seemingly adventitious juxtaposition of two historically unrelated elements.

Conclusion

I have adopted a broadly iconographic method here, applied to a single, and by no means widely disseminated, poster image, in order to reflect upon some very large themes, those of the mastering gaze over space and the imperializing imperative of global representations, on the one hand, and of imaginative reverie in the contemplation of the earth picture, on the other. The themes are by no means incompatible; they have long co-existed and indeed supported each other in shaping the European encounter with a global geography.[24] I make no claims about the conscious intentions of those who designed the image in mobilizing these conventions or about how its meanings have been received and interpreted by those who might have seen the poster. Given that copies were displayed largely inside Catholic churches, it is unlikely ever to have received the depth of critical and historical interpretation to which I have subjected it here. Its relevance to the contemporary cultural geographer is twofold. First, the poster offers evidence of continued appeal to the authority of monovocal, globalizing discourses in fields of action well outside those of commercial mass culture that geographers have so assiduously dissected in recent years, and thus of the need to extend the critical scope of geographical study into religious and missionary aspects of contemporary globalization that tend to be neglected. Second, it alerts us to the historical depth and continued fertility of imaginative responses to global geography and the cosmographic sublimities within which global geography is inevitably located. Such responses are easily discounted in our attention to the secular features of contemporary culture, but they remain vital.

In the light of this last claim, the photomontage has some appeal for Yi-Fu Tuan's project of using geography as a reflection on the examined life, a contemporary response to Anaxagoras's answer to the question of purpose in human existence: "We are born for the sake of viewing the heavens and the things there, stars, moon and sun," and the unseen order that sustains them. It offers a rather different and perhaps problematically ambiguous perspective on Tuan's cosmopolitan hearth. To adopt a postmodern textual trick in order to give Tuan the last word here, I (mis)quote the final sentence of his *Cosmos and Hearth*: "Having seen something of the splendid spaces, he or she ... will not want to return, permanently, to the ambiguous safeness of the [h]earth."[25]

Notes

1. Yi-Fu Tuan, *The Hydrological Cycle and the Wisdom of God: The Theme in Geoteleology* (Toronto: University of Toronto Press, 1968); Tuan, *Topophilia: A Study of Environmental Perception, Attitudes, and Values* (Englewood Cliffs, N.J.: Prentice-Hall, 1974).

2. Denis Cosgrove, *Apollo's Eye: A Cosmographic Genealogy of the Globe and Whole Earth in the Western Imagination* (Baltimore: Johns Hopkins University Press, forthcoming).

3. Yi-Fu Tuan, "Topophilia; or, Sudden Encounter with the Landscape," *Landscape* 11 (fall 1961): 29–32.

4. Yi-Fu Tuan, "Surface Phenomena and Aesthetic Experience," *Annals of the Association of American Geographers* 79 (1989): 233–41.

5. Ibid., 235.

6. Yi-Fu Tuan, *Cosmos and Hearth: A Cosmopolite's Viewpoint* (Minneapolis: University of Minnesota Press, 1996).

7. Stephen Toulmin, *Cosmopolis: The Hidden Agenda of Modernity* (Chicago: University of Chicago Press, 1990).

8. On the relations between cosmography and geography in the early modern world, see Marica Milanesi, "Geografia e cosmografia in Italia tra XV e XVII secolo," *Memorie della Società Astronomica Italiana* 65 (1994): 443–68.

9. Denis Cosgrove, "Contested Global Visions: One World, Whole Earth, and the Apollo Space Photographs," *Annals of the Association of American Geographers* 84 (1994): 270–94.

10. James Blaut, *The Colonizer's Model of the World: Geographical Diffusion and Eurocentric History* (London: Guilford Press, 1993); Derek Gregory, *Geographical Imaginations* (Oxford: Blackwell, 1993).

11. Donna Haraway, *Simians, Cyborgs, and Women* (London: Verso, 1994), refers to the "god-trick" whereby an implicitly Western, male reason has historically assumed au-

thority over description and explanation of the material and social world and failed to acknowledge its own partial and positioned perspective. See also Linda J. Nicholson, ed., *Feminism/Postmodernism* (London: Routledge, 1990), for discussion of positioned knowledge.

12. J. D. Spence, *The Memory Palace of Matteo Ricci* (London: Faber and Faber, 1984); P. Findlen, *Possessing Nature: Museums, Collecting, and Scientific Culture in Early Modern Italy* (Berkeley: University of California Press, 1994); Denis Cosgrove, "Global Illumination and Enlightenment in the Geographies of Vincenzo Coronelli and Athanasius Kircher," in *Enlightenment Geographies,* ed. C. Withers and D. Livingstone (Chicago: University of Chicago Press, 2000), 33–66.

13. Findlen, *Possessing Nature,* 81.

14. For further exploration of panoramic vision and geography, see Kenneth Olwig, "Landscape as a Contested Topos of Place, Community, and Self," in this volume.

15. Cicero, *De Re Publica, De Legibus,* vol. 16 of *Cicero in Twenty-Eight Volumes,* Loeb Classical Library (London: William Heineman, 1988), 269.

16. Cicero, *De Re Publica,* 273–74.

17. Tony Campbell, *The Earliest Printed Maps 1472–1500* (London: British Museum Publications, 1987).

18. David Woodward: "Medieval *Mappaemundi,*" in *The History of Cartography,* vol. 1: *Cartography in Prehistoric, Ancient, and Mediaeval Europe and the Mediterranean,* ed. Brian Harley and David Woodward (Chicago: University of Chicago Press, 1987), 286–370, esp. 300, with comprehensive bibliography.

19. For a recent commentary on Macrobius's classification and its influence on Kepler, see Fernand Hallyn, *The Poetic Structure of the World* (New York: Zone Books, 1993), 253–86, esp. 255–57.

20. Macrobius, *Commentary on the Dream of Scipio,* trans. William Harris Stahl (New York: Columbia University Press, 1952), 214.

21. Quoted in Hallyn, *Poetic Structure,* 272.

22. Cicero, *De Re Publica,* 267.

23. Macrobius, *Commentary on the Dream of Scipio,* 216.

24. I develop this argument in *Apollo's Eye.* While the role of an imperializing master narrative in shaping the Western image of global space has been exhaustively examined in critical cultural geography, most recently in Martin W. Lewis and Karen E. Wigen, *The Myth of Continents: A Critique of Metageography* (Berkeley: University of California Press, 1997), they pay scant, if any, attention to imagination and reverie in the response to the global image or map.

25. Tuan, *Cosmos and Hearth,* 188.

BONE-CRONES HAVE NO HEARTH

Some Women in the Medieval Wilderness

Marijane Osborn and Gillian R. Overing

As medievalists interested in the power and presence of the past, we have been drawn to the places of the texts and cultures that we study. As a result, we have taken — and written about — many journeys to Scandinavia and Iceland and have developed an understanding and appreciation of place that has been greatly enhanced by our contact with the field of humanist geography. The expansive perspectives offered by scholars in this field have profoundly influenced how we imagine the places of the past and have added a new dimension to our work as literary scholars in the humanities. Of particular importance are essays such as "Geography, Phenomenology, and the Study of Human Nature" and "Geographical Theory: Queries from a Cultural Geographer" by Yi-Fu Tuan, which, together with his recent *Cosmos and Hearth*, have contributed to our understanding not only of what cultural, humanistic geography actually is but of what it might offer scholars in such disparate fields. Indeed, our title is a conscious response to Tuan's.

The following essay is prompted by our experience of place, of how place interacts with story, especially in Iceland, and although we work and travel together, our essay will reflect our different voices and perspectives. As we have done before, we write in tandem, but not in unison, and thus we have divided the essay into two individually authored sections to facilitate our parallel but separate approaches. We are both inspired by the presence of the "bone-crone" in the Icelandic wilderness, but we are led in very different directions in our attempts to build a context for her. This "bone-crone" that motivates us both is, we should note initially, a pile of stones marking location in the wilderness. Such a cairn is called a *beinakerling* in Icelandic; since *kerling* means "old woman," and one meaning of *beina* (though probably not this one) is "bone," we have the evocative translation "bone-crone."[1] "She" provides a useful focus upon which to project our two different interests concerning women in the wilderness, Gillian Overing's vagrants and Marijane Osborn's "loathly ladies," women who change into trolls. Thus our bone-crone is no mere stone cairn. As she marks a human and gendered path through the wilderness, she crosses boundaries and designates them; she resists categorization on many levels and, indeed, challenges our categories. The first part of this essay, written by Gillian

Overing, will recast some oppositional categories; she will take up some of the peculiarly Icelandic challenges to binary thinking and look at some boundaries that might be crossed or reimagined. Those boundaries between wilderness and civilization, home and travel, margin and center — these are lines to be crossed before returning to the bone-crone and the cultural and literal boundaries of gender that she crosses. In the second part, Marijane Osborn will move farther afield; she will track a variety of wandering medieval women through the wilderness, discovering that the bone-crone's particular ability to straddle categories finds resonance in different literary, mythological, and geographical contexts.

I. Homeless Bone-Crones, *by Gillian R. Overing*

I begin my examination of boundary-crossing by first noting the challenge humanist geographers have made to our binary thinking as medievalists, and some boundaries we crossed. Tuan encourages us to think of self, place, and ourselves in place, as a process, one of situating the self, of negotiating and integrating information on many levels. A landscape "is not a given, a piece of reality that is simply there,"[2] but an effort of the imagination, an "ordering of reality from different angles,"[3] a combining of objective and subjective in the mind's eye. The terrain of place is then substantially internal, the picture made within the frame of individual perception. Tuan's richly developed analyses transform a self/place binary into a dialectic and require that we consider our own role in the creation of landscape: the implications of Wordsworth's "mighty world / Of eye and ear — both what they half create / And what perceive."[4] As medievalists presently contemplating the places of the past, we are presently implicated in our creation of the past; place becomes a prism of semiotic convergence, where the literary, the historical, and the cultural are in ongoing negotiation with the geographical, the material, and the personal.

Tuan's emphasis on the embodiment of the self brings home our fundamentally physical relationship to environment, and his arguments have produced some productive parallels in hypothesizing a medieval sense of place.[5] Such physical connections to space and place reveal an intimate level of bodily inscription.[6] We map our world, our spaces and places, with our bodies, even as our body is inscribed by them, and when we place this dialectic — both physical and political — in the context of medieval Iceland, some challenging anomalies emerge. The clear territorial imperative of the settlement of the island and the development of the Freestate (930–1262),[7] which provides the setting for the majority of the sagas, invites the question of to what extent the landscape is bound up with identity and how ownership and identity are connected. Indeed, what does the idea of ownership connote to a group of scattered individuals claiming and naming often hostile terrain, farming and surviving on the periphery of a vast and unforgiving wilderness that comprises the uninhabitable center of the country? The socialized margin interacts with and is conditioned by the spatial centrality of wilderness. So things are inside out, as it were, to start with. The margin is the center, and the center is the wilderness — a point I'll come back to.

The sacred nature of the homeland common in classical antiquity must be substantially revised in the context of two general observations about Iceland and Icelandic culture. The first is the nature of the terrain, something that has changed relatively little since the time of the sagas; "land of fire and ice" may sound rather like a tourist brochure (in fact, it does come from a tourist brochure), but it accurately suggests the varieties of landscapes — eerie, stark, beautiful — made possible by both volcanic and glacial activity. When one discovers in *Egil's Saga* how Egil, a notorious Icelander and Viking who started killing at the age of six, tends to calm down when he returns home to Iceland, that he is content to farm his land and leave "most men in peace,"[8] one wonders about the power of place. The larger-than-life characteristics of this most violent of Icelanders are subdued, perhaps balanced out by the exacting realities of his home. This Viking meets his match in his home.

What indeed might home be to a Viking? This leads to another general observation about Icelandic culture — the cultural and political importance of the capacity to travel. The capacity to travel, the tradition of travel, the political freedom to travel, all of which characterize the society of the sagas — How are these factors involved in defining that which is home? "Home as refuge is the reverse of challenge and strain," writes Tuan. "To travel is to take risks, to be aware of inhospitable lands and circumstances; the experience of insecurity, by providing contrast, intensifies the identification of home with security and rest."[9] But surely the connotations of negativity, of security and insecurity, must be commuted, or perhaps their relation to each other might be rearranged in the context of the medieval Icelander's experience. One might even postulate travel as a distinct cultural value, both ethical and material. Perhaps we can see the Vikings as potential "cosmopolites" — albeit a touch on the barbaric side. Their hearth possesses a truly "ambiguous safeness,"[10] an ambiguity that is communally experienced.

April Veness argues in this part against differentiating cosmos and hearth and for their inseparability and mutuality of definition. The Viking cultural experience and the cultural and cosmological imagination of the medieval Icelander "at home" bring their specific complexity to such mutuality, however. The extent to which the self must be refashioned as it moves from hearth to cosmos — a point that Veness takes up from Tuan's discussion in *Cosmos and Hearth* — raises some interesting questions. Initially, describing, indeed isolating, a self/place dynamic may also represent an arbitrary kind of carving up of the spectrum of Icelandic experience. Kirsten Hastrup asserts that "time, space, quality, society, and individuals seem to coalesce"[11] in the Icelandic notion of *veröld* (world), which combines *verr* (man) with *öld* (age, epoch). Hastrup contends that "measuring the world in Iceland was a matter of collating temporal, spatial and social realities";[12] moreover, her spatial analyses of Icelandic horizontal cosmological and vertical social models reveal a pervasive symmetry, suggesting that "concepts of cosmology and society were mutually enforcing realizations of what seem to have been a basic conceptual structure."[13] There are many ways in which temporal, spatial, and social realities merge. A brief, but key, example: the concepts of geographical place and the law merge completely in the Icelanders' single term for their land and their society: *vár lög* (our law).[14] The law is land is country is society. When the Icelandic Viking leaves "home," different rules apply — or perhaps a different purchase on the cosmos: bigamy, for example, was illegal in Iceland, but in moving to another place, and hence another time, a man could legally marry a second time.[15] On the one hand, we might postulate the Vikings as possessing dual "selves" and that hearth and cosmos are qualitatively different; on the other, the Vikings are well known for their remarkable powers of cultural assimilation — both to assimilate and be assimilated; they are "at home" in such disparate early medieval cultures as those of France, Constantinople, and England. If travel represents a vital urge to engage the cosmos, to leave home, then the Icelander's already deeply cosmologically aligned view of and from home might encourage at least a fluidity of identity and suggest that a single cultural form, here that of "home," can contain elements of both cosmos and hearth in dynamic relation.

The Icelander "at home" lives within the legal and literal confines of *vár lög*: that which is "outside" the law — literally and legally — is the opposite and the negative of the "social," that is, the "wild." This division of inside/outside permeates social and legal conceptions of space, beginning at the microlevel of domestic spatial arrangements and extending to Icelandic cosmological geography. "Outside the fence" (*útangarðs*), or beyond the periphery of the central farmhouse, the terrain of the non- and antisocial unfolds in legally gradable degrees until the *óbyggðir* takes over, the vast uninhabited center. But here too boundaries are continually challenged, and the notion of "wilderness" exists in ongoing tension with elements of the social. The famous Icelandic outlaw/hero Grettir shares this negative space with a variety of supernatural beings (trolls, giants, elves) and others on the outs, as it were, with society, or without social identity, such as runaway slaves. The boundaries between the social and the wild are not only questioned but problematized and redrawn by the enigmatic figure of Grettir, who is himself a bundle of contradictions; he is preternaturally strong and afraid of the dark; his often casual violence is offset by a talent for poetry and magic and a clearer understanding of the law than that possessed by those who have outlawed him. Grettir inhabits this *óbyggð*, the uninhabited place, revealing a remarkable talent for survival; his contradictory stance and progress speak the dialectic between the center and the margin, and the instability and reversibility of both.

One might place women closer to the "wild," too, though at the more social edge of this spatial spectrum. "Womanspace" is peripheral, on the edge: sons inherited the central farmhouse, while women inherited the "outlying lands" (*útjarðir*).[16] But it must also be noted that a traditional Western binary is disrupted in the Icelandic gendering of space — the association of the female with "nature" and the male with "culture." Recent anthropological analyses of agricultural divisions of labor suggest both a traditional and contemporary association of women with the human world, and their unambiguous relation to culture, in conjunction with an ambiguous, but continuous, male relation to the nonhuman and natural worlds. "Icelandic farm-life represents an instance of the 'wild' being associated with maleness on the general level," a "wild" that presents a threat to women who have "to remain inside the social for protection."[17]

What place, then, for the bone-crone of our title, who ranges far outside the social? Not only does she cross boundaries like outlaws, slaves, and a host of supernatural elements, but she also marks a boundary, and as such she stands for the particular complexity, social and geographical, of the Icelandic construction of the "border." She disturbs our boundaries. I think of her also as a means of asking questions about the relation of gender stereotyping to social and geographical space and of examining how different social groups — in this case the subculture represented by old(er) women — are situated in relation to the polarities of home and journey, wilderness and civilization, cosmos and hearth.

The alterity of Icelandic culture does not transcend or avoid the stereotyping of the old woman so prominent in European medieval culture.[18] Old women (a category very hard to define in terms of actual years — these are usually women past childbearing age) are associated with a spectrum of evils, from gossip to sorcery to sexual predation throughout the sagas. Such "evils" associated with old women can also be understood, according to the argument of social function, as characteristics developed most often by old women in order to retain a viable function in a community. "Threat by witchcraft or appeal to supernatural agencies, by rousing public opinion through gossip and public complaint," such are the "mechanisms used by the aged to ensure support."[19]

A vagrant woman who was not supported by any one community, but made a living providing news and gossip as she traveled from one area to another, was designated a *førukona* and perhaps is still — the death of a gossip-woman named Trippasigga being recorded as recently as 1964. Traditionally, when such women die, travelers erected a cairn in their memory and must either add a stone or write a poem in honor of the *beinakerling,* the "old bone-woman" or "bone-crone" — our preferred if more folkloric translation. There are in fact two such memorials currently documented: one is in Kaldidalur in southwest Iceland, complete with poems or rhymes — often sexualized and ribald; the second is in Sprengisandur, the very heart of the uninhabited center of

Iceland — a testimonial perhaps to the far-ranging beat of the *førukona*. The *førukona* claims a specific social function as newsbearer — though we cannot say whether her vagrancy, her homeless aspect, is chosen or otherwise. Quite how the community function of newsbearer or storyteller becomes conflated with its more negative counterpart of gossip and derogatory sexualization is a matter for speculation; so too is the nature of the complex transaction that the bone-crone enables between the "conversational" aspects of both hearth and cosmos[20] — the cosmopolitan ability, in fact, of the wandering woman to negotiate these territories and modes. What I would like to emphasize here in conclusion, however, are the material connections between actual social function and gender stereotyping.

This is *not* to suggest that deep-rooted pancultural stereotypes involving fear and hatred of the old female body may be explained away as effects of voluntary social role acquisition. The stigma attached to old women is profound and profoundly negative overall.[21] But perhaps it is possible to contextualize the stereotype and localize it within the specific geography of Icelandic social practice. The bone-crone tells a story of community, of location, and of boundary-crossing; she informs the traveler, in body and in effigy, but does not escape sexualization even as a pile of stones; her news is welcome, her tales are cautionary. This wandering woman may be both welcomed and feared by the community. She has no community of her own, but she connects one to the other. What to do with her? She creates confusion and a degree of discomfort because she does not fit. The Icelandic solution? Make a memorial to her. And in so doing, Icelanders actively, practically, and visually engage her as an oppositional model. The capacity to acknowledge, engage — even celebrate — paradox is for me peculiarly Icelandic; oppositions, especially those least reconcilable, are entirely permissible, pervasive in so many aspects of both medieval and contemporary Icelandic culture, where lines remain permanently — and wonderfully — crossed.

II. Alone in the Wild, *by Marijane Osborn*

Whereas the gossip-women of Gillian Overing's discussion traditionally travel through the wilderness in groups, going from farm to farm, my interest is in a particular boundary-crossing that is *not* permitted, the passing of a woman alone into the wilderness, perhaps to live there. The title of our essay makes reference to Yi-Fu Tuan's book *Cosmos and Hearth,* which beautifully documents two impulses innate to most of us, the wish to go out, to explore, and the comfort we find at home. The impulse to range outward into the "cosmos" has long been associated with men, whereas our culture conditions us women to believe we should stay at home, be pretty and sweet,[22] and tend the hearth. Medieval texts confirm this view. As one Anglo-Saxon poem says:

Figure 1.

> It is meet that a woman remain by her table;
> Wandering, she will stir up words....
> Often, she wrinkles early.[23]

Another Anglo-Saxon poem places even more emphasis on female stasis as a woman speaks of a man far away:

> I tracked the wide-ranging hopes of my Wulf
> when it was rainy weather and I sat weeping.[24]

He goes, she sits still, presumably by her hearth. But our title refers to someone far from home and hearth, the figure of the "bone-crone" (*beinakerling*), the pile of stones marking a human path through the central wilderness of Iceland and also serving as a mailbox for messages (nowadays mostly risqué verses). Although the translation "bone-crone" draws on a folk-etymology,[25] this type of cairn is represented as female through long tradition. The photographs in Figures 1 and 2 show an apparently female image that someone has placed on top of such a bone-crone, with Wincie Jóhannsdóttir (see note 1) standing alongside the cairn to indicate its size. This bone-crone pile of stones, in its dual function as wilderness sign and mailbox, serves as an icon for the two different but related topics that we are addressing in our essay: homeless old women who, normally traveling in groups, find a social function as bearers of messages,[26] and younger women at risk of losing their human identity when alone in the wilderness, being "transformed" into hags or trolls. Women *alone* in the

Figure 2.

wild, whether in Britain or Iceland, do not have medieval culture's permission to be there.

We see this again and again. When Thomas of Erceldoune, in the fourteenth-century romance of that title, sees a beautifully dressed woman alone in the wilderness, he claims her as his rightful prey:

> If thou be parelde moste of prysse,
> And here rydis thus in thy folye,
> Of lufe, lady, als thou erte wysse,
> Thou gyffe me leve to lye thee bye.[27]

> [If you, apparelled with such show,
> Come in your folly riding by,
> For love, lady, as you must know,
> You give me leave with you to lie.]

Even more interesting than his outrageous attitude is her response. If he rapes her, she says, she will change into a hag, a loathly lady — like the famous shape-shifting hag encountered at the forest's edge in Chaucer's "Wife of Bath's Tale."[28] Nevertheless, Thomas does rape the lovely lady, and she does change, apparently becoming "loathly" mainly because she is now disheveled, no longer ornamental. It happens elsewhere in medieval stories that ladies beautifully done up are regarded as "fair," and as soon as disheveled become "foul."[29] Crossing into the wilderness can have a similar effect upon a woman. In the following stanza of the ballad "The Marriage of Sir Gawain" (Child Ballad

31, from Bishop Percy's manuscript), the Loathly Lady, after changing back to lovely, tells how she got to be loathly. It is the usual wicked stepmother story known from "Snow White," but observe how this particular stepmother has tried to get rid of the beautiful girl. Freed from her ugliness, the now lovely lady explains:

> She witch'd me, being a faire yonge maid,
> In the green forest to dwelle;
> And there to abyde in lothlye shape,
> Most like a fiend in helle.[30]

To this ballad story may be compared the ballad "Kempion" (a version of Child Ballad 34, "Kemp Owyne"), in which the lady likewise explains that her enchanter was her "wicked stepmother" (stanza 16). In this ballad, however, she turns about and curses her stepmother — to become an animal (a wolf?) living in woods where "worms" (dragons) dwell:

> Her hairs grow rough, and her teeths grow lang,
> And on her four feet shall she gang.
> None shall take pity her upon,
> But in wormes wood she shall ay won [reside].
> (From stanzas 17 and 18)[31]

It seems that merely by cursing her to live in the forest the stepmother of "The Marriage of Sir Gawain" turns the fair young maid into "lothlye shape," and the similarly mistreated stepdaughter in "Kempion" avenges herself with poetic justice for a similar crime upon her person.

"Oft lurks a troll-woman under a fair skin," says the Icelandic proverb ("opt eru flogd í fogru skinni"; *flogd* = troll-woman). My theory is that it is not wilderness itself that has the dehumanizing effect of turning a woman into a hag but the lack of a "hearth" and all that goes with it in the way of personal human attachments, attachments that offer an emotional reason as well as the facilities for looking after one's appearance. Snow White is saved from such a curse when the seven dwarves give her a hearth and an equally warm family. The lack of attachment, and the ensuing loathliness that goes with that lack, can be terrifying. In *Skírnismál,* one of the poems of the Icelandic *Poetic Edda,*[32] the man named Skirnir goes to court the giant maiden Gerðr on behalf of his master, the lovelorn god Freyr. When she rejects his bribes of (age-defying?) apples and a magic ring, Skirnir offers her various threats including decapitation. In reply she says scornfully, "Coercion I shall never endure / at any man's desire" (stanza 24). But then he threatens her with his "taming rod" and a curse that will make her "go where the sons of men / shall never see you again . . . / on an eagle's mound,"[33] and where when captured she will be "a spectacle when you come out" (stanzas 26–28). Skirnir's serious threat and his gesture toward implementing it finally elicit Gerðr's promise to "grant love" to Freyr. To be cast alone into the wilderness, without men or the looks to attract them, is apparently the worst fate this beautiful giantess can imagine (in this probably male-authored poem). It is a worse fate than being bullied into having sex.

Skírnismál is myth. When women in Icelandic stories set in real-world geography are forced to live alone in the wilderness, there is a good chance they will become trolls. This change does not seem to happen to men; both Gisli and Grettir, heroes of their respective sagas, live for many years as outlaws without "shape-shifting" into another kind of being. Perhaps this is because, though each outlaw had a heavy price on his head, neither was wholly cut off from the nurture of family and community.[34] Perhaps if they had been more isolated, they too would have become trollish. But the stories suggest that women in the wilderness were more vulnerable to this change. I shall now briefly illustrate this thesis with two more Icelandic stories about women, Helga and Jóra, who cross that forbidden boundary between hearth and cosmos, and I will conclude with some suggestions about that greatest and scariest of all troll-women, Grendel's mother.

Helga, in the first of these stories, is the daughter of Bard of Snæfellsness, whose saga was composed around 1300.[35] She gets caught on an ice-floe and carried to Greenland, where she falls in love with a married man in Erik the Red's colony there. When her father, Bard, finds out, he goes to fetch Helga and bring her home. "She grieved and faded away ever after," says the saga, and Helga composes a poem about her longing in which, rather like the Anglo-Saxon woman quoted above, she says, "I cannot conceal my sorrow. / I sit alone and recount my misery" (35). Shortly thereafter "she went away and took to neither men, animals, or lodgings. She lived mostly in caves and mounds.... She went everywhere secretly, always far away from people" (35–37). Helga is seen only twice in later chapters of the saga, briefly as the foster-mother of her half-brother and even more briefly at a banquet in a cave, sitting on the same bench as Jóra of Júrukleif (69). The saga-writer's associations of her with cave-dwelling and with Jóra suggest that her misery and isolation have turned this woman into a troll.

Jóra clearly becomes a troll. Briefly, this is her story. Jóra is a farmer's daughter, young and promising but thought to be rather moody. One day she takes her father's horse to participate in a horse-fight. When she sees him losing, she flies into a rage, tears off his leg, and races away to hurl it into the nearby river. Then she leaps across the river at a place, the story says, that "has since been called either Troll-Woman Leap or Jóra's Leap." She climbs the cliffs (now called Júrukleif) up into a cave, makes her home there, and "she became the worst troll, and did damage to both men and beasts."[36]

The Icelandic verb "to do damage" is *granda*, which reminds one of the name of Grendel, the man-eating monster fought by Beowulf, hero of the Anglo-Saxon poem.[37] After Beowulf wins that fight by tearing off the creature's arm, Grendel's mother comes, the poet says specifically, to avenge her son (line 1278). This act of vengeance is one of several items that identifies the monsters as partly human; another is their descent from Cain (e.g., lines 1261–66). Without prolonging the discussion, I'd like to propose that such violent, alienated beings as Grendel and his mother are troll-like (or wolf-like, see lines 1506 and 1599)[38] in proportion to their alienation, their life in the wilderness, and that their mysterious and isolated lifestyle itself dilates them, makes them monstrous in others' perceptions. Their kinship with Cain perhaps curses them as Cain was cursed, to dwell "as a fugitive and a vagabond on the earth" (Genesis 4:12), that is, in the wilderness.

Life in the wilderness is hard, a matter that brings us to another interesting dichotomy attested in Old English and Old Icelandic texts. Anticipating Tuan's statement that "Home . . . is the reverse of challenge and strain," the *Old English Rune Poem* suggests that cosmos is "hard" and hearth is "soft":

> Riding is easy [*sefte:* "soft"] for warriors sitting in the hall, and very strenuous [*hwæt:* "hard"] for one who bestrides a powerful horse travelling the long roads.[39]

Writing on gender in Old Icelandic literature, Carol J. Clover asserts that "the ideal man is *hvatr* [hard] and the typical woman is *blauðr* [soft]."[40] This opposition corresponds closely to that in the *Old English Rune Poem*, *hwæt* [hard] and *sefte* [soft]; the first pair, *hwæt/hvatr*, are exactly cognate, and the second pair, *sefte/blauðr*, are semantically identical. Clover adds that "each [ideal man and woman] can, and does, slip into the territory of the other."[41] For example, in pagan Scandinavia it was the woman's duty to "whet" (Old Icelandic *hvettja*) or harden the purpose of the man in order to make him perform his murderous duty in a feud.[42]

In this context I like Clover's geographic metaphor about each slipping into the other's territory, because these examples suggest that the distinctive territories of cosmos and hearth are themselves gendered in this culture in terms of hard and soft. Unlike mournful Helga and mad Jóra, alienated from home and family, Grendel's mother apparently possesses a hearth of some kind in her hall (there is firelight in lines 1516b–17 and 1570), even though that hall is situated magically under a lake. I suggest that as soon as a woman becomes identified at all with a place and a relationship, even if it is a place in the wilderness and the relationship is with a monstrous offspring, she is likely to have a hearth, however alien her manner of living and her home. Just as home is traditionally part of the concept of being human, a hearth is associated more specifically with comfort (softness) and with the female, especially motherhood. A mother is, moreover, by definition in relationship to her child, no longer a woman alone in the wilderness. These factors, Grendel's mother's hearth and her relationship, "soften" her, complicating what would otherwise be an undilutedly evil, cannibalistic, troll-like, wolf-like, almost genderless[43] demonic force preying from "out there" upon "us," here by the hearth. While women out there in order to survive must become *hwæt* or *hvatr*, sharpened and whetted, this hardening itself makes them "unnatural"; Grendel's mother, with a hearth of her own and a son whom she seeks to avenge, gains a degree of our sympathy despite our horror. Like the other bone-crones, both vagrants and trolls, whom we have evoked in these two linked essays, she becomes liminal. Even as antagonist, she straddles our rigid categories.

Afterword

Our two perspectives on travel in medieval places, and on women "out of place," come together in the presence of the Icelandic cairn from which we have appropriated the term "bone-crone" to mark female presence in the wilderness. Gillian is concerned with old women traveling and Marijane with women transformed by wilderness exile. Such concerns prompt us to ask questions about liminality and border-crossing in terms of gender and to travel within and across disciplines ourselves. As in our imaginations we follow old women and troll-women across the enticing but dangerous and gendered terrain of the bone-crone, such a journey necessarily forces us to consider, through the lens of humanistic geography, foundational and peripheral aspects of our own discipline.

Notes

1. The evocative translation "bone-crone" is by Wincie Jóhannsdóttir in *The Visitor's Key to Iceland*, ed. Örlygur Hálfdánarson, Wincie Jóhannsdóttir, and Steinthor Steinthorsson frá Hlsöðum (Reykjavík: Íslanska Bókaútgáfan, 1996), 391 and 401; this is a revised and updated version of *The Iceland Road Guide*, ed. Steinthor Steinthorsson (Reykjavík: Örn and Örlygur, 1975). I am especially grateful to Wincie Jóhannsdóttir for her insights and suggestions throughout the various stages of this essay.

2. Yi-Fu Tuan, "Thought and Landscape: The Eye and the Mind's Eye," in *The Interpretation of Ordinary Landscapes*, ed. D. W. Meinig (Oxford: Oxford University Press, 1979), 100.

3. Ibid., 90.

4. William Wordsworth, "Lines Composed a Few Miles above Tintern Abbey," in *The Norton Anthology of English Literature* (New York: W. W. Norton, 1979), 157.

5. This was part of our intention in our previous collaborative work. See Gillian R. Overing and Marijane Osborn, *Landscape of Desire: Partial Stories of the Medieval Scandinavian World* (Minneapolis: University of Minnesota Press, 1994). The present essay takes several of its premises from the earlier work, and I shall refer the reader throughout this shorter essay to *Landscape of Desire* for more detailed discussion of Icelandic spatial characteristics.

6. See *Space and Place: The Perspective of Experience* (Minneapolis: University of Minnesota Press, 1977) for Tuan's most detailed analysis of physical relations to space. He details the many ways in which language reflects body/space connection, via folk measurements, for example, which often reflect body parts or functions, as in a "handful," a "foot," a "stone's throw," or "within shouting distance." He asks that we consider the spatial implications of a phrase like "we are close friends" or the self/other split in spatial language indicated by the parallels of we = here, they = there, and hence "us" set against "them" (*Space and Place*,

50), an early argument that reaches a new and rich complexity in the discussion of China and the United States in *Cosmos and Hearth: A Cosmopolite's Viewpoint* (Minneapolis: University of Minnesota Press, 1996).

7. For an expanded discussion of the development of the Freestate, see Overing and Osborn, *Landscape of Desire*, 50–52. The following discussion of aspects of the Icelandic relation to place refers extensively to this earlier work. See especially the section titled "Iceland and Icelanders," 48–55.

8. *Egil's Saga*, trans. Hermann Pálsson and Paul Edwards (Harmondsworth, England: Penguin, 1976), 176.

9. Yi-Fu Tuan, "Geography, Phenomenology, and the Study of Human Nature," *Canadian Geographer* 15, no. 3 (1971): 189.

10. Tuan, *Cosmos and Hearth*, 188.

11. Kirsten Hastrup, *Culture and History in Medieval Iceland* (Oxford: Clarendon Press, 1985), 68.

12. Ibid., 61. See Overing and Osborn, *Landscape of Desire*, 48–50, for examples of conceptions of time and their connection to social and legal realities and for a discussion of place-naming and directionality as these reflect the Icelanders' sense of place.

13. Kirsten Hastrup, *Island of Anthropology: Studies in Past and Present Iceland* (Odense, Denmark: Odense University Press, 1990), 25.

14. Hastrup, *Culture and History*, 121.

15. Ibid., 91.

16. Ibid., 191.

17. Hastrup, *Island of Anthropology*, 279.

18. For further discussion of old women in medieval Iceland, see Gillian R. Overing, "A Body in Question: Aging, Community, and Gender in Medieval Iceland," *Journal of Medieval and Early Modern Studies* (forthcoming).

19. Corinne N. Nydegger, "Family Ties of the Aged in Cross Cultural Perspective," *The Gerontologist* 32, no. 1 (1983): 30.

20. See Tuan, *Cosmos and Hearth*, 174–77.

21. For a discussion of medieval negative stereotyping of old women, see Shulamith Shahar, "The Old Body in Medieval Culture," in *Framing Medieval Bodies,* ed. Sarah Kay and Miri Rubin (Manchester: Manchester University Press, 1994), 160–86.

22. Tuan discusses such flower-like prettiness in *Dominance and Affection: The Making of Pets* (New Haven, Conn.: Yale University Press, 1984), in the midst of a discussion of harem and seraglio (123–28) and citing work by Eleanor Perenyi. He brings up and questions the traditional and "innocent" association of women with gardens — another enclosed space, like the home — and the prettiness of flowers: "Are these images and things so innocent? In the Western world as elsewhere, flower connotes beauty, but also a certain useless passivity and frivolity. *Du bist wie eine Blume.* You are like a flower. The 'you,' of course, is a woman and the comparison is meant to flatter her. A man, thus compared, would feel insulted" (126).

23. These lines are from a composite poem, joining several Old English texts, that I translated as "The Fates of Women," in *New Readings on Women in Old English Literature,* ed. Helen Damico and Alexandra Hennessey Olsen (Bloomington: Indiana University Press, 1990), xi–xiii. This part is from "Maxims I," lines 62–65, in *The Exeter Book,* ed. George Philip Krapp and Elliott van Kirk Dobbie (New York: Columbia University Press, 1936), 159.

24. This is my translation of lines 9–10 of the ambiguous poem "Wulf and Eadwacer," in Krapp and van Kirk Dobbie, *The Exeter Book,* 179–80. The controversy about the word *dogode* in line 9, that I here translate "tracked," is not important to the present argument. I discuss it in some detail in "*Dogode* in *Wulf and Eadwacer* and King Alfred's Hunting Metaphors," soon to be published in *American Notes and Queries.*

25. Heimir Pálsson explains that a likely etymology of *beinakerling* makes the first element *beini* (weak masc.), meaning "provisions," so that this *kerling* or cairn is simply "the

pile of stones where you eat your provisions for the day." He confesses, however, a personal liking for the folk etymology (e-mail message, July 24, 1997).

26. The most famous group of these women messengers appears in chapter 44 of *Njal's Saga*. Hallgerd, chief mischief-maker of the saga, invites these "talkative and sharp-tongued creatures" (*Njal's Saga*, trans. Magnus Magnusson and Hermann Pálsson [Harmondsworth, England: Penguin, 1960], 114) into her private room to talk. The talk provokes a man named Sigmund to make up some malicious verses about Njal, so the beggar-women go next to tell Njal's wife about the conversation. As a result, Njal's sons kill Sigmund. Though settled by compensation at the Althing, this is one of the events leading to the crisis of the story. The carrying of (chiefly malicious) messages is the primary function of socially inferior women, not necessarily old ones, in the sagas.

27. The Middle English text is from the anthology *Middle English Literature*, ed. Charles W. Dunn and Edward T. Byrnes (New York: Garland, 1990), 467. The imitative verse translation that follows is my own. Compare Child Ballad 37, "Thomas Rymer," in Francis James Child, *The English and Scottish Popular Ballads* (New York: Dover, 1965), 317–29.

28. See "The Wife of Bath's Tale" in *The Riverside Chaucer*, ed. Larry B. Benson (New York: Houghton-Mifflin, 1987), 118. "Loathly Lady" is a standard folklorists' term for the woman capable of changing shape between attractive and loathsome forms, though we usually see her first as a hag then as a beautiful young woman.

29. The present discussion merely touches on the woman's forfeiture in the wilderness of the tame and flowerlike prettiness demanded by life in a "cultivated" milieu (see Tuan's discussion of women and gardens in *Dominance and Affection*, cited in note 22). Such loss, however, is the primary symptom of her becoming a hag and is alluded to in several of the sources quoted here.

30. The stanza is from *Ancient Ballads Selected from Percy's Collection* (London: Vernor, Hood, and Sharp, 1807). We are told the ballads in the collection were selected by "A Lady."

31. These words are from Bertrand Harris Bronson, ed., *The Singing Tradition of Child's Popular Ballads* (Princeton, N.J.: Princeton University Press, 1976), 96.

32. The most recent complete English translation of the poem is in *The Poetic Edda: A New Translation*, trans. Carolyne Larrington (Oxford: Oxford University Press, 1996), 61–68. I quote from her translation, p. 65.

33. Ursula Dronke, who interprets the poem as a *hieros gamos*, observes in passing that in his curse Skirnir invokes the picture of a life that is a parody of the gods' life: "[Gerðr] will be mocked as a travesty of Heimdallr, sitting in her uncouth hideousness on the edge of hell, as he in his radiance sits at the edge of heaven; she will be given goat's urine to drink, while the gods drink the mead that flows from the udders of the goat Heiðrun. Her life will be no life but living death" ("Art and Tradition in Skírnismál," in *English and Medieval Studies Presented to J. R. R. Tolkien on the Occasion of His Seventieth Birthday*, ed. Norman Davis and C. L. Wrenn [London: Allen and Unwin, 1962], 206). P. R. Orton compares the woman's threatened situation in the Old Icelandic poem with the actual situation in the "Wife's Lament," positing a mythic source for the latter and arguing, as others have, that her cavern under an oak tree is a cult site ("*The Wife's Lament* and *Skírnismál*: Some Parallels," in *Úr Döslum til Dala: Guðbrandur Vigfússon Centenary Essays*, ed. Rory McTurk and Andrew Wawn, Leeds Texts and Monographs [Leeds: University of Leeds, 1989], 205–37). Although the speaker of "The Wife's Lament" is living in a solitary place, the fact that she weeps with anger and longing but is not "loathly" suggests that she considers herself still within the realm of human community.

34. *Gisli's Saga* is translated (as *The Saga of Gisli*) by George Johnston (London: Dent, 1963), and *Grettir's Saga* by Denton Fox and Hermann Pálsson (Toronto: University of Toronto Press, 1974).

35. *Bárðar Saga* is edited and translated by Ján Skaptason and Phillip Pulsiano (New York: Garland, 1984), to which the page numbers in parentheses refer.

36. I have copied, transcribed, and translated the brief account of *Jóra frá Júrukleif* from http://www.snerpa.is/net/thjod/jora.html. I was referred to this site by Heimir Pálsson, to whom I am most grateful. (See note 25 above.)

37. I use the text of *Beowulf and the Fight at Finnsburg,* ed. Fr. Klaeber (Boston: Heath, 1950). The association of the verb *granda* with *Grendel* is not meant to have etymological validity any more than does the evocative translation "bone-crone."

38. At line 1518, Grendel's mother is described additionally as a *grund-wyrgen* ("warg of the depths"). Association of the term *warg* with the concept of the wolf has been traced as far back as the Hittite law codes and is relevant to the present examination insofar as both words seem to be applied to persons outlawed "beyond the pale," that is, legally and geographically displaced from the human center. The term is discussed by, among others, Mary R. Gerstein, "Germanic Warg: The Outlaw as Werwolf," in *Myth in Indo-European Antiquity,* ed. Gerald James Larson (Berkeley: University of California Press, 1974), 131–50. In my opinion, by developing the werewolf associations, Gerstein over-romanticizes the meaning of *warg* (possibly influenced by Tolkien's fictions). The term is in need of further analysis from a more sophisticated juridical and geographical perspective.

39. The rune described here is called *Rad* ("Riding"). The translation of these lines by Maureen Halsall is from her volume *The Old English Rune Poem: A Critical Edition* (Toronto: University of Toronto Press, 1981), 87.

40. Carol J. Clover, "Regardless of Sex: Men, Women, and Power in Early Northern Europe," *Speculum* 68 (1993): 377. Clover goes so far as to suggest that in early Icelandic society "there was finally just one 'gender,' one standard by which persons were judged adequate or inadequate, and it was something like masculine. What finally excites fear and loathing in the Norse mind is not femaleness per se, but the condition of powerlessness, the lack or loss of volition, with which femaleness is typically, but neither inevitably nor exclusively, associated. By the same token, what prompts admiration is not maleness per se, but sovereignty" (379).

41. Ibid.

42. In *Old Norse Images of Women* (Philadelphia: University of Pennsylvania Press, 1996), Jenny Jochens devotes two full chapters (chapters 7 and 8) to the role of the female inciter, adducing many illuminating examples from both literary and historical sources.

43. The poet refers, for example, to Grendel's mother with the masculine pronouns *he* at line 1392 and *se* at line 1497. The most famous women to inhabit or at least range the wilderness of our culture, women whom our word *bone-crone* inevitably calls to mind, are the witches that reached the height of their notoriety some two centuries after the end of the medieval period addressed in this essay. They are the topic of chapter 9 of Tuan's *Landscapes of Fear* (New York: Pantheon, 1979). Much has been written since, both in anthropological discourse and in terms of Wicca apologetics, about these persecuted women. "Witches" in other cultures abound. One thinks, for example, of the Cherokee Spearfinger, who waits in the mountain valleys of North Carolina to scoop the liver out of the unwary or dying with her long, pointed fingernail.

BUT IT'S (NOT) SUPPOSED TO FEEL LIKE HOME

Constructing the Cosmopolitan Hearth

April R. Veness

Normative definitions of home have long been used to construct and legitimize geographies of inclusion and exclusion. Statements indicating that *these* are the habitats rightfully called home, or *those* are the habits appropriately practiced at home, not only set social and spatial boundaries but send strong messages. People who unwillingly or unwittingly find themselves "un-homed," because their physical and/or emotional worlds break social convention, have few options. They can defy convention, as many homeless people do when they declare that their cardboard encampments, abandoned cars, or carved-out spaces below city streets are home.[1] They can alter their appearance, attitude, or action to fit social expectations. Or they can maneuver a middle path that alternately challenges social convention, abides by expectations, and slowly assembles human experience into contexts of meaning and value.

In this essay I look at how a graduate student, while at university, ambivalently yet ambitiously negotiates a path between the known and comforting world of home, or hearth, and the unknown, not-meant-to-be-homey world of the cosmos. On the surface this transition looks like it should be a straightforward process, for the university has long been viewed as both home-away-from-home where students abide by the rules of *in loco parentis* and as a way station where students learn lessons essential to their successful exploration of the larger world. Thus the combination of resources from hearth and cosmos could be expected to smooth the way. In addition, the displacement she and others will experience in graduate school is a corollary of growing up, moving away, and going beyond what is already known. Therefore the transition would be a natural and universal experience. But, as her words will soon show, the frustrating and sometimes painful experience of being displaced from hearth while seeking emplacement in cosmos is neither natural nor evenly distributed. The experience is highly structured within the context of a particular place and time, and it is organized around assumptions and practices that unnecessarily and differentially undermine successful navigation. The institutional structure of the university, in particular graduate school, harms and hinders people — is an unhealthy and less-than-moral place — partly because it does not take seriously hearth-based knowledge.

Before I examine the experiences of a graduate student and develop my argument for hearth-based knowledge, it is beneficial to examine, however briefly, the type of place the university's academic department wants to be. Here I take my lead from Yi-Fu Tuan. His book *Cosmos and Hearth* provides us with an intellectual construct and possible name for the type of place the university might be: the "cosmopolitan hearth."[2] In the last chapter, he also begins to sort out the lineaments of such a place: what it might look like, how it might sound, and what one must do to get and stay there. Given Tuan's expressed wish in the book to move beyond traditional conceptions of cosmopolitanism so that hearth-based human attachments and diversity are regarded, the prototypical cosmopolitan hearth he offers is an exciting way into the university as a place combining cosmos and hearth. With Tuan's help, then, I might begin to understand the academy as well as the student's experiences of it.

On first glance Tuan's cosmopolitan hearth looks like a rich and equitable union. From the cosmos come the universal ideals of reason, truth, and human commonality. From the hearth come emotions, social structures and conventions, and individual/cultural differences that make us unique. Together, one presumes, they create a context within which the full breadth of one's humanity can be experienced. In the language Tuan uses to describe some of the roles performed by cosmos and hearth, however, it soon appears that what hearth brings to the partnership is provisional. For instance, Tuan urges us not to accept human emotions at face value. Though they are an inescapable part of human life, by their very nature they are dangerous. Powerful emotions we may bring to the cosmopolitan hearth must be evaluated, watched, and harnessed, so to speak, by the trustworthy half of the marriage — the rational, reflective, and imaginative mind that operates in and defines cosmopolitanism.[3] As Tuan walks us through the attitudes and actions that define his cosmopolitan hearth, cosmos or the intellect always has the upper hand. Cosmos frees us from the demands of convention and the disruptive, divisive emotions that derail conversation and undercut the ability of cosmopolites to achieve larger loyalties. Cosmos offers us critical reasoning and conversations that make mutual exploration toward a greater understanding and good possible. Without cosmos, conversation is rutted in "social talk," "gossip," and "admonition."[4] Thus, "[c]onversation," of the type critical to the cosmopolitan hearth, "is an accomplishment of the cosmos rather than of the hearth. When it does take place at the hearth, between husband and wife (for instance), it is evidence that the hearth has been infiltrated by the cosmos."[5]

Tuan's reluctance to let hearth speak for itself, with all its limitations and possibilities, regrettably weakens the overall beauty of the cosmopolitan-hearth project. His inclusion of hearth in an otherwise cosmopolitan world-order admittedly pays some attention to the attachments and commitments that people have at a nonuniversal level. This compromise inclusion even earns Tuan recognition as a leader in the political and philosophical move to redefine cosmopolitanism so that it will address the "multiple attachment[s]" that people actually hold.[6] But throttling hearth in the process, as I interpret Tuan's effort, makes his cosmopolitan-hearth project more reactive than proactive. Scholars, like Tuan, who have adhered to the modernist underpinnings of traditional cosmopolitanism have been challenged for some time by feminists, postmodernists, communitarians, and others. These critics of traditional cosmopolitanism have argued there can be no single universal truth; all knowledge is situated or relative; and ideas, just like human relationships, are shaped by power relations embedded in particular places, time frames, and social hierarchies.[7] Tuan's concerned response to this outright repudiation of cosmopolitanism by many intellectuals (intellectuals, incidentally, who were brought up on and once embraced cosmopolitan ideals, says Tuan) may help explain both his construction of the cosmopolitan hearth and his insistence that cosmos governs it.[8]

Hearth's Influence on Cosmos

Given the importance of the cosmopolitan-hearth construct to our understandings of contemporary conflicts and concerns, it is important to examine critically what hearth is and what, exactly, it can do to make the world a better place. Because hearth is rarely studied but often stereotyped, it is narrowly depicted in either cozy sentimental terms or suspicious critical terms. As the traditional domain of women, children, and marginalized people, hearth often becomes a place filled with lovable (albeit potentially evil), frisky, but ultimately trainable people. Though hearth and cosmos are both "imagined places" to some extent, hearth is a decidedly grounded and real domain. Yet because we do not examine hearth for what it is, it frequently becomes what we cannot find and do not want in cosmos. Paradoxically, in time we come to accept that the lessons learned from the head are trustworthy while the lessons learned by heart are not. As long as there is a fundamental distrust of human nature and knowledge formed in the hearth, our ability to imagine and construct possible worlds where the full range of human need and experience are accepted is impeded. Similarly, our responses to the many injustices and excesses of hearth will be partial at best, reactionary at worst.

We cannot avoid, then, the fact that real-world ideological skirmishes, unequal social positions, and emotional repertoires that cannot be erased or overcome by the reasoning mind will shape the actual experience of getting to the cosmopolitan hearth. Because people are embedded in specific contexts, any examination and evaluation of the cosmopolitan hearth as an ideal and practice would have to be grounded in concrete situations structured around place, time, hierarchically arranged social relations, hegemonic models of the universe, and the powerful import of peoples' feelings. Likewise, the cosmopolitan hearth would have to deal with "embodied" aspects of our human state: our body type, sex, race, age, physical abilities, and other social definitions of us such as class and social position.[9] These largely indelible attributes of self and identity affect how people converse, think about the world, and undertake their everyday activities in specific places.

An extensive literature, popular and academic, now informs us of the many ways that gender, for example, shapes human life. From Deborah Tannen's best-seller, *You Just Don't Understand: Women and Men in Conversation*, to Carol Gilligan's influential book, *In a Different Voice*, we learn that our conversational styles and philosophical positions are shaped by the emotional worlds we inhabit.[10] Indeed, some feminist scholars argue that the "ethic of care" women use in their daily lives and communications markedly contrasts with the more individualized rights-based ethics and exchanges used by men and that this ethic may go further toward alleviating injustice and harm than others.[11] Yet other scholars do not see the "ethic of care" as specific to women.[12] As the human skills and knowledge that people learn "at home" gain overdue recognition, they are being introduced to the classroom, workplace, and community by men and women in professions as diverse as medicine, the ministry, and higher education.[13] These developments all positively suggest that our emotional repertoire, as well as our intellectual repertoire, is valuable throughout our lives and in all walks of life.

To gain a fuller understanding of what a cosmopolitan hearth is and can be, I now turn to the thoughts, feelings, and understandings of that place from the perspective of a Ph.D. student in the first two years of her program. From her personal writings, which describe and analyze the cosmopolitan hearth that she knew, we learn about a person and place. My purpose in using her narrative, however, is not so much to expose her person — her insecurities, anxieties, and emotional or intellectual limitations. My purpose is to situate her personal experiences within the context of a concrete place in order to show how "micropolitical structures" direct the nature and flow of her ideas (knowledge), her practices (conversations), and her emotions (needs and expressions of self).[14] By demonstrating that her experiences are structured, I wish to initiate serious conversations about the nature of the academy as an institution, the possibility of designing a cosmopolitan hearth that would take emotional resources into account, and the role of place in the creation and reproduction of im/moral worlds.[15]

Most of the information I will share is recorded in the handwritten pages of the student's journal; several selections are letters given to her by others and tucked into the pages of the journal. In her writing she indirectly "speaks" to her adviser, to her department, and to her family, and, on some occasions, she passes on her thoughts in letter form to others. As we listen to her descriptions of that place and look at the difficulties she experiences adjusting to this place, I will attempt to show that all conversations, from the trivial to the most intellectual, are grounded in the emotional systems of the speakers. The cosmopolitan hearth that the student imagines and experiences is not exactly like the one outlined by Tuan. For her, an ethic of care in which emotion is central permeates all aspects of her intellectual life.

Conversations in the Cosmopolitan Hearth: A Case Study

The student described in the following narrative is both bewildered and excited by the array of highly charged ideas circulating around her. While she is keen to try them out and thus to try on the identity "professional geographer," getting into the conversations that define the cosmopolitan hearth is no simple matter. One generation removed from her family's WASP working-class background, and a woman in a male-dominated profession, she appears to have too little of the cultural and social capital that could have positioned her more securely in the cosmopolitan hearth of academia.[16] Yet the student's Middle American, small-town past — a past that insulates some young people and nurtures in them a naive belief that all is right with the world and that they are snugly centered in this world — may well have given her a shorter list of injuries and fuller sense of self-confidence when she entered university.[17] But it did not prepare her for the boot-camp environment of graduate school. Her social position in the larger society and personal baggage mark and sometimes stymie her progress. Likewise, the physical, social, and political aspects of the department itself hamper conversations and easy progress.

Obvious to anyone who visits the department where this student studied is the awkwardness of the site itself. Spread across several floors of a high-rise office building, the public spaces in the department are confined to dark, narrow hallways and small foyers outside the elevator doors. These uniformly unpleasant spaces do not invite people to pause in conversation; rather the spaces are executed with efficiency. Because there are no classrooms in the office building and no designated "lounge" space within the department, there is also none of the ebb and flow of students periodically massing and drifting past office doors. Without the background banter and movement of people to fill the hollow corridors, those conversational exchanges that do take place in the hallways run the risk of being broadcast through sound tunnels. So, instead of being granted a measure of privacy in which to try out conversation in public performance space, nearly all conversations, all interactions, require some degree of self-conscious monitoring.[18] Undefined or unprofessional engagement, then, could be construed by others as suspicious lurking, idle ambling, inappropriate emoting, or worse.

Given the physical attributes of the site, it is no wonder that the student interprets the nonverbal messages conveyed in head nods, diverted gazes, and rushed movements as "stay-away postures," "suffer-alone silencing," and "economized civilities." It is not just the site constraints that make one feel viewed and judged at all times. The place-ballet reinforces the feeling that if you are not a key actor with a clear role to play, you should quickly adopt a bit part, refrain from impromptu lines of interaction, stand aside, and passively observe what others say and do. In contrast with the emotional and social permissiveness this student apparently experienced in other departments — departments that called on a socio-emotional repertoire closer to what she learned and practiced at home — this place is ponderous: "I look around me for the glance, the warmth, the harmony. All I see are the backs of people hurrying to another spot. . . . There is no cohesion, no glue to this group. With so many 'concealed identities' it is impossible to see where our edges fit together." Some of the messages she reads from the physical and social environment — such as "you sink or swim on your own devices" — are hard and cold.[19]

Living in a Cool Climate

A number of months into her studies, the student does have a chance encounter in the hallway with a more senior female graduate student whom she rarely sees and knows only tangentially. Rather than their same-sex exchange being automatically familiar and supportive because it rests on similar assumptions, backgrounds, needs, and life goals, it is awkward and alarming to the student. In the following piece, titled "Primrose Path for Me or Thee?" the student remembers this exchange and how it affected her:

> I met Jan in the hallway one afternoon and wearily proclaimed that on completion of my dissertation I hoped that every indifferent, sterile sage would realize the senselessness of his shortsighted ways. Jan's retort was swift and sure. "Fuck them," she snapped, "I wrote mine for me, for my satisfaction, and care nothing about their thoughts."
>
> My embarrassment was immediate. Words intended to be powerful were nothing more than pin-striped pretensions poking out of a poesy-patterned pinafore. My stainless-steely reasoning that recognition should be linked to difference, fertile imaginings, and commonsensical investments in the long haul was but an old-fashioned heirloom. Self-assertion, self-fulfillment cannot be pinned to the ruffles of feeling. Surely I, a woman who entered adulthood on Norinyl 1+50 [a birth-control pill], knew better than to thread my confidence through the eye of the other.
>
> DOWN WITH THE DUSTER, IGNOBLE NEEDLES, SERVANT'S PRAYERS.
> WHY SEEK ACCREDITATION ON SOMEONE ELSE'S BACK STAIRS.
>
> When I'm sitting alone, struggling over the notes scattered across my desk, I remember that moment in the hallway and sadly consider the futility of the unrest. If the effort is to *master, claim* knowledge, *define* what

is fair, then to do "just" for me is simple: call forth verve and enact self-verification. But if the hope is to *matter, find* knowledge, *refine* fair, then such me-type justice is ultimately barren. While crossing imprisoned abstractions with courageously fought battles is hybridization visibly grand, it exists for a harvest. Next generation we all lose the stand.

Archaic forms that long served and preserved us — discarded, disembodied, demoralized. Thy balance is missing, not valued. In thoughtlessness all are denied.

Although Jan and the student each sees herself gaining recognition and acceptance by resisting a gendered expectation of politeness, they move toward this position differently. The student demonstrates her self-worth by privileging the notion that hard work and competition give her success along with the "guys" (and by smugly thinking that the guys would, one day, regret how they divorced themselves from their feelings and fuller senses). Conversely, Jan seemingly disabuses herself of both the myth of meritocracy and the mental anguish of worrying about rebuke from her professors. Jan transgresses traditionally "masculine" and "feminine" modes of making it, thereby maximizing her shared identity with feminists presumably within the academy. Her proclamations, however, effectively exclude and shame the female student who does not share Jan's ideas.[20] Embarrassed by the power of Jan's remark to put her in her place, the student examines the outdated conventions and parochialism of her own self-identity and tries to emulate a 1980s feminism she vaguely comprehends. To activate a new set of emotions, which would then initiate a new set of ideas and actions, she writes and recites an imagined feminist mantra. But any participation in the emancipation parade is halfhearted. For whether she chooses to follow this group of women into the cosmopolitan hearth, chooses to stay behind in the hearth with another group of women, or tries to adopt the footpath of the men, her sense is that all of these could well be the proverbial primrose path. None of the choices are right for her. Ignorant of ideologies, metanarratives, and identity politics that promise to package self and social salvation for the price of getting on board, she sits sullenly at the curb.

Today, years after this graduate student penned her thoughts, I wonder if she was anticipating at a very experiential level some of the limits of the modernist, feminist, and postmodernist projects that we talk about today.[21] Her gut-level objections to (modernist conceptions of) reason over emotion, (early feminist conceptions of) galvanized womanhood, and (postmodernist conceptions of) fecund hybridity may have been the "outlaw emotions" that Alison M. Jaggar urges us to accept as evidence that something is wrong with the status quo.[22] When our intellectual understandings straightjacket what we know by heart to be true, it suggests that our better guide here is our emotions and not our intellectualizations. As this example suggests, emotional acuity and confident, skillful deployment of our creative and critical emotional capital could be a trusted and valued component of the cosmopolitan hearth.

Instead of her foray into conversation with Jan being a supportive encounter, the student feels more uncertain afterward. Implicitly instructed to discount her gut feelings, she reaffirms the sociological order of the cosmopolitan hearth she inhabits and seeks truth via a process of discursive conversion. Her stowaway emotions niggle and unnerve her so much that she writes: "I am unable to continue this way. I can neither compromise nor conform, and because I am so unable to fit in I am doomed to perpetual disappointment and failure." Vulnerable to emotions that cannot be dismissed, she feels immobilized. "I cannot bring myself to see you, [my adviser]," she writes to herself, "though I had such wonderful visions of enlightenment, and helpfulness, coming from you to me." Before she can participate in the intellectual conversation she has to get herself out of an emotional bind. And that means thinking through the problem. What she sees and writes about in the next journal entry is the impossibility and unfairness of exorcising personal feelings from conversations. In "Attention and Response" the student gives a reasoned plea to bring concrete lessons of hearth to the cosmos, not as a crutch or convenience but as a matter of necessity and justice:

> I would not mind so much that attentiveness necessarily prods and peels back the illusory and protective layers that obstruct vision. Nor would I mind that the excitement, satisfaction, self-congratulation following attentiveness is momentary. I would not mind any of the many reasons we have for fostering the attentive genius . . . required to pursue truth, knowledge, and explanation, if, with equal honesty and zeal, attention to the experiential aftermath of this quest was encouraged and admissible.
>
> If only the suppressed and denigrated emotions and dissembled responses to revelation were given audience too. If gratefully released tears were allowed to wash the unsettled emotional debris of our diggings and disturbances from our eyes. If restorative, humbled yearnings were allowed to stand in for the defensive detachments and approved inattentiveness. If concerned assurances, sincere advice, and, yes, possible misunderstanding were allowed to keep the doors of dialogue open. If agile arms and emotional comfort could enclose and shelter those caught short and exposed. If we had the ability to recognize and respond to the un-attended effects of attentiveness on others and ourselves.

The student's ruminations about the emotional foundations needed to build ease and trust, recognition and mutual support, and an ethic of care in the department eventually do encourage her to seek her adviser. One afternoon she enters his office, sits down, and asks, "Why is it so unhome-like here?" Without hesitating or turning the table around to question her question, he simply and gently replies, "But it's not supposed to feel like home." She did not demand to know "why not?" or launch into an argument for home. She politely stays in her seat until she can slip out the door to compose herself. When she recounts that episode in her journal, her embarrassment, fear, and foreboding are mentioned. Because she trusts her adviser's worldliness and wisdom, as well as his kindness, she accepts the blanket explanation, feels the weight of its layered meanings, and folds it into her head and heart. She is uncertain about whether his comment is specific to the transitional nature of graduate school and its connections to personal growth. Or whether he is indicating that public settings such as workplaces, where a boundary is traditionally maintained between one's personal life and professional life, must not feel like home. Recently, scholars have shown that the boundary between work and home has been gradually erased as more and more women enter the workforce.[23] But this current understanding could not comfort her then. Instead, the message she took away was that emplacement—feeling that you belong—must be a decidedly political process.[24]

With this knowledge tucked away, the student intersperses her less frequent, less enthusiastic face-to-face conversations with her adviser with regular journal entries where she boldly, albeit secretly, speaks to him. Not only does this put distance between her not-supposed-to-be-here emotions and the institutional culture of the department, but it also gives her the separate space she needs to negotiate a viable position for her views and her self. As the next several journal entries show, the student resists a full-fledged elimination of emotion at the same time that she operates within the constraints of place. Though she insists on her individual emotional rights, insists on the value of emotions in this place, she distances her emotions by transposing them into words on a sheet of paper. Self-consciously creating a subversive conversational space closer to hearth than is institutionally sanctioned, she is both undercutting the power of *this* place and empowering a different geography, one where response-ability is part of conversation:[25]

> Sitting here, thinking about the easiness and stimulation of our talk this afternoon, I am taken by the newfound sense of encouragement and confidence I feel. Dare I hope that the interludes of awkward retreat from his office in disappointment are ended? . . . Before I had always felt cheated, stranded offshore without the supple support of the surf beneath me, guiding me to a new and instructive beach. I kept returning to the same familiar coast, always on my own power, never suspecting I had the ability to swim to a further location or that if I were patient a wave might come along to propel me to that end.
>
> If I sit quietly in that chair facing his desk and listen to the stillness, do I detect his thoughts in motion? How long should I wait? Have I mistaken this silence as thought-in-the-process-of-being projected, when, in fact, it might be the indentation separating paragraphs? Am I negligent and

late for my response? Or is he forming a transition in the communication that would relay back to me the meanings we were in the process of creating?...Knowing when to say nothing, to trust that silence is not dismissal, disinterest or dismay is one of the more difficult lessons of my life.

The student's reflections about the techniques required of conversationalists in the cosmopolitan hearth — techniques to enter, stay in, and become an equal participant — show that it is no easy matter. Part of the problem, a problem that the student understands well, is that words, silences, and body language are imbued with meanings that make sense only within a context.[26] To understand the conversational etiquette, she needs to learn about the place and people there. She also needs the confidence *not* to presume that conversational awkwardness is due to her failings. By coincidence the student's adviser gives a departmental seminar on the notion of attention that, in turn, gives her more of the information she needs to understand her dilemma. And after his talk, she apparently writes him a note. This prompts him to respond to her with the following letter:

> Thank you very much for your note. I am reassured to think that [my] talk on "attention" is not altogether without sense....I think it is true [what you say] that people ruthlessly repress their sensitivity and capacity for attention except along narrow channels. Culture — all cultures, though to different degrees — encourages, and indeed insists upon, such repression, according to (among others) the anthropologist Jules Henry....Attention, as I choose to understand the term, is unnatural — a bit antilife. It does threaten social life and cultural norms, and hence also biological life because the latter can hardly survive without the former. Thinking itself, except in the limited instrumental sense, is rather unnatural....
>
> Attention is the special calling of academicians. Tenure, by providing us with a degree of economic security, is supposed to help us to attend courageously and (if necessary) over an extended period of time. But we seldom attend, as you say. If we do attend, society will be deeply shocked and will withdraw what little support it gives us.
>
> Attention, unlike purposeful thinking, doesn't guarantee tangible results. That's why it is an act of adventure and of courage. On the other hand, attention is sure to have an effect on us, on the sort of person we are, on what we consider to be important, on our every gesture and thought.
>
> It is too difficult to attend. That's why, at the end of my talk, I suggested that when we cannot attend we should plunge through our normal state of awareness to the total indifference — the unjudging indifference — of a pebble in the sun.

Unwilling to let her adviser's ideas go unattended, she jots some thoughts on the margins of his letter. Her remarks examine the ethics of response-ability, the politics of indifference, and the impossibility of conversation without context, without dependence on something, some force in the universe. She writes: "But to rest as a pebble in the sand is to resign one's humanness and become the insensate object of outside forces beyond one's control. Even the harmless, inanimate, unjudging indifference of the pebble can become an irritant or danger to the world surrounding it. Indifference is *not* neutral. The pebble can crush sand into fine powder by its larger size, and if carried across the beach on a wave it can leave a trailing imprint — a scar — on the sandy surface. In a *social* world can we afford not to attend?"

Microgeographical Realities

Other students in the department are also thinking about the social structures and social forces that shape human thought and action, but these departmental conversations typically look at the issue only at the macro level. What makes the student's perspective a bit different is its inclusion of emotions along with thought and action and her interest in structures and forces at the institutional and interpersonal level. In another journal entry the student writes about a meeting the Chair convened with graduate students, a meeting meant to assuage student anxieties about current and future professional lives. Calling a meeting does indicate that the department was paying some attention to student needs; however, journal entries indicate that the Chair's argument that successful credentialing depended entirely on the individual merit, savvy, and actions of students was not appreciated.[27] The student also takes issue with the Chair's assessment:

> I cannot accept your conclusion that grad students are "dumb" or "undaring" if they do not actively solicit and follow faculty advice, make themselves known, and cover all the bases in the course offerings in order to make themselves more marketable. It is unfair for faculty to place responsibility for student performance and success entirely on the students' individual prowess; likewise it would be wrong [for students to attribute their insecure or unimpressive standing in the academic community] solely to the unresponsiveness and insensitivity of faculty. Somewhere between one side being guilty and the other being innocent is a possible understanding of why enthusiastic daring may be missing.

The student's response to the Chair indicates that the department's institutional culture, along with the everyday practices employed to reproduce this culture, is not being considered as a possible force in the personal and professional lives of the student body. The terms of inclusion — what students should think, do, achieve — are pitched within a model of self-determination (students as knowledgeable agents). But the actual process by which citizenship in the profession is conferred is structured both within the larger context of the job market and within the peculiarities of place-based hierarchies and politics. Meanwhile, the amount of "emotion-work" involved in moving into and through the cosmopolitan hearth of the department is substantial.[28] Refashioning self, rearranging priorities, recognizing the thoughts, actions, and limited emotions that will be vital to one's survival in the cosmopolitan hearth, and establishing a type of comportment deemed "professional" are exhausting labors. Required is a sophisticated knowledge of what Candace Clark calls the "microhierarchical arrangements of social places" and access to those resources needed for a "social actor to know what line of action to take towards others in the socioemotional economy" of a given place.[29] Significant as these microgeographical arrangements are to place and self-identity, they are rarely recognized or discussed.

Unsurprisingly, the student often wonders "Why am I where I am?" and worries about whether this place is right for her. In part her concern is generated because there is no public conversation about the significance of emotional, social, and cultural capital within the institution. Instead of seeing the structurally unequal placement of students, including her, for what it is, the department looks for deficiencies within the players. Told this enough times, she questions her own capabilities: "On every turn I seem to bump my arm or leg. Though the external bruises vanish they become points of continued sensitivity and awareness. Charging out on my own I can expect a collision of some sort. Is that because I am clumsy, or because obstacles are placed in my path? Maneuvering in the maze of the uncertain is a lonely achievement [for] no one else can share in your excitement or your misery.... Wearied, disillusioned, and alone I see little reason to uncork those emotions that drive beliefs."

Still feeling powerless to steer a passage through a strange system, in part because the emotions that would animate her beliefs and actions are largely "outlawed," she follows the path prescribed to her. Trustingly she anticipates the moment when her self-identity will be aligned with place-identity. Her impatience with a merger too slow to materialize is distressing. Confused and uncertain, in her journal she seeks solace: "Oh, adviser, I am not a geographer. I am nothing even remotely similar to the persona created in our academic institutions. A battle ensues inside me, a constant warfare for co-existence. Must I relinquish one identity to assume another, despite how regrettable that loss may be to me?" Again, the student questions both the terms of inclusion and the consequences of admission if she fully identifies with the group called "geographer."[30] Unbeknown to her, professions often do have what Eliot Freidson calls an "occupational cartel ... [that] must be able to control the number of people who enter the field so as to maintain relative scarcity and to control as well the competitive behavior of its own members."[31] Although the clubbiness and gamesmanship often elude and exclude her, she stays the course and silently complains: "How I dislike this 'game'. But it, in fact, ceases to be a game when it assumes the importance and necessity — the internal inertia — of a process all on its own. It is more like a perpetual metamorphosis, a constant alteration of self into some ill-defined 'ideal' that even long-time participants cannot fully pin down. Why is this group, or any group, so important and essential to our self-validation and ability to live? Where or what is my group, adviser? Is there a resting place where I might feel at one — at home?"

Making Home at the Margin

Over time, as the student gains some distance and critical perspective on the institutional culture of academia and the personality of her department, she is better able to evaluate this world on some of her own terms. Place-experiences and place-imaginings, along with exercises in socioemotional management, are addressed in this allusive piece of prose titled "Homecoming Day." In it she exposes and critiques the hypocrisy she perceives:

> Jaunty gusts grab corners of secured and shuttered windows
>   imploring lightness, ritual bonding, revelry.
> But too much hurt lies in this courtyard in between us,
>   the common place of which you speak I cannot see.
> Onto this scene of drifted affects, thrown open slapping madly,
>   I draft adroitly bending distant willow tree.
> Then inch by inch past patched and pointless actions
>   wish there a space which takes and makes the whole of me.
> As awesome rainbows atop taut fields and harvest bounties,
>   can sometimes hem a purple sky, hem misery.
> Could untold honesties, fair minds and human heartbeats,
>   achieve the promise that we made with these degrees?

In this striking contrast between the emotion-suppressed environment of academia and an imagined place where people give and make place for one another, the student invokes an ethic of care. Though she looks to the comforting hearth-like image of a willow tree, she never speaks of retreating to this past. Instead she attempts to link past, present, and future in a yet-known place — in her version, perhaps, of a cosmopolitan hearth.

Through her self-reflective creative writing and critical conversations this student secretly practices her intellectual and emotional skills, slowly develops a detailed assessment of the place she inhabits, and constructively imagines a cosmopolitan hearth in which the microgeographical arrangements are more humane and just. The student's journal entries suggest that although communications between students are sometimes tinged with envy and insecurity, they are nevertheless filled with respect and affection. After one conversation with a friend, she writes:

It was reassuring to know that I'm not alone in my resigned disaffiliation. Fran, too, felt the pain and bitterness, and we both agree on some of the causes. The nature of this faculty, the hierarchy within the graduate students, the in-tact and handed-down paranoia, the temporariness of grad life, the mismatch between genders and relationship statuses, and the varying degrees of cynicism and snobbery are all involved. Fran is looking forward to leaving here — her escape from emotional bondage. Such a waste of opportunity, reciprocity, and happiness.

So far my focus has been on the department as a place that shapes identity and self. But graduate students do not spend all of their time in the institutional setting; nor are all institutional settings as difficult to understand and negotiate as the one portrayed in this narrative. Each student brings her own knowledge and experience to a department, and with every coming and going there is the continual refitting of people into places and place into people. The rhythm of resignation/resistance seen in previous journal entries is broken in this next entry. After a summer largely away from the university, the student muses over some of the adaptive strategies used by students and faculty in the cosmopolitan hearth. For one, there is the seasonal change of wardrobes between summer, autumn, and winter — the addition of "layers of concealing clothing" that to her becomes a ritual burial of self and emotion. Neither blindly accepting nor boldly challenging the situation, the student sees the collective cocooning for what it is — a structural adjustment made to protect human beings from the inhospitable elements of the academic environment. "In some respects, the loss [of self] is comforting — we are back into the season of school. Institutionalized actions, routinized and regulated emotions, patterned projections of hierarchically defined roles all direct our thoughts as well as our repertoire of responses. New and returning grad students and faculty members enter with emblazoned emblems of self, but within a month or so they become fused into a standard semblance of self."

In the process of doing the emotion-work needed to survive in the cosmopolitan hearth, group identity and unity — a semblance of home — were being created. But her increasingly familiar yet ultimately contrived niche was hardly a healthy one, as she knows, deep down, when she asks: "What is left for me? I am 27 years old. While my intellectual horizon looks broad and intensely bold (if I can stake it out), my emotional concourse appears dank and dark. The tension within me has taken the form of separating my mind from my body, allowing my intellect the unbounded freedom of uncharted flight while consigning my heart to a future of restricted and predictable outcomes."

Women in academe are particularly susceptible to messages that the mind and body are separate spheres and that the mind rules in the cosmopolitan hearth.[32] The emotional deadening demanded by the cosmopolitan hearth is a problem for everyone, however, if it undermines what people can accomplish.

Too much intellectualization can cripple the human spirit, as we see in the following passage:

> I wonder if I'm truly alive. I do so much less than I am capable of and would like to do; yet at every turn where I would spurt into an enlivened gallop — hair flying wildly in the draw — I think of the destination of this romp and refrain. I don't know the destination? No, it's not that I have a fear of the unknown. Rather what holds me back is an accumulation of what I *now* know — the pragmatic concerns of effectively and efficiently guiding myself through a course laden with many implicit rules and regulations. I feel as though I am forever rehearsing.

Without unselfconscious emotion, her life feels too staged, too disciplined — too dishonest. To be the sure, savvy, and daring type of student that the department publicly endorsed meant following a path to a possibly insalubrious site and unlivable situation.[33]

As the student realizes all too painfully, each incremental step taken toward the center of a cosmos-dominated cosmopolitan hearth, each degree of relative comfort achieved there, involves a corresponding loss. The tug-of-war, between wanting to put her intellect through the exercises and needing emotions to tether her, plays itself out in the following reflections about a holiday visit with her family. In her journal the student writes that her mother, eyes welling with tears and voice trembling, muttered, "We are losing you," as she hugged her daughter goodbye. That unnerving comment, along with uncomprehending comments from her husband, siblings, and grandmother, lead the student to conclude: "What I say and write to them has no meaning." Her growing wisdom and worldliness may bring applause, but the sound of clapping hands cannot move the earth under her feet as hands clasping hers can do. She also sees how erudite pontifications can baffle and abuse.[34] No longer centered in her family's world, and stranded at the edge of a cosmopolitan hearth that she admires and yet deems amoral in some of its practices, the student defends her position while apologizing about its impact:

> Sometimes I see myself and my movements and thoughts so well. It is as if they fit into the set of data I am observing, and they reinforce whatever partial understandings [of the world] I have arrived at.... And knowing my commonality with the larger group encourages me to come forward and speak of my observations with passion and unfailing zeal. I press for audience, I demand to be heard. But why? Is it that what I have to say is so important, or that I, like others, feel that my own presentation of self takes priority?... These [words] are not pearls to be admired and accepted; I do not intend or mean to present them as such...I am not aware of any scheme in the back of my mind to usurp power or calculatingly gain attention.... [So] just because I happen upon some key that opens a door

to my awareness and understanding does not mean it is — I am — capable of doing the same for anyone else.

It is clear that moving into cosmos creates a backwash that touches people in the hearth and leaves them with experiences for which there were no plans or preparations. The ability or act of transcending the hearth is not automatically good, especially when it causes pain to others. Had the emotional resources and moral lessons learned at the hearth been more equitably paired with the intellectual ideals and commitments of the cosmos from the beginning, perhaps the impasse faced by this student and those around her would not be so striking. As it is, the student in the narrative uses the subversive spaces of her heart and mind to engineer a place that feels a bit more like home than it was supposed to, a place that is more moral than it acts.[35]

Cosmopolitan Hearth as a Healthy and Moral Place

It would be easier to dismiss the economized civilities, performance anxieties, social-intellectual cliquishness, and credentialism of academia as occupational hazards if they were not so potentially harmful to human beings and, ultimately, scholarship. When a second Harvard graduate student in two years committed suicide in 1998, the cool emotional climate of the chemistry department and the underdeveloped emotional and psychological abilities of both students and faculty were identified as factors.[36] Since then, Harvard administrators have acknowledged that the academic environment is "most stressful" and that students are "increasing[ly] fragil[e]," and they have initiated institutional changes that might better support the emotional well-being of their campus community.[37] Yes, the cosmopolitan hearth is not home. But it does not follow that emotions associated with home would be better, or could ever be, left at home. Emotions will be included in conversations of every type in and out of the hearth. Our task is to understand and tend to emotions as well as we have understood and tended to ideas.

This means that we academics must pay more attention to what is learned and brought from hearth to academic departments as well as other places. By taking seriously our emotional worlds, valuing the emotional capital that people have with them, and examining the intersection of emotions and place-based micropolitical hierarchies, we would not only discover much about this largely unexplored institutional place. We would come closer to understanding those groups and individuals who misuse and abuse hearth-based knowledge. Quite possibly, caring and responsiveness will be one of the most effective means we have to approach emotionally charged social groups who angrily and hatefully pull themselves apart from society, righteously recite recipes for exclusion, and defiantly match every reasoned argument for commonality with a reason to regroup. Success in responding to emotions will depend on whether

we can listen to, understand, and trust our own emotions enough to comprehend those of others. The challenge is how to bring hearth-based knowledge
into the world, not whether to bring it.

I wish that responsive conversations in and out of the cosmopolitan hearth
would automatically produce geographies of equality or magically restructure
reality. That is not likely. Attention to hearth in our own lives as well as in the
lives of the students we teach, the people we know, and the groups that we
wish to study and understand can be a commitment and course of action. This
will not restructure the world, but it might speed us along in redistributing
some of the human resources that support dignity, activate ideas and actions,
and allow each of us to negotiate the lives that we are given and make. And it
might bring out in us the ethic of care that is part of being human.

Notes

I fondly thank Yi-Fu Tuan for initiating and sustaining many valuable and enjoyable
conversations with me over the years.

1. For examples of how home is made in contested spaces, see Talmadge Wright, *Out
of Place: Homeless Mobilizations, Subcities, and Contested Landscapes* (Albany: State University of New York Press, 1997); Susan M. Ruddick, *Young and Homeless in Hollywood*
(New York: Routledge Press, 1996); D. A. Snow and L. Anderson, *Down on Their Luck: A
Study of Homeless Street People* (Berkeley: University of California Press, 1993); and Jen-
nifer Toth, *The Mole People: Life in the Tunnels beneath New York City* (Chicago: Chicago
Review Press, 1993).

2. Yi-Fu Tuan, *Cosmos and Hearth: A Cosmopolite's Viewpoint* (Minneapolis: University of Minnesota Press, 1996).

3. Ibid., 164.

4. Ibid., 175.

5. Ibid., 176.

6. Bruce Robbins, "Actually Existing Cosmopolitanism," in *Cosmopolitics: Thinking and Feeling beyond the Nation,* ed. Pheng Cheah and Bruce Robbins (Minneapolis:
University of Minnesota Press, 1998), 3.

7. Robbins, "Actually Existing Cosmopolitanism," as well as Seyla Benhabib, *Situating
the Self: Gender, Community, and Postmodernism in Contemporary Ethics* (Cambridge:
Polity Press, 1992), critique the traditional cosmopolitan viewpoint on the grounds that it
does not deal with context and the particularities of people's lives.

8. Tuan, *Cosmos and Hearth,* 137–41.

9. Some of the ways that class, race, as well as gender differentially position people
in various forms of communication in academia are described in Michelle M. Tokarczyk and Elizabeth A. Fay, *Working-Class Women in the Academy: Laborers in the
Knowledge Factory* (Amherst: University of Massachusetts Press, 1993). Likewise, Robyn
Longhurst, "(Dis)embodied Geographies," *Progress in Human Geography* 21 (1997): 486–
501, describes recent efforts by scholars to transcend the traditional masculinist mind/body
separation that has shaped our conceptualizations of the world. If we could identify
and transcend other similar intellectual limitations, perhaps by paying closer attention to
hearth-based understandings, we might see very different worlds out there.

10. Deborah Tannen, *You Just Don't Understand: Women and Men in Conversation*
(New York: Ballantine Books, 1990); Carol Gilligan, *In a Different Voice* (Cambridge,
Mass.: Harvard University Press, 1982).

11. Nel Noddings, *Caring: A Feminine Approach to Ethics and Moral Education* (Berkeley: University of California Press, 1984), several contributors in the edited volume by Mary Jeanne Larrabee, *An Ethic of Care: Feminist and Interdisciplinary Perspectives* (New York: Routledge Press, 1993), and, most recently, Peta Bowden, in *Caring: Gender-Sensitive Ethics* (New York: Routledge Press, 1997) all believe that the ethic of care is gendered.

12. Other contributors to the Larrabee volume, *An Ethic of Care,* as well as Joan Tronto in *Moral Boundaries: A Political Argument for an Ethic of Care* (New York: Routledge Press, 1993), argue that the ethic of care is universal.

13. For a discussion of the enlarged role for care and other emotions, see Robert Wuthnow, *Learning to Care: Elementary Kindness in an Age of Indifference* (New York: Oxford University Press, 1995); Susan S. Phillips and Patricia Benner, eds., *The Crisis of Care: Affirming and Restoring Caring Practices in the Helping Professions* (Washington, D.C.: Georgetown University Press, 1994); Barbara Jacoby et al., *Service Learning in Higher Education* (San Francisco: Jossup Bass Publishers, 1996); and Robert Rhodes, *Community Service and Higher Learning: Explorations of the Caring Self* (Albany: State University of New York Press, 1997).

14. Candace Clark, "Emotions and Micropolitics in Everyday Life: Some Patterns and Paradoxes of 'Place,' " in *Research Agendas in the Sociology of Emotions,* ed. Theodore D. Kemper (Albany: State University of New York Press, 1990), 305–33.

15. As I attempt to describe the character of the cosmopolitan hearth in the form of an academic department, I am reminded of Robert Sack's discussion of how ideas, social relationships, and physical attributes of the environment are contained and structured within places. See his *Homo Geographicus: A Framework for Action, Awareness, and Moral Concern* (Baltimore: Johns Hopkins University Press, 1997).

16. Pierre Bourdieu, in *Homo Academicus* (Stanford, Calif.: Stanford University Press, 1988), argues that "cultural capital" — language skills, aesthetic sensibilities, mannerisms — directly affects one's success in academia. Like cultural capital, social and human capital are resources connected to the social group into which a person is born and raised. These resources are tapped to enhance status and expand opportunities. The effects of such capital on individual/group advancement have been examined in fields as varied as international and regional development, public health, economics, political science, management, and education. Interestingly, studies have shown that social and human capital are gendered in the sense that women are most involved in reproducing this type of hearth-based knowledge and experience. For an example, see M. Patricia Fernandez Kelly, "Towanda's Triumph: Social and Cultural Capital in the Transition to Adulthood in the Urban Ghetto," *International Journal of Urban and Regional Research* 18 (1994): 88–111.

17. The mixed blessing of growing up in such a world is nicely depicted in Susan Allen Toth's book, *Blooming: A Small-Town Girlhood* (Boston: Little, Brown and Company, 1978).

18. The idea of social interactions being played on a stage is traced to the work of Erving Goffman, *The Presentation of Self in Everyday Life* (Garden City, N.Y.: Doubleday Books, 1959). Two recent works that discuss the theatrics of social interaction and how these performances affect place-attachments and social relationships are Melinda Milligan, "Interactional Past and Potential: The Social Construction of Place Attachment," *Symbolic Interaction* 21 (1998): 1–33, and Lyn Lofland, *The Public Realm: Exploring the City's Quintessential Social Territory* (New York: Aldine de Gruyter, 1998). Again, gender appears to play a part in how one performs in public settings. Virginia Valian, *Why So Slow? The Advancement of Women* (Cambridge, Mass.: MIT Press, 1998), details the subtle and incremental advantages accrued by men in professional presentations of self. When men and women with similar talents and skills are compared, consistently men are deemed more competent and given more status — status that translates into women's self-protective devaluation of their expectations and achievements and men's faster professional advancement.

19. J. M. Barbalet, in *Emotions, Social Theory, and Social Structure* (Cambridge: Cam-

bridge University Press, 1998), 159, contends that the emotional climate experienced by people is significant "in the formation and maintenance of political and social identities and collective behavior."

20. See Tim Cresswell, *In Place/Out of Place: Geography, Ideology, and Transgression* (Minneapolis: University of Minnesota Press, 1996). The purpose of maximizing shared identity to reinforce and empower marginalized communities is discussed in Gill Valentine, "Making Space: Separatism and Difference," in *Thresholds in Feminist Geography: Difference, Methodology, and Representation,* ed. John Paul Jones III, Heidi J. Nast, and Susan M. Roberts (New York: Rowman and Littlefield Publishers, 1997), 65–76.

21. This is an expansive literature, but several recent works in geography discuss the differences between and limitations of these projects. See Gillian Rose, *Feminism and Geography* (Cambridge: Polity Press, 1993); Jones, Nast, and Roberts, *Thresholds,* and Sack, *Homo Geographicus.*

22. Alison M. Jaggar, "Love and Knowledge: Emotion in Feminist Epistemology," in *Women, Knowledge, and Reality: Explorations in Feminist Philosophy,* ed. Ann Garry and Marilyn Pearsall (Boston: Unwin Hyman, 1989), 144.

23. Arlie Hochschild, in *The Time Bind: When Work Becomes Home and Home Becomes Work* (New York: Metropolitan Books, 1997), demonstrates that in today's labor market, where women and men spend large portions of their lives, the corporate world has begun to recognize employee needs that once were taken care of at home and deemed inappropriate to the workplace. Paradoxically, as some workplaces begin to offer hearthlike support structures (from nurseries and flexible hours to a conscious effort to build caring relationships between co-workers), business practices associated with the workplace (time routinization, task regimentation, a heightened concern for efficiency) have seeped into the home-place. The "emotion-work" discussed by Hochschild in *The Time Bind* as well as in her book *The Managed Heart* (Berkeley: University of California Press, 1983) has become part of both the private and public worlds of home and work. This labor continues to be shouldered by women.

24. The politics of emplacement is wrapped into the literature on the politics of identity. See Patricia Yaeger, ed., *The Geography of Identity* (Ann Arbor: University of Michigan Press, 1996); Michael Keith and Steve Pile, eds., *Place and the Politics of Identity* (New York: Routledge Press, 1993); as well as Linda McDowell, ed., *Undoing Place? A Geographical Reader* (New York: Arnold Publisher, 1997).

25. Allan Wade, in "Small Acts of Living: Everyday Resistance to Violence and Other Forms of Oppression," *Contemporary Family Therapy* 19 (1997): 23–39, argues that in the narrative accounts of people who have experienced the injustices of any type of oppression we can often see evidence of resistance. The words, gestures, and physical actions depicted in these accounts, as well as any imagined conversations and imagined places voiced in the accounts, may prevent or undercut the powerful effects of oppression. Likewise, refusals to take advice, or challenges to prevailing opinion, logic, or tradition, constitute spontaneous acts of resistance and may work to subvert the status hierarchies that support oppression.

26. Tokarczyk and Fay, *Working-Class Women in the Academy.* A number of the chapters in this book describe the discomfort experienced by working-class women who come to academia without the middle-class social and cultural capital that would make their acceptance easier.

27. Eliot Freidson, *Professional Powers: A Study of the Institutionalization of Formal Knowledge* (Chicago: University of Chicago Press, 1986), 63–72.

28. Hochschild, *The Managed Heart.*

29. Candace Clark, *Misery and Company: Sympathy in Everyday Life* (Chicago: University of Chicago Press, 1997), 231.

30. Liz Bondi, "Locating Identity Politics," in Keith and Pile, *Place and the Politics of Identity,* 97, argues that the identity we promote and the position we have are context-dependent. Donna Langston, "Who Am I Now? The Politics of Class Identity," in Tokarczyk and Fay, *Working-Class Women in the Academy,* 60–72, writes of the self-conscious efforts

she made during her migration into the world of academia. She also raises the important issues of how race, ethnicity, sexuality, or childhoods experienced in rural versus urban settings intersect with class position to give people different positions — privilege — in academia.

31. Freidson, *Professional Powers,* 63.

32. See Nadya Aisenberg and Mona Harrington, *Women of Academe: Outsiders in the Sacred Grove* (Amherst: University of Massachusetts Press, 1988).

33. The possibly unhealthy effects of fracturing one's identity in order to conform to expected roles are discussed by Peter E. S. Freund, "Social Performances and Their Discontents: The Biopsychosocial Aspects of Dramaturgical Stress," in *Emotions in Social Life: Critical Themes and Contemporary Issues,* ed. Gillian Bendelow and Simon J. Williams (New York: Routledge Press, 1998), 268–94. These social roles, as seen in the student's narrative, are partly defined in and by place. Thus it may be possible to identify salubrious versus insalubrious places — places that ease rather than intensify the stresses that contribute to ill health. Robert Rotenburg, in "On the Salubrity of Sites," in *The Cultural Meaning of Urban Space,* ed. Robert Rotenberg and Gary McDonogh (Westport, Conn.: Bergin and Garvey, 1993), 17–29, notes that historically elites managed to offset the stresses of urbanity by creating urban gardens. This suggests that even in the most cosmopolitan of settings, the city, there was a recognized need for self-restoration, or mind/body unity in an arena that was neither fully the work-world (cosmos) nor the home-place (hearth).

34. Though Sack, in *Homo Geographicus,* 23, indicates that "cosmopolites...often claim a more encompassing sense of moral concern and responsibility," the student account I have been sharing does not uphold such a claim. As her narrative repeatedly reveals it is immensely difficult if not impossible to detach the self from its surrounding situation and individual need. People are embedded in micropolitical place settings; in their everyday lives they must negotiate group differences, status inequalities, and local expectations. According to Sack, chapters 6–7, specific places may exhibit more or less attention to overall moral concerns. Thus it is possible that some academic departments (cosmopolitan hearths) could emphasize a "moral perspective" over either the "discursive/scientific perspective" or the "aesthetic perspective" that Sack discusses in his book.

35. bell hooks, "Homeplace: A Site of Resistance," in McDowell, *Undoing Place?* 33–38, describes the power she gains through her ties to the racially segregated home-world of her family. Likewise, research of mine on marginally homed people shows how many of them find personal power in the contested sites they inhabit and in the subversive attachments they form with place and people. See April Veness, "Neither Homed nor Homeless: Contested Definitions and the Personal Worlds of the Poor, "*Political Geography* 12 (1993): 319–40. The idea of creating moral geographies is not new. Yi-Fu Tuan has written about morality in the modern world in *Morality and Imagination: Paradoxes of Progress* (Madison: University of Wisconsin Press, 1989), and recently a number of geographers have tackled this idea under the banners of social justice, and geography and ethics. See David M. Smith, "Geography and Moral Philosophy: Some Common Ground," *Ethics, Place, and Environment* 1 (1998): 7–34, and James D. Proctor, "Ethics in Geography: Giving Moral Form to the Geographical Imagination," *Area* 30 (1998): 8–18, for a review of these developments.

36. Stephen S. Hall, "Lethal Chemistry at Harvard," *New York Times Magazine,* November 29, 1998, 118–28.

37. Carey Goldberg, "Mental Health of Students Gets New Push at Harvard," *New York Times,* December 14, 1999, A18.

CONVERSING DIVERSITY

Provincial Cosmopolitanism and America's Multicultural Heritage

Steven Hoelscher

When Sheldon Hackney became Chair of the National Endowment of the Humanities in 1993 he made it his first order of business to direct the agency toward a discussion of America's increasing cultural heterogeneity.[1] The focus of ill-tempered argument, multiculturalism had ignited "an out-of-control screaming match in the public square [and] uncivil verbal assassinations." The divide was cast frequently as one between a "traditional" and "conservative" emphasis on keeping established values of a liberal arts education (exemplified most readily perhaps by Allan Bloom's grumpy and idiosyncratic best-seller, *The Closing of the American Mind*) and a "radical" and "ethnic" demand for diversification (best seen in Lawrence Levine's *The Opening of the American Mind*, a direct and highly effective response to Bloom). Humanistic inquiry itself, Hackney felt, "is prudently, passionately pluralistic" and thus well-qualified to "bring the 'drive-by debate' on ethnic and racial difference off the mean streets of talk radio and rhetorical invective."[2]

The NEH's approach to the National Conversation on Pluralism and Identity focused on relocating the discussion of multiculturalism to a space of civil exchange. Public forums were organized that aimed to draw disparate and otherwise "noncommunicating elements" of society into conversation with one another. As might be expected, vastly divergent views on ethnic pluralism permeated the discussions. One participant said, "When multiculturalism means the extension of our concern and our education and so on to other cultures, other colors, that's fine. But when it means the efforts to establish, promote, and perpetuate separate ethnic and racial communities, that's different.... [T]hat's what the ideologists of multiculturalism are arguing for today." "No," another answered, "there are varieties of multiculturalism.... You cannot lump us all together.... I subscribe to the multiculturalism that says that the time has come for us to learn from one another."[3]

In the end, and despite considerable differences in opinion, the participants — scholars and nonacademics alike — shared a commitment to the idea and promise of pluralism. Arthur Schlesinger's shrill warnings of "multicultural zealots," "the cult of ethnicity," and a nation at the brink of "Balkanization" seemed to carry little weight in a conversation that prioritized diversity.[4] The NEH initiative, one might suggest, anticipated its own findings by creating a certain type of forum, by the inevitable selectivity of participants, and by asking the sorts of questions that it did. More than that, however, the National Conversation captured a fundamental condition of our time: as Nathan Glazer has put it recently, "We are all multiculturalists now."[5]

If multiculturalism occupies paradigmatic status among people across the ideological spectrum, the dilemmas it poses and the confusions it generates are real nonetheless. How can an individual both develop his or her intense ethnic identity while learning to respect strong ethnic sentiments in others? How much cultural diversity can a society tolerate while still pursuing economic and political equality? How does one reconcile the demands of mixed-race Americans for recognition in the U.S. census while important black politicians defend a "one drop rule" for identifying African Americans that was designed to serve slaveholders and white supremacists? How can groups as different as backward-looking Hasidim and forward-looking feminists be convinced that they are engaged in a common endeavor? Indeed, can a common goal exist in a place as culturally diverse as the United States?[6] Such questions, and the difficulty we have in answering them, point to the ambiguity of multiculturalism itself. At a time when the problem of ethnic and racial boundaries is more acute than ever — powerfully demonstrated on the streets during the 1992 Los Angeles riot (or multiethnic insurrection) and in the strikingly divergent reactions of blacks and whites to the nonguilty verdict of O. J. Simpson's 1995 criminal trial — multiculturalism, as an intellectual movement, raises more questions than it answers.[7]

Despite (or, perhaps due to) its very prodigiousness, multiculturalism's importance in promoting minorities' rights and education is diminished by the amorphousness of the movement in which it is a part. Multiculturalism, David Hollinger argues, "is like many historic movements that speak compellingly to the anxieties and aspirations of a distinctive historical moment, but are then inhibited from meeting new challenges by the generality of the commitments to which they owe their existence: it has outgrown itself."[8] We may be all multiculturalists now, but the way in which we conceive of difference and integration varies considerably. In particular, the question of whether multiculturalism should direct the American polity toward divergence or convergence is rarely addressed in the debate, which is often looking backward to various ethnic histories and rarely looking forward to a polyethnic future.[9] These failings aside, the issues behind multiculturalism and the questions that it raises are too important to be brushed aside. An appraisal of multiculturalism's intellectual and social origins — of its direct antecedent's limitations and potential — might reinvigorate its promise of pluralism and justice.

Although the term came into wide use in the United States only in the late 1980s, multiculturalism is an international phenomenon that loosely coincides with such disparate events as the dissolution of the Soviet Union and Yugoslavia, the rise of religious fundamentalism in Israel and in Muslim countries, the growing acrimony between Canada's Francophone and Anglophone populations — each reflects to some degree the refusal of ethnic communities to cast off deeply felt cultural aspirations for the sake of membership in a secular nation-state. The immediate roots of these developments can be found in the worldwide radical protests of the 1960s in which racism, sexism, and imperialism received powerful condemnations. Moreover, critics first from the left, then from the right, began to search for identities that might rescue individuality from the anonymity of mass society.[10] Groups that had once sacrificed their particular racial or ethnic identities for the sake of building a strong state and national culture were no longer willing to do so. At exactly the same time that economies became truly global in scale, the reaction against this process became acute. Ever an active conversationalist in discussions of identity and place, Yi-Fu Tuan has described the situation nicely: "the more Americans participate in, and indeed lead the world, in globalism, the more they yearn for locality, tradition, and roots — for the hearths and ethnos that they can directly experience and understand."[11]

This critical tension between the global and the local, the universal and the particular, pluralism and assimilation, ethnos and civic, or cosmos and hearth, is much deeper than simply the outcome of political and economic unrest of the last thirty years. From an American context, the divisions between, and incorporation of, diverse cultures into the body politic lies at the core of national identity.[12] Indeed, if our conception of place is expanded beyond the narrowest of scales to include the state or nation, and if place is considered less a static container than a process created by social relations, ideology, and experience, then the United States — as a place — owes its origins to the often unequal interactions between its diverse peoples.[13] From the moment of first contact, what has become the United States is unique upon the world stage: it has always been a place, as Ishmael Reed has put it, "where the cultures of the world crisscross." Even the national motto, *E Pluribus Unum,* holds the view that whatever may weld the nation it is to be forged from diverse materials.[14]

But if the long history of intergroup contact and conflict defines American nation-ness, an explicit discussion of the country as a multicultural society is relatively short and has remained largely ignored. Werner Sollors has identified the decades of the 1930s and the 1940s as decisive for the intellectual foundation of multiculturalism, the period this essay examines.[15] Pluralist thought predated these decades, of course; the popular writing of Horace Kallen and Randolph Bourne in the years around World War I in particular articulated the possibilities and desirability of maintaining group identity. Like today's multiculturalism, their cultural pluralism argued that the United States should be home to a diversity of cultures, especially those carried by ethnic and racial groups.[16] Their trenchant critiques of the "melting pot" ideology were especially pertinent during a time when any group identification beyond a narrow American patriotism was strongly condemned and, in some cases, forcibly suppressed.[17] As important as Kallen and Bourne were in developing a pluralist model of American place, however, their contributions remained confined largely to a liberal intelligentsia. Only with the popularization of their pluralism two decades later did large numbers of Americans awaken to the notion that their country was, as one leader put it, "a nation of nations" — and, importantly, that it was all the better for it.[18]

In what follows I sketch a genealogy of multiculturalism's predecessor, a popular movement that I call "provincial cosmopolitanism." Less a coherent philosophical statement than a messy, and sometimes contradictory, assemblage of ideas, provincial cosmopolitanism was a widely shared vision among many political leaders, leftist scholars, and activists, as well as a good number of ordinary people convinced of America's pluralist nature. Provincial cosmopolitanism — itself a contradiction in terms — calls attention to several components of a unique brand of pluralist thought: unlike traditional notions of cosmopolitanism, it maintained a greater sensitivity to ethnic identity; and, less positively, its ambitions in bridging cultural divides were more limited. Perhaps most significantly, however, this perspective transcended cosmopolitanism's customary elitism as it reached out to many more people than merely self-defined "citizens of the world."

Such *popular* geographies — defined here as an image of place created outside academic and scientific discourse that is available for mass public consumption — can be extremely influential in constructing nations. Travel writing, advertising, social documentaries, and fiction are several of the various media through which popular geographies are created.[19] Making good use of these media, two spokespersons for an interwar version of multiculturalism stand out. Fred Holmes and Louis Adamic, writing at different geographic scales, popularized the view of the United States as a culturally diverse place. Trained neither as professional scholars nor affiliated with academic institutions, both nevertheless became influential proponents of a provincial cosmopolitanism based on a principle of "unity in diversity," of a heritage-based structure of knowledge that diluted "difference" while seeming to support it. Knowing something of their views, and their shortcomings, can help in understanding the ways in which multiculturalism is a continuation of an old conversation and how it is also a highly distinctive episode.

Fred Holmes's Travels through Old World Wisconsin

Frederick Lionel Holmes made his living as a reporter and lawyer, but exploring and writing about his native state of Wisconsin were his real loves.[20] Born of Yankee stock and deeply involved in the state's Progressive party politics under Robert La Follette, at twenty-three he founded the Holmes News Service, a wire agency that serviced Wisconsin and national metropolitan newspapers until 1927.[21] In that year Holmes shifted professions and was admitted to the bar, a profession he followed until his death in 1946. During the final decade of his life, he increasingly turned his attention away from his law practice and toward what he called the "side roads and excursions into Wisconsin's past." These "excursions" took both physical and metaphorical form as Holmes, at least by his own calculation, drove nearly every road of Wisconsin and delved into the state's history by reading, interviewing knowledgeable people, and writing up his findings.

It was also at this time that he served as a curator at the State Historical Society. This third career, of professional traveler and amateur historian, found its outlet in three books, each seeking to convey some of the "unsung glories of the state."[22] The first two books were written to help relieve "the grim dullness of quotidian life," a condition produced by the grind of modern, urban existence. While *Alluring Wisconsin* (1937) highlighted romantic *places* to which one might escape modernity, the second book in the trilogy, *Badger Saints and Sinners* (1939), focused on the "colorful" *people* who created these cultural "shrines."[23]

The third book in Holmes's trilogy was by far his most successful and the one he believed of greatest importance.[24] *Old World Wisconsin: Around Europe in the Badger State* (1944), Holmes felt, "will grip [people] from the twenty-four nations who make up the Wisconsin melting pot. People who look at this book cannot escape the conclusion that here is a story about Wisconsin never before told."[25] Where the previous books featured distinctly Wisconsin topics, the third concentrated on the "universal appeal" of ancestry, identity, and heritage. Holmes found it remarkable that "no other state has gathered in a melting pot such a diversity of rural and urban foreign groups.... To know them from their racial backgrounds through their New World cultures is to understand more clearly the reasons for our hegemony in the family of states." Moreover, those groups could still be found on the landscape as "living history," where "each little transplanted group has its own individuality."[26] This central idea — that the state owed its unique character to its mixture of *still surviving* foreign groups — was Holmes's chief discovery and the message that he wanted to convey to the nation.

Fred Holmes knew at an early stage the book's general themes and how he wished to shape its focus. Like all travel writers, he wished to extend his personal experiences to a readership that could encounter a distant place through his — the travel writer's — eyes. In this case, the distant place was home: "wanderings though Europe have been taken by the vicarious method of trodding the byways of newer Wisconsin." As an influential and well-to-do male, Holmes never faced the dilemmas of establishing narratorial authority; unlike, say, Victorian women travel writers whose writing was often dismissed as overly emotional, Holmes's credibility was guaranteed immediately.[27] But like these and many travel writers, his privileged class and ethno-racial position precluded anything resembling critical analysis. This became an unresolved contradiction as the book intended to convey these travels as a serious historical treatment. Holmes sought to "publish the truth only" and illuminate a most important, if previously unacknowledged, aspect of the state's popular geography.[28]

"Do Any of the Swiss Farmers Yodel at Work?" Researching Nostalgia

It was only in 1940 that work on *Old World Wisconsin* began in earnest. Though trained as neither geographer, folklorist, nor historian, Holmes did boast extensive proficiency as a reporter and maintained personal contacts throughout the state from his days as newspaper man, editor, and lawyer. He made impressive use of these skills as his several dozen trips around Wisconsin enabled Holmes to conduct interviews, take fieldnotes, and collect a vast array of primary documents. From his Madison home, he wrote literally hundreds of letters to old acquaintances and potential informants soliciting information. A closer examination of his methodology is instructive, for it reveals an inquisitive, if romantic mind — two features that most succinctly summarize *Old World Wisconsin*.

In every case, Holmes began his inquiry with letters to prominent members of the community who, it was hoped, could not only provide firsthand knowledge of that community but advise him about other, knowledgeable informants. In the summer of 1941, for instance, he began work on the state's Finnish population. First, he contacted a circuit court judge and old friend who directed Holmes to the manager of the Workers Mutual Savings Bank in Superior and who then put Holmes in contact with knowledgeable informants around the region, all of whom shared a commitment to their Finnish ancestry.[29]

Once he established contact, he sent questionnaires to a handful of people in each community. Significantly, the questionnaires were not standardized but were tailored to elicit information that he deemed most important. The question list he devised for the Swiss, to take one example, consisted of twenty-seven short questions that reflected a romanticized and essentialized view of ethnic culture: "Do any of the Swiss farmers yodel while at work? At Swiss churches do men sit on one side and women on the other? Do any bands play any airs nationalistic to Switzerland? Are Tuesday and Thursday the only days in which Swiss will be married? Do women always leave the church first? and Do cattle wear bells made in Switzerland?"[30] The Finnish questions, conversely, were more general and betrayed less familiarity with an essentialized culture. One person was simply asked "what old world customs persist among the Finns," while another was given four general questions about Finnish settlement, Old World customs, political beliefs, and festivals.[31] This less-invasive method produced better results. Where the lengthy Swiss question list invoked pat answers and confirmed stereotypes, the Finns offered detailed and vivid descriptions that found their way directly into the final text.

Finally, the work on the Finns enjoyed the benefit of skilled copyediting and advice from the leading historian of the region, George Hill, who removed factual errors and strengthened certain topics — most notably, Finnish socialism and cooperative movements. But where George Hill, a sociologist at the University of Wisconsin and himself the son of Finnish immigrants, removed some stereotypes, he advocated other changes designed to put a positive spin on his ancestral group. Originally "Strange People" in Holmes's text, Finns became "Amazing People" after Hill's editing. The sociologist also wanted it known that "only a few [Finns] may be said to lack pride in their nationality."[32] The chapter on the Swiss enjoyed no comparable expert overview and, perhaps not coincidentally, is riddled with interpretive errors. Some of the errors are historical in nature — such as the questionable suggestion that the earliest settlers chose the location due to its resemblance to the "Old World" — while others were contemporary, as when Holmes devoted considerable attention to cheesemaking but failed to mention that by the mid-1940s cheese factories had, without exception, ceased operation in the surrounding region. Nor does he bother to mention the chief employer in the region, the Pet Milk Condensing factory.[33]

Yet to judge *Old World Wisconsin* as merely flawed history betrays a genre error. Or, following David Lowenthal, such a judgment mistakes "heritage" for "history." Where history remains remote and critical in its view toward the past, heritage thrives on personal immediacy and embraces the past as a foundation for identity. While neither offers a transparent window to the past, heritage willfully fabricates the past in order to bolster self-esteem and to promote an acceptable vision of the present.[34] Thus, at the same time that the *Oshkosh Northwestern* called *Old World Wisconsin* a "scholarly and thorough study," it also noted that the book is "a fascinating story, told in an easy conversational manner, so that the reader feels he is being introduced personally to the costumes, characteristics, cuisine, festivals, and lore of the many settlers who [made] their homes in a free America." The book intended to tell a fascinating story — indeed, the most fascinating story of the state's development by way of travel narrative. Its duplicity — and its power — derived from heritage masquerading as history.

"Romantic Days Are Fading": Rejecting Modernity through Provincial Cosmopolitanism

At its core, *Old World Wisconsin* sought to wrest the state's founding myth away from its Yankee political elite and place it in the hands of the descendants of immigrants from Poland, Italy, and Germany. Highlighting and appreciating the individuality and distinctiveness of the places built by these peoples became the book's raison d'être. Holmes's topophilia bursts through on every page as he recounts becoming "subtly conscious of the centuries of simple living reflected in the daily lives" at the Lake Michigan Luxemburger settlement and of the "nostalgia of exiled peoples [that] has enriched the world of music and literature." Summarizing his vision of cultural diversity, he concludes that "had it not been for the invasion of these aggressive European stocks the strong bedrock of Wisconsin civilization might have been more friable."[35]

This appreciation of cultural diversity takes on greater urgency if one believes, with Holmes, that its existence is threatened. The first chapter sets the tone for the book with its title, "Romantic Days Are Fading." The ethnic places that receive the most tender treatment are those, like the French village of Somerset, that "alone remain with many Old World customs unspoiled." The Luxemburger settlement is blessed because its "way of life" adheres to tradition over "the hurry, confusion, and insecurity found in urban districts." And the Dutch communities along Lake Michigan are favored because, "despite the dreary efforts of modern civilization to enforce conformity on all peoples, it has not succeeded."[36] In this way, *Old World Wisconsin* may be seen as a species of antimodernism, as a regionalist plea for place distinctiveness, cultural pluralism, and localist organicism against the onslaught of what Walter Lippmann called the "acids of modernity."[37]

Holmes's antimodernist reclamation project hinged on his particular vision of cultural pluralism, a vision that may be called provincial cosmopolitanism. If maintaining distinctiveness was to be admired, there was also assumed a blending between groups — what Holmes calls a "racial admixture" — whereby everyone should work together to compose a harmonious whole. Holmes hoped that nationalities would maintain their customs, but within a *shared* political and social framework. Although little interaction occurred between groups in Holmes's text — indeed, each is treated in random order, almost as a separate island unto itself — underlying each chapter is the conviction that the dreams of the many nationalities have "bloomed into a *common heritage*." More integrationist than separatist, Holmes's pluralism rested on the belief that ethnic culture could and should be maintained, but only insofar as it contributed to a composite that was, at its core, welded and unified. Distinctiveness was admirable; separation, however, was unacceptable.[38]

This cosmopolitan vision of a unified, harmonious plurality was only surpassed by its provincialism. In this way, Holmes's implicit cosmopolitanism differs significantly from that of Randolph Bourne, who celebrated the *de*-provincializing effect of immigrants on the native-born population.[39] Holmes reveled in the antimodern influence of ethnic life; cosmopolitanism for the local historian contained value precisely for its retreat from a homogenizing and modern world. His parochialism joined with his cosmopolitanism to create a vision of his beloved state's historical and geographical development that grew out of its harmonious ethnic diversity.

Provincial cosmopolitanism for Holmes was contingent upon a larger framework of consensus, a consensus achieved through tourism. This is illustrated in a letter by another *Old World* fan, Charles Gillen, who found that

> Dr. Holmes has done an extraordinary thing: he has made it possible for the widely different groups settled in Wisconsin to visit one the other within a few hours; to learn the best of their traditions, customs, artistry, and ethics; and thus to *make each group more appreciative to the others.* I can think of no finer way in which to increase the *harmony* that should prevail in America, and to keep America the wonder of civilization and the guarantor of the peace of the world.[40]

Such a reading grasped the book's subtext that Holmes's proto-multiculturalism, at its very core, revisualized ethnic place as *tourist place.* His "vicarious method" of traveling Europe in Wisconsin relied on a view of culture that was a tourist vision of culture, on an imaginative geography far removed from the reality he claimed to depict. When one looks for the essences of quaint peoples, ethnics become synonymous with their representations: the Swiss *are* yodelers, the Hungarians *are* wheat-harvesting peasants, the Welsh *are* singers of hymns (see Figure 1 on the following page). As Jonathan Culler notes, the tourist vision "is interested in everything as a sign of itself." It may be true that some people may yodel and sing hymns, but the tourist vision of culture essentializes the representation — one is seeing the essence of Swissness or Hungarianness or Welshness through these practices. The crucial role of human agency and social constructedness of that culture is effectively hidden from view.[41]

Louis Adamic and the Therapeutic Necessity of Ethnic Pride

While most readers found this approach commendable, at least one reviewer demurred. For Louis Adamic, *Old World Wisconsin*'s celebration of ethnic diversity focused too narrowly on what he disparagingly called Holmes's "tourist's eye." Although he approved of Holmes's emphasis on "Europe's past and present influence" in Wisconsin and of the author's acknowledgment of both the diversity of these peoples and their ability to work together, Adamic severely criticized the book's "lushness and sentimentality." *Old World*'s author unduly stressed "the more obvious and less lasting evidence of the transplantation" and downplayed its more important, but "less visible," aspects.[42] Adamic, however, was vague about what precisely constituted those more important, but less visible, attributes. In many respects, Adamic and Holmes had more in common than the former would admit. Though their writing styles may have been at odds, both positioned ethnic heritage as a means of overcoming what they saw to be the malaise of a modernized, increasingly homogenized America.

A Slovenian immigrant who became part of the mass migration from southeastern Europe in the early years of the twentieth century, Louis Adamic ranked

Figure 1. *Ethnic Place as Tourist Place.* By looking for the essences of quaint folk, Fred Holmes came to present Old World peoples as synonymous with their representations. This photograph of a Hungarian wheat harvest just outside Milwaukee was taken by Arthur M. Vinje and was reprinted in *Old World Wisconsin* (1944, p. 307). Photograph courtesy of the State Historical Society of Wisconsin, neg. WHi (V51) 34.

among the most popular and prolific American writers of the 1930s and 1940s. His many books, articles, and speeches grappled with the ethnic question in American life with an intensity and commitment matched by few. Perhaps other immigrants made as great an effort as Louis Adamic to understand the nature of their new country, but it is doubtful if any were as successful in reaching a broad, diverse audience. Popular discourse about ethno-racial identity during this period relied heavily on his work as both elites and nonelites alike reflected on America's cultural diversity. Called the "symbolic personification of ethnic America," Adamic extended the provincial cosmopolitanism of Fred Holmes to a much larger audience.[43] As the monumental *Harvard Encyclopedia of American Ethnic Groups* (1980) has its origins in Adamic's "Nation of Nations" project, his work directly prefigures many of the possibilities and limitations of the multiculturalism of our own time.[44]

Adamic emerged on the literary scene in the early decades of the century as an important social critic. He frequently wrote for H. L. Mencken's *American Mercury* as well as for *Harper's Magazine*, the *New Republic, Labor Age*, and even *Reader's Digest*.[45] These early articles, and especially his influential book *Dynamite: The Story of Class Violence in America* (1931), established Adamic as an important labor journalist and one of the country's foremost leftist writers. Like his good friend and protégé Carey McWilliams, Adamic's sympathies were solidly behind the factory worker, the union member, and the common laborer, whom he regarded as all-but-powerless victims of the economic chaos produced by American capitalism. His concern for the working class was deeply humanistic as Adamic devoted considerably more energy to describing the plight of ordinary people than in unlocking the systematic working of industrial capitalism. In one early article (1931) Adamic wrote with sympathy and affection of the out-of-work mill workers in the "Tragic Towns of New England" whom he described as "shabby men leaning against walls and lamp-posts, and standing on street corners ... pathetic, silent, middle-aged men in torn, frayed overcoats or even without overcoats, broken shoes ... , slumped in postures of hopeless discontent, their faces sunken and their eyes shifty and bewildered."[46] Based on the strength of such passionate description and on the critical success of *Dynamite*, Adamic was awarded a Guggenheim Fellowship the following year. He used the opportunity to return to his native Slovenia (after an absence of nineteen years) and to the new country of Yugoslavia. The results of these travels, *The Native's Return: An American Immigrant Visits Yugoslavia and Discovers His Old Country* (1934), solidified Adamic's reputation as it became a Book-of-the-Month-Club selection and enjoyed general sales of fifty thousand in the first two months.[47]

The Native's Return marked a shift in Adamic's writing. His trip to Slovenia made "a deep and lasting impression" on Adamic as it reawakened a consciousness of his own cultural roots and reoriented his writing toward ethnic conflict and tensions. Although he never abandoned his left-liberal political-economic interests, questions of the politics of identity assumed utmost importance.[48] In 1934 he set out on a lecture tour to publicize the book (and a revised edition of *Dynamite*) that brought him to no less than fifty ethnic communities where his visits were noted with considerable approval by the local newspapers and the foreign-language press serving these different communities.[49] This positive response to his message of ethnic pride, as well as the deep socioeconomic problems that he saw in many of those places, contributed to a redirected focus on questions of cultural diversity. Adamic needed a method to articulate more fully the anxieties of working-class ethnic families and communities and found it, like so many writers, filmmakers, and photographers of the period, in the social documentary.

Uniting Plymouth Rock and Ellis Island: A New Kind of Social Documentary

"The thing to do . . . is to write the truth as one feels and sees it . . . and at the same time reveal oneself sufficiently as one writes so that the reader . . . will arrive at truth of his own in his particular, significant way."[50] Thus did Adamic once describe his aesthetic. Such an approach — of focusing on experience, feeling, and human emotion — was characteristic of the principal genre of the day: the social documentary. Although "truth," Roy Stryker said, "is the objective of the documentary attitude," its truth is achieved through empathy and emotion. And with the social documentary of the 1930s, the concern was less with the "human condition" — experiences like death, chance, and the effects of hurricanes and earthquakes that are perennial and unpreventable — than with conditions neither permanent nor necessary: racial and ethnic discrimination, police brutality, unemployment, the Great Depression.[51] Whether in painting, film, writing, broadcast, or photography, this distinctly political genre aimed toward social improvement. Adamic, one of the period's most prolific and best-known social documentarians, called upon emotion and experience to help Americans reconsider their attitudes toward ethnic minorities during a period of radical social disintegration.[52]

Thus, what gave Adamic's writing so much power was his flair for the dramatic, but also a sense that what he wrote was true and derived from experience, not ethereal principles.[53] In the depth of the depression, William Stott notes, "Americans had grown skeptical of abstract promises. More than ever they became worshipers of the cult of experience and believed just what they saw, touched, handled, and — the crucial word — felt."[54] Like Holmes, Adamic sought to persuade the reader of the validity of his views by boasting his many travels: in preparation for *My America* (1938), he claimed to have "traveled perhaps 100,000 miles in America, by train, by automobile, by plane, as well as afoot, pausing here and there to look and listen, to ask questions, to get 'the feel of things.' "[55] But experience was derived equally from a second, vicarious source. More data on the lives and experiences of ethnic communities were required than his travels could provide, and so Adamic devised a lengthy questionnaire that he mailed to hundreds, if not thousands, of individuals and communities asking about their own experiences.

Sent to new immigrants and old-stock Americans (a "special questionnaire" was later sent to African Americans), the so-called Broadside was a curious method for obtaining information. Not only did it request a wide array of information about experiences and attitudes, prejudices encountered, and opinions about one's own and America's future, but it also served as a platform for Adamic to share his own views on ethnic and racial diversity. The Broadside was far from the type of scientific survey that we are accustomed to today, as it outlined, point-by-point, Adamic's vision of a pluralist society, one that acknowledged, with Whitman, that "here is not a nation, but a teeming nation of nations."[56] The questionnaire was distributed nationally by the Foreign Language Information Service through its mailing lists of fraternal organizations and newspaper subscriptions. Although it is impossible to tell exactly how many Broadsides were eventually distributed — Adamic hoped to mail thousands — his writing after 1940 frequently made use of the letters that he received from hundreds of people.[57]

Like Fred Holmes, but on the scale of the nation, Adamic sought to rewrite American history as ethnic history. "The record written into the standard textbooks," Adamic correctly noted, "portrays the U.S.A. as a White Protestant Anglo-Saxon country with a Wasp civilization patched here and there with pieces of alien civilization."[58] The cultural renewal that he sought would not be possible until "a revaluation of facts in the American Story [takes place] so that Immigration might cease to be a footnote on page 317 and become a main subject in the text, so that each group in our population would be seen as a necessary and integral thread."[59] As Holmes aimed to unite Wisconsin's Yankee and "Old World" pasts, so did Adamic wish to join "Plymouth Rock and Ellis Island." For Adamic, a proper understanding of America's past as well as its contemporary makeup required an

> intellectual-emotional synthesis of old and new America; of the Mayflower and the steerage; of the New England wilderness and the social-economic jungle of the city slums and the factory system; of the Liberty Bell and the Statue of Liberty. The old American Dream needs to be interlaced with the immigrant emotions as they saw the Statue of Liberty. The two must be made one story.[60]

Such a rewriting of history was no idle pastime but a deeply political act that was to bring about dramatic social change. In his belief that such artistic and intellectual production can in itself lead to a resolution of conflict, Adamic was hardly alone. The makers of the Harlem Renaissance, the *Partisan Review* cosmopolitans, the *New Masses* communists, and regionalists of every stripe all shared a common faith in a cultural radicalism predicated on the notion that educated reason and artistic expression could solve deep social ills.[61]

But where Holmes (the Wisconsin Yankee) sought this reconciliation as an antimodernist move to promote acceptable difference, Adamic (the Slovenian immigrant) operated on a more personal and psychological level. The resolution of emotional distress, rather than the recovery of romantic "scenes from the past," defined his mission. In an especially influential article written for the November 1934 issue of *Harper's Magazine,* Adamic outlined the distress that he detected during his visits with some of the "thirty million new Americans." Written after his nationwide tour of ethnic communities, Adamic tried to explain the emotional malaise of the second- and third-generation Americans he met. "The chief and most important fact . . . about the new Americans," he wrote, "is that the majority of them are oppressed by feelings of inferiority." Where Holmes saw "quaint" Cornish, "quiet" Luxemburgers, "thrifty" Belgians, and "strong, virile" Norwegians, Adamic encountered people who "cannot look one in the eye. They are shy. Their limp handshakes gave me creepy feelings all the way from New York to the Iron Range of Minnesota."[62]

Encountering so many working-class "new Americans" and hearing of their difficulties in the midst of the Great Depression confirmed for Adamic that something was terribly disturbing with these communities. Not one family he met was free from feelings of inferiority, and those who had embraced American culture tended toward chauvinism and shallow materialism: "This inferiority manifests itself variously. Some [ethnics] become patriotic, chauvinistic, only their patriotism is lip-service, without basis in conviction or feeling. Most of them just hang back and form a tremendous mass of neutral citizenry. Not a few turn their feeling of inferiority inside out and get tough and loud; in some cases, anti-social." These communities, Adamic contended, were "bewildered, politically neutral, economically unaggressive, culturally nowhere."[63]

"Unity in Diversity"

Such arguments reflected a new concern in discussions about ethnic diversity. While Adamic reacted strongly to the victimization of immigrants as scapegoats for unemployment, his greatest attention focused on their children and on their problems of identity. In particular, he believed that an awareness of one's cultural background would enhance self-esteem and forge a way through an "inferiority complex" that lay at the heart of "the second generation problem."[64] That problem, it seemed, hinged on the immigrant generation's inability to transmit to their children "a consciousness . . . of their being part of any sort of continuity in human or historic experience." The solution to the dilemma was a typically *therapeutic* one, namely, building a sense of belonging by passing along "a knowledge of, and pride in, their own heritage."[65]

As far apart as these two writers may seem at first, and as Adamic would have wished, a remarkably similar vision of pluralism and unity undergirded their thinking. Although Adamic insisted on the importance of ethnic studies and the necessity of ethnic pride, he equally attacked nativists who, by whipping "the seas of vague distrust," aimed "to keep the population chopped up into racial-cultural islands."[66] Rather, and very much like Holmes, Adamic called for an appreciation of each group's contribution, for tolerance of diversity en route to a unified American republic. This provincial cosmopolitanism was spelled out perhaps most succinctly in the 1939 statement of purposes of *Common Ground,* a journal edited by Adamic for one and a half years. With an editorial board composed of such notables as Van Wyck Brooks, Mary Ellen Chase, Langston Hughes, and Thomas Mann, Adamic's journal was published by the Common Council for American Unity, whose purpose was

> To help create among the American people the unity and mutual understanding resulting from a common citizenship, a common belief in democracy and the ideals of liberty, the placing of the common good before the interests of any group, and the acceptance, in fact as well as in law, of all citizens, whatever their national or racial origins, as equal partners in American society.[67]

Adamic's provincial cosmopolitanism shared with Holmes the ambition of promoting what he called "unity in diversity." It was Adamic, not Holmes, who wrote that "the pattern of America is all of a piece; it is a blend of cultures from many lands, woven of threads from many corners of the world. Diversity itself is the pattern, is the stuff and color of the fabric."[68]

The major divergence between the two stemmed more from personal background and temperament than from serious philosophical differences. Indeed, their shared provincial cosmopolitan vision transcended the critical political divide that separated the immigrant Socialist from the WASP Progressive. Where Holmes wrote with upbeat and unwavering optimism, Adamic tended to concentrate on the difficulties of adjustment. However, both had a tendency to attribute group characteristics to individuals, from which the leap to stereotyping was a very short hop. With words that might well have come from *Old World Wisconsin,* Adamic wrote that same year of "spice" added from "the flavor of cynicism and humanitarianism from the Jews, sex and sophistication from the French, and sentimentality and love of comfort from the old fashioned Germans, and you have a rough outline of essential Americanism."[69] Both were infected with the filiopietism and search for what David Lowenthal has called the need for "being first" that underscored much of ethnic writing during these decades and that is so much a part of the heritage enterprise.[70] And both regretted that, as Adamic put it, "there has been entirely too much melting away and shattering of the cultural values of the new groups," while at the same time noting with approval that "there has been more getting together among

Americans than ever before." The key rested in the view that unity could be achieved through diversity, through a provincial cosmopolitanism (Figure 2).[71]

Whiteness and the Banality of Difference

The provincial cosmopolitanism of both Adamic and Holmes contained, at its very core, an unresolvable contradiction. If distinctiveness between groups is to be maintained, this would seem to imply the maintenance of the social and geographic distance that, ultimately, both writers found unacceptable. Interaction between, and a fusion of, cultures would lead to the dissolution of an ethnically diverse America that both so revered. Louis Adamic and Fred Holmes were not alone in finding themselves at the center of this inconsistency. While anthropologists were regarding the tight cultural cohesion in "primitive groups" as healthy, other social scientists were decrying its by-product (or cause?) — ethnocentrism. Philip Gleason later stated the matter with precision when he asked: "How could diversity be a good thing if the ethnocentrism that was central to preserving ethnic distinctiveness was such a bad thing?"[72] Since the question was never put in such stark terms, no answer was given. Both must have sensed the tension inherent in their version of pluralism, however; for both Holmes and Adamic, but in slightly different ways, the way out of this contradiction was to render "difference" symbolic and inconsequential.

It is axiomatic that this reappraisal of, and appreciation for, ethnicity came at a time when these groups became ever less a potential threat. Put somewhat differently, the years surrounding World War II were the first in which the new immigrants and their descendants could lay a secure claim to whiteness. Before the 1940s, the people whom Adamic met on Minnesota's Iron Range and in Italian Harlem were considered "inbetween peoples" and of indeterminate racial status — sometimes white, sometimes not. Such a new racial formation — the beginning of replacing "white" for hyphenated identities among all European immigrant groups — is the critical element of interwar provincial cosmopolitanism. It became less difficult to discover and relish differences between, say, Poles and Italians if both were white.[73]

By emphasizing an unspoken, but nevertheless present, whiteness of their respective groups, both Holmes and Adamic tread ever so close to what Barbara Kirshenblatt-Gimblett has called the "banality of difference." The "proliferation of variation," she suggests, "has the neutralizing effect of rendering difference (and conflict) inconsequential."[74] Difference was fine as long as it was acceptable, nonthreatening, and beyond politics. Though offered by Adamic and, to a lesser extent, Holmes as an alternative to the often brutal efforts of nativists to suppress group identity, the discourse of "unity in diversity," or provincial cosmopolitanism, almost inevitably negates real political difference.[75]

Holmes took the banality of difference to an extreme as he simply wrote

Figure 2. *Unity in Diversity.* This photomontage, by Alexander Alland and published in *Common Ground*, graphically depicts Adamic's vision of a diverse yet solidly unified nation. He wrote that the collage was intended to "reflect the spirit of Whitman." Photomontage published in *Common Ground* 2 (spring 1942): 3; reprinted here with permission of the Immigration and Refugee Services of America.

African Americans and American Indians out of his celebration of Wisconsin's diversity. Indeed, *Old World Wisconsin* was premised on a thoroughly Eurocentric perspective. Although the state was home to fewer African Americans than its midwestern neighbors, Milwaukee's black population grew significantly in the first half of the century, from 980 in 1910 to more than 10,000 in 1945, creating a viable, and visible, fraction of the city's working class. Likewise, Native American communities remained firmly anchored in place — especially in the state's northern reaches — a fact evident by even the most cursory glance.[76] The result was a viewpoint where difference was not exactly colorless; it was white. "There is no feeling, reading the book, that these [white ethnics] are 'foreign' people," the *Milwaukee Journal* correctly noted. "Rather, you seem to look upon them as part of the big Wisconsin family."[77]

For Adamic, too, "difference" became banal as he found it difficult to integrate peoples of color into the structure of his thinking on American diversity. Although *Common Ground* did ultimately pick up the "Negro Question" with some vigor after he resigned his editorship, Adamic himself never really swerved from his binary linking of "Ellis Island and Plymouth Rock."[78] As he described it in 1938, his "great educational-cultural work [aimed] to reach almost everybody in this country with the fact that socially and culturally the United States, as it stands today, is an extension not only of the British Isles and the Netherlands, but, more or less, all of Europe."[79] Only later did he amend his pedagogical geography to include "and parts of Asia and Africa."[80]

The ambiguity of Adamic's pluralism is further illustrated in his conception of a multivolume encyclopedia of the immigrant experience. As the culmination of his Nation of Nations project, this encyclopedia was to help Americans realize their loftiest ideals of unity in diversity. The limitations of the project — first proposed in an address to the Progressive Education Association in 1935 — are revealed in an exchange between Adamic and Anson Phelps Stokes, a philanthropist with twenty-some years of educational work with African Americans. Upon hearing of the proposed project, Stokes wrote to Adamic informing him of his own plans for a work to be titled *Encyclopedia of the Negro*, which had just been approved at Howard University.[81] Adamic's response was dismissive: "The Negro millions are part of the United States, not separate from it, and I feel that they belong, along with the Indians, Yankees, the Dutch, and the more recent immigrant strains, in a complete racial encyclopedia, which will tell us — the people of the United States: all of us — who we are, what we have in us, etc."[82] Stokes, an old-line Progressive, was more in touch with the situation of blacks, as he disagreed with Adamic's flippant erasure of race. He admitted that the experience of African Americans shared some relation to "other racial problems," but he insisted that it was "by its character, history, and seriousness, in a class largely by itself, so that it must have special treatment."[83] One need not essentialize race to find an untenable idealism in Adamic's position; his integrationist impulses led him to forget that the melting pot operated differently for ethnic than for racial groups.[84] By lumping all groups together and finding the variance of experiences between African Americans and Swedish Americans no greater than between Norwegians and Poles, "difference" for Adamic became empty.

Conclusion: From Provincial to Rooted Cosmopolitanism

The popular geographies of Fred Holmes and Louis Adamic illustrate both the promise and limitations of multiculturalism's ancestor and, hence, of our own era's intense grappling with the tensions between cosmos and hearth. Their provincial cosmopolitanism, though pluralist, conceived of diversity in terms of ancestral origins; in the end both envisioned a fully unified culture. Equally important, both dramatically underplayed the importance of political and economic inequalities in shaping the experiences of different groups. Recognizing the profoundly different historical-geographical forces shaping the nation's many cultures — from enslavement, conquest, and immigration under widely contrasting socioeconomic conditions — renders their version of the "unity in diversity" paradigm obsolete. Finally, and most important, their brand of cosmopolitanism hinged on a tacit whiteness. Although Adamic did at least seem aware of the African American presence, his "common ground" was too provincial to include Americans from places other than Europe.

What, then, can one committed to a multiculturalist perspective learn from such popular geographies? A close reading of these two writers suggests, first, that the often well-meaning attempt to secure legitimacy in an ancestral past can lead down a spurious path. If we chastise Adamic and Holmes for their filiopietism, for their attempt to bolster self-esteem by reveling in one's cultural past, we should also be careful to recognize that this impulse remains with us. Beyond the generic, if benign, genealogical desire for noble ancestors and the pride most people take in the cultural contributions of their larger ethno-racial community, there is a sharpened and politicized version that bears close resemblance to Nietzsche's "will to power." "The will to descend," David Hollinger notes, consists of claiming, on behalf of a particular descent-community, vainglorious cultural accomplishments as a way to position one's group relative to others.[85] Claiming, as Madison Grant did famously in 1916, that Jesus Christ was "Nordic" is only one such example of how a historically privileged, but defensive, group seeks to fortify its position by the will to descend. Moreover, empowered white Americans have long appropriated the cultural creativity of black people who, in the process, have found themselves largely erased from America's cultural geography.[86] Thus, while examples of the will to descend exist for both privileged and subaltern groups, those in power and those on the verge of power (like Adamic's second-generation European immigrants) have been much more accomplished at ennobling their group through a manipulation of the past.

A second message, less a cautionary than a directional cue, derives from provincialism's second meaning. If the midcentury's cosmopolitanism suffered from a Eurocentric narrowness, it also welcomed the importance of ethnos and local culture. Such a view — radical then, accepted today — signals that the time is right for a critical renewal of cosmopolitanism, an "unfashionable term," Bruce Robbins notes, "that needs defending."[87] Among the many voices calling for a fresh look at an old idea, Yi-Fu Tuan's seems to have something unique to offer. Like Adamic and Holmes, he is wary of singular identities and acknowledges the inexorable power of local culture. Tuan's rooted cosmopolitanism — if I may call it that — recognizes, with postmodernism more generally, that ideas and values once taken to be universal are time-space specific: all cultures are rooted.[88] Such a perspective takes "difference" seriously, acknowledging that earlier notions of universalism and globalism ring hollow. Tuan's rooted cosmopolitanism is far from separatist or relativist, however, as it also looks for commonalities between diverse groups and individuals. This is the essential element of his ideal place — the cosmopolitan hearth — for without bridges between communities "the development of any large, liberating vision that encompasses the stranger" is thwarted. Perhaps it has taken someone who has always considered himself a stranger to renew the conversation of diversity in such an original manner.[89]

Notes

I would like to thank Paul Adams, Shelley Fisher Fishkin, Kent Mathewson, Mark C. Smith, Karen Till, and Yi-Fu Tuan for their helpful comments on earlier drafts of this essay.

1. Sheldon Hackney, *One America Indivisible* (Washington, D.C.: National Endowment for the Humanities, 1997).

2. Ibid., 4–5. Allan Bloom, *The Closing of the American Mind: How Higher Education Has Failed Democracy and Impoverished the Souls of Today's Students* (New York: Simon and Schuster, 1987); Lawrence Levine, *The Opening of the American Mind: Canons, Culture, and History* (Boston: Beacon Press, 1996).

3. Hackney, *One America*, 168–69.

4. Arthur Schlesinger Jr., *The Disuniting of America: Reflections on a Multicultural Society* (New York: Norton, 1992). For a provocative critique of the Balkanization metaphor, of which Schlesinger makes liberal use, see Mark Ellis and Richard Wright, "The Balkanization Metaphor in the Analysis of U.S. Immigration," *Annals of the Association of American Geographers* 88 (1998): 686–98.

5. Nathan Glazer, *We Are All Multiculturalists Now* (Cambridge, Mass.: Harvard University Press, 1997). For another, and nicely ironic, statement that claims popular victory for multiculturalism and its mainstreaming, see Janny Scott, "At Appomattox in the Culture Wars," *New York Times*, May 25, 1997, sec. 4, p. 1.

6. Gary Gerstle, "The Limits of American Universalism," *American Quarterly* 45 (1993): 230–36; Mary C. Waters, "Multiple Ethnic Identity Choices," in *Beyond Pluralism: The Conception of Groups and Group Identities in America*, ed. Wendy Katkin, Ned Landsman, and Andrea Tyree (Urbana: University of Illinois Press, 1998), 28–46; Walter Benn Michaels, *Our America: Nativism, Modernism, and Pluralism* (Durham, N.C.: Duke University Press, 1995); Avery F. Gordon and Christopher Newfield, eds., *Mapping Multiculturalism* (Minneapolis: University of Minnesota Press, 1996).

7. Mark Baldassare, ed., *The Los Angeles Riots: Lessons for the Urban Future* (Boulder, Colo.: Westview Press, 1994); David Hollinger, "How Wide the Circle of the 'We'? American Intellectuals and the Problem of the Ethnos since World War II," *American Historical Review* 98 (1993): 335–36; Michael Walzer, "Multiculturalism and Individualism," *Dissent* 41 (1994): 185–86.

8. David Hollinger, *Postethnic America: Beyond Multiculturalism* (New York: Basic Books, 1995), 2.

9. John Higham, "Multiculturalism and Universalism: A History and Critique," *American Quarterly* 45 (1993): 195–219. Among the many people who have recently problematized the notion of "difference," John Agnew has remarked that "when political identity is totally bound up with a singular social identity, the search for commonalities and common understanding...is abandoned" (John Agnew, "Democracy and Human Rights after the Cold War," in *Geographies of Global Change*, ed. R. J. Johnston, Peter J. Taylor, and Michael J. Watts [Oxford: Blackwell, 1995], 91). As with Agnew, not all of the criticisms of multiculturalism are at odds with the ideal of cultural diversity. See, for example, Michael Dyson, "Contesting Racial Amnesia: From Identity Politics to Post-Multiculturalism," in *Higher Education under Fire: Politics, Economics, and the Crisis of the Humanities*, ed. Michael Berube and Carey Nelson (New York: Routledge, 1995), 336–52; Todd Gitlin, "From Universality to Difference: Notes on the Fragmentation of the Idea of the Left," *Contention* 2 (1993): 15–40; Itabari Njeri, "Sushi and Grits: Ethnic Identity and Conflict in a Newly Multicultural America," in *Lure and Loathing: Essays on Race, Identity, and the Ambivalence of Assimilation*, ed. Gerald Early (New York: Penguin, 1994), 13–40; David Rieff, "Multiculturalism's Silent Partner: It's the New Globalized Consumer Economy, Stupid," *Harper's* (August 1993): 62–72; David Harvey, *Justice, Nature, and the Geography of Difference* (Cambridge, Mass.: Blackwell, 1996), esp. 334–65; and Michaels, *Our America*.

10. David Theo Goldberg, "Introduction: Multicultural Conditions," in *Multiculturalism: A Critical Reader*, ed. David Theo Goldberg (Oxford: Basil Blackwell, 1994), 1–41. For the classic conservative glamorization of ethnicity, see Michael Novak, *The Rise of the Unmeltable Ethnics* (New York: Macmillan, 1972).

11. Yi-Fu Tuan, *Cosmos and Hearth: A Cosmopolite's Viewpoint* (Minneapolis: University of Minnesota Press, 1996), 104. Tuan's argument is echoed in much of the vast literature on globalization and its impact on identity and place. Among the most useful from the perspective of ethnicity and multiculturalism are Benjamin Barber, *Jihad vs. McWorld* (New York: Ballantine Books, 1996); Stuart Hall, "The Local and the Global: Globalization and Ethnicity," in *Culture, Globalization, and the World-System: Contemporary Conditions for the Representation of Identity*, ed. Anthony King (Minneapolis: University of Minnesota Press, 1997), 19–40; Frederick Buell, "Nationalist Postnationalism: Globalist Discourse in Contemporary American Culture," *American Quarterly* 50 (1998): 548–91; Arjun Appadurai, *Modernity at Large: Cultural Dimensions of Globalization* (Minneapolis: University of Minnesota Press, 1996); Timothy Luke, "Identity, Meaning, and Globalization: Detraditionalization in Postmodern Space-Time Compression," in *Detraditionalization: Critical Reflections on Authority and Identity*, ed. Paul Heelas, Scott Lash, and Paul Morris (Oxford: Basil Blackwell, 1996), 109–13. See also Wilbur Zelinsky, "The World and Its Identity Crisis," in this volume, for a slightly different perspective on this dynamic.

12. Philip Gleason, *Speaking of Diversity: Language and Ethnicity in Twentieth-Century America* (Baltimore: Johns Hopkins University Press, 1992).

13. Tuan was the first to note that place exists at different scales, from "a favorite armchair" to "the whole earth" (Yi-Fu Tuan, *Space and Place: The Perspective of Experience* [Minneapolis: University of Minnesota Press, 1977]). Important statements that see place less as a static entity and more as a "process" tied to social forces and ideological movements include Alan Pred, "Place as Historically Contingent Process: Structuration and the Time-Geography of Becoming Places," *Annals of the Association of American Geographers* 74 (1984): 279–97; John Agnew, *Place and Politics: The Geographical Mediation of State*

and Society (Boston: Allen and Unwin, 1987); Doreen Massey, *Space, Place, and Gender* (Minneapolis: University of Minnesota Press, 1994); J. Nicholas Entrikin, *The Betweenness of Place* (Baltimore: Johns Hopkins University Press, 1991); and Robert David Sack, *Homo Geographicus* (Baltimore: Johns Hopkins University Press, 1997). It is clear that place remains critical to identity-formation even in an age of instability, globalization, and reflexivity. As Craig Calhoun has recently reminded us, even as people strive to establish identities that are not necessarily place-specific, they do so in a geographical "field" of shared relevance, like a state (Craig Calhoun, "Social Theory and the Politics of Identity," in *Social Theory and the Politics of Identity,* ed. Craig Calhoun [Cambridge, Mass.: Blackwell, 1994], 25).

14. Ishmael Reed, "America: The Multicultural Society," in *Multi-Cultural Literacy,* ed. Rick Simonson and Scott Walker (St. Paul: Greywolf Press, 1988), 160. An acknowledgment of cultural diversity came early in America. It stemmed not only from the need to incorporate thirteen different sovereignties into one political authority but also from the new nation's ethno-racial, social, and religious heterogeneity. See D. W. Meinig, *The Shaping of America: Atlantic America, 1492–1800,* vol. 1 (New Haven, Conn.: Yale University Press, 1986), esp. 79–254, 438–54.

15. Werner Sollors, "The Multiculturalism Debate as Cultural Text," in *Beyond Pluralism: The Conception of Groups and Group Identities in America,* ed. Wendy F. Katkin, Ned Landsman, and Andrea Tyree (Urbana: University of Illinois Press, 1998), 87–89. Carla Kaplan, likewise, emphasizes the years following World War I as offering "especially important lessons about the possibilities for multiculturalism and interracial understanding" (Carla Kaplan, "On Modernism and Race," *Modernism/Modernity* 4 [1997]: 157–69).

16. Horace M. Kallen, "Democracy versus the Melting-Pot: A Study of American Nationality," *The Nation* (February 18 and February 25, 1915): 190–94, 100, 217–20; and Randolph S. Bourne, "Trans-National America," *Atlantic Monthly* (July 1916): 86–97.

17. The foundational work on the virulent racism and xenophobia unleashed by World War I nationalism remains John Higham, *Strangers in the Land: Patterns of American Nativism, 1860–1925,* 2d ed. (New York: Atheneum, 1978).

18. Louis Adamic, *A Nation of Nations* (New York: Harper and Brothers, 1945). Stewart G. Cole and Mildred Wiese Cole put it even more clearly, almost a half-century before the current debates about multiculturalism: "The unique fact that characterizes America is that it is a multicultural society. Consider at random almost any community in the country. Its social structure reveals a variety of culture groups, which differ widely in pattern, enlisting more or less distinctive racial folkways, religious faiths, languages, Old-World or indigenous household practices, social mores, and economic class status" (Stewart G. Cole and Mildred Wiese Cole, *Minorities and the American Promise: The Conflict of Principle and Practice,* Bureau for Intercultural Education Publication Series, no. 10 [New York: Harper and Brothers, 1954], 3).

19. For example, see Felix Driver, "Geography's Empire: Histories of Geographical Knowledge," *Environment and Planning D: Society and Space* 10 (1992): 23–40; Derek Gregory, "Between the Book and the Lamp: Imaginative Geographies of Egypt, 1849–50," *Transactions of the Institute of British Geographers* 20 (1995): 29–57.

20. Information on the life of Fred Holmes is gleaned from the impressive holdings at the State Historical Society of Wisconsin's manuscript archives. The Fred L. Holmes Papers (FHP) contain nine archival boxes and six scrapbooks detailing his extensive writing and public life. This short description of his life is based also on obituaries and appreciations in *Capital Times,* July 28, 1946; Lawrence Whittet, "Frederick Lionel Holmes, 1883–1946," *Wisconsin Magazine of History* 30 (December 1946): 184–85; and "Frederick Lionel Holmes," in *Dictionary of Wisconsin Biography* (Madison: State Historical Society of Wisconsin, 1960), 174–75.

21. Robert M. La Follette, *The Political Philosophy of Robert M. La Follette as Revealed in his Speeches and Writings,* ed. Fred L. Holmes (Westport, Conn.: Hyperion, 1975 [1920]).

22. Fred L. Holmes, *Side Roads: Excursions into Wisconsin's Past* (Madison: State Historical Society of Wisconsin, 1949).

23. Fred L. Holmes, *Alluring Wisconsin* (Milwaukee: E. M. Hale, 1937), 9–10; Fred L. Holmes, *Badger Saints and Sinners* (Milwaukee: E. M. Hale, 1939), 11.

24. As a measure of the book's success, in the half-century since the publication of Fred Holmes's book, "Wisconsin culture" has come to mean "Old World culture." The most direct evidence came in 1976 with the creation of the state's most significant and ambitious museum, the Old World Wisconsin Outdoor Ethnic Museum, in Eagle. With its town hall named "Harmony" and surrounded by a constellation of Euro-American vernacular buildings, Old World Wisconsin (the museum) bears an unmistakable resemblance to its namesake, *Old World Wisconsin* (the book). As Holmes's book was a "new kind of Wisconsin book," so is the Old World Wisconsin Museum the first of its kind: the "only multinational, multicultural 'living museum' in existence." In short, to cite the Wisconsin Arts Board as it prepared to ready the state for its 1998 Sesquicentennial, "Fred Holmes's *Old World Wisconsin* established a paradigm for understanding Wisconsin's cultural geography as a mosaic of evolving but persisting ethnic cultures" (Richard March, "Statewide Folk Arts Fieldwork in Preparation for the Wisconsin Folklife Festival," National Endowment for the Arts Grant Application WAB FY95–97 [Madison: Wisconsin Arts Board, 1994], 2).

25. Fred L. Holmes to E. M. Hale, March 18, 1943, box 2, folder 2, FHP.

26. Fred L. Holmes, *Old World Wisconsin: Around Europe in the Badger State* (Eau Claire, Wis.: E. M. Hale, 1944), 9.

27. Ibid., 9–10. On travel writing, especially by British women, see Karen M. Morin and Jeanne Kay Guelke, "Strategies of Representation, Relationship, and Resistance: British Women Travelers and Mormon Plural Wives, ca. 1870–1890," *Annals of the Association of American Geographers* 88 (1998): 436–62; Cheryl McEwan, "Paradise or Pandemonium? West African Landscapes in the Travel Accounts of Victorian Women," *Journal of Historical Geography* 22 (1996): 68–83; and Alison Blunt, *Travel, Gender, and Imperialism: Mary Kingsley and West Africa* (New York: Guilford Press, 1994). A closer comparison with Holmes might be with the editor and amateur historian Charles Fletcher Lummis and his writing on the Southwest. See Martin Padget, "Travel, Exoticism, and the Writing of Region: Charles Fletcher Lummis and the 'Creation' of the Southwest," *Journal of the Southwest* 37 (1995): 421–49.

28. Fred L. Holmes to C. H. Thordarson, June 20, 1941, box 7, folder 10, FHP.

29. Fred L. Holmes to Carl H. Daley, July 8, 1941; Ilmar Kauppinen to Fred L. Holmes, October 2, 1941, both from box 7, folder 12, FHP.

30. Typeset questionnaire with handwritten responses, n.d., box 6, folder 6; and handwritten question list, n.d., box 6, folder 6, FHP.

31. Ilmar Kauppinen to Fred L. Holmes, October 2, 1941; and Fred L. Holmes to S. W. Rahr, September 14, 1942, box 7, folder 12 FHP.

32. Corrected manuscript to chapter 12 of *Old World Wisconsin*, undated, box 7, folder 12, FHP.

33. Holmes, *Old World Wisconsin*, 131–50. Steven Hoelscher, *Heritage on Stage: The Invention of Ethnic Place in America's Little Switzerland* (Madison: University of Wisconsin Press, 1998).

34. Holmes opens himself to criticism by his own admission to "publish the truth only" and by the nearly one hundred scholarly footnotes that underline his text. The State Historical Society's executive committee called Holmes "a historian who . . . appreciated the opportunity to broaden and deepen that knowledge of the lives of our pioneers." Publisher William J. Evjue believed that the book brought together "between two covers a scholarly study of the many nationalities which migrated to the state and contributed to its development," and the *Chicago Tribune* noted that, in preparation for the book, Holmes "thoroly [*sic*] studied the many nationalities which have helped to people . . . his beloved state." Finally, the editor for the *Oshkosh Northwestern* found that "in the volume . . . he had placed in type a scholarly and thorough study of the many nationalities that migrated to this state." Whittet, "Frederick Lionel Holmes"; *Capitol Times,* May 3, 1944; *Chicago Sunday Tribune,* May 28, 1944; *Oshkosh Northwestern,* May 8, 1944. See also David Lowenthal, *Possessed*

by the Past: The Heritage Crusade and the Spoils of History (New York: Free Press, 1996); John Gillis, "Heritage and History: Twins Separated at Birth," *Reviews in American History* 25 (1997): 375–78.

35. Holmes, *Old World Wisconsin,* 68, 88, 49.

36. Ibid., 26, 68, 84, 124.

37. For a discussion of regionalism and antimodernism, see Robert L. Dorman, *Revolt of the Provinces: The Regionalist Movement in America, 1920–1945* (Chapel Hill: University of North Carolina Press, 1993); and T. J. Jackson Lears, *No Place of Grace: Antimodernism and the Transformation of American Culture* (New York: Pantheon, 1981). Quote by Walter Lippmann on p. 24 of Dorman, *Revolt of the Provinces.*

38. John Higham, "Ethnic Pluralism and Modern American Thought," in *Send These to Me: Jews and Other Immigrants in Urban America* (Baltimore: Johns Hopkins University Press, 1984), 196–230.

39. David Hollinger, "Ethnic Diversity, Cosmopolitanism, and the Emergence of the American Liberal Intelligentsia," in *In the American Province: Studies in the History and Historiography of Ideas* (Bloomington: Indiana University Press, 1985), 56–73. In his provincialism, Holmes may be closer to a contemporary of, and major influence on, Bourne — Josiah Royce. For Royce, as for Holmes, modernity represented a threat to communities of descent that called for preservation. Thus, provincialism was conceived as an agency of redemption against the "levelling tendencies of modern life" (Josiah Royce, "Provincialism," in *Race Questions, Provincialism, and Other American Problems* [New York: Macmillan, 1908], 57–108). See also J. Nicholas Entrikin, "Royce's 'Provincialism': A Metaphysician's Social Geography," in *Geography, Ideology, and Social Concern,* ed. D. R. Stoddart (Oxford: Basil Blackwell, 1981), 208–26; and Sollors, *Beyond Ethnicity,* 179–95.

40. Gillen to E. M. Hale, May 3, 1944, clipping scrapbook no. 6, FHP; emphasis added.

41. Jonathan Culler, "Semiotics of Tourism," *American Journal of Semiotics* 1 (1981): 127–40; and John Frow, "Tourism and the Semiotics of Nostalgia," *October* 57 (summer 1991): 123–51. On the seemingly inevitable dissonance between the "imaginative geographies" depicted by travelers and the reality they encounter, see the various essays in James Duncan and Derek Gregory, eds., *Writes of Passage: Reading Travel Writing* (New York: Routledge, 1998).

42. Louis Adamic, typeset manuscript review of *Old World Wisconsin,* 1944, clipping scrapbook no. 6, FHP. Adamic's review was published subsequently in the *Wisconsin Magazine of History* 28 (September 1944): 87–89.

43. Richard Weiss, "Ethnicity and Reform: Minorities and the Ambiance of the Depression Years," *Journal of American History* 66 (1979): 569. A hint of Adamic's importance and national reputation comes from a telling incident during World War II. Upon his first wartime visit to the United States in the winter of 1941–42, Winston Churchill articulated a vision of an "all conquering alliance of the English speaking people," a notion that Franklin Roosevelt sought to temper. He asked Churchill to read Adamic's recently published *Two-Way Passage,* in which the United States is represented as a culturally diverse nation. Adamic, who was invited to the White House to meet with the prime minister, later recalled Roosevelt's frustration in conveying this multicultural perspective to Churchill: "My friend doesn't realize fully — really — what a mixture of races, religions and nationality backgrounds we are, and that our backgrounds persist" (Louis Adamic, *Dinner at the White House* [New York: Harper and Brothers, 1946], 66).

44. Stephan Thernstrom, Ann Orlov, and Oscar Handlin, eds., introduction to *Harvard Encyclopedia of American Ethnic Groups* (Cambridge, Mass: Harvard University Press, 1980). For useful treatments of Adamic's work, see Robert F. Harney, "E Pluribus Unum: Louis Adamic and the Meaning of Ethnic History," *Journal of Ethnic Studies* 14 (spring 1986): 29–46; Philip Gleason, "Minorities (Almost) All," in *Speaking of Diversity: Language and Ethnicity in Twentieth-Century America* (Baltimore: Johns Hopkins University Press, 1992), 91–122; Henry A. Christian, *Louis Adamic: A Checklist* (Kent, Ohio: Kent

State University Press, 1971); and Carey McWilliams, *Louis Adamic and Shadow-America* (Los Angeles: A. Whipple, 1935). On the relationship between Adamic and McWilliams, see Michael Denning, *The Cultural Front: The Laboring of American Culture in the Twentieth Century* (London: Verso, 1997), 445–54. Adamic's writing on ethnicity is approached best through his many books, the most important of which are Louis Adamic, *My America, 1928–1938* (New York: Harper and Brothers, 1938); *From Many Lands* (New York: Harper and Brothers, 1940); *Two-Way Passage* (New York: Harper and Brothers, 1941); *What's Your Name?* (New York: Harper and Brothers, 1942); and *A Nation of Nations* (New York: Harper and Brothers, 1945). Finally, any treatment of Adamic is reliant on two further sources: his papers, contained in more than one hundred boxes, are held in the Princeton University Library, Special Collections (references to these materials are hereafter cited as LAP); and the several collections at the Immigration History Research Center, University of Minnesota (hereafter cited as IHRC).

45. Christian, *Louis Adamic*, xxii–xxiv.

46. Louis Adamic, "Tragic Towns of New England," *Harper's Monthly Magazine* (May 1931): 752.

47. Sales figures on p. 137 in Adamic, *My America*.

48. McWilliams, *Louis Adamic*, 81–82. Adamic had written earlier essays on ethnicity and immigration for the *American Mercury*, and as important as these pieces were in bringing him to a national audience, none reaches the depth of his work in the 1930s and 1940s. Louis Adamic, "The Yugoslav Speech in America," *American Mercury* (November 1927): 319–21; Louis Adamic, "The Bohunks," *American Mercury* (July 1928): 318–24.

49. Adamic, *My America*, 137–38, 188. The local response in Pittsburgh was typical of the adulation bestowed upon Adamic by his ethnic admirers. See "Adamic Says 'Melting Pot' Is Seething with Prejudice," *Pittsburgh Post Gazette,* March 27, 1934; and "Anti-immigrant Propaganda Hit by Yugo-Slav Speaker," *Pittsburgh Press,* March 27, 1934.

50. Adamic, *My America*, 478.

51. William Stott, *Documentary Expression and Thirties America* (New York: Oxford University Press, 1973), 20. Roy Stryker was the head of one of the most important depression-era social documentary outlets, the Photography Unit of the Farm Security Administration. For a recent examination of the FSA, see James Curtis, *Mind's Eye, Mind's Truth: FSA Photography Reconsidered* (Philadelphia: Temple University Press, 1992). Stryker quote is from Stott, *Documentary Expression*, 14.

52. William Stott recognizes Adamic's *My America* as by far the best-selling "I've seen America" book of the 1930s (Stott, *Documentary Expression*, 252).

53. According to Carey McWilliams, Adamic "cannot write without dramatizing.... [H]e thinks of himself, in relation to the world, dramatically" (McWilliams, *Shadow America*, 53).

54. Stott, *Documentary Expression*, 73. Stott's phrase "the cult of experience" is derived from an essay by Philip Rahv of the same title. In 1940 Rahv wrote that Americans had "an intense predilection for the real: and the real appears as a vast phenomenology swept by waves of sensation and feeling" (cited in ibid., 38–39).

55. Adamic, *My America*, xiii.

56. Louis Adamic, Layout of a Broadside, box 43, folder 6, LAP. Adamic's Broadside was reprinted several places, most notably in his *From Many Lands* (1939) and *Two-Way Passage* (1941). Adamic's quote of Whitman is from the preface to *Leaves of Grass*.

57. Boxes 51–52, LAP. The responses to the Broadside varied tremendously. Some, like Edward Lewis of Winnetka, Illinois, espoused classic nativist rhetoric when he argued that "One, ten, or a hundred immigrants are lovable and appealing individuals, but millions, when they come from twenty-five different nationalities and when the total of the foreign-born and children of the foreign-born equal about one-third of our population, are a problem." Others, like an anonymous "Negro teacher" from North Carolina, responded by critiquing the hypocrisy of America's undeniable racism: "Can the people of the United States afford to criticize Germany for crushing the Jews when people in America will hang

Negroes up trees and cut off parts of their bodies for souvenirs?" Both quotes from Adamic, *From Many Lands,* 346, 339.

58. Louis Adamic, "American History as a Record and a Process," *Common Ground* 8 (1948): 21.

59. Adamic, *A Nation of Nations,* 5.

60. Louis Adamic, "Plymouth Rock and Ellis Island: A Summary of a Lecture," 1940, p. 13, manuscript no. 1007479, IHRC.

61. Edward Abrahams, *The Lyrical Left: Randolph Bourne, Alfred Stieglitz, and the Origins of Cultural Radicalism in America* (Charlottesville: University Press of Virginia, 1988). See also Richard Pells, *Radical Visions and American Dreams: Culture and Social Thought in the Depression Years* (Urbana: University of Illinois Press, 1998); Denning, *Cultural Front;* and Dorman, *Revolt of the Provinces.*

62. Adamic, "Plymouth Rock and Ellis Island," 13.

63. Adamic, *My America,* 221.

64. Weiss, "Ethnicity and Reform," 576, 580. The "second-generation problem" was a major concern of social scientists and reformers during the interwar period. Many elites feared that, due to their relative poverty and the parents' place of origin, children and grand-children of the massive wave of eastern and southern European immigrants suffered from psychic distress. This, combined with their marginal status, would then make them more apt to turn to lives of crime or the "shallow" popular culture of the dance hall and movie palace. For a sample of the extensive literature on the criminality and antisocial behavior of the second generation, see Floyd H. Allport, "Cultural Conflict vs. the Individual and Factors in Delinquency," *Social Forces* 9 (1931): 493–97; Lawrence Guy Brown, *Immigration, Cultural Conflicts, and Social Adjustment* (New York: Arno, 1969 [1933]); Louis Wirth, "Culture Conflict and Misconduct," *Social Forces* 9 (1931): 484–92. On the movie palace of this time, see Karal Ann Marling, "Fantasies in Dark Places," in this book.

65. Louis Adamic, "Thirty Million New Americans," in *My America,* 210–32.

66. Adamic, *My America,* 208.

67. Louis Adamic, "Common Council for American Unity," in *From Many Lands,* 347.

68. Adamic, *A Nation of Nations,* 6.

69. Ibid., 12.

70. Lowenthal, *Possessed by the Past,* 173–91.

71. Adamic, *From Many Lands,* 301; Adamic, *A Nation of Nations,* 5. Such sentiments were hardly Adamic's alone; he was joined by many prominent public intellectuals and scholars. See, for example, Carey McWilliams, *Diversity within National Unity* (Washington, D.C.: National Council for the Social Sciences, a Department of the National Education Association, 1945).

72. Philip Gleason, "Americans All: World War II and the Shaping of American Identity," *Review of Politics* 43 (October 1981): 493–94.

73. James Barrett and David Roediger, "Inbetween Peoples: Race, Nationality, and the 'New Immigrant' Working Class," *Journal of American Ethnic History* 16, no. 3 (1997): 3–44. Michael Denning singles out 1942 as "a turning point in our dealings with all colored minorities" and the beginning of a new racial formation, while Richard Alba, in an intensively quantitative analysis, finds strong trends toward social and economic convergence between ethnic groups at exactly this time (Denning, *Cultural Front;* and Richard Alba, *Ethnic Identity: The Transformation of White America* [New Haven, Conn.: Yale University Press, 1990]). More generally on the growing importance of whiteness as a cultural category in the United States, see Matthew Frey Jacobson, *Whiteness of a Different Color: European Immigrants and the Alchemy of Race* (Cambridge, Mass.: Harvard University Press, 1998); Shelley Fisher Fishkin, "Interrogating 'Whiteness,' Complicating 'Blackness': Remapping American Culture," *American Quarterly* 47 (1995): 428–66; Ruth Frankenberg, *Displacing Whiteness: Essays in Social and Cultural Criticism* (Durham, N.C.: Duke University Press, 1997); Robert Orsi, "The Religious Boundaries of an Inbetween People: Street Feste and the Problem of the Dark-Skinned 'Other' in Italian Harlem, 1920–1990,"

American Quarterly 44 (1992): 313–47; Gary Gerstle, "Race and the Myth of the Liberal Consensus," *Journal of American History* 82 (1995): 579–86; and Grace Elizabeth Hale, *Making Whiteness: The Culture of Segregation in the South, 1890–1940* (New York: Vintage, 1998). Much of the recent scholarship on the construction of whiteness can be traced to the seminal work of David Roediger; see his *The Wages of Whiteness: Race and the Making of the American Working Class* (London: Verso, 1991).

74. Barbara Kirshenblatt-Gimblett, *Destination Culture: Tourism, Museums, and Heritage* (Berkeley: University of California Press, 1998), 77.

75. As Jackson and Bonnet both point out, such an erasure of political difference is itself a deeply political act, and one that is consistent with the historical invisibility of whiteness as a social category (Peter Jackson, "The Construction of 'Whiteness' in the Geographic Imagination," *Area* 30 [1998]: 99–106; and Alastair Bonnett, "Geography, Race, and Whiteness: Invisible Traditions and Current Challenges," *Area* 29 [1997]: 193–99).

76. Joe Trotter, *Black Milwaukee: The Making of an Industrial Proletariat, 1915–1945* (Urbana: University of Illinois Press, 1985); Robert Bieder, *Native American Communities in Wisconsin, 1600–1960* (Madison: University of Wisconsin Press, 1995).

77. *Milwaukee Journal*, May 14, 1944.

78. Through a content analysis, Deborah Ann Overmyer found that *Common Ground* gradually shifted its coverage: in the early years, under Adamic's editorship, the majority of articles dealt with immigration and white ethnicity, whereas between 1943 and 1949 (after Adamic stepped down from the magazine), over half the articles attacked racial (primarily antiblack) prejudice. See Deborah Ann Overmyer, "*Common Ground* and America's Minorities, 1940–1949: A Study in the Changing Climate of Opinion" (Ph.D. diss., University of Cincinnati, 1984).

79. Adamic, *My America,* 219.

80. Adamic, *From Many Lands,* 302. Even the structure of *Nation of Nations* (1944) indicates the disparity between the status of white immigrant identity and African American identity. The study contains fourteen chapters arranged identically: "Americans from Italy" is followed by "Americans from France," and "Americans from Poland," and so on. The sole exception is chapter 8: "Negro Americans." Such a racially charged syntax suggests that the common ground on which the children of immigrants stand—their common experience of geographical dislocation and persecution, and their whiteness—is not large enough to include "Americans from Africa" (as the chapter might have been titled).

81. Anson Phelps Stokes to Louis Adamic, February 26, 1935, correspondence files, box 49, LAP. Stokes was pursuing a project first outlined by W. E. B. Du Bois and that, until recently, remained unfulfilled. See Kwame Anthony Appiah and Henry Louis Gates Jr., eds., *Africana: The Encyclopedia of the African and African American Experience* (New York: Basic Books, 1999).

82. Adamic to Stokes, March 3, 1935, correspondence files, box 49, LAP.

83. Stokes to Adamic, March 15, 1935, correspondence files, box 49, LAP. It should be noted that the *Harvard Encyclopedia of American Ethnic Groups* has received similar criticism. See M. G. Smith, "Ethnicity and Ethnic Groups in America: The View from Harvard," *Ethnic and Racial Studies* 5 (1982): 1–22.

84. This is the critical point in Michael Omi and Howard Winant, *Racial Formation in the United States: From the 1960s to the 1990s,* 2d ed. (New York: Routledge, 1994).

85. David Hollinger, "National Culture and Communities of Descent," *Reviews in American History* 26 (1998): 319. See also Lowenthal, *Possessed by the Past.*

86. Hollinger, "National Culture," 319. Michael Rogin, *Blackface, White Noise: Jewish Immigrants in the Hollywood Melting Pot* (Berkeley: University of California Press, 1996); George Lipsitz, *The Possessive Investment in Whiteness: How White People Profit from Identity Politics* (Philadelphia: Temple University Press, 1998).

87. Bruce Robbins, "Othering in the Academy: Professionalism and Multiculturalism," *Social Research* 58 (1991): 354–72. See also Bruce Robbins, "Actually Existing Cosmopoli-

tanism," in *Cosmopolitics: Thinking and Feeling beyond the Nation,* ed. Pheng Cheah and Bruce Robbins (Minneapolis: University of Minnesota Press, 1998), 1–19.

88. Although Tuan does not use the term *rooted cosmopolitanism,* it seems to me that this captures well his idea of the cosmopolitan hearth. It should also be noted that Tuan is far from alone in calling for a cosmopolitanism that is rooted and particular, instead of universal and free-floating. The renewed interest in a critical cosmopolitanism emerges from an interesting confluence of scholars on the political left, who invariably lend more emphasis on place, roots, and ethnos than did their earlier counterparts. Bruce Ackerman, Mitchell Cohen, Kwame Anthony Appiah, and David Hollinger all qualify their preferred form of cosmopolitanism as "rooted"; Homi Bhabha describes his as "vernacular"; and James Clifford, in his wish to avoid "the excessive localism of particularist cultural relativism, as well as the overly global vision of a capitalist or technocratic monoculture," calls for a "discrepant cosmopolitanism." Bruce Ackerman, "Rooted Cosmopolitanism," *Ethics* 104 (1994): 516–35; Mitchell Cohen, "Rooted Cosmopolitanism," *Dissent* (fall 1992): 478–83; Kwame Anthony Appiah, "Cosmopolitan Patriots," *Critical Inquiry* 23 (1997): 617–39; Hollinger, *Postethnic America;* Homi Bhabha, "Unsatisfied Notes on Vernacular Cosmopolitanism," in *Text and Narration,* ed. Peter Pfeiffer and Laura Garcia-Moreno (Columbia, S.C.: Camden House, 1996), 191–207; and James Clifford, "Traveling Cultures," in *Cultural Studies,* ed. Lawrence Grossberg, Cary Nelson, and Paula Treichler (New York: Routledge, 1992), 96–112.

89. Yi-Fu Tuan, "Cultural Pluralism and Technology," *Geographical Review* 79 (1989): 279; Tuan, *Who Am I? An Autobiography of Emotion, Mind, and Spirit* (Madison: University of Wisconsin Press, 1999).

BODY, SELF, AND LANDSCAPE

A Geophilosophical Inquiry into the Place-World

Edward S. Casey

It was to satisfy man's curiosity concerning the differences of the world from place to place that geography developed as a subject of popular interest.

— RICHARD HARTSHORNE, *Perspectives on the Nature of Geography*

Rather than immersion in the locality where we now live, our mind and emotion are ever ready to shift to other localities and times.

— YI-FU TUAN, *Cosmos and Hearth*

Setting the Scene of Place

There has been a remarkable convergence between geography and philosophy in the past two decades. It is almost as if Strabo's opening claim in his *Geographia* had finally become justified two millennia later: "The science of Geography, which I now propose to investigate, is, I think, quite as much as any other science, a concern of the philosopher."[1] What is new (and not in Strabo) is the growing conviction that philosophy is the concern of the geographer as well, or more exactly that philosophy and geography now need each other — especially when it comes to matters of place and space. This has been evident ever since the appearance of Yi-Fu Tuan's *Space and Place* just over twenty years ago. This book was epoch-making because of its stress on the experiential features of place, its "subjective" or "lived" aspects. Other pioneers of place include Edward Relph, Anne Buttimer, Edward W. Soja, and J. Nicholas Entrikin. Each of these geographers, influenced and inspired by Tuan's inaugural work, is committed to the view that a primary task of contemporary geography is to render justice to its place-based character. So much is this the case that Robert David Sack, another leading figure in this place-work, can claim unhesitatingly in his recent book *Homo Geographicus* that "[in geography] the truly important factor is place and its relationship to space."[2]

What is worrisome, however, in Sack's otherwise exemplary treatment of place is precisely its uneasy alliance with space: as is found, for example, in his assertion that the "very fact that place combines *the unconstructed physical space* in conjunction with social rules and meaning enables place to draw together the three realms, and makes place constitutive of ourselves as agents,"[3] as if space were simply there, like some kind of matériel, to be made into places. More problematic yet is Sack's claim that space is "coterminous with nature"[4] — an apparent reinstatement of the Cartesian view that reflects the modernist faith in the primacy of space, a primacy that Sack endorses in unguarded moments, as when he remarks that "I personally would think of nature as the most basic category, and thus would say that space is primary to place."[5] Even if it is true (as Sack says plausibly) that "we must transform space into places for us to exist," the logic of this very same claim imputes to space an unquestioned priority, as does the related statement that "all of the places we experience are in this universal physical space."[6]

I go to the trouble of pointing so quickly to Sack's Cartesian clay feet not in order to cavil at what is clearly a major new work but to indicate that struggling out from under the Colossus of Descartes (and other proponents of the priority of space over place) continues to be extremely difficult, even after three centuries of philosophical critique as well as two decades of assiduous efforts on the part of geographers to restore place to a position of central significance. We are no longer in the position of Archytas, who could proclaim unequivocally that place is "the first of all things."[7] He could say this without any shadow of doubt because in the ancient Greek world place had no competition from space; indeed, there was no conception of space as a ubiquitous medium that is coextensive with the natural world. Times have changed — times in which the relationship between place and space has become a most vexatious matter. In fact, the entire debate between modernism and postmodernism can be expressed in terms of this still unresolved relationship — the modernist insisting on the priority of space (whether in the form of well-ordered physical space or highly structured institutional space) and the postmodernist conversely maintaining the primacy of place and, in particular, lived place.[8]

My own view is that space and place are two different *orders* of reality between which no simple or direct comparisons are possible. If this is so, then we should not seek compromises of the sort to which both Descartes and Sack are so prone: Descartes dubs volumetric space "internal place," thereby confounding one kind of space with place, just as Sack's idea of "secondary place" is in effect a commixture of space and place.[9] Nor can we justifiably affirm that place somehow *derives* from space: that it is dependent on it and shaped by it, as on the widely held assumption that "All people undertake to change amorphous space into articulated geography."[10]

I maintain that "space" is the name for that most encompassing reality that allows for things to be located within it; and it serves in this locatory capacity whether it is conceived as absolute or relative in its own nature. "Place," on the other hand, is the immediate ambiance of my lived body and its history, including the whole sedimented history of cultural and social influences and personal interests that compose my life-history. Place is situated in physical space, but then so is everything else, events as well as material things; it has no privileged relationship to that space, either by way of exemplification or representation. Nor can it be derived from it by some supposed genealogy. To believe in such a genealogy is to buy into the modernist myth that the universe is made of pure extended space and that anything less than such infinite space, including place, follows from it by condensation or delimitation.

Thus even as we celebrate the turn to place in recent geographical theory — a turn whose single most eloquent and intrepid investigator is Yi-Fu Tuan — we must conceive of place in such a way that it can be disentangled, once and for all, from false assimilations to space.[11]

Self, Body, Landscape

In the remainder of this essay I shall consider several matters that have been of special concern to the person honored in this volume: self, body, and landscape. Each of these notions addresses a different dimension of place. The self has to do with the agency and identity of the geographical subject; body is what links this self to lived place in its sensible and perceptible features; and landscape is the presented layout of a set of places, their sensuous self-presentation as it were.

Western philosophical theories of human selfhood have for the most part tended to tie it to awareness — hence to consciousness. A paradigm instance is Locke's view that the self's "personal identity" is entirely a function of the scope of its consciousness of its own past by means of memory. "Since consciousness," writes Locke, "always accompanies thinking, and it is that which makes every one to be what he calls self, . . . in this alone consists personal identity . . . as far as this consciousness can be extended backwards to any past action or thought, so far reaches the identity of that person; it is the same self now [as] it was then."[12] For Locke, personal identity is a matter of linking up one's present consciousness with a past consciousness and has nothing whatever to do with place. Place figures only as a parameter of the sheer physical identity of something that has no consciousness whatsoever.[13]

The quintessential modernist view of the relation between place and self is thus that *there is no such relation.* Place belongs entirely to the physical world, the self to the realm of consciousness, and the twain supposedly never meet. Locke's *Essay,* published in 1690, keeps personal identity and place as far apart as mind and matter in Descartes's writings fifty years earlier in the same century.

It is a mark of late modern or postmodern thought to contest the dichotomies that hold the self apart from body and place. Contra Descartes, the body is recognized as integral to selfhood, with the result that we can no longer distinguish neatly between physical and personal identity. Against Locke, place is regarded as constitutive of one's sense of self: "place and self help construct and activate each other."[14] Places require human agents to become "primary places" in Sack's nomenclature, and these same agents require specific places if they are to be the selves they are in the process of becoming. Personal identity is no longer a matter of sheer self-consciousness but now involves intrinsically an awareness of one's place — a specifically geographical awareness.[15]

Any effort to assess the relationship between self and place should point not just to reciprocal influence (that much any ecologically sensitive account would maintain) but, more radically, to constitutive co-ingredience: each is essential to the being of the other. In effect, there is *no place without self; and no self without place.* What is needed is a model whereby the abstract truth of Sack's position — which is emblematic of many philosophically minded geographers writing today — can be given concrete articulation, without conflating place and self or maintaining the self as an inner citadel of unimplaced freedom. Just how, then, is place constitutive of the self? How does it insinuate itself into the very heart of personal identity?

Thinned-out Places

To answer difficult questions such as these, it is best to begin with what Heidegger calls the "deficient mode" of any given phenomenon — in this case, the *scattered self* of postmodern society. Let us grant that this deeply distracted self is correlated with the *disarray of place* — with what Sack calls the "thinned-out places" of our time. Moreover, as places become more attenuated in their hold upon us, they merge into an indifferent state that is reminiscent of nothing so much as *space:* the very thing that dominated the early modern period from which we are reputedly escaping. Nowadays, emphasizes Sack, "places become thinned out and *merge with space.*"[16] It is a matter of what has been called "glocalization," whereby a given locale is linked indifferently to every (or any) other place in global space.[17] This is the converse of the premodern situation in which, as Heidegger remarks, "Bare space is still veiled over. Space has [already] been split up into places."[18] What does this implicit narrative of the fate of place from premodern to postmodern times tell us about the relation between place and self?

At the very least, it tells us that certain habitual patterns of relating to place have become weakened to the point of disappearing altogether. I refer to the micropractices that tie the geographical subject to his or her place-world, one instance of which is the "work-world" (*Werkwelt*) that is Heidegger's focus in his celebrated discussion of ready-to-hand things in *Being and Time.* In this discussion, place and self are intimately interlocked in the world of practical work. Tools not only are literal "instruments" that have a functional purpose of their own — for example, a hammer to drive in nails — but create works or products that allude to the person who will make use of them: "the work is cut to [the consumer's] figure; he 'is' there along with it as the work emerges."[19]

Not just the abstract figure of the consumer, however, but the concrete form of the laboring self is at stake in the work-world. When Heidegger remarks that "our concernful absorption in whatever work-world lies closest to us has a function of *discovering*,"[20] he means that this absorption helps us to become aware of our own being-in-the-world and not just the external destination of what we create in the workplace. It helps us to actualize our "pre-ontological understanding of the world," that is, to grasp the particular place we are in as the particular person which we are.[21]

Heidegger is telling us that in a comparatively demanding place such as a workshop, the human beings who labor there are so deeply embroiled that their being-in-the-world, their very self, is part of the scene and not something that hovers above it at a transcendental remove. The purpose of the tools we employ is not exhausted in sheer production or an economic fate outside the workplace but is also closely geared into the circuit of selfhood, indeed into its ultimate "care-structure."[22] In such a circumstance, then, place and self are thoroughly enmeshed — without, however, being fused into each other in a single monolithic whole. The articulations Heidegger finds in the situation, including the "towards-which" of serviceability, the "for-which" of usability, and the various "assignments" or references that are part of the work-world, indicate that the place/self relation is here as highly ramified as it is intimate.[23]

It would follow that thinned-out places are those in which the densely enmeshed infrastructures of the kind Heidegger discerns are missing. Not only do such places not *contain* strictly, as on Aristotle's model; they do not even *hold*, lacking the rigor and substance of thickly lived places. Their very surface is attenuated, being open to continual reshaping and reconnecting with other surfaces. Think of the way in which programs on television or items on the Internet melt away into each other as we switch channels or surf at leisure. In such circumstances, there is a notable *lability of place* that corresponds to a fickle self who seeks to be entertained: the "aesthetic self" as Kierkegaard would call it. The collapse of the kind of place that is capable of *keeping something within it* — for example, by its containing surface, such as the stable "surrounder" (*periechon*) of the Aristotelian model of place — correlates with a self of infinite distractability whose own surface is continually complicated by new pleasures: in short, a self that has become (in Gilles Deleuze and Félix Guattari's arresting term) a "desiring machine."[24]

Not that all is lost. Not even in postmodernity. As M. Merleau-Ponty said trenchantly, "no one is saved and no one is totally lost."[25] The point applies to place as well as to the self. Places (if they are to remain places at all) can never become utterly thinned out; they may become increasingly uniform and unable to engage our concernful absorption, yet without ceasing to exist altogether as places for us. In particular, they will not "merge with," much less *turn into*, space, as Sack claims: this claim, or fear, confuses two orders of being that are strictly separate.[26]

The same is true of the self, which can certainly become more superficial, yet will always retain traces of integral selfhood — even under the direst of diremptions. Thinned-out places of the sort with which we are surrounded today put the self to the test, tempting it to mimic their tenuous character by becoming itself an indecisive entity incapable of the kind of resolute action that is required in a determinately structured place like a workshop. But the self is not only enfeebled by nonrobust places; it can also make a virtue of the circumstance by becoming more sensitive to differences between places, for example, by leaving one's attenuated natal place in order to appreciate and savor other places and peoples. This is the ambiguous moral of Tuan's sagacious *Cosmos and Hearth:* the skeptical cosmopolite, for all his or her unsettledness, learns much more about the larger world and becomes more reflective than does the person who refuses to leave the hearth.[27]

At stake here is what we might call "the compensatory logic of loss." All too often, we presume a different logic is at work when it comes to matters of place and self — a logic of what Freud calls the "complemental series," whereby the more of one thing, the less of the other with which it is paired. Thus, it might be thought that the stronger the self becomes — the more autonomous, self-directive, and so on — the less important place should be. Should not a stronger self be less reliant on particular places?[28] And by the same token, should not a stronger link to a given place — for example, a hearth — bring with it a weaker self, a self that is so able to count on the security of home as to have no "mind of its own," much less be capable of "thinking [in] the reflective, ironic, quizzical mode"?[29]

But I believe that rather than a logic of more from less (and, equally, less from more) what we often find in the place/self relationship is a logic of *more with more.* The more places are thinned-out, the *more,* not the less, may selves be led to seek out thick places in which their own personal enrichment can flourish. Two brief examples: (1) The proliferation of movies on video (and now on dvd) — a decisive step toward the thinness of virtual space — has not meant the end of actual movie theaters but has even managed to increase the attractiveness of such theaters as real places with their own sensuous density and social interest. (2) The remarkable success of online superstores such as Amazon.com — an enterprise that unabashedly advertises itself as the "earth's biggest bookstore" — has certainly been deeply problematic for many small local bookstores. But such rapid growth has also accompanied and paralleled the equally remarkable success of large bookstores like Borders that have become congenial places in which to browse and read and drink coffee. More has meant not just less — but also more. Place, actual place, is here strengthened and not only diminished by the challenge posed by virtual place.

By this compensatory logic, the self stands to gain as well. For it is now able to move between virtual and actual places with a leeway that, even if not exhibiting the absolute freedom dreamed of in modernism, embodies that modicum of choice that is necessary (if not sufficient) to account for the relationship between self and place. The compensatory model allows us to imagine that both self and place may prosper in the very desert of the postmodern world, that gain may accompany loss: the experience of each being enhanced, rather than simply undermined, in the wasteland of thinned-out places.

Habitus in the Middle

Whether this quasi-meliorist reading of our present predicament will prove to be right, no one can claim to know for sure. But we can make progress of a more certain sort if we are able to answer the quite basic question: What ties place and self together? What ensures that these terms are genuinely co-constitutive and not merely diremptive? Here we seek a missing term that brings place and self together in any circumstance, whether premodern, modern, or postmodern. To hold that place qua place constitutes self qua self (or vice versa) is only to deepen the mystery, not to clarify it. To be as deeply ingressive in each other as they appear to be, place and self must be mediated by a third term common to both, a term that brings them together and keeps them together.[30] What, in short, is the mediatrix of place and self?

The work-world analyzed in *Being and Time* again offers a crucial clue. The basis of the density of engagement between self and place in this world is the set of *habitualities* by which its rich fabric is woven. Customary actions of certain specific sorts ensure that the work-world counts as a coherent and lasting *world* to which recourse can be made again and again: a world that I, the worker, can continually reenter. In part, this is a matter of investing what Merleau-Ponty calls my "customary body" in such a world with its particular demands for skillful behaviors on my part.[31] But in still larger part, it is a question of engendering, in a given such world, a habitus that draws on all my resources, not only bodily but also cultural, social, intellectual, and emotional.

I take the term *habitus* from Pierre Bourdieu in his *Outline of a Theory of Practice,* where it serves as a figure of the between: above all, between nature and culture, but also between consciousness and body, self and other, mechanism and teleology, determinism and freedom, even between memory and imagination. Habitus has a genius for mediation, indeed "universalizing mediation."[32] Here I want to propose that it is equally a middle term between place and self — and, in particular, between lived place and the geographical self. This self is constituted by a core of habitudes that incorporate and continue, at both psychical and physical levels, what one has experienced in particular places.

Habitus is not to be confused with mere routine, the sheerly habitual. True, it possesses a sedimented aspect that may induce a "hysteresis effect," leading to lag and missed opportunity, and being slow on the uptake.[33] But it is also improvisational and open to innovation: Bourdieu even defines habitus at one point as an "intentionless invention of regulated improvisation."[34] His example of such improvisation is telling; it is that of "the distribution of activities and objects within the internal space of the house."[35] In short, a home-place is the scene of the regulated improvisation effected by habitus — in contrast with, say, agrarian rituals, which are "strictly regulated by customary norms and upheld by social sanctions."[36] The home-place, like Heidegger's workplace, allows for innovation within regulation; it encourages moving around freely in its ambiance, facilitating *bricolage* and other forms of improvising within the limited resources of a given place and its contents. And it is thanks to such open-ended habitudinal action within placial constraints that there occurs "the production of a commonsense world endowed with the objectivity secured by consensus on the meaning (*sens*) of practices and the world."[37] This world is ineluctably a *place-world*.

Although Bourdieu does not invoke place specifically, it is everywhere present in his discussion of habitus, indeed at both ends of the quasi-diachronic model he proposes in *Outline of a Theory of Practice*. It is there at the start as the scene of inculcation, the place of instruction that embodies "the structures constitutive of a particular type of environment (e.g., the material conditions characteristic of a class condition)."[38] Among these material conditions of existence are surely the concrete places in which members of a given class reside and which constitute "a particular type of environment." And place is there at the later point when a given habitus has been fully formed and is continually reenacted in similar circumstances, that is, when durable dispositions are "lastingly subjected to the same conditioning, and hence placed in the same material conditions of existence."[39] A given habitus is always enacted in a particular place and incorporates the regularities inherent in previous such places — all of which are linked by a habitudinal bond. It does not matter that the bond itself is often unconscious, "without explicit reason or signifying intent."[40] Indeed, its very status as *taken for granted* is what allows it to be all the more effective in its operative force. Prominent among things taken for granted is *the implacement of habitus itself,* its placial bearing as it were: a particular place gives to habitus a familiar arena for its enactment, and the lack of explicit awareness of that place as such, its very familiarity, only enhances its efficacy as a scene in which it is activated. Such a place (to adopt Bourdieu's Gallic formula) "goes without saying because it comes without saying."[41]

And the same is true for the self in all this. Its enduring interests and proclivities are incorporated into habitudes — interests and proclivities not separate from its social and historical milieu but individuated, given a personal tonality by way of incorporation into the self. If this were not to happen, the self would be a merely ephemeral entity, the creature of every passing circumstance; in fact, it has layers that are as durationally deep as the places it finds itself in are spatially thick: this is Bergson's point in positing a *moi profond* that is not subject to the usual chronometric time but the source of a distinctive nonnumerable temporality: *durée pure*.[42] Here we have to do with the temporality of habitus, whose lasting dispositions require the kind of generous outlay of time that duration alone can provide.

Habitus is mediational in its capacity to bring together the placiality of its ongoing setting and the temporality of its recurrent reenactment. Despite Kant's dogmatic effort to keep time out of geography and to confine it to history,[43] whenever the geographical subject is at stake, time and history alike reenter geographical consideration. They do so most effectively in the form of habitus, which is as ineluctably temporal as it is placial in its formation and consolidation.

Thus the very idea of habitus leads us to merge what Kant wanted to keep strictly apart: history and geography. This is all the more the case if the schemes operative within habitudes are placial as well as temporal.[44] *As they must be* if habitus is truly to mediate between place (primarily but not exclusively spatial) and the self (primarily but not only temporal). The generativity of habitudinal schemes is at once placial and temporal, and because of this double-sidedness, the geographical subject is able to insinuate himself or herself all the more completely into the place-world. Were it not so, were habitus exclusively one or the other, this subject would be schizoid within and alienated without, unable to complete the cycle that place and the self continually reconstitute thanks to the habitudinal basis that they share.[45] Such a subject would be precisely the self-riven early modern subject described by Descartes and Locke in their tendentious descriptions of human selfhood.

A corollary of this last line of thought is that if places can become thinned-out in certain historical moments such as our own, this can only mean that these places have begun to lose the habitudinal density whereby they are implicated within the selves who experience them. *The attenuation is primarily of the habitus linking places and selves* — or more exactly, of the placial and temporal schemes that generate various customary ways of being in the place-world. The consequence can only be a dessication of both self and place, the diminishing of both, a common failure to find "a matrix of perceptions, appreciations, and actions [that] makes possible the achievement of infinitely diversified tasks."[46] This doubly denuded circumstance, this diminution of habitudinal thickness, is a situation of *less with less,* less place, less self. This is an inversion of a positively compensatory logic of *more with more:* more place, more self. If the thinning-out is this inversion itself and not the prelude to a reinvestment in place and self, then we are left with the sobering prospect of a redoubled loss: loss of place, loss of self.

From Habitus to Habitation

Promising and suggestive as is the notion of habitus when transposed from social anthropology to geography,[47] Bourdieu's conception needs to be expanded in one important direction if it is to fully accomplish its role as mediatrix of place and self. As composed of internalized and sedimented schemes, and as constantly subject to hysteresis, habitus becomes deeply buried within the self as if it were an abiding possession — as is signified by Bourdieu's descriptive terms "durable," "lasting," "predisposed," and "matrix." Reinforcing this tendency to contain habitus, to alienate it from its own improvisational powers, is Bourdieu's claim that, as something taken for granted, it has nothing to do with the reproduction of "lived experiences." Instead of being the expression of subjects' intentions, the habitus is something "automatic and impersonal, significant [but] without intending to signify."[48] Recognizable in these claims is Bourdieu's effort to distance himself from phenomenology.

But in fact we do act on the basis of habitus, and action is something that is both lived (i.e., consciously experienced) and intentional (i.e., involves an aim even if this is not explicitly formulated). It is the actional dimension that needs to be added to Bourdieu's analysis. The value or virtue of a given habitus resides in the actuality of its enactment, not in its being a solidified deposition of past actions or a mere disposition to future actions. Whatever its antecedent history and subsequent fate, a habitus is something we continually *put into action;* and we do so, moreover, by means of concrete bodily behaviors that follow out the plans and projects of a self who actively intends to do something in the very "commonsense world" that is the product of "the orchestration of habitus."[49] Given that this world presents itself to us as a layout of places, the activation of habitus expresses an intentional and invested *commitment to the place-world.* Even if it is the internalization of social practices by way of origin, in its actual performance a given habitus is a reaching out to place.

The primary way in which the geographical subject realizes this commitment to place is by means of *habitation.* I am taking *habitation* in a sense capacious enough to include nomadic life as well as settled dwelling. Either way, the self relates to the place of habitation by means of concerted bodily movements that are the embodiment of habitudinal schemes, their explicitation and exfoliation in the inhabited place-world. In the word *habitation,* moreover, we hear not only living somewhere and not just the concretization of habitus but, more particularly, the active root of *habitation* itself, namely, *habere,* Latin for "to have, to hold." Both of these root verbs are performative and transitive in character and thus adumbrate the ongoing engagement that is always at stake in the place/self cycle, especially in its habitational modes. When I inhabit a place — whether by moving through it or staying in it — I *have* it in my actional purview. I also *hold* it by virtue of being in its ambiance: first in my body as it holds on to the place by various sensory and kinesthetic means, then in my memory as I hold it in mind — a mind, moreover, that includes such nonmentalistic things as language, body memory, and habitudes themselves. This is how the durability of habitus is expressed: by my active holding on to a situation so as to prolong what I experience beyond the present moment.

Thus the *in* of *inhabitation* is not Aristotle's *in* of containment; it is the active *in* of going *into,* holding *on to,* and often eventuates in moving *out of.*[50] The Aristotelian *in* here gives way to the Heideggerian *ex,* "out of": a prefix we hear equally in "ex-perience" and in "ec-stasy." Heidegger's concept of dwelling, for example, is that of an active taking hold, a reaching *out,* a sparing and preserving, a being *on* earth that implies action on its surface, a going in and out of places on this surface.[51]

In the end, we need to do justice both to habitus and to habitation. Geographical being is a matter of what Edmund Husserl liked to call "activity in passivity" — the activity of habitation and the passivity of habitus. If habitus represents a movement from the externality of established customs and norms to the internality of durable dispositions, habitation is a matter of re-externalization — of taking the habitus that has already been acquired and enacting it anew in the place-world. Just as there can be no habitus without the preexisting places of history and society, so there would be no habitation without the habitudes that make implacement possible for a given subject.[52] Thus we must acknowledge the importance of intentionality and lived experience and an active assumption of stances within the world of place, whether these stances be central or marginal vis-à-vis a given society.[53] This world is not to be confused with the realm of determinate history and collective sociality, even though both of the latter certainly influence and shape it. It is a genuine "thirdspace," to adopt Edward Soja's suggestive term for what I prefer to call "place-world," a world that is not only perceived or conceived but actively *lived.* As Soja maintains, such space, such a world, is at once social and historical — and, equally, spatial. The spatiality is a lived spatiality: which is what Bourdieu neglects and Soja celebrates in his "real-and-imagined" experiences of Los Angeles.[54]

Ingoing and Outgoing Body

What, then, is the vehicle of this lived and lively thirdspace that is neither simply material nor sheerly mental in character, a domain that we find and experience both actively and passively, both through habitation and habitude? The vehicle of being-in-place is the *body.* The body is indispensable here not just as a "practical operator" of habitudinal schemes or as the "body schema" that is the format or receptacle of such schemes.[55] Nor is it only a question of what I have referred to above as "concerted bodily movements that are the embodiment of habitudinal schemes." The body's role is much more basic. In matters of place, as Henri Lefebvre claims, "the body serves both as point of departure and as destination."[56] But how can something that is normally beneath our notice be the pivot of the place-world?

It is the pivot in at least two ways, which I shall label "outgoing" and "incoming."

1. *Outgoing.* The lived body *goes out to meet the place-world.* It does so in myriad ways, including highly differentiated and culturally freighted ways such as racial or class or gender identity, the focus of so many recent writings on the body. But it goes out in one primary way in which all more particular ways share: I refer to the "spatial framework"[57] whereby it links up most pervasively with the place-world. By means of this framework, the three inherent axes of the body, each defined by a binary opposition (i.e., up/down, front/back, right/left), lead into the primary dimensions of any given place (i.e., verticality, frontality, and horizontality) as well as the implicit directionality of that place (e.g., upward or downward, forward or backward, verging to the right or to the left).[58] It is not a matter of sheer fit — as if body and place were each, in advance, already fully formed, such that they would cohere like pieces of a jigsaw puzzle. (This way lies Aristotle's container model once again.) Neither body nor place is a wholly determinate entity; each continually evolves, and precisely in relation to the other. The place-world is energized and transformed by the bodies that inhabit it, while these bodies are in turn guided and influenced by this world's inherent structures. The dialectic between the two is so subtle that our lived sense is often that body and place come already suited for each other and that we simply belong to our current place-world and it belongs to us; yet this mutual suitability is in fact a hard-won and precarious accomplishment that includes resistance as well as agreement in its evolution.[59]

2. *Incoming.* But the body not only goes out to reach places; it also bears the traces of the places it has known. These traces are continually laid down in the body, being sedimented there, and thus becoming formative of its specific somatography. A body is shaped by the places it has come to know and that have come to it — come to take up residence in it, by a special kind of placial incorporation that is just as crucial to human experience as is the interpersonal incorporation so central to classical Freudian theory. Furthermore, places are themselves altered by our having been in them. As Elizabeth Grosz says, "The City is made and made over into the simulacrum of the body, and the body, in its turn, is transformed, 'citified,' urbanized as a distinctively metropolitan body."[60]

It is the latter action designated by Grosz — whereby the body is in effect placialized — that I am designating as "incoming." Moreover, the *coming in* of places into the body, their inscription there, is a matter of both tenacity and subjection.

a. Tenacity. Places come into us lastingly; once having been in a particular place for any considerable time — or even briefly, if our experience there has been intense — we are forever marked by that place, which lingers in us indefinitely and in a thousand ways, many too attenuated to specify. The inscription is not of edges or outlines, as if place were some kind of object; it is of the whole brute presence of the place. What lingers most powerfully is this presence and, more particularly, *how it felt to be in this presence:* how it felt to be in the Crazy Mountains that summer, how I sensed the Lower East Side during January. Proust points out that the essence of a place can be compressed into a single sensation that, being reawakened, can bring the place back to us in its full vivacity. In his own example, the feeling of a paving-stone underfoot somewhere in France evokes just how it felt to be in the foyer of St. Mark's Cathedral in Venice — a foyer whose floor is lined with stones of similar un-evenness.[61] There is an *impressionism of place* by which the presence of a given place remains lodged in our body long after we have left it; this presence is held within the body in a virtual state, ready to regain explicit awareness when the appropriate impression or sensation arises.

b. Subjection. In contrast with Kant's view that we construct space by a formal transcendental activity, we are not the masters of place but prey to it; we are subjects of place or, more exactly, *subject to place.* Such subjection ranges from docility (wherein we are the mere creatures of a place, at its whim and in its image) to appreciation (by which we enjoy being in a place, savoring it) to change (whereby we alter ourselves as a function of having been in a certain place). In every case, we are still, even many years later, *in the places to which we are subject* because (and to the exact extent that) *they are in us.* They are in us — indeed, *are us* — thanks to their in-corporation into us by a process of somatic localization whose logic is yet to be discerned. They constitute us as subjects. To be *Homo geographicus* is to be such a subject. To be (a) subject to/of place is to *be what we are as an expression of the way a place is.* The body is the primary vehicle of such expression, and precisely in Leibniz's sense of a condensed and often tacit representation: the body expresses its place-world as a monad expresses the universe. Such expression is tantamount to deep reflection: in its subjection to place, a body "reflects its region."[62]

Thanks to the inscriptive tenacity and expressive subjection of the body, places are embedded in us; they become part of our very character, what we enact and carry forward. Neither habitus nor habitation, taken alone, captures completely this factor of *persistence of place in body.* Habitus is the socially encoded core of our bodily self; habitation is the activist commitment of the same self; but to such socialism and activism we need to add a third ingredient, *idiolocalism.* Where habitus internalizes the collective subject of customary and normative structure, and habitation calls for the intentional subject of concerted action, idiolocality invokes the subject who incorporates and expresses a particular place, its *idios,* what is "peculiar" in both senses of this Greek word. And the bearer of idiolocality is none other than the body, the proper subject of place. Only such a subject can be subject to place in its idiosyncrasy; only this subject can inscribe the peculiarities of place in its very flesh, keeping them there in a state of *Parathaltung,* a condition of readiness to reappear at the flash of a mere impression.[63]

In the end, we do not have three subjects here — any more than Soja or Lefebvre would maintain that we have three separate spaces to contend with in their trialectic typologies.[64] There is only one subject of place, one body-subject who experiences, expresses, and deals with place by means of habitus, habitation, and idiolocalization. Place is shared out among these three modalities; it is a matter of "the betweenness of place," in Entrikin's striking phrase, which I here interpret as the pervasiveness of place, its permeation into every crevice of the body-subject in its habitudinal, habitational, and idiolocal modalities. Just as Entrikin argues that we need not make an exclusionary choice between existential and naturalistic conceptions of place but should address both "from a point in between"[65] that does not exclude either, so I would maintain that the three aspects of the body-in-place I have singled out should be treated inclusively, without any forced choice having to be made between them. We owe no less to place and to the body that at once bears and transforms it.

The Landscape in All This

To pursue what it means to be *Homo geographicus* is to be led, therefore, to the body in at least the three modalities I have attempted to describe. And by the same token it is to be led back to the self. The self of the place/self cycle from which we began is what Barbara Hooper calls a "body/self."[66] Only such a self can be implaced; there is no subject of place except as embodied. Locke is here doubly undone: personal identity entails body (and not just consciousness) as well as a body-in-place (rather than an unimplaced self). *The body is the heft of the self that is in place,* whose very "extensity"[67] calls for a massive and thick subject to be equal to the demanding task of existing in the place-world.

Just as there is no implaced self except as a body/self, there is no place without such a self. There may well be space and location in the absence of an embodied self, which is only contingently connected to *their* presence. But in the presence of place there can be no subject other than a corporeal subject capable of possessing habitus, undertaking habitation, and bearing the idiolocality of place itself.[68] This is the concrete self of the hearth, not the disembodied occupant of the cosmos.

The body comes first and is even first among equals when it comes to philosophical (and specifically phenomenological) meditations on geography. Yet the body is not the last word concerning an expanded sense of the geographical self. Requisite as well is *landscape,* and I want to end with some brief observations on this basic term so familiar to contemporary cultural geographers, thanks again to the seminal work of Yi-Fu Tuan, as well as J. B. Jackson, W. G. Hoskins, Edward Relph, Denis Cosgrove, and others. (Philosophers are natural predators on what is self-evident to others — not so as to undermine what is obviously true but in order to show the sometimes unsuspected complications and implications of the obvious itself. This is what I have been doing with body and will now attempt to do, much more cursorily, with landscape.)

If it is true to say that the geographical self is *deepened* by the body — drawn down into it — it is equally true to say that place is *broadened* in landscape. As Relph writes, "Landscape is both the context for places and an attribute of places."[69] In fact, body and landscape are the concretization and exfoliation, respectively, of the initially indefinite dyad of self and place. For this latter dyad is abstract as it stands — as much as is the Pythagorean indeterminate dyad (*aiostos dyas*) of same and other, like and unlike, odd and even.[70] The empty armature of place-cum-self needs to be fleshed out, and in two opposed but complementary directions: downward into body and outward into landscape. I say "needs to be" because both body and landscape are so deeply ingredient in the experience of the human subject as to pass unnoticed for the most part. The presence of the body is "pre-reflective," as Merleau-Ponty liked to say; the surrounding landscape is mostly "invisible," as Erwin Straus has argued, a matter of "spirit" in Relph's word.[71] All the more reason, then, to bring such factors into our reflective awareness — to make them as palpable as possible. To do so is to take a crucial step toward a geography that is responsive to the material conditions of the place-world: a geography so diversely enlivened by the writings of Yi-Fu Tuan.

Landscape is a cusp concept; it serves to distinguish place and space (whose difference I have taken for granted until now),[72] being the point of their most salient difference. There is no landscape of space, though there is landscape of both place and region. It is important to stress this difference, since it is easy to think of landscape as a mere middle term between place and space — as the transition between the two. In fact, it stands between cosmos and hearth. Phrases like "wide open spaces" that we apply unthinkingly to landscape only confuse the issue. But just as thinned-out places do not merge into space, so an open landscape does not fade into space. A landscape may indeed be vast; it can contain an entire region, thus a very large set of places; yet it will never *become* space. No matter how capacious a landscape may be, it remains a congeries or a composition of places, their intertangled skein. It may constitute a place-world but never a universe, that is, space as an endless, infinitized totality. Once again, the difference is categorical. Landscape is a detotalized totality of places.

The ontological difference between place and space is nowhere more evident than in the fate of a primary feature of landscape, its *horizon*. Every landscape has a horizon, yet space never does. As Straus says tellingly, "In a landscape we are enclosed by a horizon; no matter how far we go, the horizon constantly goes with us. Geographical space has no horizon."[73] The horizon is an arc wherein a given landscape comes to an end — an end of visibility, of presence, of availability. A place per se has no horizon, only an enclosure or perimeter. Only when places are concatenated in a landscape is there anything like a horizon, which is the undelimited limit, or better the *boundary,* for the landscape as a whole. As a boundary, the horizon does not merely close off the landscape; it opens it up for further exploration, that is, for bodily ingression. As Heidegger puts it: "A boundary is not that at which something stops but, as the Greeks recognized, the boundary is that from which something *begins its presencing*. That is why the concept is that of *horismos*, that is, the horizon [as] the boundary."[74] Hence we can apply to horizon the same term by which Aristotle describes the limit of a place: the *surrounder*. The horizon is the boundary that surrounds the grouping of places making up a given landscape. The outward movement of landscape — a movement out beyond any particular place and beyond any body in that place — reaches its (nonmetric) end in the horizon.

Other features of landscape include its *sensuous display* — that is, the panoply of features sensed on its surface that make it into a variegated scene of perception and action — and its *atmosphere,* the combination of air and light that gives to a landscape its special diffuseness or "glow." Ingredient as well is its *ground* — the subtending layer that need not be earth but can be sea or even asphalt — on which the concrete *things* of a given landscape repose: where "things" may be humanly constructed as well as engendered by nature. I first described these various factors in a discussion of "wild places," and it is significant that they hold up as descriptive terms of landscape in general, whether this latter be wild or cultivated.[75] But wilderness remains paradigmatic for the outreach of landscape, its openness, its uncontrollability — even as a cityscape is emblematic of dense historicity, intentional order, cultural diversity, and social complexity. The extensity and power of landscape may be such that all we can do is to glance at it, take parts of it in, and let the rest go.[76]

A landscape is nothing if not expansive. Where the body characteristically *draws in* the place-world around it — ingests it in schematized bodily behavior and in lingering body memories — the landscape *draws out* the same place-world, often to its utmost limit. It is rare, if not impossible, to experience an entirely isolated place: a place without relation to any other place, without imbrication in a region.[77] Landscape is the capacious scene wherein the coadnunation of places in a given region arises; it is the matrix of places without us, hence the antipode of habitus as the matrix of schemes within us. It is the arena in which cosmos and hearth, otherwise such disparate terms, connect and animate each other. As such, it shows hearth and cosmos to be not merely dichotomous but ultimately continuous with each other.

"In a landscape," says Straus, "we always get to one place from another place,"[78] echoing the first epigraph of this essay: "It was to satisfy man's curiosity concerning the differences of the world from place to place that geography developed as a subject of popular interest." The curiosity to which Hartshorne refers is a curiosity about landscape, for only in a coherent and concatenated landscape can we go from place to place, whether this be on land or sea or even in the air.[79] Only in the generous embrace of landscape can we go from hearth to cosmos and then, having become cosmopolitan, return to hearth once more. Landscape is the transitional domain that links cosmos and hearth, place and space, self and other.

In short summation: landscape and the body are the effective epicenters of the geographical self. The one widens out into vistas of the place-world — all the way to the horizon and beyond it to the beckoning cosmos — while the other literally incorporates this same world and acts upon it. Without landscape, we would be altogether confined to the peculiarities of a particular place, its insistent idiolocalism, its hemmed-in hearth; without the body, even this one place would pass us by without leaving a mark on us, much less inspire us to act toward it in novel ways or to transcend it toward a more extensive cosmic whole. But because we have both body and landscape, place and self alike are enriched and sustained, enabling us to become enduring denizens of the place-world to which we so fatefully belong.

Notes

1. *The Geography of Strabo,* trans. H. L. Jones (New York: Putnam's, 1917), 1.3.

2. Robert David Sack, *Homo Geographicus* (Baltimore: Johns Hopkins University Press, 1997), 34, 30.

3. Ibid., 33; emphasis added.

4. Ibid., 28 (in diagram). At p. 34 Sack says that "Space is coextensive with nature and [is] a foundation of the universe."

5. Ibid., 265 n. 7. Another testimony to the priority of space is found at p. 98: "the loops composing place are all variants of the same relation — space. Each loop simply reworks space so that it can engage material from that realm."

6. The first statement is at ibid., 265 n.7; the second at 31.

7. The complete statement is "Perhaps [place] is the first of all things." This is cited by Simplicius, *Commentary on Aristotle's Categories,* trans. S. Sambursky, in *The Concept of Place in Late Neoplatonism* (Jerusalem: Israel Academy of Sciences and Humanities, 1982), 37. Archytas, a neo-Pythagorean, lived and wrote in the late fifth and early fourth centuries B.C.

8. For this contrast, see especially David Harvey, *The Condition of Postmodernity: An Inquiry into the Origins of Cultural Change* (Oxford: Blackwell, 1989), pt. 3, and table 4.1, where modernity is encapsulated as "becoming/epistemology/regulation/urban renewal" and postmodernity as "being/ontology/deregulation/urban revitalization/place."

9. Sack's working premise is that "at the most general level, place integrates nature and culture" (*Homo Geographicus,* 166 n. 13). Not every kind of place can do this: not, for example, "secondary place," which is merely "the distribution of certain things *in space*" (ibid., 32; emphasis added). But "primary place" does bring nature and culture together, and it does so "when place, and not only the things in it, is a force — when it influences, affects, and controls" (ibid.). Primary place influences, affects, and controls because of the presence of human intention and meaning, which convert secondary places into primary places — the very places we inhabit and explore and enjoy.

10. Yi-Fu Tuan, *Space and Place: The Perspective of Experience* (Minneapolis: University of Minnesota Press, 1976), 83. Tuan and Sack are by no means the only geographers to engage in this paralogism. Compare Pred: place "always involves an appropriation and transformation of space and nature" (Allen Pred, "Place as Historically Contingent Process: Structuration and the Time-Geography of Becoming Places," *Annual of the Association of American Geographers* 74, no. 2 [1984]: 279).

11. Another such misconception is the confinement of place to the experience of human beings alone. When Sack claims that "primary places involve [only] human actions and intentions" (*Homo Geographicus,* 32), he engages in an unduly anthropocentric way of thinking that undervalues the fact that other animals (and even plants and rocks) have their

own places of habitations that are just as definitively unspatial as are distinctively human places such as homes and buildings. Nor does it help to say that "the concept of a place does not obtain in the nonhuman realm because there is no real territorial structure [there] with *rules* of in/out of place" (ibid., 132). This claim begs the question since "rules of in/out of place" are, by definition, human-created. Hidden from view in such thinking is the fact that the very idea of infinite space is a human conception. We need to reverse the usual assumptions and admit that place, the finite unit, is not (necessarily) human and that space, the more extensive notion, is the product of human thought of a particular historical era.

12. John Locke, *An Essay concerning Human Understanding,* ed. A. C. Fraser (New York: Dover, 1959), 1:449.

13. Not only is place not part of personal identity, but even in the realm of the purely physical it serves not to identify something but only to distinguish it from other things that are otherwise entirely alike: "When we see anything to be in any place in any instant of time, we are sure (be it what it will) that it is that very thing, and not another, which at that same time exists in another place, how like and undistinguishable soever it may be in all other respects; and in this consists identity [of a thing]. . . . For we never finding, nor conceiving it possible, that two things of the same kind should exist in the same place at the same time" (ibid.).

14. Sack, *Homo Geographicus,* 132. See also his statement that "the formation of personality [is] directly connected to the formation of place" (131).

15. As Sack says: "Opening our homes to new ideas, or leaving home to see the world, is essential for an enlightened *geographical awareness*" (ibid., 19; emphasis added). This claim rejoins the central thesis of Yi-Fu Tuan's *Cosmos and Hearth: A Cosmopolite's Viewpoint* (Minneapolis: University of Minnesota Press, 1996).

16. Sack, *Homo Geographicus,* 138; emphasis added. On this theme, see also ibid., 9–11.

17. "With the sudden but subtle 'inflation of the present,' of a present globalized by teletechnologies, present time occupies center stage not only of history (between past and future) but especially of the geography of the *globe.* So much so that a new term has recently been coined, *glocalization*" (Paul Virilio, *Open Sky,* trans. J. Rose [London: Verso, 1997], 135; cf. also 144). Virilio describes in temporal terms what has become true in spatial terms.

18. Martin Heidegger, *Being and Time,* trans. J. Macquarrie and E. Robinson (New York: Harper and Row, 1962), 138. Heidegger is speaking here of the "region" (*Gegend*) that gathers the ready-to-hand implements of our concrete life — gathers them in terms of "totalities of significance" that are not yet subject to modernist reductions.

19. Ibid., 100. Heidegger adds: "The work produced refers not only to the 'towards-which' of its usability and the 'whereof' of which it consists: under simple craft conditions it also has an assignment to the person who is to use it or wear it" (ibid.). For further discussion, see John Pickles, *Phenomenology, Science, and Geography: Spatiality and the Human Sciences* (Cambridge: Cambridge University Press, 1985), 160–68.

20. Heidegger, *Being and Time,* 101; emphasis added.

21. The notion of "pre-ontological understanding of the world" occurs at ibid., 102: "Does not Dasein have an understanding of the world — a pre-ontological understanding, which indeed can and does get along without explicit ontological insights?" A given work-world has for its "for-the-sake-of-which" (*Worum-willen*) the Being of Dasein itself, that is, its being-in-the-world. See ibid., 116–17.

22. Indeed, even the external fate of the product refers back to this care-structure as it belongs to those who will use it; the roof I make for a bus-stop is also "for the sake of a possibility of Dasein's Being" (ibid., 116). On the care-structure itself, see ibid., secs. 39–42.

23. Concerning the "towards-which" of serviceability and the "for-which" of usability, see ibid., sec. 18. On the character of reference at stake in the workplace, see ibid., sec. 17, "Reference and Signs." Note Heidegger's remark that "for primitive man, the sign coincides with that which is indicated" (113) — a clear rejection of a fusionist model for understanding modernity — in contrast with the signs at stake in the work-world that "always indicate primarily 'wherein' one lives, where one's concern dwells, what sort of involvement there

is with something" (111). Of special interest in this statement is the link between sign and place.

24. On the desiring machine, see Gilles Deleuze and Félix Guattari, *Anti-Oedipus: Capitalism and Schizophrenia,* trans. R. Hurley, M. Seem, and H. R. Lane (Minneapolis: University of Minnesota Press, 1983), pt. 1, "The Desiring Machines."

25. M. Merleau-Ponty, *Phenomenology of Perception,* trans. C. Smith (New York: Humanities Press, 1962), 171.

26. Which does not prevent thinned-out places from becoming something *similar to* space, thanks to taking on certain of the predicates of space such as planiformity, isotropism, isometrism, homogeneity, and so on. But this is a far cry from *becoming space*.

27. Such a situation "can link us both seriously and playfully to the cosmos — to strangers in other places and times; and it enables us to accept a human condition that we have always been tempted by fear and anxiety to deny, namely, the impermanence of our state wherever we are, our ultimate homelessness" (Tuan, *Cosmos and Hearth,* 188). Sack claims similarly that "thinned-out places with permeable boundaries help us see through the veils of culture" (*Homo Geographicus,* 138). He also points out that "thinned-out places work well when they do not intrude on our consciousness and thus allow us to attend to the things that should take place in them. This is how routinization of complex life is constructed" (ibid., 9). But the second claim is a purely functional point, and the former assertion carries with it, by Sack's own admission, this price: "in seeing through more clearly, the weight of making sense of the world falls on our shoulders, and for many this is too heavy a burden" (ibid., 138). Already Heidegger, let it be noted, insisted that at the very center of being-at-home is an uncanny unhomeliness: *Unheimlichkeit* lurks within *Heimlichkeit* (see *Being and Time,* sec. 40: "The Basic State-of-Mind of Anxiety as a Distinctive Way in Which Dasein Is Disclosed).

28. This way of thinking colors Tuan's neo-Kantian model of the cosmopolite, whose freedom to range over many places on earth reflects its greater self-reliance: "Rather than immersion in the locality where we now live, our mind and emotion are ever ready to shift to other localities and times. . . . Having seen something of the splendid spaces, he or she . . . will not want to return, permanently, to the ambiguous safeness of the hearth" (*Cosmos and Hearth,* 188). Tuan's argument here is closely affiliated with the view expressed in his book *Segmented Worlds and Self: Group Life and Individual Consciousness* (Minneapolis: University of Minnesota Press, 1982), namely, that the more differentiated a society comes to be the more opportunities there are for the development of a deeper reflective self.

29. Tuan, *Cosmos and Hearth,* 188.

30. I am not alone in calling for a mediating term between place and self. The "relational framework" set forth by Sack in *Homo Geographicus* is one in which there are at least three mediating terms: nature, meaning, and social relations. These overlap in turn and are interconnected by various loops, thus constituting a matrix of common involvement for self and place: the mediator is itself mediated, thrice over! See especially Figures 2.1 and 4.1 in *Homo Geographicus.*

31. For Merleau-Ponty's discussion of the customary body and, more generally, habit, see his *Phenomenology of Perception,* 139–47, 150–53.

32. Pierre Bourdieu, *Outline of a Theory of Practice,* trans. R. Nice (Cambridge: Cambridge University Press, 1977), 79.

33. On the hysteresis effect, see ibid., 78 and esp. 83: "the hysteresis of habitus, which is inherent in the social conditions of the reproduction of the structures in habitus, is doubtless one of the foundations of the structural lag between opportunities and the dispositions to grasp them."

34. Ibid., 79. See also ibid., 21, 54, 95. Both Dewey and Merleau-Ponty have also pointed to the way in which habit, far from discouraging innovation, fosters it — insofar as habit is not confused with routine. See John Dewey, *Human Nature and Conduct* (New York: Random House, 1950), 42, 66, 172–80; and Merleau-Ponty, *Phenomenology of Perception,* 144–45.

35. Bourdieu, *Outline of a Theory of Practice,* 21.

36. Ibid.

37. Ibid., 80. "Objectivity" is in italics. The sentence continues: "in other words the harmonization of agents' experiences and the continuous reinforcement that each of them receives from the expression, individual or collective (in festivals, for example), [is] improvised or programmed (commonplaces, sayings), of similar or identical experiences" (ibid.). A habitus is enduring, yet not permanent; it is a disposition, not a determinism; and it is the product of inculcation whereby what one learns in a given circumstance is transposable to another, like circumstance by "analogical transfers of schemes permitting the solution of similarly shaped problems" (ibid., 83).

38. Ibid., 72. A habitus is "this immanent law, *lex insita,* laid down in each agent by his earliest upbringing" (ibid., 81).

39. Ibid., 85. The full statement is: "The habitus is the product of the work of inculcation and appropriation necessary in order for those products of collective history, the objective structures (e.g., of language, economy, etc.) to succeed in reproducing themselves more or less completely, in the form of durable dispositions, in the organisms (which one can, if one wishes, call individuals) lastingly subjected to the same conditioning, and hence placed in the same material conditions of existence." The use of "placed" in this last statement, though not underlined or otherwise made thematic, can hardly be accidental.

40. Ibid., 79.

41. Ibid., 167; italics in the original. The full statement is: "Because the subjective necessity and self-evidence of the commonsense world are validated by the objective consensus on the sense of the world, what is essential *goes without saying because it comes without saying:* the tradition is silent, not least about itself as a tradition" (ibid.).

42. See Henri Bergson, *Time and Free Will: An Essay on the Immediate Data of Consciousness,* trans. F. L. Pogson (Kila, Mont.: Kessinger, n.d.), chap. 2.

43. "Description according to time is History, that according to space is Geography.... History differs from Geography only in the consideration of time and area. The former is a report of phenomena that follow one another and has reference to time. The latter is a report of phenomena beside each other in space" (from Kant's "Lectures on Physical Geography," as cited in Richard Hartshorne, *The Nature of Geography: A Critical Survey of Current Thought in the Light of the Past* [Lancaster, Pa.: Association of American Geographers, 1939], 135).

44. Not surprisingly, Bourdieu finds the inner working of habitus to lie in various "schemes" wherein it condenses its operations and holds them ready for employment. The heart of habitudinal action is found in "the generative schemes incorporated in the body schema" (*Outline of a Theory of Practice,* 167). Ironically, the idea of *scheme* stems from Kant's idea of the "schematism of the understanding" whereby categories such as causality or substance or coexistence are given temporal specificity (e.g., as "succession," "permanence," "simultaneity," etc.) (see Immanuel Kant, *Critique of Pure Reason,* trans. N. K. Smith [New York: St. Martin's, 1965], bk. 2, chap. 1: "The Schematism of the Pure Concepts of Understanding"). If Kant is right, Kant is wrong: if the geographical subject depends on a repertoire of schematized habitudes, then the experience of the geographic world will be undeniably temporal, hence historical.

45. Thus we must amend Bourdieu's claim that "the habitus, the product of history, produces individual and collective practices, and hence history, in accordance with the schemes engendered by history" (*Outline of a Theory of Practice,* 82) to a formulation more like this: the habitus, the product of geography and history, produces individual and collective practices, and hence history and geography, in accordance with the placial and temporal schemes engendered by both.

46. Bourdieu, *Outline of a Theory of Practice,* 82–83.

47. David Harvey has made a brief but effective use of habitus in his *Condition of Postmodernity* (Cambridge, Mass.: Blackwell, 1989), 319 and 345.

48. Bourdieu, *Outline of a Theory of Practice,* 80. On the same page is found Bourdieu's

critique of Dilthey's notion of the reproduction of lived experience. The "objective intention" (vs. the lived intention) of practices based on habitus "has nothing to do with the
'reproduction' (*Nachbildung,* as the early Dilthey puts it) of lived experiences and the re-
constitution, unnecessary and uncertain, of the personal singularities of an 'intention' which
is not their true origin."

49. Ibid., 80.

50. Compare Merleau-Ponty: "We must therefore avoid saying that our body is *in* space,
or *in* time. It *inhabits* space and time" (*Phenomenology of Perception,* 139; emphasis in
original). The italicizing of "inhabits" indicates its active character. For Aristotle's treatment
of *in* as a matter of passive containment, see his *Physics,* bk. 4, chap. 3.

51. Heidegger's recourse to dwelling comes both early and late in his work: early, in his
tracing of *in* to *innan,* which means "dwelling" in an active sense of caring for (as signified by the associated Latin verbs *colo* and *diligo*) (see *Being and Time,* sec. 12); later, in
his discussion of "dwelling" as a matter of sparing and preserving the earth (see "Building
Dwelling Thinking," in *Poetry, Language, Thought,* trans. A. Hofstadter [New York: Harper, 1971], 147–50). Striking for our purposes is that *both* senses of dwelling are conceived
as intentional, active issues. For Heidegger's emphasis on the *ex-,* see his discussion of the
ecstases of temporality in *Being and Time,* sec. 65, esp. the statement that Dasein's temporality is "the *ekstatikon* pure and simple. *Temporality is the primordial 'outside-of-itself' in
and for itself*" (377; emphasis in original).

52. But the place-world in which this progress ends is not the same as the social world
from which it begins. For Bourdieu, the latter is ineluctably an "*objective event* which
exerts its action of conditional stimulation calling for or demanding a determinate response"
(*Outline of a Theory of Practice,* 83). Precisely this collective and historical objectivity
contrasts with the habitus as "a matrix of perceptions, appreciations, and actions" located
within the sphere of the individual. But more than contrast is at stake here: the objectivity
of the one calls for the subjectivity of the other. Only when internalized as the basis for
habitual actions can social structure become efficacious at the level of the individual.

53. Soja's admiration for bell hooks's self-professed action of "choosing marginality" as
a place of vulnerability that can become a scene of resistance is a striking instance of what
I am here calling active/lived habitation. See Edward W. Soja, *Thirdspace: Journeys to Los
Angeles and Other Real-and-Imagined Places* (Oxford: Blackwell, 1996), 96–105.

54. Thirdspace is defined as "a knowable and unknowable, real and imagined lifeworld
of experiences, emotions, events, and political choices that is existentially shaped by the
generative and problematic interplay between centers and peripheries, the abstract and concrete, the impassioned spaces of the conceptual and the lived, marked out materially and
metaphorically in *spatial praxis,* the transformation of (spatial) knowledge into (spatial)
action in a field of unevenly developed (spatial) power" (ibid., 31). In this statement, "lifeworld" can be construed as "place-world" and "spaces" as "places." On thirdspace as not
just perceived or conceived, see ibid., 10ff.

55. For these two notions, see Bourdieu, *Outline of a Theory of Practice,* 116–19 and
167, respectively. Henri Lefebvre speaks similarly of the "practico-sensory body": "the moment the body is envisioned as a practico-sensory totality, a decentering and recentering of
knowledge occurs" (Henri Lefebvre, *The Production of Space,* trans. D. Nicholson Smith
[Oxford: Blackwell, 1991], 62). The idea of body schema derives from Paul Schilder in *The
Image and Appearance of the Human Body* (*Das Körperschema* [Berlin: Springer, 1923])
and was developed further by Merleau-Ponty in his *Phenomenology of Perception.*

56. Lefebvre, *Production of Space,* 194. Consider also Lefebvre's statement that "the
relationship to space of a 'subject' who is a member of a group or society implies his relationship to his own body and vice versa" (ibid., 40). Still more succinctly, "the whole of
(social) space proceeds from the body" (ibid., 405).

57. I take this term from the writings of Nancy Franklin and Barbara Tversky, for
example, their groundbreaking essay, "Searching Imagined Environments," *Journal of Ex-*

perimental Psychology: General 119 (1990): esp. 63–77. I have explored the relevance of the spatial framework to implacement in *Getting Back into Place*, 102–3, 110.

58. As Franklin and Tversky say, the body's spatial framework thus renders "certain directions more accessible than others, depending on the natural axes of the body and the position of the body with respect to the perceptual world" ("Searching Imagined Environments," 74). What the authors call "the perceptual world" I am inclined to call "the place-world." Note that Lefebvre had already envisioned the importance of the spatial framework in 1974: "A body so conceived, as produced and as the production of a space, is immediately subject to the determinants of that space: symmetries, interactions, and reciprocal actions, axes and planes, centers and peripheries, and concrete (spatio-temporal) oppositions" (*The Production of Space*, 195; cf. also 199).

59. This co-belonging of place to self and self to place is basic to what we nonchalantly call "orientation." Such orientation, which is part of the repertoire of the geographic self, is a condition of habitation itself. Without it, we would not be able to get into a place or to stay there, much less to understand what we are doing in that place. It is also basic to what Tuan calls "hearth," in which there is a comparable sense of mutual fit between self and place (see *Cosmos and Hearth*, chap. 1).

60. Cited in Soja, *Thirdspace*, 112.

61. See Mary C. Rawlinson, "Proust's Sensationalism," *L'esprit créateur* (1981): 123–39.

62. I take this phrase from the title of Wallace Stevens's late poem "A Mythology Reflects Its Region."

63. I borrow the term *Parathaltung* from Roman Ingarden, who employs it to describe the heteronomy of the literary work, whose various levels require vivification by the reader. See Ingarden's *The Literary Work of Art: An Investigation on the Borderlines of Ontology, Logic, and Theory of Literature*, trans. G. G. Grabowicz (Evanston, Ill.: Northwestern University Press, 1973), 265–67, 330, 331.

64. In Lefebvre's case I refer to his triple distinction between spatial practices, representations of space, and representational spaces, as developed at length in *The Production of Space*, 33ff. For Soja, the trialectic is that of perceived/conceived/lived (see *Thirdspace*, 70–82).

65. J. Nicholas Entrikin, *The Betweenness of Place: Towards a Geography of Modernity* (Baltimore: Johns Hopkins University Press, 1991), 134.

66. "A body/self, a subject, an identity: it is, in sum, a social space, a complexity involving the workings of power and knowledge *and* the workings of the body's lived unpredictabilities" (Barbara Hooper, "Bodies, Cities, Texts: The Case of Citizen Rodney King," cited in Soja, *Thirdspace*, 114). Bruce Wilshire uses the closely analogous term "body-subject" in his *Role-Playing and Identity* (Bloomington: Indiana University Press, 1983).

67. This is Bergson's term for lived space in contrast with homogeneous "extension"; it is the spatial equivalent of duration in the realm of time. See Bergson, *Time and Free Will* and especially *Matter and Memory* (trans. N. M. Paul and W. S. Palmer [New York: Doubleday, 1959]), chaps. 3 and 4.

68. It should be added that the self so conceived is not restricted to the *human* self. Animals, perhaps even plants, possess their own equivalents of embodiment and implacement. Just as we must resist an exclusively individualistic model of the human subject, so we must resist a humanocentric paradigm of implacement.

69. Edward Relph, *Place and Placelessness* (London: Pion, 1976), 123.

70. On the indefinite (*to apeiron*) as a principle (*archē*), see Plato, *Philebus* 23c–26d; on the indeterminate dyad as Plato's material principle, see Aristotle's commentary in his *Metaphysics* 1081a and 1099b.

71. On the prereflective status of the body, see Merleau-Ponty, *Phenomenology of Perception*, pt. 1, "The Body"; on the invisibility of landscape, see Erwin Straus, *The Primary World of Senses*, trans. J. Needleman (New York: Free Press, 1963), 318–23. Relph states that "the spirit of a place resides in its landscape" (*Place and Placelessness*, 30).

72. I should also make it clear that by "place" I mean something very close to what Soja

calls "spatiality" in his important essay entitled "The Spatiality of Social Life: Towards a Transformative Retheorisation," in *Social Relations and Spatial Structures,* ed. D. Gregory and J. Urry (Basingstoke, Eng.: Macmillan, 1985), 91–127. Like spatiality as interpreted by Soja, place is neither physical space nor the mental representation of space (see ibid., 93–94). I prefer the language of "place," however, because of its higher degree of contrast with "space": a contrast I treat at length in my *Fate of Place,* pts. 1 and 2. I thank David DeLaney of Amherst College for urging me to clarify this contrast and for bringing Soja's essay to my attention.

73. Straus, *Primary World of Senses,* 319.

74. M. Heidegger, "Building Dwelling Thinking," 154.

75. See Edward Casey, *Getting Back into Place,* pt. 3, "Wild Places," especially 202–22, where I give a much more complete description of a somewhat different list of basic features.

76. On cityscape and the glance, see my unpublished paper, "Cityscape and Landscape."

77. This is what Whitehead calls "simple location" (see Alfred North Whitehead, *Science and the Modern World* [New York: Free Press, 1973], 52, 58).

78. Straus, *Primary World of Senses,* 319.

79. On the anomalous — and revealing — case of traveling in the air, especially the upper stratosphere, see Paul Virilio, *Open Sky,* passim.

GEOGRAPHER AS HUMANIST

J. Nicholas Entrikin

Philosophical meditations about life present a *portrait*, not a theory.
— ROBERT NOZICK, *The Examined Life*

To learn means to make everything we do answer to whatever essentials address themselves to us at a given time....A cabinet-maker's apprentice...will serve as an example. He is learning not mere practice, to gain facility in the use of tools. Nor does he merely gather knowledge about the customary forms of the things he is to build. If he is to become a true cabinetmaker, he makes himself answer and respond above all to the different kinds of wood and to the shapes slumbering within wood — to wood as it enters into man's dwelling with all the hidden riches of its nature. In fact, this relatedness to wood is what maintains the whole craft. Without that relatedness, the craft will never be anything but empty busywork.   — MARTIN HEIDEGGER, *What Is Called Thinking*

The humanist tradition in geography has had many important contributors, but its principal contemporary architect has been Yi-Fu Tuan. His geographical project displays the humanist's faith in the power of reason and habit of mind that looks for the universal in the particular. Since the publication of his now classic 1976 article, humanistic geography has taken numerous and not always consistent directions, from a hermeneutic social science to an antiscientific romanticism, but Tuan's broadly exploratory and innovative writings form an expansive and creative center for this diverse collective enterprise.[1] He has offered insights into the ways in which language, imagination, and culture work to create worlds out of nature, but his main goal has been to use these insights of humanistic geography to help gain an understanding of the nature of the good life.

Geography as Bridging the Sciences and the Humanities

Tuan's choice of topics has sometimes puzzled geographers who as a rule tend to characterize their work in utilitarian terms. The traditional disciplinary training of geographers did not put philosophy and geography together. When these subjects have been joined as in recent years, the goal has usually been epistemological and/or methodological. Tuan's philosophical goals, however, extend into the unfamiliar territories of metaphysics, ethics, and aesthetics. His model of learning is that of liberal education that expands the range of experience to extend beyond one's immediate milieu, the here and the now, to engage intellectually the experiences of past and distant cultures.

He has been a critical voice and liberating spirit in contemporary geography. His writings have stimulated geographers to explore topics left relatively underexamined in the disciplinary literature, topics such as environmental perception, symbolic landscapes, geographical aesthetics, environmental ethics, and cultural fantasy and escapism. His peripatetic existence as the son of a Chinese diplomat, born in China, educated in China, Australia, England, and the United States, and employed as a professor at several North American universities, has given him the unique perspective of being both insider and outsider to Eastern (Chinese) and Western cultures.

Few if any contemporary geographers can match his intellectual range. This observation may seem to contradict the carefully crafted image of geography as a synthetic discipline in which practitioners draw together nature and culture. Yet even the most optimistic enthusiast for geography would want to distinguish between the synthetic quality of the collective work versus that of any single individual. The ideal standard set in the nineteenth century by members of the geographic pantheon, for example, Alexander von Humboldt, is occasionally invoked but rarely approached or even attempted in twentieth-century geography.

In contemporary American geography, only two names come readily to mind as possible examples of this ideal: Karl Butzer, who offers a naturalistic or ecological conception of the human, and Yi-Fu Tuan, who presents a humanized conception of the natural. Both were trained as physical geographers, but each recognized the calling of the geographer to study relations between the earth and its human inhabitants. It is Tuan, however, who has led geography more directly into the realm of the humanities. What follows is a consideration of his humanistic geography and its ambiguous place in the narratives of contemporary geographic thought.

Tuan the Humanist

Tuan offers a generally hopeful view of humanity based upon the latent power of human imagination and creativity. His humanistic vision is tempered by an underlying naturalism, which recognizes that the evolutionary and biological are never far from the aesthetic and the moral. Like the American Transcendentalists Ralph Waldo Emerson and Henry David Thoreau, Tuan's concern has been to use the relationship of humans to nature as a means of understanding the human spirit. Such a spiritual naturalism is well suited to the geographical imagination but represents a fundamental shift from Tuan's original training in the natural science tradition of geography.

Tuan's first publications in the late 1950s and early 1960s were predominantly about geomorphology, but from the start one sees the glimmerings of the humanistic orientation that would be his legacy in geography. Early in his professional career he began to cross disciplinary and subdisciplinary boundaries, mixing sediments and similes, mountains and melancholy.[2] The standard and oft-repeated narrative about Yi-Fu Tuan that describes him as a geomorphologist turned humanist misses the true professional *bildung,* the emergence of a unique voice in geography that gradually evolved from the blending of parts into a more complex whole. The relative balance of the parts shifts over time, but the basic elements are evident throughout and form a uninterrupted story of development. In Tuan's own words: "The life of thought is a continuous story, like life itself; one book grows out of another as in the world of political commitment one action leads to another."[3]

Many natural scientists will in private moments express the moral commitments and aesthetic tastes that led them to their academic specialization. Tuan's humanistic project involves seeing these elements as a necessary part of his intellectual project and not as matters for private rumination. He is, as he once described Lewis Mumford, a "profound generalist of discrete specialisms whose central concern is of immediate relevance to a persistent though usually private interest among geographers."[4]

In keeping with his broadly humanistic spirit, Tuan has considered fundamental and sometimes taken-for-granted aspects of the human condition. What does it mean to be human? How have humans changed themselves as they have adapted to and transformed nature in making the earth their home? What is the dynamic tension between nature and culture? To address such questions, he has had to explore beyond the restrictive domain of naturalized social science, in which the rational is reduced to the utilitarian. He has also had to move beyond the human geographer's traditional object domains and expand the geographic horizon to include a wide range of human experiences, including the realm of the intimate and private. His topics include not only cities and landscapes but also sexuality and religion, food and music, pets and wilderness. The complex humans that Tuan describes are not only utility maximizers but also cultural agents and moral and aesthetic beings.

The philosophy guiding Tuan's geographic project is best expressed through his own words. Indeed, one of the benefits of Tuan's pursuit of an examined life is the reflexive quality of his writings, in which his personal and professional biographies merge into a single story. This weaving together of the personal and the professional has become especially evident in his more recent works. Thus in his 1998 Charles Homer Haskins Lecture to the American Council of Learned Societies, he explains that

> early in life, in the midst of war and poverty, I had a taste of the True, the Beautiful, and the Good, culled from different civilizations. It excited

in me a yearning for the great triad, especially for the Good, that has lasted into old age. I began the search for what good means to different peoples in the facts of human geography. Good, I was to find out, means at the bottom nurturance and stability. Nature provides nurturance, though rather meagerly; and it provides stability, though not one that is utterly reliable. Culture is how humans, by imagination and skill, escape into more predictable, responsive, and flattering worlds of their own making. These worlds are immensely varied. On the material plane, they range from grass hut to skyscraper, village to metropolis; on the mental plane, from magical beliefs to great systems of religion and metaphysics. They are all, in different ways, aspirations to the Good.[5]

Some take this orientation as characteristic of a naive optimism about the modern human condition that is at odds with their sense of a troubled modern world. Certainly Tuan is hopeful, but he is not naively optimistic. Much has been made of his seemingly romantic references to the warmth of human connections to community and place, but little notice has been taken of his criticisms of nostalgia for community and of his call for the need to return from the close attachments of place to the clear view offered from a more detached and distanced spatial perspective.[6] He has been consistently critical of both extremes and has warned of the "twin errors of excessive rationalism and excessive sentimentality."[7] His writings are replete with references to the imperfectibility of the human condition and to the presence of evil. Thus he attaches the human aspiration for the good to the opposing forces of violence and destruction, misuse of power, and self-deception in his complex and nuanced portrait of the human condition. His writing brilliantly captures both the light and dark side of culture and depicts a thoroughly humanized earth, an earth transformed for better and for worse.[8]

One might legitimately place Tuan's work in the realm of cultural geography, as, indeed, he has done in several of his books and essays.[9] However, in doing so it is necessary to avoid the tendency evident in contemporary geography of too narrowly defining cultural geography in order to fit the current fashion toward specialization. Tuan's cultural geography, like Carl Sauer's vision of this field, should be interpreted broadly, less like a subfield and more as a synonym for human geography. His cultural geography is characterized by its perspective rather than its particular object realm.

Like the wood of Heidegger's apprentice cabinetmaker, human experience is the raw material for Tuan's cultural geography and descriptive psychology. Rather than shaping this experience in the manner of the social scientist to fit within particular concepts and categories, Tuan seeks to expose, not simplify, its semantically rich and complex character. He observes and writes about the commonplace and, in doing so, captures the inherent tensions and ambiguities that exist just beneath the apparent concreteness and certainty of the customary rhythms of everyday life. As David Ley has noted, an important quality of the humanistic cultural geography inspired by Tuan is its aspiration "to speak the language of human experience."[10]

Tuan's form of presentation is one of taking a general theme and exploring its various dimensions through extended analysis of several concrete examples. For the social scientist such a method is anecdotal; to the humanist it is a means of interpreting the particulars of experience in search of the universal. This style in contemporary geography has engendered a new adjective, "tuanian," which has become part of the lexicon of the professional geographer. It is applied to texts displaying a lucid prose style, a subtle probing of the human experience of the environment, and a sophisticated mix of wit, irony, and high-mindedness. His texts are often relatively short, inevitably well written, and deceptively complex. The examples that he uses to illuminate his themes range from the material to the mental, from actual landscapes to fables and fairy tales. Learning as conversation and dialogue is not merely an abstract ideal for Tuan but rather one that he incorporates into his writing.

Tuan in Geography

Human geography has followed the course marked by Tuan's intellectual journey, from environmental perception to the rediscovery of place and the reinvigoration of cultural geography. Yet the basic challenge for anyone who wishes to discuss Tuan's role in modern geography remains that of addressing why this seemingly unambiguous influence and intellectual leadership is not evident in obvious sorts of measures. The issue is further complicated by the knowledge that Yi-Fu Tuan is one of the most recognized voices for geography outside of the discipline. Curiously, his ambiguous relation to the geographical profession is a theme that could be repeated in discussing other marginalized yet acclaimed humanists in geography, such as David Lowenthal and Donald Meinig.

It is ironic, and a little disquieting, that several well-attended conferences have recently taken place (such as the one that gave birth to this volume) that have been dedicated to the many and diverse themes found in Tuan's impressive oeuvre, but most so-called disciplinary surveys discuss Tuan as an interesting yet isolated figure in the evolution of modern paradigms. The greatest emphasis is given to his one textbook, *Topophilia*, certainly an original and imaginative work, but in the end more descriptive of the work of others than is generally the case in his books.[11]

A similar story is told through the increasingly popular yet notoriously vague genre of citation studies. Beyond the usual difficulties of making inferences from citations, these studies seem to be especially unreliable in gauging the influence of the humanistic geographer, except to suggest that humanists such as Tuan often work outside of the circuits of disciplinary power that Michael Curry has shown to be such an important element in these flawed measures of intellectual influence.[12]

Disciplinary overviews are inevitably selective in a manner similar to Karl Popper's characterization of scientific theories. Theories for Popper are like searchlights that illuminate parts of natural systems but that leave most sections in the dark.[13] Selectivity leading to such partial illumination is as much a feature of modern historicist texts, such as David Livingstone's *The Geographical Tradition,* as it is of rational reconstructions, such as Richard Hartshorne's *The Nature of Geography.*[14] This perspectival quality is reduced somewhat by committee-written and edited books, such as the recent disciplinary surveys *Geography in America* and *Rediscovering Geography.*[15] However, these volumes introduce a new set of questions about selection through consensus in which the natural tendency is toward expanding surface coverage at the expense of striving for greater depth. In either case the question remains the same, Why do disciplinary surveys so consistently underplay the intellectual leadership of Tuan in geography?

To address this seeming mismatch between the level of Tuan's influence on human geography and its recording in contemporary accounts of the field, it is necessary to proceed to the larger issue of the present and future path of humanism in contemporary geography and the current trends in the writing of disciplinary surveys and histories of geographic thought.

Utility and Specialization

What is and will be the role of the humanist in our increasingly pragmatic, instrumentalist, and fragmented discipline? There seems to be a basic incompatibility between the direction of contemporary trends in geography and the goals of humanist scholarship. Tuan predicted this outcome in his 1976 article on humanistic geography by stating that despite the positive services of humanism to the discipline, "the humanist's approach will never be really popular," because it exposes too much that is uncomfortable to view.[16] He foretold the challenges to humanism that would come from pressures to provide immediately useful knowledge and to be more scientific, but he could not foresee some of the other challenges that would come from the humanities themselves.

As noted earlier, Tuan's humanism comes out of the tradition of humanities as liberal education, a term one hesitates to use because of its increasingly banal quality in contemporary popular and political discourse. In its classical origins, however, it is a critical reflection on the nature of a good life. The political philosopher Michael Oakeshott described it as a form of learning that allows one "to disentangle oneself, for a time, from the urgencies of the here and now and to listen to the conversation in which human beings forever seek to understand themselves."[17] In contemporary debates in the humanities and the social sciences, critics charge that such a view smacks of elitism and political conservatism. In fact, however, it has at its core a concern to liberate thought from the here and the now, from the easily obtained consensus and the taken-for-granted quality that characterize everyday life.

In geography this liberal education model has been both undermined and attacked. It has been undermined by the utilitarian turn in a geography that wishes to highlight the geographer's credentials as a problem-solver in possession of a unique and powerful set of disciplinary tools. And, from another direction, it has been attacked by postmodern and postcolonial critics who associate liberal education models with arguments in defense of "human nature" and the politics of imperial domination and cultural hegemony. In the first, the utilitarian, emphasis shifts from learning to teaching and to a sophisticated vocational and technical training. In the second, the postmodern, the conversation of the liberal humanist is construed as limited to too few participants, leading to the criticism that underneath its polished, learned exterior is a form of cultural manipulation and repression in which the privileged tell others how to understand themselves.

To the humanist the consequences of the utilitarian turn have been exacerbated by a related but somewhat independent tendency toward specialization. Both trends are, of course, larger than any one discipline and reflect the increasing intellectual fragmentation and subdisciplinarity found throughout academic life. In a field such as geography, however, in which practitioners range from natural scientists to moral philosophers, this specialization results not in a tidy breakdown of parts to a whole but rather in a set of often unrelated or marginally related parts. Such fragmentation limits the audience and potential impact for a more disciplinary- and multidisciplinary-scale humanistic scholarship.

The rapid rise of specialty groups in geography is evident to all who have regularly attended the annual meetings of the Association of American Geographers or the Institute of British Geographers. Like all changes in the academy and in academically oriented professional organizations, this shift has both an intellectual and a political function. Academics are aware of the advantages of such groupings and of how sharply and positively they contrast with the relatively closed professional associations of the past, for example, the Association of American Geographers, in an earlier era when membership was by invitation only and when one's contributions to a common geographic canon were part of the price of admission. These recent specialized groupings, whose membership requires only a check mark on a membership form and an occasional fee, provide the voluntary associations and loose organizational structure that shape late-twentieth-century American geography. This structure has been further reinforced by the seemingly unlimited willingness of publishers to support the development of new subdisciplinary journals.

The concern of these specialty groups to codify their respective subfields has contributed to a situation in which contemporary geographic thought is increasingly filtered through the classifications and concepts of specializations rather than through discipline-wide categories. The result is the creation of significant scale-disparities. The humanist, such as Tuan, speaks to what it is to be a geographer and a human being, a fully dimensional human being, one that requires consideration of economic and social agency, biological constraint, and moral and aesthetic judgment.

In contemporary histories of the field, however, Tuan's legacy in geography cannot escape the categories of this culture of specialization. His work is treated as a contribution to a subfield. It becomes "a part of a part," a component of a subfield most often identified as humanistic geography (or, less frequently, environmental perception), with the normalizing label of "specialization." Even in some of the more thoughtful examples of this genre, one is struck by the thinness of the image of Tuan as the builder of a subfield, compared to his almost boundless project of understanding the nature of the good life.[18]

In this parts-to-whole model, humanistic geography contributes one part to a contemporary history of geography that is no more than the sum of its parts. The history of the field thus becomes equivalent to the combined histories of different specialities. Some may view the resulting variety as a positive aspect of the field, but it in fact weakens one of the strongest arguments in support of geography — its integrative and synthetic character — and thus marginalizes the principal aims of the humanist geographer.

The scale-mismatch becomes evident in two ways, both of which tend to diminish the contributions of the humanist geographer. At the scale of disciplinary history the dominant trope becomes one of connecting the parts, as subsystems of disciplinary practices among larger systems, human geography to physical geography, economic geography to cultural geography, or political ecology to cultural ecology. The difficulty of presenting humanistic geography as one such subsystem leads to it being either left out of the story altogether or redefined as one competing method or approach within, say, "human/environment relations" or "cultural geography." At the scale of the specialty group, the humanistic literature of authors such as Tuan becomes too broad, or in a certain sense too "undisciplined," to be encapsulated within subdisciplinary categories.

This tendency is evident even in some of the most ecumenical treatments of subdisciplinary debates. For example, in B. L. Turner's inclusive diagram of current schools of thought working within the geographic tradition of human/environment relations, competing and complementary research cores swirl through a spiral that moves between the natural sciences and the humanities. Tuan is retired to a footnote, with other broadly based humanistic thinkers such as David Lowenthal and Ann Buttimer — too small in number and, one could add, too broad in vision to merit their own research core.[19]

The same quality may be seen in the recent volume *Re-reading Cultural Geography,* an equally ecumenical and fair-minded presentation of the contemporary contributions of cultural geographers. This is an impressive and ambitious volume in many ways, not the least of which is its attempt to reconcile the many warring factions within cultural geography. Tuan's contributions are recognized by some of the various authors and editors. However, his role is never seen as central to the project of contemporary cultural geography, in spite of his very clear position as an innovator in this field and the importance of culture to his conception of geography.[20]

For some, the utilitarian and specialist turn offers a path of salvation for the field. The attractiveness of the model of geographer as problem-solver is enhanced by geography's relatively weak institutional position within the American university system. Geography departments for much of the 1990s felt the sometimes intense pressure to highlight the usefulness of geography and increasingly succumbed to these pressures, as is especially evident in the sometimes blind rush toward the current bandwagon, Geographic Information Systems (GIS). To be useful is indeed a good thing, but unfortunately "usefulness" is often too narrowly defined. What is referred to as the "real world" is misnamed. It is not actually the "real world," for that world, so well described in Tuan's writings, is a complex mix of the natural, the economic, the moral, and the aesthetic. It is a world composed of many of the elements that so-called applied geographers eliminate from their organizational charts. It is not the real world that they face, but rather the highly schematized and ritualized world of the intellectual marketplace, a form of life that often devalues humanism and is sometimes threatened by the ideals of liberal education.

The Politics of Theory

I do not want to overstate the travails of the humanist in geography, because by some definitions their numbers and influence appear to be growing. There has, for example, been an increase in self-identified cultural studies within geography. Concerns of modernity, aesthetics, morality and ethics, cultural attitudes toward the environment, and other themes originally addressed or resuscitated in geography by Tuan have become increasingly evident in the expanded topical range of geographical journals. Their authors, however, tend not to acknowledge an intellectual ancestry in the humanistic model associated with Tuan. The difference is in part associated with questions of the politics of theory and the politics of representation and Tuan's association with the humanities tradition of liberal education.

One of the most dramatic instances of this growth of research on humanist topics has been the humanizing of Marxian geography as illustrated in the recent discovery of the concept of place. For example, David Harvey, who previously dismissed place as a concept for the ideologically blinded and deceived, now trumpets place as the potential site for the development of political consciousness, or what he refers to as "militant particularism."[21] His acknowledged intellectual sources for this political attachment to place are found, not surprisingly, in the cultural materialism of Raymond Williams and the social space of Henri Lefebvre, and not the humanistic geography of Tuan. The Left in geography has discovered the world of everyday life, the terrain of humanist geography once so roundly criticized as irrelevant to earlier, more structurally minded forms of Marxian analysis. However, even in this cultural turn, geographical Marxism differs from Tuan's humanistic project in its assignment of cultural power to the social relations of production rather than to the more fundamental ability of humans to create meaning through language.[22]

In spite of the divide separating geographical Marxism and Tuan's geographical humanism, both Harvey and Tuan share an underlying belief in the potential for human progress, a belief missing from the postmodernist arguments. In *Cosmos and Hearth,* Tuan presents an understanding of cultural progress illustrated by the move from the circumscribed view of the provincial to the universalism of the cosmopolite. The relativism and particularism of postmodernism are for Tuan a modernist construction, an artifice that obscures the conditions of its own possibility.[23] To the postmodernist, poststructuralist, and postcolonialist, Tuan apparently fails to recognize the insights gained from the appropriate mix of politics and theory. This view may be illustrated by the brief and in many ways quite accurate portrait of Tuan's work presented by Derek Gregory, who in the end draws a relatively extreme conclusion about the supposed atheoretical quality of Tuan's humanistic geography. He states that Tuan offers a sophisticated exploration of human experience, but one with a "philosophical anthropology" that relies on a concept of the whole of humanity and of a "we" that shares a "common sense" and a "common experience."[24] In Gregory's words, Tuan's "humanistic geography is, in essence, a moral-aesthetic discourse; it is contemplative, at once reflective and speculative, and yet — despite the model of ideal conversation — is at best studiously indifferent to the wider conversations that might be made *through the theoretical.*"[25] This same point is made in a recent text on contemporary geographic thought coedited by Gregory and Trevor Barnes in which Tuan's dialogic model is characterized as follows:

> In Yi-Fu Tuan's more idiosyncratic essays, the argument is conducted through an imaginary (or "ideal") conversation between the author and the reader, in which Tuan offers a series of "ironic observations on familiar and exotic forms of geographical knowledge and experience" based on his contemplation of the world around him. Tuan's writings are hardly typical, but he shares with many other humanistic geographers whose concerns also circle around the moral, the aesthetic, and the experiential, a reticence towards the conjunction of formal theory and analytical style that characterizes both spatial science and mainstream social science. Writers like these worried that such formalisation would get in the way

of their attentiveness to the world, that it would both limit their openness and diminish their responsiveness to the human condition.[26]

The dialectically achieved moral to their story is that this and other early forms of humanistic geography were supplanted by a more theoretical cultural geography, one that combined the spatial analyst's concern for theory with the humanist's sensitivity to culture and meaning. But who among the so-called theorists of contemporary geography could not themselves be labeled as idiosyncratic? The response generally is that such works are "theoretically informed," a term that has been used so promiscuously that it is almost empty of meaning. It is hard to even imagine a major work in human geography that could not be described as informed by theory.

Tuan does not appear to be "studiously indifferent to theory," but such an assessment would in the end rest on the increasingly fuzzy semantics associated with the term *theory*. It is clear, however, that Tuan is not a theorist, but it is important to add that his work is neither innocent nor deliberately neglectful of theory. His relation to theoretical work is best described not in "Humanistic Geography," to which Gregory refers and in which Tuan situates himself in relation to science and thus a natural science model of theory, but rather in a 1991 *Annals* article, "Language and the Making of Place: A Narrative Descriptive Approach." In this article Tuan describes his narrative-descriptive approach as one in which theories "hover supportively in the background" to allow the complex phenomenon under study, human experience, to take center stage.[27] For Tuan, theory is unable in the last analysis to explain human creativity and imagination, the central focus of his humanistic approach.

One can see evidence of theory "hover[ing] supportively in the background" in many of his texts, most notably *Segmented Worlds and Self* and *Cosmos and Hearth*, which are clearly informed by and inform social and political theory. One could point to additional examples, such as the concern with social disorder that frames *Landscapes of Fear* and the analysis of human power and control that forms the core of *Dominance and Affection*.[28] For evidence of the theoretical fruitfulness of Tuan's ideas, one need only look as far as the important and original contributions to geographic theory of Tuan's colleague Robert Sack.[29]

Tuan's description of the existential isolation of the self in the modern world, in which cultural beliefs and religion no longer offer the sense of connectedness to other human beings or to nature that they once did, has profound theoretical consequences for the social scientist. Even those who insist on the necessity of associating individual identity with group identity and who emphasize ethnic, gender, national, or other forms of modern solidarities are adding support to Tuan's own thesis concerning the struggle between modern individualism and the desire for reconnection to the group.[30] The dominant genre of contemporary social scientific writing is one that highlights the forces of social and cultural disintegration. Tuan recognizes these forces and takes them into account but in the end emphasizes the equally powerful binding potential of culture and the individual's desire for community.[31]

How could a body of work so broad in its consideration of the cultural world of humans not connect with theory at numerous points? One need only consider the importance of power as a theme in Tuan's writing, especially the power to create meaning through language, to control and manipulate nature, and to create landscapes, in order to see potential theoretical significance. As one sociologist reviewer, David Franks, states about *Segmented Worlds*: "Though Tuan's book focuses on the range of social psychological processes covered by 'culture and personality,' he is not attempting a 'social scientific treatise.' Sociologists will usually have to supply their own theoretical context and references."[32] Franks goes on to add that to do so would not be difficult, for Tuan offers insights of direct relevance to theoretical debate, in this instance, Marxian concerns of alienation, Weberian arguments about disenchantment in modern societies, and Mead's symbolic interactionism.

Tuan's work is both theoretically informed and informing. He is indeed not a theorist nor has he ever claimed to be one. As Robert Nozick observes in the epigram cited above, philosophical meditation on life produces a portrait, not a theory.

The Perfect Humanistic Geographer

Other themes could be highlighted in speculating about the apparent mismatch between the enormity of Tuan's contributions and the narratives of contemporary geographic thought. Similar to the ones that I have discussed, each gives us a mirror-like reflected image of the current state of geography and the complex relationship of Tuan to his chosen field. He has acknowledged his intellectual debt to geography, which has given him the freedom to roam between descriptions of nature and cultural interpretations. However, he is also cognizant of his being isolated as a geographer, both from philosophers who would share in his concern for the examined life and from geographers who work with similar concepts but who ask different types of questions and search for answers in quite disparate realms.[33] To some extent this position may be viewed as a foreseeable consequence of a decision to follow a largely untraveled academic path.

However, a more troubling sign from these reflected images is the suspicion that Tuan's ambiguous relation to much of contemporary social and cultural geography is a consequence of his relative hopefulness and his belief in human progress. By this, I do not mean the twentieth-century vision of progress, a vision linked to the expansion of capitalism and the increased role of technology that makes life easier for a certain proportion of the earth's population. It is not the progress of facsimile machines and satellite dishes but rather a moral progress, a belief in the spiritual growth of humans that takes place through learning. It is a growth and development that has been in part associated with a knowledge and mastery of the material world but that also emphasizes self-knowledge through conversations with those from present and past generations and other civilizations who have pursued similar aims.

The goal of such knowledge is to develop the whole person, to create a good person, and in this way to cultivate humanity.[34] Such a cultivating process is based upon a belief in the power of human reason. As Tuan has demonstrated in so many different ways, the application of reason in human affairs creates a sometimes uncomfortable and isolating critical distance from cultural tradition and custom and a separation from nature. The goal of cultivating humanity then becomes a struggle to overcome this isolation without forsaking reason.

It is this goal that defines Tuan's perfect geographer. In his inaugural Alexander von Humboldt Lecture, Tuan discussed the life and work of von Humboldt in relation to this ideal. His underlying theme was that of making a good human being. The perfect geographer, according to Tuan, could be created by combining the attributes of Alexander and his brother Wilhelm and thus achieving a completeness as a result of putting together complementary sides of the two brothers. From Wilhelm, one draws the appreciation of language and the importance of the human bond, and from Alexander, the bond to the natural world. It is that combination that makes the perfect geographer and, by implication, defines the ideal geography. Tuan makes clear, however, that Wilhelm and his interests might better coincide with his idea of the perfect humanistic geographer.

One could say of Yi-Fu Tuan what he has said about Alexander von Humboldt (but changed to the present tense): "his spirit promotes cooperation, enthusiasm, and creativity. He is both a great geographer and a fine person."[35] Yi-Fu Tuan has helped to bring the conversation of the humanities to geography. Geographers could benefit by listening more carefully.

Notes

1. Yi-Fu Tuan, "Humanistic Geography," *Annals of the Association of American Geographers* 66 (1976): 266–76; Stephen Daniels, "Arguments for a Humanistic Geography," in *The Future of Geography*, ed. R. J. Johnston (London: Methuen, 1985), 143–58.

2. Yi-Fu Tuan, "Use of Simile and Metaphor in Geographical Description," *Professional Geographer* 9 (1957): 8–11; Tuan, "The Desert and the Sea: A Humanistic Interpretation," *New Mexico Quarterly* 33 (1963): 329–31; Tuan, "Mountains, Ruins, and the Sentiment of Melancholy," *Landscape* 14 (1964): 27–30; Tuan, *The Hydrologic Cycle and the Wisdom of God: A Theme in Geoteleology* (Toronto: University of Toronto Department of Geography Research Publications, 1968).

3. Yi-Fu Tuan, *Space and Place: The Perspective of Experience* (Minneapolis: University of Minnesota Press, 1977), v.

4. Yi-Fu Tuan, "Lewis Mumford and the Quality of Life," *Geographical Review* 58 (1968): 671.

5. Yi-Fu Tuan, *The Life of Learning,* Charles Homer Haskins Lecture, no. 42 (New York: American Council of Learned Societies, 1998), 14.

6. Yi-Fu Tuan, "Community and Place: A Skeptical View," in *Person Place and Thing: Interpretative and Empirical Essays in Cultural Geography,* ed. Shue Tuck Wong (Baton Rouge: LSU Geoscience Publications, 1992), 47–59; Tuan, *Cosmos and Hearth: A Cosmopolite's Viewpoint* (Minneapolis: University of Minnesota Press, 1996); Tuan, "Review of *Senses of Place* Edited by Steven Feld and Keith Basso," *Western Folklore* 56 (1997): 92–94.

7. Yi-Fu Tuan, "Geopiety: A Theme in Man's Attachment to Nature and to Place," in *Geographies of the Mind: Essays in Honor of John Kirkland Wright,* ed. David Lowenthal and Martyn Bowden (New York: Oxford University Press, 1976), 13.

8. For example, Yi-Fu Tuan, *Escapism* (Baltimore: Johns Hopkins University Press, 1998), xi–xvii; Tuan with Steven Hoelscher, "Disneyland: Its Place in World Culture," in *Designing Disney Theme Parks: The Architecture of Reassurance,* ed. Karal Ann Marling (Paris: Flammarion, 1997), 191–96.

9. Yi-Fu Tuan, " 'Environment' and 'World,' " *Professional Geographer* 17 (1965): 6–7; Tuan, *Passing Strange and Wonderful: Aesthetics, Nature, and Culture* (Washington, D.C.: Island Press, 1993), 227–43.

10. David Ley, "Fragmentation, Coherence, and Limits to Theory in Human Geography," in *Remaking Human Geography,* ed. Audrey Kobayashi and Suzanne MacKenzie (Boston: Unwin Hyman, 1989), 227.

11. Yi-Fu Tuan, *Topophilia: A Study of Environmental Perception Attitude and Values* (Englewood Cliffs, N.J.: Prentice-Hall, 1974).

12. David Lowenthal, "Geography Misconstrued as Social Science," *Area* 24 (1992): 158–60; Michael Curry, *The Work in the World: Geographical Practice and the Written Word* (Minneapolis: University of Minnesota Press, 1996), 143–49.

13. Karl Popper, *The Open Society and Its Enemies* (Princeton, N.J.: Princeton University Press, 1950), 443–63.

14. David Livingstone, *The Geographical Tradition: Episodes in the History of a Contested Enterprise* (London: Oxford University Press, 1992); Richard Hartshorne, *The Nature of Geography: A Critical Survey of Current Thought in Light of the Past* (Lancaster, Pa.: Association of American Geographers, 1939).

15. Gary Gaile and Cort Wilmott, eds., *Geography in America* (Columbus, Ohio: Merrill Publishing, 1989); National Research Council, *Rediscovering Geography: New Relevance for Science and Society* (Washington, D.C.: National Academy Press, 1997).

16. Tuan, "Humanistic Geography," 275.

17. Michael Oakeshott, "A Place of Learning," in *The Voice of Liberal Learning: Michael Oakeshott on Education,* ed. Timothy Fuller (New Haven, Conn.: Yale University Press, 1989), 41; cited in René Arcilla, *For the Love of Perfection: Richard Rorty and Liberal Education* (New York: Routledge, 1995), 3.

18. For example, see Paul Cloke, Chris Philo, and David Sadler, *Approaching Human Geography: An Introduction to Contemporary Theoretical Debates* (New York: Guilford 1991), 57–92; Timothy Unwin, *The Place of Geography* (London: Longman, 1992); Carville Earle, Kent Mathewson, and Martin Kenzer, eds., *Concepts in Human Geography* (Lanham, Md.: Rowman and Littlefield, 1996).

19. B. L. Turner, "Spirals, Bridges, and Tunnels: Engaging Human-Environment Perspectives in Geography," *Ecumene* 4 (1997): 196–217.

20. Kenneth Foote et al., eds., *Re-reading Cultural Geography* (Austin: University of Texas Press, 1994).

21. David Harvey, "Between Space and Time: Reflections on the Geographical Imagination," *Annals of the Association of American Geographers* 80 (1990): 431–32; David Harvey, *Justice, Nature, and the Geography of Difference* (London: Blackwell, 1996).

22. Yi-Fu Tuan, "Language and the Making of Place: A Narrative-Descriptive Approach," *Annals of the Association of American Geographers* 81 (1991): 684–96.

23. Tuan, *Cosmos and Hearth*, 8, 179, 185.

24. Derek Gregory, *Geographical Imaginations* (Cambridge: Blackwell, 1994), 79.

25. Ibid., 79–80.

26. Trevor Barnes and Derek Gregory, eds., *Reading Human Geography: Poetics and Politics of Inquiry* (London: Arnold, 1997), 356–57.

27. Tuan, "Language and the Making of Place," 686.

28. Tuan, *Cosmos and Hearth;* Tuan, *Segmented Worlds and Self: Group Life and Individual Consciousness* (Minneapolis: University of Minnesota Press, 1982); Tuan, *Landscapes of Fear* (New York: Pantheon, 1979); Tuan, *Dominance and Affection: The Making of Pets* (New Haven, Conn.: Yale University Press, 1984).

29. Robert D. Sack, *Homo Geographicus: A Framework for Action, Awareness, and Moral Concern* (Baltimore: Johns Hopkins University Press, 1997).

30. Yi-Fu Tuan, "Place and Culture: Analeptic for Individuality and the World's Indifference," in *Mapping American Culture*, ed. Wayne Franklin and Michael Steiner (Iowa City: University of Iowa Press, 1992), 27–49; Tuan, *Segmented Worlds and Self.*

31. Yi-Fu Tuan, foreword to Anne Buttimer, *Geography and the Human Spirit* (Baltimore: Johns Hopkins University Press, 1993), x–xi.

32. David Franks, "Contributions from Cultural Geography to Community, Self, and Meaning," *Contemporary Sociology* 12 (1983): 607.

33. Tuan, "A Life of Learning," 15.

34. Martha Nussbaum, *Cultivating Humanity: A Classical Defense of Reform in Liberal Education* (Cambridge, Mass.: Harvard University Press, 1997), 9.

35. Yi-Fu Tuan, *Alexander von Humboldt and His Brother: Portrait of an Ideal Geographer in Our Time,* Alexander von Humboldt Lecture (Los Angeles: Department of Geography, 1997), 12.

CONTRIBUTORS

PAUL C. ADAMS has held teaching positions at Virginia Polytechnic Institute and State University, University at Albany, SUNY, and Texas A&M University. His research addresses topics in all areas of communication and geography, including popular culture, globalization, the geographical implications of technological change, spatial aspects of identity and agency, and communication practices in the urban landscape. His publications include articles in *Political Geography, Urban Geography, Geographical Review,* and *Annals of the Association of American Geographers.* A monograph titled *Geography and Communication* is nearing completion.

ANNE BUTTIMER is professor and head of the Department of Geography at University College Dublin. She has held research and teaching positions in Belgium, Canada, France, Scotland, Sweden, and the United States. She is author of several books and articles on subjects ranging from social space and urban planning to the history of ideas and environmental policy. Her work has been published in translation in Dutch, French, German, Japanese, Latvian, Polish, Portuguese, Spanish, Swedish, and Russian. She has received the Association of American Geographers' Honors Award (1986), the Ellen Semple Award (1990), and the Murchison Medal from the Royal Geographical Society (1997). She was elected member of Academia Europaea (1993), council member of the Royal Geographical Society/Institute of British Geographers (1996), and vice president of the International Geographical Union (1996) and was awarded an honorary doctorate in philosophy from the University of Joensuu, Finland (1999). In 2000, she was elected president of the International Geographical Union.

EDWARD S. CASEY is professor and Chair of the Department of Philosophy at the State University of New York, Stony Brook, where he has taught during the past two decades. His research interests include aesthetics, philosophy of perception, philosophy of mind, philosophy of space and time, and psychoanalytic theory. He has written *Imagining* and *Remembering,* two studies in the phenomenology of mind, and, more recently, *Getting Back into Place* and *The Fate of Place. Representing Place in Landscape Paintings and Maps* is forthcoming from the University of Minnesota Press.

DENIS COSGROVE is Alexander von Humboldt Professor of Geography at the University of California, Los Angeles. His recent writings, which pursue the themes of landscape, mapping, and the visual arts in geography, include *Mappings; Apollo's Eye: A Cosmographic Genealogy of the Globe;* and the essay "Global Illumination," in *Geography and Enlightenment,* edited by David Livingstone and Charles W. J. Withers.

TIM CRESSWELL teaches at the University at Wales, Aberystwyth. He is author of *In Place/Out of Place: Geography, Ideology, and Transgression* (Minnesota, 1996) and *The Tramp in America;* coauthor (with Ulf Strohmayer) of *Urban Culture;* and coeditor (with Deborah Dixon) of *Engaging Film: Geographies of Mobility and Identity.* His current research focuses on the cultural politics of mobility.

MICHAEL CURRY is professor of geography at the University of California, Los Angeles. His research is on the geographical implications of information technologies. He is author of *The Work in the World: Geographical Practice and the Written Word* (Minnesota, 1996) and *Digital Places: Living with Geographic Information Technologies.* He is currently working on books about the interrelationships between the concepts of privacy and of place and on the history of technologies of individual identification, from the surname to the passport to biometrics.

DYDIA DELYSER is assistant professor of geography at Louisiana State University and coeditor of the journal *Historical Geography.* Her book *Ramona Memories* is forthcoming, and she is currently at work on a second book, *The Good, the Bad, and the Ugly: Landscape and Social Memory in Three Western Ghost Towns.*

JAMES S. DUNCAN is a fellow of Emmanuel College and university lecturer in geography at the University of Cambridge. A cultural geographer who has studied the role of landscapes in the reproduction of cultural systems in North America and South Asia, he is author of several books, including *The City as Text: The Politics of Landscape Interpretation in the Kandyan Kingdom; Writing Worlds: Discourse, Text, and Metaphor in the Representation of Landscape* (with Trevor Barnes); and *Writes of Passage: Reading Travel Writing* (with Derek Gregory).

NANCY G. DUNCAN is a fellow of Fitzwilliam College and affiliated lecturer in geography at the University of Cambridge. She is a cultural geographer with an interest in landscapes of power. She has written numerous publications on landscape interpretation and methodology, including *BodySpace: Destabilizing Geographies of Gender and Sexuality.*

J. NICHOLAS ENTRIKIN is professor of geography at the University of California, Los Angeles. He is a Guggenheim fellow and has served as a visiting director of research with CNRS in France. His research concerns the role of place and community in modern societies and has been presented in numerous articles and monographs, most notably *The Betweenness of Place: Towards a Geography of Modernity*. He is currently writing on place in democratic theory.

STEVEN HOELSCHER is assistant professor of American studies and geography at the University of Texas at Austin. A former editor of *Historical Geography*, he is author of *Heritage on Stage*, and his writings on ethnicity and place have appeared in such publications as *Ecumene, Journal of Historical Geography, The Geographical Review*, and *American Quarterly*.

WILLIAM HOWARTH is professor of English at Princeton University. He has written and edited numerous works on American literature, including *The Book of Concord, Thoreau in the Mountains*, and *The John McPhee Reader*. His current interests lie in ecocriticism, environmental history, and theories of place and evolution.

JOHN PAUL JONES III is professor of geography and codirector of the Committee on Social Theory at the University of Kentucky. He has served as editor of the *Annals of the Association of American Geographers* since 1996. His research interests lie in poststructuralist theory, feminist theory, cultural studies, and geographic thought and methodology. He is coeditor, with Heidi Nast and Sue Roberts, of *Thresholds in Feminist Geography*.

DAVID LEY is professor of geography at the University of British Columbia and codirector of the Vancouver Centre of Excellence for Immigration Studies. His current research is concerned with the social geographies of immigration. His most recent books are *The New Middle Class and the Remaking of the Central City* and *Neighbourhood Organizations and the Welfare State* (with Shlomo Hasson).

DAVID LOWENTHAL is emeritus professor of geography at University College London and visiting professor of heritage studies at St. Mary's University College, Strawberry Hill, Twickenham. His books include *West Indian Societies; The Past Is a Foreign Country; Possessed by the Past: The Heritage Crusade and the Spoils of History;* and *George Perkins Marsh, Prophet of Conservation*.

KARAL ANN MARLING is professor of art history and American studies at the University of Minnesota. Among her many books on American culture are *Norman Rockwell* and *Designing Disney's Theme Parks: The Architecture of Reassurance*. New editions of *The Colossus of Roads* (her first excursion into the domain of cultural geography) and *Wall-to-Wall America* have recently been published by the University of Minnesota Press.

PATRICK MCGREEVY is professor of geography and Chair of the Department of Anthropology, Geography, and Earth Science at Clarion University. His interest in the historical and cultural geography of North America is increasingly cross-disciplinary. He is the author of numerous articles and a book, *Imagining Niagara: Meaning and the Making of Niagara Falls*.

KENNETH R. OLWIG has worked at university institutions in Denmark, Sweden, and Norway and is presently a professor in the geography department at the University in Trondheim, Norway. His list of publications includes *Nature's Ideological Landscape* and *Landscape, Nature, and the Body Politic.*

MARIJANE OSBORN is professor of English at the University of California at Davis, where she is the faculty adviser for the interdepartmental medieval research consortium. She has published many articles and translations on subjects ranging from Nahuatl poetry to Nathaniel Hawthorne, with an emphasis on Old and Middle English poetry. Among other books, she has authored or coauthored three that emphasize place and material culture: *Beowulf: A Verse Translation with Treasures of the Ancient North; Beowulf: A Likeness* (with Randolf Swearer and Raymond Oliver); and *Landscape of Desire: Partial Stories of the Medieval Scandinavian World* (with Gillian R. Overing; Minnesota, 1994). Her most recent book, *Romancing the Goddess: Three Middle English Verse-Romances about Women,* focuses on women and women's religion.

GILLIAN R. OVERING is professor of English at Wake Forest University, where she teaches Old English, linguistics, and women's studies and coordinates the medieval studies program. In addition to coediting two anthologies, she has published articles on Old English literature, literary history, and contemporary theory and is author of *Language, Sign, and Gender in Beowulf.* She is coauthor, with Marijane Osborn, of *Landscape of Desire: Partial Stories of the Medieval Scandinavian World* (Minnesota, 1994). She is currently engaged in several collaborative projects on women in Anglo-Saxon and medieval Icelandic culture.

EDWARD RELPH is professor of geography and associate principal, University of Toronto at Scarborough. His books include *Place and Placelessness* and *The Modern Urban Landscape.*

MILES RICHARDSON is presently the Doris Z. Stone Professor in Latin American Studies in the Department of Geography and Anthropology at Louisiana State University, Baton Rouge. He received his doctorate in anthropology from Tulane University in 1965. He is approaching the final draft of a manuscript titled "Being-in-Christ and Putting Death in Its Place in Spanish America and in the American South: An Anthropologist's Account." In preparation is a restatement of the humanistic metanarrative titled "Reclaiming Anthropocentrism in a Postmodern World."

ROBERT D. SACK is the Clarence Glacken and John Bascom Professor of Geography and Integrated Liberal Studies at the University of Wisconsin, Madison. His books include *Conceptions of Space in Social Thought; Human Territoriality; Place, Modernity, and the Consumer's World;* and *Homo Geographicus.* He is currently working on *A Geographical Guide to the Real and the Good.*

JONATHAN M. SMITH is associate professor of geography at Texas A&M University. He is a cultural geographer with interests in the history of geography and geographical representation. He is coeditor of the journal *Philosophy and Geography* and a contributing editor to the recent books *Worldview Flux: Perplexed Values among Postmodern Peoples* and *American Space/American Place: Geographies of the Contemporary U.S.A.*

KAREN E. TILL is assistant professor of geography at the University of Minnesota. She is the former coeditor of *Historical Geography* and the recipient of the Warren J. Nystrom Dissertation Award from the Association of American Geographers (1998). She is author of several articles and book chapters, including "Staging the Past: Landscape Designs, Cultural Identity, and *Erinnerungspolitik* at Berlin's Neue Wache" in *Ecumene* (1999), and is currently working on a book titled *Memory in Place.*

YI-FU TUAN was born in Tientsin, China. He attended school in China, Australia, and the Philippines, and earned degrees from the University of Oxford and the University of California at Berkeley. He has taught at Indiana University, the University of New Mexico, the University of Toronto, the University of Minnesota, and the University of Wisconsin, Madison, where he retired in 1998 from his position as Vilas Professor of Geography. He is author of *Escapism* and *Who Am I? An Autobiography of Emotion, Mind, and Spirit,* as well as ten other books and more than one hundred articles and book chapters. His interests span the range of the social sciences, with a focus on the central geographical themes of space and place.

APRIL R. VENESS is associate professor of geography at the University of Delaware. Her research, teaching, and service often focus on the meaning and experience of home as well as the politics of who claims what as home. She has been addressing local conflicts over the "proper placement" of homeless people, (im)migrant laborers, and university students.

WILBUR ZELINSKY is professor emeritus of geography at the Pennsylvania State University, where he has roosted since 1963. He has suffered from an insatiable curiosity about the nature of his native land and the many meanings of being an American, and most of his research publications have dealt with various cultural, social, demographic, historical/geographic, and landscape questions set in North America. His books include *The Cultural Geography of the United States* and *Exploring the Beloved Country: Geographic Forays into American Society and Culture.*

Index

Abbey, Edward, 193, 195

Absence, xiv, 227; and construction of the past, 24, 29–38, 288; deconstructionist theory of, 263; and presence, xxiv, 226, 230, 263. *See also* Presence

Academy. *See* University

Acquisitive Society, The (Tawney), 208

Action, political, 375–77; and preservation of place, 41–46, 53; provincial cosmopolitanism as, 378, 389–93; social documentary as, 386–88

Adamic, Louis, 378, 383, 385–93

Adams, Paul C., xxv, 125–26, 186–206

Adler, Jeffrey S., 171

Advertising, 26, 126, 378; and the walker, 193, 195–96, 197, 200

Aesthetics: and attachment to place, xxiii, 41–54; and death, 266; in description of the world, 151, 327; in humanistic geography, 427, 434, 435; in literary criticism, 56; of social documentary, 386; of urban landscape, 202; of walking, 190

Aestheticization: of place and landscape, 41; of poverty, 47. *See also* Aesthetics

Agency: of citizens, emergence of, 108–9; and control of social memory, 274–77, 290–94; and development of place-identity, 111–12, 383, 404, 405–6; geographical, 232–41; in human geography, xxxii n38, 433; limits of human, 252, 366; loss of, in the professions, 216–18; of place, 232, 239. *See also* Identity; Self

Agnew, John, 395 n9

Alienation, 4, 41, 196, 437; from community, 343–45, 348–51, 355, 359–71; from nature, 61, 66; postmodern, 61; urban, 48, 52

Alluring Wisconsin (Holmes), 379

Alpers, Svetlana, 109, 110

Althusser, Louis, 7, 106–7

American Dream, 21, 387

American studies, xviii

Anavagoras, 327, 328, 338

Anderson, Benedict, xxi, 293. *See also* "Imagined Communities"

Anderson, Nels, 169, 176, 178–79

Anthropology, xviii, 411

Architecture, 247, 248; and borrowing from history, 161; deceptiveness in, 162; development of perspective in, 95; and framing of experience, 5, 8–18, 100, 280, 284, 285, 359; of postmodern landscape, 154

Archytas, 404

Arendt, Hannah, 226, 251, 254

Aristotle, 115 n35, 163–64, 335, 407, 413, 414

Artifacts: display of, 27, 31–32, 34, 273–99; leaving of, 227, 257–69; place as, xviii; significance of, 263, 267, 270 n4, 275, 276

Artifice, xxi; in architecture, 4, 9–13, 16, 18, 30, 31; city as, 48; in corporations, 162; in landscape, 162, 164; postmodern, 155, 435

Assimilation, cultural, 132, 137, 145; barriers to, 392–93; critiques of, 146, 377–78, 388, 389

Association of American Geographers, 432

Attention, xiv; character of, 250–54; to emotions, 362, 364–65, 370–71; inspired by place, xxv, 24, 239; to surroundings, 225, 226, 249–50, 435–36; to textual places, 58; to the void, 247, 253, 254. *See also* Awareness

Audubon, John James, 69

Augustine, 224

Authenticity, 53, 127; of identity, 139; landscapes of, 125, 155, 162–63

Authority, xvii; challenges to, xxvi, 133; and place, xxiv, 218. *See also* Power relations, social; Status

Awareness: "geographical," 405–7, 415; moral aspects of, xxviii, 232–45; of reality, 224, 233–34, 238–44; of the self in nature, 193–94. *See also* Attention; Perception

"Away" (Frost), 200

Bachelard, Gaston, 59

Badger Saints and Sinners (Holmes), 379

Bakhtin, Mikhail, 254

Bancroft, George, 86–87, 89

Barnes, Trevor, 435

Barthes, Roland, 104, 107

Bartram, William, 68–69

Bates, Marston, 84

Baudelaire, Charles, 199

Bauman, Zygmunt, 136, 143

Baym, Nina, 64

Beckett, Samuel, 246

Bedford Village, New York, xxiii, 5–6, 41–54

Behavior, criminal, 33, 64, 74, 170–76, 202, 297 n25, 400 n64

Beier, A. L., 170–71

Being and Time (Heidegger), 268, 406–7, 423 n51

Being, gift of, 265. *See also* Presence

Benjamin, Walter, 213

Bentham, Jeremy, 213–14

Bergson, Henri, 410–11